OUT OF MANY

VOLUME II

OUT OF MANY

A HISTORY
OF THE
AMERICAN PEOPLE

BRIEF THIRD EDITION

JOHN MACK FARAGHER
Yale University

MARI JO BUHLE
Brown University

DANIEL CZITROM
Mount Holyoke College

SUSAN H. ARMITAGE
Washington State University

Prentice
Hall

Upper Saddle River, New Jersey 07458

A Library of Congress has catalogued
the (single volume) edition as follows:
Out of many: a history of the American people / John Mack Faragher. . . [et al.]. —
    Combined ed., brief 3rd ed.
        p.   cm.
    Includes bibliographical references and index.
    ISBN 0-13-017704-0
    1. United States—History.   I. Faragher, John Mack

E178.1.0935   2001   00–029273
973—dc21   CIP

Editorial Director: Charlyce Jones Owen
Editor-in-Chief of Development: Susanna Lesan
Development Editor: Robert Weiss
Creative Director: Leslie Osher
Art Director: Ximena Tamvakopoulos
Interior Designer: Thomas Nery
Cover Designer: Ximena Tamvakopoulos
Cover Photo Researcher: Karen Sanatar
Cover Art: Gifford Beal (1879–1956), "Elevated Columbus Avenue,
    New York," oil on canvas, 36½" x 48½". Photo by Michael Agee.
    Source: New Britain Musuem of American Arts, Connecticut,
    Charles F. Smith Fund.
Marketing Manager: Sheryl Adams

AVP, Director of Production and Manufacturing: Barbara Kittle
Manufacturing Manager: Nick Sklitsis
Prepress and Manufacturing Buyer: Lynn Pearlman
Production Editor: Jean Lapidus
Photo Permissions Coordinator: Michelina Viscusi
Formatting & Art Manager: Guy Ruggiero
Artist: Mirella Signoretto
Copy Editor: Sylvia Moore
Indexer: Murray Fisher
Text Permissions Specialist: Irene Hess
Proofreader: Helena DeKeukelaere

Credits and acknowledgments for materials borrowed from other sources and reproduced,
with permission, in this textbook appear on pages C1–C2.

This book was set in 11/12 Weiss by Carlisle Communications, Ltd.
and was printed and bound by Webcrafters, Inc.
The cover was printed by Phoenix Color Corp.

Printed in the United States of America
10 9 8 7 6 5 4 3 2 1

ISBN 0-13-017703-2

Prentice-Hall International (UK) Limited, *London*
Prentice-Hall of Australia Pty. Limited, *Sydney*
Prentice-Hall Canada Inc., *Toronto*
Prentice-Hall Hispanoamericana, S.A., *Mexico*
Prentice-Hall of India Private Limited, *New Delhi*
Prentice-Hall of Japan, Inc., *Tokyo*
Pearson Education Asia Pte. Ltd., *Singapore*
Editora Prentice-Hall do Brasil, Ltda., *Rio de Janeiro*

To our students,

our sisters,

and our brothers

BRIEF CONTENTS

CONTENTS

30 The Overextended Society, 1974–1980   568

MAPS

CHARTS, GRAPHS, AND TABLES

PREFACE

Out of Many, A History of the American People, Brief Third Edition, offers a distinctive and timely approach to American history, highlighting the experiences of diverse communities of Americans in the unfolding story of our country. These communities offer a way of examining the complex historical forces shaping people's lives at various moments in our past. The debates and conflicts surrounding the most momentous issues in our national life—independence, emerging democracy, slavery, westward settlement, imperial expansion, economic depression, war, technological change—were largely worked out in the context of local communities. Through communities we focus on the persistent tensions between everyday life and those larger decisions and events that continually reshape the circumstances of local life. Each chapter opens with a description of a representative community. Some of these portraits feature American communities struggling with one another: African slaves and English masters on the rice plantations of colonial Georgia, or Tejanos and Americans during the Texas war of independence. Other chapters feature portraits of communities facing social change: the feminists of Seneca Falls, New York, in 1848; the sitdown strikers of Flint, Michigan, in 1934; and the African Americans of Montgomery, Alabama, in 1955. As the story unfolds we find communities growing to include ever larger groups of Americans: The soldiers from every colony who forged the Continental Army into a patriotic national force at Valley Forge during the American Revolution; the movie-goers who dreamed a collective dream of material prosperity and upward mobility during the 1920s; and the Americans linked in ever-growing numbers in the virtual communities of cyberspace as the twenty-first century begins.

We prepared this brief edition to serve the needs of one-semester courses, teachers who assign supplemental readings, or anyone interested in a more condensed narrative of American history. While this volume is about two-thirds the length of the full-length version, it retains the distinct point of view that makes it unique among all college-level American history texts. The community focus remains fully in place as the integrating perspective that allows us to combine political, social, and cultural history.

Out of Many is also the only American history text with a truly continental perspective. With community vignettes from New England to the South, the Midwest to the far West, we encourage students to appreciate the great expanse of our nation. For example, a vignette of seventeenth-century Santa Fé, New Mexico, illustrates the founding of the first European settlements in the New World. We present territorial expansion into the American West from the point of view of the Mandan villagers of the upper Missouri River of North Dakota. We introduce the policies of the Reconstruction era through the experience of African Americans in the Sea Island of South Carolina. This continental perspective drives home to students that American history has never been the preserve of any particular region.

In these ways *Out of Many* breaks new ground, but without compromising its coverage of the traditional turning points that we believe are critically important to an understanding of the American past. Among these watershed events are the Revolution and the struggle over the Constitution, the Civil War and Reconstruction, and the Great Depression and World War II. In *Out of Many,* however, we seek to *integrate* the narrative of national history with the story of the nation's many diverse communities. The Revolutionary and Constitutional period tried the ability of local communities to forge a new unity, and success depended on their ability to build a nation without compromising local identity. The Civil War and Reconstruction formed a second great test of the balance between the national ideas of the revolution and the power of local and sectional communities. The Depression and the New Deal demonstrated the impotence of local communities and the growing power of national institutions during the greatest economic challenge in our history. *Out of Many* also looks back in a new and comprehensive way—from the vantage point of the beginning of a new century and the end of the Cold War—at the salient events of the last fifty years and their impact on American communities. The community focus of *Out of Many* weaves the stories of the people and of the nation into a single compelling narrative.

SPECIAL FEATURES

With each edition of *Out of Many* we have sought to strengthen its unique integration of the best of traditional American history with its innovative community-based focus and strong continental perspective. A wealth of special features and pedagogical aids reinforces our narrative and helps students grasp key issues.

- **Community and Diversity.** *Out of Many,* Brief Third Edition, opens with an introduction, titled "Community and Diversity," that acquaints students with the major themes of the book, providing them with a framework for understanding American history.

- **Immigration and Community: The Changing Face of Ethnicity in America.** This feature, new to this edition, highlights the impact of the immigrant experience on the formation of American communities. There are four Immigration and Community features in the book. The first covers the colonial period through 1800, the second covers from 1800 to 1860, the third covers from 1860 to 1930, and the last covers the period since 1930. Each is four pages long and opens with an overview of the character of immigration during the period in question. This overview is followed by a section called "In Their Own Words" that consists of extracts from primary sources written by immigrants themselves and by native-born Americans in response to the new arrivals. Study questions at the end of each Immigration and Community feature ask students to relate issues raised in the overview and documents to broader issues in American history.

- **History and the Land.** These features focus on the geographical dimension of historical change to give students an appreciation of the relationship between geography and history. Each elucidates an important historical trend or process with a map and a brief explanatory essay.

- **American Communities.** Each chapter opens with an American Communities vignette that relates the experience of a particular community to the broader issues discussed in the chapter.

- **Maps.** *Out of Many,* Brief Third Edition, has more maps than any other American history textbook. Many maps include topographical detail that helps students appreciate the impact of geography on history.

- **Overview tables.** Overview tables, also new to this edition, provide students with a summary of complex issues.

- **Graphs, charts, and tables.** Every chapter includes one or more graphs, charts, or tables that help students understand important events and trends.

- **Photos and illustrations.** The abundant illustrations in *Out of Many,* Brief Third Edition, include many images that have never before been used in an American history text. None of the images is anachronistic—each one dates from the historical period under discussion. Extensive captions treat the images as visual primary source documents from the American past, describing their source and explaining their significance.

- **Chapter-opening outlines and key topics lists.** These pedagogical aids provide students with a succinct preview of the material covered in each chapter.

- **Chronologies.** A chronology at the end of each chapter helps students build a framework of key events.

- **Review Questions.** Review questions help students review, reinforce, and retain the material in each chapter and encourage them to relate the material to broader issues in American history.

- **Recommended Reading and Additional Bibliography.** The works on the annotated Recommended Reading list at the end of each chapter have been selected with the interested introductory student in mind.

CLASSROOM ASSISTANCE PACKAGE

In classrooms across the country, many instructors encounter students who perceive history as merely a jumble of names, dates, and events. The key to bringing dimension to our dynamic past for students is a scholarship-laden, pedagogically rich text accompanied by a multimedia classroom assistance package that brings the 1600s through the 1990s alive. The package that accompanies *Out of Many,* Brief Edition, includes print and multimedia supplements that are designed to reinforce and enliven the richness of our past and inspire students with the excitement of studying the field of history.

PRINT SUPPLEMENTS
Instructor's Resource Manual
The *Instructor's Resource Manual* contains chapter outlines, detailed chapter overviews, activities, discussion questions, readings, and information on audio-visual resources that can be used in developing and preparing lecture presentations.

Test Item File

The *Test Item File* offers more than 1,500 multiple-choice, true-false, and essay test questions. It also includes multiple choice and map questions from the study guide that can be used for quizzes.

Prentice Hall Custom Test

This commercial-quality computerized test management program, for Windows and Macintosh environments, allows users to create their own tests using items from the printed Test Item File. The program allows users to edit the items in the Test Item File and to add their own questions. Online testing is also available.

Transparency Pack

This collection of over 160 full-color transparency acetates provides the maps, charts, and graphs from the text for use in classroom presentations.

Study Guide, Volumes I and II

The *Study Guides* are designed according to an SQ3R (Survey-Question-Read-Recite-Review) methodology. Each chapter includes a brief overview, a list of chapter objectives, an extensive questioning technique applied to chapter topics, study skills exercises, identification of terms, multiple-choice, fill-in-the-blank, matching, short answer, and essay questions. In addition, each chapter includes two to three pages of map questions and exercises.

Documents Set, Volumes I and II

Prepared by John Mack Faragher, Yale University, and Daniel Czitrom, Mount Holyoke College.

The authors have selected and carefully edited more than 300 documents that relate directly to the theme and content present in the text and organized them into five general categories: community, social history, government, culture, and politics. Each document includes a brief introduction as well as a number of questions to encourage critical analysis of the reading and to relate it to the content of the text. The documents are available for a nominal fee to the student with the purchase of the textbook.

Retrieving the American Past: A Customized U.S. History Reader

Written and developed by leading historians and educators, this reader is an on-demand history database that offers 59 compelling modules on topics in American History. Approximately 35 pages in length, each module includes an introduction, several primary source documents, secondary source documents, follow-up questions, and recommendations for further reading. By deciding which modules to include and the order in which they will appear, instructors can compile the reader they want to use. Instructor-originated material—other readings, exercises—can be included. Contact your local Prentice Hall Representative for more information about this exciting custom publishing option.

Understanding and Answering Essay Questions

Prepared by Mary L. Kelley, San Antonio College.

This brief guide suggests helpful study techniques as well as specific analytical tools for understanding different types of essay questions and provides precise guidelines for preparing well-crafted essay answers. This guide is available free to students upon adoption by the instructor.

Reading Critically About History: A Guide to Active Reading

Prepared by Rose Wassman and Lee Ann Rinsky.

This guide focuses on the skills needed to learn the essential information presented in college history textbooks. Material covered includes vocabulary skills, recognizing organizational patterns, critical thinking skills, understanding visual aids, and practice sections. This guide is available free to students upon adoption by the instructor.

Themes of the Times

The New York Times and Prentice Hall are sponsoring *Themes of the Times*, a program designed to enhance student access to current information of relevance in the classroom. Through this program, the core subject matter provided in the text is supplemented by a collection of current articles from one of the world's most distinguished newspapers, *The New York Times*. These articles demonstrate the vital, ongoing connection between what is learned in the classroom and what is happening in the world around us. To enjoy the wealth of information of the *The New York Times* daily, a reduced subscription rate is available. For information call toll-free: (800) 631–1222.

Prentice Hall and *The New York Times* are proud to co-sponsor *Themes of the Times*. We hope it will make the reading of both textbooks and newspapers a more dynamic, involving process.

MULTIMEDIA SUPPLEMENTS

History on the Internet: A Critical Thinking Guide

This guide focuses on developing the critical thinking skills necessary to evaluate and use online sources. The guide also provides a brief introduction to navigating the Internet, along with complete references related specifically to the History discipline and how to use the *Companion Website*™ available for *Out of Many*, Brief Edition. This 96-page supplementary book is free to students with the purchase of the textbook.

Mapping American History: Interactive Explorations CD ROM

Prepared by Gerald Danzer, University of Illinois—Chicago.

This unique multimedia resource provides over 150 interactive map activities and exercises organized by the chapters in the text. Designed to develop map reading, analysis, and literacy skills, the program also helps reinforce and review the content of each chapter. Available for Windows and Macintosh environments, the program uses audio, video, photographs, and illustrations to provide a complete multimedia experience. The software is available for a nominal fee with the purchase of the textbook.

Companion Website™

Address: www.prenhall.com/faragher

Students can now take full advantage of the World Wide Web to enrich their study of American history through the *Out of Many Companion Website*™. Features of the website include, for each chapter in the text, objectives, study questions, map labeling exercises, related links, and document exercises. A faculty module provides material from the Instructor's Resource Manual and the maps and charts from the text in Powerpoint™ format.

Powerpoint™ Images CD ROM

Available for Windows and Macintosh environments, this resource includes the maps, charts, graphs, and other illustrations from the text for use in Powerpoint™ as well as over 200 color photographs. Organized by chapters in the text, this collection of images is useful for classroom presentations and lectures.

ACKNOWLEDGMENTS

In the years it has taken to bring *Out of Many* from idea to reality and to improve it in successive editions, we have often been reminded that although writing history sometimes feels like isolated work, it actually involves a collective effort. We want to thank the dozens of people whose efforts have made the publication of this book possible.

At Prentice Hall, Charlyce Jones Owen, Editorial Director, gave us her full support and oversaw the entire publication process. Bob Weiss, Senior Development Editor, greatly helped to strengthen the book's most distinctive features with his careful attention to detail and clarity. Susanna Lesan, now Editor-in-Chief of Development, worked with us on the first edition of the text; without her efforts this book would never have been published. Jean Lapidus, Production Editor, oversaw the entire complicated production process in an exemplary fashion. Barbara Salz, our photo researcher, expertly tracked down the many pertinent new images that appear in this edition.

Among our many other friends at Prentice Hall we also want to thank: Phil Miller, President; Sheryl Adams, Marketing Manager; Leslie Osher, Creative Design Director; and Ximena Tamvakopoulos, Art Director.

Although we share joint responsibility for the entire book, the chapters were individually authored: John Mack Faragher wrote chapters 1–8; Mari Jo Buhle wrote chapters 18–20, 25–26, 29–30; Daniel Czitrom wrote chapters 17, 21–24, 27–28, 31; and Susan Armitage wrote chapters 9–16.

Historians around the country greatly assisted us by reading and commenting on our chapters for this and previous editions. We want to thank each of them for the commitment of their valuable time.

Donald Abbe, Texas Tech University, TX
Richard H. Abbott, Eastern Michigan University, MI
Guy Alchon, University of Delaware, DE
Don Barlow, Prestonsburg Community College, KY
William Barney, University of North Carolina, NC
Alwyn Barr, Texas Tech University, TX
Debra Barth, San Jose City College, CA
Peter V. Bergstrom, Illinois State University, IL
William C. Billingsley, South Plains College, TX
Peter H. Buckingham, Linfield College, OR
Bill Cecil-Fronsman, Washburn University of Topeka, KS
Victor W. Chen, Chabot College, CA
Jonathan M. Chu, University of Massachusetts, MA
P. Scott Corbett, Oxnard College, CA
Matther Coulter, Collin Country Community College, TX
Virginia Crane, University of Wisconsin, Oshkosh, WI
Jim Cullen, Harvard University, MA
Thomas J. Curran, St. John's University, NY
Richard V. Damms, Ohio State University, OH
Elizabeth Dunn, Baylor University, TX
Emmett G. Essin, Eastern Tennessee State Unversity, TN
Mark F. Fernandez, Loyola University, IL
Leon Fink, University of North Carolina, Chapel Hill, NC

Michael James Foret, University of Wisconsin, Stevens Point, WI

Joshua B. Freeman, Columbia University, NY

Glenda E. Gilmore, Yale University, CT

Don C. Glenn, Diablo Valley College, CA

Lawrence Glickman, University of South Carolina, SC

Kenneth Goings, Florida Atlantic University, FL

Mark Goldman, Tallahassee Community College, FL

Gregory L. Goodwin, Bakersfield College, CA

Gretchen Green, University of Missouri, Kansas City, MO

Emily Greenwald, University of Nebraska at Lincoln, NE

Mark W. T. Harvey, North Dakota State University, ND

James A. Hijiya, University of Massachusetts at Dartmouth, MA

Raymond M. Hyser, James Madison University, VA

John Inscoe, University of Georgia, GA

John C. Kesler, Lakeland Community College, OH

Peter N. Kirstein, Saint Xavier University, IL

Frank Lambert, Purdue University, IN

Susan Rimby Leighow, Millersville University, PA

Janice M. Leone, Middle Tennessee University, TN

Glenn Linden, Southern Methodist University, Dallas, TX

George Lipsitz, University of California, San Diego, CA

Judy Barrett Litoff, Bryant College, RI

Jesus Luna, California State University, CA

Larry Madaras, Howard Community College, MD

Lynn Mapes, Grand Valley State University, MI

John F. Marszalek, Mississippi State University, MS

Scott C. Martin, Bowling Green State University, OH

Robert L. Matheny, Eastern New Mexico University, NM

Thomas Matijasic, Prestonsburg Community College, KY

M. Delores McBroome, Humboldt State University, CA

Gerald McFarland, University of Massachusetts, Amherst, MA

Sam McSeveney, Vanderbilt University, TN

Warren Metcalf, Arizona State University, AZ

M. Catherine Miller, Texas State University, TX

Norman H. Murdoch, University of Cincinnati, OH

Gregory H. Nobles, Georgia Institute of Technology, GA

Dale Odom, University of Texas at Denton, TX

Sean O'Neill, Grand Valley State University, MI

Edward Opper, Greenville Technical College, Greenville, SC

Charles K. Piehl, Mankato State University, MN

Carolyn Garrett Pool, University of Central Oklahoma, OK

Christie Farnham Pope, Iowa State University, IA

Susan Porter-Benson, University of Missouri, MO

Russell Posner, City College of San Francisco, CA

John Powell, Penn State University, Erie, PA

Sarah Purcell, Central Michigan University, MI

Joseph P. Reidy, Howard University, DC

Marilyn D. Rhinehart, North Harris College, TX

Leo P. Ribuffo, George Washington University, DC

Judy Ridner, California State University at Northridge, CA

Neal Salisbury, Smith College, MA

Roberto Salmon, University of Texas-Pan American, TX

Steven Schuster, Brookhaven Community College, TX

Megan Seaholm, University of Texas, Austin, TX

Nigel Sellars, University of Oklahoma, Norman, OK

John David Smith, North Carolina State University, NC

Patrick Smith, Broward Community College, FL

Mark W. Summers, University of Kentucky, KY

John D. Tanner, Jr., Palomar College, CA

Robert R. Tomes, St. John's University, NY

Michael Miller Topp, University of Texas at El Paso, TX

John Trickel, Richland Community College, IL

Steve Tripp, Grand Valley State University, MI

Fred R. Van Hartesveldt, Fort Valley State University, GA

Philip H. Vaughan, Rose State College, OK

Robert C. Vitz, Northern Kentucky University, KY

F. Michael Williams, Brevard Community College, FL

Charles Regan Wilson, University of Mississippi, MS

Harold Wilson, Old Dominion University, VA

William Woodward, Seattle Pacific University, WA

Loretta E. Zimmerman, University of Florida, FL

Each of us depended on a great deal of support and assistance with the research and writing that went into this book. We want to thank: Kathryn Abbott, Nan Boyd, Krista Comer, Crista DeLuzio, Keith Edgerton, Carol Frost, Jesse Hoffnung Garskof, Jane Gerhard, Todd Gernes, Melani McAlister, Cristiane Mitchell, J. C. Mutchler, Tricia Rose, Gina Rourke, and Jessica Shubow.

Our families and close friends have been supportive and ever so patient over the many years we have devoted to this project. But we want especially to thank Paul Buhle, Meryl Fingrutd, Bob Greene, and Michele Hoffnung.

ABOUT THE AUTHORS

Chris Freitag

JOHN MACK FARAGHER

John Mack Faragher is Arthur Unobskey Professor of American History at Yale University. Born in Arizona and raised in southern California, he received his B.A. at the University of California, Riverside, and his Ph.D. at Yale University. He is the author of *Women and Men on the Overland Trail* (1979), which won the Frederick Jackson Turner Award of the Organization of American Historians, *Sugar Creek: Life on the Illinois Prairie* (1986), and *Daniel Boone: The Life and Legend of an American Pioneer* (1992). He is also the editor of *The American Heritage Encyclopedia* (1988).

DANIEL CZITROM

Daniel Czitrom is Professor and Chair of History at Mount Holyoke College. He received his B.A. from the State University of New York at Binghamton and his M.A. and Ph.D. from the University of Wisconsin, Madison. He is the author of *Media and the American Mind: From Morse to McLuhan* (1982), which won the First Books Award of the American Historical Association. His scholarly articles and essays have appeared in the *Journal of American History*, *American Quarterly*, *The Massachusetts Review*, and *The Atlantic*. He is currently completing *Mysteries of the City: Culture, Politics, and the Underworld in New York, 1870–1920*.

MARI JO BUHLE

Mari Jo Buhle is Professor of American Civilization and History at Brown University, specializing in American women's history. She is the author of *Women and American Socialism, 1870–1920* (1981) and *Feminism and its Discontents: A Century of Struggle with Psychoanalysis* (1998). She is also coeditor of *Encyclopedia of the American Left*, second edition (1998). She currently serves as an editor of a series of books on women and American history for the University of Illinois Press. Professor Buhle held a fellowship (1991–1996) from the John D. and Catherine T. MacArthur Foundation.

SUSAN H. ARMITAGE

Susan H. Armitage is Professor of History at Washington State University. She earned her Ph.D. from the London School of Economics and Political Science. Among her many publications on western women's history are three coedited books, *The Women's West* (1987), *So Much To Be Done: Women on the Mining and Ranching Frontier* (1991), and *Writing the Range: Race, Class, and Culture in the Women's West* (1997). She is the editor of *Frontiers: A Journal of Women's Studies*.

COMMUNITY & DIVERSITY

One of the most characteristic features of our country has always been its astounding variety. The American people include the descendants of native Indians, colonial Europeans, Africans, and migrants from virtually every country and continent. Indeed, as we enter the new century the nation is absorbing a tide of immigrants from Latin America and Asia that rivals the great tide of immigrants from eastern and southern Europe that arrived at the beginning of the twentieth century. The struggle to make a nation out of our many communities is what much of American history is all about. That is the story told in this book.

Every human society is made up of communities. A community is a set of relationships that link men, women, and their families into a coherent social whole, more than the sum of its parts. In a community people develop the capacity for unified action. In a community people learn, often through trial and error, how to transform and adapt to their environment. The sentiment that binds the members of a community together is the origin of group identity and ethnic pride. In the making of history, communities are far more important than even the greatest of leaders, for the community is the institution most capable of passing a distinctive historical tradition to future generations.

Communities bind people together in multiple ways. They can be as small as the local neighborhood, in which people maintain face-to-face relations, or as large as the imagined entity of the nation. This book examines American history from the perspective of community life—an ever widening frame that has included larger and larger groups of Americans.

For years there have been persistent laments about the "loss of community" in modern America. But community has not disappeared—it is continually being reinvented. Until the late eighteenth century, community was defined primarily by space and local geography. The closer one gets to the present, the more community is reshaped by new and powerful historical forces such as the nation state, the marketplace, industrialization, the corporation, mass immigration, and electronic media.

The title for our book was suggested by the Latin phrase selected by John Adams, Benjamin Franklin, and Thomas Jefferson for the Great Seal of the United States: *E Pluribus Unum*—"Out of Many Comes Unity." These men understood that unity could not be imposed by a powerful central authority but had to develop out of mutual respect among Americans of different backgrounds. The revolutionary leadership expressed the hope that such respect could grow on the basis of a remarkable proposition: "We hold these truths to be self-evident, that all men are created equal; that they are endowed by their Creator with certain unalienable rights; that among these are life, liberty, and the pursuit of happiness." The national government of the United States would preserve local and state authority but would guarantee individual rights. The nation would be strengthened by guarantees of difference.

Out of Many—that is the promise of America, and the premise of this book. The underlying dialectic of American history, we believe, is that as a people we need to locate our national *unity* in the celebration of the *differences* that exist among us; these differences can be our strength, as long as we affirm the promise of the Declaration. Protecting the "right to be different," in other words, is absolutely fundamental to the continued existence of democracy, and that right is best protected by the existence of strong and vital communities. We are bound together as a nation by the ideal of local and cultural differences protected by our common commitment to the values of our revolution.

Today—with the many social and cultural conflicts that abound in the United States—some Americans have lost faith in that vision. But our history shows that the promise of American unity has always been problematic. Centrifugal forces have been powerful in the American past, and at times the country has seemed about to fracture into its component parts. Our transformation from a collection of groups and regions into a nation has been marked by painful and often violent struggles. Our past is filled with conflicts between Indians and colonists, masters and slaves, Patriots and Loyalists, Northerners and Southerners, Easterners and Westerners, capitalists and workers, and sometimes the government and the people. Americans often appear to be little more than a contentious collection of peoples with conflicting interests, divided by region and background, race and class.

Our most influential leaders also sometimes suffered a crisis of faith in the American project of "liberty and justice for all." Thomas Jefferson not only believed in the inferiority of African Americans, but he feared that immigrants from outside the Anglo-American tradition might "warp and bias" the development of the nation "and render it a heterogeneous, incoherent, distracted mass." We have not always lived up to the American promise, and there is a dark side to our history. It took the bloodiest war in American history to secure the human rights of African Americans, and the struggle for full equality continues nearly a century and a half later. During the great influx of immigrants in the early twentieth century, fears much like Jefferson's led to movements to *Americanize* the foreign born by forcing them, in the words of one leader, "to give up the languages, customs, and methods of life which they have brought with them across the ocean, and adopt instead the language, habits, and customs of this country, and the general standards and ways of American living." Similar thinking motivated Congress at various times to bar the immigration of Asians and other ethnic groups into the country, and to force assimilation on American Indians by denying them the freedom to practice their religion or even to speak their own language. Such calls for restrictive unity resound in our own day.

But other Americans have argued for a more idealistic version of *Americanization*. "What is the American, this new man?" asked the French immigrant Michel Crévecoeur in 1782. "A strange mixture of blood which you will find in no other country," he answered; in America, "individuals of all nations are melted into a new race of men." A century later Crévecoeur was echoed by historian Frederick Jackson Turner, who believed that "in the crucible of the frontier, the immigrants were Americanized, liberated, and fused into a mixed race, English in neither nationality nor characteristics. The process has gone on from the early days to our own."

The process by which diverse communities have come to share a set of common American values is one of the most fundamental aspects of our history. It did not occur, however, because of compulsory *Amer-icanization* programs, but because of free public education, popular participation in democratic politics, and the impact of popular culture. Contemporary America does have a common culture: we laugh at the same television sitcoms and share the same aspirations to own a home and send our children to college—all unique American traits.

To a degree that too few Americans appreciate, this common culture resulted from a complicated process of mutual discovery that took place when different ethnic and regional groups encountered one another. Consider just one small and unique aspect of our culture, the barbecue. Americans have been barbecuing since before the beginning of written history. Early settlers adopted this technique of cooking from the Indians—the word itself comes from a native term for a framework of sticks over a fire on which meat was slowly cooked. Colonists typically barbecued pork, fed on Indian corn. African slaves lent their own touch by introducing the use of hot sauces. Thus the ritual that is a part of nearly every American family's Fourth of July silently celebrates the heritage of diversity that went into making our common culture.

The American educator John Dewey recognized this diversity early in this century. "The genuine American, the typical American is himself a hyphenated character," he declared, "international and interracial in his make-up." The point about our "hyphenated character," Dewey believed, "is to see to it that the hyphen connects instead of separates." We, the authors of *Out of Many*, share Dewey's perspective on American history. "Creation comes from the impact of diversity," wrote the American philosopher Horace Kallen. We also endorse Kallen's vision of the American promise: "A democracy of nationalities, cooperating voluntarily and autonomously through common institutions, . . . a multiplicity in a unity, an orchestration of mankind." And now, let the music begin.

CHAPTER SEVENTEEN

RECONSTRUCTION
1863–1877

AMERICAN COMMUNITIES
Hale County, Alabama: From Slavery to Freedom in a Black Belt Community

On a bright Saturday morning in May 1867, 4,000 former slaves eagerly streamed into the town of Greensboro, bustling seat of Hale County in west-central Alabama. They came to hear speeches from two delegates to a recent freedmen's convention in Mobile and to find out about the political status of black people under the Reconstruction Act just passed by Congress. In the days following this unprecedented gathering of African Americans, tension mounted throughout the surrounding countryside. Military authorities had begun supervising voter registration for elections to the upcoming constitutional convention that would rewrite the laws of Alabama. On June 13, John Orrick, a local white man, confronted Alex Webb, a politically active freedman, on the streets of Greensboro. Webb had recently been appointed a voter registrar for the district. Orrick swore he would never be registered by a black man, and shot Webb dead. Hundreds of armed and angry freedmen formed a posse to search for Orrick, but they failed to find him. Webb's murder galvanized 500 local freedmen to form a local Union League chapter, which functioned as both a militia company and a forum to agitate for political rights.

The Civil War had destroyed slavery and the Confederacy, but the political and economic status of newly emancipated African Americans remained to be worked out. The 4 million freed people constituted roughly one-third of the total southern population, but the black–white ratio in individual communities varied enormously. In some places the Union army had been a strong presence during the war, hastening collapse of the slave system and encouraging experiments in free labor. Other areas remained untouched by the fighting.

West-central Alabama had emerged as a fertile center of cotton production just two decades before the Civil War. There African Americans constituted more than three-quarters of the population, as they did throughout the South's black belt. The region was virtually untouched by fighting until the very end of the Civil War. But with the arrival of federal troops in the spring of 1865, African Americans in Hale County, like their counterparts elsewhere, began to challenge the traditional organization of plantation labor.

Above all, freed people wanted more autonomy. Overseers and owners thus grudgingly allowed them to work the land "in families," letting them choose their own supervisors and find their own provisions. The result was a shift from the gang labor characteristic of the antebellum period, in which large groups of slaves worked under the harsh and constant supervision of white overseers, to the sharecropping system, in which African American families worked small plots of land in exchange for a small share of the crop. This shift represented less of a victory for newly freed African Americans than a defeat for plantation owners, who resented even the limited economic independence it forced them to concede to their black workforce.

Only a small fraction—perhaps 15 percent—of African American families were fortunate enough to be able to buy land. The majority settled for some version of sharecropping, while others managed to rent land from owners, becoming tenant farmers. Still, planters throughout Hale County had been forced to change the old routines of plantation labor.

Local African Americans also organized politically. In 1866 Congress had passed the Civil Rights Act and sent the Fourteenth Amendment to the Constitution to the states for ratification; both promised full citizenship rights to former slaves. Hale County freedmen joined the Republican Party and local Union League chapters, which operated as the Republican Party's organizational arm in the South. Freedmen used their new political power to press for better labor contracts, demand greater autonomy for the black workforce, and agitate for the more radical goal of land confiscation and redistribution. Two Hale County former slaves, Brister Reese and James K. Green, won election to the Alabama state legislature in 1869.

It was not long before these economic and political gains prompted a white counterattack. In the spring of 1868, the Ku Klux Klan—a secret organization devoted to terrorizing and intimidating African Americans and their white Republican allies—came to Hale County. Disguised in white sheets, armed with guns and whips, and making nighttime raids on horseback, Klansmen flogged, beat, and murdered free people. They intimidated voters and silenced political activists. Planters used Klan terror to dissuade former slaves from leaving plantations or organizing for higher wages.

An 1871 congressional investigation led to passage of the Ku Klux Klan Act. Federal intervention did manage to break the power of the Klan temporarily in parts of the former Confederacy. But no serious effort was made to stop Klan terror in the west Alabama black belt. Planters thus reestablished much of their social and political control.

The events in Hale County illustrate the struggle that beset communities throughout the South during the Reconstruction era after the Civil War. The destruction of slavery and the Confederacy forced African Americans and white people to renegotiate their old economic and political roles. These community battles both shaped and were shaped by the victorious and newly expansive federal government in Washington. In the end, Reconstruction was only partly successful. Not until the "Second Reconstruction" of the twentieth-century civil rights movement would the descendants of Hale County's African Americans begin to enjoy the full fruits of freedom— and even then not without challenge.

Greensboro

KEY TOPICS

- Competing political plans for reconstructing the defeated Confederacy

- African Americans make the difficult transition from slavery to freedom

- The political and social legacy of Reconstruction in the southern states

- Post-Civil War transformations in the economic and political life of the North

THE POLITICS OF RECONSTRUCTION

When General Robert E. Lee's men stacked their guns at Appomattox, the bloodiest war in American history ended. Although President Abraham Lincoln insisted early on that the conflict was to preserve the Union, by 1863 the contest had evolved into a war of African American liberation. Indeed, slavery—as a political, economic, and moral issue—was the root cause of the war. The Civil War ultimately destroyed slavery, though not racism, once and for all.

The Civil War also settled the constitutional crisis provoked by the cecession of the Confederacy and its justification in appeals to states' rights. The name *United States* would from now on be understood as a singular rather than a plural noun, signaling an impor-

tant change in the meaning of American nationality. The old notion of the United States as a voluntary union of sovereign states gave way to the new reality of a single nation in which the federal government took precedence over the individual states.

The Defeated South

The white South paid an extremely high price for secession, war, and defeat. In addition to the battlefield casualties of 260,000, the Confederate states sustained deep material and psychological wounds. Much of the best agricultural land was destroyed. Many towns and cities, including Richmond, Atlanta, and Columbia, South Carolina, lay in ruins. By 1865 the South's most precious commodities, cotton and African American slaves, no longer were measures of wealth and prestige. Retreating Confederates destroyed most of the South's cotton to prevent its capture by federal troops. What remained was confiscated by Union agents as contraband of war. The former slaves, many of whom had fled to Union lines during the latter stages of the war, were determined to chart their own course in the reconstructed South as free men and women.

It would take the South's economy a generation to overcome the severe blows dealt by the war. In 1860 the South held roughly 25 percent of the nation's wealth; a decade later it controlled only 12 percent.

Many white Southerners resented their conquered status, and white notions of race, class, and "honor" died hard. A white North Carolinian, for example, who had lost almost everything dear to him in the war—his sons, home, and slaves—recalled in 1865 that despite the tragedy he still retained one thing. "They've left me one inestimable privilege—to hate 'em. I git up at half-past four in the morning, and sit up till twelve at night, to hate 'em."

Emancipation proved the bitterest pill for white Southerners to swallow, especially the planter elite. Conquered and degraded, and in their view robbed of their slave property, white people responded by tending more than ever to perceive African Americans as vastly

Charleston, South Carolina, in 1865, after Union troops had burned the city. In the aftermath of the Civil War, scenes like this were common throughout the South. The destruction of large portions of so many southern cities and towns contributed to the postwar economic hardships faced by the region.

inferior to themselves. However, emancipation forced white people to redefine their world. The specter of political power and social equality for African Americans made racial order the consuming passion of most white Southerners during the Reconstruction years. In fact, racism can be seen as one of the major forces driving Reconstruction and, ultimately, undermining it.

Abraham Lincoln's Plan

By late 1863 Union military victories had convinced President Lincoln of the need to fashion a plan for the reconstruction of the South (see Chapter 16). He based his reconstruction program on bringing the seceded states back into the Union as quickly as possible. His Proclamation of Amnesty and Reconstruction of December 1863 offered full pardon and the restoration of property, not including slaves, to white Southerners willing to swear an oath of allegiance to the United States and its laws, including the Emancipation Proclamation. Prominent Confederate military and civil leaders were excluded from Lincoln's offer, although he indicated that he would freely pardon these officers.

The president also proposed that when the number of any Confederate state's voters who took the oath of allegiance reached 10 percent of the number who had voted in the election of 1860, this group could establish a state government that Lincoln would recognize as legitimate. Fundamental to this Ten Percent Plan was acceptance by the reconstructed governments of the abolition of slavery. Lincoln's plan was designed less as a blueprint for Reconstruction than as a way to shorten the war and gain white people's support for emancipation.

Lincoln's amnesty proclamation angered Radical Republicans, who advocated not only equal rights for the freedmen but a tougher stance toward the white South as well. In July 1864 Senator Benjamin F. Wade of Ohio and Congressman Henry W. Davis of Maryland sought to substitute a harsher alternative to the Ten Percent Plan. The Wade–Davis bill required that 50 percent of the white male citizens had to take a loyalty oath before elections for new state constitutional conventions could be held in the seceded states. The Radicals saw Reconstruction as a chance to effect a fundamental transformation of southern society. They thus wanted to delay the process until war's end and to limit participation to a smaller number of southern Unionists. Lincoln viewed Reconstruction as part of the larger effort to win the war and abolish slavery. He wanted to weaken the Confederacy by creating new state governments that could win broad support from southern white people. The Wade–Davis bill threat-

FREEDOM TO SLAVES!

Whereas, the President of the United States did, on the first day of the present month, issue his *Proclamation* declaring "that *all persons held as Slaves in certain designated States, and parts of States, are, and henceforward shall be free,*" and that the Executive Government of the United States, including the Military and Naval authorities thereof, would recognize and maintain the freedom of said persons. *And Whereas,* the county of *Frederick* is included in the territory designated by the Proclamation of the President, in which the *Slaves should become free,* I therefore hereby notify the citizens of the city of Winchester, and of said County, of said Proclamation, and of my intention to maintain and enforce the same.

I expect all citizens to yield a ready compliance with the Proclamation of the Chief Executive, and I admonish all persons disposed to resist its peaceful enforcement, that upon manifesting such disposition by acts, they will be regarded as rebels in arms against the lawful authority of the Federal Government and dealt with accordingly.

All persons liberated by said Proclamation are admonished to abstain from all violence, and immediately betake themselves to useful occupations.

The officers of this command are admonished and ordered to act in accordance with said proclamation and to yield their ready co-operation in its enforcement.

R. H. Milroy,
Brig. Gen'l Commanding.

Winchester Va.
Jan. 5th, 1863.

A Union commander notifies the citizens of Winchester, Virginia, of President Abraham Lincoln's Emancipation Proclamation. Union officers throughout the South had to improvise arrangements for dealing with African Americans who streamed into Union army camps. For many newly freed slaves, the call for taking up "useful occupations" meant serving the Union forces in their neighborhoods as laborers, cooks, spies, and soldiers.

ened his efforts to build political consensus within the southern states, so Lincoln vetoed it.

As Union armies occupied parts of the South, commanders improvised a variety of arrangements involving confiscated plantations and the African American labor force. For example, in 1862 General Benjamin F. Butler initiated a policy of transforming slaves on Louisiana sugar plantations into wage laborers under the close supervision of occupying federal troops. Butler's policy required slaves to remain on the estates of loyal planters, where they would receive wages according to a fixed schedule, as well as food and medical care for the aged and sick. Abandoned plantations would be leased to northern investors.

In January 1865 General William T. Sherman issued Special Field Order No. 15, setting aside the Sea Islands off the Georgia coast and a portion of the South Carolina low-country rice fields for the exclusive settlement of freed people. Each family would receive forty acres of land and the loan of mules from the army—the origin, perhaps, of the famous "forty acres and a mule" idea that would soon capture the imagination of African Americans throughout the South. Sherman's intent was to relieve the demands placed on his army by the thousands of impoverished African Americans who followed his march to the sea. By the summer of 1865 some 40,000 freed people, eager to take advantage of the general's order, had been settled on 400,000 acres of "Sherman land."

Conflicts within the Republican party prevented the development of a systematic land distribution program. In March 1865 Congress established the Freedmen's Bureau. Along with offering provisions, clothing, and fuel to destitute former slaves, the bureau was charged with supervising and managing "all the abandoned lands in the South and the control of all subjects relating to refugees and freedmen." The act that established the bureau also stated that forty acres of abandoned or confiscated land could be leased to freed slaves or white Unionists, who would have an option to purchase after three years and "such title thereto as the United States can convey."

On April 14, 1865, while attending the theater in Washington, President Lincoln was shot by John Wilkes Booth. At the time of his assassination, Lincoln's Reconstruction policy remained unsettled and incomplete. In its broad outlines the president's plans had seemed to favor a speedy restoration of the southern states to the Union and a minimum of federal intervention in their affairs. But with his death the specifics of postwar Reconstruction would have to be hammered out by a new president, Andrew Johnson of Tennessee, a Democrat whose personality, political background, and racist leanings put him at odds with a Republican-controlled Congress.

Andrew Johnson and Presidential Reconstruction

Andrew Johnson, a Democrat and former slaveholder, was a most unlikely successor to the martyred Lincoln. By trade a tailor, educated by his wife, Johnson overcame his impoverished background and served as state legislator, governor, and U.S. senator. Throughout his career he had championed yeoman farmers and viewed the South's plantation aristocrats with contempt.

In 1864 the Republicans, determined to broaden their appeal to include northern and border state "War Democrats," nominated Johnson, the only southern member of the U.S. Senate to remain loyal to the Union, for vice president. But despite Johnson's success in the 1864 campaign, many Radical Republicans distrusted him. In the immediate aftermath of Lincoln's murder, however, Johnson appeared to side with those Radical Republicans who sought to treat the South as a conquered province.

But support for Johnson quickly faded as the new president's policies unfolded. Johnson defined Reconstruction as the province of the executive, not the legislative, branch, and he planned to restore the Union as quickly as possible. He blamed individual Southerners—the planter elite—rather than entire states for leading the South down the disastrous road to secession.

In the spring of 1865 Johnson granted amnesty and pardon, including restoration of property rights except slaves, to all Confederates who pledged loyalty to the Union and support for emancipation. Fourteen classes of Southerners, mostly major Confederate officials and wealthy landowners, were excluded. But these men could apply individually for presidential pardons. During his tenure Johnson pardoned roughly 90 percent of those who applied. Significantly, he instituted this plan while Congress was not in session. Johnson also appointed provisional governors for several former Confederate states and set highly favorable terms for readmission to the Union. By the fall of 1865 ten of the eleven Confederate states claimed to have met Johnson's requirements to reenter the Union.

Andrew Johnson used the term *restoration* rather than *reconstruction*. A lifelong Democrat with ambitions to be elected president on his own in 1868, Johnson hoped to build a new political coalition composed of northern Democrats, conservative Republicans, and southern Unionists. Firmly committed to white supremacy, he opposed political rights for the freedmen. Johnson's open sympathy for his fellow white Southerners, his antiblack bias, and his determination to control the course of Reconstruction placed him on a collision course with the powerful Radical wing of the Republican party.

The Radical Republican Vision

Most Radicals were men whose careers had been shaped by the slavery controversy. At the core of their thinking lay a deep belief in equal political rights and equal economic opportunity, both guaranteed by a powerful national government. They argued that once free labor, universal education, and equal rights were implanted in the South, that region would be able to share in the North's material wealth, progress, and social mobility.

In the Radicals' view, the power of the federal government would be central to the remaking of southern society, especially in guaranteeing civil rights and suffrage for freedmen. In the most far-reaching proposal, Representative Thaddeus Stevens of Pennsylvania called for the confiscation of 400 million acres belonging to the wealthiest 10 percent of Southerners, to be redistributed to black and white yeomen and northern land buyers.

Northern Republicans were especially outraged by the "Black Codes" passed by southern states to restrict the freedom of the black labor force and keep freed people as close to slave status as possible. Laborers who left their jobs before contracts expired would forfeit wages already earned and be subject to arrest by any white citizen. Vagrancy, very broadly defined, was punishable by fines and involuntary plantation labor. Apprenticeship clauses obliged black children to work without pay for employers. Some states attempted to bar African Americans from land ownership. Other laws specifically denied African Americans equality with white people in civil rights, excluding them from juries and prohibiting interracial marriages.

The Black Codes underscored the unwillingness of white Southerners to accept the full meaning of freedom for African Americans. The Radicals, although not a majority of their party, were joined by moderate Republicans as growing numbers of Northerners grew suspicious of white southern intransigence and the denial of political rights to freedmen. When the Thirty-Ninth Congress convened in December 1865, the large Republican majority prevented the seating of the white Southerners elected to Congress under President Johnson's provisional state governments. Republicans also established the Joint Committee on Reconstruction. After hearing extensive testimony from a broad range of witnesses, it concluded that not only were old Confederates back in power in the South, but that Black Codes and racial violence necessitated increased protection for African Americans.

As a result, in the spring of 1866 Congress passed two important bills designed to aid African Americans. The landmark Civil Rights bill, which bestowed full citizenship upon African Americans, overturned the 1857 *Dred Scott* decision and the Black Codes. It defined all people born in the United States (except Indian peoples) as national citizens, and it enumerated various rights, including the rights to make and enforce contracts, to sue, to give evidence, and to buy and sell property. Under this bill, African Americans acquired "full and equal benefit of all laws and proceedings for the security of person and property as is enjoyed by white citizens."

Congress also voted to enlarge the scope of the Freedmen's Bureau, empowering it to build schools and pay teachers, and also to establish courts to prosecute those charged with depriving African Americans of their civil rights. The bureau achieved important, if limited, success in aiding African Americans. Bureau-run schools helped lay the foundation for southern public education. The bureau's network of courts allowed freed people to bring suits against white people in disputes involving violence, nonpayment of wages, or unfair division of crops.

An angry President Johnson vetoed both of these bills. But his intemperate attacks on the Radicals—he damned them as traitors unwilling to reunite the Union—rallied the united moderate and Radical Republicans, and they succeeded in overriding the vetoes. Congressional Republicans, led by the Radical faction, were now united in challenging the president's power to direct Reconstruction and in using national authority to define and protect the rights of citizens.

In June 1866, fearful that the Civil Rights Act might be declared unconstitutional and eager to settle the basis for the seating of southern representatives, Congress passed the Fourteenth Amendment. The amendment defined national citizenship to include former slaves ("all persons born or naturalized in the United States") and prohibited the states from violating the privileges of citizens without due process of law. It also empowered Congress to reduce the representation of any state that denied the suffrage to males over twenty-one. Republicans adopted the Fourteenth Amendment as their platform for the 1866 congressional elections and suggested that southern states would have to ratify it as a condition of readmission. President Johnson, meanwhile, took to the stump in August to support conservative Democratic and Republican candidates. His unrestrained speeches often degenerated into harangues, alienating many voters and aiding the Republican cause.

For their part, the Republicans began an effective campaign tradition known as "waving the bloody shirt"—reminding northern voters of the hundreds of thousands of Yankee soldiers left dead or maimed by the war. In November 1866 the Republicans increased their majority in both the House and the Senate and gained control of all the northern states.

Congressional Reconstruction and the Impeachment Crisis

United against Johnson, Radical Republicans and their moderate allies took control of Reconstruction early in 1867. In March Congress passed the First Reconstruction Act over Johnson's veto. This act divided the South into five military districts subject to martial law. To achieve restoration, southern states were first required to call new constitutional conventions, elected by universal manhood suffrage. Once these states had drafted new constitutions, guaranteed African Ameri-

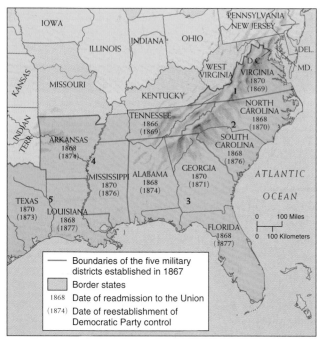

Reconstruction of the South, 1866–1877 *Dates for the readmission of former Confederate states to the Union and the return of Democrats to power varied according to the specific political situation in those states.*

can voting rights, and ratified the Fourteenth Amendment, they were eligible for readmission to the Union.

Congress also passed several laws aimed at limiting Johnson's power. One of these, the Tenure of Office Act, stipulated that any officeholder appointed by the president with the Senate's advice and consent could not be removed until the Senate had approved a successor. In this way, congressional leaders could protect Republicans, such as Secretary of War Edwin M. Stanton, entrusted with implementing Congressional Reconstruction. In August 1867, with Congress adjourned, Johnson suspended Stanton and appointed General Ulysses S. Grant interim secretary of war. This enabled the president to remove generals in the field that he judged to be too radical and replace them with men who were sympathetic to his own views. It also served as a challenge to the Tenure of Office Act. In January 1868, when the Senate overruled Stanton's suspension, Grant broke openly with Johnson in a bitter dispute. Stanton resumed his position and barricaded himself in his office when Johnson attempted to remove him once again.

Outraged by Johnson's relentless obstructionism and seizing upon his violation of the Tenure of Office Act as a pretext, Radical and moderate Republicans in the House of Representatives again joined forces and voted to impeach the president by a vote of 126 to 47 on February 24, 1868. To ensure the support of moderate Republicans, the articles of impeachment focused on violations of the Tenure of Office Act, leaving unstated the Republicans' real reasons for wanting the president removed: Johnson's political views and his opposition to the Reconstruction Acts.

Behind the scenes during his Senate trial, Johnson agreed to abide by the Reconstruction Acts. An influential group of moderate Senate Republicans feared the damage a conviction might do to the constitutional separation of powers. They also worried about the political and economic policies that might be pursued by the man who would succeed Johnson: Benjamin Wade, the Radical president pro tem of the Senate. In May the Senate voted thirty-five for conviction, nineteen for acquittal—one vote shy of the two-thirds necessary for removal from office. Johnson's narrow acquittal established the precedent that only criminal actions by a president—not political disagreements—warranted removal from office.

The Election of 1868

Sobered by the close impeachment vote, Johnson cooperated with Congress for the remainder of his term. In 1868 seven states (Arkansas, Alabama, Florida, Georgia, Louisiana, North Carolina, and South Carolina) ratified the revised constitutions, elected Republican governments, and ratified the Fourteenth Amendment. Having done so, they rejoined the Union. Although Mississippi, Texas, and Virginia still awaited readmission to the Union, the presidential election of 1868 offered some hope that the Civil War's legacy of sectional hate and racial tension might finally ease.

Republicans nominated Ulysses S. Grant, the North's foremost military hero. Grant enjoyed tremendous popularity after the war, especially when he broke with Johnson. Totally lacking in political experience, Grant admitted after receiving the nomination that he had been forced into it in spite of himself.

Significantly, at the very moment that the South was being forced to enfranchise former slaves as a prerequisite for readmission to the Union, the Republicans rejected a campaign plank endorsing black suffrage in the North. Their platform left "the question of suffrage in all the loyal States . . . to the people of those States." State referendums calling for black suffrage failed in eleven northern states between 1865 and 1868, succeeding only in Iowa and Minnesota. The Democrats, determined to reverse congressional Reconstruction, nominated Horatio Seymour, former governor of New York and a long-time foe of emancipation and supporter of states' rights.

OVERVIEW

RECONSTRUCTION AMENDMENTS TO THE CONSTITUTION, 1865–1870

Amendment and Date Passed by Congress	Main Provisions	Ratification Process (3/4 of all states including ex-Confederate states required)
13 (January 1865)	Prohibited slavery in the United States	December 1865 (27 states, including 8 southern states)
14 (June 1866)	• Conferred national citizenship on all persons born or naturalized in the United States • Reduced state representation in Congress proportionally for any state disfranchising male citizens • Denied former Confederates the right to hold state or national office • Repudiated Confederate debt.	July 1868 (after Congress makes ratification a prerequisite for readmission of ex-Confederate states to the Union)
15 (February 1869)	Prohibited denial of suffrage because of race, color, or previous condition of servitude	March 1870 (ratification required for readmission of Virginia, Texas, Mississippi, and Georgia)

The Ku Klux Klan, founded as a Tennessee social club in 1866, threatened, whipped, and murdered black and white Republicans to prevent them from voting. This terrorism enabled the Democrats to carry Georgia and Louisiana, but such tactics ultimately cost the Democrats votes in the North. In the final tally, Grant carried twenty-six of the thirty-four states for an electoral college victory of 214 to 80. But he received a popular majority of less than 53 percent, beating Seymour by only 306,000 votes. Significantly, more than 500,000 African American voters cast their ballots for Grant, demonstrating their overwhelming support for the Republican party. The Republicans also maintained overwhelming majorities in both houses of Congress.

In February 1869 Congress passed the Fifteenth Amendment, providing that "the right of citizens of the United States to vote shall not be abridged . . . on account of race, color, or previous condition of servitude." To enhance the chances of ratification, Congress required the three remaining unreconstructed states—Mississippi, Texas, and Virginia—to ratify both the Fourteenth and Fifteenth Amendments before readmission. They did so and rejoined the Union in early 1870. The Fifteenth Amendment was ratified in February 1870. In the narrow sense of simply readmitting the former confederate states to the Union, Reconstruction was complete.

Woman Suffrage and Reconstruction

Many women's rights advocates had long been active in the abolitionist movement. The Fourteenth and Fifteenth amendments, which granted citizenship and the vote to freedmen, both inspired and frustrated these activists. For example, Elizabeth Cady Stanton and Susan B. Anthony, two leaders with long involvement in both the antislavery and feminist movements, objected to the inclusion of the word *male* in the Fourteenth Amendment. "If that word 'male' be inserted," Stanton predicted in 1866, "it will take us a century at least to get it out."

Insisting that the causes of the African American vote and women's vote were linked, Stanton, Anthony, and Lucy Stone founded the Equal Rights Association in 1866. The group launched a series of lobbying and petition campaigns to remove racial and sexual restrictions on voting from state constitutions. Throughout the nation, the old abolitionist organizations and the Republican party emphasized passage of the Fourteenth and Fifteenth Amendments and withdrew funds and support from the cause of

Susan B. Anthony (1820–1906) and Elizabeth Cady Stanton (1815–1902), the two most influential leaders of the woman suffrage movement, c. 1892. Anthony and Stanton broke with their longtime abolitionist allies after the Civil War when they opposed the Fifteenth Amendment. They argued that the doctrine of universal manhood suffrage it embodied would give constitutional authority to the claim that men were the social and political superiors of women. As founders of the militant National Woman Suffrage Association, Stanton and Anthony established an independent woman suffrage movement with a broader spectrum of goals for women's rights and drew millions of women into public life during the late nineteenth century.

woman suffrage. Disagreements over these amendments divided woman suffragists for decades.

The radical wing, led by Stanton and Anthony, opposed the Fifteenth Amendment, arguing that ratification would establish an "aristocracy of sex," enfranchising all men while leaving women without political privileges. They argued for a Sixteenth Amendment that would secure the vote for women. Other women's rights activists, including Lucy Stone and Frederick Douglass, asserted that "this hour belongs to the

Negro." They feared a debate over woman suffrage at the national level would jeopardize passage of the two amendments.

By 1869 woman suffragists had split into two competing organizations: the moderate American Woman Suffrage Association (AWSA), which sought the support of men, and the more radical all-female National Woman Suffrage Association (NWSA). For the NWSA, the vote represented only one part of a broad spectrum of goals inherited from the Declaration of Sentiments manifesto adopted at the first women's convention held in 1848 at Seneca Falls (see Chapter 13).

Although women did not win the vote in this period, they did establish an independent suffrage movement that eventually drew millions of women into political life. The NWSA in particular demonstrated that self-government and democratic participation in the public sphere were crucial for women's emancipation. The failure of woman suffrage after the Civil War was less a result of factional fighting than of the larger defeat of Radical Reconstruction and the ideal of expanded citizenship.

THE MEANING OF FREEDOM

The deep desire for independence from white control formed the underlying aspiration of newly freed slaves. For their part, most southern white people sought to restrict the boundaries of that independence. As individuals and as members of communities transformed by emancipation, former slaves struggled to establish economic, political, and cultural autonomy. They built upon the twin pillars of slave culture—the family and the church—to consolidate and expand African American institutions and thereby laid the foundation for the modern African American community.

Emancipation greatly expanded the choices available to African Americans. It helped build confidence in their ability to effect change without deferring to white people. Freedom also meant greater uncertainty and risk. But the vast majority of African Americans were more than willing to take their chances.

Moving About

The first impulse of many emancipated slaves was to test their freedom. The simplest, most obvious way to do this involved leaving home. By walking off a plantation, coming and going without restraint or fear of punishment, African Americans could taste freedom. Throughout the summer and fall of 1865, observers in the South noted the enormous numbers of freed people on the move.

"Leaving for Kansas," Harper's Weekly, May 17, 1879. *This drawing depicts a group of southern freed people on their way to Kansas. Black disillusionment following the end of Reconstruction led thousands of African Americans to migrate to Kansas, where they hoped to find the political rights, economic opportunities, and freedom from violence denied them in the South. Most of these "Exodusts" (after the biblical story of the Israelite Exodus from Egypt) lacked the capital or experience to establish themselves as independent farmers on the Great Plains. Yet few chose to go back to the South, where their former masters had returned to political and economic power.*

Many freed people went out of their way to reject the old subservience. Moving about freely was one way of doing this, as was refusing to tip one's hat to white people, ignoring former masters or mistresses in the streets, and refusing to step aside on sidewalks.

The African American Family

Emancipation allowed freed people the chance to strengthen family ties. For many former slaves, freedom meant the opportunity to reunite with long-lost family members. To track down relatives, freed people trekked to faraway places, put ads in newspapers, sought the help of Freedmen's Bureau agents, and questioned anyone who might have information about loved ones. Many thousands of family reunions took place after the war.

Thousands of African American couples who had lived together under slavery streamed to military and civilian authorities and demanded to be legally married. By 1870 the two-parent household was the norm for a large majority of African Americans.

Emancipation brought changes to gender roles within the African American family as well. Black men could now serve on juries, vote, and hold office; black women, like their white counterparts, could not. Freedmen's Bureau agents designated the husband as household head and established lower wage scales for women laborers. African American editors, preachers, and politicians regularly quoted the biblical injunction that wives submit to their husbands.

African American men asserted their male authority, denied under slavery, by insisting their wives work at home instead of in the fields. Yet African American women continued to work outside the home, engaging in seasonal field labor for wages or working a family's rented plot. Most rural black families barely eked out a living, so the labor of every family member was essential to survival. The key difference from slave times was that African American families themselves, not white masters and overseers, decided when and where women and children worked.

Yet many who left their old neighborhoods returned soon afterward to seek work in the general vicinity, or even on the plantation they had left. Many wanted to separate themselves from former owners, but not from familial ties and friendships. Others moved away altogether, seeking jobs in nearby towns and cities. A large number of former slaves left predominantly white counties, where they felt more vulnerable and isolated, for new lives in the relative comfort of predominantly black communities. Many African Americans, attracted by schools, churches, and fraternal societies as well as the army, preferred the city. Between 1865 and 1870, the African American population of the South's largest ten cities doubled while the white population increased by only 10 percent.

Disgruntled planters had difficulty accepting African American independence. During slavery, they had expected obedience, submission, and loyalty from African Americans. Now, many could not understand why so many former slaves wanted to leave despite urgent pleas to continue working at the old place.

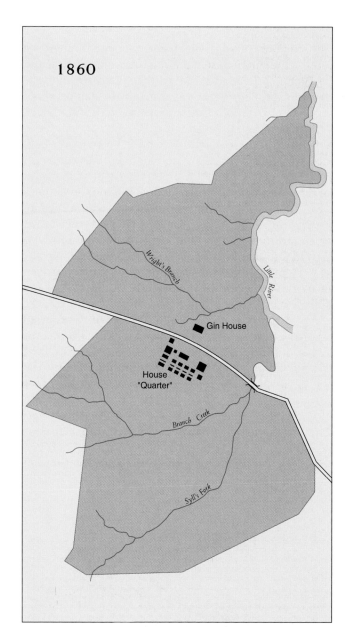

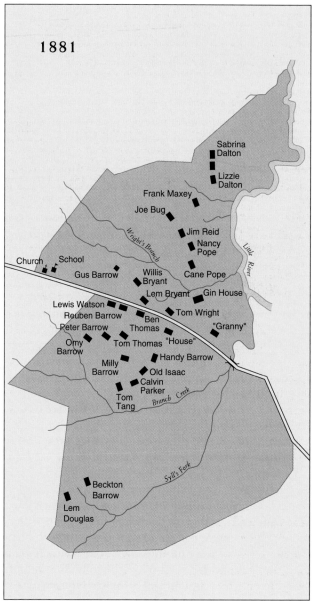

The Barrow Plantation, Oglethorpe County, Georgia, 1860 and 1881 (approx. 2,000 acres)   *These two maps, based on drawings from* Scribner's Monthly, *April 1881, show some of the changes brought by emancipation. In 1860 the plantation's entire black population lived in the communal slave quarters, right next to the white master's house. In 1881 black sharecropper and tenant families lived on individual plots, spread out across the land. The former slaves had also built their own school and church.*

Labor and Land After Slavery

Most newly emancipated African Americans aspired to quit the plantations and to make new lives for themselves. Leaving the plantation was not as simple as walking off. Some freed people did find jobs in railroad building, mining, ranching, or construction work. Others raised subsistence crops and tended vegetable gardens on squatters' land. The majority hoped to become self-sufficient farmers. Many former slaves believed they were entitled to the land they had worked throughout their lives. This was not a pipe dream. Frequent reference in the Congress and the press to the question of land distribution made the idea of "forty acres and a mule" a matter of serious public debate.

Above all, African Americans sought economic autonomy, and ownership of land promised the most independence. But by 1866 the federal government had already pulled back from the various wartime experiments involving the breaking up of large plantations and the leasing of small plots to individual families. President Johnson directed General Oliver O. Howard of the Freedmen's Bureau to evict tens of thousands of freed people settled on confiscated and abandoned land in southeastern Virginia, southern Louisiana, and the Georgia and South Carolina low country. These evictions created a deep sense of betrayal among African Americans. A former Mississippi slave, Merrimon Howard, bitterly noted that African Americans had been left with "no land, no house, not so much as a place to lay our head. . . . We were friends on the march, brothers on the battlefield, but in the peaceful pursuits of life it seems that we are strangers."

By the late 1860s, sharecropping had emerged as the dominant form of working the land. Sharecropping represented a compromise between planters and former slaves. Under sharecropping arrangements, individual families contracted with landowners to be responsible for a specific plot. Large plantations were thus broken into family-sized farms. Generally, sharecropper families received one-third of the year's crop if the owner furnished implements, seed, and draft animals, or one-half if they provided their own supplies. African Americans preferred sharecropping to gang labor—a system in which large groups of freedmen worked under labor contracts for planters, who often cheated them—as it allowed families to set their own hours and tasks and offered freedom from white supervision and control. For planters, the system stabilized the work force by requiring sharecroppers to remain until the harvest and to employ all family members. It also offered a way around the chronic shortage of cash and credit that plagued the postwar South.

By 1880 about 80 percent of the land in the black belt states—Mississippi, Alabama, and Georgia—had been divided into family-sized farms. Nearly three-quarters of black southerners were sharecroppers. Through much of the black belt, family and community were one. Often several families worked adjoining parcels of land in common, pooling their labor in order to get by. Men usually oversaw crop production. Women went to the fields seasonally during planting or harvesting, but they mainly tended to household chores and child care. In addition, women often held jobs that might bring in cash, such as raising chickens or taking in laundry. The cotton harvest engaged all members of the community, from the oldest to the youngest.

African American Churches and Schools

The creation of separate African American churches proved the most lasting and important element of the energetic institution building that went on in post-Emancipation years. Before the Civil War southern Protestant churches had relegated slaves and free African Americans to second-class membership. Black worshipers were required to sit in the back during services, they were denied any role in church governance, and they were excluded from Sunday schools. Even in larger cities, where all-black congregations sometimes built their own churches, the law required white pastors. In rural areas, slaves preferred their own preachers to the sermons of local, white ministers who quoted scripture to justify slavery and white supremacy.

In communities around the South, African Americans now pooled their resources to buy land and build their own churches. Before these structures were completed, they might hold services in a railroad boxcar, where Atlanta's First Baptist Church began, or in an outdoor arbor, the original site of the First Baptist Church of Memphis. Churches became the center not only for religious life but for many other activities that defined the African American community: schools, picnics, festivals, and political meetings. They also helped spawn a host of organizations devoted to benevolence and mutual aid, such as burial societies, Masonic lodges, temperance clubs, and trade associations.

"Electioneering at the South," Harper's Weekly, July 25, 1868. Throughout the Reconstruction-era South, newly freed slaves took a keen interest in both local and national political affairs. The presence of women and children at these campaign gatherings illustrates the importance of political issues to the entire African American community.

The church became the first social institution fully controlled by African Americans. In nearly every community ministers, respected for their speaking and organizational skills, were among the most influential leaders. By 1877 the great majority of black Southerners had withdrawn from white-dominated churches and belonged to black Baptist or Methodist churches.

African American communities received important educational aid from outside organizations. By 1869 the Freedmen's Bureau was supervising nearly 3,000 schools serving more than 150,000 students throughout the South. Over half the roughly 3,300 teachers in these schools were African Americans, many of whom had been free before the Civil War. Other teachers included dedicated northern white women volunteers. Throughout the South in 1865 and 1866, African Americans raised money to build schoolhouses, buy supplies, and pay teachers. Black artisans donated labor for construction, and black families offered room and board to teachers. By 1870 black Southerners, most of them impoverished, had managed to raise over $1 million for education, a feat that long remained a source of collective pride.

The Origins of African American Politics

Inclusion rather than separation formed the keynote of early African American political activity. In 1865 and 1866 African Americans throughout the South organized scores of mass meetings, parades, and petitions that demanded civil equality and the right to vote. In the cities the growing web of churches and fraternal societies helped bolster early efforts at political organization.

Hundreds of African American delegates, selected by local meetings or churches, attended statewide political conventions held throughout the South in 1865 and 1866. Convention debates sometimes reflected the tensions within African American communities, such as friction between poorer former slaves and better-off free black people, or between lighter- and darker-skinned African Americans. But most of these state gatherings concentrated on passing resolutions on issues that united all African Americans. The central concerns were suffrage and equality before the law.

The passage of the First Reconstruction Act in 1867 encouraged even more political activity among African Americans. The military started registering the South's electorate, ultimately enrolling approximately 735,000 black and 635,000 white voters in the ten unreconstructed states. Five states—Alabama, Florida, Louisiana, Mississippi, and South Carolina—had black electoral majorities. Fewer than half the registered white voters participated in the elections for state constitutional conventions in 1867 and 1868. In contrast, four-fifths of the registered black voters cast ballots in these elections.

The Union League, begun during the war, became the political voice of the former slaves. Union League chapters brought together local African Americans, soldiers, and Freedmen's Bureau agents to demand the vote and an end to legal discrimination against African Americans. It brought out African American voters, instructed freedmen in the rights and duties of citizenship, and promoted Republican candidates.

In 1867 and 1868 the promise of Radical Reconstruction enlarged the scope of African American political participation and brought new leaders to the fore. Many were teachers, preachers, or others possessing useful skills, such as literacy. For most ordinary African Americans, politics was inseparable from

This poster, ca. 1880, honored seven prominent ex-slaves, including U.S. Senators Hiram R. Revels and Blanche K. Bruce, both representing Mississippi. In the center is Frederick Douglass. This poster was typical of many other Reconstruction-era prints celebrating the entry of African Americans into state and national legislatures.

economic issues, especially the land question. Grassroots political organizations often intervened in local disputes with planters over the terms of labor contracts. African American political groups closely followed the congressional debates over Reconstruction policy and agitated for land confiscation and distribution. Perhaps most important, politics was the only arena where black and white Southerners might engage each other on an equal basis.

SOUTHERN POLITICS AND SOCIETY

By the summer of 1868, when the South had returned to the Union, the majority of Republicans believed the task of Reconstruction to be finished. Ultimately, they put their faith in a political solution to the problems facing the vanquished South. That meant nurturing a viable two-party system in the southern states, where no Republican party had ever existed. If that could be accomplished, Republicans and Democrats would compete for votes, offices, and influence, just as they did in northern states.

Yet over the next decade the political structure created in the southern states proved too restricted and fragile to sustain itself. Federal troops were needed to protect Republican governments and their supporters from violent opposition. Congressional action to monitor southern elections and protect black voting rights became routine. Despite initial successes, southern Republicanism proved an unstable coalition of often conflicting elements, unable to sustain effective power for very long. By 1877 Democrats had regained political control of all the former Confederate states.

Southern Republicans

Three major groups composed the fledgling Republican coalition in the postwar South. The first group, African American voters, made up a large majority of southern Republicans throughout the Reconstruction era.

The second group consisted of white Northerners, derisively called *carpetbaggers* by native white Southerners. Most carpetbaggers combined a desire for personal gain with a commitment to reform the "unprogressive" South by developing its material resources and introducing Yankee institutions such as free labor and free public schools. Most were veterans of the Union Army who stayed in the South after the war. Others included Freedmen's Bureau agents and businessmen who had invested capital in cotton plantations and other economic enterprises. Although they made up a tiny percentage of the population, carpetbaggers played a disproportionately large role in southern politics. They won a large share of Reconstruction offices, particularly in Florida, South Carolina, and Louisiana and in areas with large African American constituencies.

The third major group of southern Republicans comprised native whites perjoratively called *scalawags*. They had more diverse backgrounds and motives than the northern-born Republicans. Loyalists during the war, traditional enemies of the planter elite (most were small farmers), these white Southerners looked to the Republican party for help in settling old scores and relief from debt and wartime devastation.

Deep contradictions strained the alliance of these three groups. Republican state conventions in 1867 and 1868 voiced support for internal improvements, public schools, debt relief, and railroad building. Yet few white Southerners identified with the political and economic aspirations of African Americans. Nearly every party convention split between "confiscation radicals" (generally African Americans) and moderate elements committed to white control of the party and to economic development that offered more to outside investors than to impoverished African Americans and poor whites.

Reconstructing the States: A Mixed Record

With the old Confederate leaders barred from political participation, and with carpetbaggers and newly enfranchised African Americans representing many of the plantation districts, Republicans managed to dominate the ten southern constitutional conventions of 1867–69. Most of these conventions produced constitutions that expanded democracy and the public role of the state. The new documents guaranteed the political and civil rights of African Americans, and they abolished property qualifications for officeholding and jury service, as well as imprisonment for debt. They created the first state-funded systems of education in the South, to be administered by state commissioners. The new constitutions also mandated establishment of orphanages, penitentiaries, and homes for the insane. In 1868, only three years after the end of the war, Republicans came to power in most of the southern states. By 1869 new constitutions had been ratified in all the old Confederate states. "These constitutions and governments," one South Carolina Democratic newspaper vowed bitterly, "will last just as long as the bayonets which ushered them into being, shall keep them in existence, and not one day longer."

Republican governments in the South faced a continual crisis of legitimacy that limited their ability to legislate change. They had to balance reform urges against ongoing efforts to gain acceptance, especially by white Southerners. Their achievements were thus mixed. In the realm of race relations there was a clear thrust toward equal rights and against discrimination. Republican legislatures followed up the federal Civil Rights Act of 1866 with various antidiscrimination clauses in new constitutions and laws prescribing harsh penalties for civil rights violations. African Americans could now be employed in police forces and fire departments, serve on juries, school boards, and city councils, and hold public office at all levels of government.

However, segregation became the norm in public school systems. African American leaders often accepted segregation because they feared that insistence on integrated education would jeopardize funding for the new school systems. African Americans opposed constitutional language requiring racial segregation in schools, but most were less interested in the abstract ideal of integrated education than in ensuring educational opportunities for their children and employment for African American teachers.

Segregation in railroad cars and other public places was more objectionable to African Americans. By the early 1870s, as black influence and assertiveness grew, laws guaranteeing equal access to transportation and public accommodation were passed in many states. By and large, though, such civil rights laws were difficult to enforce in local communities.

In economic matters, Republican governments failed to fulfill African Americans' hopes of obtaining land. Few former slaves had the cash to buy land in the open market, so they looked to the state for help. Republicans tried to weaken the plantation system and promote black ownership by raising taxes on land. Yet even when state governments seized land for nonpayment of taxes, the property was never used to create black homesteads.

Republican leaders envisioned promoting northern-style capitalist development—factories, large towns, and diversified agriculture—in the South through state aid. Much Republican state lawmaking was devoted to encouraging railroad construction. Between 1868 and 1872 the southern railroad system was rebuilt and more than 3,000 new miles of track added, an increase of almost 40 percent. But despite all the new laws, it proved impossible to attract significant amounts of northern and European investment capital. The obsession with railroads drew resources from education and other programs. As in the North, it also opened the doors to widespread corruption and bribery of public officials. Railroad failures eroded public confidence in the Republicans' ability to govern. The "gospel of prosperity" ultimately failed to modernize the economy or solidify the Republican party in the South.

White Resistance and "Redemption"

The emergence of a Republican party in the reconstructed South brought two parties but not a two-party system. The opponents of Reconstruction, the Democrats, refused to acknowledge Republicans' right to participate in southern political life. In these southern Democrats' view, the Republican party was the partisan instrument of the northern Congress, and its support was based primarily upon the votes of former slaves. Because Republicans controlled state governments, this denial of legitimacy meant, in effect, a rejection of state authority itself.

From 1870 to 1872 a resurgent Ku Klux Klan fought an ongoing terrorist campaign against Reconstruction governments and local leaders. Although not centrally organized, the Klan was a powerful presence in nearly every southern state. It acted as a kind of guerrilla military force in the service of the Democratic party, the planter class, and all those who sought the restoration of white supremacy. In October 1870, after Republicans carried Laurens County in South Carolina, bands of white people drove 150 African Americans from their homes and murdered 13 black and white Republican activists. In March 1871 three African Americans were arrested in Meridian, Mississippi, for giving "incendiary" speeches. At their court hearing, Klansmen killed two of the defendants and the Republican judge; thirty more African Americans were murdered in a day of rioting. The single bloodiest episode of Reconstruction era violence took place in Colfax, Louisiana, on Easter Sunday 1873. Nearly 100 African Americans were murdered during a contested election.

Southern Republicans looked to Washington for help. In 1870 and 1871 Congress passed three Enforcement Acts designed to counter racial terrorism. These declared interference with voting a federal offense, provided for federal supervision of voting, and authorized the president to send the army and suspend the writ of habeas corpus in districts declared to be in a state of insurrection. The most sweeping measure was the Ku Klux Klan Act of April 1871, which made the violent infringement of civil and political rights a federal crime punishable by the national government. Attorney General Amos T. Akerman prosecuted hundreds of Klansmen in North Carolina and Mississippi. In October 1871 President Grant sent federal

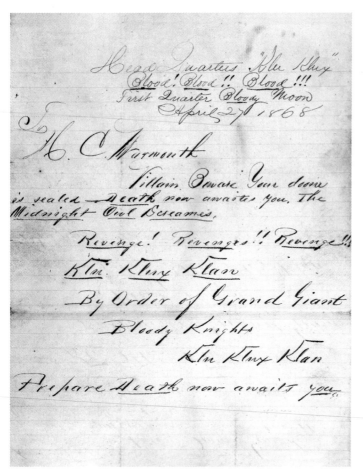

The Ku Klux Klan emerged as a potent political and social force during Reconstruction, terrorizing freed people and their white allies. An 1868 Klan warning threatens Louisiana governor Henry C. Warmoth with death. Warmoth, an Illinois-born "carpetbagger," was the state's first Republican governor. Two Alabama Klansmen, photographed in 1868, wear white hoods to conceal their identities.

troops to occupy nine South Carolina counties and round up thousands of Klan members. By the election of 1872 the federal government's intervention had helped break the Klan's hold and restored relative law and order.

As wartime idealism faded, however, northern Republicans had too much trouble retaining political control in the North to intervene in the South. In 1874 the Democrats gained a majority in the House of Representatives for the first time since 1856. Key northern states also began to fall to the Democrats. Northern Republicans slowly abandoned the freedmen and their white allies in the South.

Gradually, conservative Democrats "redeemed" one state after another. Virginia and Tennessee led the way in 1869, followed by North Carolina in 1870, Georgia in 1871, Texas in 1873, and Arkansas and Alabama in 1874. In Mississippi white conservatives used violence and intimidation to wrest control in 1875 and "redeemed" the state the following year. Republican infighting in Louisiana in 1873 and 1874 led to a series of contested election results, including bloody clashes between black militia and armed whites, and finally to "redemption" by the Democrats in 1877. Once these states returned to Democratic control, African Americans faced obstacles to voting, more stringent controls on plantation labor, and deep cuts in social services.

Several Supreme Court rulings involving the Fourteenth and Fifteenth Amendments effectively constrained federal protection of African American civil rights. In the so-called Slaughterhouse cases of 1873, the Court issued its first ruling on the Fourteenth Amendment. The cases involved a Louisiana charter that gave a New Orleans meat-packing company a monopoly over the city's butchering business, on the grounds of protecting public health. A rival group of butchers had sued, claiming the law violated the Fourteenth Amendment, which prohibited states from depriving any person of life, liberty, or property without due process of law. The Court held that the Fourteenth Amendment protected only the former slaves, not butchers, and that it protected only *national* citizenship rights, not the regulatory powers of states. The ruling in effect denied the original intent of the Fourteenth Amendment: to protect against state infringement of national citizenship rights as spelled out in the Bill of Rights.

Three other decisions curtailed federal protection of black civil rights. In *U.S. v. Reese* (1876) and *U.S. v. Cruikshank* (1876) the Court restricted congressional power to enforce the Ku Klux Klan Act by holding that the Fourteenth Amendment extended the federal power to protect civil rights only in cases involving discrimination by states; discrimination by individuals or groups was not covered. The Court also ruled that the Fifteenth Amendment did not guarantee a citizen's right to vote; it only barred certain specific grounds for denying suffrage: "race, color, or previous condition of servitude." This opened the door for southern states to disfranchise African Americans for allegedly nonracial reasons. States back under Democratic control began to limit African American voting by passing laws restricting voter eligibility through poll taxes and property requirements. "Grandfather clauses," which restricted voting to those descended from a grandfather who had voted, became an effective tool for limiting black suffrage, because most African Americans had been slaves before Reconstruction. Finally, in the 1883 *Civil Rights Cases* decision, the Court declared the Civil Rights Act of 1875 unconstitutional, holding that the Fourteenth Amendment gave Congress the power to outlaw discrimination by states, but not by private individuals. Together, these Supreme Court decisions marked the end of federal attempts to protect African American rights until well into the next century.

"King Cotton" and the Crop Lien System

The Republicans' vision of a "New South" remade along the lines of the northern economy failed to materialize. Instead, the South declined into the country's poorest agricultural region. Cotton growing had defined the economic life of the large plantations. In the post–Civil War years "King Cotton" expanded its realm, as even greater numbers of small white farmers were forced to switch from substance crops to growing cotton for market.

The spread of the crop lien system as the South's main form of agricultural credit forced more and more farmers, both white and black, into cotton growing. A chronic shortage of capital and banking institutions made local merchants and planters the sole source of credit. They advanced loans to sharecroppers and tenant farmers only in exchange for a lien, or claim, on the year's cotton crop, and they often charged usurious interest rates on advances, while marking up the prices of the goods they sold in their stores. Thus at the end of the year, sharecroppers and tenants found themselves deep in debt to stores (many owned by Northerners) for seed, supplies, and clothing.

The near total dominance of "King Cotton" inhibited economic growth across the region. Unlike midwestern and western farm towns burgeoning from trade in wheat, corn, and livestock, southern communities found themselves almost entirely dependent on the price of one commodity as more and more farmers turned to cotton growing as the only way to obtain credit. Expanding production depressed prices. Competition from new cotton centers in the world market, such as Egypt and India, accelerated the downward spiral. As cotton prices declined alarmingly, from roughly eleven cents per pound in 1875 to five cents in 1894, per capita wealth in the South fell steadily; by the 1890s it equaled only one-third that of the East, Midwest, or West. Cotton dependency also prevented planters from acquiring the capital to purchase the farm equipment needed to profitably cultivate wheat or corn.

By 1880 about one-third of white farmers and nearly three-quarters of African American farmers in the cotton states were sharecroppers or tenants. Many former slaves and poor white people had tried subsistence farming in the undeveloped backcountry. Yet to obtain precious credit, most found themselves forced to produce cotton for market and thus became enmeshed in the debt-ridden crop lien system. In the up-country and newer areas of cultivation, cotton-dominated commercial agriculture, with landless tenants and sharecroppers as the main workforce, had replaced the more diversified subsistence economy of the antebellum era.

RECONSTRUCTING THE NORTH

Abraham Lincoln liked to cite his own rise as proof of the superiority of the northern system of free labor over

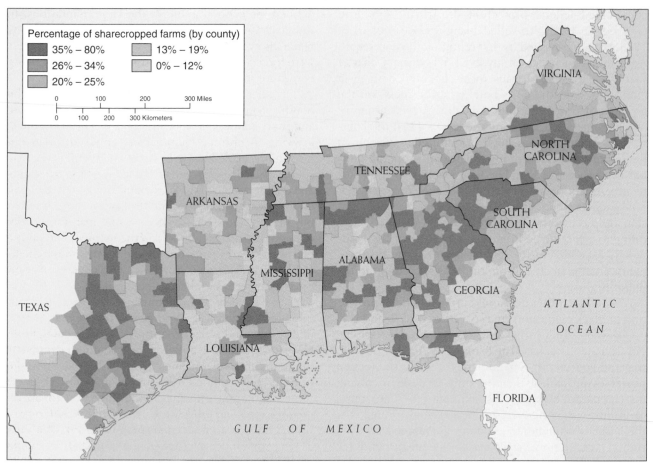

Southern Sharecropping and the Cotton Belt, 1880   *The economic depression of the 1870s forced increasing numbers of southern farmers, both white and black, into sharecropping arrangements. Sharecropping was most pervasive in the cotton belt regions of South Carolina, Georgia, Alabama, Mississippi, and east Texas.*

slavery. But the triumph of the North in the war brought with it fundamental changes in the economy, labor relations, and politics that called Lincoln's ideal vision into question. The spread of the factory system, the growth of large and powerful corporations, and the rapid expansion of capitalist enterprise all hastened the development of a large unskilled and routinized workforce. Rather than becoming independent producers, more and more workers found themselves consigned to a permanent position of wage labor.

The old Republican ideal of a society bound by a harmony of interests had become overshadowed by a grimmer reality of class conflict. A violent national railroad strike in 1877 was broken only with the direct intervention of federal troops. Northern society, like the society of the South, appeared more hierarchical than equal. That same year, the last federal troops withdrew from their southern posts, marking the end of the Reconstruction era. By then, the North had undergone its own reconstruction.

The Age of Capital

In the decade following Appomattox, the North's economy continued the industrial boom begun during the Civil War. By 1873 America's industrial production had grown 75 percent over the 1865 level. By that time, too, the number of nonagricultural workers in the North had surpassed the number of farmers. Between 1860 and 1880 the number of wage earners in manufacturing and construction more than doubled, from 2 million to over 4 million.

COMPLETION OF THE PACIFIC RAILROAD—MEETING OF LOCOMOTIVES OF THE UNION AND CENTRAL PACIFIC LINES: THE ENGINEERS SHAKE HANDS.

Completion of the transcontinental railroad, May 10, 1869, as building crews for the Union Pacific and Central Pacific meet at Promontory Point, Utah. The two locomotive engineers salute each other, while the chief engineers for the two railroads shake hands. Construction had begun simultaneously from Omaha and Sacramento in 1863, with the help of generous subsidies from Congress. Work crews, consisting of thousands of ex-soldiers, Irish immigrants, and imported Chinese laborers, laid nearly 1,800 miles of new track.

The railroad business both symbolized and advanced the new industrial order. Shortly before the Civil War, enthusiasm mounted for a transcontinental line. Private companies took on the huge and expensive job of construction. The federal government funded the project, providing the largest subsidy in American history. An 1864 act bestowed a subsidy of $15,000 per mile of track laid over smooth plains country and varying larger amounts, up to $48,000 per mile, in the foothills and mountains of the Far West. Gangs of Irish American and African American workers were employed to lay track heading west from Omaha, while 10,000 men from China were brought in to handle the difficult work in the Sierra Nevada mountain region. On May 10, 1869, the governor of California, Leland Stanford, traveled to Promontory Point, Utah, to hammer a ceremonial golden spike, marking the finish of the first transcontinental line.

Railroad corporations became America's first big businesses. Railroads required huge outlays of investment capital, and their growth increased the economic power of banks and investment houses centered in Wall Street. Bankers often gained seats on boards of directors, and their access to capital sometimes gave them the real control of lines. A new breed of aggressive entrepreneur sought to ease cutthroat competition by absorbing smaller companies and forming "pools" that set rates and divided the market. A small group of railroad executives, including Cornelius Vanderbilt, Jay Gould, Collis P. Huntington, and James J. Hill, amassed unheard-of fortunes. When he died in 1877, Vanderbilt left his son $100 million. By comparison, a decent annual wage for working a six-day week was around $350.

Railroad promoters, lawyers, and lobbyists became ubiquitous figures in Washington and state capitals, wielding enormous influence among lawmakers. Railroads benefited greatly from government subsidies. Between 1862 and 1872 Congress awarded more than 100 million acres of public lands to railroad companies and provided over $64 million in loans and tax incentives.

Some of the nation's most prominent politicians routinely accepted railroad largesse. The worst scandal of the Grant administration grew out of corruption involving railroad promotion. As a way of diverting funds for the building of the Union Pacific Railroad, an inner circle of Union Pacific stockholders created the dummy Crédit Mobilier construction company. In return for political favors, a group of prominent Republicans received stock in the company. When the scandal broke in 1872, it ruined Vice President Schuyler Colfax politically and led to the censure of two congressmen.

Other industries also boomed in this period as railroad growth stimulated expansion in the production of coal, iron, stone, and lumber. These industries also received significant government aid. For example, under the National Mineral Act of 1866, mining companies received millions of acres of free public land. Oil refining enjoyed a huge expansion in the 1860s and 1870s. As with railroads, an early period of fierce competition soon gave way to concentration. By the late 1870s John D. Rockefeller's Standard Oil

Company controlled almost 90 percent of the nation's oil-refining capacity.

Liberal Republicans and the Election of 1872

With the rapid growth of large-scale, capital-intensive enterprises, Republicans increasingly identified with the interests of business rather than the rights of freedmen or the antebellum ideology of "free labor." The old Civil War–era Radicals had declined in influence. State Republican parties now organized themselves around the spoils of federal patronage rather than grand causes such as preserving the Union or ending slavery. Despite the Crédit Mobilier affair, Republicans had no monopoly on political scandal. In 1871 New York City newspapers reported the shocking story of how Democratic party boss William M. Tweed and his friends had systematically stolen millions of dollars from the city treasury. The Tweed Ring had received enormous bribes and kickbacks from city contractors and businessmen. But to many, the scandal represented only the most extreme case of the routine corruption that now plagued American political life.

By the end of President Grant's first term, a large number of disaffected Republicans sought an alternative. The Liberal Republicans, as they called themselves, emphasized the doctrines of classical economics, stressing the law of supply and demand, free trade, defense of property rights, and individualism. They called for a return to limited government, arguing that bribery, scandal, and high taxes all flowed from excessive state interference in the economy.

Liberal Republicans were also suspicious of expanding democracy. They believed that politics ought to be the province of "the best men"—educated and well-to-do men like themselves, devoted to the "science of government." They proposed civil service reform as the best way to break the hold of party machines on patronage.

Although most Liberal Republicans had enthusiastically supported abolition, the Union cause, and equal rights for freedmen, they now opposed continued federal intervention in the South. The national government had done all it could for the former slaves; they must now take care of themselves. "Root, Hog, or Die" was the harsh advice offered by Horace Greeley, editor of the *New York Tribune*. In the spring of 1872 a diverse collection of Liberal Republicans nominated Greeley to run for president. A longtime foe of the Democratic party, Greeley nonetheless won that party's presidential nomination as well. He made a new policy for the South the center of his campaign against Grant. All Americans, Greeley urged, must put the Civil War behind them and "clasp hands across the bloody chasm."

Grant easily defeated Greeley, carrying every state in the North and winning 56 percent of the popular vote. Most Republicans were not willing to abandon the regular party organization, and waving the bloody shirt was still a potent vote-getter. But the 1872 election accelerated the trend toward federal abandonment of African American citizenship rights. The Liberal Republicans quickly faded as an organized political force, but their ideas helped define an increasingly popular conservative agenda in the North. This agenda included retreat from the ideal of racial justice, fear of trade unions, suspicion of working-class and immigrant political power, celebration of competitive individualism, and opposition to government intervention in economic affairs.

The Depression of 1873

In the fall of 1873 the postwar boom came to an abrupt halt as a severe financial panic triggered a deep economic depression. The collapse resulted from commercial overexpansion, especially speculative investing in the nation's railroad system. By 1876 half the nation's railroads had defaulted on their bonds. Over the next two years over 100 banks folded and 18,000 businesses shut their doors. The depression that began in 1873 lasted 65 months—the longest economic contraction in the nation's history up to that time.

The human toll of the depression was enormous. As factories closed across the nation, the unemployment rate soared to about 15 percent. In many cities the jobless rate was much higher; roughly one-quarter of New York City workers were unemployed in 1874. Many thousands of men took to the road in search of work, and the "tramp" emerged as a new and menacing figure on the social landscape. The Pennsylvania Bureau of Labor Statistics noted that never before had "so many of the working classes, skilled and unskilled . . . been moving from place to place seeking employment that was not to be had." Farmers were also hard hit by the depression. Agricultural output continued to grow, but prices and land values fell sharply. As prices for their crops fell, farmers had a more difficult time repaying their fixed loan obligations; many sank deeper into debt.

Mass meetings of workers in New York and other cities issued calls to government officials to create jobs through public works. But these appeals were rejected. Indeed, many business leaders and political figures denounced even meager efforts at charity.

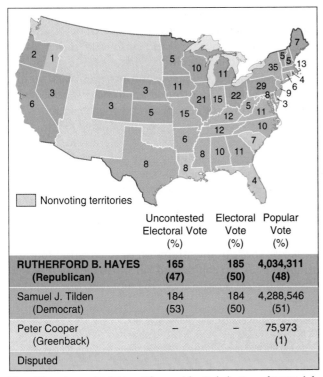

	Uncontested Electoral Vote (%)	Electoral Vote (%)	Popular Vote (%)
RUTHERFORD B. HAYES (Republican)	**165 (47)**	**185 (50)**	**4,034,311 (48)**
Samuel J. Tilden (Democrat)	184 (53)	184 (50)	4,288,546 (51)
Peter Cooper (Greenback)	–	–	75,973 (1)
Disputed			

Nonvoting territories

The Election of 1876   *The presidential election of 1876 left the nation without a clear-cut winner.*

They saw the depression as a natural, if painful, part of the business cycle, one that would allow only the strongest enterprises (and workers) to survive.

The depression of the 1870s prompted workers and farmers to question the old free-labor ideology that celebrated a harmony of interests in northern society. More people voiced anger at and distrust of large corporations that exercised great economic power from outside their communities.

The Electoral Crisis of 1876

With the economy mired in depression, Democrats looked forward to capturing the White House in 1876. New scandals plaguing the Grant administration had weakened the Republican party. In 1875 there surfaced a conspiracy between distillers and U.S. revenue agents to cheat the government out of millions in tax revenues. The government secured indictments against over 200 members of this "Whiskey Ring," including Orville E. Babcock, Grant's private secretary. Though acquitted thanks to Grant's deposition, Babcock resigned in disgrace. In 1876 Secretary of War William W. Belknap was impeached for receiving bribes for the sale of trading posts in Indian Territory.

Democrats nominated Governor Samuel J. Tilden of New York, who brought impeccable reform credentials to his candidacy for president. In 1871 he had helped expose and prosecute the "Tweed Ring" in New York City. As governor he had toppled the "Canal Ring," a graft-ridden scheme involving inflated contracts for repairs on the Erie Canal. In their platform the Democrats linked the issue of corruption to Republican Reconstruction policies that had encouraged "a corrupt centralism."

Republican nominee Rutherford B. Hayes, governor of Ohio, also sought the high ground. As a lawyer in Cincinnati he had defended runaway slaves. Later he had distinguished himself as a general in the Union Army. Hayes promised, if elected, to support an efficient civil service system, to vigorously prosecute officials who betrayed the public trust, and to introduce a system of free universal education.

On an election day marred by widespread vote fraud and violent intimidation, Tilden received 250,000 more popular votes than Hayes. But Republicans refused to concede victory, challenging the vote totals in the electoral college. Tilden garnered 184 uncontested electoral votes, one shy of the majority required to win, while Hayes received 165. The problem centered in 20 disputed votes from Florida, Louisiana, South Carolina, and Oregon. In each of the three southern states, two sets of electoral votes were returned. In Oregon, which Hayes had unquestionably carried, the Democratic governor illegally replaced a Republican elector with a Democrat.

The crisis was unprecedented. In January 1877 Congress moved to settle the deadlock, establishing an Electoral Commission composed of five senators, five representatives, and five Supreme Court justices; eight were Republicans and seven were Democrats. The commission voted along strict partisan lines to award all the contested electoral votes to Hayes. Outraged by this decision, Democratic congressmen threatened a filibuster to block Hayes's inauguration. Violence and stalemate were avoided when Democrats and Republicans struck a compromise in February. In return for Hayes's ascendance to the presidency, the Republicans promised to appropriate more money for southern internal improvements, to appoint a southerner to Hayes's cabinet, and to pursue a policy of noninterference ("home rule") in southern affairs.

Shortly after assuming office, Hayes ordered removal of the remaining federal troops in Louisiana and South Carolina. Without this military presence to sustain them, the Republican governors of those two states quickly lost power to Democrats. "Home rule" meant Republican abandonment of freed people, Radicals, carpetbaggers, and scalawags. It also effectively nullified the Fourteenth and Fifteenth Amendments and the Civil Rights Act of 1866. The Compromise of 1877 completed repudiation of the idea, born during the Civil War and pursued during congressional Reconstruction, of a powerful federal government protecting the rights of all American citizens.

CONCLUSION

Reconstruction succeeded in the limited political sense of reuniting a nation torn apart by civil war. But the freed people's political and civil equality proved only temporary. The Radical Republicans' vision of racial justice, equal civil and political rights guaranteed by the Fourteenth and Fifteen Amendments, and a new Southern economy organized around independent small farmers never enjoyed the support of the majority of the party or the northern public. The federal government's failure to pursue land reform left former slaves without the economic independence needed for full emancipation. Yet the newly autonomous black family, along with black-controlled churches, schools, and other social institutions, provided the foundations for the modern African American community.

Even as the federal government retreated from the defense of equal rights for black people, it took a more aggressive stance as the protector of business interests. The Hayes administration responded decisively to one of the worst outbreaks of class violence in American history by dispatching federal troops to several northern cities to break the Great Railroad Strike of 1877. In the aftermath of Reconstruction, the struggle between capital and labor had clearly replaced "the southern question" as the number one political issue of the day.

CHRONOLOGY

1865	Freedmen's Bureau established			Suffragists split into National Woman Suffrage Association and American Woman Suffrage Association
	Abraham Lincoln assassinated			
	Andrew Johnson begins Presidential Reconstruction		1870	Fifteenth Amendment ratified
	Black Codes begin to be enacted in southern states		1871	Ku Klux Klan Act passed
	Thirteenth Amendment ratified			"Tweed Ring" in New York City exposed
1866	Civil Rights Act passed		1872	Liberal Republicans break with Grant and Radicals, nominate Horace Greeley for president
	Congress approves Fourteenth Amendment			Crédit Mobilier scandal
	Ku Klux Klan founded			Grant reelected president
1867	Reconstruction Acts, passed over President Johnson's veto, begin Congressional Reconstruction		1873	Financial panic and beginning of economic depression
	Tenure of Office Act			Slaughterhouse cases
	Southern states call constitutional conventions		1874	Democrats gain control of House for first time since 1856
1868	President Johnson impeached by the House, but acquitted in Senate trial		1875	Civil Rights Act
	Fourteenth Amendment ratified		1876	Disputed election between Samuel Tilden and Rutherford B. Hayes
	Most southern states readmitted to Union		1877	Electoral Commission elects Hayes president
	Ulysses S. Grant elected president			Hayes dispatches federal troops to break Great Railroad Strike and withdraws last remaining federal troops from the South
1869	Congress approves Fifteenth Amendment			
	Union Pacific and Central Pacific tracks meet at Promontory Point in Utah Territory			

REVIEW QUESTIONS

1. How did various visions of a "reconstructed" South differ? How did these visions reflect the old political and social divisions that had led to the Civil War?

2. What key changes did emancipation make in the political and economic status of African Americans? Discuss the expansion of citizenship rights in the post–Civil War years. To what extent did women share in the gains made by African Americans?

3. What role did such institutions as the family, the church, schools, and political parties play in the African American transition to freedom?

4. How did white Southerners attempt to limit the freedom of former slaves? How did these efforts succeed, and how did they fail?

5. Evaluate the achievements and failures of Reconstruction governments in the southern states.

6. What were the crucial economic changes occurring in the North and South during the Reconstruction era?

RECOMMENDED READING

Michael Les Benedict, *The Impeachment and Trial of Andrew Johnson* (1973). The best history of the impeachment crisis.

Laura F. Edwards, *Gendered Strife & Confusion: The Political Culture of Reconstruction* (1997). An ambitious analysis of how gender ideologies played a key role in shaping the party politics and social relations of the Reconstruction-era South.

Michael W. Fitzgerald, *The Union League Movement in the Deep South* (1989). Uses the Union League as a lens through which to examine race relations and the close connections between politics and economic change in the post–Civil War South.

Eric Foner, *Reconstruction: America's Unfinished Revolution, 1863–1877* (1988). The most comprehensive and thoroughly researched overview of the Reconstruction era.

William Gillette, *Retreat from Reconstruction: A Political History, 1867–1878* (1979). Covers the national political scene, with special attention to the abandonment of the ideal of racial equality.

Jacqueline Jones, *Labor of Love, Labor of Sorrow* (1985). Includes excellent material on the work and family lives of African American women in slavery and freedom.

Leon Litwack, *Been in the Storm So Long: The Aftermath of Slavery* (1979). A richly detailed analysis of the transition from slavery to freedom; excellent use of African American sources.

Michael Perman, *Emancipation and Reconstruction, 1862–1879* (1987). A short but very useful overview of Reconstruction, emphasizing racial issues and the end of slavery.

Edward Royce, *The Origins of Southern Sharecropping* (1993). A sophisticated, tightly argued work of historical sociology that explains how sharecropping emerged as the dominant form of agricultural labor in the post–Civil War South.

Mark W. Summers, *Railroads, Reconstruction, and the Gospel of Prosperity* (1984). The best study of the economic and political importance of railroad building in this era.

Allen W. Trelease, *White Terror: The Ku Klux Klan Conspiracy and Southern Reconstruction* (1971). The most complete account of Klan activity and the efforts to suppress it.

CHAPTER EIGHTEEN

CONQUEST AND SURVIVAL IN THE TRANS-MISSISSIPPI WEST

1860–1900

AMERICAN COMMUNITIES
The Oklahoma Land Rush

Decades after the event, cowboy Evan G. Barnard vividly recalled the preparations made by settlers when Oklahoma territorial officials announced the opening of No Man's Land to the biggest "land rush" in American history. "Thousands of people gathered along the border. . . . As the day for the race drew near the settlers practiced running their horses and driving cart." Finally the morning of April 22, 1889, arrived. "At ten o'clock people lined up . . . ready for the great race of their lives."

What was to become the state of Oklahoma in 1907 had been reserved since the 1830s for the Five Civilized Tribes (Cherokees, Chickasaws, Choctaws, Creeks, and Seminoles), who had been forcibly removed from their eastern lands. All five tribes had reestablished themselves as sovereign republics in Indian Territory.

However, the Civil War took a heavy toll on their success. Some tribes, slaveholders themselves, sided with the Confederacy; others pledged loyalty to the Union. When the war ended, more than 10,000 people—nearly one-fifth of the total population of Indian Territory—had died. To make matters worse, new treaties required the Five Tribes to cede the entire western half of the territory for the resettlement of tribes from other regions, including the former northern Indian territory of Nebraska and Kansas.

Western Oklahoma thereby became a new home for thousands more displaced peoples, including the Pawnees, Peorias, Ottawas, Wyandots, and Miamis. But not all tribes agreed to settle peacefully. Nomadic by tradition, the buffalo-hunting Kiowas, Cheyennes, Comanches, and Arapahoes continued to traverse the plains until the U.S. Army forced them onto reservations. Eventually, more than 80,000 tribespeople were living on twenty-one separate reservations in western Oklahoma, all governed by agents appointed by the federal government.

The fate of both the tribal reservations and Indian Territory to the east was tied to one small strip of unassigned land: No Man's Land. To many non-Indians, this so-called Promised Land seemed just perfect for dividing up into thousands of small farms. African Americans, many former slaves of Indian planters, appealed to the federal government for the right to stake claims there. Another group of would-be homesteaders, known as "Boomers," quickly tired of petitioning and invaded the district in 1880, only to be booted out by the Tenth Cavalry. Meanwhile, the railroads, seeing the potential for lucrative commerce, put constant pressure on the federal government to open No Man's Land for settlement. In 1889 the U.S. Congress finally gave in.

Cowboy Barnard was just one of the thousands who would mark the historic opening of almost 2 million acres of the far western district of Oklahoma to homesteading. Many homesteaders simply crossed the border from Kansas, but Southerners, dispossessed by warfare and economic ruin in their own region, were also well represented. By nightfall of April 22, 1889, tent cities had been set up along railroad lines as market-minded settlers claimed the land located nearest to transportation routes. In a little over two months, after 6,000 homestead claims had been filed, the first houses, built of blocks of grass and dirt and

Indian Territory (Oklahoma)

known as "soddies," sheltered growing communities of non-Indian farmers, ranchers, and other entrepreneurs.

Dramatic as it was, the land rush of 1889 was only one in a series that opened all of Oklahoma, including Indian Territory, to homesteaders. The Five Tribes held on until 1898, when Congress passed the Curtis Act, which formally dissolved Indian Territory. Members of the former Indian nations were directed to dismantle their governments, abandon their estates, and join the ranks of other homesteaders. By 1907, tribespeople were outnumbered in Oklahoma by a ratio of ten to one. They nevertheless retained many of their tribal customs and managed to regain sovereign status in 1977.

By this time also, nearly one-quarter of the entire population of the United States lived west of the Mississippi River. The new residents of the region successfully displaced communities that had formed centuries earlier. They also drastically transformed the physical landscape. Through their activities and the support of Easterners, the United States realized an ambition that John L. O'Sullivan had described in 1845 as the nation's "manifest destiny to overspread the continent" and remake it in a new image.

KEY TOPICS

- The impact of western expansion on Indian societies

- The West as an "internal empire" and the development of new technologies and new industries

- The creation of new communities and the displacement of old communities

- The West as myth and legend

INDIAN PEOPLES UNDER SIEGE

The tribespeople living west of the Mississippi River keenly felt the pressure of the gradual incorporation of the West into the nation. The Oregon Trail opened the Northwest to large numbers of non-Indian settlers. The following year, the United States reached an agreement with Great Britain for the division of the Oregon Country. Then came the addition of territories taken from Mexico following the Mexican–American War. Congress consolidated the national domain in the next decades by granting territorial status to Utah, New Mexico, Washington, Dakota, Colorado, Nevada, Arizona, Idaho, Montana, and Wyoming. (California and Oregon quickly became states.) The purchase of Alaska in 1867 added an area twice the size of Texas and extended the nation beyond its contiguous borders so that it reached almost to Russia and the North Pole. The federal government made itself the custodian of all these thinly settled regions, permitting limited self-rule, with appointed governors supervising the transition from territorial status to statehood. The federal government also took it upon itself to mediate disputes between the new settlers and the old residents (Indian peoples, Hispanic peoples, and Mormons), who were now forced to compete for power and influence.

Tribespeople struggled to preserve their ways of life under these changing conditions, but their prospects dimmed considerably following the discovery of gold in California in 1848 and the completion of the transcontinental railroad in 1869. White settlers rushed into these territories and repeatedly invaded Indian lands west of the Mississippi. Violent outbreaks between white emigrants and Indian peoples became increasingly commonplace. Since the Jefferson administration, federal officials had promoted the assimilation of Indian peoples. They now became even more determined to break up the Indians' tribal councils and to bring Indians into the American mainstream.

On the Eve of Conquest

Before the European colonists reached the New World, tribespeople of the Great Plains, Southwest, and Far West had occupied the lands for more than 20,000 years. Hundreds of tribes totaling perhaps a million members had adapted to such extreme climates as the desert aridity of present-day Utah and Nevada, the bitter cold of the northern plains, and the seasonally heavy rain of the Pacific Northwest. Many cultivated maize (corn), foraged for wild plants, fished, or hunted game. Several tribes built cities with several thousand inhabitants and traded across thousands of miles of western territory.

Invasion by the English, Spanish, and other Europeans brought disease, religious conversion, and new patterns of commerce. But geographic isolation still gave many tribes a margin of survival unknown in the East. At the close of the Civil War, approximately 360,000 Indian people still lived in the trans-Mississippi West, the majority of them in the Great Plains.

The surviving tribes adapted to changing conditions. The Plains Indians learned to ride the horses and shoot the guns introduced by Spanish and British traders. Some tribes took dramatic steps toward accommodation with white ways. Even before they were uprooted and moved across the Mississippi River, the Cherokees had established a constitutional republic, converted to Christianity, and become a nation of farmers.

Legally, the federal government had long regarded Indian tribes as autonomous nations residing within American boundaries and had negotiated numerous treaties with them over land rights and commerce. But pressured by land-hungry whites, several states had violated these federal treaties so often that the U.S. Congress passed the Indian Removal Act of 1830, which provided funds to relocate all eastern tribes by force if necessary. The Cherokees challenged this legislation, and the Supreme Court ruled in their

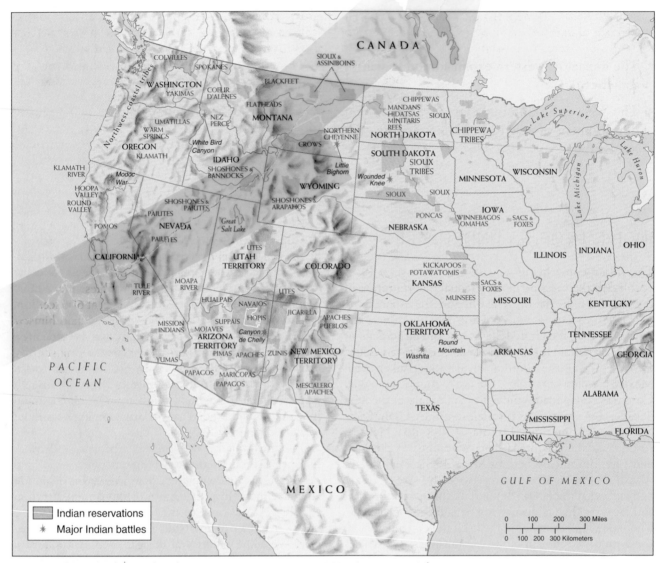

Major Indian Battles and Indian Reservations, 1860–1900 *As commercial routes and white populations passed through and occupied Indian lands, warfare inevitably erupted. The displacement of Indians to reservations opened access by farmers, ranchers, and investors by natural resources and to markets.*

favor in *Cherokee Nation v. Georgia* (1831). Ignoring the Court's ruling, President Andrew Jackson forced many tribes to cede their land and remove to Indian Territory. There, it was believed, they might live undisturbed by whites and gradually adjust to "civilized" ways. But soon, the onslaught of white settlers, railroad entrepreneurs, and prospectors for gold pressured tribes to cede millions of their acres to the United States. In 1854, to open the Kansas and Nebraska territories for white settlement, the federal government simply abolished the northern half of Indian Territory. As demand for resources and land accelerated, the entire plan for a permanent Indian Territory fell apart.

Reservations and the Slaughter of the Buffalo

As early as the 1840s, officials outlined a plan to subdue the intensifying rivalry over natural resources and land. Under the terms of their proposal, individual tribes would agree to live within clearly defined zones and, in exchange, the Bureau of Indian Affairs would provide guidance while U.S. military forces ensured protection. The reservation policy also reflected the vision of many educators and Protestant missionaries who aspired to "civilize the savages."

Several tribes did sign treaties, although often under duress. High-handed officials, such as governor Isaac Stevens of Washington Territory, made no attempt at legitimate negotiations, choosing instead to intimidate or deceive Indian peoples into signing away their lands. State officials moved the Indians onto three reservations after their leaders signed away 45,000 square miles of tribal land. The Suquamish leader Seattle admitted defeat but warned the governor: "Your time of decay may be distant, but it will surely come."

Tribes that moved to reservations often found federal policies inadequate. The Medicine Lodge Treaty of 1867 assigned reservations in existing Indian Territory to Comanches, Plains (Kiowa) Apaches, Kiowas, Cheyennes, and Arapahoes, bringing these tribes together with Sioux, Shoshones, Bannocks, and Navajos. All told, more than 100,000 people found themselves competing intensely for survival. Over the next decade, a group of Quakers appointed by President Ulysses S. Grant attempted to mediate differences among the tribes and to supply the starving peoples with food and seed. At the same time, white prospectors and miners continued to flood the Dakota Territory. Corrupt officials of the Bureau of Indian Affairs routinely diverted funds for their own use and reduced food supplies, a policy promoting malnutrition, demoralization, and desperation.

The nomadic tribes that traditionally hunted and gathered over large territories saw their freedom sharply curtailed. The Lakota, or Sioux, a loose confederation of bands scattered across the northern Great Plains, were one of the largest and most adaptive of all Indian nations. Seizing buffalo-hunting territory from their rivals, the Pawnees and the Crows, the Sioux had learned to follow the herds on horseback. The Sioux were also widely known as vision seekers. Encouraging young men and women to seek dreams that would provide them guidance for a lifetime, Sioux elders themselves followed dreams that might guide the destiny of the entire tribe or nation.

The crisis reached its peak with the mass slaughter of the buffalo, the basis of tribal livelihood. In earlier eras, vast herds of buffalo had literally darkened the western horizon. As gunpowder and the railroad came to the range, the number of buffalo fell rapidly. Non-Indian traders avidly sought buffalo fur for coats, hide for leather, and heads for trophies. New rifles, such as the .50 caliber Sharps, could kill at 600 feet; one sharpshooter bragged of killing 3,000 buffalo himself. Army commanders encouraged the practice, accurately predicting that starvation would prove the most effective means of breaking down tribal resistance to the reservation system. Their food sources practically destroyed and their way of life undermined, many Great Plains tribes, including many Sioux, concluded that they could only fight or die.

The Indian Wars

Under these pressures, a handful of tribes organized themselves and their allies to resist both federal policies and the growing wave of white settlers. The overwhelming majority of tribespeople did not take up arms. But settlers, thousands of them Civil War veterans with weapons close at hand, responded to real or imaginary threats with their own brands of violence.

Large-scale war erupted in 1864. Having decided to terminate all treaties with tribes in eastern Colorado, territorial governor John Evans encouraged a group of white civilians, the Colorado Volunteers, to stage repeated raids through Cheyenne campgrounds. Seeking protection, chief Black Kettle brought a band of 800 Cheyennes to a U.S. fort and received orders to set up camp at Sand Creek. Secure in this

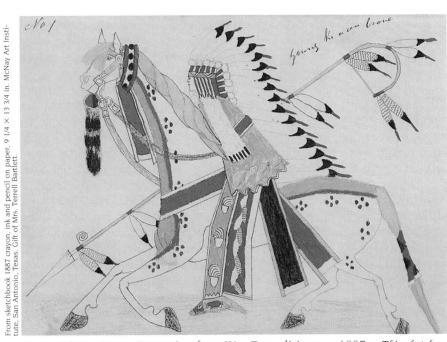

From sketchbook 1887 crayon, ink and pencil on paper, 9 1/4 × 13 3/4 in. McNay Art Institute, San Antonio, Texas. Gift of Mrs. Terrell Bartlett.

Young Kiowa Brave Preparing for a War Expedition, *ca. 1887.   This sketch on paper was made by an Indian artist, Silver Horns, who had himself taken part in the final revolt of the Kiowas in 1874. He later became a medicine man, and then served as a private in the U.S. Cavalry at Fort Sill, Oklahoma Territory.*

arrangement, Black Kettle sent out most of his men to hunt. The next morning, on November 29, 1864, the Colorado Volunteers attacked. While Black Kettle held up a U.S. flag and a white truce banner, the disorderly group of 700 men, many of whom were drunk, slaughtered 105 Cheyenne women and children and 28 men. They proceeded to mutilate the Indian corpses and took scalps back to Denver to exhibit them as trophies. One Cheyenne woman, Iron Teeth, lived with the memory of a woman "crawling along on the ground, shot, scalped, crazy, but not yet dead." Months after the Sand Creek Massacre, bands of Cheyennes, Sioux, and Arapahoes were still retaliating, burning civilian outposts and sometimes killing whole families.

The Sioux played the most dramatic roles in these wars. In 1851, believing that the U.S. government would recognize their own rights of conquest over other Indian tribes, the Sioux relinquished large tracts of land as a demonstration of good faith. But within a decade, a mass invasion of miners and the construction of military forts along the Bozeman Trail in Wyoming, the Sioux's principal buffalo range, threw the tribe's future into doubt. During the Great Sioux War of 1865–67, Sioux chief Red Cloud fought the U.S. Army to a stalemate and forced the government to abandon its forts, which the Sioux then burned to the ground. The Treaty of Fort Laramie, signed in 1868, created the Great Sioux Reservation, which included the present state of South Dakota west of the Missouri River, but restored only a temporary peace to the region.

The Treaty of Fort Laramie granted the Sioux the right to occupy the Black Hills, or *Paha Sapa*, their sacred land, "as long as the grass shall grow." The discovery of gold, however, soon undermined this guarantee. As white prospectors invaded the territory, Lieutenant Colonel George Armstrong Custer led a surveying expedition to the Black Hills during the summer of 1874. After Custer described rich veins of ore that could be cheaply extracted, the U.S. Congress pushed to acquire the territory for Americans. To protect their land, Sioux, Cheyenne, and Arapaho warriors moved into war camps during the summer of 1876.

After several skirmishes, Custer decided to rush ahead of other army regiments to a site that was known to white soldiers as Little Bighorn and to Lakotas as Greasy Grass. This foolhardy move offered the allied Cheyenne and Sioux warriors a perfect opportunity to cut off Custer's logistical and military support. On June 25, 1876, Custer and his troops fell before one of the largest Indian contingents ever assembled, an estimated 2,000 to 4,000 warriors.

"Custer's Last Stand" gave Indian haters the emotional ammunition to whip up public excitement. After Custer's defeat, Sioux Chief Sitting Bull reportedly said, "Now they will never let us rest." The U.S. Army tracked down the disbanded Indian contingents one by one. By 1877 Sioux leadership in the Indian Wars was ended.

Among the last to hold out against the reservation system were the Apaches in the Southwest. Apache bands, unable to tolerate the harsh conditions on the reservation, returned to their old ways of seizing territory and stealing cattle. For the next ten years, Geronimo led intermittent raids against white outposts in the rough Arizona terrain.

Pursued by the U.S. Army, the Apaches earned reputations as intrepid warriors. Lightning-swift raids followed by quick disappearances made legends of their brilliant strategists and horse-riding braves. The Kiowas and the Comanches, both powerful tribes, joined the Apaches in one of the bloodiest conflicts, the Red River War of 1874–75. At last the U.S. Army scored a decisive victory, less by military might than by denying Indians access to food. Still, small-scale warfare sputtered on. His band reduced to only thirty people, Geronimo surrendered in September 1886. The Indian Wars were over.

The Nez Percé

The Nez Percé (pierced nose), given their name by French Canadian trappers who thought they had seen members of the tribe wearing shells in their septums, for generations regarded themselves as good friends to white traders and settlers. Living in the plateau where Idaho, Washington, and Oregon now meet, they saved the Lewis and Clark expedition from starvation. Large numbers converted to Christianity, and they occasionally assisted U.S. armies against hostile tribes.

The discovery of gold on Nez Percé territory in 1860 changed their relations with whites for the worse. Pressed by prospectors and mining companies, government commissioners, in the treaty of 1863, demanded the Nez Percé cede 6 million acres, nine-tenths of their land, at less than ten cents per acre. Some of the Nez Percé leaders agreed to the terms of the treaty, which had been fraudulently signed on behalf of the entire tribe, but others refused. At first federal officials listened to Nez Percé complaints against the defective treaty and decided to allow the Nez Percé to remain on their land. Responding to pressure from settlers and politicians, however, they almost immediately reversed their decision, ordering the Nez Percé, including Chief Joseph and his followers, to sell their land and to move onto the reservation.

Chief Joseph's band set out from the Wallowa Valley with all their livestock and the possessions they could carry. They soon were drawn into conflict with U.S. troops, which fired on the Nez Percé truce team. The Nez Percé fought back, killed one-third of the soldiers, and outmaneuvered the subsequent military forces sent to intercept them.

Before U.S. troops surrounded them in northern Montana, Nez Percé braves had fought 2,000 regular U.S. troops and eighteen Indian auxiliary detachments, in eighteen separate engagements and two major battles, over three and a half months. General Sherman remarked admiringly at the Nez Percé's ingenious tactics, courage, and avoidance of cruelty. The Nez Percé were finally trapped in the Bear Paw Mountains, where, suffering from hunger and cold, they surrendered.

Promised they would be returned to Oregon, the Nez Percé were sent instead to disease-ridden bottomland near Fort Leavenworth in Kansas, and then to Oklahoma. Arguing for the right of his people to return to their Oregon reservation, Joseph spoke eloquently, through an interpreter, to Congress in 1879. "Treat all men alike. Give them all the same law. Give them all an even chance to live and grow. All men were made by the same Great Spirit Chief," Joseph pleaded. Government officials appeared willing to give in until Idaho's white settlers protested. The last members of Joseph's band were deported under guard to a non–Nez Percé reservation in Washington, where his descendants continue to live in exile to this day.

THE INTERNAL EMPIRE

Since the time of Christopher Columbus, Europeans had looked for a land of incredible wealth, free for the taking. In the nineteenth century, the North American continent, stretching across scarcely populated territories toward the Pacific Ocean, revived this dream. Determined to make their fortunes, be it from copper in Arizona, wheat in Montana, or oranges in California, adventurers traveled west, the largest migration and greatest commercial expansion in American history.

But the settlers themselves also became the subjects of a huge internal empire whose financial, political, and industrial centers of power remained in the East. Only a small number of settlers actually struck it rich. Meanwhile, older populations—Indian peoples, Hispanic peoples, and more recently settled communities such as the Mormons—struggled to create places for themselves in this new order.

Mining Communities

The discovery of gold in California in 1848 roused fortune seekers from across the United States, Europe, and as far away as China and Chile. Within a year, prospecting parties overran the western territories, setting a pattern for intermittent rushes for gold, silver, and copper that extended from the Colorado mountains to the Arizona deserts to California, Oregon,

Washington, and Alaska to the Black Hills of South Dakota. Mining camps and boomtowns soon dotted what had once been thinly settled regions. The population of California alone jumped from 14,000 in 1848 to 223,856 just four years later. More than any other industry or commercial enterprise, mining fostered western expansion.

The mining industry quickly grew from its treasure-hunt origins into a grand corporate enterprise. The most successful mineowners bought out the smaller claims and built an entire industry around their stakes. They found investors to finance their expansion and used the borrowed capital to purchase the latest in extractive technology, such as new explosives, compressed-air or diamond-headed rotary drills, and wire cable. They gained access to timber to fortify their underground structures and water to feed the hydraulic pumps that washed down mountains. They built smelters to refine the crude ore into ingots and often financed railroads to transport the product to distant markets. By the end of the century, the Anaconda Copper Mining Company had expanded into hydroelectricity to become one of the most powerful corporations in the nation.

The mining corporations laid the basis for a new economy as well as an interim government and established many of the region's first white settlements. Before the advent of railroads, ore had to be brought out of and supplies brought into mining areas by boats, wagons, and mules traveling hundreds of miles over rough territory. The railroad made transportation of supplies and products easier and faster. The shipping trade meanwhile grew into an important industry of its own, employing thousands of merchants, peddlers, and sailors. Gold Hill and nearby Virginia City, Nevada, began as a cluster of small mining camps and by the early 1860s became a thriving urban community of nearly 6,000 people. A decade later, the population had quadrupled, but it subsequently fell sharply as the mines gave out.

Men outnumbered women by as much as ten to one, and very few lived with families or stayed very long. They often bunked with male kin and worked alongside friends or acquaintances from their hometown. Some lived unusually well, feasting on oysters trucked in at great expense. The town center was usually the saloon, where, as one observer complained, men "without the restraint of law, indifferent to public opinion, and unburdened by families, drink whenever they feel like it, whenever they have the money to pay for it, and whenever there is nothing else to do."

The western labor movement began in these camps, partly as a response to dangerous working conditions. In the hardrock mines of the 1870s, one of every thirty workers was disabled, one of eighty killed.

Miners began to organize in the 1860s, demanding good pay for dangerous and life-shortening work. By the end of the century they had established the strongest unions in the West.

When mineowners' private armies "arrested" strikers or fought their unions with rifle fire, miners burned down the campsites, seized trains loaded with ore, and engaged in many acts of sabotage against company property. The miners' unions also helped to secure legislation mandating a maximum eight-hour day for certain jobs and workmen's compensation for injuries. Such bills, which were enacted in Idaho, Arizona, and New Mexico before 1920, long preceded similar laws adopted in most eastern states.

The unions fought hard, but they did so exclusively for the benefit of white workers. The native-born and the Irish and Cornish immigrants (from Cornwall, England) far outnumbered other groups before the turn of the century, when Italians, Slavs, and Greeks began to replace them. Labor unions eventually admitted these new immigrants, but refused Chinese, Mexican, and Indian workers.

When prices and ore production fell sharply, not even unions could stop the owners from shutting down the mines and leaving behind ghost towns. Often they also left behind an environmental disaster. Hydraulic mining, which used water cannons to blast hillsides and expose gold deposits, drove tons of rock and earth into the rivers and canyons. By the late 1860s southern California's rivers were clogged, producing floods that wiped out towns and agriculture. In 1893 Congress finally passed the Caminetti Act, giving the state the power to regulate the mines. (The act also created the Sacramento River Commission, which began to replace free-flowing rivers with canals and dams.) Underground mining continued unregulated, using up whole forests for timbers and filling the air with dangerous, sulfurous smoke.

Mormon Settlements

The Mormons (members of the Church of Jesus Christ of Latter-Day Saints) had fled western New York in the 1830s for Illinois and Missouri, only to face greater persecution in the Midwest. After their founder, Joseph Smith, was lynched after proclaiming the doctrine of polygamy (multiple wives), the community sought refuge in the West. Led by their new prophet, Brigham Young, the Mormons migrated in 1846–47 to the Great Basin in present-day Utah and formed an independent theocratic state, called Deseret. However, their dream was cut short in 1850 when Congress set up Utah Territory. In 1857 President James Buchanan declared the Mormons to be in "a state of substantial rebellion" (for being an independent state in U.S. territory) and sent the U.S. Army to occupy the territory.

Although federal troops remained until the outbreak of the Civil War in 1861, the Mormon population continued to grow. By 1860 more than 40,000 Mormons lived in Utah Territory. Contrary to federal law, church officials forbade the selling of land and instead held property in common. They created sizable settlements complemented by satellite villages joined to communal farmlands and a common pasture. Relying on agricultural techniques learned from local Indian tribes, the Mormons built dams for irrigation and harvested a variety of crops from desert soil. Eventually nearly 500 Mormon communities spread from Oregon to Idaho to Arizona.

But as territorial rule tightened, the Mormons saw their unique way of life once again threatened. Preceded by prohibitory federal laws enacted in 1862 and 1874, the Supreme Court finally ruled against polygamy in the 1879 case of *United States v. Reynolds*, which granted the freedom of belief but not the freedom of practice. In 1882 Congress passed the Edmunds Act, which effectively disfranchised those who believed in or practiced polygamy and threatened them with fines and imprisonment. Equally devastating was the Edmunds–Tucker Act, passed five years later, which destroyed the temporal power of the Mormon Church by confiscating all assets over $50,000 and establishing a federal commission to oversee all elections in the territory. By the early 1890s Mormon leaders officially renounced plural marriage.

The Southwest

The Treaty of Guadalupe Hidalgo, which ended the Mexican–American War, allowed the Hispanic people north of the Rio Grande to choose between immigrating to Mexico or staying in what was now the United States. But the new Mexican–American border, one of the longest unguarded boundaries in the world, could not sever communities that had been connected for centuries. What gradually emerged was an economically and socially interdependent zone, the Anglo–Hispanic borderlands linking the United States and Mexico.

Although under the treaty all Hispanics were formally guaranteed citizenship and the "free enjoyment of their liberty and property," local *Anglos* (as the Mexicans called white Americans) often violated these provisions and, through fraud or coercion, took control of the land. The Sante Fe Ring, a group of lawyers, politicians, and land speculators, stole millions of acres from the public domain and grabbed over 80 percent of the *Mexicano* land holdings in New Mexico alone. More often, Anglos used new federal laws to their own benefit.

For a time, Arizona and New Mexico seemed to hold out hopes for a mutually beneficial interaction between Mexicanos and Anglos. A prosperous class of Hispanic landowners, with long-standing ties to

Anglos through marriage, had established itself in cities such as Albuquerque and Tucson, old Spanish towns that had been founded in the seventeenth and eighteenth centuries. In Las Cruces, New Mexico, an exceptional family such as the wealthy Amadors could shop by mail from Bloomingdales, travel to the World's Fair in Chicago, and send their children to English-language Catholic schools. These Mexican elites, well integrated into the emerging national economy, continued to wield political power as ranchers, landlords, and real estate developers until the end of the century. They secured passage of bills for education in their regions and often served as superintendents of local schools. Several prominent merchants became territorial delegates to Congress.

The majority of Mexicans who had lived in the mountains and deserts of the Southwest for well over two centuries were less prepared for these changes. Most had worked outside the commercial economy, farming and herding sheep for their own subsistence. Before 1848 they had few contacts with the outside world. With the Anglos came land closures as well as commercial expansion prompted by railroad, mining, and timber industries. Many poor families found themselves crowded onto plots too small for subsistence farming. Large numbers turned to seasonal labor on the new Anglo-owned commercial farms, where they became the first of many generations of poorly paid migratory workers. Other Mexicans adapted by taking jobs on the railroad or in the mines. By the end of the century Mexicanos had become a predominantly urban population, dependent on wages for survival.

Women were quickly drawn into the expanding network of market and wage relations. They tried to make ends meet by selling produce from their backyard gardens; more often they worked as seamstresses or laundresses. Formerly at the center of a communal society, Mexicanas found themselves with fewer options in the cash economy. What wages they could now earn fell below even the low sums paid to their husbands, and women lost status within both the family and community.

Occasionally, Mexicanos organized to reverse these trends or at least to limit the damage done to their communities. In south Texas in 1859, Juan Cortina and sixty of his followers pillaged white-owned stores and killed four Anglos who had gone unpunished for their murder of several Mexicans. "Cortina's War" marked the first of several sporadic rebellions. Other Mexicanos organized more peacefully. *El Alianzo Hispano–Americano* (the Hispanic–American Alliance) was formed "to protect and fight for the rights of Spanish Americans" through political action. *Mutualistes* (mutual aid societies) provided sickness and death benefits to Mexican families.

Despite many pressures, Mexicanos preserved much of their cultural heritage. The Roman Catholic Church retained its influence in the community, and most Mexicans continued to turn to the church to baptize infants, celebrate the feast days of their patron saints, marry, and bury the dead. Special saints such as the Virgin of Guadalupe and distinctive holy days such as the Day of the Dead survived along with *fiestas* celebrating the change of seasons. Many communities continued to commemorate Mexican national holidays such as *Cinco de Mayo* (May 5), marking the Mexican victory over French invaders in the battle of Puebla in 1862. Spanish language and Spanish place names continued to distinguish the Southwest.

Americans had brought in commercial capitalism, their political and legal systems, and many of their social and cultural institutions. Ironically, though, even after statehood, white settlers would still be only distant representatives of an empire whose financial, political, and industrial centers remained in the Northeast. Embittered Westerners, along with Southerners, formed the core of a nationwide discontent that would soon threaten to uproot the American political system.

THE CATTLE INDUSTRY

The slaughter of the buffalo made way for the cattle industry, one of the most profitable businesses in the West. Texas longhorns, introduced by the Spanish, numbered over 5 million at the close of the Civil War and represented a potentially plentiful supply of beef for eastern consumers. The Kansas Pacific Railroad provided crucial transportation links to slaughtering and packing houses and commercial distributors in Kansas City, St. Louis, and Chicago.

Drovers pushed herd after herd north from Texas through Oklahoma on the trail marked out by part-Cherokee trader Jesse Chisholm. Great profits were made on Texas steers bought for $7–$9 a head and sold in Kansas for $30 or more. In 1880 nearly 2 million cattle were slaughtered in Chicago alone. For two decades, cattle represented the West's bonanza industry.

Cowboys

The great cattle drives depended on the cowboy, a seasonal or migrant worker. After the Civil War, cowboys—one for every 300–500 head on the trail—rounded up herds of Texas cattle and drove them as much as 1,500 miles north to grazing ranches or to the stockyards, where they were readied for shipping by rail to eastern markets. The boss supplied the horses, the cowboy his own bedroll, saddle, and spurs. The workday lasted from sunup to sundown, with short night shifts for guarding the cattle. Scurvy, a widespread ailment, could be traced to the basic chuckwagon menu of sowbelly, beans, and coffee, a diet bereft of fruits and vegetables. The cowboy worked without protection from rain or hail, and severe dust storms could cause temporary blindness.

In return for his labor, the cowboy received at the best of times about $30 per month. Wages were usually paid in one lump sum at the end of a drive, a policy that encouraged cowboys to spend their money quickly and recklessly. When wages began to fall along with the price of beef in 1883, many Texas cowboys struck for higher wages; nearly all Wyoming cowboys struck in 1886. Aided by the legendary camaraderie fostered in the otherwise desolate conditions of the long drive, cowboys, along with miners, were among the first western workers to organize against employers.

Like other parts of the West, the cattle range was ethnically diverse. Between one-fifth and one-third of all workers were Indian, Mexican, or African American. Some African American cowboys were sons of former slaves who had been captured from the African territory of Gambia, where cattle-raising was an age-old art. Unlike Mexicans, they earned wages comparable to those paid to Anglos, and especially during the early years they worked in integrated drover parties. By the 1880s, as the center of the cattle industry shifted to the more settled regions around the northern ranches, African Americans were forced out and turned to other kinds of work. The majority of Anglo cowboys also came from the South and usually remained loyal to the racial standards of the Confederacy.

Cowgirls and Prostitutes

Although few women worked as trail hands, they did find jobs on the ranches, usually in the kitchen or laundry. The majority of women attended to domestic chores, caring for children and maintaining the household. Their daughters, however, enjoyed better prospects. By the end of the century, women reared on ranches were riding astride, "clothespin style," roping calves, branding cattle, and castrating bulls.

In cattle towns, many women worked as prostitutes. During the first cattle drive to Abilene in 1867, a few women there were so engaged, but by the following spring, Cowman Joseph McCoy's assistant recalled, "they came in swarms, & as the weather was warm 4 or 5 girls could huddle together in a tent very comfortably." The best-paid prostitutes congregated in "brothel districts" or "tenderloins." Dodge City had two: one with white prostitutes for white patrons, another with black prostitutes for both white and black men.

Perhaps 50,000 women engaged in prostitution west of the Mississippi during the second half of the nineteenth century. Like most cowboys, most prostitutes were young, in their teens or twenties. Often fed up with underpaid jobs in dressmaking or domestic service, they realized that few alternatives awaited women in the cattle towns, where the cost of food and lodging was notoriously high. Still, earnings in prostitution were slim. At best a fully employed Wichita prostitute might earn $30 per week, but nearly two-thirds of that would go for room and board.

Race shaped the character of prostitution, as it did that of cattle herding. Near U.S. Army forts, Indian women figured prominently in the trade, providing a source of income for an increasingly impoverished people. Across the Southwest, Mexican women occupied the next lowest level of status, pay, and conditions. Black prostitutes were only slightly better off. All prostitutes, even the Anglo women who earned the highest wages, risked injury or even death from violent clients.

Community and Conflict on the Range

The combination of prostitution, gambling, and drinking discouraged the formation of stable communities. Personal violence was notoriously common on the streets and in the barrooms of cattle towns and mining camps populated mainly by young, single men. But contrary to popular belief, gunfights were rare. Local police officers, such as Wyatt Earp and "Wild Bill" Hickok, worked mainly to keep order among drunken cowboys.

After the Civil War, violent crime, assault, and robbery took a sharp turn upward throughout the United States. In the West, the most prevalent crimes were horse theft and cattle rustling, which both rose sharply during the peak years of the open range and then dwindled by the 1890s. Capital punishment by legal hanging—or illegally by lynching, or "necktie parties," in which the victims were "jerked to Jesus"—was the usual sentence.

The "range wars" of the 1870s produced violent conflicts. By this time, both farmers and sheep herders were encroaching on the fields where cattle had once grazed freely. Shepherds who guided their flocks through grasslands knew that sheep chewed the grass down to the roots, practically destroying land use for cattle. Farmers meanwhile set about building fences to protect their domestic livestock and property. Great cattle barons fought back against farmers by ordering cowboys to cut the new barbed-wire fences.

The cattle barons, eager for greater profits and often backed by foreign capital, overstocked their herds, and eventually the cattle began to deplete the limited supply of grass. Finally, in 1885–87, a combination of summer drought and winter blizzards killed 90 percent of the cattle. Many big ranchers fell into bankruptcy. Along the way, they often took out their grievances against the former cowboys who had gathered small herds for themselves. They charged these small ranchers with cattle rustling, taking them to court or, in some cases, rounding up lynching parties. As one historian has written, violence was "not a mere sideshow" but "an intrinsic part of western society."

FARMING COMMUNITIES ON THE PLAINS

The vision of a huge fertile garden extending from the Appalachians to the Pacific Ocean had inspired Americans since the early days of the republic. But the first explorers who actually traveled through the Great Plains quashed this dream. "The Great Desert" was the name they gave to the region stretching west from Kansas and Nebraska, north to Montana and the Dakotas, and south again to Oklahoma and Texas. Few trees fended off the blazing sun of summer or promised a supply of lumber for homes and fences. The occasional river or stream flowed with "muddy gruel" rather than pure, sweet water. Economically, the entire region appeared as hopelessly barren as it was vast. It took massive improvements in both transportation and farm technology—as well as unrelenting advertising and promotional campaigns—to open the Great Plains to wide-scale agriculture.

The Homestead Act

The Homestead Act of 1862 offered the first incentive to prospective white farmers. This act granted a quarter section (160 acres) of the public domain free to any settler who lived on the land and improved it for at least five years; a settler could buy the land for $1.25 per acre after only six months' residence. Approximately 605 million acres of public domain became available for settlement.

Homesteaders achieved their greatest success in the central and upper Midwest, where the soil was rich and weather moderate. But settlers lured to the Great Plains by descriptions of land "carpeted with soft grass—a sylvan paradise"—found themselves locked in a fierce struggle with the harsh climate and arid soil.

Rather than filing a homestead claim with the federal government, most settlers acquired their land outright. State governments and land companies usually held the most valuable land near transportation and markets, and the majority of farmers were willing to pay a hefty price for these benefits. Before the turn of the century, farm acreage west of the Mississippi had tripled, but perhaps only 10 percent of all farmers got their start under homestead provisions. The big land speculators gained the most, plucking choice locations at bargain prices. Although the Homestead Act did spark the largest migration in American history, it did not lay the foundation for a nation of prosperous family farms.

Populating the Plains

The rapid settlement of the West could not have taken place without the railroad. Although the Homestead Act offered prospective farmers free land, it was the railroad that promoted settlement, brought people to their new homes, and carried crops and cattle to eastern markets. The railroads therefore wielded tremendous economic and political power throughout the West. Their agents, reputed to know every cow in the district, made major decisions regarding territorial welfare. In designing routes and locating depots, railroad companies put whole communities on the map, or left them behind.

The western railroads directly encouraged settlement. Unlike the railroads built before the Civil War, which followed the path of villages and towns, the western lines preceded settlement. Bringing people west became their top priority, and the railroad companies conducted aggressive promotional and marketing campaigns. Agents enticed Easterners and Europeans alike with long-term loans and free transportation by rail to distant points in the West. The railroads also sponsored land companies to sell parcels of their own huge allotments from the federal government.

More than 2 million Europeans, many recruited by professional promoters, settled the Great Plains between 1870 and 1900. Some districts in Minnesota seemed to be virtual colonies of Sweden; others housed the largest number of Finns in the New World. Nebraska, whose population as early as 1870 was 25 percent foreign-born, concentrated Germans, Swedes, Danes, and Czechs. A smaller portion of European immigrants reached Kansas, still fewer the territories to the south where Indian and Hispanic peoples and African Americans remained the major ethnic populations. But Germans outnumbered all other immigrants by far.

Many immigrants found life on the Great Plains difficult but endurable. The German Russians who settled the Dakotas discovered soil similar to that of their homeland but weather that was even more severe. Having earlier fled religious persecution in Germany for Russia, they brought with them heavy coats and the technique of using sun-dried bricks to build houses in areas where lumber was scarce. These immigrants often provided examples for other settlers less familiar with such harsh terrain.

Having traveled the huge distance with kin or members of their Old World villages, immigrants tended to form tight-knit communities on the Great Plains. Many married only within their own group. For example, only 3 percent of Norwegian men married women of a different ethnic background. Like many Mexicanos in the Southwest, several immigrant groups retained their languages well into the twentieth

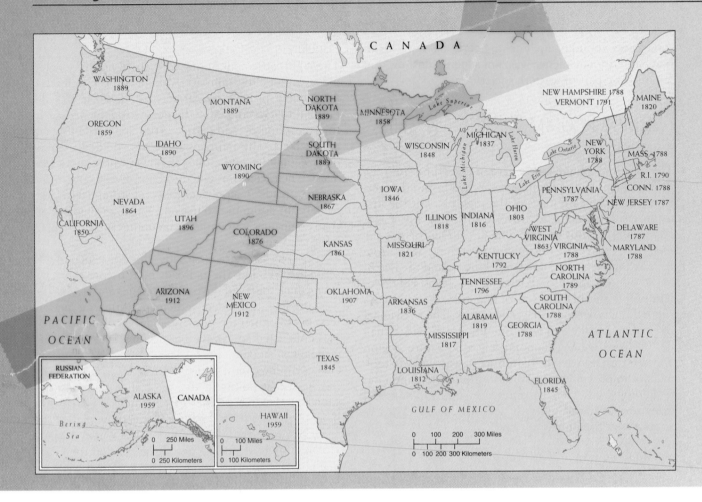

century, usually by sponsoring parochial school systems and publishing their own newspapers. A few groups closed their communities to outsiders. The Poles who migrated to central Nebraska in the 1880s, for example, formed an exclusive settlement; and the German Hutterites, who disavowed private property, lived as much as possible in seclusion in the Bon Homme colony of South Dakota, established in 1874.

Among the native-born settlers of the Great Plains, the largest number had migrated from states bordering the Mississippi River, all of which lost population in the decade after the enactment of the Homestead Act. Settling as individual families rather than as whole communities, they faced an exceptionally solitary life on the Great Plains. The prospect of doing better, which brought most homesteaders to the Great Plains in the first place, caused many families to keep seeking greener pastures. Mobility was so high that between one-third and one-half of all households pulled up stakes within a decade.

Communities eventually flourished in prosperous towns such as Grand Island, Nebraska; Coffeyville, Kansas; and Fargo, North Dakota, that served the larger agricultural region. Built alongside the railroad,

they grew as commercial centers, home to banking, medical, legal, and retail services. But closeness did not necessarily promote social equality or even deep friendship. Individuals and families in farm districts arranged themselves in a social hierarchy on the basis of education (for the handful of doctors and lawyers) and, more important, investment property (held mainly by railroad officers and bankers). Reinforced by family ties and religious and ethnic differences, this hierarchy often persisted across several generations.

Work, Dawn to Dusk

By the 1870s the Great Plains, once the home of buffalo and Indian hunters, was becoming a vast farming region populated mainly by immigrants from Europe and white Americans from east of the Mississippi. In place of the first one-room shanties, sod houses, and log cabins stood substantial frame farmhouses, along with a variety of other buildings such as barns, smokehouses, and stables. But the built environment took nothing away from the predominating vista—the expansive fields of grain.

Most farm families survived, and prospered if they could, through hard work, often from dawn to

Statehood and Ethnic Settlement

The process for admitting new states to the Union was established by Congress in the Northwest Ordinance of 1787, before the ratification of the Constitution. Although the pace at which this process operated and the way it was controlled varied from region to region and over time, its formal rules changed little. Each new state was admitted when its free population reached 60,000 and its constitution was approved by Congress, entitling those citizens eligible to vote to become full participants in the political system.

Each of the western states that entered the Union in the late nineteenth and early twentieth centuries had its own distinctive ethnic and racial composition. North Dakota, which became a state in 1889, had long had a large Native American population. An influx of newcomers, many of them European immigrants, boosted its population quickly by 1900. As the map at the right indicates, ethnic groups of European background tended to settle in clusters, mainly where they had purchased large blocs of fertile land from promoters. Nonwhites sought (or were confined to) remote locations. Much of the state remained practically uninhabited.

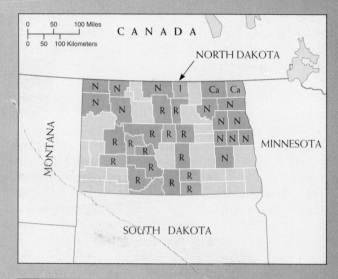

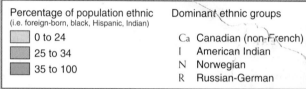

Percentage of population ethnic
(i.e. foreign-born, black, Hispanic, Indian)

- 0 to 24
- 25 to 34
- 35 to 100

Dominant ethnic groups

Ca Canadian (non-French)
I   American Indian
N   Norwegian
R   Russian-German

Source: From "The Great Plains" by James R. Shortridge, *Encyclopedia of American Social History*, Vol. II, Mary Kupiec Cayton, Elliot J. Gorn and Peter W. Williams, Editors. Copyright © 1993 by Charles Scribner's Sons. Reprinted by permission of The Gale Group.

dusk. Men's activities in the fields tended to be seasonal, with heavy work during planting and harvest; at other times, their labor centered on construction or repair of buildings and on taking care of livestock. Women's activities were cooking and canning of seasonal fruit and vegetables, washing, ironing, churning cream for butter, and keeping chickens for their eggs. Women might occasionally take in boarders, usually young men working temporarily in railroad construction, and they tended to the young children. Many women complained about the ceaseless drudgery, especially when they watched their husbands invest in farm equipment rather than domestic appliances. Others relished the challenge.

Milking the cows, hauling water, and running errands to neighboring farms could be done by the children, once they had reached the age of nine or so. The one-room school, where all grades learned together,

Crop	Time Worked		Labor Cost	
	Hand	Machine	Hand	Machine
Wheat	61 hours	3 hours	$3.55	$0.66
Corn	39 hours	15 hours	3.62	1.51
Oats	66 hours	7 hours	3.73	1.07
Loose hay	21 hours	4 hours	1.75	0.42
Baled hay	35 hours	12 hours	3.06	1.29

HAND VS. MACHINE LABOR ON THE FARM, CA. 1880

taught the basics of literacy and arithmetic that a future farmer or commercial employee would require.

The harsh climate and unyielding soil nevertheless forced all but the most reclusive families to seek out friends and neighbors. Neighbors might agree to work together haying, harvesting, and threshing grain. They also traded their labor, calculated by the hour, with families needing help with machinery or with small children in the household. The well-to-do farmer might rent his reaper in exchange for a small cash fee and, for instance, three days' labor. Women routinely

341

traded among themselves, exchanging garden produce for bread and milk or for assistance during childbirth or disability.

Much of this informal barter, however, resulted from lack of cash rather than a lasting desire to cooperate. When annual harvests were bountiful, even the farm woman's practice of bartering goods with neighbors and local merchants—butter and eggs in return for yard goods or seed—diminished sharply, replaced by cash transactions. Still, wheat production proved unsteady in the last half of the nineteenth century, and few farm families could remain reliant wholly on themselves.

For many farmers, the soil simply would not yield a livelihood, and they often owed more money than they took in. Start-up costs, including a quarter section of good land (perhaps $500) and agricultural equipment (perhaps $700), had put many farmers deep in debt to local creditors. Many eventually mortgaged their property; a sizable portion lost their land altogether. At the turn of the century, more than one-third of all farmers in the United States were tenants on someone else's land.

Again and again foreclosures wiped out the small landowner through dips in commodity prices, bad decisions, natural disasters, or illness. The swift growth of rural population soon ended. Although writers and orators alike continued to celebrate farming as the source of virtue and economic well-being, the hard reality of big money and political power told a far different story.

THE WORLD'S BREADBASKET

During the second half of the nineteenth century western farms employed the most intensive and extensive methods of agricultural production in the world. The region itself, unexcelled in its vastness, allowed farmers to bring huge numbers of acres into cultivation, while new technologies allowed them to achieve unprecedented levels of efficiency in the planting and harvesting of crops. As a result, western agriculture became increasingly integrated into international trade relations, and modern capitalism soon ruled western farms, as it did the mining and cattle industries.

New Production Technologies

Only after the trees had been cleared and grasslands cut free of roots could the soil be prepared for planting. But as farmers on the Great Plains knew so well, the sod west of the Mississippi did not yield readily to cultivation and often broke the cast-iron plows typically used by eastern farmers. Farther west, some farmers resorted to drills to plant seeds for crops such as wheat and oats. Even in the best locations, where loamy, fertile ground had built up over centuries into eight or more inches of

decayed vegetation, the preliminary breaking, or "busting," of the sod required hard labor. But as a North Dakota settler wrote to his wife back in Michigan, after the first crop the soil became as "soft as can be, any team [of men and animals] can work it."

In 1837 John Deere had designed his famous "singing plow" that easily turned prairie grasses under and turned up even highly compacted soils. Around the same time, Cyrus McCormick's reaper began to be used for cutting grain; by the 1850s his factories were turning out reapers in mass quantities. The harvester, invented in the 1870s, drew the cut stalks upward to a platform, where two men could bind them into sheaves; by the 1880s an automatic knotter tied them together. Drastically reducing the number of people traditionally required for this work, the harvester increased the pace many times over. The introduction of mechanized corn planters and mowing or raking machines for hay all but completed the technological arsenal.

In the 1890s, the U.S. commissioner of labor measured the impact of technology on farm productivity. Before the introduction of the wire binder in 1875, he reported, a farmer could not plant more than eight acres of wheat if he were to harvest it successfully without help; by 1890 the same farmer could rely on his new machine to handle 135 acres with ease and without risk of spoilage. The improvements in the last half of the century allowed an average farmer to produce up to ten times more than was possible with the old implements.

Scientific study of soil, grain, and climatic conditions was another factor in the record output. Beginning in the mid-nineteenth century, federal and state governments added inducements to the growing body of expertise, scientific information, and hands-on advice. Through the Morrill Act of 1862, land-grant colleges acquired space for campuses in return for promising to institute agricultural programs. The Department of Agriculture, which attained cabinet status in 1889, and the Weather Bureau (transferred from the War Department in 1891) also made considerable contributions to farmers' knowledge. The federal Hatch Act of 1887, which created a series of experimental agricultural stations, passed along new information, especially in the areas of soil minerals and plant growth. Many states added their own agricultural stations, usually connected with state colleges and universities.

Nevertheless, nature often reigned over technological innovation and seemed in places to take revenge against these early successes. West of the 98th meridian—a north–south line extending through western Oklahoma, central Kansas and Nebraska, and eastern Dakota—perennial dryness due to an annual rainfall of less than 28 inches constantly threatened to turn soil into dust and to break plows on the hardened ground. Summer heat burned out crops and ignited grass fires. Mountains of winter snows turned rivers into spring torrents that flooded fields; heavy fall rains washed crops away. Even good weather invited worms and flying insects to infest the crops. During the 1870s grasshoppers in clouds a mile long ate everything organic, including tree bark and clothes.

Producing for the Market

Farming changed in important ways during the last third of the nineteenth century. By 1900 few families still raised all their own provisions. Although they tended vegetable gardens and often kept fowl or livestock for household consumption, farmers raised crops mainly for the market and measured their own success or failure in terms of cash profits earned.

Wheat farmers in particular prospered. With the world population increasing at a rapid rate, the international demand for wheat was enormous, and American farmers made huge profits from the sale of this crop. Wheat production ultimately served as a barometer of the agricultural economy in the West. Farmers in all corners of the region, from Nebraska to California, expanded or contracted their holdings and planned their crops according to the price of wheat.

The new machines and expanding market did not necessarily guarantee success. Land, draft animals, and equipment remained very expensive, and start-up costs could keep a family in debt for decades. A year of good returns often preceded a year of financial disaster. Weather conditions, international markets, and railroad and steamship shipping prices all proved equally unpredictable and heartless.

The new technology and scientific expertise favored the large, well-capitalized farmer over the small one. The majority of farmers with fewer resources expanded at modest rates. Between 1880 and 1900 average farm size in the seven leading grain-growing states increased from 64.4 acres to more than 100 acres.

California

The trend toward big farms reached an apex in California, where farming as a business quickly superseded farming as a way of life. Farms of nearly 500 acres dominated the California landscape in 1870; by the turn of the century, two-thirds of the state's arable land was in 1,000-acre farms. As land reformer and social commentator Henry George noted, California was "not a country of farms but a country of plantations and estates."

This scale of production made California the national leader in wheat production by the mid-1880s. But it also succeeded dramatically with fruit and vegetables. Large- and medium-sized growers, shrewdly combined in cooperative marketing associations during the 1870s–80s, used the new refrigerator cars to ship their produce in large quantities to the East and even to Europe. By 1890, cherries, apricots, and oranges, loaded down with mountains of ice, made their way into homes across the United States.

By 1900, California had become the model for American agribusiness, not the home of self-sufficient homesteaders but the showcase of heavily capitalized farm factories. Machines soon displaced animals and even many people. Many Californios tried to hold onto their traditional forms of labor if not their land, only to become the backbone of the state's migrant work force. Intense battles in the state legislature over land and irrigation rights underscored the message that powerful forces had gathered in California to promote large-scale agricultural production.

The Toll on the Land

The new inhabitants often looked past the existing flora and fauna toward a landscape remade strictly for commercial purposes. The changes they produced in some areas were nearly as cataclysmic as those that occurred during the Ice Age.

Banishing many existing species, farmers "improved" the land by introducing exotic plants and animals—that is, biological colonies indigenous to other regions and continents. Farmers also unintentionally introduced new varieties of weeds, insect pests, and rats. Surviving portions of older grasslands and meadows eventually could be found only alongside railroad tracks, in graveyards, or inside national parks.

Numerous species disappeared altogether or suffered drastic reduction. The grizzly bear could once be found in large numbers from the Great Plains to California and throughout much of Alaska; by the early decades of the twentieth century, one nature writer estimated that only 800 survived, mostly in Yellowstone National Park. At the same time the number of wolves declined from perhaps as many as 2 million to just 200,000. By the mid-1880s, no more than 5,000 buffalo survived in the entire United States.

The slaughter of the buffalo had a dramatic impact, not only on the fate of the species but also on the grasslands of the Great Plains. Overall, the biological diversity of the region had been drastically reduced. Having killed off the giant herds, ranchers and farmers quickly shifted to cattle and sheep production. Unlike the roaming buffalo, these livestock did not range widely and soon devoured the native grasses down to their roots. With the ground cover destroyed, the soil eroded and became barren. By the end of the century, huge dust storms formed across the windswept plains.

In 1873 the U.S. Congress passed the Timber Culture Act, which allotted homesteaders an additional 160 acres of land in return for planting and cultivating forty acres of trees. Because residence was not required, and because tree planting could not be assessed for at least thirteen years, speculators filed for several claims at once, then turned around and sold the land without having planted a single tree. Although some forests were restored, neither the weather nor the soil improved.

Large-scale commercial agriculture also took a heavy toll on inland bodies of water. Before white settlement, rainfall had drained naturally into lakes and underground aquifers, and watering spots were abundant throughout the Plains. As farmers mechanically rerouted and dammed water to irrigate their crops, many bodies of water disappeared and the water table dropped. Farmers pressed for ever greater supplies of water. In 1887 the state of California formed irrigation districts, securing bond issues for construction of canals, and other western states followed. But by the 1890s, irrigation had seemed to reach its limit without federal support. The Newlands or National Reclamation Act of 1902 added 1 million acres of irrigated land, and state irrigation districts added more than 10 million acres. Expensive to taxpayers, and ultimately benefitting corporate farmers rather than small landowners, these projects further diverted water and totally transformed the landscape.

Although western state politicians and federal officials debated water rights for decades, they rarely considered the impact on the environment. The need to maintain the water supply indirectly led to the creation of national forests and the Forest Service. Western farmers supported the General Land Revision Act of 1891, which gave the president the power to establish forest reserves to protect watersheds against the threats posed by lumbering, overgrazing, and forest fires. In the years that followed, President Benjamin Harrison established 15 forest reserves exceeding 16 million acres, and President Grover Cleveland added more than 21 million acres. But only in 1897 did the secretary of the interior finally gain the authority to regulate the use of these reserves.

The Forest Management Act of 1897 and the National Reclamation Act of 1902 set the federal government on the path of large-scale regulatory activities. The Forest Service was established in 1905, and in 1907 forest reserves were transferred from the Department of the Interior to the Department of Agriculture. The federal government would now play an even larger role in economic development of the West, dealing mainly with corporate farmers and ranchers eager for improvements.

THE WESTERN LANDSCAPE

The public east of the Mississippi craved stories about the West and visual images of its sweeping vistas. Artists and photographers built their reputations on what they saw and imagined. Scholars, from geologists and botanists to historians and anthropologists, toured the trans-Mississippi West in pursuit of new data. The region and its peoples came to represent what was both unique and magnificent about the American landscape.

Nature's Majesty

By the end of the century, scores of writers had described spectacular, breathtaking natural sites of the American West such as the Grand Tetons and High Sierras, vast meadows of waving grasses and beautiful flowers, expansive canyons and rushing white rivers, and exquisite deserts covered with sagebrush or dotted with flowering cactus and enticing precisely for their stark qualities.

Moved by such reveries, the federal government began to set aside huge tracts of land as nature reserves. In 1864 Congress passed the Yosemite Act, which placed the spectacular cliffs and giant sequoias under the management of the state of California. Meanwhile, explorers returned to the East awestruck by the varied terrain of the Rocky Mountains, the largest mountain chain in North America. In 1872 Congress named Yellowstone the first national park. Yosemite and Sequoia in California, Crater Lake in Oregon, Mount Ranier in Washington, and Glacier in Montana all became national parks between 1890 and 1910.

Landscape painters, particularly the group that became known as the Rocky Mountain School, also piqued the public's interest in western scenery. In the 1860s German-born Albert Bierstadt, equipped with a camera, traveled the Oregon Trail. Using his photographs as inspiration, Bierstadt painted mountains so wondrous that they became nearly surreal, projecting a divine aura behind the majesty of nature. His huge canvases with exacting details of animals and plants thrilled viewers and sold for tens of thousands of dollars.

The Legendary Wild West

By the end of the century, many Americans, rich and poor alike, imagined the West as a land of promise and opportunity and, above all, of excitement and adventure. Future president Theodore Roosevelt, soon after his election to the New York state assembly in 1882, was horrified to see himself lampooned in the newspapers as a dandy and weakling. A year later, he bought a ranch in South Dakota. To reconstruct his public image, he wrote three books recounting his adventures in the West, claiming that they had instilled in him not only personal bravery and "hardihood" but self-reliance. The West, as Roosevelt insisted, meant "vigorous manhood."

This imagery appeared in the first westerns, the dime novels that sold in the 1860s in editions of 50,000

Buffalo Bill's "Wild West Show" poster from 1899. William Cody's theatrical company toured the United States and Europe for decades, reenacting various battles and occasionally switching to football (cowboys versus Indians).

or more. Competing against stories about pirates, wars, crime, and sea adventures, the Western genre outsold the others. Edward Zane Carroll Judson's *Buffalo Bill, the King of the Border Men*, first published in 1869, spawned hundreds of other novels, thousands of stories, and an entire magazine devoted to Buffalo Bill. Real-life African American cowboy Nat Love lived on in the imaginations of many generations as Edward L. Wheeler's dime-novel hero Deadwood Dick, who rode the range as a white cowboy in black clothes in over thirty stories. His girlfriend, Calamity Jane, "the most reckless buchario in ther Hills," also took on mythic qualities.

Railroad promoters and herd owners actively encouraged these romantic and heroic images. Cowman Joseph McCoy staged Wild West shows in St. Louis and Chicago, where Texas cowboys entertained prospective buyers by roping calves and breaking horses. Many cowboys played up this imaginary role, dressing and talking to match the stories told about them. The first professional photographers often made their living touring the West, setting up studios where cowboys and prostitutes posed in elaborate costumes.

Former Pony Express rider, army scout, and famed buffalo hunter William F. Cody hit upon the idea of an extravaganza that would bring the legendary West to those who could never experience it in person. "Buffalo Bill" Cody made sharpshooter Annie Oakley a star rodeo performer. Entrancing crowds with her stunning accuracy with pistol or rifle, Oakley shot dimes in midair and cigarettes from her husband's mouth. Cody also hired hundreds of cowboys and large numbers of

Sioux Indians to perform in mock stagecoach robberies and battles. With far less fanfare, many veteran cowboys enlisted themselves on dude ranches for tourists or performed as rope twirlers or yodeling singers in theaters across the United States.

The "American Primitive"

New technologies of graphic reproduction encouraged painters and photographers to provide new images of the West, authentic as well as fabricated. A young German American artist, Charles Schreyvogel, saw Buffalo Bill's tent show in Buffalo and decided to make the West his life's work. His canvases depicted Indian warriors and U.S. cavalry fighting furiously but without blood and gore. Charles Russell, a genuine cowboy, painted the life he knew, but also indulged in imaginary scenarios, producing paintings of buffalo hunts and first encounters between Indian peoples and white explorers.

Frederic Remington, the most famous of all the western artists, left Yale Art School to visit Montana in 1881, became a Kansas sheepherder and tavern owner, and then returned to painting. Painstakingly accurate in physical details, especially of horses, his paintings were fictionalized, celebrating the "winning of the West" from the Indian peoples.

Painters and photographers led the way for scholarly research on the various Indian societies. An early ethnographer and pioneer of fieldwork in anthropology, Lewis Henry Morgan, devoted his life to the study of Indian family or kinship patterns, mostly of eastern tribes such as the Iroquois, who adopted him into their Hawk Clan.

One of the most influential interpreters of the cultures of living tribespeople was Alice Cunningham Fletcher, an archaeologist. In 1879 she met Suzette (Bright Eyes) La Flesche of the Omaha tribe, who was on a speaking tour to gain support for her people, primarily to prevent their removal from tribal lands. Well known as an expert on Omaha music, Fletcher also supported the Omahas' campaign to gain individual title to tribal lands, eventually drafting legislation that was enacted by Congress as the Omaha Act of 1882.

While white settlers and the federal government continued to threaten the survival of tribal life, Indian lore became a major pursuit of scholars and amateurs alike. Adults and children delighted in turning up arrowheads. Fraternal organizations such as the Elks and Eagles borrowed tribal terminology. The Boy Scouts and Girl Scouts, the nation's premier youth organizations, instilled strength of character through large doses of tribal lore. And the U.S. Treasury stamped images of tribal chiefs and buffalo on the nation's most frequently used coins.

THE TRANSFORMATION OF INDIAN SOCIETIES

In 1871 the U.S. government formally ended the treaty system, eclipsing without completely abolishing the sovereignty of Indian nations. Still, the tribes persisted. Using a mixture of survival strategies from farming and trade to the leasing of reservation lands, they both adapted to changing conditions and maintained old traditions and lore.

Reform Policy and Politics

For decades, reformers, mainly from the Protestant churches, had lobbied Congress for a program of salvation through assimilation, and they looked to the Board of Indian Commissioners, created in 1869, to carry out this mission. The board often succeeded in mediating conflicts among the various tribes crowded onto reservations but made far less headway in converting them to Christianity or transforming them into prosperous farming communities. The majority of Indian peoples lived in poverty and misery, deprived of their traditional means of survival and more often than not subjected to fraud by corrupt government officials and private suppliers. Reformers who observed these conditions firsthand nevertheless remained unshaken in their belief that tribespeople must be raised out of the darkness of ignorance into the light of civilization.

Some reformers were genuinely outraged by the government's continuous violation of treaty obligations and the military enforcement of the reservation policy. One of the most influential was Helen Hunt Jackson, a noted poet and author of children's stories. Her book-length exposé, *A Century of Dishonor*, published in 1881, detailed the mistreatment of Indian peoples.

The Dawes Severalty Act, passed by Congress in 1887, incorporated many of these measures and established federal Indian policy for decades to come. The act allowed the president to distribute land not to tribes but to individuals legally "severed" from their tribes. Those who accepted the land allotment of 160 acres and agreed to allow the government to sell unallotted tribal lands (with some funds set aside for education) could petition to become citizens of the United States. A little over a decade after its enactment, many reformers believed that the Dawes Act had resolved the

"Indian problem." Hollow Horn Bear, a Sioux chief, offered a different opinion, judging the Dawes Act to be "only another trick of the whites."

The Dawes Act successfully undermined tribal sovereignty but offered little compensation. Indian religions and sacred ceremonies were banned, the telling of legends and myths forbidden, and shaman and medicine men imprisoned or exiled for continuing their traditional practices. "Indian schools" forbade Indian languages, clothing styles, and even hair fashions in order to "kill the Indian . . . and save the man," as one schoolmaster put it.

Treated as savages, Indian children fled most white schools. Government agencies allotted adults inferior farmland, inadequate tools, and little training for agricultural self-sufficiency. Seeing scant advantage in assimilating, only a minority of adults dropped their tribal religion for Christianity or their communal ways for the accumulation of private property. Within the next forty years, the Indian peoples lost 60 percent of the reservation land remaining in 1887 and 66 percent of the land allotted to them as homesteaders. The tenets of the Dawes Act were not reversed until 1934. In that year, Congress passed the Indian Reorganization Act, which affirmed the integrity of Indian cultural institutions and returned some land to tribal ownership (See Chapter 24).

The Ghost Dance

After the passage of the Dawes Severalty Act, one more cycle of rebellion remained for the Sioux. In 1888, Paiute prophet Wovoka, ill with scarlet fever, had a vision during a total eclipse of the sun. In his vision, the Creator told him that if the Indian peoples learned to love each other, they would be granted a special place in the afterlife. The Creator also gave him the Ghost Dance, which the prophet performed for others and soon spread throughout the tribe. The Sioux came to believe that when the day of judgment came, all Indian peoples who had ever lived would return to their lost world and white peoples would vanish from the earth.

White Americans took the Ghost Dance as a warning of tribal retribution rather than a religious ceremony. As thousands of Sioux danced to exhaustion, local whites demanded the practice be stopped. A group of the Sioux, now fearing mass murder, moved into hiding in the Bad Lands of South Dakota.

The U.S. Seventh Cavalry, led in part by survivors of the battle of Little Bighorn, pursued them. Three hundred undernourished Sioux, freezing and without horses, agreed to accompany the troops to Wounded Knee Creek on the Pine Ridge Reservation. There, on December 29, 1890, they were surrounded by soldiers armed with automatic guns. While the peace-seeking Chief Big Foot, who had personally raised a white flag of surrender, lay dying of pneumonia, the U.S. troops expected the Sioux to surrender their few remaining weapons, but an accidental gunshot from one deaf brave who misunderstood the command caused panic on both sides.

Within minutes, 200 Sioux had been cut down, and dozens of soldiers wounded, mostly in their own cross fire. Although the battle had ended, for two hours soldiers continued to shoot at anything that moved, mostly women and children straggling away.

Black Elk later recalled, "I can see that something else died there in the bloody mud, and was buried in the blizzard. A people's dream died there. It was a beautiful dream. . . . The nation's hoop is broken and scattered. There is no center any longer, and the sacred tree is dead."

Endurance and Rejuvenation

Not even an insular, peaceful agricultural existence on semi-arid, treeless terrain necessarily provided protection. Nor did a total willingness to accept white offers peacefully prevent attack. The Pimas of Arizona, for instance, had a well-developed agricultural system adapted to a scarce supply of water, and they rarely warred with other tribes. After the arrival of white settlers, they integrated Christian symbolism into their religion, learned to speak English, and even fought with the U.S. cavalry against the Apaches. Still, the Pimas saw their lands stolen, their precious waterways diverted, and their families impoverished.

A majority of tribes, especially smaller ones, sooner or later reached numbers too low to maintain their collective existence. The Quapaws, for example, formally disbanded in the aftermath of the Dawes Severalty Act. Later generations petitioned the federal government and regained tribal status, established ceremonial grounds and cultural centers (or bingo halls), and built up one of the most durable powwows in the state. Even so, much of the tribal lore that had underpinned distinct identity had vanished.

A small minority of tribes, grown skillful in adapting to dramatically changing circumstances, managed to persist and even grow. The Cheyennes had found themselves caught geographically between aggressive tribes in the Great Lakes region and had migrated into the Missouri area, where they split into small village-sized communities. By the mid-nineteenth century they had become expert horse traders on the Great Plains, well prepared to meet the massive influx of white settlers by shifting their location frequently. They avoided the worst of the pestilence that spread from the diseases white people carried, and likewise survived widespread intermarriage with the Sioux in the 1860s and 1870s. Instructed to settle, many Cheyenne took up elements of the Christian religion and became farmers, also without losing their tribal identity.

The Navajos experienced an extraordinary renewal, largely because they built a life in territory considered worthless by whites. Having migrated to the Southwest from the northwestern part of the continent perhaps 700 years earlier, the *Diné* ("the People," as they called themselves) had already survived earlier invasions by the Spanish. In 1863 they had been conquered again through the cooperation of hostile tribes led by the famous Colonel Kit Carson. Their crops burned, their fruit trees destroyed, 8,000 Navajo were forced along the 300-mile "Long Walk" to the desolate Bosque Redondo reservation, where they

This 1916 photograph of Chief American Horse shows the Oglala Sioux leader accepting his tribe's allotment from government agents at Pine Ridge, South Dakota. A veteran of the "Fetterman Massacre" during Red Cloud's war for the Bozeman Trail during the 1860s, American Horse had seen his people's territory reduced in size from more than 2.5 million acres to less than 150,000.

nearly starved. Four years later, the Indian Bureau allowed the severely reduced tribe to return to a fraction of its former lands.

By 1880 the Navajos' numbers approached the levels reached before their conquest by white Americans. But as they were hemmed in, they quickly depleted the deer and antelope, so that sheep alone remained to serve as a food reserve for years of bad crops. Increasingly, the Navajo turned to wool crafts of rugs and blankets, much in demand in the East, and eventually to silver jewelry as well. The Navajos lived on the economic margin, but they persevered to become by far the largest Indian nation in the United States.

The Hopis, like the Navajos, survived by stubbornly clinging to lands unwanted by white settlers and by adapting to drastically changing conditions. The Hopis had lived for centuries in their cliff cities. Their highly developed theological beliefs, peaceful social system, sand paintings, and kachina dolls helped them gather the public supporters and financial resources to fend off further threats to their reservations.

Fortunate northwestern tribes remained relatively isolated from white settlers until the early twentieth century, although they had begun trading with white visitors centuries earlier. Northwestern peoples relied largely on salmon and other resources of the region's rivers and bays. In *potlatch* ceremonies, leaders redistributed tribal wealth and maintained their personal status and the status of their tribe by giving lavish gifts to invited guests. Northwest peoples also made intricate wood carvings, including commemorative *totem* poles, that recorded their history and identified their regional status. Northwestern peoples maintained their cultural integrity in part through connections with kin in Canada, as did southern tribes with kin in Mexico. In these countries native populations suffered less pressure from new populations and retained more tribal authority than in the United States.

Indian nations approached their nadir as the century came to a close. The descendants of the great pre-Columbian civilizations had been conquered by foreigners, their population reduced to fewer than 250,000. Under the pressure of assimilation, the remaining tribespeople became known to non-Indians as the vanishing Americans. It would take several generations before Indian sovereignty experienced a resurgence.

CONCLUSION

In 1890 the director of the U.S. Census announced that the nation's "unsettled area has been so broken into by isolated bodies of settlement that there can hardly be said to be a frontier line." The development of the West met the nation's demand for mineral resources for its expanding industries and agricultural products for the people of the growing cities. Envisioning the West as a cornucopia whose boundless treasures would offer themselves to the willing pioneer, most of the new residents failed to calculate the odds against their making a prosperous livelihood as miners, farmers, or petty merchants. Nor could they appreciate the long-term consequences of the violence they brought with them from the battlefields of the Civil War to the far reaches of the West.

CHRONOLOGY

1848	Treaty of Guadalupe Hidalgo	1873	Timber Culture Act Red River War
1849–1860s	California Gold Rush	1874–75	Sioux battles in Black Hills of Dakotas
1853	Gadsden Purchase		
1858	Comstock Lode discovered	1876	Custer's Last Stand
1859	Cortina's War in South Texas	1877	Defeat of the Nez Percé
1862	Homestead Act makes free land available	1881	Helen Hunt Jackson, *A Century of Dishonor*
	Morrill Act authorizes land-grant colleges	1882	Edmunds Act outlaws polygamy
1865–67	Great Sioux War	1885–87	Droughts and severe winters cause the collapse of the cattle boom
1866	Texas cattle drives begin		
	Medicine Lodge Treaty establishes reservation system	1887	Dawes Severalty Act
	Alaska purchased	1890	Sioux Ghost Dance movement
1869	Board of Indian Commissioners created		Massacre of Lakota Sioux at Wounded Knee
	Buffalo Bill, the King of the Border Men sets off "Wild West" publishing craze		Census Bureau announces the end of the frontier line
1870s	Grasshopper attacks on the Great Plains	1897	Forest Management Act gives the federal government authority over forest reserves
1872	Yellowstone National Park created		

REVIEW QUESTIONS

1. Discuss the role of federal legislation in accelerating and shaping the course of westward expansion.

2. How did the incorporation of western territories into the United States affect Indian nations such as the Sioux or the Nez Percé? Discuss the causes and consequences of the Indian Wars. Discuss the significance of reservation policy and the Dawes Severalty Act for tribal life.

3. What were some of the major technological advances in mining and in agriculture that promoted the development of the western economy?

4. Describe the unique features of Mexicano communities in the Southwest before and after the mass immigration of Anglos. How did changes in the economy affect the patterns of labor and the status of women in these communities?

5. What role did the Homestead Act play in western expansion? How did farm families on the Great Plains divide chores among their members? What factors determined the likelihood of economic success or failure?

6. Describe the responses of artists, naturalists, and conservationists to the western landscape. How did their photographs, paintings, and stories shape perceptions of the West in the East?

RECOMMENDED READING

Alfred L. Bush and Lee Clark Mitchell, *The Photograph and the American Indian* (1994). A comprehensive study of photos of Indians from 1840 to the present.

William Cronon, George Miles, and Jay Gitlin, eds., *Under an Open Sky: Rethinking America's Western Past* (1992). A useful collection of essays stressing the bitter conflicts over territory, the racial and gender barriers against democratic community models, and the tragic elements of western history.

Jon Gjerde, *The Minds of the West: Ethnocultural Evolution in the Rural Middle West, 1830–1914* (1997). A combination cultural and economic history that weighs the importance of ethnicity in shaping of American identities in the farming regions of the Middle West. Gjerde pays close attention to the religious institutions and systems of belief of European immigrants as the basis of community formation.

John C. Hudson, *Making the Corn Belt: A Geographical History of Middle-Western Agriculture* (1994). An ecologically oriented study of corn growing that traces its development.

Ellizabeth Jameson and Susan Armitage, eds., *Writing the Range* (1997). A collection of essays on women in the U.S. West that present an inclusive historical narrative based on the experiences of women of differing backgrounds, races, and ethnic groups.

Patricia Nelson Limerick, *The Legacy of Conquest: The Unbroken Past of the American West* (1987). A controversial and popular revisionist history of the West. Focused on conflict, Limerick's study shows the frontier most of all as a site of racial antagonism.

Frederick C. Luebke, ed., *Ethnicity on the Great Plains* (1980). Essays on Germans, Czechs, Russians, and other Europeans resettling in agricultural districts. These essays show that the immigrants, rather than assimilating, often sought to recreate their homeland communities within the United States.

John G. Neihardt, *Black Elk Speaks: Being the Life Story of a Holy Man of the Oglala Sioux* (1961). Published originally in 1932. Black Elk recalls the tragedy of his tribe's destruction with the events around General George A. Custer and the battle of Little Bighorn.

Thomas E. Sheridan, *Los Tucsonenses: The Mexican Community in Tucson, 1854–1941* (1986). A highly readable account of Mexican-American communities in the Southwest. Sheridan shows how a mid-century accommodation of Anglos and Mexicanos faded with the absorption of the region into the national economy and with the steady displacement of Mexicano community from its agricultural landholdings.

Robert M. Utley, *The Lance and the Shield: The Life and Times of Sitting Bull* (1993). A careful reinterpretation of a leading chief's attempt to demand religious freedom for Indians.

Richard White, *"It's Your Misfortune and None of My Own": A History of the American West* (1991). A wide-ranging history of the West with emphasis on cultural contact and the environment. White shows that conflicting cultures with little understanding of each other clashed tragically, with great losses to the environment and the hopes of a democratic American community.

CHAPTER NINETEEN

THE INCORPORATION OF AMERICA

1865–1900

AMERICAN COMMUNITIES
Packingtown, Chicago, Illinois

Approaching Packingtown, the neighborhood adjoining the Union Stockyards, the center of Chicago's great meat-packing industry, one noticed first the pungent odor, a mixture of smoke, fertilizer, and putrid flesh, blood, and hair from the slaughtered animals. A little closer, the stench of the uncovered garbage dump blended in. Finally one crossed "Bubbly Creek," a lifeless offshoot of the Chicago River aptly named for the effect of the carbolic acid gas that formed from the decaying refuse poured in by the meat-packing plants. Railroads crisscrossed the entire area, bringing in thousands of animals each day and carrying out meat for sale in markets across the country.

Packingtown occupied about one square mile of land bounded by stockyards, packing plants, and freight yards. With a population of 30,000–40,000 at the end of the nineteenth century, it was a rapidly growing community of old and new immigrants who depended on the meat-packing industry for their livelihood. An average household included six or seven people—parents, two or three children, and two or three boarders. They lived typically in wooden houses divided into four or more flats. Although Irish, Germans, Bohemians, Poles, Lithuanians, and Slovaks were squeezed together in this solidly working-class neighborhood, strong ethnic identities persisted. Few households included residents of more than one nationality, and interethnic marriages were rare. Nearly everyone professed the Roman Catholic faith, yet each ethnic group maintained its own church and often its own parochial school, where children were taught in their parents' language. Political organizations, fraternal societies, and even gymnastic clubs and drama groups reflected these ethnic divisions.

The one local institution that bridged the different groups was the saloon. Located on virtually every street corner, saloons offered important services to the community, hosting weddings and dances, providing meeting places for trade unions and fraternal societies, and cashing paychecks. During the frequent seasons of unemployment, Packingtown workers spent a lot of time in saloons. Here they often made friends across ethnic divisions, an extension of their common work experience in the nearby stockyard and packinghouses.

Most of the meat-packing industry's first "knife men"—the skilled workers in the "killing gangs" that managed the actual slaughtering and cutting operations—were German and Irish. Many had learned their butcher's craft in the Old Country. Below them were the common laborers, mainly recent immigrants from Eastern Europe. Having no previous experience in meat packing, these workers found themselves in the lowest-paid jobs, such as the by-product manufacturing of glue and oleo. A sizable portion had never before earned wages. They soon discovered, as one Lithuanian laborer put it, that "money was everything and a man without money must die." But the money available—even a daily wage of $2 (or less)—was often not enough. The death rate from tuberculosis in Packingtown was thought to be the highest in Chicago and among the highest in the nation.

The Packingtown community was bound into an elaborate economic network that reached distant parts of the United States, transforming the way farmers raised livestock and grains, railroads operated, and consumers ate their meals. These workers helped make Chicago a gateway city, a destination point for raw materials coming in from the West as well as a point of export for products of all kinds.

Chicago meat packers, led by the "big five" of Armour, Cudahy, Morris, Schwarzschild and Sulzberger, and Swift, expanded more than 900 percent between 1870 and 1890, dominating the national market for meat and establishing a standard for monopoly capitalism in the late nineteenth century. In the process, they also became the city's largest manufacturing employer. They built huge, specialized factories during the 1860s and 1870s that speeded the killing process and—thanks to mountains of ice brought by rail from ponds and lakes—operated year round. The introduction of an efficiently refrigerated railroad car in the 1880s made it possible to ship meat nationwide. Consumers had long believed that only meat butchered locally was safe to eat, but now cheap Chicago-packed beef and pork began to appear on every meat eater's table. Local packinghouses throughout the Midwest succumbed to the ruthless competition from Chicago.

Chicago's control of the mass market for meat affected all aspects of the industry. Midwestern farmers practically abandoned raising calves on open pastures. Instead, they bought two-year-old steers from the West and fattened them on home-grown corn in feedlots, making sure that bulk went into edible parts rather than muscle and bone. The feedlot—a kind of rural factory—replaced pasture just as pasture had earlier supplanted prairie grasslands.

Few of the workers in Chicago's stockyards had seen a farm since they left their homelands. But as the working hands of what poet Carl Sandburg would later call the "City of the Big Shoulders" and "Hog Butcher for the World," they played their part, along with the farmer, the grain dealer, the ironworker, the teamster, and many others in bringing together the neighboring countryside, distant regions, and the city in a common endeavor.

Chicago

KEY TOPICS

- The rise of big business and the formation of the national labor movement
- The growth of cities
- The transformation of southern society

- The Gilded Age
- Changes in education
- Commercial amusements and organized sports

THE RISE OF INDUSTRY, THE TRIUMPH OF BUSINESS

At the time of the Civil War, the typical American business was a small enterprise, owned and managed by a single family and producing goods for a local or regional market. By the turn of the century, businesses depending on large-scale investments had organized as corporations and grown to unforeseen size. These mammoth firms could afford to mass-produce goods for national and even international markets. At the helm stood unimaginably wealthy men such as Andrew Carnegie, Philip Danforth Armour, Jay Gould, and John D. Rockefeller, all powerful leaders of a new national business community.

A Revolution in Technology

In the decades after the Civil War, American industry transformed itself into a new wonder of the world. The Centennial Exposition of 1876, held in Philadelphia, celebrated not so much the American Revolution 100 years earlier as the industrial and technological promise of the century to come. Its central theme was *power*. In the main building—at the time the largest on Earth—the visiting emperor of Brazil marked the opening day by throwing a switch on a giant steam engine. Examining the telephone, which he had never before seen in operation, he gasped, "My God, it talks!" Patented that year by Alexander Graham Bell, the telephone signaled the rise of the United States to world leadership in industrial technology.

The year 1876 also marked the opening of Thomas Alva Edison's laboratory in Menlo Park, New Jersey. Three years later, his research team hit upon its most marketable invention, an incandescent lamp that burned for more than thirteen hours. By 1882 the Edison Electric Light Company had launched its service in New York City's financial district.

By this time American inventors, who had filed nearly half a million patents since the close of the Civil War, were previewing the marvels of the next century. Henry Ford, working as an electrical engineer for the Detroit Edison Company, was already experimenting with the gasoline-burning internal combustion engine and designing his own automobile. By 1900 American companies had produced more than 4,000 automobiles. In 1903 Wilbur and Orville Wright staged the first airplane flight near Kitty Hawk, North Carolina.

A major force behind economic growth was the vast transcontinental railroad, completed in 1869. The addition of three more major lines (the Southern Pacific, the Northern Pacific, and the Atchison, Topeka, and Santa Fe) in the early 1880s and the Great Northern a decade later completed the most extensive transportation network in the world. The nation's first big business, railroads linked cities in every state and served a nationwide market for goods. Freight trains carried the bountiful natural resources, such as iron, coal, and minerals that supplied the raw materials for industry, as well as food for the growing urban populations.

The monumental advances in transportation and communication facilitated the progressively westward relocation of industry. The geographic center of manufacturing (as computed by the gross value of products) was near the middle of Pennsylvania in 1850, in western Pennsylvania by 1880, and near Mansfield, Ohio, in 1900.

Industry grew at a pace that was not only unprecedented but previously unimaginable. In 1865 the annual production of goods was estimated at $2 billion; by 1900 it stood at $13 billion, transforming the United States from fourth to first in the world in terms of productivity.

Mechanization Takes Command

This second industrial revolution depended on many factors, but none was more important than the application of new technologies to increase the productivity of labor and the volume of goods. Machines, factory managers, and workers together created a system of continuous production by which more could be made, and faster, than anywhere else on earth. Higher productivity depended not only on machinery and technology but on economies of scale and speed, reorganization of factory labor and business management, and the unparalleled growth of a market for goods of all kinds.

All these changes depended in turn on a new source of fuel, anthracite coal, which was widely used after 1850. Reliable and inexpensive sources of energy made possible dramatic changes in the industrial uses of light, heat, and motion. Equally important, coal fueled the great open-hearth furnaces and mills of the iron and steel industry. By the end of the century, the United States steel industry was the world's largest.

New systems of mass production replaced wasteful and often chaotic practices and speeded up the delivery of finished goods. In the 1860s meat packers set up one of the earliest production lines. This "disassembly line" displaced patterns of hand labor that were centuries old. The production line became standard in most areas of manufacturing.

Sometimes the invention of a single machine could instantly transform production, mechanizing every stage from processing the raw material to packaging the product. The cigarette-making machine, patented in 1881, shaped the tobacco, encased it in an endless paper tube, and snipped off the tube at cigarette-length intervals. This machine could produce more than 7,000 cigarettes per hour, replacing the worker, who at best made 3,000 per day. After a few more improvements, fifteen machines could meet the total demand for American cigarettes. Within a generation, continuous production also revolutionized the making of furniture, cloth, grain products, soap, and canned goods; the refining, distilling, and processing of animal and vegetable fats; and eventually the manufacture of automobiles.

The Expanding Market for Goods

To distribute the growing volume of goods, businesses demanded new techniques of marketing and merchandising. For generations, legions of sellers, or "drummers," had worked their routes, pushing goods, especially hardware and patent medicines, to individual buyers and retail stores. The appearance of mail-order houses after the Civil War accompanied the consolidation of the railroad lines and the expansion of the postal system. Rates were lowered for freight and postage alike, and railroad stations opened post offices and sold money orders. By 1896 rural free delivery had reached distant communities.

Growing directly out of these services, the successful Chicago-based mail-order houses drew rural and urban consumers into a common marketplace. Sears, Roebuck and Company and Montgomery Ward offered an enormous variety of goods, from shoes to buggies to gasoline stoves and cream separators. The Sears catalogue offered Armour's summer sausage as well as Aunt Jemima's Pancake Flour and Queen Mary

Scotch Oatmeal, both made of grains that came from the agricultural heartland. In turn, the purchases made by farm families through the Sears catalogue sent cash flowing into Chicago.

The chain store achieved similar economies of scale. By 1900, a half-dozen grocery chains had sprung up. The largest was A&P, originally named the Great Atlantic and Pacific Tea Company to celebrate the completion of the transcontinental railroad. Frank and Charles Woolworth offered inexpensive variety goods in five-and-ten-cent stores. Hurt financially by this competition, community-based retailers headed the lobby for antichain legislation.

Opening shortly after the Civil War, department stores began to take up much of the business formerly enjoyed by specialty shops, offering a spectrum of services that included restaurants, rest rooms, ticket agencies, nurseries, reading rooms, and post offices. Elegantly appointed with imported carpets, sweeping marble staircases, and crystal chandeliers, the department store raised retailing to new heights. By the close of the century, the names of Marshall Field of

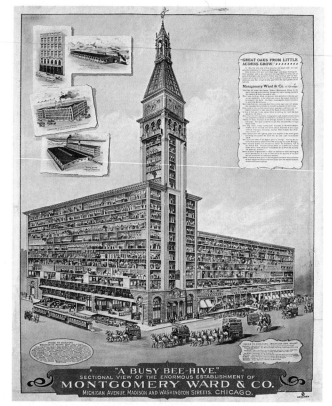

Montgomery Ward Company, Chicago, ca. 1870s. This sectional view imaginatively strips away exterior walls to show the activity of each department of the great mail-order firm. The artist suggests that all who work at the Ward Company must be overwhelmingly busy simply to meet customer demand.

Source: Lithograph ICHi-01622. "A Busy Bee-Hive" Montgomery Ward & Co., Michigan Avenue, Madison and Washington Streets, Chicago, Boston, MA; ca. 1899, printed by Forbes Company.

Chicago, Filene's of Boston, the Emporium of San Francisco, Wanamaker's of Philadelphia, and Macy's of New York had come to represent the splendors of those great cities as well as the apex of mass retailing.

Advertising lured customers to the department stores, the chains, and the independent neighborhood shops. The advertising revolution began in 1869, when Francis Wayland Ayer founded the first advertising agency. With the help of this new sales tool, gross revenues of retailers raced upward from $8 million in 1860 to $102 million in 1900.

Integration, Combination, and Merger

The business community aspired to exercise greater control of the economy and to enlarge the commercial empire. From the source of raw material to the organization of production, from the conditions of labor to the climate of public opinion, business leaders acted shrewdly. Economic cycles alternating between rapid growth and sharp decline also promoted the rise of big business. Major setbacks in 1873 and 1893 wiped out weak competitors, allowing the strongest firms to rebound swiftly and to expand their sales and scale of operation during the recovery period.

Businesses grew in two distinct, if overlapping, ways. Through *vertical integration* a firm gained control of production at every step of the way, from raw materials through processing to transport and merchandising of the finished items. In 1899 the United Fruit Company began to build a network of wholesale houses, and within two years it had opened distribution centers in twenty-one major cities. Eventually, it controlled an elaborate system of Central American plantations and temperature-controlled shipping and storage facilities for its highly perishable bananas. The firm became one of the nation's largest corporations.

The second means of growth, *horizontal combination*, entailed gaining control of the market for a single product. The most famous case was the Standard Oil Company, founded by John D. Rockefeller in 1870. Operating out of Cleveland in a highly competitive but lucrative field, Rockefeller first secured preferential rates from railroads eager to ensure a steady supply of oil. He then convinced or coerced other local oil operators to sell their stock to him. The Standard Oil Trust, established in 1882, controlled over 90 percent of the nation's oil-refining industry.

In 1890 Congress passed the Sherman Antitrust Act to restore competition by encouraging small business. Ironically, the courts interpreted the law in ways that hindered the organization of trade unions (on grounds that unions restricted the free flow of labor) and actually helped the consolidation of business. Over 2,600 firms vanished between 1898 and 1902 alone. By 1910 the industrial giants that would dominate the American economy until the last half of the twentieth century—U.S. Rubber, Goodyear, American Smelting and Refining, Anaconda Copper, General Electric, Westinghouse, Nabisco, Swift and Company, Armour, International Harvester, Eastman-Kodak, and American Can—had already formed.

The Gospel of Wealth

Ninety percent of the nation's business leaders were churchgoing Protestants. They attributed their personal achievement to hard work and perseverance. Ironically, their faith had much in common with the secular theories of naturalist Charles Darwin. They believed that the rise of big business, like the evolution of the species, depended on the survival of the fittest.

One version of this "gospel of wealth" justified the ruthless behavior of entrepreneurs who accrued wealth and power through shady deals and conspiracies. Speculator Jay Gould wrung his fortune, it was widely believed, from the labor of others. He rose quickly from his modest origins through a series of unsavory financial maneuvers and such high-handed measures as sending armed strike-breakers to seize a factory.

Speculation in railroads proved Gould's forte. He took over the Erie Railroad, paying off New York legislators to get the state to finance its expansion. He acquired the U.S. Express Company by pressuring and tricking its stockholders. When threatened with arrest, Gould sold off his shares for $9 million and moved on to the Union Pacific, where he cut wages, precipitated strikes, and manipulated elections in western and plains states. Tired of being caricatured in the press as a great swindler, Gould bought the leading newspapers.

Andrew Carnegie offered a strikingly different model. A poor immigrant from Scotland, Carnegie spent his boyhood studying bookkeeping at night while working days in a textile mill. In 1852 he became the personal secretary of the superintendent of the Pennsylvania Railroad's western division. He learned quickly and soon stepped into the superintendent's position. While improving passenger train service, he invested brilliantly to build funds for his next venture.

Carnegie built an empire in steel. A genius at vertical integration, he undercut his competitors by using the latest technology and designing his own systems of cost analysis. By 1900 Carnegie managed the most efficient steel mills in the world and accounted for one-third of the nation's output. When he sold out to J. P. Morgan's new United States Steel Corporation in 1901, his personal share of the proceeds came to $225 million.

Carnegie was well known as a civic leader. From one point of view, he was a despot who underpaid his employees and ruthlessly managed their working conditions. But to the patrons of the public libraries, art museums, concert halls, colleges, and universities that he funded, Carnegie appeared to be the greatest single philanthropist of the age. By the time he died, he had given away his massive personal fortune.

LABOR IN THE AGE OF BIG BUSINESS

Like the gospel of wealth, the "gospel of work" affirmed the dignity of hard work, thrift, and the importance of individual initiative. But unlike business leaders, the philosophers of American working people did not believe in riches as the proof of work well done, or in the lust for power as the driving force of progress. On the contrary, they contended that honesty and competence should become the badge of the morally responsible.

This faith inspired a slender minority, less than 3 percent of the workforce, to form unions in various trades and industries. Despite its small size, the labor movement represented the most significant and lasting response of workers to the rise of industry and the consolidation of corporate power.

The Changing Status of Labor

The accelerating growth of industry, especially the steady mechanization of production, dramatically changed employer–employee relations and created new categories of workers. Both in turn fostered competition among workers and created conditions often hazardous to health.

For most craft workers, the new system destroyed long-standing practices and chipped away at their customary authority. Frederick Winslow Taylor, the pioneer of scientific management, explained that managers should "take all the important decisions . . . out of the hands of workmen." Teams of ironworkers, for example, had previously set the rules of production as well as wages while the company supplied raw materials and equipment. Once steel replaced iron, most companies gradually introduced a new managerial structure. Workers now faced constant supervision, higher production quotas, and new, faster machinery. Highly skilled cabinet makers, who had traditionally brought their own tools to the factory, were often replaced with "green hands": immigrants, including many women, who with minimal training and close supervision could operate new woodworking machines.

Not all trades conformed to this pattern. The garment industry, for example, retained older systems of labor alongside the new. The new, highly mechanized factories employed hundreds of thousands of young immigrant women, while the outwork system, established well before the Civil War, contracted ever-larger numbers of families to work in their homes on sewing machines or by hand. Paid by the piece, all workers worked faster and longer to forestall a dip in wages.

Industrial expansion also offered new opportunities for women to work outside the home. African American and immigrant women found employment in the trades least affected by technological advances, such as domestic service. In contrast, English-speaking white women moved into clerical and sales positions in the rapidly expanding business sector. After the typewriter and telephone came into widespread use in the 1890s, the number of women employed in office work rose even faster. At the turn of the century, 8.6 million women worked outside their homes—nearly triple the number in 1870.

By contrast, African American men found themselves excluded from many fields. In Cleveland, for example, the number of black carpenters declined after 1870, just as the volume of construction was rapidly increasing. African American men were also systematically driven from restaurant service and barred from newer trades such as boilermaking, plumbing, electrical work, and paperhanging, which European immigrants secured for themselves.

Discriminatory or exclusionary practices fell hardest on workers recruited earlier from China to work in railroad construction. Once their contracts expired and they sought other jobs, white workers and small business proprietors viewed them chiefly as competitors and called for their deportation. White San Franciscans staged a major riot in 1877 that destroyed many Chinese neighborhoods. In 1882 Congress passed the Chinese Exclusion Act, which suspended Chinese immigration, limited the civil rights of resident Chinese, and forbade their naturalization.

For even the best-placed wage earners, the new workplace could be unhealthy, even dangerous. Meat packing produced its own hazards, from the dampness of the pickling room, the sharp blade of the slaughtering knife, and the noxious odors of the fertilizer department. Factory owners often failed to mark high-voltage wires, locked fire doors, and allowed the emission of toxic fumes. Extractive workers, such as coal and copper miners, labored in mine shafts where the air could turn suddenly poisonous and where cave-ins were possible. Except for federal employees, who had been granted the eight-hour day in 1868, most workers still toiled upwards of ten or twelve hours daily.

Moreover, steady employment was rare. Between 1866 and 1897, fourteen years of prosperity stood against seventeen of hard times. The two major depressions of 1873–79 and 1893–97 were the worst in the nation's history up to that time. Three "minor" recessions (1866–67, 1883–85, and 1890–91) did not seem insignificant to the millions who lost their jobs.

Mobilization Against the Wage System

The National Labor Union (NLU) formed in 1866 to combat the new wage system. William Sylvis, its founder and president, insisted that through "cooperation we will become a nation of employers—the employers of our own labor. The wealth of the land will pass into the hands of those who produce it." The NLU grew to nearly 300,000 members but disintegrated soon after Sylvis's death.

The Noble and Holy Order of the Knights of Labor, founded by a group of Philadelphia garment cutters in 1869, grew to become the largest labor organization in the nineteenth century. Led by Grand Master Workman Terence V. Powderly, the order sought to bring together all wage earners regardless of skill. The knights endorsed a variety of reform measures—child labor reform, a graduated income tax, more land set aside for homesteading, the abolition of contract labor, and monetary reform—to offset the power of the industrialists. They believed that the "producing classes," once freed from the grip of corporate monopoly and the curses of ignorance and alcohol, would transform the United States into a genuinely democratic society. Organizing slowly at first, the Knights of Labor had become the largest labor assembly in the nation by the 1880s.

The Knights promoted economic cooperation as the alternative to the wage system and advocated a system of producers' cooperatives. In these factories workers collectively made all decisions on prices and wages and shared all profits. The Knights also ran small cooperative cigar shops and grocery stores, often housed in their own assembly buildings. Successful for a time, most cooperatives could not compete against heavily capitalized enterprises and ultimately failed.

The Knights reached their peak during a great campaign for a shorter workday. The Eight-Hour League, led by Ira Steward, advocated a "natural" rhythm of eight hours for work, eight for sleep, and eight for leisure. After staging petition campaigns, marches, and a massive strike in New York City, the movement collapsed during the economic recession of the 1870s. The Knights helped revive it in the next decade, and this time the campaign aroused widespread support from consumers, who boycotted brands of beer, bread, and other products made in longer-hour shops. Finally, during the first weeks of May 1886, more than a third of a million workers walked off their jobs; approximately 200,000 won shorter hours.

The eight-hour campaign swelled the ranks of the Knights of Labor. The organization grew from a few thousand in 1880 to nearly three-quarters of a million six years later. Nearly 3,000 women formed their own "ladies' assemblies" or joined mixed locals. Leonora Barry, appointed to organize women, helped to increase their share of membership to 10 percent. African Americans also joined the Knights—20,000 to 30,000 nationally—mainly in separate assemblies within the organization. Like the NLU, the Knights excluded Chinese laborers and supported further restrictions on immigration.

The shorter-hours campaign ended in tragedy. On May 4, 1886, following a series of confrontations between strikers and authorities, a protest against police violence at Chicago's Haymarket Square seemed to be ending quietly until someone threw a bomb that killed one policeman and left seven others fatally wounded. Police responded by firing wildly into the crowd, killing an equal number. During the next few weeks, newspaper editorials warned of revolution in the nation's streets. After Chicago authorities arrested anarchist leaders, a sensational trial ended in death sentences, although no evidence linked them to the bombing. Four of the convicted were hanged, one committed suicide, and three other "Haymarket Martyrs," as they were called, remained jailed until pardoned in 1893 by Illinois governor John Peter Altgeld.

The labor movement had suffered an irreparable setback. Employers' associations successfully pooled funds to rid their factories of troublesome organizers and announced that they would no longer bargain with unions. The wage system had triumphed.

The American Federation of Labor

The events of 1886 also signaled the rise of a very different kind of organization, the American Federation of Labor (AFL). Unlike the NLU or the Knights, the AFL accepted the wage system. Following a strategy of "pure and simple unionism," the AFL sought to gain recognition of its union status to bargain with employers for better working conditions, higher wages, and shorter hours. In return it offered compliant firms the benefit of amenable day-to-day relations with the most highly skilled wage earners. Only if companies refused to bargain in good faith would union members strike.

The new federation, with twelve national unions and 140,000 affiliated members, declared war on the Knights of Labor. In the wake of the Haymarket tragedy and collapse of the eight-hour movement, the AFL pushed ahead of its rival by organizing craft workers. AFL president Samuel Gompers refused to include unskilled workers, racial minorities, women, and immigrants, believing that they were impossible to organize and even unworthy of equal status. Under his leadership, the AFL member became the "aristocrat" of the factory, the best-paid manual laborer in the world.

By the end of the century, the AFL had enrolled only 10 percent of the nation's workers. It could not slow the steady advance of mechanization, which diminished the craft worker's autonomy and eliminated some of the most desirable jobs. But the AFL had achieved a degree of respectability that the Knights of Labor had commanded only briefly. Local politicians courted AFL members' votes, and Labor Day became a national holiday in 1894.

THE INDUSTRIAL CITY

Before the Civil War, manufacturing had centered in the nation's countryside, in burgeoning factory towns such as Lowell, Massachusetts, and Troy, New York. By century's end, 90 percent of all manufacturing took place in cities. The metropolis stood at the center of the growing industrial economy, a magnet drawing raw material, capital, and labor. It became the key distribution point for manufactured goods. The industrial city dominated the nation's economic, social, and cultural life. Civic leaders often bragged about its size and rate of growth; immigrants wrote their countryfolk of its pace, both exciting and exhausting.

Populating the City

The population of cities grew at double the rate of the nation's population as a whole. In 1860 only 16 cities had more than 50,000 residents. By 1890 one-third of all Americans were city-dwellers. Eleven cities claimed more than 250,000 people.

The major cities—New York, Chicago, Philadelphia, St. Louis, Boston, and Baltimore— achieved international fame for the size and diversity of their populations. Many of their new residents had migrated from rural communities in the United States. Between 1870 and 1910, an average of nearly 7,000 African Americans from the South moved north each year, hoping to escape poverty and oppression and find better-paying jobs. By the end of the century, nearly 80 percent of African Americans in the North lived in urban areas.

Whereas the countryside attracted the majority of first-wave immigrants before the Civil War, the industrial city drew the "new immigrants" from Europe, Japan, Latin America, and Canada. At the turn of the century Chicago had more Germans than all but a few German cities and more Poles than most Polish cities; New York had more Italians than all but a handful of the largest Italian cities; and Boston had nearly as many Irish as Dublin. By 1885 immigrants constituted a majority in all major cities outside the South, and in almost every group except the Irish, men outnumbered women.

Like rural in-migrants, immigrants came to take advantage of the expanding opportunities for employment. Many hoped to build a new home in the land of plenty, but a large number intended to work hard, save money, and return to their families in the Old Country.

In the 1880s nearly half of all Italian, Greek, and Serbian men, for example, returned to their native lands. Others could not, or did not wish to, return to their homelands. Jews, for instance, had emigrated mainly to escape persecution. A Yiddish critic later called this generation "Jews without Jewish memories. . . . They shook them off in the boat when they came across the seas. They emptied out their memories."

Of all the immigrant groups, Jews had the most experience with urban life. Forbidden to own land in most parts of Europe and boxed into *shtetls* (villages), Jews had helped form the thriving urban communities of Vilna, Berlin, London, and Vienna. A large number had worked in garment manufacturing in, for example, London's East End, and followed a path to American cities such as New York, Rochester, Philadelphia, and Chicago, where the needle trades flourished.

Bohemians settled largely in Chicago, Pittsburgh, and Cleveland. French Canadians, a group of a few hundred thousand, emigrated from Quebec and settled almost exclusively in New England and upper New York State. Finding work mainly in textile mills, they transformed smaller industrial cities such as Woonsocket, Rhode Island, into French-speaking communities. Cubans, themselves often first- or second-generation immigrants from Spain, moved to Ybor City, a section of Tampa, Florida, to work in cigar factories. Still other groups tended toward cities dominated by fishing, shoemaking, or even glassblowing, a craft carried directly from the Old Country. Italians, the largest segment of the immigrant population, settled mainly in the northeastern cities, constructing railroads, subways, and the city's buildings.

Resettlement in an American city did not necessarily mark the end of the journey. Newcomers, both native-born and immigrant, moved frequently from neighborhood to neighborhood and between cities. Cities experienced a total population turnover three or four times during each decade of the last half of the century.

The Urban Landscape

Faced with a population explosion and an unprecedented building boom, the cities encouraged the creation of many beautiful and useful structures, including commercial offices, sumptuous homes, and efficient public services. At the same time, cities did little to improve the conditions of the majority of the population, who worked in dingy factories and lived in crowded tenements. Open space rapidly decreased as American cities grew.

American streets customarily followed a simple gridiron pattern. Builders leveled hills, filled ponds, and pulled down any farms or houses in the way. City officials usually lacked any master plan save the idea of

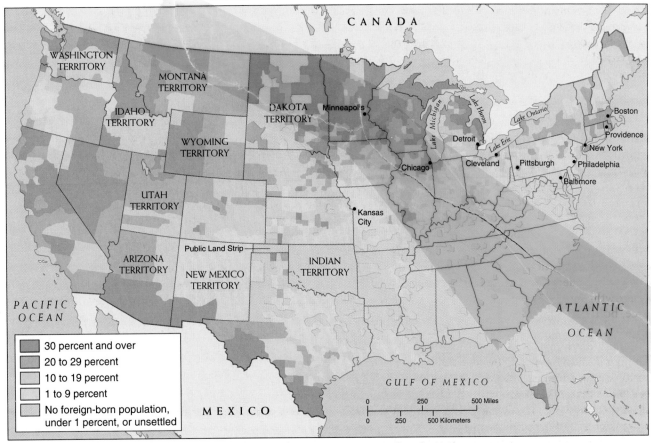

Population of Foreign Birth by Region, 1880   *European immigrants after the Civil War settled primarily in the industrial districts of the northern Midwest and parts of the Northeast. French Canadians continued to settle in Maine, Cubans in Florida, and Mexicans in the Southwest, where earlier immigrants had established thriving communities.*

Source: Public Domain.

endless expansion. Factories often occupied the best sites, typically near waterways, where goods could be easily transported and chemical wastes dumped.

Built by the thousands after the Civil War, the tenement was designed to maximize the use of space. A typical tenement sat on a lot 25 feet by 100 feet and rose to five stories. There were four families on each floor, each with three rooms. By 1890 New York's Lower East Side packed more than 700 people per acre in back-to-back buildings, producing one of the highest population densities in the world.

At the other end of the urban social scale, New York's Fifth Avenue, St. Paul's Summit Avenue, Chicago's Michigan Avenue, and San Francisco's Nob Hill gleamed with new mansions and townhouses. Commonwealth Avenue marked Boston's fashionable Back Bay district, built on a filled-in 450-acre tidal flat. State engineers planned this community, with its magnificent boulevard, uniform five-story brown-

stones, and back alleys designed for deliveries. Back Bay opened to Fenway Park, designed by the nation's premier landscape architect, Frederick Law Olmstead.

The industrial city established a new style of commercial and civic architecture. Using fireproof materials, expanded foundations, and internal metal construction, the era's talented young architects focused on the factory and office building. Concentrating as many offices as possible in the downtown areas, they fashioned hundreds of buildings from steel, sometimes decorating them with elaborate wrought-iron facades. The office building could rise seven, ten, even twenty stories high.

In the 1890s, influenced by American wealth and its enhanced role in the global economy, city planners turned to the monumental or imperial style, laying grand concrete boulevards at enormous public cost. New sports amphitheaters spread pride in the city's accomplishments, and huge new art galleries, museums,

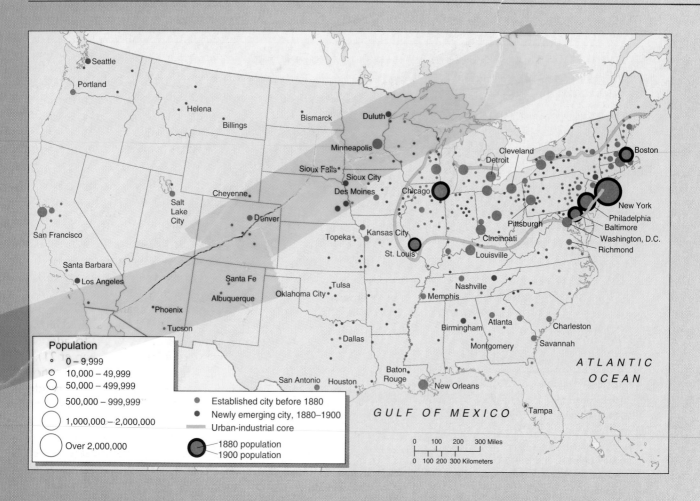

Patterns in Urban Growth in Turn-of-the-Century America

By the turn of the century, the ten largest cities in the United States were located in the Northeast and the Midwest. The rapid growth of these cities reflected the rise of industry and commerce in the nation's urban-industrial core and the demand for labor that accompanied it. New York City, Chicago, Philadelphia, St. Louis, and Boston, for example, attracted new immigrants who found jobs in these cities' huge ready-to-wear clothing industries and other light manufacturing shops. Chicago, Pittsburgh, Detroit, and Buffalo became the home of working-class families who looked for their livelihood to these cities' giant steel mills and packing-house plants.

The growth of the cities in the western and southern states reflected the expansion of the nation's railroads in those regions and the efficient transportation of goods and people that expansion made possible. The growth of Atlanta, for example, was tied to the expansion of the southern rail system. Like Chicago in the Midwest and Los Angeles in the West, Atlanta became a hub and distribution center for regionally produced goods.

and concert halls promoted urban excitement as well as cultural uplift. The imperial style also increased congestion and noise, making the city a more desirable place to visit than to live in.

The city inspired other architectural marvels. The Brooklyn Bridge won wide acclaim as the most original American construction of all. Designed by John Roebling, who died on the job, and by his son Washington, who became an invalid while completing it, the bridge opened in 1883. Its steel piers, arches, and cables were immediately considered an aesthetic and practical wonder.

Like the railroad but on a smaller scale, streetcars changed business dramatically, carrying traffic of many different kinds—information, people, and goods—swifter and farther. By 1895 over 800 communities operated electrically powered cars or trolleys. In 1902 New York opened its subway system, which would grow to become the largest in the nation.

In his watercolor The Bowery at Night, *painted in 1895, W. Louis Sonntag Jr. shows a New York City scene transformed by electric light. Electricity transformed the city in other ways as well, as seen in the electric streetcars and elevated railroad.*

The City and the Environment

By making it possible for a great number of workers to live in communities distant from their place of employment, mass transportation also allowed cities to increase their size dramatically. In 1880 New York City's surface transit system accommodated more than 150 million riders annually, a large proportion traveling into Manhattan from the boroughs of Queens and Brooklyn.

The electric trolley systems eliminated tons of waste from the horsecars that had fouled city streets for decades. But they also brought congestion and safety hazards for pedestrians. Elevated trains, designed to avoid these problems, placed entire communities in the shadow of noisy and rickety wooden platforms.

Modern sewer systems became part of a hidden city of pipes and wires, mirroring the growth of the visible city above ground. Electric lights began to replace gas in streetlights and in house illumination, improving the environment for evening education, leisure, and more intensive factory labor.

These advances did not in themselves eradicate serious environmental problems. Most cities continued to dump sewage in nearby bodies of water. Rather than outlawing factory dumping and cleaning rivers at their sources, municipal governments usually moved to establish separate clean water systems through the use of reservoirs.

The unrestricted burning of coal to fuel the railroads and to heat factories and homes after 1880 greatly intensified urban air pollution. Noise levels continued to rise in the most compacted living and industrial areas. Overcrowded conditions and inadequate sanitary facilities continued to breed tuberculosis, smallpox, scarlet fever, and other communicable diseases. Children's diseases such as whooping cough and measles swept many poor neighborhoods. Only after the turn of the century, amid an intensive campaign against municipal corruption, did laws and administrative practices begin to address these problems (see Chapter 21).

Meanwhile, the distance between city and countryside closed. Naturalists had hoped for large open spaces—a buffer zone—to preserve farmland and wild areas, protect future water supplies, and diminish regional air pollution. However, nearby rural lands not destined for private housing or commercial development had already begun to house water treatment and sewage plants, garbage dumps, and graveyards, services essential to the city's growing population.

THE NEW SOUTH

At the turn of the century southern industries lagged far behind enterprises in other regions of the country. Their progress was held back by northern business and finance capital, continued dependence on cotton, and the legacy of slavery.

Industrialization

In the 1870s a vocal and powerful new group of Southerners headed by Henry Woodfin Grady, editor of the *Atlanta Constitution*, insisted that the region enjoyed great potential in its abundant natural resources of coal, iron, turpentine, tobacco, and lumber. Arguing against planters who aspired to rejuvenate the agricultural economy by cultivating a few staple crops, the group forcefully promoted industrial development and welcomed northern investors.

Northern investors secured huge concessions from state legislatures, including land, forest, and mineral rights and large tax exemptions. Exploiting the incentives, railroad companies laid over 22,000 miles of new track, connecting the region with national markets and creating new cities. By 1890 a score of large companies, centered mainly in New York, held more than half of all southern track.

Northerners also used various means to protect their investments from southern competition. By the late 1870s southern merchants had begun to run iron factories around Birmingham, Alabama. Southern iron production was soon encroaching on the northeastern market. To stave off this competition, Andrew Carnegie ordered railroads to charge higher freight fees to Birmingham's iron producers. New York bankers later succeeded in expatriating Birmingham's profits through stock ownership in southern firms. After the turn of the century, U.S. Steel took over much of Birmingham's production.

The production of cotton textiles followed a similar course. Powerful merchants and large landowners, realizing they could make high profits by controlling the cotton crop from field to factory, promoted the vertical integration of the cotton industry. The number of cotton mills grew from 161 in 1880 to 400 in 1900. Southern investors supplied large amounts of the capital for industrial expansion and technological improvements. The latest machines ran the new mills, and the South boasted the first factory fully equipped with electricity. Production in the four leading cotton-manufacturing states—North Carolina, South Carolina, Alabama, and Georgia—skyrocketed, far outpacing the New England mills.

Recognizing the potential for great profit in these new factories with their cheap labor, northern manufacturers, including many New England mill owners, shifted their investments to the South. By the 1920s northern investors held much of the South's wealth, including the major textile mills, but returned only a small share of the profits to the region's people.

The governing role of capital investments reinforced long-standing relationships. Even rapid industrialization—in iron, railroads, and textiles—did not carry the same consequences achieved in the North. The rise of the New South after Reconstruction reinforced, rather than diminished, the region's status as the nation's internal colony.

Southern Labor

The advance of southern industry did little to improve the working lives of African Americans. African American men did find work with the railroads; in booming cities like Atlanta they even gained skilled positions in the construction trades and worked as bricklayers, carpenters, and painters. For the most part, however, African Americans were limited to unskilled, low-

paying jobs. In the textile mills and cigarette factories, African Americans were assigned mainly to janitorial jobs and rarely worked alongside the white workers who tended the machines. Nearly all African American women who earned wages did so as household workers.

Locals of the all-white carpenters' union maintained a segregation policy so absolute that if too few members were available for a job, the union would send for out-of-town white workers rather than employ local members of the black carpenters' union. In an Atlanta mill in 1897, 1,400 white women went on strike when the company proposed to hire two black spinners.

Only at rare moments did southern workers unite across racial lines. In the 1880s the Knights of Labor briefly organized both black and white workers. But when white politicians and local newspapers began to raise the specter of black domination, the Knights were forced to retreat. Across the region their assemblies collapsed. Other unions remained the exclusive preserve of white skilled workers.

Wages throughout the South were low for both black and white workers. Southern textile workers' wages were barely half those of New Englanders. In the 1880s, when investors enjoyed profits ranging from 30 to 75 percent, southern millworkers earned as little as 12 cents per hour. Black men earned at or below the poverty line of $300; black women rarely earned more than $120 and white women about $220 annually. The poorest paid workers were children, a mainstay of southern mill labor.

As industry expanded throughout the nation, so did the number of children earning wages. This was especially so in the South. In 1896, only one in twenty Massachusetts millworkers was younger than sixteen, but one in four cotton mill operatives in North Carolina was. Traditions rooted in the agricultural economy reinforced the practice of using the labor of all family members, even the very young. Seasonal labor, such as picking crops or grinding sugar cane, put families on the move, making formal education all but impossible. Not until well into the twentieth century did compulsory school laws effectively restrict child labor in the South.

A system of convict labor also thrived in the South. Public work projects of all kinds, especially in remote areas, created living and working conditions reminiscent of slavery. African Americans made up 90 percent of the convict work force. Transported and housed like animals—chained together by day and confined in portable cages at night—these workers suffered high mortality rates. Southern leaders took pride in what they called the "good roads movement"— the chief use of convict labor—as proof of regional progress.

The Transformation of Piedmont Communities

The impact of the New South was nowhere greater than in the Piedmont, the region extending from southern Virginia and the central Carolinas into northern Alabama and Georgia. After 1870 long-established farms and plantations gave way to railroad tracks, textile factories, numerous mill villages, and a few sizable cities. By the turn of the century, five Piedmont towns topped 10,000 in population. Even more dramatic was the swell in the number of small towns with populations between 1,000 and 5,000—from fourteen in 1870 to fifty-two in 1900. Once the South's backcountry, the Piedmont now surpassed New England in the production of yarn and cloth to stand first in the world.

Rural poverty encouraged many farm families to strike out for a new life in the mill town. Those with the least access to land and credit—mainly widows and their children and single women—were first to go into the mills. Then families sent their children. As the agricultural crisis deepened, more and more people abandoned the countryside entirely for what they called "public work."

A mill community typically comprised rows of single-family houses, a small school, several churches, a company-owned store, and the home of the superintendent, who governed everyone's affairs. Mill workers often complained that they had no private life. A federal report published shortly after the turn of the century concluded that "all the affairs of the village and the conditions of living of all the people are regulated entirely by the mill company. Practically speaking, the company owns everything and controls everything, and to a large extent controls everybody in the mill village."

Mill superintendents relied on schoolteachers and clergy to set the tone of community life. They hired Baptist and Methodist ministers to preach a faith encouraging workers to be thrifty, orderly, temperate, and hard-working. The schools, similarly subsidized by the company, reinforced these lessons and encouraged students to follow their parents into the mill. It was mainly young children between six and eight years old who attended school. But when more hands were needed in the mill, superintendents plucked out these youngsters and sent them to join their older brothers and sisters, who were already at work.

Piedmont mill villages such as Greenville, South Carolina and Burlington, Charlotte, and Franklinville, North Carolina nevertheless developed a cohesive character more typical of rural than urban communities. The new residents maintained many aspects of their agricultural pasts, tilling small gardens and keeping chickens, pigs, and cows in their yards.

Factory owners rarely paved roads or sidewalks or provided adequate sanitation. Mud, flies, and diseases such as typhoid fever flourished. Millworkers endured poverty and health hazards by strengthening community ties through intermarriage. Within a few generations most village residents had, according to one study, "some connection to each other, however distant, by marriage," blood, or both. Even the men and women without families boarded in households where privacy was scarce and collective meals created a family-like atmosphere. Historians have called this complex of intimate economic, family, and community ties the *customs of incorporation.*

CULTURE AND SOCIETY IN THE GILDED AGE

The growth of industry and spread of cities had a profound impact on all regions of the United States. During the final third of the century the standard of living climbed, although unevenly and erratically. Real wages (pay in relation to the cost of living) rose, fostering improvements in nutrition, clothing, and housing. More and cheaper products appeared within the reach of all but the very poor. Food from the farms became more abundant and varied: grains for bread or beer; poultry, pork, and beef; and fresh fruits and vegetables from California. Although many Americans continued to acknowledge the moral value of hard work, thrift, and self-sacrifice, the explosion of consumer goods and services promoted sweeping changes in behavior and beliefs.

Conspicuous Consumption

Labeled the "Gilded Age" by humorist and social critic Mark Twain, the era favored the growth of a new class united in its pursuit of money and leisure. The well-to-do enjoyed great status throughout the nineteenth century, but only after the Civil War did upper-class Americans form national networks to consolidate their power. Business leaders built diverse stock portfolios and often served simultaneously on the boards of several corporations. Similarly, they intertwined their interests by joining the same religious, charitable, athletic, and professional societies. Their wives and children vacationed together in the sumptuous new seashore and mountain resorts, while they themselves made deals at their leisure at the new downtown social clubs and on the golf links of suburban country clubs. Just as *Dun and Bradstreet* ranked the nation's leading corporations, the *Social Register* identified the 500 families that controlled most of its wealth.

According to economist and social critic Thorstein Veblen, the rich had created a new style of conspicuous consumption. A vice president of the Chicago & Northwestern Railroad, Perry H. Smith, built his palatial marble home in the classical Greek style. Its ebony staircase was trimmed in gold, and its butler's pantry was equipped with faucets, not only for hot and cold water but for iced champagne as well. The women who oversaw elaborate households such as Smith's served as measures of their husband's status, according to Veblen, by adorning themselves in jewels, furs, and dresses of the latest Paris design.

Perhaps no display of wealth matched the ostentation of the "cottages" of Newport, Rhode Island, where the rich created a summer community of consumption. Architect H. H. Richardson and his protégés built exquisite manor houses more magnificent than the English originals. Here, wealthy young men and women engaged in new amateur sports such as polo, rowing, and lawn tennis. Young and old alike joined in yachting and golf tournaments.

The nation's wealthy also became the leading patrons of the arts as well as the chief importers of art treasures from Europe and Asia. They provided the bulk of funds for the new symphonies, operas, and ballet companies, which soon rivaled those of continental Europe. Nearly all the major museums and art galleries were founded during the last decades of the nineteenth century.

Gentility and the Middle Class

A new middle class formed during the last half of the century. The older middle class comprised the owners or superintendents of small businesses, as well as doctors, lawyers, teachers, and ministers and their families. The new middle class included these professionals but also the growing number of salaried employees: the managers, technicians, clerks, and engineers who worked in the complex web of corporations and government. Long hours of labor earned their families a modest status and sufficient income to live securely in style and comfort.

For as little as $10 a month, a family could finance the construction of a suburban house in which to retreat from the noise, filth, and dangers of the city. Assisted by modern transportation systems, men often traveled an hour or two a day, five or six days a week, to their city offices and back again. Women and children stayed behind.

Middle-class women found themselves devoting a large part of their day to home care. They often employed one or two servants but relied increasingly on the many new household appliances to get their work done. Improvements in the kitchen stove, such as the conversion from wood fuel to gas, saved a lot of time. Yet with the widespread circulation of cookbooks and recipes in newspapers and magazines, as well as the availability of new foods, the preparation of meals became more complex and time-consuming. Similarly, the new carpet sweepers surpassed the broom in efficiency, but the fashionable high-napped carpeting demanded more care. Rather than diminishing with technological innovation, household work expanded to fill the time.

Almost exclusively white, Anglo-Saxon, and Protestant, the new middle class embraced "culture" not for purposes of conspicuous consumption but as a means of self-improvement and moral uplift. Whole families visited the new museums and art galleries, constituting the majority who used these new cultural institutions. The middle class also provided the bulk of patrons for the new public libraries.

Middle-class families applied the same standards to their other leisure activities. Hiking was a favorite activity among both men and women. Roller skating was available in specially designed rinks in almost every major town. By the 1890s the "safety" bicycle had replaced the large-wheel variety, which was difficult to ride. A good bike cost $100; as in the case of the piano, ownership signaled middle-class status.

Leisure became the special province of middle-class childhood. Removed from factories and shops and freed of many domestic chores, children enjoyed a new age of creative play and physical activity. The toy market boomed, and lower printing prices helped children's literature flourish. Uplifting classics such as *Little Women* and *Black Beauty* were popular.

Life in the Streets

Immigrants often weighed the material abundance they found in the United States against their memories of the Old Country. One could live better here, but only by working much harder. In letters back home, they described the riches of the new country but warned friends and relatives not to send weaklings, who would surely die of stress and strain amid the alien and intense commercialism of American society. In many immigrant communities, alcoholism and suicide rates soared. Embittered German immigrants called their new land *Malbuerica*, misfortune; Jews called it *Ama Reka*, Hebrew for "without soul"; and Slavs called it *Dollerica*.

Many newcomers, having little choice about their place of residence, were concentrated in districts marked off by racial or ethnic lines. In San Francisco city ordinances prevented Chinese from operating laundries in most of the city's neighborhoods, effectively confining the population to Chinatown. In Los Angeles and San Antonio, Mexicans lived in distinctive *barrios*. In most cities African American families were compelled to live in the most vicious, crime-ridden, and dangerous sections of town.

The intersection of Orchard and Hester Streets on New York's Lower East Side, photographed ca. 1905. Unlike the middle classes, who worked and played hidden away in offices and private homes, the Jewish lower-class immigrants who lived and worked in this neighborhood spent the greater part of their lives on the streets. Here children and adults mingle partaking in both business and conversation.

For working-class families, income levels and social customs were so complex and varied that no single pattern emerged. In the city tenements families often shared their rooms with other families or, when finances demanded, paying boarders. During the summer heat, adults, children, and boarders alike competed for a sleeping place on the fire escape or roof, and all year round, noises raced through paper-thin walls. Packingtown's Slovaks, Lithuanians, and Poles, for example, often took in boarders, yet Bohemians rarely did. But skilled ironrollers who worked at the Carnegie Steel Company in Homestead, Pennsylvania, often owned their own homes, with parlors and even imported Belgian carpets on their floors. At the other extreme, Italian immigrants, who considered themselves fortunate to get work with a shovel, usually lived in overcrowded rented apartments, one paycheck from eviction.

Whether a small cottage or a tenement flat, the working-class home was generally devoid of the new mechanical innovations. In addition to cooking and cleaning, women used the cramped domestic space for homework. They gathered their children—and their husbands after a hard day's work—to sew garments, wrap cigars, string beads, or paint vases for a contractor who paid them small wages by the piece. And they cooked and cleaned for the boarder whose rent supplemented the family income.

Despite working people's slim resources, their combined buying power created new and important markets for consumer goods. Often they bought shoddy replicas of products sold to the middle class: cheaper canned goods, inferior cuts of meat, and partially spoiled fruit. Several leading clothing manufacturers specialized in inexpensive ready-to-wear items, usually copied from patterns designed for wealthier consumers but constructed hastily from flimsy materials. Patent medicines advertised for ailments caused by working long periods in cramped conditions sold well in working-class communities, where money for doctors was scarce. Their high alcohol content lifted spirits, if only temporarily.

The close quarters of the urban neighborhood allowed immigrants to preserve many Old World customs. In immigrant communities such as Pittsburgh's Poletown and New York's Lower East Side, people usually spoke their native language while visiting their friends and relatives. In good weather they walked and talked, an inexpensive pastime common in the great European walking cities. Immigrants also re-created Old World religious institutions such as the church and synagogue, or secular institutions such as German family-style taverns and Russian Jewish tearooms. They replicated their native cuisine and married, baptized children, and buried the dead by Old World customs.

Ultimately, working-class people helped to shape the emerging popular culture by being innovative entrepreneurs as well as the best customers. Ragtime, for example, quickly found its way north from the Storyville red-light district of New Orleans, where the African American and Creole bands of Buddy Bolden and other early giants first popularized the music. Those who rushed to the dancehalls to hear the new tunes were mainly the teenage offspring of immigrants.

When developers realized that "wholesome fun" for the masses could pay better than upper-class leisure or lower-class vice, they decided to transform Coney Island into a magnificent working-class resort filled with ingenious amusements such as water slides, mechanized horse races, rollercoasters, and funhouses. Here, millions of working-class people enjoyed cheap thrills, offsetting their hard working lives.

CULTURES IN CONFLICT, CULTURE IN COMMON

The new commercial entertainments gave Americans from various backgrounds more in common than they might have otherwise imagined. On New York's Lower East Side, for instance, theater blossomed with dramas that Broadway would adopt years later, while children dreamed of going uptown, where the popular songs they heard on the streets were transcribed onto sheet music and then sold in stores throughout the city.

Education

Business and civic leaders realized that the welfare of society now depended on an educated population, one with the skills and knowledge needed to keep both industry and government running. In the last three decades of the nineteenth century, the idea of universal, free schooling at the primary level, at least for white children, took hold. The St. Louis public school system opened the first kindergarten in 1873, and by the turn of the century more than 4,000 similar programs took in children between the ages of three and seven. The number of public high schools also increased, from 160 in 1870 to 6,000 by century's end.

Agricultural colleges formed earlier in the century developed into institutes of technology and took their places alongside the prestigious liberal arts colleges. The Morrill Federal Land Grant Act of 1862 funded a system of state colleges and universities for teaching agriculture and mechanics "without excluding other scientific and classic studies." One of the most important developments occurred in the area of research and graduate studies, pioneered in this country in 1876 by Johns Hopkins University. By the end of the century several American universities, including Stanford and Chicago, had adopted the Johns Hopkins model and expanded beyond the undergraduate curriculum to offer advanced degrees in the arts and sciences.

This expansion benefitted women, who previously had little access to higher education. After the Civil War, a number of women's colleges were founded. The first, Vassar College, founded to educate women in 1865, established high academic standards. Smith and Wellesley followed in 1875, Bryn Mawr in 1885. By the end of the century 125 women's colleges offered a first-rate education comparable to that given men at Harvard, Yale, and Princeton. Meanwhile, coeducation grew at an even faster rate; women constituted 21 percent of undergraduate enrollments by 1870, 32 percent by 1880, and 40 percent by 1910.

Outside the women's colleges were institutions that served an entirely different clientele. Boston's first training school for nurses opened in 1873, followed in 1879 by a diet kitchen that trained women as cooks for the city's hospitals. Founded in 1877 by middle-class women, the Boston Women's Educational and Industrial Union offered a multitude of classes to Boston's wage-earning women, ranging from French and German to painting to dressmaking to carpentry. In the early 1890s, when the entering class at a large women's college such as Vassar still averaged under 100, the Union reported that its staff of 83 served an estimated 1,500 clients per day. By that time, one of its most well-funded programs was a training school for domestic servants.

The leaders of the business community had begun to promote manual training for working-class and immigrant boys. Craft unionists in several cities actively opposed this development, preferring their own methods of apprenticeship to training programs they could not control. But local associations of merchants and manufacturers lobbied hard for "industrial education" and raised funds themselves to supplement the public school budget. By 1895 all elementary and high schools in Chicago offered courses training working-class boys for jobs in industry and business.

The expansion of education did not benefit all Americans or benefit them all the same way. Because African Americans were prohibited from enrolling in colleges attended by white students, special colleges were founded in the southern states shortly after the Civil War. Atlanta opened in 1865, Fisk the following year; both offered a rigorous curriculum in the liberal arts. Educator Booker T. Washington encouraged African Americans to resist "the craze for Greek and Latin learning" and to strive for practical instruction. In 1881 he founded the Tuskegee Institute in Alabama to provide industrial education and moral uplift. By the end of the century black colleges, including Tuskegee, had trained so many teachers that the majority of black schools were staffed by African Americans.

Leisure and Public Space

Most large cities set aside open land for common leisure-time use by residents. New York's Central Park opened in 1858 for ice skating and provided a model for urban park systems across the United States. The parks were rolling expanses cut across by streams, pathways, and footbridges and set off by groves of trees, ornamental shrubs, and neat flower gardens. According to the designers' vision, the urban middle-class could renew themselves and find relief from the stress of modern life by strolling through the picturesque, semirural grounds.

The working classes had their own ideas about the use of parks and open land. Trapped in overcrowded tenements, they wanted space for sports, picnics, and lover's trysts. Young people openly defied ordinances that prohibited playing on the grassy knolls of parks, while their elders routinely voted against municipal bonds that did not include funds for more recreational space. Immigrant ward representatives on the Pittsburgh city council, for instance, argued that band shells for classical music meant little to their constituents, but spaces suitable for sports meant much.

Public drinking of alcoholic beverages, especially on Sunday, provoked similar disputes. Pittsburgh Blue Laws forbidding businesses to open on Sunday were rigidly enforced when it came to neighborhood taverns, while large firms such as the railroads enjoyed exemptions. Nevertheless, many working people, particularly the beer-loving German immigrants, continued to treat Sunday as their one day of relaxation, and gathered for picnics in the city's parks.

National Pastimes

After the turn of the century, middle-class urbanites sought out ragtime bands and congregated on the rooftops of posh hotels and uptown restaurants to listen and dance and even to drink.

Vaudeville, the most popular form of commercial entertainment since the 1880s, also bridged middle- and working-class tastes. Drawing on a variety show tradition of singers, dancers, comedians, jugglers, and acrobats who had entertained Americans since colonial days, "vaude" became a big business that made ethnic and racial stereotypes and the daily frustrations of city life into major topics of amusement.

Sports outdistanced all other commercial entertainments in appealing to all kinds of fans and creating a sense of national identity. No doubt the most popular parks in the United States were the expanses of green surrounded by grandstands and marked by the unique diamond shape: the baseball fields. Baseball clubs formed in many cities, and shortly after the Civil War traveling teams made baseball a professional sport. The formation of the National League in 1876 encouraged other spectator sports, but for generations baseball remained the most popular.

Rowdy behavior flavored the game with a working-class ambiance. Team owners, themselves often proprietors of local breweries, counted heavily on liquor sales in the parks. To attract more subdued middle-class fans, the National League raised admission prices and banned the sale of alcohol. Catering to a more working-class audience, the American Association kept the price of admission low, sold liquor, and played ball on Sunday.

Entrepreneur Albert G. Spalding brought order to often chaotic baseball, but at a price. Manager and then president of the Chicago White Stockings, Spalding quickly came to see baseball as a source of multiple profits. He procured exclusive rights to manufacture the official ball and rule book. Meanwhile, he built impressive baseball parks in Chicago, with seating for 10,000 and private boxes for the wealthy above the grandstands.

Spalding also tightened the rules of employment. He prevented players from negotiating a better deal and leaving the team that had originally signed them. Spalding refused to allow the White Stockings to play any team with an African American, effectively setting a segregation standard for professional baseball. African Americans organized their own traveling teams, and in the 1920s formed the Negro Leagues, which produced some of the nation's finest ballplayers.

As attendance continued to grow, the enthusiasm for baseball straddled important cultural divisions, bringing Americans of many kinds together, if only on a limited basis. Although interesting few women, sports news riveted the attention of men from all social classes. Loyalty to the home team helped to create an urban identity, and individual players became national heroes.

CONCLUSION

By the end of the nineteenth century, industry and the city had opened a new world for Americans. Fresh from Europe or from the American countryside, ordinary urban dwellers struggled to form communities of fellow newcomers through work and leisure—at the factory and the ballpark, in the neighborhood and the public school. Meanwhile, the wealthy members of the business community and the new middle class made and carried out the decisions of industry and marketing, established the era's grand civic institutions, and set the tone for high fashion and art.

Rich and poor alike bore witness to many developments that inspired fascination and confidence in the emerging order. Yet inequalities increased. Indeed, they were as much a part of the new order as the construction of the Brooklyn Bridge or the appearance of advertising. During the mostly prosperous 1880s, optimists believed that unfair treatment based on region, class, and even race and gender might ease in time. By the depressed 1890s, these hopes had worn thin. The lure of an overseas empire, symbol of manifest destiny, was one of the few goals that seemed to unite a suffering and otherwise divided nation.

CHRONOLOGY

1862	Morrill Act authorizes land-grant colleges	1882	Peak of immigration to the United States (1.2 million) in the nineteenth century
1866	National Labor Union founded		Chinese Exclusion Act passed
1869	Knights of Labor founded		Standard Oil Trust founded
1870	Standard Oil founded	1886	Campaigns for eight-hour workday peak
1871	Chicago Fire		Haymarket riot and massacre discredit the Knights of Labor
1873	Financial panic brings severe depression		American Federation of Labor founded
1876	Baseball's National League founded	1890	Sherman Antitrust Act passed
	Alexander Graham Bell patents the telephone	1893	Stock market panic precipitates severe depression
1879	Thomas Edison invents incandescent bulb	1895	Coney Island opens
	Depression ends	1896	Rural free delivery begins
1881	Tuskegee Institute founded	1901	U.S. Steel Corporation formed

REVIEW QUESTIONS

1. Discuss the sources of economic growth in the decades after the Civil War. Historians often call this period the era of the second industrial revolution. Do you agree with this description?

2. Describe the impact of new technologies and new forms of production on the routines of industrial workers. How did these changes affect African American and women workers in particular? What role did trade unions play in this process?

3. Choose one major city, such as Boston, New York, Chicago, Birmingham, or San Francisco, and discuss changes in its economy, population, and urban space in the decades after the Civil War.

4. Discuss the role of northern capital in the development of the New South. How did the rise of industry affect the lives of rural southerners? Analyze these changes from the point of view of African Americans.

5. How did urban life change during the Gilded Age? How did economic development affect residential patterns? How did the middle class aspire to live during the Gilded Age? How did their lifestyles compare with those of working-class urbanites?

6. How did the American educational system change to prepare children for their adult roles in the new industrial economy?

7. How did the rise of organized sports and commercial amusements reflect and shape social divisions at the end of the century? Which groups were affected most (or least) by new leisure activities?

RECOMMENDED READING

James R. Barrett, *Work and Community in the Jungle* (1987). A very close study of the Packingtown district of Chicago, Illinois, at the turn of the century. Barrett describes the transformation of animals to meat in great stockyards and processing plants. He also provides rich documentation of neighborhood life.

Alfred D. Chandler Jr., *The Visible Hand: The Managerial Revolution in American Business* (1977). A highly acclaimed study of corporate management. Chandler shows how the rapid growth in the scale of business, as well as its influence on public life, brought about a new type of executive with skills for national decision making and close links with others of his kind.

William Cronon, *Nature's Metropolis* (1991). Analyzes the changing economic and political relationship between the city of Chicago and the surrounding countryside. Cronon demonstrates through a variety of evidence the tight interdependence of urban and rural regions.

Herbert G. Gutman, *Work, Culture and Society in Industrializing America: Essays in American Working-Class and Social History* (1977). Influential essays on the formation of working-class communities in the nineteenth century. Gutman focuses on the role of immigrants in transforming the values and belief systems of working-class Americans in the throes of industrialization.

John F. Kasson, *Amusing the Million: Coney Island at the Turn of the Century* (1978). A heavily illustrated account of America's favorite amusement park. Kasson sees Coney Island as the meeting point for shrewd entrepreneurs and pleasure-seeking immigrants, its amusements and architectural styles emblematic of a special era in American history.

Alice Kessler-Harris, *Out To Work: A History of Wage-Earning Women in the United States* (1982). A comprehensive survey of women's increasing participation in the labor force. Kessler-Harris documents women's role in trade unions and the impact on family patterns and ideas about women's role in American society.

Kenneth L. Kusmer, *A Ghetto Takes Shape: Black Cleveland, 1870–1930* (1976). A keen analysis of a long-standing African American community. Kusmer shows how blacks suffered downward mobility and increased segregation as their skilled jobs and small-business opportunities were given to European immigrants.

Lawrence H. Larsen, *The Rise of the Urban South* (1985). Studies of the changing South. In Larsen's view, the true New South was the city, for few had lived there before the late nineteenth century, but rural values remained vital, especially in religious life and voting patterns.

David F. Noble, *America by Design: Science, Technology and the Rise of Corporate Capitalism* (1977). A view of scientific advancement and its connections with the expanding economy. Noble shows how scientific breakthroughs were often created for, but especially adapted to, corporate purposes.

Dave Roediger and Franklin Rosemont, eds., *Haymarket Scrapbook* (1986). A large, beautifully illustrated book about the events and consequences of the Haymarket tragedy.

Roy Rosenzweig, *Eight Hours for What We Will: Workers and Leisure in an Industrial City, 1870–1920* (1983). Analyzes class and cultural conflicts over recreational space. This valuable book treats the city park as the arena for conflict over whether public community life should be uplifting (devoted to nature walks and concerts) or entertaining (for drinking, courting, and amusement).

Alan Trachtenberg, *The Incorporation of America: Culture and Society in the Gilded Age* (1982). One of the best and most readable overviews of the post–Civil War era. Trachtenberg devotes great care to describing the rise of the corporation as the defining institution of national life and the reorientation of culture to reflect the new middle classes employed by the corporation.

CHAPTER TWENTY

COMMONWEALTH AND EMPIRE

1870–1900

AMERICAN COMMUNITIES
The Cooperative Commonwealth

Edward Bellamy's *Looking Backward* (1888), the century's best-selling novel after Harriet Beecher Stowe's *Uncle Tom's Cabin*, tells the story of a young man who awakens in the year 2000 after a sleep lasting more than 100 years. He is surprised to learn that Americans had solved their major problems. There is no poverty, no crime, war, taxes, air pollution, or even housework. Nor are there politicians, capitalists, bankers, or lawyers. Most amazing, gone is the great social division between the powerful rich and the suffering poor. In the year 2000 everyone lives in material comfort, happily and harmoniously.

Community and cooperation are the key concepts in Bellamy's utopian tale. The nation's businesses, including farms and factories, have been given over to the collective ownership of the people. Elected officials now plan the production and distribution of goods for the common well-being. With great efficiency, they even manage huge department stores and warehouses full of marvelous manufactured goods and oversee majestic apartment complexes with modern facilities for cooking, dining, and laundering. To get the necessary work done, an industrial army enlists all adult men and women, but automated machinery has eliminated most menial tasks. Moreover, the workday lasts only four hours; vacations extend to six months of each year. At age forty-five everyone retires to pursue hobbies, sports, and culture.

Bellamy designed his technological utopia to promote the "highest possible physical, as well as mental, development for everyone." There was nothing fantastic in this plan, the author insisted. It simply required Americans to share equally the abundant resources of their land and live up to their democratic ideals.

Bellamy, a journalist and writer of historical fiction from Chicopee Falls, Massachusetts, moved thousands of his readers to action. His most ardent fans endorsed his program for a "new nation" and formed the Nationalist movement, which by the early 1890s reached an apex of 165 clubs. Many leaders of the woman suffrage movement threw in their support. They endorsed *Looking Backward's* depiction of marriage as a union of "perfect equals."

Bellamy's disciples established a settlement in Point Loma, California, in 1897. Situated on 330 acres, with avenues winding through gardens and orchards newly planted with groves of eucalyptus trees, Point Loma was known for its physical beauty. Many young married couples chose to live in small bungalows, which were scattered throughout the colony's grounds; others opted for private rooms in a large communal building. Either way, they all met twice daily to share meals and usually spent their leisure hours together. On the ocean's edge the residents constructed an outdoor amphitheater and staged plays and concerts.

No one earned wages, but all 500 residents lived comfortably. They dressed simply in clothes manufactured by the community's women. The majority of the men worked in agriculture. They conducted horticultural experiments that yielded new types of avocados and tropical fruits and eventually produced over half of the community's food supply. Children, who slept in a special dormitory from the time they reached school age, enjoyed an education so outstanding that they often demonstrated their talents to audiences in nearby San Diego. They excelled in the fine arts, including music and drama.

The Point Loma community never met all its expenses but managed to remain solvent for decades. Admirers across the country sent donations. Baseball entrepreneur Albert Spalding, who lived there during his retirement, helped to make up the financial deficit. As late as the 1950s some seventy-five members still lived on about 100 acres of land.

Even the establishment of successful cooperative communities such as Point Loma could not bring about the changes that Bellamy hoped to see, and he knew it. Only a mobilization of citizens nationwide could overturn the existing hierarchies and usher in the egalitarian order depicted in *Looking Backward*. Without such a rigorous challenge, the economic and political leadership that had been emerging since the Civil War would continue to consolidate its power and become even further removed from popular control.

The last quarter of the nineteenth century saw just such a challenge, producing what one historian calls "a moment of democratic promise." Ordinary citizens sought to renew the older values of community through farm and labor organizations, philanthropic and charitable societies. However, they did not see that the fate of the nation depended increasingly on events beyond its territorial boundaries. Business leaders and politicians had proposed their own vision of the future: an American empire extending to far distant lands.

Point Loma

KEY TOPICS

- The growth of federal and state governments and the consolidation of the modern two-party system

- The development of mass protest movements

- Economic and political crisis in the 1890s

- The United States as a world power

- The Spanish–American War

TOWARD A NATIONAL GOVERNING CLASS

The basic structure of government changed dramatically in the last quarter of the nineteenth century. Mirroring the fast-growing economy, public administration expanded at all levels—municipal, county, state, and federal—and took on greater responsibility for regulating society, especially market and property relations.

This expansion offered ample opportunities for politicians, who were eager to compete against one another for control of the new mechanisms of power. Political campaigns, especially those staged for the presidential elections, became mass spectacles, and votes became precious commodities. The most astute politicians attempted to rein in the growing corruption and to promote both efficiency and professionalism in the expanding structures of government.

The Growth of Government

Before the Civil War, local governments attended mainly to the promotion and regulation of trade and relied on private enterprise to supply vital services such as fire protection and water supply. As cities became more responsible for their residents' well-being, they introduced professional police and firefighting forces and began to finance school systems, public libraries, and parks. This expansion demanded huge increases in local taxation.

At the national level, mobilization for the Civil War and Reconstruction had demanded an unprecedented degree of coordination, and the federal government continued to expand under the weight of new tasks and responsibilities. Federal revenues also skyrocketed, from $257 million in 1878 to $567 million in 1900. The administrative bureaucracy also grew dramatically, from 50,000 employees in 1871 to 100,000 only a decade later.

The modern apparatus of departments, bureaus, and cabinets took shape amid this upswing. The Department of Agriculture was established in 1862 to provide information to farmers and consumers of farm products. The Department of the Interior, which had been created in 1849, grew into the largest and most important federal department after the Post Office. It came to comprise more than twenty agencies, including the Bureau of Indian Affairs, the U.S. Geological Survey, and the Bureau of Territorial and International Affairs. The Department of the Treasury, responsible for collecting federal taxes and customs as well as printing money and stamps, grew from 4,000 employees in 1873 to nearly 25,000 in 1900.

The nation's first independent regulatory agency, the Interstate Commerce Commission (ICC), was created in 1887 to bring order to the growing patchwork of state laws concerning railroads. The five-member commission appointed by the president approved freight and passenger rates set by the railroads. The ICC could take public testimony on possible violations, examine company records, and generally oversee enforcement of the law. This set a precedent for future regulation of trade as well as for positive government—that is, for the intervention of the government into the affairs of private enterprise.

The Machinery of Politics

Only gradually did Republicans and Democrats adapt to the demands of governmental expansion. The Republican Party continued to run on its Civil War record, pointing to its achievements in reuniting the nation and in passing new reform legislation. Democrats, by contrast, sought to reduce the influence of the federal government, slash expenditures, repeal legislation, and protect states' rights. While Republicans held on to their long-time constituencies, Democrats gathered support from southern white voters and immigrants newly naturalized in the North. But neither party commanded a clear majority of votes until the century drew to a close.

Presidents in the last quarter of the century—Rutherford B. Hayes (1877–81), James A. Garfield (1881), Chester A. Arthur (1881–85), Grover Cleveland (1885–89), Benjamin Harrison (1889–93), and Cleveland again (1893–97)—did not espouse a clear philosophy of government. They willingly yielded power to Congress and the state legislatures. Only 1 percent of the popular vote separated the presidential candidates in three of five elections between 1876 and 1892. Congressional races were equally tight, less than 2 percentage points separating total votes for Democratic and Republican candidates in all but one election in the decade before 1888.

Both political parties operated essentially as state or regional organizations. Successful politicians responded primarily to the particular concerns of their constituents. To please local voters, Democrats and Republicans repeatedly cross-cut each other by taking identical positions on controversial issues.

The rising costs of maintaining local organizations and orchestrating mammoth campaigns drove party leaders to seek ever-larger sources of revenue. Winners often seized and added to the spoils of office through an elaborate system of payoffs. Legislators who supported government subsidies for railroad corporations, for instance, commonly received stock in return and sometimes cash bribes. At the time few politicians or business leaders regarded these practices as unethical.

At the local level, powerful bosses and political machines dominated both parties. Democrats William Marcy Tweed of New York's powerful political organization, Tammany Hall, and Michael "Hinky Dink" Kenna of Chicago specialized in giving municipal jobs to loyal voters and holiday food baskets to their families.

A large number of federal jobs, meanwhile, changed hands each time the presidency passed from one party to another. More than 50 percent of all federal jobs were patronage positions—nearly 56,000 in 1881—that could be awarded to loyal supporters as part of the spoils of the winner. Observers estimated the decisions about congressional patronage filled one-third of all legislators' time. No wonder Bellamy's utopian community operated without politicians and political parties.

One Politician's Story

A typical politician of the age was James Garfield, the nation's twentieth president. Born in a frontier Ohio log cabin in 1831, he briefly worked as a canal boat driver, experiences he later exploited as proof of his humble origins. While serving in Congress, Garfield seemed at first committed to social reform. He introduced a bill to create a Department of Education, arguing that public education would prove the best stepping-stone to equality. He denounced his own Republican Party for allowing corruption to flourish during Ulysses S. Grant's administration.

With the failure of Reconstruction, Garfield shifted his stance. Nearly defeated by the 1874 Democratic congressional landslide, he concluded that "the intelligence of the average American citizen" fell short of the demands of the democratic system. As a result, he came out against universal suffrage. Garfield now looked to the probusiness faction of the Republican Party as a vehicle for realizing his personal ambition. After six years of trading votes and favors to build his reputation, Garfield became the party's candidate for the 1880 presidential election, a mediocre race with no outstanding issues. Garfield won by less than 40,000 popular votes out of 9 million cast.

Garfield the idealist had grown into Garfield the machine politician and lackluster president. He had already shown himself indecisive and even indifferent to governing when a bullet struck him down just 200 days after his inauguration. Like other presidents of his era, Garfield assumed that the nation's chief executive served as his party's titular leader and played mainly a ceremonial role in office.

The Spoils System and Civil Service Reform

As early as 1865, Republican representative Thomas A. Jenckes of Rhode Island proposed a bill for civil service reform. However, Congress feared that such a measure would hamper candidates in their relentless pursuit of votes. Finally, a group consisting of mainly professors, newspaper editors, lawyers, and ministers organized the Civil Service Reform Association and enlisted Democratic senator George H. Pendleton to sponsor legislation.

In January 1883, a bipartisan congressional majority passed the Pendleton Civil Service Reform Act. This measure allowed the president to create, with Senate approval, a three-person commission to draw up a set of guidelines for executive and legislative appointments. The commission established a system of standards for various federal jobs. The Pendleton Act also barred political candidates from soliciting campaign contributions from government workers. Patronage did not disappear, but public service did improve.

Many departments of the federal government took on a professional character similar to that which doctors, lawyers, and scholars were imposing on their fields through regulatory societies such as the American Medical Association and the American Historical Association. At the same time, the federal judiciary began to act more aggressively to establish the parameters of government. Through the Circuit Courts of Appeals Act of 1891, the U.S. Supreme Court gained the right to review all cases at will.

Despite these reforms, many observers still viewed government as a reign of insiders, people pulling the levers of the party machinery or spending money to influence important decisions. Edward Bellamy agreed. He advised Americans to organize their communities for the specific purpose of wresting control of government from the hands of politicians.

FARMERS AND WORKERS ORGANIZE THEIR COMMUNITIES

In the late 1860s farmers and workers began to organize their respective communities. Though short on financial resources, farmers and workers waged the most significant challenge to the two-party system since the Civil War: the populist movement.

The Grange

In many farming communities, the headquarters of the local chapter of the Patrons of Husbandry, known as the Grange (a word for " farm"), became the center of social activity, serving as the site of summer dinners and winter dances.

The Grange movement spread rapidly, especially in areas where farmers were experiencing their greatest hardships. Great Plains farmers barely survived the blizzards, grasshopper infestations, and droughts of the early 1870s. Meanwhile, farmers throughout the trans-Mississippi West and the South watched the prices for grains and cotton fall year by year in the face of growing competition from producers in Canada, Australia, Argentina, Russia, and India. In the hope of improving their condition through collective action, many farmers joined their local Grange. The Patrons of Husbandry soon swelled to more than 1.5 million members.

Grangers blamed their hard times on a band of "thieves in the night"—especially railroads and banks—that charged exorbitant fees for services. They fumed at American manufacturers, such as Cyrus McCormick, who sold farm equipment more cheaply in Europe than in the United States. To purchase equipment and raw materials, farmers borrowed money and accrued debts averaging twice that of Americans not engaged in business.

Grangers mounted their greatest assault on the railroad corporations. By bribing state legislators, railroads enjoyed a highly discriminatory rate policy, commonly charging farmers far more to ship their crops short distances than over long hauls. In 1874 several midwestern states responded to pressure and passed a series of so-called Granger laws establishing maximum shipping rates. Grangers also complained to their lawmakers about the price-fixing policies of grain wholesalers, warehousers, and operators of grain elevators. In 1873 the Illinois legislature passed a Warehouse Act, establishing maximum rates for storing grains.

Determined to buy less and produce more, Grangers established local grain elevators, set up retail stores, and even manufactured some of their own farm machinery.

The deepening depression of the late 1870s wiped out most of these cooperative programs. By 1880 Grange membership had fallen to 100,000. Meanwhile, the Supreme Court overturned most of the key legislation regulating railroads. Despite these setbacks, the Patrons of Husbandry had promoted a model of cooperation that would remain at the heart of agrarian protest movements until the end of the century.

The Farmers' Alliance

Agrarian unrest did not end with the downward turn of the Grange but instead moved south. In the 1880s farmers organized in communities where both poverty and the crop-lien system prevailed (see Chapter 17).

In 1889, several regional organizations joined forces to create the National Farmers' Alliance and Industrial Union. The combined movement claimed 3 million white members. Separately, the National Colored Farmers' Alliance and Cooperative Union grew from its beginnings in Texas and Arkansas in 1888

The symbols chosen by Grange artists represented their faith that all social value could be traced to the honest labor of the entire farm family. The hardworking American required only the enlightenment offered by the Grange to build a better community.

Source: The *Kingfisher Reformer,* May 3, 1894.

and quickly spread across the South to claim more than a million members of its own.

In the South, the falling price of cotton underlined the need for action, and farmers readily translated their anger into intense loyalty to the one organization pledged to the improvement of their lot. With more than 500 chapters in Texas alone, and cooperative stores complemented by cooperative merchandising of crops, the Southern Farmers' Alliance became a viable alternative to the capitalist marketplace—if only temporarily.

The Northern Farmers' Alliance took shape in the Plains states, drawing upon large organizations in Minnesota, Nebraska, Iowa, Kansas, and the Dakota Territory. During 1886 and 1887, summer drought followed winter blizzards and ice storms, reducing wheat harvests by one-third. Locusts and cinch bugs ate much of the rest. As if this were not enough, prices on the world market fell sharply for what little remained. By 1890 the Kansas Alliance alone boasted 130,000 members.

Grangers had pushed legislation that would limit the salaries of public officials, provide public school students with books at little or no cost, establish a program of teacher certification, and widen the admissions policies of the new state colleges. But only rarely did they put up candidates for office. In comparison, the Farmers' Alliance had few reservations about taking political stands or entering electoral races. By 1890 the alliances had gained control of the Nebraska legislature and held the balance of power in Minnesota and South Dakota.

Workers Search for Power

Like farmers, urban workers organized their communities in protest movements during the 1870s. The depression following the Panic of 1873, which

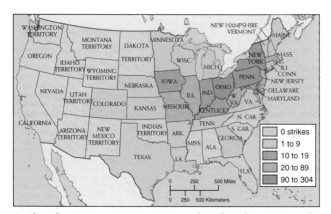

Strikes by State, 1880 *Most strikes after the Uprising of 1877 could be traced to organized trades, concentrated in the manufacturing districts of the Northeast and Midwest.*

Source: Reprinted from *Geographical Inquiry and American Historical Problems* by Carville Earle with the permission of the publishers, Stanford University Press, © 1992 by the Board of Trustees of the Leland Stanford Junior University.

produced 25 percent unemployment in many cities, served as a catalyst for organization.

The railroad industry, probably the nation's single largest employer, became the focus of protests by workers and farmers alike. Nonetheless, the railroad corporations were unprepared for the Great Uprising of 1877, the first nationwide strike. In Martinsburg, West Virginia, a 10 percent wage cut prompted workers to uncouple all engines. No trains would run, they promised, until wages were restored. Within a few days, the strike had spread along the railroad routes to New York, Buffalo, Pittsburgh, Chicago, Kansas City, and San Francisco. In all these cities workers in various industries and masses of the unemployed formed angry crowds, defying armed militia ordered to disperse them by any means. Meanwhile, strikers halted train traffic. They seized carloads of food for hungry families, and in St. Louis workers even took over the city's administration.

The rioting persisted for nearly a week. Fearing a "national insurrection," President Hayes set a precedent by calling in the U.S. Army to suppress the strike. In Pittsburgh, federal troops equipped with semiautomatic machine guns fired into a crowd and killed more than 20 people. By the time the strike finally ended, more than 100 people were dead.

Memories of the Uprising of 1877 haunted business and government officials for decades, prompting the creation of the National Guard and the construction of armories in working-class neighborhoods. Workers also drew lessons from the events. Before the end of the century, more than 6 million workers would strike in industries ranging from New England textiles to southern tobacco factories to western mines. While the Farmers' Alliance put up candidates in the South and Plains states, workers launched labor parties in dozens of industrial towns and cities.

In New York City, popular economist and land reformer Henry George, with the ardent support of the city's Central Labor Council and the Knights of Labor, put himself forward in 1886 as candidate for mayor on the United Labor Party ticket. His best-selling book, *Progress and Poverty* (1879), advocated a sweeping tax on all property to generate enough revenue to allow all Americans to live in comfort.

Tammany Hall delivered many thousands of the ballots cast for George straight into the Hudson River. Nevertheless, George managed to finish a respectable second with 31 percent of the vote, running ahead of young patrician Theodore Roosevelt. Although his campaign ended in defeat, George had issued a stern warning to the entrenched politicians and his impressive showing encouraged labor groups in other cities to form parties.

In the late 1880s labor parties won seats on many city councils and state legislatures. The Milwaukee People's Party elected the mayor, a state senator, six assemblymen, and one member of Congress. In smaller industrial towns where workers outnumbered the middle classes, labor parties did especially well.

Women Build Alliances

Women helped to build both the labor and agrarian protest movements while campaigning for their own rights as citizens. Women in the Knights of Labor endorsed the order's political planks while putting forth their own set of demands. In 1886 sixteen women attending the national convention lobbied for the creation of a special department "to investigate the abuses of which our sex is subjected by unscrupulous employers, to agitate the principles which our Order teaches of equal pay for equal work and the abolition of child labor." The delegates accepted the plan with little dissent. With perhaps 65,000 women members at its peak, the Knights ran daycare centers for the children of wage-earning mothers and occasionally even set up bakery cooperatives to reduce the drudgery of cooking.

Women made a similar mark on farmers' organizations. The Patrons of Husbandry issued a charter to a local chapter only when women were well represented on its rolls, and in the 1870s delegates to its conventions routinely gave speeches endorsing woman suffrage and even dress reform. The Farmers' Alliance continued this policy, enjoining women to assist their fathers, husbands, or sons in agitation efforts. In both the Northern and Southern Alliances, women made up perhaps one-quarter of the membership, and several advanced through the ranks to become leading speakers and organizers.

Women in both the Knights of Labor and the Farmers' Alliance found their greatest leader in Frances E. Willard, the most famous woman of the century. From 1878 until her death in 1897, Willard presided over the Woman's Christian Temperance Union (WCTU), at the time the largest organization of women in the world. She mobilized nearly 1 million women to, in her words, "make the whole world HOMELIKE." WCTU members preached moderation in the consumption of alcoholic beverages, but they also worked to reform the prison system, eradicate prostitution, and eliminate the wage system. Willard drew up plans for a new system of government whereby all offices, right up to the presidency, would be shared jointly by men and women.

The WCTU grew into the major force behind the campaign for woman suffrage, far surpassing the American Woman Suffrage Association and the National Woman Suffrage Association. By 1890, when the two rival associations merged to form the National American Woman Suffrage Association, the WCTU had already pushed the heart of the suffrage campaign into the Plains states and the West. Agitation for the right to vote provided a political bridge among women organized in the WCTU, Farmers' Alliance, Knights of Labor, and various local suffrage societies.

Farmer–Labor Unity

In December 1890 the Farmers' Alliance called a meeting at Ocala, Florida, to press for a national third-party movement. This was a risky proposition because the Southern Alliance hoped to capture control of the Democratic Party, whereas many farmers in the Plains states voted Republican. In some areas, though, the Farmers' Alliance established its own parties, put up full slates of candidates for local elections, won majorities in state legislatures, and even sent a representative to Congress. Reviewing these successes, delegates at Ocala decided to push ahead and form a national party, and they appealed to other farm, labor, and reform organizations to join them.

In February 1892, representatives from the Farmers' Alliance, the Knights of Labor, and the National Colored Farmers' Alliance, among others, met in St. Louis. The 1,300 delegates adopted a platform for the new People's Party. It called for government ownership of railroads, banks, and telegraph lines, prohibition of large landholding companies, a graduated income tax, an eight-hour workday, and restriction of immigration. The People's Party convened again in Omaha in July 1892 and nominated James Baird Weaver of Iowa for president and, to please the South, Confederate veteran James Field from Virginia for vice-president.

The Populists, as supporters of the People's Party styled themselves, quickly became a major factor in American politics. Although Democrat Grover Cleveland regained the presidency in 1892 (he had previously served from 1885 to 1889), Populists scored a string of local victories. They elected three governors, ten representatives to Congress, and five senators. Despite poor showings among urban workers east of the Mississippi, Populists looked forward to the next round of state elections in 1894. But the great test would come with the presidential election in 1896.

THE CRISIS OF THE 1890s

A series of events in the 1890s shook the confidence of many citizens in the reigning political system. But nothing was more unsettling than the severe economic depression that consumed the nation. Many feared—while others hoped—that the entire political system would topple.

Financial Collapse and Depression

The collapse of the Philadelphia and Reading Railroad in March 1893, followed by the downfall of the National Cordage Company, precipitated a crisis in the stock market and sent waves of panic splashing over banks across the country. In a few months, more than 150 banks went into receivership and hundreds more closed; nearly 200 railroads and more than 15,000 businesses also slipped into bankruptcy. In the steel industry alone thirty companies collapsed within six months of the panic. Agricultural prices plummeted to new lows. Subsequent bank failures and stock market declines held back recovery until 1897, when the economy slowly began to pick up again. The new century arrived before prosperity returned.

In many cities, unemployment rates reached 20 to 25 percent; Samuel Gompers, head of the American Federation of Labor (AFL), estimated nationwide unemployment at 3 million. Few people starved, but millions suffered from malnutrition. Inadequate diets prompted a rise in communicable diseases such as tuberculosis and pellagra. Unable to buy food, clothes, or household items, families learned to survive with the barest minimum.

Tens of thousands "rode the rails" or went "on the tramp" to look for work, hoping that their luck might change in a new city or town. Vagrancy laws (enacted during the 1870s) forced many into prison. In New York City alone, with more than 20,000 homeless people, thousands ended up in jail. Newspapers warned against this "menace" and blamed the growing crime rates on the "dangerous classes."

Another Populist, Jacob Sechler Coxey, decided to gather the masses of unemployed into a huge army and then to march to Washington, D.C., to demand from Congress a public works program. On Easter Sunday, 1894, Coxey left Massillon, Ohio, with several hundred followers, hoping to attract more. Communities across the country welcomed the marchers, but U.S. attorney general Richard C. Olney, a former lawyer for the railroad companies, conspired with state and local officials to halt them. Only 600 men and women reached the nation's capital, where the police first clubbed and then arrested the leaders for trespassing on the grass. Coxey's Army quickly disbanded, but not before voicing the public's growing impatience with government apathy toward the unemployed.

Strikes and Labor Solidarity

Meanwhile, in several locations the conflict between labor and capital had escalated to the brink of civil war. Wage cuts in the silver and lead mines of northern Idaho led to one of the bitterest conflicts of the decade.

To put a brake on organized labor, mineowners had formed a "protective association," and in March 1892 they announced a lower wage scale throughout the Coeur d'Alene district. After the miners' union refused to accept the cut, the owners locked out all union members and brought in strikebreakers by the trainload. Unionists tried peaceful methods of protest. But after three months of stalemate, they loaded a railcar with explosives and blew up a mine. Strikebreakers fled while mineowners appealed to the Idaho governor for assistance. More than 300 union members were herded into bullpens, where they were kept under unsanitary conditions for several weeks before their trial. Ore production meanwhile resumed, and by November, when troops were withdrawn, the mineowners declared a victory. But the miners' union survived, and most members eventually regained their jobs.

At Homestead, Pennsylvania, members of the Amalgamated Iron, Steel and Tin Workers, the most powerful union of the AFL, had carved out an admirable position for themselves in the Carnegie Steel Company. Well paid, proud of their skills, the unionists customarily directed their unskilled helpers without undue influence of company supervisors. Determined to gain control over every stage of production, Carnegie and his chairman, Henry C. Frick, decided not only to lower wages but to break the union.

In 1892, when the Amalgamated's contract expired, Frick announced a drastic wage cut. He also ordered a wooden stockade built around the factory, with grooves for rifles and barbed wire on top. When Homestead's city government refused to assign police to disperse strikers, Frick dispatched a barge carrying a private army armed to the teeth. Gunfire broke out and continued throughout the day. After the governor sent the Pennsylvania National Guard to restore order, Carnegie's factory reopened, with strikebreakers doing the work.

After four months, the union was forced to concede a crushing defeat, not only for itself but in effect for all steelworkers. The Carnegie company reduced its work force by a quarter, lengthened the workday, and cut wages 25 percent for those who remained on the job. If the Amalgamated Iron, Steel and Tin Workers, known throughout the industry as the "aristocrats of labor," could be brought down, less skilled workers could expect little from the corporate giants. Within a decade, every major steel company operated without union interference.

But the spirit of labor solidarity did not die. Just two years after strikes at Coeur d'Alene and Homestead, the most earthshaking railway strike since 1877 again dramatized the extent of collusion between the government and corporations to crush the labor movement.

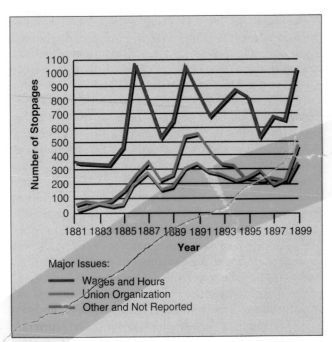

Work Stoppages, 1881–1899 *The number of strikes over wages and hours peaked in the years of 1886, 1890, and 1899, as workers in various trades and industries acted to protect or better their situations. By contrast, strikes for union recognition by employees—waged mostly by skilled workers—rose slowly but steadily until the economic depression of the 1890s. As the depression eased, strikes again increased.*

Source: United States Bureau of the Census, *Historical Statistics of the United States, Colonial Times to 1957* (Washington, D.C.: Bureau of the Census, 1960), p. 99.

Like Lowell, Massachusetts, sixty years earlier, the town of Pullman, Illinois, just south of Chicago, had been regarded as a model industrial community. Its creator and proprietor, George Pullman, had manufactured luxurious sleeping cars for railroads since 1881. He built his company as a self-contained community, with the factory at the center, surrounded by modern cottages, a library, churches, an independent water supply, and even its own cemetery. The Pullman Palace Car Company deducted rent, library fees, and grocery bills from each worker's weekly wages. In good times workers enjoyed a decent livelihood, although many resented Pullman's autocratic control of their daily affairs.

When times grew hard, the company cut wages by as much as one-half, in some cases down to less than $1 a day. Charges for food and rent remained unchanged. Furthermore, factory supervisors sought to make up for declining profits by driving workers to produce greater volume. In May 1894, after Pullman fired members of a committee that had drawn up a list of grievances, workers voted to strike.

Pullman workers found their champion in Eugene V. Debs, who had recently formed the Ameri-

can Railway Union (ARU) to bring all railroad workers into one organization. Debs, the architect of the ARU's victory over the Great Northern rail line just one month earlier, advised caution, but delegates to an ARU convention voted to support a nationwide boycott of all Pullman cars. This action soon turned into a sympathy strike by railroad workers across the country. Support for the strike was especially strong in the western states.

Compared to the Uprising of 1877, the orderly Pullman strike at first produced little violence. ARU officials urged strikers to ignore all police provocations and hold their ground peacefully. But Attorney General Olney, claiming that the ARU was disrupting mail shipments (actually Debs had banned such interference), issued a blanket injunction against the strike. On July 4, President Cleveland sent federal troops to Chicago, over Illinois governor John Peter Altgeld's objections. After a bitter confrontation that left thirteen people dead and more than fifty wounded, the army dispersed the strikers. For the next week, railroad workers in twenty-six other states resisted federal troops, and a dozen more people were killed. On July 17, the strike finally ended when federal marshals arrested Debs and other leaders.

Assailing the arrogance of class privilege that encouraged the government to use brute force against its citizens, Debs concluded that the labor movement could not regain its dignity under the present system. An avid fan of Bellamy's *Looking Backward*, Debs came out of jail committed to the ideals of socialism and in 1898 moved on to help form a political party dedicated to its principles.

Tens of thousands of people supported Debs. Declining nomination on the Populist ticket in 1896, Debs ran for president as a Socialist in 1900 and in four subsequent elections. The odds against him grew with the scale of the booming economy, but Debs made his point on moral grounds.

The Social Gospel

Like Edward Bellamy, a growing number of Protestant and Catholic clergy and lay theologians noted a discrepancy between the ideals of Christianity and prevailing attitudes toward the poor. Like Bellamy, they could no longer sanction an economic system that allowed large numbers of its citizens to toil long hours under unhealthy conditions and for subsistence wages. They demanded that the church lead the way to a new cooperative order.

Ministers called for civil service reform and the end of child labor. Supporting labor's right to organize and, if necessary, to strike, they petitioned government officials to regulate corporations and place a limit on profits. Local Protestant ministers and community leaders sought to restore what they considered the true spirit of Christianity. Although the social gospel spread most rapidly through the northern industrial cities, southern African Americans espoused their own version. They reinterpreted the Gospel as Jesus' promise to emancipate their race from satanic white power brokers. The biblical republic of "Beulahland" became their model of redemption.

Catholics, doctrinally more inclined than Protestants to accept poverty as a natural condition, joined the social gospel movement in smaller numbers. In the early 1880s Polish Americans broke away from the Roman Catholic Church to form the Polish National Church, which was committed to the concerns of working people. Irish Americans encouraged priests to ally themselves with the labor movement. Pope Leo XIII's encyclical *Rerum Novarum* (1891) endorsed the right of workers to form trade unions.

Women guided the social gospel movement in their communities. In nearly every city, groups of women affiliated with various evangelical Protestant sects raised money to establish small, inexpensive residential hotels for working women, whose small wages rarely covered the price of safe, comfortable shelter. Federated as the Young Women's Christian Association, by the turn of the century the YWCA incorporated more than 600 local chapters. The "Y" sponsored a range of services for needy Christian women, ranging from homes for the elderly and for unmarried mothers to elaborate programs of vocational instruction and physical fitness. Meanwhile, Catholic lay women and nuns served the poor women of their faith, operating numerous schools, hospitals, and orphanages.

POLITICS OF REFORM, POLITICS OF ORDER

The severe hardships of the 1890s, following decades of popular unrest and economic uncertainty, led to a crisis in the two-party system and pointed to the presidential election of 1896 as a likely turning point in American politics. Populists showed surprising ingenuity and courage in breaking down barriers against political insurgents.

The Free Silver Issue

Grover Cleveland owed his victory in 1892 over Republican incumbent Benjamin Harrison to the predictable votes of the Democratic "solid South" and to the unanticipated support of such northern states as Illinois and Wisconsin, whose German-born voters turned against the increasingly nativist Republicans. But when the economy collapsed the following year, Cleveland and the Democrats who controlled

Congress faced a public eager for action. Convinced that the economic crisis was "largely the result of financial policy . . . embodied in unwise laws," the president called a special session of Congress to reform the nation's currency.

For generations, reformers had advocated "soft" currency—that is, an increase in the money supply that would loosen credit. During the Civil War the federal government took decisive action, replacing state bank notes with a national paper currency popularly called "greenbacks" (from the color of the bills). In 1873 President Grant signed a Coinage Act that added silver to gold as the precious metal base of currency, presumably lowering the value of currency by adding to its supply. This measure had little real impact on the economy but opened the door to more tinkering.

The Sherman Silver Purchase Act of 1890 directed the Treasury to increase the amount of currency coined from silver mined in the West and also permitted the U.S. government to print paper currency backed by the silver. Eastern members of Congress supported this measure when Westerners agreed, in turn, to support the McKinley tariff, which established the highest import duties yet on foreign goods.

With the economy in ruins, a desperate President Cleveland now demanded the repeal of the Sherman Act, insisting that only the gold standard could pull the nation out of depression. By exerting intense pressure on congressional Democrats, Cleveland succeeded in October 1893, but not without ruining his chances for renomination. The midterm elections in 1894 brought the largest shift in congressional power in American history: the Republicans gained 117 seats, and the Democrats lost 113. The "Silver Democrats" of Cleveland's own party vowed revenge and began to look to the Populists, mainly Westerners and farmers who favored "free silver"—that is, the unlimited coinage of silver. Republicans confidently began to prepare for the presidential election of 1896, known as the "battle of the standards."

Populism's Last Campaigns

Populists had been buoyed by the 1894 election, which delivered to their candidates nearly 1.5 million votes, a gain of 42 percent over their 1892 totals. They made impressive inroads into several southern states. Still, even in the Midwest where Populists doubled their vote, they managed to win less than 7 percent of the total.

As Populists prepared for the 1896 election, they found themselves at a crossroad: What were they to do with the growing popularity of Democrat William Jennings Bryan? A spellbinding orator, Bryan won a congressional seat in 1890. After seizing the Populist slogan "Equal Rights to All, Special Privilege to

None," Bryan became a major contender for president of the United States.

Noting the surging interest in free silver, Bryan became its champion. For two years before the 1896 election, Bryan wooed potential voters in a speaking tour that took him to every state in the nation. Pouring new life into his divided party, Bryan pushed Silver Democrats to the forefront.

At the 1896 party convention, the thirty-six-year-old orator thrilled delegates with his evocation of agrarian ideals. What became one of the most famous speeches in American political history closed on a dramatic note. Spreading his arms to suggest the crucified Christ figure, Bryan pledged to answer all demands for a gold standard by saying, "You shall not press down upon the brow of labor this crown of thorns, you shall not crucify mankind upon a cross of gold." The next day, Bryan won the Democratic presidential nomination.

The Populists feared that the growing emphasis on currency would overshadow their more important planks calling for government ownership of the nation's railroads and communication systems. As the date of their own convention approached, delegates divided over strategy: they could endorse Bryan and give up their independent status; or they could run an independent campaign and risk splitting the silver vote.

In the end, the Populists nominated Bryan for president and chose one of their own ranks, the popular Georgian Tom Watson, for the vice-presidential candidate. However, most state Democratic Party organizations refused to put the "fusion" ticket on the ballot, and Bryan and his Democratic running mate, Arthur Sewall, simply ignored the Populist campaign.

The Republican Triumph

After Cleveland's blunders, Republicans anticipated an easy victory in 1896, but Bryan's nomination, as party stalwart Mark Hanna warned, "changed everything." Luckily, they had their own handsome, knowledgeable, courteous, and ruthless candidate, Civil War veteran William McKinley. Equally important, the Republicans enjoyed an efficient and well-financed machine. Hanna raised up to $7 million and outspent Bryan more than ten to one. The sheer expense and skill of coordination outdid all previous campaigns and established a precedent for future presidential elections. In the campaign's final two weeks, organizers dispatched 1,400 speakers to spread the word. Fearful of divisions in their own ranks, Republicans played down the silver issue while emphasizing the tariff and consistently cast Bryan as a dangerous naysayer.

McKinley triumphed in the most important presidential election since Reconstruction. Bryan won 46 percent of the popular vote but failed to carry the Midwest, West Coast, or Upper South. Moreover, the

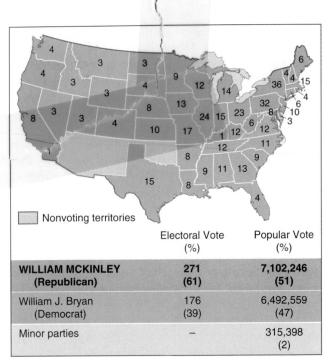

	Electoral Vote (%)	Popular Vote (%)
WILLIAM MCKINLEY (Republican)	**271 (61)**	**7,102,246 (51)**
William J. Bryan (Democrat)	176 (39)	6,492,559 (47)
Minor parties	–	315,398 (2)

Election of 1896, by States　*Democratic candidate William Jennings Bryan carried most of rural America but could not overcome Republican William McKinley's stronghold in the populous industrial states.*

free silver campaign rebuffed traditionally Democratic urban voters, who feared that soft money would bring higher prices. Neither the reform-minded middle classes nor impoverished blue-collar workers were convinced that Bryan's grand reform vision really included them. The Populist following, disappointed and disillusioned, dwindled away.

Once in office, McKinley promoted a mixture of probusiness and expansionist measures. He supported the Dingley tariff of 1897, which raised import duties to an all-time high and favored the passage of the Gold Standard Act of 1900. In 1897 McKinley also encouraged Congress to create the United States Industrial Commission, which would plan business regulation; in 1898 he promoted a bankruptcy act that eased the financial situation of small businesses; he proposed the Erdman Act of the same year, which established a system of arbitration to avoid rail strikes. The Supreme Court ruled in concert with the president, finding eighteen railways in violation of antitrust laws and granting states the right to regulate hours of labor under certain circumstances.

McKinley's triumph ended the popular challenge to the nation's governing system. With prosperity returning by 1898 and nationalism rising swiftly, McKinley encouraged Americans to go for "a full dinner pail," the winning Republican slogan of the 1900 presidential election.

The Limits of Democracy

Campaign rhetoric aside, McKinley and Bryan differed only slightly on the major problems facing the nation in 1896. Neither Bryan the reformer nor McKinley the prophet of prosperity addressed the escalation of racism and nativism (anti-immigrant feeling) throughout the nation.

Toward the end of the century, the nation's patriotic fervor took on a strongly nationalistic and antiforeign tone. Striking workers and their employers alike tended to blame immigrants for the hard times. Semisecret organizations such as the American Protective Association sprang up to defend American institutions. Fourth of July orators continued to celebrate freedom and liberty but more often boasted about the might and power of their nation.

White southern local and state governments codified racist ideology by passing discriminatory and segregationist legislation, which became known as Jim Crow laws. Wealthy planters, merchants, and farmers organized to disfranchise black voters and extend the practice of segregation to cover facilities such as restaurants, public transportation, and even drinking fountains. The United States Supreme Court upheld the new discriminatory legislation. Its decisions in the *Civil Rights Cases* (1883) overturned the Civil Rights Act of 1875, and in *Plessy v. Ferguson* (1896) the Court upheld a Louisiana state law formally segregating railroad cars on the basis of the "separate but equal" doctrine. In *Cumming v. Richmond County Board of Education* (1899), the Court allowed separate schools for blacks and whites, even where facilities for African American children did not exist.

Southern states enacted new literacy tests and property qualifications for voting, demanding proof of property and the ability to read and write. Loopholes permitted poor whites to vote even under these conditions, except where they threatened the Democratic Party's rule. Grandfather clauses, invented in Louisiana, exempted from all restrictions those who had been entitled to vote on January 1, 1867, together with their sons and grandsons. In 1898 the Supreme Court ruled that poll taxes and literacy requirements enacted in order to prevent blacks (and some poor whites) from voting were a proper means of restricting the ballot to "qualified" voters. By this time, only 5 percent of the southern black electorate voted, and African Americans were barred from public office and jury service.

Racial violence escalated. Not only race riots but thousands of lynchings took place. Between 1882 and the turn of the century, the number of lynchings usually exceeded 100 each year; 1892 produced a record 230 deaths (161 black, 69 white). Announced in local newspapers, lynchings became public spectacles for entire white families, and railroads sometimes offered special excursion rates for travel to these events.

After three local black businessmen were lynched in 1892, Ida B. Wells, young editor of a black newspaper in Memphis, vigorously denounced the outrage, blaming white business competitors of the victims. Her stand fanned the tempers of local whites, who destroyed her press and forced the outspoken editor to leave the city.

Wells launched an international movement against lynching, lecturing across the country and in Europe, demanding an end to the silence about this barbaric crime. Her work also inspired the growth of a black women's club movement. The National Association of Colored Women was founded in 1896.

"IMPERIALISM OF RIGHTEOUSNESS"

Many Americans attributed the economic crisis of 1893–97 not simply to the collapse of the railroads and the stock market but to basic structural problems: an overbuilt economy and an insufficient market for goods. Profits from total sales of manufactured and agricultural products had grown substantially over the level achieved in the 1880s, but output increased even more rapidly. While the number of millionaires shot up from 500 in 1860 to more than 4,000 in 1892, the majority of working people lacked enough income to buy back a significant portion of what they produced. As Republican Senator Albert J. Beveridge of Indiana put it, "We are raising more than we can consume . . . making more than we can use. Therefore, we must find new markets for our produce, new occupation for our capital, new work for our labor."

The White Man's Burden

In 1893 historian Frederick Jackson Turner read his famous essay, "The Significance of the Frontier in American History," in which he said that Americans required a new frontier if democracy were to survive, at the meeting of the American Historical Association. The meeting was held in Chicago at the time of the World's Fair, less than two months after the nation's economy collapsed. A complex of more than 400 buildings, newly constructed in beaux arts design, commemorated the four hundredth anniversary of Columbus's landing.

Agriculture Hall showcased the production of corn, wheat, and other crops and featured a gigantic globe encircled by samples of American-manufactured farm machinery. The symbolism was evident: all eyes were on worldwide markets for American products. Another building housed a model of a canal cut across Nicaragua, suggesting the ease with which American traders might reach Asian markets if transport ships could travel directly from the Caribbean to the Pacific.

The World's Fair also "displayed" representatives of the people who populated foreign lands. The Midway Plaisance, a strip nearly a mile long and more than 600 feet wide, was an enormous sideshow of recreated Turkish bazaars and South Sea island huts. There were Javanese carpenters, Dahomean drummers, Egyptian swordsmen, and Hungarian Gypsies as well as Eskimos, Syrians, Samoans, and Chinese. Very popular was the World Congress of Beauty, parading "40 Ladies from 40 Nations" dressed in native costume.

By celebrating the brilliance of American industry and simultaneously presenting the rest of the world's people as a source of exotic entertainment, the planners of the fair delivered a powerful message. Former abolitionist Frederick Douglass, who attended the fair on "Colored People's Day," objected to the stark contrast setting off Anglo-Saxons from people of color, an opposition between "civilization" and "savagery."

The Chicago World's Fair gave shape to prevalent ideas about the superiority of American civilization and its racial order. At the same time, by showcasing American industries, it made a strong case for commercial expansion abroad. Social gospeler Josiah Strong, a Congregational minister who had begun his career trying to convert Indians to Christianity, provided a timely synthesis. Linking economic and spiritual expansion, Strong advocated an "imperialism of righteousness" by the white Americans, who were best suited to "Christianizing" and civilizing others with their "genius for colonizing." It was the white American, Strong argued, who had been "divinely commissioned to be, in a peculiar sense, his brother's keeper." Many newspaper reporters and editorialists agreed that it would be morally wrong for Americans to shirk what the British poet Rudyard Kipling called the "White Man's Burden."

Foreign Missions

The push for overseas expansion coincided with a major wave of religious evangelism and foreign missions. Early in the nineteenth century, Protestant missionaries, hoping to fulfill what they believed to be a divine command to carry God's message to all peoples and to win converts for their church, had focused on North America. Many disciples, such as Strong himself, headed west and stationed themselves on Indian reservations. Others worked among the immigrant populations of the nation's growing cities. As early as the 1820s, however, a few missionaries had traveled to the Sandwich Islands (Hawai'i) in an effort to supplant the indigenous religion with Christianity. After the Civil War, following the formation of the Women's Union Missionary Society of Americans for Heathen Lands, the major evangelical Protestant denominations all sponsored missions directed at foreign lands, funded by wealthy men.

By the 1890s college campuses blazed with missionary excitement, and the intercollegiate Student Volunteers for Foreign Missions spread rapidly. Young Protestant women rushed to join foreign missionary societies. By 1915, more than 3 million women had enrolled in forty denominational missionary societies, surpassing in size all other women's organizations in the United States.

By 1898 Protestants claimed to have made Christians of more than 80,000 Chinese, a tiny portion of the population but a significant stronghold for American interests in their nation. The missionaries did more than spread the gospel. They taught school, provided rudimentary medical care, offered vocational training programs, and sometimes encouraged young men and women to pursue a college education in preparation for careers in their homelands.

Outside the churches proper, the YMCA and YWCA, which had set up nondenominational missions for the working poor in many American cities, also embarked on a worldwide crusade to reach non-Christians. A close observer ironically suggested that the United States had three great occupying forces: the army, the navy, and the "Y."

Missionaries played an important role both in generating public interest in foreign lands and in preparing the way for American economic expansion. As Josiah Strong aptly put it, "Commerce follows the missionary."

An Overseas Empire

Business and political leaders also had set their sights on distant lands. In the 1860s William Henry Seward, secretary of state under Abraham Lincoln and then under Andrew Johnson, correctly predicted that foreign trade would play an increasingly important part in the American economy. Between 1870 and 1900 exports more than tripled, from about $400 million to over $1.5 billion. But as European markets for American goods began to contract, business and political leaders looked more eagerly to Asia as well as to lands closer by.

Since the American Revolution, many Americans had regarded all nearby nations as falling naturally within their own territorial realm, destined to be acquired when opportunity allowed. Seward advanced these imperialist principles in 1867 by negotiating the purchase of Alaska (known at the time as Seward's Icebox) from Russia for 7.2 million dollars. Meanwhile, with European nations launched on their own imperialist missions in Asia and Africa, the United States increasingly viewed the Caribbean as an "American lake" and all of Latin America as a vast potential market for U.S. goods. The crisis of the 1890s transformed this long-standing desire into a perceived economic necessity. Unlike European imperialists, powerful Americans

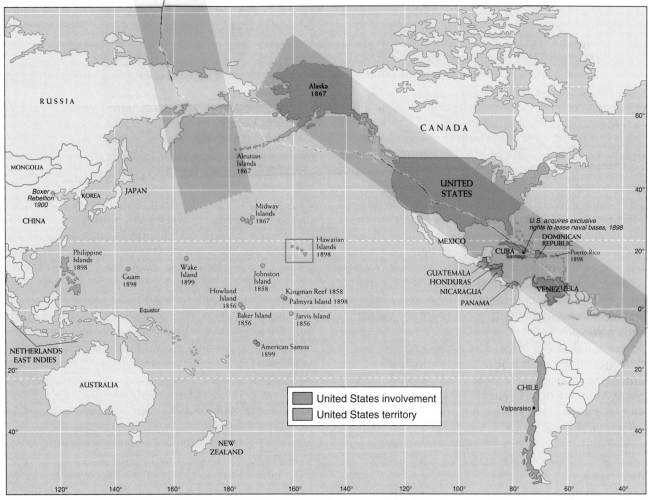

The American Domain, ca. 1900 *The United States claimed numerous islands in the South Pacific and intervened repeatedly in Latin America to secure its economic interests.*

dreamed of empire without large-scale permanent military occupation and costly colonial administration.

Americans focused their expansionist plans on the Western Hemisphere, determined to dislodge the dominant power, Great Britain. In 1867, when Canada became a self-governing dominion, American diplomats hoped to annex their northern neighbor, believing that Great Britain would gladly accede in order to concentrate its imperial interests in Asia. But Great Britain refused to give up Canada, and the United States backed away. Central and South America proved more accommodating.

Republican stalwart James G. Blaine, secretary of state under presidents Garfield and Harrison, determined to work out a Good Neighbor policy (a phrase coined by Henry Clay in 1820). Bilateral treaties with Mexico, Colombia, the British West Indies, El Salvador, and the Dominican Republic allowed American business to dominate local economies, importing their raw materials at low prices and flooding their local markets with goods manufactured in the United States. Often American investors simply took over the principal industries of these small nations, undercutting national business classes.

The Good Neighbor policy depended, Blaine knew, on peace and order in the Latin American states. In 1883, wishing to enforce treaties and protect overseas investments, Congress appropriated funds to build up American seapower. Beginning with ninety small ships, over one-third of them wooden, the navy grew quickly to become known as the Great White Fleet.

The annexation of Hawai'i on July 7, 1898, followed nearly a century of economic penetration and diplomatic maneuver. American missionaries, who had arrived in the 1820s to convert Hawai'ians to Christianity, began to buy up huge parcels of land and to subvert the existing feudal system of landholding. They also encouraged American businesses to buy into sugar plantations, and by 1875 U.S. corporations dominated the sugar trade. In 1887 a new treaty allowed the

United States to build a naval base at Pearl Harbor on the island of Oahu.

The next year, American planters went a step further, arranging the overthrow of a weak king, Kalakaua, and securing a new government allied to their economic interests. In 1891, the new queen, Lili-uokalani, struck back by issuing a constitution granting her more discretionary power. The U.S. minister, prompted by the pineapple magnate Sanford B. Dole, responded by calling for military assistance. On January 16, 1893, U.S. sailors landed on Hawai'i to protect American property. Liliuokalani was deposed, a new provisional government was installed, and Hawai'i was proclaimed an American protectorate (a territory protected and partly controlled by the United States). President Cleveland refused to consider annexation, but five years later McKinley affirmed a joint congressional resolution under which Hawai'i would become an American territory in 1900. The residents of Hawai'i were not consulted about this momentous change in their national identity.

Hawai'i was often viewed as a stepping-stone to the vast Asian markets. To accelerate railroad investment and trade, a consortium of New York bankers created the American China Development Company in 1896. However, they feared that the tottering Manchu dynasty would fall to European, Russian, and Japanese colonial powers, which would then prohibit trade with the United States. Secretary of State John Hay responded in 1899 by proclaiming the Open Door policy. According to this doctrine, outlined in notes to six major powers, the United States enjoyed the right to advance its commercial interests anywhere in the world, at least on terms equal to those of the other imperialist nations. The Chinese marketplace, although still small, was too important to lose.

THE SPANISH–AMERICAN WAR

During his 1896 campaign, William McKinley firmly committed himself to the principle of economic expansion. It was for him the proper alternative to Edward Bellamy's program for a cooperative commonwealth. Indeed, he once described his greatest ambition as achieving American supremacy in world markets. As president, McKinley not only reached out for markets but took his nation into war.

A "Splendid Little War" in Cuba

Cuba had long tempted American investors. As early as the 1840s, advocates of expansion described the nearby Caribbean island, still owned by Spain, as a fruit ripe for picking. After the Civil War Americans invested heavily in sugar mills, tobacco plantations, and mines, and by the early 1890s they held nearly $50 million worth of prop-

erty on Cuba. In 1894, however, the Wilson–Gorman tariff placed stiff restrictions on Cuban imports to the United States, cutting the volume of trade by as much as 50 percent. The Cuban economy, along with American investments, went into a deep recession, setting the stage for revolution.

As unemployment and unrest spread, nationalist leader José Martí declared that "Cuba must be free from Spain and the United States." Cubans rallied under his leadership until Spanish troops ambushed and killed Martí in May 1895. Martí's martyrdom fueled the flames of rebellion.

Many Americans supported the movement for *Cuba Libre*. President Cleveland refused to back the Cuban revolutionaries but urged Spain to grant the island a limited autonomy. Even when Congress passed a resolution in 1896 welcoming the future independence of Cuba, Cleveland and his advisers demurred, determined to avoid war with Spain.

When McKinley took over the presidency, he immediately perceived that the insurrection harmed U.S. investments and might destroy the entire Cuban economy. He nevertheless drew back. In his inaugural address he declared, "We want no wars of conquest; we must avoid the temptation of territorial aggression." The tide turned, however, when Spain appeared unable to maintain order. In early 1898 American newspapers published a private letter written by a Spanish diplomat in Washington characterizing the president as weak and opportunistic. Public indignation, whipped up by tabloid press headlines and sensational stories, turned into frenzy five days later, on February 15, when an explosion ripped through the battleship USS *Maine*, stationed in Havana harbor ostensibly to rescue American citizens living in Cuba.

McKinley, suspecting that war was close, had already begun to prepare for intervention. While newspapers ran banner headlines charging a Spanish conspiracy, the president established a commission to investigate the explosion, which proved to be an accident rather than an act of Spanish aggression. The impatient public meanwhile demanded revenge for the death of 266 American sailors.

Finally, on April 11 McKinley asked Congress for a declaration of war against Spain. Yet the Senate barely passed the war resolution by a vote of 42 to 35, and only with the inclusion of an amendment by Republican senator Henry Teller of Colorado that disclaimed "any disposition or intention to exercise sovereignty, jurisdiction or control over said island, except for the pacification thereof." McKinley, who opposed any plan to annex Cuba, signed the declaration of war on April 29, 1898.

Ten weeks later the war was all but over. On land, Lieutenant Colonel Theodore Roosevelt—who boasted of killing Spaniards "like jackrabbits"—led his Rough Riders to victory. On July 3, the main Spanish fleet near Santiago Bay was destroyed, two weeks later Santiago itself surrendered and the war drew to a close. Although fewer than 400 Americans died in battle, disease and the inept treatment of the wounded claimed more than 5,000 lives. Roosevelt nevertheless felt invigorated by the conflict, agreeing with John Hay that it had been a "splendid little war."

On August 12, at a small ceremony in McKinley's office marking Spain's surrender, the United States secured Cuba's independence but nevertheless denied the island an official role in the proceedings. American businesses tightened their hold on Cuban sugar plantations, while U.S. military forces oversaw the formation of a constitutional convention that made Cuba a protectorate of the United States. Under the Platt Amendment, sponsored by Republican senator Orville H. Platt of Connecticut in 1901, Cuba promised to provide land for American bases, devote national revenues to paying back debts to the United States, sign no treaty that would be detrimental to American interests, and acknowledge the right of the United States to intervene at any time to protect its interests in Cuba. After American troops withdrew from Cuba, the amendment was incorporated into the Cuban–American Treaty of 1903. This treaty, which remained in place until 1934, paved the way for American domination of the island's sugar industry and contributed to anti-American sentiment among Cuban nationalists.

The United States further advanced its interests in the Caribbean to include Puerto Rico, ceded by Spain, and eventually the Virgin Islands of St. Thomas and St. John, purchased from Denmark in 1917. The acquisition of Pacific territories, including Guam, marked the emergence of the United States as a global colonial power.

War in the Philippines

The Philippines, another of Spain's colonies, seemed an especially attractive prospect, its 7,000 islands a natural way station to the markets of mainland Asia. In 1897 Assistant Secretary of the Navy Theodore Roosevelt and President McKinley had discussed the merits of taking the Pacific colony in the event of war with Spain. At the first opportunity, McKinley acted to bring these islands into the U.S. strategic orbit. Shortly after Congress declared war on Spain, on May 4, the president dispatched 5,000 troops to occupy the Philippines. George Dewey, a Civil War veteran who commanded the American Asiatic Squadron, demolished the Spanish fleet in Manila Bay in seven hours. Once the war ended, McKinley pledged "to educate the Filipinos, and to uplift and civilize and Christianize them." But after centuries of Spanish rule, the majority

"Uncle Sam Teaches the Art of Self-Government," editorial cartoon, 1898. Expressing a popular sentiment of the time, a newspaper cartoonist shows the rebels as raucous children who constantly fight among themselves and need to be brought into line by Uncle Sam.

of islanders—already Christians—were eager to create their own nation.

The Filipino rebels, like the Cubans, at first welcomed American troops and fought with them against Spain. But when the war ended and they perceived that American troops were not preparing to leave, the rebels, led by Emilio Aguinaldo, turned against their former allies and attacked the American base of operations in Manila in February 1899. Predicting a brief skirmish, American commanders seriously underestimated the population's capacity to endure great suffering for the sake of independence.

U.S. troops had provoked this conflict in various ways. Military leaders, the majority veterans of the Indian wars, commonly described the natives as "gugus," and reported themselves, as one said, as "just itching to get at the niggers." While awaiting action, American soldiers repeatedly insulted or physically abused civilians, raped Filipino women, and otherwise whipped up resentment.

The resulting conflict took the form of modern guerrilla warfare, with brutalities on both sides. Instructed to regard every male Filipino over ten years of age as a potential enemy who could be shot without provocation, U.S. troops attacked civilians and destroyed their food, housing, and water supplies. Many

American soldiers appeared indifferent to the sight of bloodshed. Ordered to take no prisoners, American soldiers forced Filipino civilians to dig their own graves and bragged about killing the wounded. By the time the fighting slowed down in 1902, 4,300 American lives had been lost, and one of every five Filipinos had died in battle or from starvation or disease. On some of the Philippine islands, intermittent fighting lasted until 1935.

The conquest of the Philippines, which remained a U.S. territory until 1946, evoked for its defenders the vision of empire. Once again, Josiah Strong proclaimed judgment over an era. His famous treatise *Expansion* (1900) roundly defended American overseas involvements by carefully distinguishing between freedom and independence. People could achieve freedom, he argued, only under the rule of law. And because white Americans had proven themselves superior in the realm of government, they could best bring "freedom" to nonwhite peoples by setting aside the ideal of national independence for a period of enforced guidance. Many began to wonder, however, whether the United States could become an empire without sacrificing its democratic spirit, and to ask whether the subjugated people were so fortunate under the rule of the United States.

Critics of Empire

No mass movement formed to forestall U.S. expansion, but distinguished figures such as Mark Twain, Andrew Carnegie, William Jennings Bryan, and Harvard philosopher William James voiced their opposition strongly. Organized protest to military action, especially against the widely reported atrocities in the Philippines, owed much to the Anti-Imperialist League, which was founded by a small group of prominent Bostonians. In historic Faneuil Hall, which had witnessed the birth of both the American Revolution and the antislavery movement, a mass meeting was convened in June 1898 to protest the "insane and wicked ambition which is driving the nation to ruin." Within a few months, the league reported 25,000 members. Most supported American economic expansion but advocated free trade rather than political domination as the means to reach this goal.

A few outspoken anti-imperialists, such as former Illinois governor John Peter Altgeld, openly toasted Filipino rebels as heroes. Morrison Swift, leader of the Coxey's Army contingent from Massachusetts, formed a Filipino Liberation Society and sent antiwar materials to American troops. Others, such as Samuel Gompers, a league vice-president, felt no sympathy for conquered peoples, but simply wanted to prevent colonized nonwhites from immigrating to the United States and "inundating" American labor.

Military leaders and staunch imperialists did not distinguish between racist and nonracist anti-imperialists. They called all dissenters "unhung traitors" and demanded their arrest. Newspaper editors accused universities of harboring antiwar professors, although college students as a group were enthusiastic supporters of the war.

Most Americans put aside their doubts and welcomed the new era of aggressive nationalism. Untouched by the private tragedies of dead or wounded American soldiers and the mass destruction of civilian society in the Philippines, the vast majority could approve Theodore Roosevelt's defense of armed conflict: "No triumph of peace is quite so great as the supreme triumphs of war."

CONCLUSION

The conflicts marking the last quarter of the nineteenth century that pitted farmers, workers, and the proprietors of small businesses against powerful outside interests had offered Americans an important moment of democratic promise. By the end of the century, however, the rural and working-class campaigns to retain a large degree of self-government in their communities had been defeated, their organizations destroyed, their autonomy eroded. The rise of a national governing class and its counterpart, the large bureaucratic state, established new rules of behavior, new sources of prestige, and new rewards for the most successful citizens.

But the nation would pay a steep price, in the next era, for the failure of democratic reform. Regional antagonisms, nativist movements against the foreign-born, and deepening racial tensions blighted American society. As the new century opened, progressive reformers moved to correct flaws in government while accepting the framework of a corporate society and its overseas empire.

CHRONOLOGY

1867 Patrons of Husbandry (Grange) founded

Secretary of State William H. Seward negotiates the purchase of Alaska

1873 Coinage Act adds silver to gold as the precious metal base of currency

Panic of 1873 initiates depression

1874 Tompkins Square Riot inaugurates era of labor violence

Granger laws begin to regulate railroad shipping rates

1877 Rutherford B. Hayes elected president

Great Uprising of 1877

1879 Henry George publishes *Progress and Poverty*

1881 President James A. Garfield assassinated; Chester A. Arthur becomes president

1883 Pendleton Civil Service Reform Act passed

1884 Grover Cleveland elected president

1887 Interstate Commerce Act creates the Interstate Commerce Commission

1888 Edward Bellamy publishes *Looking Backward*

National Colored Farmers' Alliance and Cooperative Union formed

Benjamin Harrison elected president

1889 National Farmers' Alliance and Industrial Union formed

1890 Sherman Silver Purchase Act

McKinley tariff enacted

National American Woman Suffrage Association formed

1891 National Women's Alliance formed

Populist (People's) Party formed

1892 Grover Cleveland elected to second term as president

Coeur d'Alene miners' strike

Homestead, Pennslvania, steelworkers strike

Ida B. Wells begins crusade against lynching

1893 Western Federation of Miners formed

Financial panic and economic depression begin

World's Columbian Exhibition opens in Chicago

1894 "Coxey's Army" marches on Washington, D.C.

Pullman strike

1896 *Plessy v. Ferguson* upholds segregation

William McKinley defeats William Jennings Bryan for president

1897 Dingley tariff again raises import duties to an all-time high

1898 Eugene V. Debs helps found Social Democratic Party

Hawai'i is annexed

War is declared against Spain; Cuba and Philippines seized

Anti-Imperialist League formed

1899 *Cumming v. Richmond County Board of Education* sanctions separate schools for black and white children

Secretary of State John Hay announces Open Door policy

Guerrilla war begins in the Philippines

1900 Gold Standard Act

Josiah Strong publishes *Expansion*

McKinley reelected

REVIEW QUESTIONS

1. Discuss some of the problems accompanying the expansion of government during the late nineteenth century. What role did political parties play in this process? Explain how a prominent reformer such as James Garfield might become a leading machine politician.

2. What were the major causes and consequences of the populist movement of the 1880s and 1890s? Why did the election of 1896 prove so important to the future of American politics?

3. Discuss the role of women in both the Grange and the People's Party. What were their specific goals?

4. Discuss the causes and consequences of the financial crisis of the 1890s. How did various reformers and politicians respond to the event? What kinds of programs did they offer to restore the economy or reduce poverty?

5. How did the exclusion of African Americans affect the outcome of populism? Explain the rise of Jim Crow legislation in the South, and discuss its impact on the status of African Americans.

6. Describe American foreign policy during the 1890s. Why did the United States intervene in Cuba and the Philippines? What were some of the leading arguments for and against overseas expansion?

RECOMMENDED READING

Ruth Bordin, *Woman and Temperance: The Quest for Power and Liberty, 1873–1900* (1981). Relates the history of the WCTU to other campaigns for women's emancipation in the late nineteenth century and highlights the leadership of Frances E. Willard.

John G. Cawelti, *Apostles of the Self-Made Man* (1965). Examines the popular cultural obsession with the idea of success: both the myths behind the notion of equal opportunity for all and the methods of popularizing success in the various media of the time.

Lawrence Goodwyn, *Democratic Promise: The Populist Movement in America* (1976). The most detailed study of populism, this book focuses on the economic cooperation and visionary schemes that preceded the populist electoral actions of the 1890s.

Lewis L. Gould, *The Presidency of William McKinley* (1980). A biography and political study of the president who represented a new kind of national leader in several key ways. Gould presents McKinley as a model Republican, product of machine politics.

Michael Kazin, *The Populist Persuasion: An American History* (1995). A fresh interpretation of populist-style movements through the nineteenth and twentieth century that suggests such movements can be either "right" or "left" depending on circumstances.

Walter LaFeber, *The New Empire: An Interpretation of American Expansion, 1860–1898* (1963). The best overview of U.S. imperial involvement in the late nineteenth century. LaFeber shows how overseas commitments grew out of the economic expansionist assumptions of American leaders.

Nell Irvin Painter, *Standing at Armageddon: The United States, 1877–1919* (1987). Presents a broad overview of racial and industrial conflicts and the political movements that formed in their wake.

Thomas C. Reeves, *Gentleman Boss: The Life of Chester Alan Arthur* (1975). A detailed treatment of President Arthur as a product of a particular stage in the American political system.

Emily S. Rosenberg, *Spreading the American Dream: American Economic and Cultural Expansion, 1890–1945* (1982). Insightfully examines the significance of expansionist ideology.

William Appleman Williams, *Empire as a Way of Life: An Essay on the Causes and Character of America's Present Predicament* (1982). A lucid general exploration of American views of empire. Williams shows that Americans allowed the idea of empire and, more generally, economic expansion, to dominate their concept of democracy.

C. Vann Woodward, *The Strange Career of Jim Crow*, 3d rev. ed. (1974). The classic study of southern segregation. Woodward shows how racist laws and customs tightened in the South and in many parts of the North in the last decades of the nineteenth century and how southern society encouraged the rise of Jim Crow legislation.

CHAPTER TWENTY-ONE

URBAN AMERICA AND THE PROGRESSIVE ERA

1900–1917

AMERICAN COMMUNITIES
The Henry Street Settlement House: Women Settlement House Workers Create a Community of Reform

A shy and frightened young girl appeared in the doorway of a weekly home nursing class for women on Manhattan's Lower East Side. The girl pleaded in broken English for the teacher to come home with her. "Mother," "baby," "blood," she kept repeating. The teacher gathered up the sheets that were part of the interrupted lesson in bedmaking. The two hurried through narrow, garbage-strewn, foul-smelling streets, then groped their way up a pitch-dark, rickety staircase. They reached a cramped, two-room apartment occupied by an immigrant family of seven and several boarders. There, in a vermin-infested bed, encrusted with dried blood, lay a mother and her newborn baby. The mother had been abandoned by a doctor because she could not afford his fee.

The teacher, Lillian Wald, was a twenty-five-year-old nurse at New York Hospital. Years later she recalled this scene as her baptism of fire and the turning point in her life. Born in 1867, Wald enjoyed a comfortable upbringing in a middle-class German Jewish family in Rochester. Against her parents' objections, she moved to New York City to become a professional nurse. Wald resented the disdainful treatment nurses received from doctors, and she was horrified by the inhumane conditions she witnessed in her job at a juvenile asylum. She was determined to find a way of caring for the sick more directly, in their neighborhoods and in their homes. Along with her nursing school classmate Mary Brewster, Wald rented a fifth-floor walk-up apartment on the Lower East Side and established a visiting nurse service. The two women offered professional care in the home to hundreds of families for a nominal fee of ten to twenty-five cents. They also offered each family they visited information on basic health care, sanitation, and disease prevention. In 1895 philanthropist Jacob Schiff donated a red brick Georgian house on Henry Street as a new base of operation.

The Henry Street settlement stood in the center of perhaps the most overcrowded neighborhood in the world, New York's Lower East Side. Roughly 500,000 people were packed into an area only as large as a midsized Kansas farm. Population density was about 500 per acre, roughly four times the figure for the rest of New York City and far more concentrated than even the worst slums of London or Calcutta. A single block might have as many as 3,000 residents. Home for most Lower East Siders was a small tenement apartment that might include paying boarders squeezed in alongside the immediate family. Residents were mostly immigrants from southern and eastern Europe: Jews, Italians, Germans, Greeks, Hungarians, Slavs. Men, women, and children toiled in the garment shops, small factories, retail stores, breweries, and warehouses to be found on nearly every street. An Irish-dominated machine controlled local political affairs.

The Henry Street Settlement became a model for a new kind of reform community. It was essentially a community of college-educated women who encouraged and supported one another in a wide variety of humanitarian, civic, political, and cultural activities. As a living arrangement, settlement houses closely resembled the dormitory atmosphere found at such new women's colleges as Smith, Wellesley, and Vassar. Like these colleges, the settlement house was an "experiment," but one designed, in Jane Addams's words, "to aid in the solution of the social and industrial problems which are engendered by the modern conditions of urban life." Settlement house residents were committed to living in the midst of poor neighborhoods and working for immediate improvements in the health and welfare of the community.

The college-educated women were beneficiaries as well. The settlement house allowed them to preserve a collegial spirit, satisfy the desire for service, and apply their academic training.

In 1891 there were 6 settlements in the United States, in 1897 there were 74, by 1900 over 200, and by 1910 over 400. Few made settlement work a career; the average stay was less than five years. Those who did make a career of this work typically chose not to marry, and most lived together with female companions. As the settlements flourished, the residents described the plight of their neighbors in countless articles and lectures, which helped build sympathy for the plight of the poor and fostered respect for different cultural heritages.

By 1909 Henry Street had over forty residents, supported by the donations of well-to-do New Yorkers. In addition to the nursing service, Wald and her allies convinced the New York Board of Health to assign a nurse to every public school in the city. They lobbied the Board of Education to create the first school lunch programs. They persuaded the city to set up municipal milk stations to ensure the purity of milk. Henry Street also pioneered tuberculosis treatment and prevention. Its leaders became powerful advocates for playground construction, improved street cleaning, and tougher housing inspection. The settlement's Neighborhood Playhouse became an internationally acclaimed center for innovative theater, music, and dance. Henry Street was a meeting place for the National Negro Conference in 1909, out of which emerged the National Association for the Advancement of Colored People. It was no cliché for Wald to say, as she did on many occasions, "The whole world is my neighborhood."

New York City

such as Timothy Sullivan, Robert Wagner, and Al Smith worked with middle-class progressive groups to pass child labor laws, factory safety regulations, worker compensation plans, and other efforts to make government more responsive to social needs. Urban machines also began to champion cultural pluralism, opposing prohibition and immigration restrictions and defending the contributions made by new ethnic groups in the cities.

Political Progressives and Urban Reform

Political progressivism originated in the cities. City governments, especially in the Northeast and industrial Midwest, hardly seemed capable of providing the basic services needed to sustain large populations. For example, an impure water supply left Pittsburgh with one of the world's highest rates of death from typhoid, dysentery, and cholera. Most New York City neighborhoods rarely enjoyed street cleaning, and playgrounds were nonexistent.

Reformers placed much of the blame for urban ills on the machines and looked for ways to restructure city government. Reformers revised city charters in favor of stronger mayoral power and expanded use of appointed administrators and career civil servants.

Business and professional elites became the biggest boosters of structural reforms in urban government. In the summer of 1900 a hurricane in the Gulf of Mexico unleashed a disastrous tidal wave on Galveston, Texas. Leading businessmen convinced the state legislature to replace the mayor–council government with a small board of commissioners. Each commissioner was elected at large and each was responsible for a different city department. Under this plan voters could more easily identify and hold accountable those responsible for city services. The city commission, enjoying both policy-making and administrative powers, proved very effective in rebuilding Galveston. By 1917 nearly 500 cities had adopted the commission form of government. Another approach, the city manager plan, gained popularity in small and midsized cities. In this system, a city council appointed a professional, nonpartisan city manager to handle the day-to-day operations of the community.

Progressive politicians who focused on the human problems of the industrial city championed a different kind of reform, one based on changing policies rather than the political structure. In Cleveland a wealthy businessman, Thomas L. Johnson, served as mayor from 1901 to 1909. He emphasized both efficiency and social welfare. His popular program included lower streetcar fares, public baths, milk and meat inspection, and an expanded park and playground system.

Progressivism in the Statehouse

Their motives and achievements were mixed, but progressive politicians became a powerful force in many state capitols. In Wisconsin Republican dissident Robert M. La Follette forged a coalition of angry farmers, ethnic minorities, and workers with his fiery attacks on railroads and other large corporations. As governor he pushed through tougher corporate tax rates, a direct primary, an improved civil service code, and a model railroad commission. La Follette used faculty experts at the University of Wisconsin to help research and write his bills. Other states began copying the "Wisconsin Idea"—the application of academic scholarship and theory to the needs of the people.

In practice, La Follette's railroad commission accomplished far less than progressive rhetoric claimed. Ordinary consumers did not see lower passenger fares or reduced food prices. Commissioners also began to see that state regulation was often ineffective as long as the larger railroads had a national reach. Although La Follette championed a more open political system, he also enrolled state employees in a tight political machine of his own. The La Follette family would dominate Wisconsin politics for forty years.

Western progressives displayed the greatest enthusiasm for institutional political reform. The Oregon System was in many ways the essence of western progressivism. In the early 1900s Oregon voters approved a series of constitutional amendments designed to strengthen direct democracy. The two most important were the initiative, which gave the people a direct vote on specific measures put on the state ballot by petition, and the referendum, which allowed voters to decide upon bills referred to them by the legislature. Other reforms included the direct primary, which allowed voters to cross party lines, and the recall, which gave voters the right to remove elected officials by popular vote. Widely copied throughout the West, all these measures intentionally weakened political parties.

In the South, progressivism drew upon the agrarian program and flamboyant oratory of populism. Southern progressives made genuine improvements in educational facilities, regulation of corporations, and reform of city governments. But southern progressivism was for whites only. A strident racism accompanied reform campaigns against entrenched conservative Democratic machines, reinforcing racial discrimination and segregation.

New Journalism: Muckraking

The mass media drew the attention of millions to urban poverty, political corruption, the plight of industrial workers, and immoral business practices. As early as

1890, journalist Jacob Riis had shocked the nation with his landmark book *How the Other Half Lives*, a portrait of New York City's poor. A Danish immigrant who arrived in New York City in 1871, Riis became a newspaper reporter, covering the police beat and learning about the city's desperate underside. For his book, Riis made a remarkable series of photographs in tenements, lodging houses, sweatshops, and saloons, which made a powerful impact on a whole generation of urban reformers.

Within a few years, magazine journalists had turned to uncovering the seamier side of American life. The key innovator was S. S. McClure, a young midwestern editor who in 1893 started America's first large-circulation magazine, *McClure's*. Charging only a dime for his monthly, McClure effectively combined popular fiction with articles on science, technology, travel, and recent history. He attracted a new readership among the urban middle class.

In 1902 McClure began hiring talented reporters to write detailed accounts of the nation's social problems. Lincoln Steffens's series *The Shame of the Cities* revealed the widespread graft at the center of American urban politics. He showed how big-city bosses routinely worked hand in glove with businessmen seeking lucrative municipal contracts for gas, water, electricity, and mass transit. Ida Tarbell, in her *History of the Standard Oil Company*, thoroughly documented how John D. Rockefeller ruthlessly squeezed out competitors with unfair business practices.

McClure's and other magazines discovered that "exposure journalism" paid off handsomely in terms of increased circulation. Series such as Steffens's fueled reform campaigns that swept individual communities. Between 1902 and 1908, magazines were full of articles exposing insurance scandals, patent medicine frauds, and stock market swindles. Upton Sinclair's 1906 novel *The Jungle*, a socialist tract set among Chicago packinghouse workers, exposed the filthy sanitation and abysmal working conditions in the meat-packing industry. In an effort to boost sales, Sinclair's publisher devoted an entire issue of a monthly magazine it owned, *The World's Work*, to articles and photographs that substantiated Sinclair's devastating portrait.

SOCIAL CONTROL AND ITS LIMITS

Many middle- and upper-class Protestant progressives feared that immigrants threatened the stability of American democracy, and they worried that alien cultural practices were disrupting what they viewed as traditional American morality. Many progressives saw themselves as part of what sociologist Edward A. Ross called the "ethical elite." They believed they had a mission to frame laws and regulations for the social control of immigrants, industrial workers, and African Americans. This moralistic and often xenophobic side of progressivism provided a powerful source of support for the regulation of drinking, prostitution, leisure activities, and schooling. Organizations devoted to social control constituted other versions of reform communities. These attempts at moral reform met with mixed success.

The Prohibition Movement

During the last two decades of the nineteenth century, the Women's Christian Temperance Union had grown into a powerful mass organization. The WCTU appealed especially to women angered by men who used alcohol and then abused their wives and children. But local WCTU chapters put their energy into nontemperance activities as well, including homeless shelters, Sunday schools, prison reform, child nurseries, and woman suffrage. By 1911 the WCTU, with a quarter-million members, was the largest women's organization in American history.

Other temperance groups had a narrower focus. The Anti-Saloon League, founded in 1893, began by organizing local-option campaigns in which rural counties and small towns could ban liquor within their geographic limits. It drew much of its financial support from local businessmen who saw a link between closing a community's saloons and increasing the productivity of workers. The league was a one-issue pressure group that played effectively on anti-urban and anti-immigrant prejudice.

The battle to ban alcohol revealed the deep ethnic and cultural divides within America's urban communities. Opponents of alcohol generally viewed the world from a position of moral absolutism. These included native-born, middle-class Protestants associated with evangelical churches, along with some old-stock Protestant immigrant denominations. Opponents of prohibition had less arbitrary notions of personal morality. These were largely new-stock, working-class Catholic and Jewish immigrants, along with some Protestants, such as German Lutherans.

The Social Evil

Many of the same reformers who battled saloons and drinking also engaged in efforts to eradicate prostitution. Crusades against "the social evil" reached a new level of intensity between 1895 and 1920.

Between 1908 and 1914 exposés of the "white slave" traffic became a national sensation. Dozens of books, articles, and motion pictures alleged an international conspiracy to seduce and sell girls into prostitution. Most of these materials exaggerated the practices they attacked. They also made foreigners, especially Jews and southern Europeans, scapegoats for the sexual anxieties of native-born whites. In 1910 Congress passed legislation that permitted the deportation of foreign-born prostitutes or any foreigner convicted of procuring or employing them. That same year, the Mann Act made it a federal offense to transport women across state lines for "immoral purposes."

The progressive bent for defining social problems through statistics was nowhere more evident than in reports on prostitution. Vice commission investigators combed red-light districts, tenement houses, hotels, and dancehalls, drawing up detailed lists of places where prostitution took place. They interviewed prostitutes, pimps, and customers. These reports agreed that commercialized sex was a business run by and for the profit and pleasure of men. They also documented the dangers of sexually transmitted disease to the larger community. The highly publicized vice reports were effective in forcing police crackdowns in urban red-light districts.

For wage-earning women, however, prostitution was a rational choice in a world of limited opportunities. Maimie Pinzer, a prostitute, summed up her feelings in a letter to a wealthy female reformer: "I don't propose to get up at 6:30 to be at work at 8 and work in a close, stuffy room with people I despise, until dark, for $6 or $7 a week! When I could, just by phoning, spend an afternoon with some congenial person and in the end have more than a week's work could pay me." Ultimately, the antivice crusades succeeded in closing down many urban red-light districts and larger brothels, but these were replaced by the streetwalker and call girl, who were more vulnerable to harassment and control by policemen and pimps.

The Redemption of Leisure

For large numbers of working-class adults and children, leisure meant time and money spent at vaudeville and burlesque theaters, amusement parks, dancehalls, and motion picture houses. For many cultural traditionalists, the flood of new urban commercial amusements posed a grave threat: "Commercialized leisure must be controlled by the community, if it is to become an agency of civilization rather than the reverse," warned Cleveland progressive Frederick C. Howe in 1914.

Movies became the most popular form of cheap entertainment. By 1911 an estimated 11,500 movie theaters attracted 5 million patrons each day. For five or ten cents one could see a program that might include a slapstick comedy, a Western, a travelogue, and a melodrama. Early movies were most popular in the tenement and immigrant districts of big cities, and with children. As the films themselves became more sophisticated and as "movie palaces" began to replace cheap storefront theaters, the new medium attracted a large middle-class clientele as well.

Progressive reformers seized on the new medium as an alternative to the older entertainment traditions, such as concert saloons and burlesque theater, that had been closely allied with machine politics and the vice economy. In 1909 New York City movie producers and exhibitors joined with the reform-minded People's Institute to establish the voluntary National Board of Censorship (NBC). Movie entrepreneurs, most of whom were themselves immigrants, sought to shed the stigma of the slums, attract more middle-class patronage, and increase profits. A revolving group of civic activists reviewed new movies, passing them, suggesting changes, or condemning them. Local censoring committees all over the nation subscribed to the board's weekly bulletin. By 1914 the NBC was reviewing 95 percent of the nation's film output.

WORKING-CLASS COMMUNITIES AND PROTEST

The industrial revolution, which had begun transforming American life and labor in the nineteenth century, reached maturity in the early twentieth. In 1900, out of a total labor force of 28.5 million, 16 million people worked at industrial occupations and 11 million on farms. By 1920, in a labor force of nearly 42 million, almost 29 million were in industry, but farm labor had declined to 10.4 million. The world of the industrial worker included large manufacturing towns in New England, barren mining settlements in the Far West, primitive lumber and turpentine camps in the Deep South, steel and coal-mining cities in Pennsylvania and Ohio, and densely packed immigrant ghettos from New York to San Francisco, where workers toiled in garment trade sweatshops.

All of these industrial workers shared the need to sell their labor for wages in order to survive. At the same time, differences in skill, ethnicity, and race proved powerful barriers to efforts at organizing trade unions that could bargain for improved wages and working conditions. So too did the economic and political power of the large corporations that dominated much of American industry. These years saw many labor struggles that created effective trade unions or laid the groundwork for others. Industrial workers also became a force in local and national politics, adding a chorus of insistent voices to the calls for social justice.

The New Immigrants

On the eve of World War I, close to 60 percent of the industrial labor force was foreign-born. In the nineteenth century much of the overseas migration had come from the industrial districts of northern and western Europe. English, Welsh, and German artisans had brought with them skills critical for emerging industries such as steelmaking and coal mining. Unlike their predecessors, the new Italian, Polish, Hungarian, Jewish, and Greek immigrants nearly all lacked industrial skills. They thus entered the bottom ranks of factories, mines, mills, and sweatshops.

These new immigrants had been driven from their European farms and towns by several forces. These included the undermining of subsistence farming by commercial agriculture, a falling death rate that brought a shortage of land, and religious and political persecution. American corporations also sent agents to recruit cheap labor. Except for Jewish immigrants, a majority of whom fled virulent anti-Semitism in Russia and Poland, most newcomers planned on earning a stake and then returning home.

The low-paid, backbreaking work in basic industry became nearly the exclusive preserve of the new immigrants. In 1907, of the 14,359 common laborers employed at the Carnegie steel mills, 11,694 were eastern Europeans. For twelve-hour days and seven-day weeks, two-thirds of these workers made less than $12.50 a week, far less than the $15.00 that the Pittsburgh Associated Charities had set as the minimum for providing necessities for a family of five. Small wonder that the new immigration was disproportionately male: one-third of the immigrant steelworkers were single. Workers with families generally supplemented their incomes by taking in single men as boarders.

Between 1898 and 1907 more than 80,000 Japanese entered the United States. The vast majority were young men working as contract laborers in the West. American law prevented Japanese immigrants (the Issei) from obtaining American citizenship because they were not white. Most Japanese settled near Los Angeles, where they established small communities centered around fishing, truck farming, and the flower and nursery business. In 1920 Japanese farmers produced 10 percent of the dollar volume of California agriculture on 1 percent of the farm acreage.

Mexican immigration also grew in these years, providing a critical source of labor for the West's farms, railroads, and mines. Economic and political crises spurred tens of thousands of Mexico's rural and urban poor to emigrate to the north. Large numbers of seasonal agricultural workers regularly came up from Mexico to work in the expanding sugar beet industry and then returned. But between 1900 and 1914, the number of people of Mexican descent living and working in the United States tripled, from roughly 100,000 to 300,000.

Company Towns

Cities such as Lawrence, Massachusetts; Gary, Indiana; and Butte, Montana, revolved around the industrial enterprises of Pacific Woolen, U.S. Steel, and

IMMIGRATION TO THE UNITED STATES, 1901–1920

Total: 14,532,000		% of Total
Italy	3,157,000	22%
Austria–Hungary	3,047,000	21
Russia and Poland	2,524,000	17
Canada	922,000	6
Great Britain	867,000	6
Scandinavia	709,000	5
Ireland	487,000	3
Germany	486,000	3
France and Low Countries (Belgium, Netherlands, Switz.)	361,000	2
Mexico	268,000	2
West Indies	231,000	2
Japan	213,000	2
China	41,000	*
Australia and New Zealand	23,000	*

*Less than 1% of total

Source: U.S. Bureau of the Census, *Historical Statistics of the United States from Colonial Times to* 1970, Washington, D.C., 1975.

Anaconda Copper. Workers had little or no influence over the economic and political institutions of these cities. But they did maintain some community control in other ways. Family and kin networks, ethnic lodges, saloons, benefit societies, churches and synagogues, and musical groups affirmed traditional forms of community in a setting governed by individualism and private capital.

In Gary, immigrant steelworkers suffered twice the accident rate of English-speaking employees, who could better understand safety instructions and warnings. A 1910 study of work accidents revealed that nearly a fourth of all new steelworkers were killed or injured each year.

In steel and coal towns, women not only maintained the household and raised the children, but also boosted the family income by taking in boarders, sewing, and laundry. Many women also tended gardens and raised chickens, rabbits, and goats. This helped reduce dependence on the company store. Working-class women felt the burdens of housework more heavily than their middle-class sisters. Running water, indoor plumbing, and sewage disposal were often available only on a pay-as-you-go basis. The daily drudgery endured by working-class women far outlasted the "man-killing" shift worked by the husband.

The adjustment for immigrant workers was not so much a process of assimilation as one of adaptation and resistance. Efficiency experts such as Frederick Taylor carefully observed and analyzed the time and energy needed for each job, then set standard methods for each worker. But the newcomers learned from more skilled and experienced British and American workers that "slowing down" or "soldiering" spread out the work. As new immigrants became less transient and more permanently settled in company towns, they increased their involvement in local politics and union activity.

The Colorado Fuel and Iron Company (CFI) employed roughly half of the 8,000 coal miners who labored in that state's mines. In mining towns such as Ludlow and Trinidad, the CFI thoroughly dominated the lives of miners and their families. About one-fifth of CFI miners spoke no English. Frequent mine explosions and poor housing made for extremely harsh living conditions.

In September 1913 the United Mine Workers led a strike in the Colorado coal fields, calling for improved safety, higher wages, and recognition of the union. In October the governor ordered the Colorado National Guard into the tense strike region to keep order. The troops proceeded to ally themselves with the mine operators. By spring the strike had bankrupted the state, forcing the governor to remove most of the troops. The coal companies then brought in large numbers of private mine guards, who were extremely hostile toward the strikers. On April 20, 1914, a combination of guardsmen and private guards surrounded the largest of the tent colonies at Ludlow, where over a thousand mine families lived. After a pitched battle that lasted until the poorly armed miners ran out of ammunition, the troops burned the tent village to the ground, routing the families and killing fourteen, including eleven children. Enraged strikers attacked mines throughout southern Colorado in an armed rebellion that lasted ten days, until President Wilson ordered the U.S. Army into the region. News of the Ludlow Massacre aroused widespread protests against the policies of CFI and its owner, John D. Rockefeller, Jr.

Urban Ghettos

By 1920 immigrants and their children constituted almost 60 percent of the population of cities over 100,000. The sheer size and dynamism of these cities made the immigrant experience more complex there than in the company town. Immigrant workers in the urban garment trades toiled for low wages and suffered layoffs, unemployment, and poor health. But conditions in the small, labor-intensive shops of the clothing industry differed significantly from those in the large-scale capital-intensive industries such as steel.

New York City had become the center of both Jewish immigration and America's huge ready-to-wear clothing industry. The city's Jewish population was 1.4 million in 1915, almost 30 percent of its inhabitants. In small factories, lofts, and tenement apartments, some 200,000 people, most of them Jews, some of them Italians, worked in the clothing trades. Most of the industry operated on the grueling piece-rate, or task, system, in which manufacturers and subcontractors paid individuals or teams of workers to complete a certain quota of labor within a specific time.

The garment industry was highly seasonal. A typical work week was sixty hours, with seventy common during the busy season. But there were long stretches of unemployment in slack times. Even skilled cutters—all men—earned an average of only $16 per week. Unskilled workers—nearly all of them young single women—made only $6 or $7 a week.

In November 1909 two New York garment manufacturers responded to strikes by unskilled women workers by hiring thugs and prostitutes to beat up picketers. The strikers won the support of the Women's Trade Union League, a group of female reformers that included Lillian Wald, Mary Drier, and prominent society figures. At a dramatic mass meeting in Cooper Union Hall, Clara Lemlich, a teenage working girl speaking in Yiddish, made an emotional plea for a general strike. She called for everyone in the crowd to take an old Jewish oath: "If I turn traitor to the cause I now pledge, may this hand wither from the arm I now raise." The "uprising of the 20,000" swept through the city's garment district.

The strikers demanded union recognition, better wages, and safer and more sanitary conditions. Hundreds of them were arrested, and many were beaten by police. After three cold months on the picket line the strikers returned to work without union recognition. But the International Ladies Garment Workers Union (ILGWU), founded in 1900, did gain strength and negotiated contracts with some of the city's shirtwaist makers. The strike was an important breakthrough in the drive to organize unskilled workers into industrial unions.

On March 25, 1911, the issues raised by the strike took on new urgency when a fire raced through three floors of the Triangle Shirtwaist Company. Workers found themselves trapped by exit doors locked from the outside. Within half an hour, 146 people, mostly young Jewish women, had been killed by smoke or had leaped to their death. In the bitter aftermath, women progressives led by Florence Kelley and Frances Perkins of the National Consumers League joined with Tammany Hall leaders Al Smith, Robert Wagner, and Timothy Sullivan to create a New York State Factory Investigation Commission (FIC). Under Perkins's vigorous leadership, the FIC conducted an unprecedented round of public hearings and on-site inspections, leading to a series of state laws that dramatically improved safety conditions and limited the hours for working women and children.

The AFL: "Unions, Pure and Simple"

Following the depression of the 1890s, the American Federation of Labor emerged as the strongest and most stable organization of workers. Samuel Gompers's strategy of recruiting skilled labor into unions organized by craft had paid off. Union membership climbed from under 500,000 in 1897 to 1.7 million by 1904. The national unions—the United Mine Workers of America, the Brotherhood of Carpenters and Joiners, the International Association of Machinists—represented workers of specific occupations in collective bargaining. Trade autonomy and exclusive jurisdiction were the ruling principles within the AFL.

But the strength of craft organization also gave rise to weakness. In 1905 Gompers told a union gathering in Minneapolis that "Caucasians" would not "let their standard of living be destroyed by negroes, Chinamen, Japs, or any others." Each trade looked mainly to the welfare of its own. Many explicitly barred women and African Americans from membership. There were some important exceptions. The United Mine Workers of America followed a more inclusive policy, recruiting both skilled underground pitmen and the unskilled above-ground workers. The UMWA even tried to recruit strikebreakers brought in by coal operators. With 260,000 members in 1904, the UMWA became the largest AFL affiliate.

AFL unions had a difficult time holding on to their gains. Economic slumps, technological changes, and aggressive counterattacks by employer organizations could be devastating. Trade associations using management-controlled efficiency drives fought union efforts to regulate output and shop practices. The National Association of Manufacturers, a group of smaller industrialists founded in 1903, launched an open shop campaign to eradicate unions altogether. "Open shop" was simply a new name for a workplace where unions were not allowed.

Unfriendly judicial decisions also hurt organizing efforts. In 1906 a federal judge issued a permanent injunction against an iron molders strike at the Allis Chalmers Company of Milwaukee. In the so-called Danbury Hatters' Case (*Loewe v. Lawlor*, 1908), a federal court ruled that secondary boycotts, aimed by strikers at other companies doing business with their employer, were illegal. Not until the 1930s would unions be able to count on legal support for collective bargaining and the right to strike.

The IWW: "One Big Union"

Some workers developed more radical visions of labor organizing. In company towns miners suffered from low wages, poor food, and primitive sanitation, as well as injuries and death from frequent cave-ins and explosions.

In response to the brutal realities of labor organizing in the West, the Western Federation of Miners embraced socialism and industrial unionism. In 1905 leaders of the WFM, the Socialist party, and various radical groups gathered in Chicago to found the Industrial Workers of the World (IWW). The IWW charter proclaimed bluntly, "The working class and the employing class have nothing in common. . . . Between these two classes a struggle must go on until the workers of the world unite as a class, take possession of the earth and the machinery of production, and abolish the wage system."

William D. "Big Bill" Haywood, an imposing, one-eyed hard-rock miner, emerged as the most influential and flamboyant spokesman for the IWW, or Wobblies, as they were called. Haywood, a charismatic speaker and effective organizer, regularly denounced the conservative craft consciousness of the AFL. The Wobblies concentrated their efforts on miners, lumberjacks, sailors, "harvest stiffs," and other casual laborers. Openly contemptuous of bourgeois respectability, the IWW stressed the power of collective direct action on the job: strikes and, occasionally, sabotage.

The IWW briefly became a force among eastern industrial workers, tapping the rage and growing militance of the immigrants and unskilled. In 1909 an IWW-led steel strike at McKees Rocks, Pennsylvania, challenged the power of U.S. Steel. In the 1912 "Bread and Roses" strike in Lawrence, Massachusetts, IWW organizers turned a spontaneous walkout of textile workers into a successful struggle for union recognition.

These battles gained the IWW a great deal of sympathy from radical intellectuals, along with public scorn from the AFL and employers' groups. The IWW failed to establish permanent organizations in the eastern cities, but it remained a force in the lumber camps, mines, and wheat fields of the West. Despite its militant rhetoric, the IWW concerned itself with practical gains. But when the United States entered World War I, the Justice Department used the IWW's anticapitalist rhetoric and antiwar stance to crush it.

WOMEN'S MOVEMENTS AND BLACK AWAKENING

The New Woman

The settlement house movement was just one of the new avenues of opportunity for Progressive-era women. Single-sex associations had existed throughout the nineteenth century, but their rapid expansion by the 1890s reflected the changing conditions of middle-class women. With more men working in offices, with more children attending school, and with family size declining, the middle-class home was emptier. At the same time, more middle-class women were graduating from high school and college.

The new women's club movement combined an earlier focus on self-improvement and intellectual pursuits with newer benevolent efforts on behalf of working women and children. The Chicago Women's Club helped settlement workers found the Legal Aid Society, the Public Art Association, and the Protective Agency for Women and Children. For many middle-class women the club movement provided a new kind of female-centered community.

Other women's associations made even more explicit efforts to bridge class lines between middle-class homemakers and working-class women. The National Consumers League (NCL), started in 1898 by Maud Nathan and Josephine Lowell, sponsored a "white label" campaign in which manufacturers who met safety and sanitary standards could put NCL labels on their food and clothing. Under the dynamic leadership of Florence Kelley, the NCL took an even more aggressive stance by publicizing labor abuses in department stores and lobbying for maximum hour and minimum wage laws in state legislatures. In its efforts to protect home and housewife, worker and consumer, the NCL embodied the ideal of "social housekeeping."

Birth Control

The phrase "birth control," coined by Margaret Sanger around 1913, described her campaign to provide contraceptive information and devices for women. In 1910 Sanger was a thirty-year-old nurse and housewife living with her husband and three children in a New York City suburb. Excited by a socialist lecture she had attended, Sanger convinced her husband to move to the city, where she threw herself into the bohemian milieu. She became an organizer for the IWW, and in 1912 she wrote a series of articles on female sexuality for a socialist newspaper.

When postal officials confiscated the paper for violating obscenity laws, Sanger left for Europe to learn more about contraception. She returned to New York determined to challenge the obscenity statutes with her own magazine, *The Woman Rebel*. Sanger's journal celebrated female autonomy, including the right to sexual expression and control over one's body. When she distributed her pamphlet *Family Limitation*, postal inspectors confiscated copies and she found herself facing forty-five years in prison. In October 1914 she fled to Europe again.

An older generation of feminists had advocated the right to say no to a husband's sexual demands. The new birth control advocates embraced contraception as a way of advancing sexual freedom for middle-class women as well as responding to the misery of working-class women who bore numerous children while living in poverty. Sanger returned to the United States in October 1915. After the government dropped the obscenity charges she embarked on a national speaking tour. In 1916 she again defied the law by opening a birth control clinic in a working-class neighborhood in Brooklyn and offering birth control information without a physician present. Arrested and jailed, she gained more publicity for her crusade. Within a few years, birth control leagues and clinics could be found in every major city and most large towns in the country.

Racism and Accommodation

African Americans endured a deeply racist popular culture that made hateful stereotypes of black people a normal feature of political debate and everyday life. White southern politicians and writers claimed that African Americans had undergone a natural "reversion to savagery" upon the end of slavery. In northern cities "coon songs," based on gross caricatures of black life, were extremely popular in theaters and as sheet music. Like the antebellum minstrel shows, these songs reduced African Americans to creatures of pure appetite for food, sex, alcohol, and violence.

In this political and cultural climate, Booker T. Washington won recognition as the most influential black leader of the day. Born a slave in 1856, Washington was educated at Hampton Institute in Virginia, one of the first freedmen's schools devoted to industrial education. In 1881 he founded Tuskegee Institute, a black school in Alabama devoted to industrial and moral education. He became the leading spokesman for racial accommodation, urging blacks to focus on economic improvement and self-reliance, as opposed to political and civil rights. His widely read autobiography, *Up from Slavery* (1901), stands as a classic narrative of an American self-made man. Written with a shrewd eye toward cementing his support among white Americans, it stressed the importance of learning values such as frugality, cleanliness, and personal morality. But Washington also gained a large following among African Americans, especially those who aspired to business success. Publicly he insisted that "agitation of questions of social equality is the extremest folly." But privately Washington also spent money and worked behind the scenes trying to halt disfranchisement and segregation.

Racial Justice and the NAACP

Washington's focus on economic self-help remained deeply influential in African American communities long after his death in 1915. But alternative black voices challenged his racial philosophy while he lived. In the early 1900s scholar and activist W. E. B. Du Bois created a significant alternative to Washington's leadership. A product of the black middle class, Du Bois had been educated at Fisk University and Harvard, where in 1895 he became the first African American to receive a Ph.D. Through essays on black history, culture, education, and politics, Du Bois explored the concept of "double consciousness." Black people, he argued, would always feel the tension between an African heritage and their desire to assimilate as Americans.

Du Bois criticized Booker T. Washington's philosophy for its acceptance of "the alleged inferiority of the Negro." The black community, he argued, must fight for the right to vote, civic equality, and higher education for the "talented tenth" of their youth. In 1905 Du Bois and editor William Monroe Trotter brought together a group of educated black men to oppose Washington's conciliatory views. Discrimination they encountered in Buffalo, New York, prompted the men to move their meeting to Niagara Falls, Ontario. The Niagara movement protested legal segregation, the exclusion of blacks from labor unions, and the curtailment of voting and other civil rights.

The Niagara movement failed to generate much change. But in 1909 many of its members, led by Du Bois, attended a National Negro Conference held at the Henry Street Settlement in New York. A new, interracial organization emerged from this conference: the National Association for the Advancement of Colored People. Du Bois was the only black officer of the original NAACP.

NATIONAL PROGRESSIVISM
Theodore Roosevelt and Presidential Activism

The assassination of William McKinley in 1901 made forty-two-year-old Theodore Roosevelt the youngest man ever to hold the office of president. Born to a moderately wealthy New York family in 1858, Roosevelt overcame a sickly childhood through strenuous physical exercise and rugged outdoor living. After graduating from Harvard he immediately threw himself into a career in the rough and tumble of New York politics. He won election to the state assembly, ran an unsuccessful campaign for mayor of New York, served as president of the New York City Board of Police Commissioners, and went to Washington as assistant secretary of the navy. During the Spanish–American War, he won national fame as leader of the Rough Rider regiment in Cuba. Upon his return, he was elected governor of New York and then in 1900 vice president. Roosevelt viewed the presidency as a "bully pulpit" and aimed to make the most of it.

Roosevelt was a uniquely colorful figure, a shrewd publicist, and a creative politician. He preached the virtues of "the strenuous life" and believed that educated and wealthy Americans had a special responsibility to serve, guide, and inspire those less fortunate. In style, Roosevelt made key contributions to national progressivism. He knew how to inspire and guide public opinion. He stimulated discussion and aroused curiosity like no president before him. In 1902 Roosevelt demonstrated his unique style of activism when he personally intervened in a bitter strike by anthracite coal miners. Using public calls for conciliation, a series of White House bargaining sessions, and private pressure on the mine owners, Roosevelt secured a settlement that won better pay and working conditions for the miners, but without recognition of their union. Roosevelt also pushed for efficient government as the solution to social problems. Unlike most nineteenth-century Republicans, who had largely denied economic and social differences, Roosevelt frankly acknowledged them. Administrative agencies run by experts, he believed, could find rational solutions that could satisfy everyone.

Photographs and Print Division, Schomburg Center for Research in Black Culture, The New York Public Library, Astor, Lenox, and Tilden Foundations.

In July 1905 a group of African American leaders met in Niagara Falls, Ontario, to protest legal segregation and the denial of civil rights to the nation's black population. This portrait was taken against a studio backdrop of the Falls.

Trustbusting and Regulation

One of the first issues Roosevelt faced was growing public concern with the rapid business consolidations taking place in the American economy. In 1902 he directed the Justice Department to begin a series of prosecutions under the Sherman Anti-Trust Act. The first target was the Northern Securities Company, a huge merger of transcontinental railroads brought about by financier J. P. Morgan. The deal would have created a giant holding company controlling nearly all the long-distance rail lines from Chicago to California. The Justice Department fought the case all the way through a hearing before the Supreme Court. In *Northern Securities v. U.S.* (1904) the Court held that the stock transactions constituted an illegal combination in restraint of interstate commerce.

This case established Roosevelt's reputation as a trustbuster. During his two terms, the Justice Department filed forty-three cases under the Sherman Anti-Trust Act to restrain or dissolve business monopolies. Roosevelt viewed these suits as necessary to publicize the issue and assert the federal government's ultimate authority over big business. But he did not really believe in the need to break up large corporations. Unlike many progressives, who were nostalgic for smaller companies and freer competition, Roosevelt accepted centralization as a fact of modern economic life and considered government regulation the best way to deal with big business.

After easily defeating Democrat Alton B. Parker in the 1904 election, Roosevelt felt more secure in pushing for regulatory legislation. In 1906 he responded to public pressure for greater government intervention and, overcoming objections from a conservative Congress, signed three important measures into law. The Hepburn Act strengthened the Interstate Commerce Commission (ICC), established in 1887 as the first independent regulatory agency, by authorizing it to set maximum railroad rates and inspect financial records. The Pure Food and Drug Act established the Food and Drug Administration (FDA), which tested and approved drugs before they went on the market. The Meat Inspection Act (passed with help from the shocking publicity surrounding Upton Sinclair's muckraking novel *The Jungle*) empowered the Department of Agriculture to inspect and label meat products.

As a naturalist and outdoorsman, Roosevelt also believed in the need for government regulation of the natural environment. He worried about the destruction of forests, prairies, streams, and the wilderness. In 1905 he created the U.S. Forest Service and named conservationist Gifford Pinchot to head it. Pinchot recruited a force of forest rangers to manage the reserves. By 1909 total timber and forest reserves had increased from 45 to 195 million acres, and more than 80 million acres of mineral lands had been withdrawn from public sale.

Republican Split

By the end of his second term, Roosevelt had moved beyond the idea of regulation to push for the most far-reaching federal economic and social programs ever proposed. He saw the central problem as "how to exercise . . . responsible control over the business use of vast wealth."

In 1908 Roosevelt kept his promise to retire after a second term. He chose Secretary of War William Howard Taft as his successor. Taft easily defeated Democrat William Jennings Bryan in the 1908 election. During Taft's presidency, the gulf between "insurgent" progressives and the "stand pat" wing split the Republican party wide open. To some degree, the battles were as much over style as substance. Compared with Roosevelt, the reflective and judicious Taft brought a much more restrained concept of the presidency to the White House. He supported some progressive measures, including the Sixteenth Amendment legalizing a graduated income tax (ratified in 1913), safety codes for mines and railroads, and the creation of a federal Children's Bureau. But in a series of bitter political fights involving tariff, antitrust, and conservation policies, Taft alienated Roosevelt and many other progressives.

After returning from an African safari and a triumphant European tour in 1910, Roosevelt threw himself back into national politics. He directly challenged Taft for the Republican party leadership. In a dozen bitter state presidential primaries (the first ever held), Taft and Roosevelt fought for the nomination. Although Roosevelt won most of these contests, the old guard still controlled the national convention and narrowly renominated Taft in June 1912. Roosevelt's supporters stormed out, and in August the new Progressive party nominated Roosevelt and Hiram Johnson of California as its presidential ticket. The platform called for woman suffrage, the eight-hour day, prohibition of child labor, minimum wage standards for working women, and stricter regulation of large corporations.

The Election of 1912: A Four-Way Race

With the Republicans so badly divided, the Democrats sensed a chance for their first presidential victory in twenty years. They chose Governor Woodrow Wilson of New Jersey as their candidate. Although not nearly as well known nationally as Taft and Roosevelt, Wilson had built a strong reputation as a reformer. The son of a Virginia Presbyterian minister, Wilson spent most of his early career in academia. He studied law at the University of Virginia and then earned a Ph.D. in political science from Johns Hopkins. After teaching history and political science at several schools, he became president of Princeton University in 1902. In 1910 he won election as New Jersey's governor. He won the Democratic nomination for president with the support of many of the party's progressives, including William Jennings Bryan.

Wilson declared himself and the Democratic Party to be the true progressives. Crafted largely by progressive lawyer Louis Brandeis, Wilson's New Freedom platform was far more ambiguous than Roosevelt's. It emphasized restoring conditions of free competition and equality of economic opportunity. Wilson did favor a variety of progressive reforms for workers, farmers, and consumers. But in sounding older, nineteenth-century Democratic themes of states' rights and small government, Wilson argued against allowing the federal government to become as large and paternalistic as Roosevelt advocated.

Socialist party nominee Eugene Debs offered the fourth and most radical choice to voters. The Socialists had more than doubled their membership since 1908, to over 100,000. On election days Socialist

strength was far greater than that, as the party's candidates attracted increasing numbers of voters. By 1912 more than a thousand Socialists held elective office in thirty-three states and 160 cities. Geographically, Socialist strength had shifted to the trans-Mississippi South and West. Debs and the Socialists could also take credit for pushing both Roosevelt and Wilson further toward the Left. Both the Democratic and Progressive party platforms contained proposals considered extremely radical only ten years earlier.

In the end, the divisions in the Republican party gave the election to Wilson. He won easily, polling 6.3 million votes to Roosevelt's 4.1 million. Taft came in third with 3.5 million. Eugene Debs won 900,000 votes, 6 percent of the total, for the strongest Socialist showing in American history. Even though he won with only 42 percent of the popular vote, Wilson swept the electoral college with 435 votes to Roosevelt's 88 and Taft's 8, giving him the largest electoral majority ever to that time. In several respects, the election of 1912 was the first modern presidential race. It featured the first direct primaries, challenges to traditional party loyalties, an issue-oriented campaign, and a high degree of interest group activity.

Woodrow Wilson's First Term

As president, Wilson followed Roosevelt's lead in expanding the activist dimensions of the office. He became more responsive to pressure for a greater federal role in regulating business and the economy. This pressure came from hundreds of local and national reform groups, Washington-based lobbies, and the new Progressive party. With the help of a Democratic-controlled Congress, Wilson pushed through a significant battery of reform proposals.

The Underwood–Simmons Act of 1913 substantially reduced tariff duties on a variety of raw materials and manufactured goods, including wool, sugar, agricultural machinery, shoes, iron, and steel. Taking advantage of the newly ratified Sixteenth Amendment, it also imposed the first graduated tax (up to 6 percent) on personal incomes. The Federal Reserve Act that same year restructured the nation's banking and currency system. It created twelve Federal Reserve Banks regulated by a central board in Washington. By giving central direction to banking and monetary policy, the Federal Reserve Board diminished the power of large private banks.

Wilson also supported the Clayton Antitrust Act of 1914, which replaced the old Sherman Act of 1890 as the nation's basic antitrust law. Clayton reflected the growing political clout of the American Federation of Labor. It exempted unions from being construed as illegal combinations in restraint of trade, and it forbade federal courts to issue injunctions against

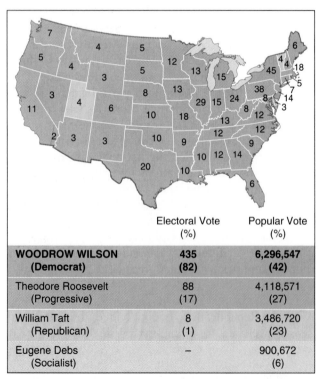

	Electoral Vote (%)	Popular Vote (%)
WOODROW WILSON (Democrat)	**435** **(82)**	**6,296,547** **(42)**
Theodore Roosevelt (Progressive)	88 (17)	4,118,571 (27)
William Taft (Republican)	8 (1)	3,486,720 (23)
Eugene Debs (Socialist)	–	900,672 (6)

The Election of 1912   *The split within the Republican Party allowed Woodrow Wilson to become only the second Democrat since the Civil War to be elected president. Eugene Debs's vote was the highest ever polled by a Socialist candidate.*

CURRENTS OF PROGRESSIVISM

	Key Figures	Issues	Institutions/Achievements
Local Communities	Jane Adams, Florence Kelley, Lillian Wald, Frederic C. Howe, Samuel Jones	Improving health, education, welfare in urban immigrant neighborhoods Child labor, eight hour day Celebrating immigrant cultures Reforming urban politics Municipal ownership/regulation of utilities	Hull House Settlement Henry Street Settlement National Consumers Loan New York Child Labor Committee Bureau of Municipal Research
State	Robert M. LaFollette, Hiram Johnson, Al Smith	Limiting power of railroads, other corporations Improving civil service Direct democracy Applying academic scholarship to human needs	"Wisconsin Idea" State Workmen's Compensation, Unemployment Insurance Public utility regulation
	James K. Vardaman, Hoke Smith	Disfranchisement of African Americans	Legalized segregation
National	Theodore Roosevelt	Trustbusting Conservation and Western development National regulation of corporate and financial excesses	Reclamation Bureau (1902) U.S. Forest Service (1905) Food and Drug Administration (1906) Meat Inspection Act (1906) Hepburn Act—ICC (1906)
	Woodrow Wilson	National regulation of corporate and financial excesses Reform of national banking	Graduated Income Tax (1913) Federal Reserve Act (1913) Clayton Antitrust Act (1914) Federal Trade Commission (1914)
Intellectual/Cultural	Jacob Riis Lincoln Steffens Ida Tarbell Upton Sinclair S.S. McClure	Muckraking	*How the Other Half Lives* (1890) *The Shame of the Cities* (1904) *History of Standard Oil* (1904) *The Jungle* (1906) *McClure's Magazine*
	John Dewey	Education reform	*Democracy and Education* (1916)
	Louis Brandeis	Sociological jurisprudence	*Muller v. Oregon*
	Edward A. Ross	Empowering the "ethical elite"	*Social Control* (1901)

strikers. But Wilson adopted the view that permanent federal regulation was necessary for checking the abuses of big business. The Federal Trade Commission (FTC), established in 1914, sought to give the federal government the same sort of regulatory control over corporations that the ICC had over railroads.

On social issues, Wilson proved more cautious. His initial failure to support federal child labor legislation and rural credits to farm banks angered many progressives. A Southerner, Wilson also sanctioned the spread of racial segregation in federal offices. As the reelection campaign of 1916 approached, Wilson worried about defections from the labor and social justice wings of his party. He proceeded to support a rural credits act providing government capital to federal farm banks, as well as federal aid to agricultural extension programs in schools. He also came out in favor of child labor reform and a worker compensation bill for federal employees. But by 1916 the dark cloud of the European War had already begun to cast its long shadow over progressive reform.

CONCLUSION

The American political and social landscape was significantly altered by progressivism, but these changes reflected the tensions and ambiguities of progressivism itself. Nearly every new election law had the effect of excluding some people from voting while including others. For African Americans, progressivism largely meant disfranchisement from voting altogether. Direct primary laws eliminated some of the most blatant abuses of big-city machines, but they left party leaders in substantial control of candidate selection. Stricter election laws made it more difficult for third parties to get on the ballot. Voting itself steadily declined in these years.

Overall, party voting became a less important form of political participation. Interest group activity, congressional and statehouse lobbying, and direct appeals to public opinion gained currently as ways of influencing government. Business groups such as the National Association of Manufacturers and individual trade associations were among the most active groups pressing their demands on government. Political action often shifted from legislatures to the new administrative agencies and commissions created to deal with social and economic problems. Popular magazines and journals grew significantly in both number and circulation, becoming more influential in shaping and appealing to national public opinion.

Social progressives and their allies could point to significant improvements in the everyday lives of ordinary Americans. On the state level, real advances had been made through a range of social legislation covering working conditions, child labor, minimum wages, and worker compensation. Social progressives, too, had discovered the power of organizing into extra-party lobbying groups such as the NCL and the National Woman Suffrage Association. Yet the tensions between fighting for social justice and the urge toward social control remained unresolved. The emphasis on efficiency, uplift, and rational administration often collided with humane impulses to aid the poor, the immigrant, the slum dweller. The large majority of African Americans, blue-collar workers, and urban poor remained untouched by federal assistance programs.

Progressives had tried to confront the new realities of urban and industrial society. What had begun as a discrete collection of local and state struggles had by 1912 come to redefine state and national politics. Politics itself had been transformed by the calls for social justice. Federal and state power would now play a more decisive role than ever in shaping work, play, and social life in local communities.

CHRONOLOGY

1889	Jane Addams founds Hull House in Chicago
1890	Jacob Riis publishes *How the Other Half Lives*
1895	Booker T. Washington addresses Cotton States Exposition in Atlanta, emphasizing an accommodationist philosophy
	Lillian Wald establishes Henry Street Settlement in New York
1898	Florence Kelley becomes general secretary of the new National Consumers' League
1900	Robert M. La Follette elected governor of Wisconsin
1901	Theodore Roosevelt succeeds the assassinated William McKinley as president
1904	Lincoln Steffens publishes *The Shame of the Cities*
1905	President Roosevelt creates U.S. Forest Service and names Gifford Pinchot head
	Industrial Workers of the World founded in Chicago
1906	Upton Sinclair's *The Jungle* exposes conditions in the meat-packing industry
	Congress passes Pure Food and Drug Act and Meat Inspection Act and establishes Food and Drug Administration
1908	In *Muller v. Oregon* the Supreme Court upholds a state law limiting maximum hours for working women
1909	Uprising of the 20,000 in New York City's garment industries helps organize unskilled workers into unions
	National Association for the Advancement of Colored People founded
1911	Triangle Shirtwaist Company fire kills 146 garment workers in New York City
	Socialist critic Max Eastman begins publishing *The Masses*
1912	Democrat Woodrow Wilson wins presidency, defeating Republican William H. Taft, Progressive Theodore Roosevelt, and Socialist Eugene V. Debs
	Bread and Roses strike involves 25,000 textile workers in Lawrence, Massachusetts
	Margaret Sanger begins writing and speaking in support of birth control for women
1913	Sixteenth Amendment, legalizing a graduated income tax, is ratified
1914	Clayton Antitrust Act exempts unions from being construed as illegal combinations in restraint of trade
	Federal Trade Commission established
	Ludlow Massacre
1916	National Park Service established

REVIEW QUESTIONS

1. Discuss the tensions within progressivism between the ideals of social justice and the urge for social control. What concrete achievements are associated with each wing of the movement? What were the driving forces behind them?

2. Describe the different manifestations of progressivism at the local, state, and national levels. To what extent did progressives redefine the role of the state in American politics?

3. What gains were made by working-class communities in the progressive era? What barriers did they face?

4. How did the era's new immigration reshape America's cities and workplaces? What connections can you draw between the new immigrant experience and progressive era politics?

5. Analyze the progressive era from the perspective of African Americans. What political and social developments were most crucial, and what legacies did they leave?

6. Evaluate the lasting impact of progressive reform. How do the goals, methods, and language of progressives still find voice in contemporary America?

RECOMMENDED READING

John D. Buenker, *Urban Liberalism and Progressive Reform* (1973). Explores the contributions of urban ethnic voters and machine-based politicians to the progressive movement.

Robert M. Crunden, *Ministers of Reform: The Progressives' Achievement in American Civilization, 1889–1920* (1982). Emphasizes the moral and religious traditions of middle-class Protestants as the core of the progressive ethos.

Alan Dawley, *Struggles for Justice: Social Responsibility and the Liberal State* (1991). Offers an important interpretation of progressivism that focuses on how the working class and women pushed the state toward a more activist role in confronting social problems.

Susan A. Glenn, *Daughters of the Shtetl: Life and Labor in the Immigrant Generation* (1990). A sensitive analysis of the experiences of immigrant Jewish women in the garment trades.

Dewey Grantham, *Southern Progressivism: The Reconciliation of Progress and Tradition* (1982). Examines the contradictions within the southern progressive tradition.

James R. Green, *The World of the Worker: Labor in Twentieth Century America* (1980). Includes a fine overview of life and work in company towns and urban ghettos in the early twentieth century.

Morton Keller, *Regulating a New Society: Public Policy and Social Change in America, 1900–1930* (1994). A comprehensive study of public policy making on local and national levels in early twentieth-century America.

Arthur Link and Richard L. McCormick, *Progressivism* (1983). The best recent overview of progressivism and electoral politics.

Kathryn Kish Sklar, *Florence Kelley and the Nation's Work* (1995). The first installment in a two-volume biography, this book brilliantly brings Florence Kelley alive within the rich context of late nineteenth-century women's political culture.

Robert Wiebe, *The Search for Order, 1877–1920* (1967). A pathbreaking study of how the professional middle classes responded to the upheavals of industrialism and urbanization.

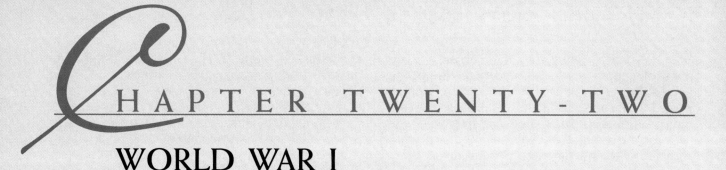

CHAPTER TWENTY-TWO

WORLD WAR I

1914–1920

AMERICAN COMMUNITIES
Vigilante Justice in Bisbee, Arizona

Early in the morning of July 12, 1917, two thousand armed vigilantes swept through Bisbee, Arizona, acting on behalf of the Phelps-Dodge mining company and Bisbee's leading businessmen to break a bitter strike that had crippled Bisbee's booming copper industry. The vigilantes seized miners in their homes, on the street, and in restaurants and stores. Any miner who wasn't working or willing to work was herded into Bisbee's downtown plaza, where two machine guns commanded the scene. From the Plaza more than 2,000 were marched to the local baseball park. There, mine managers gave them a last chance to return to work. Hundreds accepted and were released. The remaining 1,400 were forced at gunpoint onto a freight train, which took them 173 miles east to Columbus, New Mexico, where they were dumped in the desert.

The Bisbee deportation occurred against a complex backdrop. America had just entered World War I, corporation were seeking higher profits, and labor militancy was on the rise. Bisbee was only one of many American communities to suffer vigilantism during the war. Any number of offenses—not displaying a flag, failing to buy war bonds, criticizing the draft, alleged spying, any apparently "disloyal" behavior—could trigger vigilante action. In western communities like Bisbee, vigilantes used the superpatriotic mood to settle scores with labor organizers and radicals.

Arizona was the leading producer of copper in the United States. With a population of 8,000, Bisbee lay in the heart of the state's richest mining district. The giant Phelps-Dodge Company dominated Bisbee's political and social life. It owned the town's hospital, department store, newspaper, library, and largest hotel. With the introduction of new technology and open pit mining after 1900, unskilled laborers—most of them Slavic, Italian, Czech, and Mexican immigrants—had increasingly replaced skilled American and English-born miners in Bisbee's workforce.

America's entry into the war pushed the price of copper to an all-time high, prompting Phelps-Dodge to increase production. Miners viewed the increased demand for labor as an opportunity to flex their own muscle and improve wages and working conditions. Two rival union locals, one affiliated with the American Federation of Labor (AFL), the other with the more radical Industrial Workers of the World (IWW), or "Wobblies," sought to organize Bisbee's workers. On June 26, 1917, Bisbee's Wobblies went on strike. They demanded better mine safety, an end to discrimination against union workers, and a substantial pay increase. The IWW, making special efforts to attract lower-paid foreign-born workers to their cause, even hired two Mexican organizers. Although the IWW had only 300 or 400 members in Bisbee, more than half the town's 4,700 miners supported the strike.

The walkout was peaceful, but Walter Douglas, district manager for Phelps-Dodge, was unmoved. "There will be no compromise," he declared, "because you cannot compromise with a rattlesnake." Douglas, Cochese County Sheriff Harry Wheeler, and Bisbee's leading businessmen met secretly to plan the July 12 deportation. The approximately 2,000 men they deputized to carry it out were members of Bisbee's Citizens' Protective League and the Workers Loyalty League. These vigilantes included company officials, small businessmen, professionals, and anti-union workers. Local telephone and telegraph offices agreed to isolate Bisbee by censoring outgoing messages. The El Paso and Southwestern Railroad, a subsidiary of Phelps-Dodge, provided the waiting boxcars.

The participants in this illegal conspiracy defended themselves by exaggerating the threat of organized labor. They also appealed to patriotism and played on racial fears. The IWW opposed American involvement in the war, making it vulnerable to charges of disloyalty. Sheriff Wheeler told a visiting journalist he worried that Mexicans "would take advantage of the disturbed conditions of the strike and start an uprising, destroying the mines and murdering American women and children."

An army census of the deportees, who had found temporary refuge at an army camp in Columbus, New Mexico, offered quite a different picture. Of the 1,400 men, 520 owned property in Bisbee. Nearly 500 had already registered for the draft, and more than 200 had purchased Liberty Bonds. More than 400 were married with children; only 400 were members of the IWW. Eighty percent were immigrants, including nearly 400 Mexicans. A presidential mediation committee concluded that "conditions in Bisbee were in fact peaceful and free from manifestations of disorder or violence." The deported miners nonetheless found it difficult to shake the accusations that their strike was anti-American and foreign inspired.

At their camp, the miners organized their own police force and elected an executive committee to seek relief. In a letter to President Wilson, they claimed "Common American citizens here are now convinced that they have no constitutional rights." They promised to return to digging copper if the federal government operated the nation's mines and smelters. The presidential mediation committee criticized the mine companies and declared the deportation illegal. But, it also denied the federal government had any jurisdiction in the matter. Arizona's attorney general refused to offer protection for a return to Bisbee.

In September, the men began gradually to drift away from Columbus. Only a few ever returned to Bisbee. The events convinced President Wilson that the IWW was a subversive organization and a threat to national security. The Justice Department began planning an all-out legal assault that would soon cripple the Wobblies. But Wilson could not ignore protests against the Bisbee outrage from such prominent and patriotic Americans as Samuel Gompers, head of the American Federation of Labor. To demonstrate his administration's commitment to harmonious industrial relations, the president appointed a special commission to investigate and mediate wartime labor conflicts. But Arizona's mines would remain union free until the New Deal era of the 1930s.

America's entry into the war created a national sense of purpose and an unprecedented mobilization of resources. Unifying the country and winning the war now took precedence over progressive reforms. The war also aroused powerful political emotions and provided an excuse for some citizens to try to cleanse their communities of anyone who did not conform.

Bisbee

KEY TOPICS

- America's expanding international role
- From neutrality to participation in the Great War
- Mobilizing the society and the economy for war
- Dissent and its repression
- Woodrow Wilson's failure to win the peace

BECOMING A WORLD POWER

Roosevelt: The Big Stick

Like many of his class and background, Theodore Roosevelt took for granted the superiority of Protestant Anglo-American culture and the goal of spreading its values and influence. He also believed that to maintain and increase its economic and political stature, America must be militarily strong. In 1900 Roosevelt summarized his activist views, declaring, "I have always been fond of the West African proverb, 'Speak softly and carry a big stick, you will go far.' "

Roosevelt brought the "big stick" approach to several disputes in the Caribbean region. Since the 1880s, several British, French, and American companies had pursued various plans for building a canal across the Isthmus of Panama, thereby connecting the Atlantic and Pacific oceans. Roosevelt tried to negotiate a leasing agreement with Colombia, of which Panama was a province. But when the Colombian Senate rejected a final American offer in the fall of 1903, Roosevelt invented a new strategy. A combination of native Panamanian forces and foreign promoters associated with the canal project plotted a revolt against Colombia. Roosevelt kept in touch with at least one leader of the revolt, Philippe Bunau-Varilla, an engineer and agent for the New Panama Canal Company, and let him know that U.S. warships were steaming toward Panama.

On November 3, 1903, just as the USS *Nashville* arrived in Colón harbor, the province of Panama declared itself independent of Colombia. America immediately recognized the new Republic of Panama. Less than two weeks later, Bunau-Varilla, serving as a minister from Panama, signed a treaty granting the United States full sovereignty in perpetuity over a ten-mile-wide canal zone. America guaranteed Panama's independence and agreed to a downpayment of $10 million and a regular installment of $250,000 per year. Years after the canal was completed, the U.S. Senate voted another $25 million to Colombia as compensation.

The Panama Canal was a triumph of modern engineering and gave the United States a tremendous strategic and commercial advantage in the Western Hemisphere. The actual building of the canal took eight years and cost hundreds of badly paid manual workers their lives. The United States avoided the failure of earlier attempts at canal building by using better equipment and mounting a vigorous campaign against disease. Finally, in 1914, after $720 million in construction costs, the first merchant ships sailed through the canal.

"The inevitable effect of our building the Canal," wrote Secretary of State Elihu Root in 1905, "must be to require us to police the surrounding premises." Roosevelt agreed with the necessity for "proper policing of the world." He was especially concerned that European powers might step in if America did not. In 1903 Great Britain, Germany, and Italy had imposed a blockade on Venezuela in a dispute over debt payments owed to private investors. To prevent armed intervention by the Europeans, Roosevelt proclaimed what became known as the Roosevelt Corollary to the Monroe Doctrine. "Chronic wrongdoing, or an impotence which results in a general loosening of the ties of civilized society," the statement read, justified "the exercise of an international police power" anywhere in the hemisphere. Roosevelt invoked the corollary to justify U.S. intervention in the region. He and later presidents cited it to justify armed intervention in the internal affairs of Cuba, Haiti, Nicaragua, and Mexico.

With the outbreak of the Russo–Japanese War in 1904, Roosevelt worried about the future of the Open Door policy in Asia. In a series of diplomatic notes Secretary of State John Hay in 1899 had won approval for the so-called Open Door approach, giving all nations equal access to trading and development rights in China. A total victory by Russia or Japan could upset the balance of power in the Far East and threaten American business enterprises. Roosevelt became especially concerned after the Japanese scored a series of military victories over Russia and began to loom as a dominant power in the Far East.

Roosevelt mediated a settlement of the Russo–Japanese War at Portsmouth, New Hampshire, in 1905 (for which he was awarded the 1906 Nobel Peace Prize). In this settlement Japan won recognition of its dominant position in Korea and consolidated its economic control over Manchuria. Yet American–Japanese relations remained strained over anti-Japanese racism in California. Roosevelt built up American naval strength in the Pacific, and in 1908 he sent battleships to visit Japan in a muscle-flexing display of sea power. But in that same year, the two burgeoning Pacific powers reached a reconciliation. The Root–Takahira Agreement affirmed the territorial status quo in Asia and the Open Door trade policy in China.

Wilson: Moralism and Realism

Right after he took office in 1913, President Woodrow Wilson had to face international crises of a scope and complexity unprecedented in U.S. history. Wilson had no experience in diplomacy, but he brought to foreign affairs a set of fundamental principles that combined a moralist's faith in American democracy with a realist's understanding of the power of international commerce. He believed that American economic expansion, accompanied by democratic principles and Christianity, was a civilizing force in the world.

Wilson, like most corporate and political leaders of the day, emphasized foreign investments and industrial exports as the keys to the nation's prosperity. He believed that the United States, with its superior industrial efficiency, could achieve supremacy in world commerce if artificial barriers to free trade were removed. He championed and extended the Open Door policy of John Hay, advocating strong diplomatic and military measures "for making ourselves supreme in the world from an economic point of view." Wilson often couched his vision of a dynamic, expansive American capitalism in terms of a moral crusade. Yet he quickly found that the complex realities of power politics could interfere with moral vision.

Wilson's policies toward Mexico, which foreshadowed the problems he would encounter in World War I, best illustrate his difficulties. The 1911 Mexican Revolution had overthrown the brutally corrupt dictatorship of Porfirio Diaz, and popular leader Francisco Madero had won wide support by promising democracy and economic reform for millions of landless peasants. U.S. businessmen, however, were nervous about the future of their Mexican investments, which totaled over $1 billion—greater than Mexico's own investment and more than all other foreign investment in that country combined. Wilson at first gave his blessing to the revolutionary movement, but right before he took office, he

was stunned by the ousting and murder of Madero by his chief lieutenant, General Victoriano Huerta. Other nations, including Great Britain and Japan, recognized the Huerta regime, but Wilson would not. An armed opposition to Huerta, known as the Constitutionalists and led by Venustiano Carranza, emerged in northern Mexico. Wilson tried to broker a compromise between the two factions, but both sides refused his offer. Carranza, an ardent nationalist, pressed for the right to buy U.S. arms, which he won in 1914. Wilson also isolated Huerta diplomatically by persuading the British to withdraw their support in exchange for American guarantees of English property interests in Mexico.

But Huerta stubbornly remained in power. In April 1914 Wilson used a minor insult to U.S. sailors in Tampico as an excuse to invade. American naval forces bombarded and then occupied the port of Veracruz, the main entry for arms shipments to Huerta. Wilson accepted the offer of the ABC Powers—Argentina, Brazil, and Chile—to mediate the dispute. Huerta rejected a plan for him to step aside in favor of a provisional government, but Carranza managed to overthrow Huerta in August. Far from expressing gratitude, Carranza himself denounced Wilson's intervention.

As war loomed in Europe, Wilson found himself frustrated by his inability to control Mexico's revolutionary politics. For a brief period he threw his support behind Pancho Villa, Carranza's former ally who now led a rebel army of his own in the north. But Carranza defeated Villa's army, and in October 1915, with more attention being given to the war in Europe, the Wilson administration finally recognized Carranza as Mexico's *de facto* president. Meanwhile Pancho Villa, feeling betrayed, turned on the United States and tried to provoke a crisis that might draw Washington into war with Mexico. Villa led several raids in Mexico and across the border in early 1916 that killed a few dozen Americans. The man once viewed by Wilson as a fighter for democracy was now dismissed as a dangerous bandit.

In March 1916, enraged by Villa's defiance, Wilson dispatched General John J. Pershing and an army that eventually numbered 15,000. For a year, Pershing's troops chased Villa in vain, penetrating 300 miles into Mexico. The invasion made Villa a symbol of national resistance in Mexico. Skirmishes between Pershing and Carranza's army brought the two nations to the brink of war in June 1916. Wilson prepared a message to Congress in which he requested permission for American troops to occupy all of northern Mexico. But he never delivered it. The possibility of a Mexican–American war aroused fierce opposition around the United States. Perhaps more important, Wilson feared such a war because of mounting tensions with Germany. He told an aide that "Germany is anxious to

Mexican revolutionary leaders and sometime allies Francisco "Pancho" Villa (center) and Emiliano Zapata (right) are shown at the National Palace in Mexico City, c. 1916. Zapata's army operated out of a base in the southern agricultural state of Morelos, while Villa's army controlled large portions of Mexico's north. In 1914 Villa captured the imagination of American reformers, journalists, and movie makers with his military exploits against the oppressive Huerta regime. But in 1916, after several border clashes, President Wilson dispatched a punitive expedition in pursuit of Villa.

have us at war with Mexico, so that our minds and our energies will be taken off the great war across the sea." Wilson thus accepted negotiations by a face-saving international commission.

Wilson's attempt to guide the course of Mexico's revolution and protect U.S. interests left a bitter legacy. It also suggested the limits of a foreign policy tied to a moral vision of American exceptionalism. Militarism and imperialism, Wilson had believed, were hallmarks of the old European way. American liberal values—rooted in capitalist development, democracy, and free trade—were the wave of the future. Wilson declared that he had no desire to interfere with Mexican sovereignty. But that is exactly what he did. The United States, he argued, must actively use its enormous moral and material power to create a new international system based on peaceful commerce and political stability. That principle would soon engage America in Europe's bloodiest war and its most momentous revolution.

THE GREAT WAR

The Guns of August

Only a complex and fragile system of alliances had kept the European powers at peace with one another since 1871. Two great competing camps had evolved by 1907: the Triple Alliance (also known as the Central Powers), which included Germany, Austria-Hungary, and Italy; and the Triple Entente (also known as the Allies), which included Great Britain, France, and Russia. At the heart of this division was the competition between Great Britain, long the world's dominant colonial and commercial power, and Germany, which had powerful aspirations for an empire of its own.

The alliance system managed to keep small conflicts from escalating into larger ones for most of the late nineteenth and early twentieth centuries. But its inclusiveness was also its weakness: it had the potential for drawing many nations into any war that erupted. On June 28, 1914, Archduke Franz Ferdinand, heir to the throne of the unstable Austro–Hungarian empire, was assassinated in Sarajevo, Bosnia. The archduke's killer was a Slavic nationalist who believed the Austro–Hungarian province of Bosnia ought to be annexed to neighboring Serbia. Germany pushed Austria–Hungary to retaliate against Serbia, and the Serbians in turn asked Russia for help in defense.

By early August both sides had exchanged declarations of war and begun mobilizing their forces. Germany invaded Belgium and prepared to move across the French border. But after the German armies were stopped at the River Marne in September, the war settled into a long, bloody stalemate. New and grimly efficient weapons, such as the machine gun and the tank, and the horrors of trench warfare meant unprecedented casualties. Centered in northern France, the fighting killed 5 million people over the next two and a half years.

American Neutrality

The outbreak of war in Europe shocked Americans, but they could at least take comfort in the long-established tradition of staying out of far-away European wars. President Wilson issued a formal proclamation of neutrality and urged citizens to be "impartial in thought as well as in action."

Both sides bombarded the United States with vigorous propaganda campaigns. The British effectively exploited their natural advantage of common language and heritage. Reports of German looting, raping, and killing of innocent civilians circulated widely in the press. Many of these were exaggerated. German propagandists blamed the war on Russian expansionism and France's desire to avenge its defeat by Germany in 1870–71. It is difficult to measure the impact of war propaganda on American public opinion. As a whole, though, it highlighted the terrible human costs of the war and thus strengthened the conviction that America should stay out of it.

Economic ties between the United States and the Allies, however, were a great barrier to true neutrality. A key tactic for the British was a naval blockade on all shipping to Germany. Theoretically, Wilson's neutrality meant that, as a nonbelligerent, the United States had the right to trade with both sides. In practice, although he protested the blockade, the president had to accept the situation and allow trade with the Allies to continue while commerce with Germany all but ended. As war orders poured in from Britain and France, the value of American trade with the Allies shot up from $824 million in 1914 to $3.2 billion in 1916. Increased trade with the Allies helped produce a great economic boom at home, and the United States became neutral in name only.

Preparedness and Peace

Germany used submarine warfare to break the British blockade. In February 1915 Germany declared the waters around the British Isles to be a war zone. Previously, the procedure had been for submarines to surface, stop a ship, check its cargo, and unload all passengers before attacking. Now, all enemy shipping was subject to surprise submarine attack. Neutral powers were warned that the problems of identification at sea put their ships at risk.

On May 7, 1915, a German U-boat sank the Cunard liner *Lusitania* off the coast of Ireland. Among the 1,198 people who died were 128 American citizens. The *Lusitania* was in fact secretly carrying war materials, and passengers had been warned about a possible attack. Wilson nevertheless denounced the sinking as illegal and inhuman, and the American press loudly condemned the act as barbaric. Secretary of State William Jennings Bryan resigned in protest against a policy he thought too warlike.

Then, in March 1916, a German U-boat torpedoed the *Sussex*, an unarmed French passenger ship, injuring four Americans. President Wilson threatened to break off diplomatic relations with Germany unless it abandoned its methods of submarine warfare. Germany promised that all vessels would be visited before attack, but this crisis prompted Wilson to begin preparing for war. The National Security League, active in large eastern cities and bankrolled by conservative banking and commercial interests, helped push for a bigger army and navy, and, most important, a system of universal military training.

In June 1916 Congress passed the National Defense Act, which more than doubled the size of the regular army. In August Congress passed a bill that dramatically increased spending for new battleships, cruisers, and destroyers.

Not all Americans supported these preparations for battle, and opposition to military buildup found expression in scores of American communities. As early as August 29, 1914, 1,500 women clad in black marched down New York's Fifth Avenue in the Woman's Peace Parade. Out of this gathering evolved the American Union Against Militarism, which lobbied against the preparedness campaign and intervention in Mexico. Antiwar feeling was especially strong in the South and Midwest. A group of thirty to fifty House Democrats, led by majority leader Claude Kitchin of North Carolina, stubbornly opposed Wilson's buildup.

A large reservoir of popular antiwar sentiment flowed through the culture in various ways. Movie director Thomas Ince's 1916 film *Civilization* depicted Christ returning to reveal the horrors of war to world leaders. Two of the most popular songs of 1915 were "Don't Take My Darling Boy Away" and "I Didn't Raise My Boy to Be a Soldier."

Wilson acknowledged the strong opposition to involvement in the war by adopting in the 1916 presidential campaign the winning slogan "He Kept Us Out of War." He made a point of appealing to progressives of all kinds, stressing his support for the eight-hour day and his administration's efforts on behalf of farmers. The war-induced prosperity no doubt helped him to defeat conservative Republican Charles Evans Hughes in a very close election. But Wilson knew that the peace was as fragile as his victory.

Safe for Democracy

By the end of January 1917 Germany's leaders had decided their only hope lay in a final decisive offensive against the Allies. On February 1, 1917, Germany announced a new policy of unrestricted submarine warfare, with no warnings, knowing that it might bring America into the conflict. In effect, German leaders were gambling that they could destroy the Allies before the United States would be able to mobilize troops and resources.

Wilson was indignant and disappointed. Germany had made it impossible for him to preserve his twin goals of U.S. neutrality and freedom of the seas. He broke off diplomatic relations with Germany and called upon Congress to approve the arming of U.S. merchant ships. On March 1 the White House shocked the country when it made public a recently intercepted coded message from German foreign secretary Arthur Zimmerman to the German ambassador in

Mexico. The Zimmerman note proposed that an alliance be made between Germany and Mexico if the United States entered the war. Zimmerman suggested that Mexico take up arms against the United States and receive in return the "lost territory in New Mexico, Texas, and Arizona." The specter of a German–Mexican alliance helped turn the tide of public opinion in the Southwest, where opposition to U.S. involvement in the war had been strong.

Revelation of the Zimmerman note stiffened Wilson's resolve. He issued an executive order in mid-March authorizing the arming of all merchant ships and allowing them to shoot at submarines. In that month German U-boats sank seven U.S. merchant ships, leaving a heavy death toll. Anti-German feeling increased, and thousands took part in prowar demonstrations in New York, Boston, Philadelphia, and other cities. Wilson finally called a special session of Congress to ask for a declaration of war.

On April 2, on a rainy night before a packed and very quiet assembly, Wilson made his case. He reviewed the escalation of submarine warfare, and said that neutrality was no longer feasible or desirable. But the conflict was not merely about U.S. shipping rights, Wilson argued. "The world must be made safe for democracy. Its peace must be planted upon the tested foundations of political liberty."

Wilson's eloquent speech won over the Congress, most of the press, and even his bitterest political critics, such as Theodore Roosevelt. On April 6 President Wilson signed the declaration of war. All that remained was to win over the American public.

AMERICAN MOBILIZATION

Selling the War

Just a week after signing the war declaration, Wilson created the Committee on Public Information (CPI) to organize public opinion. It was dominated by its civilian chairman, journalist and reformer George Creel. Creel transformed the CPI from its original function as coordinator of government news to a much more aggressive role in promoting the war. In his drive to create what he called "a national ideology," Creel raised the art of public relations to new heights.

The CPI led an aggressively negative campaign against all things German. Its posters and advertisements depicted the Germans as Huns, bestial monsters outside the civilized world. German music and literature—indeed, the German language itself—were suspect, and were banished from the concert halls, schools, and libraries of many communities. The CPI also urged ethnic Americans to abandon their Old World ties, to become "unhyphenated Americans."

"You're in the Army Now"

Traditionally, the United States had relied upon volunteer forces organized at the state level for its army. But volunteer rates after April 6 were less than they had been for the Civil War or the Spanish–American War, reflecting the softness of prowar sentiment. The administration thus introduced the Selective Service Act, which provided for the registration and classification for military service of all men between ages twenty-one and thirty-five. To prevent the widespread opposition to the draft that had occurred during the Civil War, the new draft had no unpopular provision allowing draftees to buy their way out of service by paying for a substitute.

On June 5, 1917, nearly 10 million men registered for the draft. There was scattered organized resistance, but overall, registration records offered evidence of national support. A supplemental registration in August 1918 extended the age limits to eighteen and forty-five. Of the 2.8 million men eventually called up for service, about 340,000, or 12 percent, failed to show up. Another 2 million Americans volunteered for the various armed services.

The vast, polyglot army posed unprecedented challenges of organization and control. But progressive elements within the administration also saw opportunities for pressing reform measures involving education, alcohol, and sex. Army psychologists gave the new Stanford-Binet intelligence test to all recruits and were shocked to find illiteracy rates as high as 25 percent. Low test scores among many recent immigrants and rural African Americans no doubt resulted from difficulty with language and from the cultural biases embedded in the tests.

African Americans were organized into segregated units, barred entirely from the marines and the Coast Guard, and largely relegated to working as cooks, laundrymen, stevedores, and the like in the army and navy. Thousands of black soldiers endured humiliating, sometimes violent treatment, particularly from white southern officers. African American servicemen faced hostility from white civilians as well, North and South, often being denied service in restaurants and admission to theaters near training camps.

Over 200,000 African Americans eventually served in France, but only about one in five saw combat, as opposed to two out of three white soldiers. Black combat units served with distinction in various divisions of the French army, however. The all-black 369th U.S. Infantry, for example, saw the first and longest service of any American regiment deployed in a foreign army, serving in the trenches for 191 days. The French government awarded the *Croix de Guerre* to the entire regiment, and 171 officers and enlisted men were cited individually for exceptional bravery in

The military reinforced old patterns of racism in American life by segregating African American troops and assigning most of them to menial and support tasks. Yet African Americans generally supported the war effort.

action. African American soldiers by and large enjoyed a friendly reception from French civilians as well. The contrast with their treatment at home would remain a sore point with these troops upon their return to the United States.

Americans in Battle

President Wilson appointed General John J. Pershing, recently returned from pursuing Pancho Villa in Mexico, as commander of the American Expeditionary Force (AEF). Pershing insisted that the AEF maintain its own identity, distinct from that of the French and British armies. He was also reluctant to send American troops into battle before they had received at least six months' training. The AEF's combat role would be brief but intense: not until early 1918 did AEF units reach the front in large numbers; eight months later the war was over.

In the early spring of 1918 the Germans launched a major offensive that brought them to within fifty miles of Paris. In early June about 70,000 AEF soldiers helped the French stop the Germans in the battles of Château-Thierry and Belleau Wood. In July Allied forces, led by Marshal Foch of France, began a counteroffensive designed to defeat Germany once and for all. American reinforcements began flooding the ports of Liverpool in England and Brest and Saint-Nazaire in France. The "doughboys" streamed in at a rate of over 250,000 a month. By

September General Pershing had more than a million Americans in his army.

In late September 1918 the AEF took over the southern part of a 200-mile front in the Meuse–Argonne offensive. In seven weeks of fighting, most through terrible mud and rain, the U.S. army used more ammunition than the entire Union Army had in four years of the Civil War. The Germans, exhausted and badly outnumbered, began to fall back and look for a cease-fire. On November 11, 1918, the war ended with the signing of an armistice.

The massive influx of American troops and supplies no doubt hastened the end of the war. About two-thirds of the U.S. soldiers saw at least some fighting, but even they managed to avoid the horrors of the sustained trench warfare that had marked the earlier years of the war. For most Americans at the front, the war experience was a mixture of fear, exhaustion, and fatigue. Their time in France would remain a decisive moment in their lives. In all, over 52,000 Americans died in battle. Another 60,000 died from influenza and pneumonia, half of these while still in training camp. More than 200,000 Americans were wounded in the war. These figures, awful as they were, paled against the estimated casualties (killed and wounded) suffered by the European nations: 9 million for Russia, more than 6 million for Germany, nearly 5 million for France, and more than 2 million each for Great Britain and Italy.

OVER HERE

Organizing the Economy

In the summer of 1917 President Wilson established the War Industries Board (WIB) as a clearing house for industrial mobilization. Led by successful Wall Street speculator Bernard M. Baruch, the WIB proved a major innovation in expanding the regulatory power of the federal government. The WIB had to balance price controls against war profits. Only by ensuring a fair rate of return on investment could it encourage stepped-up production.

The WIB eventually handled 3,000 contracts worth $14.5 billion with various businesses. Standardization of goods effected large savings and streamlined production. Baruch continually negotiated with business leaders, describing the system as "voluntary cooperation with the big stick in the cupboard." When Elbert Gary of U.S. Steel refused to accept the government's price for steel, and when Henry Ford balked at limiting private car production, Baruch warned that he would instruct the military to take over their plants. Both industrialists backed down.

In August 1917 Congress passed the Food and Fuel Act, authorizing the president to regulate the production and distribution of food and fuel necessary

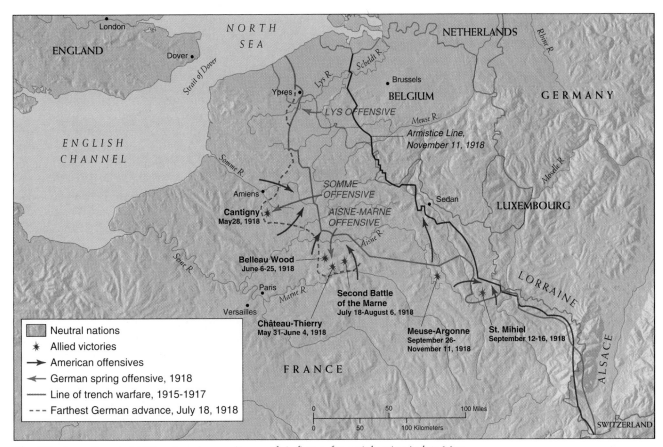

The Western Front, 1918   *American units saw their first substantial action in late May, helping to stop the German offensive at the battle of Cantigny. By September, more than 1 million American troops were fighting in a counteroffensive campaign at St. Mihiel, the largest single American engagement of the war.*

Source: Reprinted by permission of Mountain High Maps, Digital Wisdom, Inc., Tappahannock, VA.

for the war effort. To lead the Food Administration (FA), Wilson appointed Herbert Hoover, a millionaire engineer who had already won fame for directing the Belgian relief effort. He became one of the best-known figures of the war administration. Hoover enacted price controls on certain agricultural commodities, such as sugar, pork, and wheat. These were purchased by the government and then sold to the public through licensed dealers. The FA also raised the purchase price of grain so that farmers would increase production. But Hoover stopped short of imposing mandatory food rationing, preferring to rely on persuasion and voluntary controls.

Hoover's success, like George Creel's at the CPI, depended on mobilizing hundreds of thousands of volunteers in thousands of American communities. The FA coordinated the work of local committees that distributed posters and leaflets urging people to save food, recycle scraps, and use substitutes for scarce produce. Hoover exhorted Americans to "go back to simple food, simple clothes, simple pleasures." These efforts resulted in a sharp cutback in the consumption

of sugar and wheat, as well as a boost in the supply of livestock. The resultant increase in food exports helped sustain the Allied war effort.

The enormous cost of fighting the war, about $33 billion, meant unprecedentedly large expenditures for the federal government. The entire structure of American taxation shifted during the war as taxes on incomes and profits replaced excise and customs levies as the major sources of revenue. A graduated federal income tax had been in effect only since 1913. Lowering the minimum level of taxable income to $1,000 brought many more households into the federal tax system. Thus, in 1916 only 437,000 Americans paid income tax; by 1918 the figure was 4,425,000. Tax rates were as steep as 70 percent in the highest brackets.

The bulk of war financing came from government borrowing, especially in the form of the popular Liberty Bonds sold to the American public. Bond drives became highly organized patriotic campaigns that ultimately raised a total of $23 billion for the war effort. The administration also used the new Federal Reserve Banks to expand the money supply, making borrowing easier. The federal debt jumped from $1 billion in 1915 to $20 billion in 1920.

The Business of War

Overall, the war meant expansion and high profits for American business. Between 1916 and 1918 Ford Motor Company increased its workforce from 32,000 to 48,000, General Motors from 10,000 to 50,000. Total capital expenditure in U.S. manufacturing jumped from $600 million in 1915 to $2.5 billion in 1918. Corporate profits as a whole nearly tripled between 1914 and 1919, and many large businesses did much better than that. Expanded farm acreage and increased investment in farm machinery led to a jump of 20 to 30 percent in overall farm production.

The most important and long-lasting economic legacy of the war was the organizational shift toward corporatism in American business. Never before had business and the federal government cooperated so closely. Under war administrators such as Baruch and Hoover, entire industries (such as radio manufacturing) and economic sectors (such as agriculture and energy) were organized, regulated, and subsidized as never before. War agencies used both public and private power—legal authority and voluntarism—to hammer out and enforce agreements. Here was the genesis of the modern bureaucratic state.

Labor and the War

The expansion of the wartime economy often meant severe disruptions and discomfort for America's workers. Overcrowding, rapid work force turnover, and high inflation rates were typical in war-boom communities. In Bridgeport, Connecticut, a center for small-arms manufacturing, the population grew by 50,000 in less than a year. In 1917 the number of families grew by 12,000, but available housing stock increased by only 6,000 units. Chronic congestion became common in many cities.

That same economic expansion, combined with army mobilization and a decline in immigration from Europe, caused a growing wartime labor shortage, so that working people generally enjoyed higher wages and a better standard of living. Trade unions, especially those affiliated with the American Federation of Labor (AFL), enjoyed a sharp rise in membership.

Organized labor's power and prestige, though by no means equal to business's or government's, clearly grew during the war. Samuel Gompers, president of the AFL, pledged the AFL's patriotic support to the war effort, and in April 1918 President Wilson appointed him to the National War Labor Board (NWLB). During 1917 the nation had seen thousands of strikes involving more than a million workers. Wages were usually at issue, reflecting workers' concerns with spiraling infla-

tion and higher prices. The NWLB, cochaired by labor attorney Frank Walsh and former president William H. Taft, acted as a supreme court for labor, arbitrating disputes and working to prevent disruptions in production. The great majority of these interventions resulted in improved wages and reduced hours of work.

Most important, the NWLB supported the right of workers to organize unions and furthered the acceptance of the eight-hour day for war workers—central aims of the labor movement. It also backed time-and-a-half pay for overtime, as well as the principle of equal pay for women. AFL unions gained over a million new members during the war, and overall union membership rose from 2.7 million in 1914 to over 5 million by 1920.

If the war boosted the fortunes of the AFL, however, it spelled the end for more radical elements of the U.S. labor movement. The Industrial Workers of the World (IWW), unlike the AFL, had concentrated on organizing unskilled workers into all-inclusive industrial unions. The Wobblies denounced capitalism as an unreformable system based on exploitation, and they opposed U.S. entry into the war. IWW leaders advised their members to refuse induction for "the capitalists' war." In September 1917 the Wilson administration responded to appeals from western business leaders for a crackdown on the Wobblies. Justice Department agents, acting under the broad authority of the recently passed Espionage Act, swooped down on IWW offices in over sixty towns and cities, arresting over 300 people and confiscating files. The mass trials and convictions that followed broke the back of America's radical labor movement and marked the beginning of a powerful wave of political repression.

Women at Work

For many of the 8 million women already in the labor force, the war meant a chance to switch from low-paying jobs, such as domestic service, to higher-paying industrial fields. About a million women joined the labor force for the first time. Female munitions plant workers, train engineers, drill press operators, streetcar conductors, and mail carriers became a common sight around the country.

In response to the widened range of female employment, the Labor Department created the Women in Industry Service (WIS). The service advised employers on using female labor and formulated general standards for the treatment of women workers. Although these goals had no legal force, they marked the first time the federal government had taken a practical stand on improving working conditions for women. Gains included the eight-hour day, equal pay for equal work, a minimum wage, the prohibition of night work, and the provision of rest periods, meal breaks, and restroom facilities. WIS inspectors found that despite their recommendations women were often employed for long hours in difficult and dangerous occupations. Women also suffered discrimination over pay. Government surveys found that women's average earnings were roughly half of men's in the same industries.

At war's end, women lost nearly all their defense-related jobs. By 1920 more women who worked outside the home did so in white-collar occupations—such as telephone operators, secretaries, and clerks—than in manufacturing or domestic service. The new awareness of women's work led Congress to create the Women's Bureau in the Labor Department, which continued the WIS wartime program of education and investigation through the postwar years.

Woman Suffrage

Along with the presence of so many new women wage workers, the highly visible volunteer efforts of millions of middle-class women helped finally to secure the vote for women. These women played a key role in the success of the Food Administration, and the Women's Committee of the Council of National Defense included a variety of women's organizations.

Until World War I, the fight for woman suffrage had been waged largely within individual states. Western states and territories had led the way. Ethnocultural divisions between Catholics and Protestants hindered suffrage efforts in the East. The close identification in the East between suffrage and Prohibition led many Catholic immigrants and German Lutherans to oppose the vote for women because they feared it would lead to prohibition.

The U.S. entry into the war provided a unique opportunity for suffrage groups to shift their strategy to a national campaign for a constitutional amendment granting the vote to women. Under the leadership of Carrie Chapman Catt, the National American Woman Suffrage Association (NAWSA), threw its support behind the war effort and doubled its membership to 2 million. Catt gambled that a strong show of patriotism would help clinch the century-old fight to win the vote for women. The NAWSA pursued a moderate policy of lobbying Congress for a constitutional amendment and calling for state referendums on woman suffrage.

A young Quaker activist, Alice Paul, injected new energy and more radical tactics into the movement. Dissatisfied with the NAWSA's conservative strategy of quiet lobbying and orderly demonstrations, Paul joined forces with western women voters to form the National Woman's Party. Borrowing from English suffragists, the NWP pursued a more aggressive and dramatic strategy of agitation. Paul and her supporters picketed the White House, publicly burned President Wilson's speeches,

Members of the National Woman's Party picketed President Wilson at the White House in 1917. Their militant action in the midst of the war crisis aroused both anger and sympathy. The NWP campaign helped push the President and the Congress to accept woman suffrage as "a war measure."

and condemned the president and the Democrats for failing to produce an amendment. Although some in the NAWSA objected to these tactics, Paul's radical approach helped make the NAWSA position—passage of the woman suffrage amendment as a "war measure"— more acceptable to Wilson. In 1917 the president urged Congress to pass a woman suffrage amendment as "vital to the winning of the war." The House did so in January 1918 and a more reluctant Senate approved it in June 1919. Another year of hard work was spent convincing the state legislatures. In August 1920 Tennessee gave the final vote needed to ratify the Nineteenth Amendment to the Constitution, finally making woman's vote legal nationwide.

Prohibition

Another reform effort closely associated with women's groups triumphed at the same time. The movement to eliminate alcohol from American life had attracted large numbers of Americans, especially women, since before the Civil War. Temperance advocates saw drinking as the source of many of the worst problems faced by the working class, including family violence, unemployment, and poverty. By the early twentieth century the Women's Christian Temperance Union, with a quarter million members, had become the single largest women's organization in American history.

The moral fervor that accompanied America's entry into the war provided a crucial boost to the cause. With so many breweries bearing German names, the movement also benefitted from the strong anti-German feeling of the war years. Outlawing beer and whiskey would also help to conserve precious grain, prohibitionists argued.

In 1917 a coalition of progressives and rural fundamentalists in Congress pushed through a constitutional amendment making the ban national. The Eighteenth Amendment was ratified by the states in January 1919 and became the law of the land one year later. The postwar years would show that Prohibition created a host of new problems, especially its encouragement of organized crime. At the time, however, many Americans, particularly native Protestants, considered Prohibition a worthy moral reform.

REPRESSION AND REACTION

Muzzling Dissent: The Espionage and Sedition Acts

The Espionage Act of June 1917 became the government's key tool for the suppression of antiwar sentiment. It set severe penalties (up to twenty years' imprisonment and a $10,000 fine) for anyone found guilty of aiding the enemy, obstructing recruitment, or causing insubordination in the armed forces. The act also empowered the postmaster general to exclude from the mails any newspapers or magazines he thought treasonous. Within a year, the mailing rights of forty-five newspapers had been revoked.

To enforce the Espionage Act, the government had to increase its overall police and surveillance machinery. Civilian intelligence was coordinated by the newly created Bureau of Investigation in the Justice Department. This agency was reorganized after the war as the Federal Bureau of Investigation (FBI). In May 1918 the Sedition Act, an amendment to the Espionage Act, outlawed "any disloyal, profane, scurrilous, or abusive language intended to cause contempt, scorn, contumely, or disrepute" to the government, Constitution, or flag.

These acts became a convenient vehicle for striking out at Socialists, pacifists, radical labor activists, and others who resisted the patriotic tide. The most celebrated prosecution came in June 1918 when federal agents arrested Eugene Debs in Canton, Ohio, after he gave a speech defending antiwar protesters. Debs served thirty-two months in federal prison before being pardoned by President Warren G. Harding on Christmas Day, 1921.

The Supreme Court upheld the constitutionality of the acts in several 1919 decisions. In *Debs* v. *United States* the Court affirmed the guilt of Eugene Debs for his antiwar speech in Canton, even though he had not explicitly urged violation of the draft laws. In *Abrams* v. *United States* the Court upheld Sedition Act convictions of four Russian immigrants who had printed pamphlets denouncing American military intervention in the Russian Revolution.

The Great Migration and Racial Tensions

Economic opportunity brought on by war prosperity triggered a massive migration of rural black Southerners to northern cities. From 1914 to 1920 between 300,000 and 500,000 African Americans left the rural South for the North. Chicago's black population increased by 65,000, or 150 percent; Detroit's by 35,000, or 600 percent. Acute labor shortages led northern factory managers to recruit black migrants to the booming industrial centers. The Pennsylvania Railroad alone drew 10,000 black workers from Florida and south Georgia. Black workers eagerly left low-paying jobs as field hands and domestic servants for the chance at high-paying work in meat-packing plants, shipyards, and steel mills.

Kinship and community networks were crucial in shaping what came to be called the Great Migration. They spread news about job openings, urban residential districts, and boardinghouses in northern cities. Black clubs, churches, and fraternal lodges in southern communities often sponsored the migration of their members, as well as return trips to the South. Single African American women often made the trip first because they could more easily obtain steady work as maids, cooks, and laundresses. Few African American men actually secured high-paying skilled jobs in industry or manufacturing. Most had to settle for work as construction laborers, teamsters, janitors, porters, or other lower-paid jobs.

The persistence of lynching and other racial violence in the South no doubt contributed to the Great Migration. But racial violence was not limited to the South. On July 2, 1917, in East St. Louis, Illinois, a ferocious mob of whites attacked African Americans, killing at least 200. Some of the city's manufacturers had been steadily recruiting black labor as a way to keep local union demands down. In Chicago, on July 27, 1919, antiblack rioting broke out on a Lake Michigan beach. For two weeks white gangs hunted African Americans in the streets and burned hundreds out of their homes. Twenty-three African Americans and 15 whites died, and over 500 were injured.

In both East St. Louis and Chicago, local authorities held African Americans responsible for the violence, even though the latter were largely victims, not aggressors. President Wilson refused requests for federal intervention or investigation.

Blacks' disillusionment grew quickly after the war, which they had faithfully supported. A heightened sense of race consciousness and activism was evident among black veterans and the militant growing black communities of northern cities. Taking the lead in the fight against bigotry and injustice, the NAACP held a national conference in 1919 on lynching. It pledged to

OVERVIEW

THE GREAT MIGRATION: BLACK POPULATION GROWTH IN SELECTED NORTHERN CITIES, 1910–1920					
	1910		**1920**		
	No.	**Percent**	**No.**	**Percent**	**Percent Increase**
New York	91,709	1.9%	152,467	2.7%	66.3%
Chicago	44,103	2.0	109,458	4.1	148.2
Philadelphia	84,459	5.5	134,229	7.4	58.9
Detroit	5,741	1.2	40,838	4.1	611.3
St. Louis	43,960	6.4	69,854	9.0	58.9
Cleveland	8,448	1.5	34,451	4.3	307.8
Pittsburgh	25,623	4.8	37,725	6.4	47.2
Cincinnati	19,739	5.4	30,079	7.5	53.2
Indianapolis	21,816	9.3	34,678	11.0	59.0
Newark	9,475	2.7	16,977	4.1	79.2
Kansas City	23,566	9.5	30,719	9.5	30.4
Columbus	12,739	7.0	22,181	9.4	74.1
Gary	383	2.3	5,299	9.6	1,283.6
Youngstown	1,936	2.4	6,662	5.0	244.1
Buffalo	1,773	.4	4,511	.9	154.4
Toledo	1,877	1.1	5,691	2.3	203.2
Akron	657	1.0	5,580	2.7	749.3

Source: U.S. Department of Commerce.

defend persecuted African Americans, publicize the horrors of lynch law, and seek federal legislation against "Judge Lynch." By 1919 membership in the NAACP had reached 60,000 and the circulation of its journal, *Crisis*, exceeded half a million.

Labor Strife

The relative labor peace of 1917 and 1918 dissolved after the armistice. Most of the modest wartime wage gains were wiped out by spiraling inflation and high prices for food, fuel, and housing. With the end of government controls on industry, many employers withdrew their recognition of unions. Difficult working conditions were still routine in some industries, such as the twelve-hour day in steel mills. The quick return of demobilized servicemen to the labor force meant layoffs and new concerns about job security.

Several postwar strikes received widespread national attention. They seemed to be more than simply economic conflicts, and they provoked deep fears about the larger social order. In February 1919 a strike in the shipyards in Seattle, Washington, over

wages escalated into a general citywide strike involving 60,000 workers. A strike committee coordinated the city's essential services for a week in a disciplined, nonviolent fashion. But the local press and the mayor denounced the strikers as revolutionaries, and the strike was ended by federal troops.

In September Boston policemen went out on strike when the police commissioner rejected a citizens' commission study that recommended a pay raise. Massachusetts governor Calvin Coolidge called in the National Guard to restore order and won a national reputation by crushing the strike. The entire police force was fired.

From September 1919 to January 1920 some 350,000 steelworkers went on strike. The major demands were union recognition, the eight-hour day, and wage increases. The steel companies used black strikebreakers and armed guards to keep the mills running. Elbert Gary, president of U.S. Steel, tied the strikers to revolutionaries. Public opinion turned against the strike and condoned the widespread use of state and federal troops. A violent riot in Gary, Indiana, left eighteen strikers dead. The failed steel strike

The General Strike Committee of Seattle distributed groceries to union families in February 1919. The Seattle General Strike had been triggered when shipyard workers walked off the job after failing to gain wage hikes to offset spiraling postwar inflation. The conservative Los Angeles Times *saw the strike as evidence that Bolshevism was a "right-here now American menace."*

proved to be the era's most bitter and devastating defeat for organized labor.

AN UNEASY PEACE

The Fourteen Points

President Wilson arrived in Paris to take part in the peace conference in January 1919. He brought with him a plan for peace that he had outlined a year earlier in a speech to Congress on U.S. war aims. The Fourteen Points, as they were called, had originally served wartime purposes: to appeal to wartime opponents in Austria–Hungary and Germany, to convince Russia to stay in the war, and to help sustain Allied morale. As a blueprint for peace, they contained three main elements. First, Wilson offered a series of specific proposals for setting postwar boundaries in Europe and creating new countries out of the collapsed Austro–Hungarian and Ottoman empires. Second, Wilson listed general principles for governing international conduct, including freedom of the seas, free trade, open covenants instead of secret treaties, reduced armaments, and mediation for competing colonial claims. Third, and most important, Wilson

called for a League of Nations to help implement these principles and resolve future disputes.

The most controversial element, both at home and abroad, would prove to be the League, whose covenant called for collective security as the ultimate method of keeping the peace. In the United States, Wilson's critics focused on this provision of the covenant as an unacceptable surrender of the nation's sovereignty and independence in foreign affairs.

Wilson in Paris

Despite Wilson's devotion to "open covenants," much of the negotiating at Versailles was done in secret among the Big Four: Great Britain, France, the United States, and Italy. (Italy had defected from the Central Powers to the Allies in 1915.) Wilson was unable to win support for most of his broad principles, such as freedom of the seas, free trade, and open covenants. The ideal of self-determination found limited expression. The independent states of Austria, Hungary, Poland, Yugoslavia, and Czechoslovakia were carved out of the homelands of the beaten Central Powers. But the Allies resisted Wilson's call for independence for the colonies of the defeated nations. A compromise mandate system of protectorates gave the French and British control of parts of the old German and Turkish empires in Africa and the Middle East. Japan won control of former German colonies in China. Among those trying, but failing, to influence the treaty negotiations were the sixty-odd delegates to the first Pan-African Congress, held in Paris at the same time as the peace talks.

Another disappointment for Wilson came with the issue of war guilt. He strongly opposed the extraction of harsh economic reparations from the Central Powers. But the French and British, with their awful war losses fresh in mind, insisted on making Germany pay. Bitter resentment in Germany over the punitive treaty helped sow the seeds for the Nazi rise to power in the 1930s.

Hovering over the proceedings was the specter of the Russian Revolution. The repressive and corrupt regime of Czar Nicholas II had been overthrown in March 1917 by a coalition of forces demanding change. The new provisional government, headed by Alexander Kerensky, vowed to keep Russia in the fight against Germany. But the war had taken a terrible toll on Russian soldiers and civilians, and had become very unpopular. The radical Bolsheviks, led by V. I. Lenin, gained a large following by promising "peace, land, and bread," and they began plotting to seize power. The Bolsheviks followed the teachings of German revolutionary Karl Marx, emphasizing the inevitability of class struggle and the replacement of capitalism by communism. In November 1917 the Bolsheviks took control of the Russian government.

The final treaty was signed on June 28, 1919, in the Hall of Mirrors at the Versailles palace. The Germans had no choice but to accept its harsh terms. President Wilson had been disappointed by the secret deals and the endless compromising of his ideals, no doubt underestimating the stubborn reality of power politics in the wake of Europe's most devastating war. He had nonetheless won a commitment to the League of Nations, the centerpiece of his plan, and he was confident that the American people would accept the treaty. The tougher fight would be with the Senate, where a two-thirds vote was needed for ratification.

The Treaty Fight

Preoccupied with peace conference politics in Paris, Wilson had neglected politics at home. His troubles had actually started earlier. Republicans had captured both the House and the Senate in the 1918 elections. Wilson had then made the tactical error of including no prominent Republicans in the U.S. peace delegation. He therefore faced a variety of tough opponents to the treaty he brought home.

His most extreme enemies in the Senate were a group of about sixteen "irreconcilables," opposed to a treaty in any form. Some were isolationist progressives, who opposed the League as steadfastly as they had opposed American entry into the war. Others were racist xenophobes.

The less dogmatic but more influential opponents were led by Republican Henry Cabot Lodge of Massachusetts, powerful majority leader of the Senate. They had strong reservations about the League of Nations, especially the provisions for collective security in the event of a member nation being attacked. Lodge argued that this provision impinged on congressional authority to declare war and placed unacceptable restraints on the nation's ability to pursue an independent foreign policy. Lodge proposed a series of amendments that would have weakened the League. But Wilson refused to compromise, motivated in part by the long-standing hatred he and Lodge felt toward each other. The president decided instead to take his case directly to the American people.

In September Wilson set out on a speaking tour across the country to drum up support for the League and the treaty. The crowds were large and responsive, but the strain of the fight took its toll. On September 25, after speaking in Pueblo, Colorado, the sixty-three-year-old Wilson collapsed from exhaustion. His doctor canceled the rest of the trip. A week later, back in Washington, the president suffered a stroke that left him partially paralyzed. In November Lodge brought the treaty out of committee for a vote, having appended to it fourteen reservations, or recommended changes. A bedridden Wilson stubbornly refused to compromise and instructed Democrats to vote against the Lodge version of the treaty. On November 19, Democrats joined with the "irreconcilables" to defeat the amended treaty, fifty-five to thirty-nine.

Wilson refused to budge. In January he urged Democrats to either stand by the original treaty or vote it down. The 1920 election, he warned, would be "a great and solemn referendum" on the whole issue. In the final vote, on March 19, 1920, twenty-one Democrats broke with the president and voted for the Lodge version, giving it a majority of forty-nine to thirty-five. But this was seven votes short of the two-thirds needed for ratification. As a result, the United States never signed the Versailles treaty, nor did it join the League of Nations. The absence of the United States weakened the League and made it more difficult for the organization to realize Wilson's dream of a peaceful community of nations.

The Red Scare

The revolutionary changes taking place in Russia became an important backdrop for domestic politics. In the United States it became common to blame socialism, the IWW, and trade unionism in general on foreign radicals and alien ideologies. The accusation of Bolshevism became a powerful weapon for turning public opinion against strikers and political dissenters of all kinds.

In truth, by 1919 the American radical Left was already weakened and badly split by factions. The Socialist Party had around 40,000 members. Two small Communist Parties, made up largely of immigrants, had a total of perhaps 70,000. In June 1919 simultaneous bombings in eight cities killed two people and damaged the residence of Attorney General A. Mitchell Palmer. With public alarm growing, state and federal officials began a coordinated campaign to root out subversives and their alleged Russian connections.

The 1918 Alien Act enabled the government to deport any immigrant found to be a member of a revolutionary organization before or after coming to the United States. In a series of raids in late 1919, Justice Department agents in eleven cities arrested and roughed up several hundred members of the IWW and the Union of Russian Workers. Little evidence of revolutionary intent was found, but 249 people were deported, including prominent anarchists Emma Goldman and Alexander Berkman. In early 1920 some 6,000 people in thirty-three cities, including many U.S. citizens and noncommunists, were arrested and herded into prisons and bullpens. Again, no evidence of a grand plot was found, but another 600 aliens were deported. The Palmer raids had a ripple effect around the nation, encouraging other repressive measures against radicals.

A report prepared by a group of distinguished lawyers, including Felix Frankfurter and Zechariah Chafee, questioned the legality of the attorney general's tactics. Palmer's popularity had waned by the spring of 1920, when it became clear that his predictions of revolutionary uprisings were wildly exaggerated. But the Red Scare left an ugly legacy: wholesale violations of constitutional rights, deportations of hundreds of innocent people, fuel for the fires of nativism and intolerance. Business groups, such as the National Association of Manufacturers, found "redbaiting" to be an effective tool in postwar efforts to keep unions out of their factories. Indeed, the government-sanctioned Red Scare was to return as a key element in the century's politics.

The Election of 1920

Woodrow Wilson had wanted the 1920 election to be a referendum on the League of Nations and his conduct of the war. Ill and exhausted, Wilson did not run for reelection. A badly divided Democratic party compromised on Governor James M. Cox of Ohio as their candidate. A proven vote-getter, Cox distanced himself from Wilson's policies, which had come under attack from many quarters.

The Republicans nominated Senator Warren G. Harding of Ohio. A political hack, the handsome and genial Harding had virtually no qualifications to be president, except that he looked like one. Harding's campaign was vague and ambiguous about the Versailles treaty and almost everything else. "America's present need," he said, "is not heroics but healing; not nostrums but normalcy; not revolution but restoration."

The notion of a "return to normalcy" proved very attractive to voters exhausted by the war, inflation, big government, and social dislocation. Harding won the greatest landslide in history to that date, carrying every state outside the South and taking the popular vote by 16 million to 9 million. Republicans retained their majorities in the House and Senate as well. Socialist Eugene Debs, still a powerful symbol of the dream of radical social change, managed to poll 900,000 votes from jail. But the overall vote repudiated Wilson and the progressive movement. Americans seemed eager to pull back from moralism in public and international controversies. Yet many of the underlying economic, social, and cultural changes wrought by the war would accelerate during the 1920s. In truth, there would never be a "return to normalcy."

CONCLUSION

Compared to the casualties and social upheavals endured by the European powers, World War I's impact on American life might appear slight. Yet the war helped reshape American life long after Armistice Day. Republican administrations invoked the wartime partnership between government and industry to justify an aggressive peacetime policy fostering cooperation between the state and business. Wartime production needs contributed to what economists later called "the second industrial revolution." Patriotic fervor and the exaggerated specter of Bolshevism could be used to repress radicalism, organized labor, feminism, and the entire legacy of progressive reform. The wartime measure of national prohibition evolved into perhaps the most contentious social issue of peacetime. Sophisticated use of sales techniques, psychology, and propaganda during the war helped define the newly powerful advertising and public relations industries of the 1920s. The growing visibility of immigrants and African Americans, especially in the nation's cities, provoked a xenophobic and racist backlash in the politics of the 1920s. The desire for "normalcy" reflected the deep anxieties evoked by America's wartime experience.

CHRONOLOGY

1903 United States obtains canal rights in Panama

1904 Roosevelt Corollary to the Monroe Doctrine justifies U.S. intervention in Central and South America

1905 President Theodore Roosevelt mediates peace treaty between Japan and Russia at Portsmouth Conference

1908 Root–Takahira Agreement with Japan affirms status quo in Asia and Open Door policy in China

1911 Mexican Revolution begins

1914 U.S. forces invade Mexico

Panama Canal opens

World War I begins in Europe

President Woodrow Wilson issues proclamation of neutrality

1915 Germany declares war zone around Great Britain

German U-boat sinks *Lusitania*

1916 Pancho Villa raids New Mexico and is pursued by General John J. Pershing

Wilson is reelected

National Defense Act establishes preparedness program

1917 February: Germany declares new policy of unrestricted submarine warfare

March: Zimmermann note, suggesting an alliance between Germany and Mexico, shocks Americans

April: United States declares war on the Central Powers

Committee on Public Information established

May: Selective Service Act passed

June: Espionage Act passed

July: Race riot in East St. Louis, Illinois

War Industries Board established

August: Food Administration and Fuel Administration established

November: Bolshevik Revolution begins in Russia

1918 January: Wilson unveils Fourteen Points

April: National War Labor Board established

May: Sedition Act passed

June: Eugene Debs arrested for defending antiwar protesters

U.S. troops begin to see action in France

U.S. troops serve in Russia

November: Armistice ends war

1919 January: Eighteenth Amendment (Prohibition) ratified

Wilson serves as Chief U.S. negotiator at Paris Peace Conference

June: Versailles Treaty signed in Paris

July: Race riot breaks out in Chicago

Steel strike begins in several midwestern cities

September: Wilson suffers stroke while touring country in support of Versailles Treaty

November: Henry Cabot Lodge's version of the Versailles Treaty is rejected by the Senate

Palmer raids begin

1920 March: Senate finally votes down Versailles Treaty and League of Nations

August: Nineteenth Amendment (woman suffrage) ratified

November: Warren G. Harding is elected president

REVIEW QUESTIONS

1. What central issues drew the United States deeper into international politics in the early years of the century? How did American presidents justify a more expansive role? What diplomatic and military policies did they exploit for these ends?

2. Compare the arguments for and against American participation in the Great War. Which Americans were most likely to support entry? Which were more likely to oppose it?

3. How did mobilizing for war change the economy and its relationship to government? Which of these changes, if any, spilled over to the postwar years?

4. How did the war affect political life in the United States? What techniques were used to stifle dissent? What was the war's political legacy?

5. To what extent was the war an extension of progressivism?

6. Analyze the impact of the war on American workers. How did the conflict affect the lives of African Americans and women?

7. What principles guided Woodrow Wilson's Fourteen Points? How would you explain the United States' failure to ratify the Treaty of Versailles?

RECOMMENDED READING

Robert H. Ferrell, *Woodrow Wilson and World War I* (1985). A close analysis of Wilson's handling of wartime diplomacy and domestic politics.

Martin Gilbert, *The First World War: A Complete History* (1994). An ambitious overview of World War I from a global perspective.

Maureen Greenwald, *Women, War, and Work* (1980). The best account of the impact of the war on working women.

David M. Kennedy, *Over Here* (1980). The best, most comprehensive one-volume history of the political and economic impact of the war on the domestic front.

Thomas J. Knock, *To End All Wars: Woodrow Wilson and the Quest for a New World Order* (1992). A fine analysis of Wilson's internationalism, its links to his domestic policies, and his design for the League of Nations.

Walter LaFeber, *The American Age* (1989). A comprehensive survey of the history of U.S. foreign policy that includes an analysis of the pre–World War I era.

Paul L. Murphy, *World War I and the Origin of Civil Liberties* (1979). A good overview of the various civil liberties issues raised by the war and government efforts to suppress dissent.

Ronald Schaffer, *America in the Great War: The Rise of the War Welfare State* (1991). Excellent material on how the war transformed the relationship between business and government and spurred improved conditions for industrial workers.

Joe William Trotter Jr., ed., *The Great Migration in Historical Perspective* (1991). An excellent collection of essays examining the Great Migration, with special attention to issues of class and gender within the African American community.

Neil A. Wynn, *From Progressivism to Prosperity: World War I and American Society* (1986). An illuminating account of the social impact of the war on American life. Effectively connects the war experience both with progressive era trends and with postwar developments in the 1920s.

CHAPTER TWENTY-THREE

THE TWENTIES

1920–1929

AMERICAN COMMUNITIES
The Movie Audience and Hollywood: Mass Culture Creates a New National Community

Inside midtown Manhattan's magnificent new Roxy Theater, a sellout crowd eagerly settled in for opening night. Outside, thousands of fans cheered at the arrival of movie stars such as Charlie Chaplin, Gloria Swanson, and Harold Lloyd. The audience marveled at the huge gold-and-rose-colored murals, classical statuary, plush carpeting, and Gothic-style windows. It was easy to believe newspaper reports that the theater had cost $10 million to build. Suddenly, a flood of illumination lit up a pit orchestra of 110 musicians playing "The Star Spangled Banner." An array of 100 dancers then took the stage, performing ballet numbers and singing old southern melodies. Congratulatory telegrams from President Calvin Coolidge and other dignitaries were projected onto a screen. Finally, the evening's feature presentation, *The Love of Sunya*, starring Gloria Swanson, began.

The movie palaces of the 1920s were designed to transport patrons to exotic places and different times. Every large community boasted at least one opulent movie theater. Houston's Majestic was built to represent an ancient Italian garden; it had a ceiling made to look like an open sky, complete with stars and cloud formations. The Tivoli in Chicago featured opulent French Renaissance decor, Grauman's Egyptian in Los Angeles re-created the look of a pharaoh's tomb, and Albuquerque's Kimo drew inspiration from Navaho art and religion.

The remarkable popularity of motion pictures, and later radio, forged a new kind of community. The same entertainment could be enjoyed virtually anywhere in the country by just about everyone. Movies emerged as the most popular form of entertainment in the new mass culture, and the appeal extended far beyond the films themselves, or even the theaters. Americans embraced the cult of celebrity, consuming fan magazines, gossip columns, and news of the stars. By the 1920s, the production center for this dream world was Hollywood, California, a suburb of Los Angeles that had barely existed in 1890.

Motion picture companies found Hollywood an alluring alternative to the East Coast cities where they had been born. The reliably sunny and dry climate was ideal for the year-round shooting of film. The unique physical environment offered a perfect variety of scenic locations—mountains, desert, ocean—and downtown Los Angeles was only an hour away. Los Angeles was the leading nonunion, open shop city in the country, and lower labor costs also provided a powerful incentive to relocate. By the early 1920s Hollywood was producing over 80 percent of the nation's motion pictures, and the myth of this new community was already emerging. The physical isolation of the town, its great distance from the eastern cities, the absence of traditional sources of culture and learning, all contributed to movie folk looking at life in a self-consciously "Hollywood" way.

Hollywood attracted a young, cosmopolitan group of people lured by an ideal of urban mobility and a new way of life. Most of the top studio executives were Jewish immigrants from eastern and central Europe. More than half of the writers, directors, editors, and actors in Hollywood were born in large cities of over 100,000, at a time when most Americans hailed from rural areas or small towns. Two-thirds of the performers were under thirty-five, and three-fourths of the actresses were under twenty-five. More than 90 percent of the writers had either higher education or journalism experience. Women made up one-third to one-half of this key group.

In the 1920s Hollywood achieved a mythic power in American life. Film stars became popular idols as much for their highly publicized private lives as for their work lives. Movie folk built luxurious mansions in a variety of architectural styles and outfitted them with swimming pools, tennis courts, golf courses, and lavish gardens. The lines between movie roles and private lives blurred in the public eye.

Ordinary Americans found it easy to identify with movie stars, many of whom had achieved enormous wealth and status. Unlike traditionally powerful people, such as industrialists or politicians, movie stars had no social authority over large groups of employees or voters. They too had to answer to a boss, and most had risen from humble beginnings. But above all, Hollywood, like the movies it churned out, represented for millions of Americans new possibilities: freedom, material success, upward mobility, and the chance to remake one's very identity. Only a few Americans actually realized these during the 1920s. But by the end of the decade the Hollywood dream factory had helped forge a national community whose collective aspirations and desires were increasingly defined by those possibilities.

Hollywood

Key Topics

- A second industrial revolution transforms the economy

- The promise and limits of prosperity in the 1920s

- New mass media and the culture of consumption

- Republican Party dominance

- Political and cultural opposition to modern trends

THE PRICE OF PROSPERITY

The Second Industrial Revolution

The prosperity of the 1920s rested on what historians have called the "second industrial revolution" in American manufacturing, in which technological innovations led the way to increasing industrial output without expansion of the labor force. Electricity replaced steam as the main power source for industry in these years. The spread of electricity enabled companies to use machinery that was far more efficient and flexible than steam- or water-powered equipment.

Much of the newer, automatic machinery could be operated by unskilled and semiskilled workers, and that boosted the overall efficiency of American industry. Thus, in 1929 the average worker in manufacturing produced roughly three-quarters more per hour than he or she had in 1919. The machine industry itself employed more workers than any other manufacturing sector—some 1.1 million in 1929—and not only satisfied a growing home market but also provided 35 percent of the world's export of machinery.

During the late nineteenth century heavy industries such as machine tools, railroads, iron, and steel had pioneered mass-production techniques. These were what economists call "producer-durable goods." In the 1920s modern mass-production techniques were increasingly applied as well to newer "consumer-durable goods" such as automobiles, radios, washing machines, and telephones. With more efficient management, greater mechanization, intensive product research, and ingenious sales and advertising methods, the consumer-based industries helped to nearly double industrial production in the 1920s.

The Modern Corporation

In the late nineteenth century individual entrepreneurs such as John D. Rockefeller in oil and Andrew Carnegie in steel had provided a model for success. They maintained both corporate control (ownership) and business leadership (management) in their enterprises. In the 1920s a managerial revolution increasingly divorced ownership of corporate stock from the everyday control of businesses. The new corporate ideal was to be found in men such as Alfred P. Sloan of General Motors and Owen D. Young of the Radio Corporation of America. These executives made their reputations as bureaucratic managers who coordinated production and sales, concentrated on long-range planning, and emphasized scientific research and development.

During the 1920s the most successful corporations were those that led the way in three key areas: the thorough integration of production and distribution; diversification of products; and the expansion of industrial research. For example, through World War I the Du Pont Company was a chemical manufacturer that had long specialized in explosives such as gunpowder. After the war Du Pont aggressively diversified its production, branching out to manufacture a variety of consumer goods. Similarly, the great electrical manufacturers—General Electric and Westinghouse—which had previously concentrated on manufacturing lighting and power equipment, now diversified into household appliances such as radios, washing machines, and refrigerators. The chemical and electrical industries also led the way in industrial research, hiring personnel to develop new products and test their commercial viability.

By 1929 the 200 largest corporations owned nearly half the nation's corporate wealth—that is, physical plant, stock, and property. Half the total industrial income was concentrated in 100 corporations. Oligopolies, where a few large producers controlled the market for a product, became the norm. Four companies packed almost three-quarters of all American meat. Another four rolled nine out of every ten cigarettes. Grocery, clothing, and drugstore national chains began squeezing out local neighborhood businesses. One grocery chain alone, the Great Atlantic and Pacific Tea Company (A&P), accounted for 10 percent of all retail food sales in America.

A growing class of salaried executives, plant managers, and engineers formed a new elite who made corporate policy without owning the business. They stressed scientific management and adapted the latest theories of behavioral psychology in their effort to make their workplaces more productive, stable, and profitable.

Welfare Capitalism

The wartime gains made by organized labor and the sympathy shown to trade unions by the government war boards troubled most corporate leaders. Large employers aggressively promoted a variety of new programs designed to improve worker well-being and morale and thereby challenge the power and appeal of trade unions and collective bargaining. These schemes, collectively known as "welfare capitalism," became a key part of corporate strategy in the 1920s.

One approach encouraged workers to acquire property through stock-purchasing plans or, less often, home ownership plans. Other programs offered workers insurance policies covering accidents, illness, old age, and death. Many plant managers and personnel departments consciously worked to improve safety conditions, provide more medical services, and establish sports and recreation programs for workers. But welfare capitalism could not solve the most chronic problems faced by industrial workers: seasonal unemployment, low wages, long hours, and unhealthy factory conditions.

Large corporations also mounted an effective antiunion campaign in the early 1920s called "the American plan," a tactic to associate unionism with foreign and un-American ideas. Backed by powerful business lobbies such as the National Association of Manufacturers and the Chamber of Commerce, campaign leaders called for the open shop, in which no employee would be compelled to join a union. If a union existed, nonmembers would still get whatever wages and rights the union had won—a policy that put organizers at a disadvantage in signing up new members.

The open shop undercut the gains won in a union shop, where new employees had to join an existing union, or a closed shop, where employers agreed to hire only union members. As alternatives, large employers such as U.S. Steel and International Harvester began setting up company unions. Here largely symbolic employee representation in management conferences was meant to substitute for collective bargaining.

These management strategies contributed to a sharp decline in the ranks of organized labor. Total union membership dropped from about 5 million in 1920 to 3.5 million in 1926. A large proportion of the remaining union members were concentrated in the skilled crafts of the building and printing trades. A conservative and timid union leadership was also responsible for the trend. The federal government, which had provided limited wartime support for unions, now reverted to a more probusiness posture.

The Supreme Court in particular was very unsympathetic toward unions, consistently upholding the use of injunctions to prevent strikes, picketing, and other union activities.

The Auto Age

No single development could match the automobile explosion of the postwar years for changing how Americans worked, lived, and played. The auto industry offered the clearest example of the rise to prominence of consumer durables. During the 1920s America made approximately 85 percent of all the world's passenger cars. By 1929 motor vehicle producers were the most productive industry in the United States in terms of value, producing some 4.8 million cars that year.

This extraordinary new industry had mushroomed in less than a generation. Its great pioneer, Henry Ford, had shown how the use of a continuous assembly line could drastically reduce the number of worker-hours required to produce a single vehicle. In 1914, at his sprawling new Highland Park assembly plant just outside Detroit, Ford's system finished one car every ninety minutes. By 1925, cars were rolling off his assembly line at the rate of one every ten seconds.

In 1914 Ford startled American industry by inaugurating a new wage scale: five dollars for an eight-hour day. This was roughly double the going pay rate for industrial labor, and a shorter workday as well. But in defying the conventional economic wisdom of the day, Ford acted less out of benevolence than out of shrewdness. He understood that workers were consumers as well as producers, and the new wage scale helped boost sales of Ford cars. It also reduced the high turnover rate in his labor force and increased worker efficiency. Ford's mass production system and economies of scale meant he could progressively reduce the price of the automobile, bringing it within the reach of millions of Americans. The famous Model T, thoroughly standardized and available only in black, cost just under $300 in 1924—about three months' wages for the best-paid factory workers.

The auto industry provided a large market for makers of steel, rubber, glass, and petroleum products. It stimulated public spending for good roads and extended the housing boom to new suburbs. Showrooms, repair shops, and gas stations appeared in thousands of communities. New small enterprises, from motels to billboard advertising to roadside diners, sprang up as motorists took to the highway. The rapid development of Florida and California, in particular, was partly a response to the growing influence of the automobile.

Automobiles widened the experiences of millions of Americans. They made the exploration of the world outside one's local community easier and more attractive than ever. Leisure became a more regular part of everyday life. Young people took advantage of the car to gain privacy and distance from their parents, and for many the car became the site of their first sexual experiences.

Exceptions: Agriculture, Ailing Industries

Amid prosperity and progress, there were large pockets of the country that lagged behind. Advances in real income and improvements in the standard of living for workers and farmers were uneven at best. During the 1920s one-quarter of all American workers were employed in agriculture, yet the farm sector failed to share in the general prosperity. The years 1914–19 had been a golden age for the nation's farmers. But with the war's end American farmers began to suffer from a chronic worldwide surplus of agricultural commodities.

Prices began to drop sharply in 1920. Cotton, which sold at 37 cents a pound in mid-1920, fell to 14 cents by year's end. By 1921 net farm income was down more than half from the year before. Land values also dropped, wiping out billions in capital investment. Behind these aggregate statistics were hundreds of thousands of individual human tragedies on the nation's 6 million farms.

Large sectors of American industry also failed to share in the decade's prosperity. As oil and natural gas gained in importance, America's coal mines became a less important source of energy. Economic hardship was widespread in many mining communities dependent on coal, particularly in Appalachia and the southern Midwest. Miners who did work earned lower hourly wages.

The number of miles of railroad track actually began to decrease after 1920 as automobiles and trucks began to displace trains. In textiles, the women's fashions of the 1920s generally required less material for dresses, and competition from synthetic fibers such as rayon depressed demand for cotton textiles. To improve profit margins, textile manufacturers in New England and other parts of the Northeast began a long-range shift of operations to the South, where nonunion shops and substandard wages became the rule. Older New England manufacturing centers, such as Lawrence, Lowell, Nashua, Manchester, and Fall River, were hard hit by this shift. Southern mills increased their work force from 220,000 to 257,000 between 1923 and 1933. By 1933 they employed nearly 70 percent of the workers in the industry. Southern mills generally operated night and day, used the newest labor-saving machinery, and cut back on the wage gains of the World War I years.

THE NEW MASS CULTURE

Advertising Modernity

A thriving advertising industry both reflected and encouraged the growing importance of consumer goods in American life. Earlier efforts at advertising products had been confined mostly to staid newspaper and magazine spreads that offered basic information about products. The successful efforts of the government's Committee on Public Information, set up to "sell" World War I to Americans, suggested that new techniques using modern communication media could convince people to buy a wide range of goods and services. As a profession, advertising reached a higher level of respectability, sophistication, and economic power in American life during the 1920s.

Advertisers began focusing on the needs, desires, and anxieties of the consumer rather than on the qualities of the product. Ad agencies and their clients invested extraordinary amounts of time, energy, and money trying to discover and, to some extent, shape people's beliefs. One of the more spectacular examples of advertising effectiveness involved an old product, Listerine, which had been marketed as a general antiseptic for years by Lambert Pharmaceuticals. A new ad campaign touting Listerine as a cure for halitosis—a scientific-sounding term for bad breath— boosted Lambert's profits from $100,000 in 1922 to over $4 million in 1927.

Until 1924 Henry Ford had disdained national advertising for his cars. But as General Motors gained a competitive edge by making yearly changes in style and technology, Ford was forced to pay more attention to advertising. This ad was directed at "Mrs. Consumer," combining appeals to both female independence and motherly duties.

Above all, advertising celebrated consumption itself as a positive good. In this sense the new advertising ethic was a therapeutic one, promising that products would contribute to the buyer's physical, psychic, or emotional well-being. Well-financed ad campaigns were especially crucial for marketing newer consumer goods such as cars, electrical appliances, and personal hygiene products. Total advertising volume in all media—newspapers, magazines, radio, billboards—jumped from $1.4 billion in 1919 to $3 billion in 1929.

Radio Broadcasting

In the fall of 1920 Westinghouse executive Harry P. Davis noticed that amateur broadcasts from the garage of an employee had attracted attention in the local Pittsburgh press. A department store advertised radio sets capable of picking up these "wireless concerts." Davis converted this amateur station to a stronger one at the Westinghouse main plant. Beginning with the presidential election returns that November, station KDKA offered regular nightly broadcasts that were probably heard by only a few hundred people. Radio broadcasting, begun as a service for selling cheap radio sets left over from World War I, would soon sweep the nation.

Before KDKA, wireless technology had been of interest only to the military, the telephone industry, and a few thousand "ham" (amateur) operators who enjoyed communicating with each other. By 1923 nearly 600 stations had been licensed by the Department of Commerce and about 600,000 Americans had bought radios. Most of the early stations were owned by radio equipment manufacturers, newspapers, department stores, and universities. Early programs included live popular music, phonograph records, talks by college professors, church services, and news and weather reports. For millions of Americans, especially in rural areas and small towns, radio provided a new and exciting link to the larger national community of consumption.

Who would pay for radio programs? By the end of the decade commercial (or "toll") broadcasting emerged as the answer. The dominant corporations in the industry—General Electric, Westinghouse, RCA, and AT&T—settled on the idea that advertisers would foot the bill for radio. Sponsors advertised directly or indirectly to the mass audience through such shows as the *Eveready Hour*, the *Ipana Troubadors*, and the *Taystee Loafers*.

Radio broadcasting created a national community of listeners, just as motion pictures created one of viewers. NBC and CBS led the way in creating popular radio programs that relied heavily on older cultural forms. Variety shows, hosted by vaudeville comedians, became the first important style of network radio. Radio's first truly national hit, *The Amos 'n' Andy Show* (1928), was a direct descendant of nineteenth-century blackface minstrel entertainment. Radio did more than any previous medium to publicize and commercialize previously isolated forms of American music, such as country-and-western, blues, and jazz. Broadcasts of baseball and college football games proved especially popular; millions of fans closely followed the exploits of new heroes such as Babe Ruth.

Movie-Made America

The early movie industry, centered in New York and a few other big cities, had made moviegoing a regular habit for millions of Americans, especially immigrants and the working class. They flocked to cheap storefront theaters, called "nickelodeons," to watch short Westerns, slapstick comedies, melodramas, and travelogues. With the shift of the industry westward to Hollywood, movies entered a new phase of business expansion.

Large studios such as Paramount, Fox, MGM, Universal, and Warner Brothers dominated the business with longer and more expensively produced movies: feature films. These companies were founded and controlled by immigrants from Europe. Adolph Zukor, the Hungarian-born head of Paramount, had been a furrier in New York City. Samuel Goldwyn, a founder of MGM, had been a glove salesman. William Fox, of Fox Pictures, began as a garment cutter in Brooklyn. Most of the immigrant moguls had started in the business by buying or managing small movie theaters and then entering the production phase.

Each studio combined the three functions of production, distribution, and exhibition, and each controlled hundreds of movie theaters around the country. With *The Jazz Singer* in 1927, starring Al Jolson, Hollywood added sound to its movies. Musicals, gangster films, and screwball comedies soon became popular. The higher costs associated with "talkies" also increased the studios' reliance on Wall Street investors and banks for working capital.

At the heart of Hollywood's success was the star system and the accompanying cult of celebrity. Stars such as Charlie Chaplin, Mary Pickford, Douglas Fairbanks, Rudolph Valentino, and Greta Garbo became vital to the fantasy lives of millions. For many fans, there was only a vague line separating the on-screen and off-screen adventures of the stars. Studio publicity, fan magazines, and gossip columns reinforced this ambiguity. Young Americans in particular looked to movies to learn how to dress, wear their hair, talk, and kiss.

A New Morality?

Movie stars, radio personalities, sports heroes, and popular musicians became the elite figures in a new culture of celebrity defined by the mass media. They were the ultimate consumers and the model for achievement in the new age. Great events and abstract issues were made real through movie close-ups, radio interviews, and tabloid photos.

One of the most enduring images of the Roaring Twenties is the flapper. She was usually portrayed on screen, in novels, and in the press as a young, sexually aggressive woman with bobbed hair, rouged cheeks, and short skirt. She loved to dance to jazz music, enjoyed smoking cigarettes, and drank bootleg liquor in cabarets and dance halls. She could also be competitive, assertive, and a good pal.

Was the flapper a genuine representative of the 1920s? Did she embody the "new morality" that was so widely discussed and chronicled in the media of the day? Historians have discovered that the flapper certainly did exist, but she was neither as new nor as widespread a phenomenon as the image would suggest. The delight in sensuality, individual pleasure, and rhythmically complex dance and music had long been key elements of subcultures on the fringes of middle-class society. In the 1920s these activities became normative for a growing number of white middle-class Americans, including women. Jazz, sexual experimentation, heavy use of makeup, and cigarette smoking spread to college campuses.

Several sources, most of them rooted in earlier years, can be found for the more open and widespread treatment of sexuality in the 1920s. The writings of Havelock Ellis, Ellen Key, and Sigmund Freud stressed the central role of sexuality in human experience, arguing that sex was a positive, healthy impulse and repression could be damaging to mental and emotional health. The pioneering efforts of Margaret Sanger in educating women about birth control had begun before World War I (see Chapter 21).

Advertisers routinely used sex appeal to sell products. Tabloid newspapers exploited sex with "cheesecake" photos, but they also provided features giving advice on sex hygiene and sexually transmitted disease. And movies, of course, featured powerful sex symbols such as Rudolph Valentino, Gloria Swanson, John Gilbert, and Clara Bow. Movies also taught young people the etiquette of sex. This was clear in many motion picture diaries kept by young people, part of the movie research conducted by social scientists. One typical eighteen-year-old college student wrote, "These passionate pictures stir such longings, desires, and urges as I never expected any person to possess. Just the way the passionate lover held his sweetheart suggests so many beautiful and intimate relations, which even my reenacting a scene does not satisfy any more."

Sociological surveys also suggested that genuine changes in sexual behavior occurred, beginning in the prewar years, for both married and single women. Katherine Bement Davis's pioneering study of 2,200 middle-class women, carried out in 1918 and published in 1929, revealed that most used contraceptives and described sexual relations in positive terms. Women born after the turn of the century were more than twice as likely to have experienced premarital sex as those born before 1900. The critical change took place in the generation that came of age in the late teens and early 1920s. By the 1920s, male and female sexual norms were becoming more alike.

THE STATE AND BUSINESS
Harding and Coolidge

Handsome, genial, and well-spoken, Warren Harding looked the part of a president. He was a product of small-town Marion, Ohio, and the machine politics in his native state. Republican party officials kept Senator Harding, a compromise choice, as removed from the public eye as possible in the 1920 election. They saw that active campaigning could only hurt their candidate by exposing his shallowness and intellectual weakness. Harding sadly told one visitor to the White House shortly after taking office, "I knew that this job would be too much for me."

Harding surrounded himself with a close circle of friends, "the Ohio gang," delegating to them a great deal of administrative power. The president often conducted business as if he were in the relaxed, convivial, and masculine confines of a small-town saloon.

Soon after Harding's death in 1923, a series of congressional investigations revealed a deep pattern of corruption in the Harding administration. Attorney General Harry M. Daugherty had received bribes from violators of the Prohibition statutes. He had also failed to investigate graft in the Veterans Bureau, where Charles R. Forbes had pocketed a large chunk of the $250 million spent on hospitals and supplies. The worst affair was the Teapot Dome scandal, involving Interior Secretary Albert Fall. Fall received hundreds of thousands of dollars in payoffs when he secretly leased navy oil reserves in Teapot Dome, Wyoming, and Elk Hills, California, to two private oil developers. He became the first Cabinet officer ever to go to jail.

The Harding administration's legacy was not all scandal. Andrew Mellon, an influential Pittsburgh banker, served as secretary of the Treasury under all three Republican presidents of the 1920s. Mellon believed government ought to run on the same conservative principles as a corporation. His tax program cut taxes for both higher-income brackets and businesses. By 1926 a person earning $1 million a year paid less than a third of the income tax paid in 1921. Overall, Mellon's policies succeeded in rolling back much of the progressive taxation associated with Woodrow Wilson.

When Calvin Coolidge succeeded to the presidency in 1923, he seemed to most people the

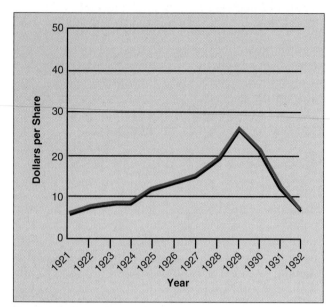

Stock Market Prices, 1921–1932 *Common stock prices rose steeply during the 1920s. Although only about 4 million Americans owned stocks during the period, "stock watching" became something of a national sport.*

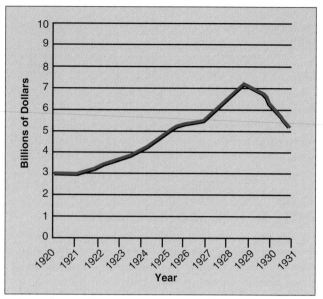

Consumer Debt, 1920–1931 *The expansion of consumer borrowing was a key component of the era's prosperity. These figures do not include mortgages or money borrowed to purchase stocks. They reveal the great increase in "installment buying" for such consumer durable goods as automobiles and household appliances.*

temperamental opposite of Harding. Born and raised in rural Vermont, elected governor of Massachusetts, and coming to national prominence only through the 1919 Boston police strike, "Silent Cal" was the quintessential New England Yankee. Taciturn, genteel, and completely honest, Coolidge believed in the least amount of government possible. He spent only four hours a day at the office. He was in awe of wealthy men such as Andrew Mellon, and he thought them best suited to make society's key decisions.

Coolidge easily won election on his own in 1924. He benefited from the general prosperity and the contrast he provided with the disgraced Harding. Coolidge defeated little-known Democrat John W. Davis.

In his full term, Coolidge showed most interest in reducing federal spending, lowering taxes, and blocking congressional initiatives. His saw his primary function as clearing the way for American businessmen. After all, they were the agents of the era's unprecedented prosperity.

Herbert Hoover and the "Associative State"

The most influential figure of the new era was Herbert Hoover, who as secretary of commerce dominated the cabinets of Harding and Coolidge before becoming president himself in 1928. As an administrator, intellectual, and politician, Hoover effectively embodied the belief that enlightened business, encouraged and informed by the government, would act in the public interest. In the modern industrial age, Hoover believed, the government needed only to advise private groups about what national or international policies to pursue.

Unlike an earlier generation of Republicans, Hoover wanted not just to create a favorable climate for business but to actively assist the business community. He spoke of creating an "associative state," in which the government would encourage voluntary cooperation among businesses and social groups. This became the central occupation of the Department of Commerce under Hoover's leadership. Under Hoover, the Bureau of Standards became one of the nation's leading research centers. It was especially involved with setting engineering standards for key American industries such as machine tools and automobiles. The bureau also helped standardize the styles, sizes, and designs of many consumer products, such as canned goods and refrigerators.

Hoover actively encouraged the creation and expansion of national trade associations. By 1929 there were about 2,000 of them. To some this practice violated the spirit of antitrust laws, but in the 1920s the Justice Department's Anti-Trust Division took a very lax view of its responsibility. In addition, the Supreme Court consistently upheld the legality of trade associations. Hoover also influenced presidential appointments to regulatory commissions; most of these went to men who had worked for the very firms the commissions had been designed to supervise. Regulatory commissions thus benefited from the technical expertise brought by industry leaders, but they in turn tended to remain uncritical of the industries they oversaw.

The government thus provided an ideal climate for the concentration of corporate wealth and power. The trend toward large corporate trusts and holding companies had been well under way since the late nineteenth century, but it accelerated in the 1920s. By 1929 the 200 largest American corporations owned almost half the total corporate wealth and about a fifth of the total national wealth.

Commerce and Foreign Policy

Throughout the 1920s, Republican leaders pursued policies designed to expand American economic activity around the world. The focus was on friendly nations and investments that would help foreign citizens to buy American goods. Toward this end Republican leaders urged close cooperation between bankers and government as a strategy for expanding American investment and economic influence abroad. For Hoover and other policy makers, American business abroad was simply rugged individualism at work around the globe.

American oil, autos, farm machinery, and electrical equipment supplied a growing world market. Much of this expansion took place through the establishment of branch plants overseas by American companies. America's overall direct investment abroad increased from $3.8 billion in 1919 to $7.5 billion by 1929.

The strategy of maximum freedom for private enterprise, backed by limited government advice and assistance, significantly boosted the power and profit levels of American overseas investors. But in Central and Latin America, in particular, aggressive U.S. investment also fostered chronically underdeveloped economies, dependent on a few staple crops (sugar, coffee, cocoa, bananas) grown for export. U.S. economic dominance in the hemisphere also hampered the growth of democratic politics by favoring autocratic, military regimes that could be counted upon to protect U.S. investments.

RESISTANCE TO MODERNITY

Prohibition

The Eighteenth Amendment, banning the manufacture and sale of alcoholic beverages, took effect in January 1920. Prohibition was the culmination of a long campaign that associated drinking with the degradation of working-class family life and the worst evils of urban politics. Supporters, a coalition of women's temperance groups, middle-class progressives, and rural Protestants, hailed the new law as "a noble experiment." But it became clear rather quickly that enforcing the new law would be extremely difficult. The

Volstead Act of 1919 established a federal Prohibition Bureau to enforce the Eighteenth Amendment. The bureau was severely understaffed, with only about 1,500 agents to police the entire country.

The public demand for alcohol, especially in the big cities, led to widespread lawbreaking. Illegal stills and breweries, as well as liquor imported from Canada, supplied the needs of Americans who continued to drink. Nearly every town and city had at least one speakeasy, where people could drink and be entertained. Local law enforcement personnel, especially in the cities, were easily bribed to overlook these illegal establishments. By the early 1920s many eastern states no longer made even a token effort at enforcing the law.

Prohibition gave an enormous boost to violent organized crime. The pattern of organized crime in the 1920s closely resembled the larger trends in American business: smaller operations gave way to more complex and carefully organized combinations. Successful organized crime figures, such as Chicago's Al "Scarface" Capone, became celebrities in their own right and received heavy coverage in the mass media.

Organized crime, based on its huge profits from liquor, also made significant inroads into legitimate businesses, labor unions, and city government. By the time Congress and the states ratified the Twenty-first Amendment in 1933, repealing Prohibition, organized crime was a permanent feature of American life.

Immigration Restriction

Sentiment for restricting immigration, growing since the late nineteenth century, reached its peak immediately after World War I. Anti-immigrant feeling reflected major shifts in both the size and makeup of the immigrant stream. The "new immigrants" were mostly Catholic and Jewish, and were darker-skinned than the "old immigrants." To many Americans they seemed more exotic, more foreign, and less willing and able to assimilate the nation's political and cultural values. They were also poorer, more physically isolated, and less politically strong than earlier immigrants. In the 1890s the anti-Catholic American Protective Association called for a curb on immigration, and by exploiting the economic depression of that decade, it reached a membership of 2.5 million. In 1894 a group of prominent Harvard graduates, including Henry Cabot Lodge and John Fiske, founded the Immigration Restriction League, providing an influential forum for the fears of the nation's elite. The league used newer arguments, based on Darwinism and genetics, to support its call for immigration restrictions.

Theories of scientific racism had become more popular in the early 1900s, and they reinforced anti-immigrant bias. Eugenicists, who enjoyed a large vogue in these years, held that heredity determined almost all of a person's capacities, and that genetic inferiority

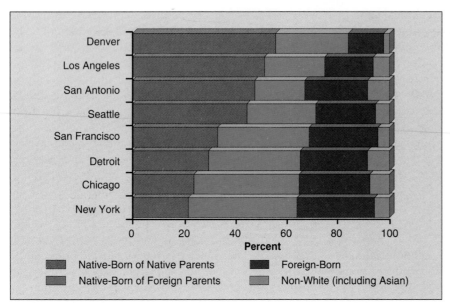

Population Composition of Selected Cities, 1920 *By 1920 the demographic impact of several decades of heavy immigration was especially evident in the nation's cities. The combined population of the foreign-born and those born of foreign parents often surpassed that of the native-born of native parents.*

predisposed people to crime and poverty. Such pseudo-scientific thinking sought to explain historical and social development solely as a function of racial differences.

Against this background, the war and its aftermath provided the final push for immigration restriction. The postwar depression coincided with the resumption of massive immigration, bringing much hostile comment on the relationship between rising unemployment and the new influx of foreigners. Sensational press coverage of organized crime figures, many of them Italian or Jewish, also played a part.

In 1921 Congress passed the Immigration Act, setting a maximum of 357,000 new immigrants each year. Restrictionists complained that the new law still allowed too many southern and eastern Europeans in. The Johnson–Reed Immigration Act of 1924 set quotas limiting annual immigration from any European country to 2 percent of its natives counted in the U.S. census for 1890, when few southern or eastern Europeans were present in the United States. The maximum total allowed each year was also halved, to 164,000. The quota laws did not apply to Canada, Mexico, or any other nation in the western hemisphere. The immigration restriction laws reversed earlier practices and became a permanent feature of national policy.

The Ku Klux Klan

If immigration restriction was resurgent nativism's most significant legislative expression, a revived Ku Klux Klan was its most effective mass movement. The original Klan had died out in the 1870s. The new

Klan, born in Stone Mountain, Georgia, in 1915, was inspired by D. W. Griffith's racist spectacle *The Birth of a Nation*, a film that depicted the original KKK as a heroic organization. The new Klan patterned itself on the secret rituals and antiblack hostility of its predecessor.

When Hiram W. Evans, a racist dentist from Dallas, became imperial wizard in 1922, he hired professional fundraisers and publicists and directed an effective recruiting scheme that paid a commission to sponsors of new members. The Klan advocated "100 percent Americanism" and "the faithful maintenance of White Supremacy." It staunchly supported Prohibition and patriotism and attacked birth control and Darwinism.

By 1924 the new Klan counted over 3 million members across the country. Its slogan, "Native, White, Protestant Supremacy," proved especially attractive in the Midwest and South. Klansmen boycotted businesses, threatened families, and sometimes resorted to violence (public whippings, arson, and lynching) against its chosen enemies.

The Klan had a strong presence among delegates to the 1924 Democratic National Convention. It began to fade in 1925 when its Indiana leader, Grand Dragon David C. Stephenson, became involved in a sordid personal affair. Stephenson had picked up a young secretary at a party, got her drunk on bootleg liquor, and then assaulted her on a train. After the woman took poison and died, Stephenson was convicted of manslaughter. With one of its most famous leaders disgraced and in jail, the new Klan began to lose members and influence.

PROMISES POSTPONED

Feminism in Transition

The achievement of the suffrage removed the central issue that had given cohesion to the disparate forces of female reform activism. In addition, female activists of all persuasions found themselves swimming against a national tide of hostility to political idealism. During the 1920s the women's movement split into two main wings over a fundamental disagreement about female identity. Should activists stress women's differences from men—their vulnerability and the double burden of work and family—and continue to press for protective legislation? Or should they emphasize the ways that women were like men—sharing similar aspirations—and push for full legal and civil equality?

In 1920 the National American Woman Suffrage Association reorganized itself as the League of Women Voters. The League represented those who believed that the vote for women would bring a nurturing sensibility and a reform vision to American politics. Most League members continued working in a variety of reform organizations, and the League itself concentrated on educating the new female electorate, encouraging women to run for office, and supporting laws for the protection of women and children.

A newer, smaller, and more militant group was the National Woman's Party, founded in 1916 by suffragist Alice Paul. The NWP argued that women were still subordinate to men. It opposed protective legislation for women, claiming that such laws reinforced sex stereotyping and prevented women from competing with men in many fields. Largely representing the interests of professional and business women, the NWP focused on passage of a brief Equal Rights Amendment to the Constitution, introduced to Congress in 1923: "Men and women shall have equal rights throughout the United States and every place subject to its jurisdiction."

Many of the older generation of women reformers opposed the ERA as an elitist idea, arguing that far more women benefited from the protective laws it would outlaw than were injured by them. ERA supporters countered that maximum hours laws and laws prohibiting women from night work prevented women from getting many lucrative jobs. But most women's groups opposed the ERA. These included the League of Women Voters, the National Consumers League, and the Women's Trade Union League. ERA supporters stressed individualism, competition, and the abstract language of equality and rights. They dreamed of a labor market that might be—one where women would have the widest opportunity. Anti-ERA forces looked at the labor market that was and insisted that it was more important to protect women from existing exploitation. The NWP campaign failed to get the ERA passed by Congress, but the debates it sparked would be echoed during the feminist movement of the 1970s.

During the 1920s a small number of professional women made real gains in the fields of real estate, banking, and journalism. The press regularly announced new "firsts" for women, such as Amelia Earhart's 1928 airplane flight across the Atlantic. As business expanded, a greater percentage of working women were employed in white-collar positions, as opposed to manufacturing and domestic service. But men still dominated in the higher-paid and managerial white-collar occupations.

Mexican Immigration

The 1920s brought a dramatic influx of Mexicans to the United States. (Mexico was not included in the immigration laws of 1921 and 1924.) The outbreak of the Mexican Revolution in 1911 caused political instability and economic hardships and provided incentives to cross the border to *El Norte*. According to the U.S. Immigration Service, an estimated 459,000 Mexicans entered the United States between 1921 and 1930. Yet many Mexicans shunned the main border crossings and thus avoided paying the $8 head tax and $10 visa fee.

The primary pull was the tremendous agricultural expansion occurring in the American Southwest. Irrigation and large-scale agribusiness had begun transforming California's Imperial and San Joaquin valleys from arid desert into lucrative fruit and vegetable fields. Cotton pickers were needed in the vast plantations of the Lower Rio Grande Valley in Texas and the Salt River Valley in Arizona. The sugar beet fields of Michigan, Minnesota, and Colorado also attracted large numbers of Mexican farm workers. Moreover, American industry had begun recruiting Mexican workers, first to fill wartime needs and later to stop the gap left by the decline in European immigration.

The new Mexican immigration appeared more permanent than previous waves—that is, more and more newcomers stayed. By 1930 San Antonio's Mexican community accounted for roughly 70,000 people

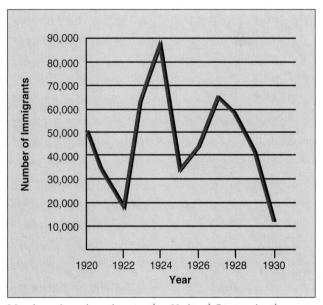

Mexican Immigration to the United States in the 1920s *Many Mexican migrants avoided official border crossing stations so they would not have to pay visa fees. Thus these official figures probably underestimated the true size of the decade's Mexican migration. As the economy contracted with the onset of the Great Depression, immigration from Mexico dropped sharply.*

out of a total population of a quarter million. Around 100,000 Mexicans lived in Los Angeles. Substantial Mexican communities also flourished in midwestern cities. Many of the immigrants alternated between agricultural and factory jobs, depending on seasonal availability of work. Mexican women often worked in the fields with their husbands. They also toiled as domestics and seamstresses, or took in laundry and boarders.

Racism and local patterns of residential segregation confined most Mexicans to barrios. Housing conditions were generally poor, particularly for recent arrivals, who lived in rude shacks without running water or electricity. Disease and infant mortality rates were much higher than average, and most Mexicans worked at low-paying, unskilled jobs and received inadequate health care. Legal restrictions passed by states and cities made it difficult for Mexicans to enter teaching, legal, and other professions. Mexicans were routinely banned from local public works projects as well. Many felt a deep ambivalence about applying for American citizenship. Loyalty to the old country was strong, and many cherished dreams of returning to live out their days in Mexico.

Ugly racist campaigns against Mexicans were common in the 1920s, especially when "cheap Mexican labor" was blamed for local unemployment or hard times. Stereotypes of Mexicans as "greasers" or "wetbacks" were prevalent in newspapers and movies of the day. Nativist efforts to limit Mexican immigration were thwarted by the lobbying of powerful agribusiness interests.

The *mutualistas*, mutual aid societies in Mexican communities of the Southwest and Midwest that provided death benefits and widow's pensions for members, also served as centers of resistance to civil rights violations and discrimination. In 1928, the Federation of Mexican Workers Unions formed in response to a large farm labor strike in the Imperial Valley. Meanwhile, a group of middle-class Mexican professionals in Texas organized the League of United Latin American Citizens. These organizations marked the beginnings of a long struggle to bring economic, social, and racial equality to Mexican Americans.

The "New Negro"

The Great Migration spurred by World War I showed no signs of letting up during the 1920s, and African American communities in northern cities grew rapidly.

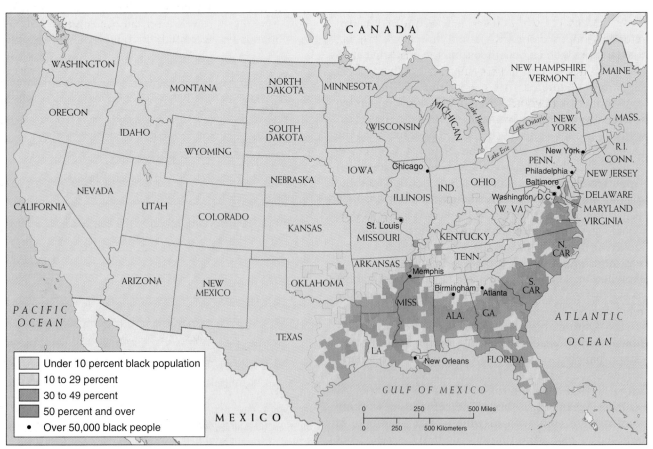

Black Population, 1920 *Although the Great Migration had drawn hundreds of thousands of African Americans to the urban north, the southern states of the former Confederacy still remained the center of the African American population in 1920.*

New York City's Harlem, the demographic and cultural capital of black America, began attracting middle-class African Americans in the prewar years. After the war, heavy migration from the South and the Carribbean encouraged real estate speculators and landlords to remake Harlem as an exclusively black neighborhood.

The demand for housing in this restricted geographic area led to skyrocketing rents. Most Harlemites held low-wage jobs. This combination led to extremely overcrowded apartments, unsanitary conditions, and the rapid deterioration of housing stock. Disease and death rates were abnormally high. Yet Harlem also boasted a large middle-class population and supported a wide array of churches, theaters, newspapers and journals, and black-owned businesses. It became a magnet for African American intellectuals, artists, musicians, and writers from all over the world.

Harlem became the political and intellectual center for what writer Alain Locke called the "New Negro." Locke was referring to a new spirit in the work of black writers and intellectuals, an optimistic faith that African Americans should develop and celebrate their distinctive culture. This was the common denominator uniting the disparate figures associated with the Harlem Renaissance. The assertion of cultural independence resonated in the poetry of Langston Hughes and Claude McKay, the novels of Zora Neale Hurston and Jessie Fauset, the essays of Countee Cullen and James Weldon Johnson, the acting of Paul Robeson, and the blues singing of Bessie Smith.

The newly militant spirit that black veterans had brought home from World War I matured and found a variety of expression in the Harlem of the 1920s. New leaders and movements began to appear alongside established organizations such as the NAACP. A. Philip Randolph began a long career as a labor leader, socialist, and civil rights activist in these years. Harlem was also headquarters to Marcus Garvey's Universal Negro Improvement Association. Garvey created a mass movement that stressed black economic self-determination, pride, and unity among the black communities of the United States, the Caribbean, and Africa. His newspaper, *Negro World*, spoke to black communities around the world, urging black businesses to trade among themselves.

Garvey's best-publicized project was the Black Star Line, a black-owned and -operated fleet of ships that would link people of African descent around the world. But insufficient capital and serious financial mismanagement resulted in the failure of the enterprise. In 1923 Garvey was found guilty of mail fraud in his fundraising efforts; he went to jail and was subsequently deported to England.

Harlem in the 1920s also became a popular tourist attraction for "slumming" whites. Nightclubs such as the Cotton Club were often controlled by white organized-crime figures. They featured bootleg liquor, floor shows, and the best jazz bands of the day, led by Duke Ellington, Fletcher Henderson, Cab Calloway, and Louis Armstrong. Black dancers, singers, and musicians provided the entertainment, yet no African Americans were allowed in the audience. Chronicled in novels and newspapers, Harlem became a potent symbol to white America of the ultimate good time. For the vast majority of Harlem residents, the day-to-day reality was depressingly different.

The Election of 1928

The 1928 campaign featured two politicians who represented profoundly different sides of American life. Al Smith, the Democratic nominee for president, was a pure product of New York City's Lower East Side. Smith came from a background that included Irish, German, and Italian ancestry, and he was raised as a Roman Catholic. He rose through the political ranks of New York's Tammany Hall machine. A personable man with a deep sympathy for poor and working-class people, Smith served four terms as governor of New York, pushing through an array of laws reforming factory conditions, housing, and welfare programs.

Herbert Hoover easily won the Republican nomination after Calvin Coolidge announced that he would not run for reelection. Hoover epitomized the successful and forward-looking American. An engineer

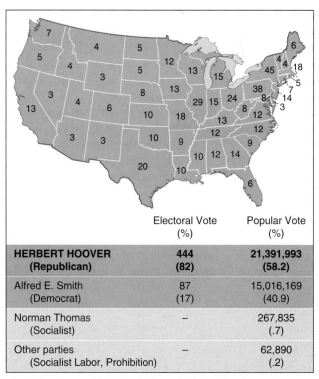

	Electoral Vote (%)	Popular Vote (%)
HERBERT HOOVER (Republican)	**444** **(82)**	**21,391,993** **(58.2)**
Alfred E. Smith (Democrat)	87 (17)	15,016,169 (40.9)
Norman Thomas (Socialist)	–	267,835 (.7)
Other parties (Socialist Labor, Prohibition)	–	62,890 (.2)

The Election of 1928   *Although Al Smith managed to carry the nation's twelve largest cities, Herbert Hoover's victory in 1928 was one of the largest popular and electoral landslides in the nation's history.*

CHRONOLOGY

1920	Prohibition takes effect
	Warren G. Harding elected president
	Station KDKA in Pittsburgh goes on the air
	Census reports that urban population is greater than rural population for first time
1921	First immigration quotas established by Congress
	Sheppard–Towner Act establishes first federally funded health care program
1922	Washington conference produces Five-Power Treaty, scaling down navies
1923	Equal Rights Amendment first introduced in Congress
	Harding dies in office; Calvin Coolidge becomes president
1924	Ku Klux Klan is at height of its influence
	Dawes Plan for war reparations stabilizes European economies
	Johnson–Reed Immigration Act tightens quotas established in 1921
1925	Scopes trial pits religious fundamentalism against modernity
	F. Scott Fitzgerald publishes *The Great Gatsby*
1926	National Broadcasting Company establishes first national radio network
1927	McNary–Haugen Farm Relief bill finally passed by Congress but is vetoed by President Coolidge as unwarranted federal interference in the economy
	Warner Brothers produces *The Jazz Singer,* the first feature-length motion picture with sound
	Charles Lindbergh makes first solo flight across the Atlantic Ocean
1928	Kellogg–Briand Pact renounces war
	Herbert Hoover defeats Al Smith for the presidency
1929	Robert and Helen Lynd publish their classic community study, *Middletown*

and self-made millionaire, he offered a unique combination of experience in humanitarian war relief, administrative efficiency, and probusiness policies. Hoover was one of the best-known men in America, and he promised to continue the Republican control of national politics.

Smith himself quickly became the central issue of the campaign. His sharp New York accent marked him clearly as a man of the city. So did his brown derby and fashionable suits, as well as his promise to work for the repeal of Prohibition. As the first Roman Catholic nominee of a major party, Smith also drew a torrent of anti-Catholic bigotry, especially in the South and Midwest.

Hoover polled 21 million votes to Smith's 15 million and swept the electoral college 444 to 87, including New York State. The incumbent majority party would not lose during prosperous times. Even the Solid South, reliably Democratic since the Civil War, gave five states to Hoover—a clear reflection of the ethnocultural split in the party. Yet the election offered important clues to the future of the Democrats. Smith ran better in the big cities of the North and East than any Democrat in modern times.

CONCLUSION

The presidential election of 1928 served as a national referendum on the Republican "new age." It also revealed just how important ethnic and cultural differences had become in defining American politics. The contest reflected many of the tensions and conflicts that marked American society in the 1920s: native-born versus immigrant, Protestant versus Catholic, Prohibition versus legal drinking, small-town life versus the cosmopolitan city, traditional sources of culture versus the new mass media. Al Smith, quintessential voice of the city, failed to win the presidency. But even in defeat, he embodied the growing political and cultural strength of urban America.

REVIEW QUESTIONS

1. Describe the impact of the "second industrial revolution" on American business, workers, and consumers. Which technological and economic changes had the biggest impact on American society?
2. Analyze the uneven distribution of the decade's economic prosperity. Which Americans gained the most, and which were largely left out?
3. How did an expanding mass culture change the contours of everyday life in the decade following World War I? What role did new technologies of mass communication play in shaping these changes? What connections can you draw between the culture of consumption, then and today?
4. What were the key policies and goals articulated by Republican political leaders of the 1920s? How did they apply these to domestic and foreign affairs?
5. How did some Americans resist the rapid changes taking place in the post–World War I world? What cultural and political strategies did they use?
6. Discuss the 1928 election as a mirror of the divisions in American society.

RECOMMENDED READING

John Braemer et al., eds., *Change and Continuity in Twentieth Century America: The 1920s* (1968). A wide-ranging collection of essays on the period, with especially good studies of the resistance to modernity.

Nancy F. Cott, *The Grounding of American Feminism* (1987). Includes a sophisticated analysis of the debates among feminists during the 1920s.

Lynn Dumenil, *The Modern Temper: America in the 1920s* (1995). Contains important new material on previously neglected social movements and minority groups.

James J. Flink, *The Car Culture* (1975). The best single volume on the history of the automobile and how it changed American life.

Ellis W. Hawley, *The Great War and the Search for Modern Order* (1979). An influential study of the relations between the state and business and the growth of mass consumer society.

Nancy Maclean, *Behind the Mask of Chivalry: The Making of the Second Ku Klux Klan* (1994). A fine case study of the KKK in Athens, Georgia, with important insights on the Klan's relationship to issues involving gender and class difference.

Roland Marchand, *Advertising the American Dream: Making Way for Modernity, 1920–1940* (1985). A superb, beautifully illustrated account of the rise of the modern advertising industry.

Geoffrey Perrett, *America in the Twenties* (1982). A useful overview of the decade with very good anecdotal material.

Emily S. Rosenberg, *Spreading the American Dream* (1982). A fine study of American economic and cultural expansion around the world from 1890 to 1945.

Susan Smulyan, *Selling Radio: The Commercialization of American Broadcasting, 1920–1934* (1994). The best analysis of the rise of commercial radio broadcasting in the 1920s.

The Changing Face of Ethnicity in America

1860 – 1930

Annual immigration to the United States, which had declined during the late 1850s from a peak of more than 400,000 in 1854, dropped sharply at the onset of the Civil War. But even before the war ended, the pace of immigration revived. From the late nineteenth century until World War I, as America's unprecedented industrial expansion created an unprecedented demand for labor, the rate of immigration increased dramatically, surpassing 1,000,000 in 1905. At the same time, the ethnic background of the immigrants changed, creating a corresponding change in the nation's ethnic landscape.

Before the Civil War most immigrants came from Ireland and Germany. After the war immigrants from Germany and northwestern Europe continued at first to predominate, but by 1896 they had been overtaken by the so-called "New Immigrants" from the countries of southern and eastern Europe. Immigration from Latin America and many Asian countries, although far lower than that from Europe, also increased. Immigration from China, however, slowed considerably after the passage of the Chinese Exclusion Act of 1882.

Overall, between 1860 and 1920 about 28.2 million people immigrated to the United States, and by 1920 these immigrants and their children represented more than one-third of the nation's population. The vast majority of New Immigrants sought better lives for themselves and their families. Driven by economic dislocation, political turmoil, and overpopulation at home, millions of people left their villages for opportunity in distant lands, including Canada, Argentina, Brazil, Australia, and New Zealand as well as the United States. Italians were the largest group among the New Immigrants: between 1880 and 1930 nearly 5 million came to the United States. Of them, 80 percent were peasants from southern Italy left landless by an agricultural depression.

Religious and ethnic persecution combined with economic hardship to drive the Jews of Russia, Poland, and other eastern European countries to emigrate. Laws in Russia dictated where Jews could live and restricted their opportunities for employment and education. Beginning in 1881, the Russian government encouraged violent attacks known as *pogroms* on Jewish communities. These hardships made the United States appear a beacon of salvation. As a result, the Jewish population of the United States grew from 250,000 in 1877 to more than 4 million in 1927.

Most New Immigrants settled in the nation's urban manufacturing centers, not on farms. Generally poorly educated and lacking industrial skills, they entered the bottom ranks in factories, mines, mills, slaughterhouses, and garment shops. Employers benefited from their numbers to reorganize the workplace and reduce their reliance on highly paid skilled workers. Jews, however, were an exception to this pattern. Many had come from cities and were skilled in craft work and business. Nearly 77 percent of immigrant Jewish men qualified for skilled work in such specialized trades as cigar manufacturing, printing, carpentry, and garment manufacturing. Japanese immigrants—more than 111,000 by 1920—likewise fared well. They had a literacy rate of 99 percent and were able to translate the agricultural experience they brought from Japan to establish themselves as successful farmers of market garden crops in California, where the majority settled.

Most New Immigrants were unmarried young men, and many did not intend to settle permanently in the United States. They hoped instead to earn enough money to return home and buy land or set up a small business. Italian immigrants, nearly 80 percent of them male, and Greek immigrants, more than 90 percent male, had the highest rate of remigration—almost 50 percent. Jews, facing persecution at home, were the least likely to return home. Only 5 percent remigrated. Instead, they saved their wages to bring other family members to the United States. As a result, Jews were the most evenly distributed by sex of the New Immigrants. Only among the Irish did women form the majority of newcomers.

Whether they planned to remigrate or stay, the New Immigrants quickly established distinctive communities, mainly in the nation's large cities or along the West Coast. In 1920 three-quarters of the foreign-born lived in cities. The vast majority of Italians, for example, entered through the port of New York, and nearly one-quarter of them settled nearby. By 1920, 400,000 Italian immigrants were living in sizable communities in Manhattan, Brooklyn, the Bronx, Queens, and Staten Island. In Chicago, one-third of all Italians lived in a single neighborhood on the city's West Side. Across the continent in Califor-

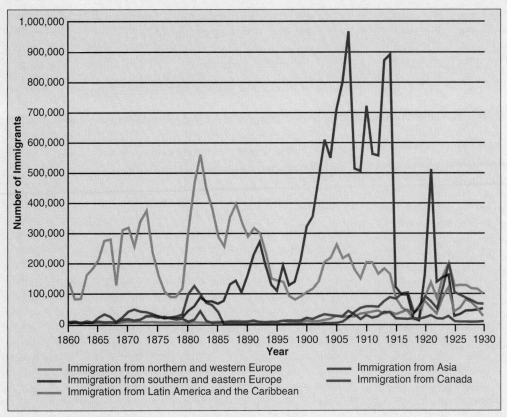

Annual Immigration to the United States, 1860–1930

nia, where Italians represented the single largest immigrant group, they gave North Beach in San Francisco a special ethnic flavor.

In many cities the New Immigrants became the numerical majority and dominated political and social institutions. By 1910 in Passaic, New Jersey, for example, 52 percent of the population was foreign-born, most from Russia, Austria-Hungary, or Italy; 32 percent was second-generation (the children of foreign-born); and only 14 percent native-born whites. The immigrant population reshaped Passaic's political landscape, eventually forcing a sweeping reorganization of city government.

Although all New Immigrants tended to concentrate in neighborhoods near the factories or the steel mills where they worked, Italians were the most likely to cluster in so-called ethnic ghettos. Here, in "Little Italy," they spoke their native language, ate familiar foods, and helped their compatriots find jobs and housing. As immigrant communities grew, they sought to recreate Old World cultural patterns through schools, businesses, mutual-aid societies, and fraternal orders. Religious institutions—church and temple—provided the most important link to cultural traditions. Foreign-language newspapers—Germans and Jews produced the largest number—likewise helped forge community solidarity.

Although most old-stock Americans welcomed immigrant labor, many feared the "alien" cultural values and mores of the immigrants themselves. Before the Civil War, nativist, or anti-immigrant, sentiment was directed primarily against Catholics; shortly after the war, its focus was the Chinese. As the new immigration gathered steam in the 1880s, nativist sentiment increasingly turned against *all* immigrants. The nativist reaction to the new immigration found justification in certain intellectual currents of the late nineteenth century. So-called "scientific racism" purported to demonstrate that some racial groups were inherently superior to others, with western Europeans, especially Anglo-Saxons, inevitably ranked at the top, Africans at the bottom, and southern and eastern Europeans not much above them. Social Darwinism similarly claimed to justify social ranking with evolutionary theory.

Until the late nineteenth century, the federal government did little to regulate immigration and instead allowed state governments to set their own policies. But a turning point was reached with the Immigration Act of 1882, which gave the federal government the right to regulate immigration in cooperation with the states. The act laid the foundation for the kind of selective immigration based on race or ethnicity that the Chinese Exclusion Act, also passed in 1882, put into practice. The Immigration Act of 1891 gave the federal government the exclusive power to regulate immigration. The following year, in 1892, the newly centralized immigration reception center opened on Ellis Island.

In 1896, in the midst of a severe economic depression, a bipartisan majority in Congress passed a law requiring all immigrants to pass a literacy test, but it was vetoed by President McKinley. Subsequent efforts to enact such a law met a similar fate until 1917, when fear that the nation would face a wave of immigrants fleeing Europe at the end of World War I generated enough support for Congress to override President Wilson's veto and enact the Immigration Act of 1917. This landmark legislation implemented a literacy test and created an "Asiatic Barred Zone" to deny admission to people from India, Burma, Siam, Afghanistan, Arabia, the Malay Islands, and Polynesia. Foreshadowing the Red Scare that followed World War I, it also tightened restrictions on radicals to exclude members of anarchist and revolutionary organizations.

The era of open-door immigration came to a decisive end in the 1920s. Bills were introduced in Congress to suspend immigration altogether, but legislators compromised on a quota plan based on national origins, which was incorporated into the emergency restriction law passed in 1921. After a series of modifications and heated debates, Congress enacted a law on May 26, 1924, limiting immigration of specific groups to 2 percent of the number recorded by the 1890 census. The consequences were dramatic. European immigration dropped from more than 800,000 in 1921 to less than 150,000 by 1929. In that year, Congress passed the National Origins Act that put the quota system in place on a permanent basis, which, along with the Great Depression, reduced immigration to the United States in the 1930s to the lowest level since 1820.

■ IN THEIR OWN WORDS

In 1910 the U.S. Immigration Commission opened the Angel Island detention center, off the coast of San Francisco, for the few Chinese who were allowed to enter the United States following a loosening of the Exclusion Act of 1882. Modeled after Ellis island, the point of entry for most European immigrants, Angel Island housed new arrivals until U.S. immigration inspectors determined whether they were eligible to settle in the United States. The experience made a lasting, often unpleasant impression on the nearly 175,000 Chinese who were detained there before 1940, when the center shut down. In the following passage, a woman immigrant recalls her detention at Angel Island in 1913 when she was nineteen years old.

There was not much for us to do on the island. In the morning we got up and washed our faces. Afterwards, we had breakfast. After we ate, we napped or washed our own clothes. At lunch time we had congee in a large serving bowl with some cookies. Then at night we had rice with a main dish. You picked at some of it . . . and that was that. We ate in a huge dining hall. . . . They allowed us to go outside to the yard or even out to the dock, where there were grass and trees, tall and fan-like. The women were allowed to wander around, jump around, and stick our hands or feet into the water to fish out seaweed. Otherwise, the day would have been hard to pass. . . .

I was interrogated one day for several hours. They asked me so much, I broke out in a sweat. Sometimes they would try to trip you: "Your husband said such-and-such and now you say this?" But the answer was out already and it was too late to take it back, so I couldn't do anything about it. If they said you were wrong, then it was up to them whether to land you or not. Later, upon landing, I noticed a white man kept coming around to my husband's laundry and looking at me through the glass window. That was how they checked you out to make sure you didn't go elsewhere.[1]

Rose Schneiderman (1882–1972), who became a prominent trade union organizer, emigrated from Russia with her family. In this account, published in a popular magazine, *The Independent*, in 1905, she recounts with pride the ups and downs of her family's fortunes and her response to the burdens that fell upon her.

My name is Rose Schneiderman, and I was born in some small city of Russian Poland. I don't know the name of the city, and have no memory of that part of my childhood. When I was about five years of age my parents brought me to this country and we settled in New York.

So my earliest recollections are of living in a crowded street among the East Side Jews, for we also are Jews.

My father got work as a tailor, and we lived in two rooms on Eldridge Street, and did very well,

Italian immigrants, ca. 1900, on Ellis Island, the main receiving station for nearly three-fourths of all the immigrants from its opening in 1892 until its closing in 1954. Italians were the largest group among the new immigrants.

though not so well as in Russia, because mother and father both earned money, and here father alone earned the money, while mother attended to the house. There were then two other children besides me, a boy of three and one of five.

I went to school until I was nine years old, enjoying it thoroughly and making great progress, but then my father died of brain fever and mother was left with three children and another one coming. So I had to stay at home to help her and she went out to look for work. . . .

I was the house worker, preparing the meals and looking after the other children—the baby, a little girl of six years, and a boy of nine. I managed very well, tho the meals were not very elaborate. I could cook simple things like porridge, coffee and eggs, and mother used to prepare the meat before she went away in the morning, so that all I had to do was to put it in the pan at night. . . .

I was finally released by my little sister being taken by an aunt, and the two boys going to the Hebrew Orphan Asylum, which is a splendid institution, and turns out good men. One of these brothers is now a student in the City College, and the other is a page in the Stock Exchange.

When the other children were sent away mother was able to send me back to school, and I stayed in this school (Houston Street Grammar) till I had reached the Sixth Grammar Grade.

Then I had to leave in order to help support the family. I got a place in Hearn's as a cash girl, and after working there three weeks changed to Ridley's, where I remained for two and a half years. I finally left because the pay was so very poor and there did not seem to be any chance of advancement, and a friend told me that I could do better making caps.[2]

Questions

1. Identify the major groups known as the "New Immigrants."
2. Why did the New Immigrants leave their homelands, and why did they choose to settle in particular regions of the United States?
3. What were the major changes in immigration law during 1860–1930 period?
4. How did old-stock Americans greet the New Immigrants?

Sources

1. Him Mark Lai, Genny Lim, and Judy Yung, eds., *Island: Poetry and History of Chinese Immigrants on Angel Island, 1910–1940* (Seattle: University of Washington Press, 1980), 72, 117
2. Rose Schneiderman, "A Cap Maker's Story," *The Independent*, 58 (April 27, 1905), pp. 935–936

CHAPTER TWENTY-FOUR

THE GREAT DEPRESSION AND THE NEW DEAL

1929–1940

AMERICAN COMMUNITIES
Sit-Down Strike at Flint: Automobile Workers Organize a New Union

In the gloomy evening of February 11, 1937, 400 tired, unshaven, but very happy strikers marched out of the sprawling automobile factory known as Fisher Body Number 1. Most carried American flags and small bundles of clothing. A makeshift banner on top of the plant announced "Victory is Ours." A wildly cheering parade line of a thousand supporters greeted the strikers at the gates. Shouting with joy, honking horns, and singing songs, the celebrants marched to two other factories to greet other emerging strikers. After forty-four days, the great Flint sit-down strike was over.

Flint, Michigan, was the heart of production for General Motors, the largest corporation in the world. In 1936 GM's net profits had reached $285 million, and its total assets were $1.5 billion. Originally a center for lumbering and then carriage making, Flint had boomed with the auto industry during the 1920s. Thousands of migrants streamed into the city, attracted by assembly line jobs averaging about $30 a week. By 1930 Flint's population had grown to about 150,000 people, 80 percent of whom depended on work at General Motors. A severe housing shortage made living conditions difficult. Tar-paper shacks, tents, even railroad cars were the only shelter available for many. Parts of the city resembled a mining camp.

The Great Depression had hit Flint very hard. Employment at GM fell from a 1929 high of 56,000 to fewer than 17,000 in 1932. As late as 1938 close to half the city's families were receiving some kind of emergency relief. By that time, as in thousands of other American communities, Flint's private and county relief agencies had been overwhelmed by the needs of the unemployed and their families. Two new national agencies based in Washington, D.C., the Federal Emergency Relief Administration and the Works Progress Administration, had replaced local sources of aid during the economic crisis.

The United Automobile Workers (UAW) came to Flint in 1936 seeking to organize GM workers into one industrial union. The previous year, Congress had passed the National Labor Relations Act (also known as the Wagner Act), which made union organizing easier by guaranteeing the right of workers to join unions and bargain collectively. The act established the National Labor Relations Board to oversee union elections and prohibit illegal anti-union activities by employers. But the obstacles to labor organizing were still enormous. Unemployment was high, and GM had maintained a vigorous anti-union policy for years. By the fall of 1936, the UAW had signed up only a thousand members. The key moment came with the seizure of two Flint GM plants by a few hundred auto workers on December 30, 1936. The idea was to stay in the factories until strikers could achieve a collective bargaining agreement with General Motors. "We don't aim to keep the plants or try to run them," explained one sit-downer to a reporter, "but we want to see that nobody takes our jobs."

The sit-down strike was a new and daring tactic that gained popularity among American industrial workers during the 1930s. In 1936 there were 48 sit-downs involving nearly 90,000 workers, and in 1937 some 400,000 workers participated in 477 sit-down strikes. Sit-downs expressed the militant exuberance of the rank and file.

The Flint strikers carefully organized themselves into what one historian called "the sit down community." Each plant elected a strike committee and appointed its own police chief and sanitary engineer. Strikers were divided into "families" of fifteen, each with a captain. No alcohol was allowed, and strikers were careful not to destroy company property. Committees were organized for every conceivable purpose: food, recreation, sanitation, education, and contact with the outside. A Women's Emergency Brigade—the strikers' wives, mothers, and daughters—provided crucial support preparing food and maintaining militant picket lines.

As the sit-down strike continued through January, support in Flint and around the nation grew. Overall production in the GM empire dropped from 53,000 vehicles per week to 1,500. Reporters and union supporters flocked to the plants. On January 11, in the so-called Battle of Running Bulls, strikers and their supporters clashed violently with Flint police and private GM guards. Michigan governor Frank Murphy, sympathetic to the strikers, brought in the National Guard to protect them. He refused to enforce an injunction obtained by GM to evict the strikers.

In the face of determined unity by the sit-downers, GM gave in and recognized the UAW as the exclusive bargaining agent in all sixty of its factories. The strike was perhaps the most important in American labor history, sparking a huge growth in union membership in the automobile and other mass production industries.

Out of the tight-knit, temporary community of the sit-down strike emerged a looser yet more permanent kind of community: a powerful, nation-wide trade union of automobile workers. The UAW struggled successfully to win recognition and collective bargaining rights from other carmakers, such as Chrysler and Ford. The national UAW, like other new unions in the mass-production industries, was composed of locals around the country. The permanent community of unionized auto workers won significant improvements in wages, working conditions, and benefits. Locals also became influential in the political and social lives of their larger communities—industrial cities such as Flint, Detroit, and Toledo. Nationally, organized labor became a crucial component of the New Deal political coalition and a key power broker in the Democratic Party. The new reality of a national community of organized labor would alter the national political and economic landscape for decades to come.

KEY TOPICS

- Causes and consequences of the Great Depression

- The politics of hard times

- Franklin D. Roosevelt and the two New Deals

- The expanding federal sphere in the West

- American cultural life during the 1930s

- Legacies and limits of New Deal reform

HARD TIMES

The Crash

Only about 4 million Americans out of a total population of 120 million owned any stocks when the tumbling of prices on the New York Stock Exchange ended the speculative mania of the 1920s. Many of these stock buyers had been lured into the market through easy-credit, margin accounts. These allowed investors to purchase stocks by making a small down payment (as low as 10 percent), borrowing the rest from a broker, and using the shares as collateral, or security, on the loan.

Though often portrayed as a one- or two-day catastrophe, the Wall Street Crash of 1929 was in reality a steep downward slide. The bull market peaked in early September, and prices drifted downward. On October 23 the Dow Jones industrials lost twenty-one points in one hour, and many large investors concluded that the boom was over. The boom itself rested on expectations of continually rising prices; once those expectations began to melt, the market had to decline. On Monday, October 28, the Dow lost thirty-eight points, or 13 percent of its value. On October 29, "Black Tuesday," the bottom seemed to fall out. Over 16 million shares, more than double the previous record, were traded as panic selling took hold. For many stocks no buyers were available at any price.

The situation worsened. The market's fragile foundation of credit, based on the debts incurred by margin accounts, quickly crumbled. Many investors with margin accounts had no choice but to sell when stock values fell. Because the shares themselves represented the security for their loans, more money had to be put up to cover the loans when prices declined. By mid-November about $30 billion in the market price of stocks had been wiped out. Half the value of the stocks listed in *The New York Times* index was lost in ten weeks.

The nation's political and economic leaders downplayed the impact of Wall Street's woes. "The fundamental business of the country," President Herbert Hoover told Americans in late October, "is on a sound and prosperous basis." Secretary of the Treasury Andrew Mellon spoke for many in the financial world when he spoke of the benefits of the slump: "It will purge the rottenness out of the system." At the end of 1929 hardly anyone was predicting that a depression would follow the stock market crash.

Underlying Weaknesses

It would be too simplistic to say that the stock market crash caused the Great Depression. But like a person who catches a chill, the economy after the crash became less resistant to existing sources of disease. The resulting sickness revealed underlying economic weaknesses left over from the previous decade. First of all, workers and consumers by and large received too small a share of the enormous increases in labor productivity.

Better machinery and more efficient industrial organization had increased labor productivity enormously. But wages and salaries did not rise nearly as much. Between 1923 and 1929 manufacturing output per worker-hour increased by 32 percent. Wages during the same period rose only 8 percent, or one-quarter the rise in productivity. Moreover, the rise in productivity itself had encouraged overproduction in many industries. The farm sector had never been able to regain its prosperity of the World War I years. Farmers suffered under a triple burden of declining prices for their crops, a drop in exports, and larger debts incurred because of wartime expansion.

The most important weakness in the economy was the extremely unequal distribution of income and wealth. In 1929 the top 0.1 percent of American families (24,000 families) had an aggregate income equal to that of the bottom 42 percent (11.5 million families). The top 5 percent of American families received 30 percent of the nation's income; the bottom 60 percent got only 26 percent. Nearly 80 percent of the nation's families (21.5 million households) had no savings; the top 0.1 percent held 34 percent of all savings.

The stock market crash undermined the confidence, investment, and spending of businesses and the well-to-do. Manufacturers decreased their production and began laying off workers, which brought further declines in consumer spending, and another round of production cutbacks. A spurt of consumer spending might have checked this downward spiral, but consumers had less to spend as industries laid off workers and reduced hours. With a shrinking market for products, businesses were hesitant to expand. A large proportion of the nation's banking funds was tied to the speculative bubble of Wall Street stock buying. Many banks began to fail as anxious depositors withdrew their funds, which were uninsured. An 86 percent plunge in agricultural prices between 1929 and 1933, compared to a decline in agricultural production of only 6 percent, brought suffering to America's farmers.

Mass Unemployment

At a time when unemployment insurance did not exist and public relief was terribly inadequate, the loss of a job could mean economic catastrophe for workers and their families. Massive unemployment across America became the most powerful sign of a deepening depression. By 1933, 12.6 million workers—over one-quarter of the labor force—were without jobs. Other sources put the figure that year above 16 million, or nearly one out of every three workers. None of these statistics tells us how long people were unemployed or how many Americans found only part-time work.

What did it mean to be unemployed and without hope in the early 1930s? Figures give us only an outline of the grim reality. Many Americans, raised believing that they were responsible for their own fate, blamed themselves for their failure to find work. Contemporary journalists noted the common feelings of shame and guilt expressed by the unemployed.

Joblessness proved especially difficult for men between the ages of thirty-five and fifty-five, the period in their lives when family responsibilities were heaviest. Nathan Ackerman, a psychiatrist who went to Pennsylvania to observe the impact of prolonged unemployment on coal miners, found an enormous sense of "internal distress." "They gave each other solace. They were loath to go home because they were indicted, as if it were their fault for being unemployed. The women punished the men for not bringing home the bacon, by withholding themselves sexually. . . . These men suffered from depression."

Women found it easier to hold onto jobs since their labor was cheaper. Female clerks, secretaries, maids, and waitresses were more likely than male factory workers to survive hard times. Unemployment upset the psychological balance in many families by undermining the traditional authority of the male breadwinner. Male responses to unemployment varied: some withdrew emotionally, others became angry or took to drinking. A few committed suicide over the shame of extended unemployment. One Chicago social worker, writing about unemployment in 1934, summed up the strains she found in families: "Fathers feel they have lost their prestige in the home; there is much nagging, mothers nag at the fathers, parents nag at the children. Children of working age who earn meager salaries find it hard to turn over all their earnings and deny themselves even the greatest necessities and as a result leave home."

Pressures on those lucky enough to have a job increased as well. Anna Novak, a Chicago meatpacker, recalled the degrading harassment at the hands of foremen: "You could get along swell if you let the boss slap you on the behind and feel you up." Fear of unemployment and a deep desire for security marked the Depression generation. A sanitation worker told an interviewer many years later, "I'm what I call a security cat. I don't dare switch [jobs]. 'Cause I got too much whiskers on it, seniority."

Hoover's Failure

The Depression overwhelmed traditional sources of relief. In most communities across America these sources were a patchwork of private agencies and local government units, such as towns, cities, or counties. They simply lacked the money, resources, and staff to deal with the worsening situation. One West Virginia coal mining county with 1,500 unemployed miners had only $9,000 to meet relief needs for that year. Unemployed transients, attracted by warm weather, posed a special problem for communities in California and Florida. By the end of 1931 Los Angeles had 70,000 nonresident jobless and homeless men; new arrivals numbered about 1,200 a day.

There was great irony, even tragedy, in President Hoover's failure to respond to human suffering. He had administered large-scale humanitarian efforts during World War I with great efficiency. Yet he failed to face the facts of the Depression. He resisted the growing calls from Congress and local communities for a greater federal role in relief efforts or public works projects. He worried, as he told Congress after vetoing one measure, about injuring "the initiative and enterprise of the American people." The President's Emergency Committee for Unemployment, established in 1930, and its successor, the President's Organization for Unemployment Relief, created in 1931, did little more than encourage local groups to raise money to help the unemployed.

Hoover's plan for recovery centered on restoring business confidence. His administration's most important institutional response to the Depression was the Reconstruction Finance Corporation, established in early 1932. The RFC was designed to make government credit available to ailing banks, railroads, insurance companies, and other businesses, thereby stimulating economic activity. The key assumption here was that the credit problem was one of supply (for businesses) rather than demand (from consumers). The RFC managed to save numerous banks and other businesses from going under, but its approach did not hasten recovery.

Protest and the Election of 1932

By 1932, direct, at times violent expressions of protest, widely covered in the press, reflected the desperate mood of many Americans. On March 7 several thousand Detroit auto workers and unemployed, led by communist organizers, marched to the Ford River Rouge factory in nearby Dearborn. When the demonstrators refused orders to turn back, Ford-controlled police fired tear gas and bullets, killing four and seriously wounding fifty others. Some 40,000 people attended a tense funeral service a few days later. Desperate farmers in Iowa organized the Farmers' Holiday Association, aimed at raising prices by refusing to sell produce. In August some 1,500 farmers turned back cargo trucks outside Sioux City, Iowa, and made a point by dumping milk and other perishables into ditches.

That spring, the "Bonus Army" began descending upon Washington, D.C., to demand the cash bonuses that Congress had promised in 1924. By summer, around 20,000 of these World War I veterans and their families were camped out all over the capital city. Their lobbying convinced the House to pass a bill for immediate payment, but the Senate rejected the bill and most of the veterans left. At the end of July U.S. Army troops led by Chief of Staff General Douglas MacArthur forcibly evicted the remaining 2,000 veterans from their encampment. The spectacle of these unarmed and unemployed men, the heroes of 1918, driven off by bayonets and bullets provided the most disturbing evidence yet of the failure of Hoover's administration.

In 1932 Democrats nominated Franklin D. Roosevelt, governor of New York, as their candidate. Roosevelt stressed the need for reconstructing the nation's economy. "I pledge you, I pledge myself," he said, "to a new deal for the American people." But his plans for recovery were vague. Hoover bitterly condemned Roosevelt's ideas as a "radical departure" from the American way of life. But with the Depression growing worse every day, probably any Democrat would have defeated Hoover. Roosevelt carried forty-two states, taking the electoral college 472 to 59 and the popular vote by about 23 million to 16 million.

FDR AND THE FIRST NEW DEAL

FDR the Man

No president of this century had a greater impact on American life and politics than Franklin Delano Roosevelt. He was born in 1882 in Dutchess County,

New York, where he grew up an only child, secure and confident, on his family's vast estate. Franklin's father, James, had made a fortune through railroad investments, but he was already in his fifties when Franklin was born, and his mother, Sara Delano, was the dominant figure in his childhood. Roosevelt's education at Groton, Harvard, and Columbia Law School reinforced the aristocratic values of his family.

In 1905 he married his distant cousin, Anna Eleanor Roosevelt, niece of President Theodore Roosevelt; she would later emerge as an influential adviser and political force on her own. Franklin turned to politics as a career early on. He was elected as a Democrat to the New York State Senate in 1910, served as assistant navy secretary from 1913 to 1920, and was nominated for vice president by the Democrats in the 1920 campaign.

A turning point came in the summer of 1921 when Roosevelt was stricken with polio at his summer home. He was never to walk again without support. The disease strengthened his relationship with Eleanor, who encouraged him not only to fight his handicap but also to continue with his political career. His patience and determination in fighting the disease transformed him. The wealthy aristocrat, for whom everything had come relatively easy, now personally understood the meaning of struggle and hardship.

Elected governor of New York in 1928, Roosevelt served two terms and won a national reputation for reform. In Albany his achievements included

The presidential succession, 1932. A glum Herbert Hoover (left) avoids conversation with Franklin D. Roosevelt as the two ride from the White House to the Capitol.

OVERVIEW

KEY LEGISLATION OF THE FIRST NEW DEAL ("HUNDRED DAYS," MARCH 9–JUNE 16, 1933)

Legislation	Purpose
Emergency Banking Relief Act	Enlarged federal authority over private banks Government loans to private banks
Civilian Conservation Corps	Unemployment relief Conservation of natural resources
Federal Emergency Relief Administration	Direct federal moneys for relief, funneled through state and local governments
Agricultural Adjustment Administration	Federal farm aid based on parity pricing and subsidy
Tennessee Valley Authority	Economic development and cheap electricity for Tennessee Valley
National Industrial Recovery Act	Self-regulating industrial codes to revive economic activity
Public Works Administration	Federal public works projects to increase employment and consumer spending

unemployment insurance, improved child labor laws, farm tax relief, and old age pensions. As the Depression hit the state he slowly increased public works and set up a Temporary Emergency Relief Administration. With his eye on the White House, he began assembling a group of key advisers, the Brain Trust, who would follow him to Washington. The "brain trusters" shared a faith in the power of organized intelligence to set the economy right, and a basic belief in government–business cooperation. They rejected the old progressive dream of re-creating an ideal society of small producers. Structural economic reform, they argued, must accept the modern reality of large corporate enterprise based on mass-production and distribution.

Restoring Confidence

In the first days of his administration Roosevelt conveyed a sense of optimism and activism that helped restore the badly shaken confidence of the nation. "First of all," he told Americans in his inaugural address on March 4, 1933, "let me assert my firm belief that the only thing we have to fear is fear itself." The very next day he issued an executive order calling for a four-day "bank holiday" to shore up the country's ailing financial system. Contemporary investigations had revealed a disquieting pattern of stock manipulation, illegal loans to bank officials, and tax evasion that helped erode public confidence in the banking system. Between election day and the inauguration, the banking system had come alarmingly close to shutting down alto-

gether due to widespread bank failures and the hoarding of currency.

Roosevelt therefore called for a special session of Congress to deal with the banking crisis, as well as unemployment aid and farm relief. On March 12 he broadcast his first "fireside chat" to explain the steps he had taken to meet the financial emergency. These radio broadcasts became a standard part of Roosevelt's political technique, and they proved enormously successful. They communicated a genuine sense of compassion from the White House.

Congress immediately passed the Emergency Banking Act, which gave the president broad discretionary powers over all banking transactions and foreign exchange. It authorized healthy banks to reopen under licenses from the Treasury Department, and it proved for greater federal authority in managing the affairs of failed banks. By the middle of March about half the country's banks, holding about 90 percent of the nation's deposits, were open for business again. Banks began to attract new currency from depositors who had held back. The bank crisis had passed.

The Hundred Days

From March to June 1933—"the Hundred Days"—FDR pushed through Congress an extraordinary number of acts designed to combat various aspects of the Depression. What came to be called the New Deal was no unified program to end the Depression, but rather an improvised series of reform and relief measures, some of which seemed to contradict each other. Roosevelt responded to pressures from Congress, business, and organized labor, but he also used his own considerable power over public opinion to get his way.

Five measures were particularly important and innovative. The Civilian Conservation Corps, established in March as an unemployment relief effort, provided work for jobless young men in protecting and conserving the nation's natural resources. Road construction, reforestation, flood control, and national park improvements were some of the major projects performed in work camps across the country. CCC workers received room and board and $30 each month, up to $25 of which had to be sent home to dependents.

In May Congress authorized $500 million for the Federal Emergency Relief Administration (FERA). Half the money went as direct relief to the states; the balance was distributed on the basis of $1 of federal aid for every $3 of state and local funds spent for relief. This system of outright federal grants differed significantly from Hoover's approach, which provided only for loans. Establishment of work relief projects, however, was left to state and local governments. To direct the FERA Roosevelt turned to Harry Hopkins, an experienced reformer from the world of New York social work. A brilliant administrator with a special commitment to ending discrimination in relief work, Hopkins became the New Deal's most influential figure in relief policies and one of Roosevelt's most trusted advisers.

The Agricultural Adjustment Administration (AAA) was set up to provide immediate relief to the nation's farmers. It established parity prices for seven basic farm commodities based on the purchasing power farmers had enjoyed during the prosperous years of 1909 to 1914. That period now became the benchmark for setting the prices of farm commodities. The AAA also incorporated the principle of subsidy, whereby farmers received benefit payments in return for reducing acreage or otherwise cutting production where surpluses existed. The funds for these payments were to be raised from new taxes on food processing.

The AAA raised total farm income and was especially successful in pushing up the prices of wheat, cotton, and corn. But it had some troubling side effects as well. Landlords often failed to share their AAA payments with tenant farmers, and they often used benefits to buy tractors and other equipment that displaced sharecroppers. Many Americans were disturbed by the sight of surplus crops, livestock, and milk being destroyed while millions went hungry.

The Southern Tenant Farmers Union, founded in 1934, protested these AAA policies. The STFU, half of whose members were black, managed to draw attention to the plight of sharecroppers, but failed to influence national farm policy.

The Tennessee Valley Authority proved to be one of the most unique and controversial projects of the New Deal era. The TVA, an independent public corporation, built dams and power plants, produced cheap fertilizer for farmers, and, most significantly, brought cheap electricity for the first time to thousands of people in six southern states. Denounced by some as a dangerous step toward socialism, the TVA stood for decades as a model of how careful government planning could dramatically improve the social and economic welfare of an underdeveloped region.

On the very last of the Hundred Days, Congress passed the National Industrial Recovery Act, the closest attempt yet at a systematic plan for economic recovery. In theory, each industry would be self-governed by a code hammered out by representatives of business, labor, and the consuming public. Once approved by the National Recovery Administration (NRA) in Washington, the codes would have the force of law. In practice, almost all the NRA codes were written by the largest firms in any given industry; labor and consumers got short shrift. The sheer administrative complexities involved in compliance made many people unhappy with the NRA's operation.

The Public Works Administration, led by Secretary of the Interior Harold Ickes, authorized $3.3 billion for the construction of roads, public buildings, and other projects. The idea was to provide jobs and thus stimulate the economy through increased consumer spending. Eventually the PWA spent over $4.2 billion building roads, schools, post offices, bridges, courthouses, and other public buildings around the country. In thousands of communities today, these structures remain the most tangible remnants of the New Deal era.

LEFT TURN AND THE SECOND NEW DEAL

Roosevelt's Critics

Criticism of the New Deal came from the right and the left. On the right, conservative newspapers and the American Liberty League, organized in 1934, denounced Roosevelt and his advisers. Dominated by wealthy executives of Du Pont and General Motors, the league attracted support from a group of conservative Democrats, including Al Smith, who declared the New Deal's laws "socialist." The league supported anti–New Dealers for Congress, but in 1934 Democrats built up their majorities from 310 to 319 in the House and from 60 to 69 in the Senate—an unusually

VERVIEW

KEY LEGISLATION OF THE SECOND NEW DEAL (1935–1938)	
Legislation	**Purpose**
Emergency Relief Appropriations Act (includes Works Progress Administration) (1935)	Large-scale public works program for jobless
Social Security Act (1935)	Federal old age pensions and unemployment insurance
National Labor Relations Act (1935)	Federal guarantee of right to organize trade unions and collective bargaining
Resettlement Administration (1935)	Relocation of poor rural families; reforestation and soil erosion projects
National Housing Act (1937)	Federal funding for public housing and slum clearance
Fair Labor Standards Act (1938)	Federal minimum wage and maximum hours

strong showing for the incumbent party in a midterm election.

More troublesome for Roosevelt and his allies were the vocal and popular movements on the left. In California well-known novelist and Socialist Upton Sinclair entered the 1934 Democratic primary for governor. He proposed a $50-a-month pension for all poor people over age sixty. Sinclair shocked local and national Democrats by winning the primary easily. He lost a close general election only because the Republican candidate received heavy financial and tactical support from wealthy Hollywood figures and frightened regular Democrats.

Huey Long, Louisiana's flamboyant backcountry orator, posed the greatest potential threat to Roosevelt's leadership. Long had captured Louisiana's governorship in 1928 by attacking the state's entrenched oil industry and calling for a radical redistribution of wealth. In office, he significantly improved public education, roads, medical care, and other public services, winning the loyalty of the state's poor farmers and industrial workers. Elected to the U.S. Senate in 1931, Long came to Washington with national ambitions. He at first supported Roosevelt, but in 1934 he began denouncing the New Deal as a failure and organized the Share Our Wealth Society. Long promised that limiting the size of large fortunes would mean a homestead worth $5,000 and a $2,500 annual income for everyone. Although Long's economics were fuzzy at best, he undoubtedly touched a deep nerve with his "Every Man a King" slogan. The Democratic National Committee was shocked when a secret poll in the summer of 1935 revealed that Long might attract 3 or 4 million votes. Only his assassination that September prevented Long's third-party candidacy, which might have proved disastrous for FDR.

A newly militant labor movement also loomed as a force to be reckoned with. Section 7a of the National Industrial Recovery Act required that workers be allowed to bargain collectively with employers, through representatives of their own choosing. Although this provision of the NIRA was not enforced, it did help raise expectations and spark union organizing. Almost 1.5 million workers took part in some 1,800 strikes in 1934. But employers resisted unionization nearly everywhere, often with violence and the help of local and state police.

The Second Hundred Days

The popularity of leaders such as Sinclair and Long suggested that Roosevelt might be losing electoral support among workers, farmers, the aged, and the unemployed. In early 1935 Roosevelt and his closest advisers responded by turning left and concentrating on a new program of social reform. What came to be called "the Second Hundred Days" marked the high point of progressive lawmaking in the New Deal.

In April the administration pushed through the Emergency Relief Appropriations Act, which allocated $5 billion for large-scale public works programs for the jobless. The major responsible agency here was the Works Progress Administration, led by Harry Hopkins. Over the next seven years Hopkins oversaw the employment of over 8 million Americans on a vast array of construction projects: roads, bridges, dams, airports, and sewers. Among the most innovative WPA programs were community service projects that employed thousands of jobless artists, musicians, actors, and writers.

The landmark Social Security Act of 1935 provided for old-age pensions and unemployment insurance. A payroll tax on workers and their employers created a fund from which retirees received monthly pensions after age sixty-five. The unemployment compensation plan established a minimum weekly payment and a minimum number of weeks during which those who lost jobs could collect. The original law had flaws. It failed to cover farm workers and domestics, many of whom were Latinos and African Americans. And to collect unemployment, one had to have had a job. But the law, which has since been amended many times, established the crucial principle of federal responsibility for America's most vulnerable citizens.

Another 1935 law, the National Labor Relations Act (often called the Wagner Act for its chief sponsor, Democratic senator Robert F. Wagner of New York), guaranteed the right of American workers to join or form independent labor unions and bargain collectively for improved wages, benefits, and working conditions. The National Labor Relations Board would conduct secret-ballot elections in shops and factories to determine which union, if any, workers desired as their sole bargaining agent. The law also defined and prohibited unfair labor practices by employers, including firing workers for union activity.

Finally, the Resettlement Administration produced one of the most utopian New Deal programs, one designed to create new kinds of model communities. The RA helped destitute farm families relocate to more productive areas. It granted loans for purchasing land and equipment, and it directed reforestation and soil erosion projects, particularly in the hard-hit Southwest. Because of lack of funds and poor administration, however, only about 1 percent of the projected 500,000 families were actually moved.

Labor's Upsurge: Rise of the CIO

In 1932 the American labor movement was nearly dead. Yet by 1942 unions claimed over 10.5 million members, nearly a third of the total nonagricultural work force. This remarkable turnaround was one of the key events of the Depression era. The growth in the size and power of the labor movement permanently changed the work lives and economic status of millions, as well as the national and local political landscapes.

At the core of this growth was a series of dramatic successes in the organization of workers in large-scale, mass-production industries such as automobiles, steel, rubber, electrical goods, and textiles. Workers in these fields had largely been ignored by the conservative, craft-conscious unions that dominated the American Federation of Labor. At the 1935 AFL convention, a group of more militant union officials led by John L. Lewis (of the United Mine Workers) and Sidney Hillman (of the Amalgamated Clothing Workers) formed the Committee for Industrial Organization (CIO). They emphasized the need for opening the new unions to all, regardless of a worker's level of skill. And they differed from nearly all old-line AFL unions by calling for the inclusion of black and women workers. In 1938 the CIO unions withdrew from the AFL and reorganized themselves as the Congress of Industrial Organizations.

The gruff son of a Welsh miner, Lewis was articulate, ruthless, and very ambitious. He saw the new legal protection given by the Wagner Act as a historic opportunity. Despite the Wagner Act, whose constitutionality was unclear until 1937, Lewis knew that establishing permanent unions in the mass industries would be a bruising battle. He committed the substantial resources of the United Mine Workers to a series of organizing drives, focusing first on the steel and auto industries. Many CIO organizers were communists or radicals of other persuasions, and their dedication, commitment, and willingness to work within disciplined organizations proved invaluable in the often dangerous task of creating industrial unions.

Militant rank-and-file unionists were often ahead of Lewis and other CIO leaders. After the dramatic breakthrough in the Flint sit-down strike at General Motors, membership in CIO unions grew rapidly. In eight months membership in the United Automobile Workers alone soared from 88,000 to 400,000. CIO victories in the steel, rubber, and electrical industries followed, but often at a very high cost. One bloody example of the perils of union organizing was the 1937 Memorial Day Massacre in Chicago. In a field near the Republic Steel Mill in South Chicago, police fired into a crowd of union supporters, killing ten workers and wounding scores more.

Overall, the success of the CIO organizing drives was remarkable. For the first time ever, the labor movement gained a permanent place in the nation's mass-production industries. Organized labor took its place as a key power broker in Roosevelt's New Deal and the national Democratic party. Frances Perkins, FDR's secretary of labor and the first female Cabinet member, captured the close relationship between the new unionism and the New Deal: "Programs long thought of as merely labor welfare, such as shorter hours, higher wages, and a voice in the terms of conditions of work, are really essential economic factors for recovery."

The New Deal Coalition at High Tide

Did the American public support Roosevelt and his New Deal policies? Both major political parties looked forward to the 1936 elections as a national referendum, and the campaign itself was an exciting and hard-fought contest. Very few political observers predicted its lopsided result.

Republicans nominated Governor Alfred M. Landon of Kansas, an easygoing, colorless man with little personal magnetism who emphasized a nostalgic appeal to traditional American values. Landon's campaign served as a lightning rod for all those, including many conservative Democrats, who were dissatisfied with Roosevelt and the direction he had taken.

Roosevelt attacked the "economic royalists" who denied that government "could do anything to protect the citizen in his right to work and his right to live." At the same time, FDR was careful to distance himself from radicalism. As Roosevelt's campaign crossed the country, his advisers were heartened by huge and enthusiastic crowds, especially in large cities such as Chicago and Pittsburgh. Still, the vast majority of the nation's newspapers endorsed Landon. And a widely touted "scientific" poll by the *Literary Digest* forecast a Republican victory in November.

On Election Day Roosevelt carried every state but Maine and Vermont, polling 61 percent of the popular vote. The *Literary Digest* poll, it turned out, had been based upon telephone directories and car registration records, which provided a very unrepresentative sample weighted toward wealthier Americans and others more likely to vote Republican. In 1936 the Democrats drew millions of new voters and forged a new coalition of voters that would dominate national politics for two generations.

The "New Deal coalition," as it came to be known, included traditional-minded white southern Democrats, big-city political machines, industrial workers of all races, trade unionists, and many Depression-hit farmers. Roosevelt was especially popular among first- and second-generation immigrants of Catholic and Jewish descent. Organized labor put an unprecedented amount of money and people power into Roosevelt's reelection. Black voters in the North and West, long affiliated with the party of Lincoln, went Democratic in record numbers. The Depression was by no means over. But the New Deal's active response to the nation's misery, particularly the bold initiatives taken in 1935, had obviously struck a powerful chord with the American electorate.

THE NEW DEAL AND THE WEST
The Dust Bowl

The southern Great Plains had suffered several drought years in the early 1930s as rainfall fell far below normal levels. Such dry spells occurred regularly in roughly twenty-year cycles. But this time the parched earth became swept up in violent dust storms. Black blizzards of dust a mile and a half high rolled across the landscape, darkening the sky and whipping the earth into great drifts that settled over hundreds of miles. Dust storms made it difficult for humans and livestock to breathe and destroyed crops and trees over vast areas. The hardest-hit regions were western Kansas, eastern Colorado, western Oklahoma, the Texas Panhandle, and eastern New Mexico. A Denver journalist coined the phrase "Dust Bowl" to describe the calamity he had witnessed on the southern plains. Dust storms turned day into night, terrifying those caught in them. "Dust pneumonia" and other respiratory infections afflicted thousands, and many travelers found themselves stranded in automobiles and trains unable to move.

The dust storms were largely the result of years of stripping the landscape of its natural vegetation. During World War I wheat fetched record-high prices

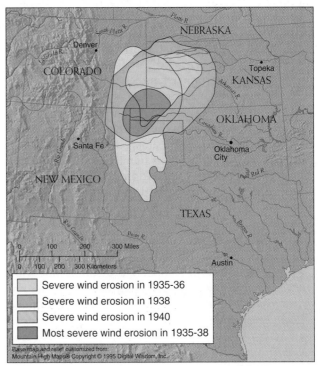

The Dust Bowl, 1935–1940 *This map shows the extent of the Dust Bowl in the southern Great Plains. Federal programs designed to improve soil conservation, water management, and farming practices could not prevent a mass exodus of hundreds of thousands out of the Great Plains.*

on the world market, and for the next twenty years Great Plains farmers turned the region into a vast wheat factory. With native grasses destroyed for the sake of wheat growing, there was nothing left to prevent soil erosion. The dust storms blew away tens of millions of acres of rich topsoil, and thousands of farm families left the region. Those who stayed suffered deep economic and psychological losses from the calamity.

The Department of Agriculture, under Secretary Henry A. Wallace, sought to change farming practices to relieve the distress. The Soil Conservation Service conducted research into controlling wind and water erosion, set up demonstration projects, and offered technical assistance, supplies, and equipment to ranchers and farmers. The SCS pumped additional federal funds into the Great Plains and created a new rural organization, the soil conservation district, which administered conservation regulations locally.

By 1940 the acreage subject to blowing in the Dust Bowl area of the southern plains had been reduced from roughly 50 million acres to less than 4 million acres. In the face of the Dust Bowl disaster New Deal farm policies had restricted market forces in agriculture.

Whereas large landowners and ranchers reaped large benefits from AAA subsidies and other New Deal programs, tenant farmers and sharecroppers received very little. Many farmers used AAA cash payments to buy tractors and other machinery and evicted their tenants. In the cotton lands of Texas, Oklahoma, Missouri, and Arkansas, thousands of tenant and sharecropper families were forced off the land. They became part of a stream of roughly 300,000 people, disparagingly called "Okies," who migrated to California in the 1930s. Most Okies could find work only as poorly paid agricultural laborers in the fertile San Joaquin and Imperial valley districts. There they faced discrimination and scorn as "poor white trash" as they struggled to create communities amid the squalor of migrant labor camps. Only with the outbreak of World War II and the pressing demand for labor were migrants able to significantly improve their situation.

Mexican farm laborers faced stiff competition from the Dust Bowl refugees. Southwestern communities, responding to racist hostility from unemployed whites, campaigned to deport Mexicans and Mexican Americans.

Water Policy

The New Deal ushered in the era of large-scale water projects constructed and controlled by the federal government. The long-range impact of these undertakings on western life would be difficult to overestimate. The key government agency in this realm was the Bureau of Reclamation of the Department of the Interior, established under the National Reclamation Act of 1902. Until the late 1920s the bureau had irrigated only a very small portion of the West. But its fortunes changed when it shifted its focus to building huge multi-purpose dams designed to control entire river systems.

The first of these projects was the Boulder Dam (later renamed the Hoover Dam). The dam, begun during the Hoover administration, was designed to harness the Colorado River, wildest and most isolated of the major western rivers. The benefits would be flood prevention, irrigation of California's Imperial Valley, domestic water for Southern California, and cheap electricity for Los Angeles and southern Arizona. Hoover, however, had come out against the public power aspect of the project, arguing that the government ought not compete with private utility companies. Roosevelt's support for public power was a significant factor in his winning the political backing of the West in 1932 and subsequent election years.

The success of Boulder Dam transformed the Bureau of Reclamation into a major federal agency with huge resources at its disposal. In 1938 it completed the All-American Canal—an 80-mile channel connecting the Colorado River to the Imperial Valley, with a 130-mile branch to the Coachella Valley. Over a million acres of desert land were opened up to the cultivation of citrus fruits, melons, vegetables, and cotton. Irrigation districts receiving water promised to repay, without interest, the cost of the canal over a forty-year period. This interest-free loan was in effect a huge government subsidy to the private growers who benefited from the canal.

The largest power and irrigation project of all was the Grand Coulee Dam, northwest of Spokane, Washington. Completed in 1941, it was designed to convert the power of the Columbia River into cheap electricity, irrigate previously uncultivated land, and thereby stimulate the economic development of the Pacific Northwest. The construction of Grand Coulee employed tens of thousands of workers and pumped millions of dollars into the region's badly depressed economy. Grand Coulee provided the cheapest electricity in the United States and helped attract new manufacturing to a region previously dependent on the export of raw materials, such as lumber and metals.

The Grand Coulee and smaller dams nearby reduced the Columbia River, long a potent symbol of the western wilderness, to a series of lakes. Spawning salmon no longer ran the river above the dam. In California the federal guarantee of river water made a handful of large farmers fabulously wealthy. But tens of thousands of farm workers, mostly of Mexican descent, labored in the newly fertile fields for very low wages, and their health suffered from contact with pesticides. The Colorado River, no longer emptying into the Pacific, began to build up salt deposits, making its water increasingly unfit for drinking or irrigation. Water pollution in the form of high salinity continues to be a problem along the 2,000-mile Colorado River to this day.

DEPRESSION-ERA CULTURE

A New Deal for the Arts

The depression hit America's writers, artists, and teachers just as hard as blue-collar workers. In 1935 the WPA allocated $300 million for the unemployed in these fields. Over the next four years, Federal Project No. 1, an umbrella agency covering writing, theater, music, and the visual arts, proved to be one of the most innovative and successful New Deal programs. Federal One, as it was called, offered work to artists and intellectuals, enriched the cultural lives of millions, and left a substantial legacy of artistic and cultural production.

The Federal Writers Project employed 5,000 writers at its height on a variety of programs. Most notably, it produced a popular series of state and city guidebooks, each combining history, folklore, and tourism. The 150-volume *Life in America* series included valuable oral histories of former slaves, studies of ethnic cultures and Indians, and pioneering collections of American songs and folk tales. Work on the Writers Project helped many American writers to survive, hone their craft, and go on to great achievement and prominence. These included Ralph Ellison, Richard Wright, Margaret Walker, John Cheever, Saul Bellow, and Zora Neale Hurston.

The Federal Theater Project reached as many as 30 million Americans with its productions. Tickets were cheap, and a variety of dramatic forms were made available. Among the most successful were the "Living Newspaper" plays based on contemporary controversies and current events.

The Federal Music Project, under Nikolai Sokoloff of the Cleveland Symphony Orchestra, employed 15,000 musicians. It financed hundreds of thousands of low-priced public concerts by touring orchestras. The Composers' Forum Laboratory supported new works by American composers such as Aaron Copland and William Schuman.

Among the painters who received government assistance through the Federal Art Project were Willem de Kooning, Jackson Pollock, and Louise Nevelson. The FAP employed painters and sculptors to teach studio skills and art history in schools, churches, and settlement houses. It also commissioned artists to paint hundreds of murals on the walls of post offices, meeting halls, courthouses, and other government buildings.

The Documentary Impulse

During the 1930s an enormous number of artists, novelists, journalists, photographers, and filmmakers tried to document the devastation wrought by the Depression in American communities. They also depicted people's struggles to cope with and reverse hard times.

"The documentary impulse" became a prominent style in 1930s cultural expression. The most direct and influential expression of the documentary style was the photograph. In 1935 Roy Stryker, chief of the Historical Section of the Resettlement Administration (later part of the Farm Security Administration), gathered a remarkable group of photographers to help document the work of the agency. These photographers, including Dorothea Lange, Walker Evans, Arthur Rothstein, Russell Lee, Ben Shahn, and Marion Post Walcott, left us the single most significant visual record of the Great Depression.

That double vision, combining a frank portrayal of pain and suffering with a faith in the possibility of overcoming disaster, could be found in many other cultural works of the period. John Steinbeck's *The Grapes of Wrath* (1939) sympathetically portrayed the hardships of Oklahoma Dust Bowl migrants on their way to California. A similar, if more personal, portrayal of hardships endured and overcome could be found in Margaret Mitchell's 1936 best-seller *Gone with the Wind*. Although this romantic novel was set in the Civil War–era South, many Americans identified with Scarlett O'Hara's determination to overcome the disaster of war.

Waiting for Lefty

The appalling social and economic conditions of the 1930s shook the confidence of many artists and intellectuals. Few Americans became communists or socialists in the 1930s (at its height, the Communist Party of the United States had perhaps 100,000 members), and many of these remained active for only a brief time. Yet Marxist analysis, with its emphasis on class conflict and the failures of capitalism, had a wide influence on the era's thought and writing.

Some writers joined the Communist Party as the best hope for political revolution. They saw in the Soviet Union an alternative to an American system that appeared mired in exploitation, racial inequality, and human misery. Communist writers, such as novelist Michael Gold and poet Meridel LeSueur, sought to radicalize art and literature, and celebrated collective struggle over individual achievement.

A more common pattern for intellectuals, especially when they were young, was flirtation with communism. Many African American writers, attracted by the Communist Party's militant opposition to lynching, job discrimination, and segregation, briefly joined the Party or found their first supportive audiences there. These included Richard Wright, Ralph Ellison, and Langston Hughes. Many playwrights and actors associated with New York's influential Group Theater were part of the Communist Party orbit in those years. That group's production of Clifford Odets's *Waiting for Lefty* (1935), depicted a union organizing drive among taxi drivers. At the play's climax, the audience was invited to join the actors in shouting "Strike!" A commercial and political success, it offered perhaps the most celebrated example of radical, politically engaged art.

Left-wing influence reached its height after 1935 during the "Popular Front" period. Alarmed by the rise of fascism in Europe, communists around the world followed the Soviet line of uniting with liberals and all other antifascists. Communists became strong supporters of Roosevelt's New Deal, and their influence was especially strong within the various WPA arts projects. Some 3,200 Americans volunteered for the Communist-organized Abraham Lincoln Brigade, which fought in the Spanish civil war on the Republican side against the fascists led by Francisco Franco.

Film and Radio in the 1930s

Several film genres proved enormously popular during the 1930s. Gangster films did very well in the early Depression years. They depicted violent criminals brought to justice by society—but along the way audiences could vicariously enjoy the pleasures of wealth, power, and lawbreaking. Social disorder was treated comically in Marx Brothers films. Mae West's popular comedies made people laugh by subverting expectations about sex roles. West was an independent woman, not afraid of pleasure. When her leading man Cary Grant asked her, "Haven't you ever met a man who could make you happy?" she replied, "Sure, lots of times."

Movie musicals such as Busby Berkeley's *Gold Diggers of 1933* and *42nd Street* (1933) offered audiences extravagant song-and-dance spectacles. Screwball comedies featured sophisticated, fast-paced humor and usually paired popular male and female stars: Clark Gable and Claudette Colbert in *It Happened One Night* (1934), Katharine Hepburn and Cary Grant in *Bringing Up Baby* (1938). A few movies, notably from the Warner Brothers studio, offered a more socially conscious view of Depression-era life. By and large, however, Hollywood avoided confronting controversial social or political issues.

The Depression helped radio expand as an influx of talent arrived from the weakened worlds of vaudeville, ethnic theater, and the recording industry. The well-financed networks offered an attractive outlet to advertisers seeking a national audience. Radio programming achieved a regularity and professionalism absent in the 1920s, making it easier for a listener to identify a show with its sponsor.

Much of network radio was based on older cultural forms. The variety show, based on the vaudeville format, was the first important style. It featured stars such as Eddie Cantor, Ed Wynn, Kate Smith, and Al Jolson, who constantly plugged the sponsor's product. The use of a studio audience re-created the human interaction so necessary in vaudeville. The popular comedy show *Amos 'n' Andy* adapted the minstrel blackface tradition to the new medium. White comedians Freeman Gosden and Charles Correll used only their two voices to invent a world of stereotyped African Americans for their millions of listeners.

The spectacular growth of the daytime serial, or soap opera, dominated radio drama. Aimed mainly at women working in the home, "soaps" revolved around strong, warm female characters who provided advice and strength to weak, indecisive friends and relatives. Thrillers such as *Inner Sanctum* and *The Shadow* emphasized crime and suspense. Very popular on evening radio, they made great use of music and sound effects to sharpen their impact.

THE LIMITS OF REFORM
Court Packing

In May 1935, in *Schecter v. United States*, the Supreme Court found the National Recovery Administration unconstitutional in its entirety. Its ruling in *Butler v. United States* in early 1936 did the same for the Agricultural Adjustment Administration. The Court was composed mostly of Republican appointees, six of whom were over seventy. Roosevelt looked for a way to get more friendly judges on the high court.

In February 1937 FDR asked Congress for legislation that would expand the Supreme Court from nine to a maximum of fifteen justices. The president would be empowered to make a new appointment whenever an incumbent judge failed to retire upon reaching age seventy. Roosevelt argued that age prevented justices from keeping up with their workload, but not many really believed this logic. Newspapers almost unanimously denounced FDR's "court-packing bill."

Even more damaging was the determined opposition from a coalition of conservatives and outraged New Dealers in the Congress, such as Democratic senator Burton K. Wheeler of Montana. As the battle dragged on through the spring and summer, FDR's claims weakened. Conservative justice Willis Van Devanter announced plans to retire, giving Roosevelt the chance to make his first Court appointment.

More important, the Court upheld the constitutionality of some key laws from the second New

Deal, including the Social Security Act and the National Labor Relations Act. At the end of August, FDR backed off from his plan and accepted a compromise bill that reformed lower court procedures but left the Supreme Court untouched. FDR may have won the war for a more responsive Court, but the Court fight badly weakened his relations with Congress. Many more conservative Democrats now felt free to oppose further New Deal measures.

The Women's Network

The Depression and the New Deal did bring about some significant changes for women in American economics and politics. Although most women continued to perform unpaid domestic labor within their homes, a growing number also worked for wages and salaries outside the home. By 1940, 25 percent of the paid workforce was female. But sexual stereotyping still routinely forced women into low-paying and low-status jobs.

The New Deal brought a measurable, if temporary, increase in women's political influence. For those associated with social reform, the New Deal opened up possibilities to effect change. A women's network, linked by personal friendships and professional connections, made its presence felt in national politics and government. Most of the women in this network had long been active in movements promoting suffrage, labor law reform, and welfare programs.

Eleanor Roosevelt on a campaign tour with her husband in Nebraska, 1935. Long active in women's organizations and Democratic party circles, she used political activity both to maintain her independence and make herself a valuable ally to FDR. "The attitude of women toward change in society," she argued, "is going to determine to a great extent our future in this country."

Eleanor Roosevelt became a powerful political figure, actively using her prominence as First Lady to fight for the liberal causes she believed in. She revolutionized the role of the political wife. Privately, she enjoyed great influence with her husband. She was a strong supporter of protective labor legislation for women, and her overall outlook owed much to the social reform tradition of the women's movement.

One of her first public acts as First Lady was to convene a White House Conference on the Emergency Needs of Women, in November 1933. She helped Ellen Woodward, head of women's projects in the Federal Emergency Relief Administration, find jobs for 100,000 women, ranging from nursery school teaching to sewing. Roosevelt worked vigorously for antilynching legislation, compulsory health insurance, and child labor reform and fought racial discrimination in New Deal relief programs. She saw herself as a buffer between Depression victims and government bureaucracy. She often testified before legislative committees, lobbied her husband privately and the Congress publicly, and wrote a widely syndicated newspaper column.

New Deal agencies opened up spaces for scores of women in the federal bureaucracy. In addition, the social work profession, which remained roughly two-thirds female in the 1930s, grew enormously in response to the massive relief and welfare programs. Yet despite the best efforts of the women's network, women never constituted more than 19 percent of those employed by work relief programs, even though they made up 37 percent of the unemployed. In sum, although the 1930s saw no radical challenges to existing male and female roles, working-class women and professional women held their own and managed to make some gains.

A New Deal for Minorities?

The old saying among blacks that they were "last hired, first fired" was never more true than during times of high unemployment. With jobs made scarce by the Depression, even traditional "Negro occupations"—domestic service, cooking, janitorial work, and elevator operating—were coveted. One white clerk in Florida expressed a widely held view among white Southerners when he defended a lynch mob attack on a store that employed blacks: "A nigger hasn't got no right to have a job when there are white men who can do the work and are out of work."

The Roosevelt administration, worried about offending the powerful southern Democratic congressmen who were a key element in FDR's political coalition, made little overt effort to combat racism and segregation. Local administration of many federal programs meant that most early New Deal programs routinely accepted discrimination. The CCC established separate camps for African Americans. The NRA labor codes tolerated lower wages for black workers doing the same jobs as whites. African Americans could not get jobs with the TVA. Finally, the Social Security Act excluded domestics and casual laborers—workers whose ranks were disproportionately African Americans—from old-age insurance.

Yet some limited gains were made. President Roosevelt issued an executive order in 1935 banning discrimination in WPA projects. In the cities the WPA, paying minimum wages of $12 a week, enabled thousands of African Americans to survive. Between 15 and 20 percent of all WPA employees were black, although African Americans made up less than 10 percent of the nation's population. The Public Works Administration (PWA), under Harold Ickes, constructed a number of integrated housing complexes and employed more than its share of black workers in construction.

The New Deal record for minorities was mixed at best. African Americans, especially in the cities, benefited from New Deal relief and work programs, although the New Deal made no explicit attempt to attack the deeply rooted patterns of racism and discrimination in American life. The deteriorating conditions faced by Mexicans and Mexican Americans resulted in a mass reverse exodus. Yet by 1936, a majority of black voters had switched their political allegiance to the Democrats. This was the most concrete evidence that they supported the directions taken by FDR's New Deal.

The Roosevelt Recession

The nation's economy had improved significantly by 1937. Unemployment had declined to 14 percent (9 million people), farm prices had improved to 1930 levels, and industrial production was slightly higher than the 1929 mark. Roosevelt, uneasy about the federal deficit, which had grown to over $4 billion, called for large reductions in federal spending, particularly in WPA and farm programs. Federal Reserve System officials, worried about inflation, tightened credit policies.

The retrenchment brought about a steep recession. The stock market collapsed in August 1937, and industrial output and farm prices plummeted. By March 1938 the jobless rate hovered around 20 percent. As conditions worsened, Roosevelt began to blame the "new depression" on a "strike of capital," claiming businessmen had refused to invest because they wanted to hurt his prestige. In truth, the administration's own severe spending cutbacks were more responsible for the decline.

The blunt reality was that even after five years the New Deal had not brought about economic recov-

ery. Throughout 1937 and 1938 the administration drifted. Roosevelt received conflicting advice on the economy. Some advisers, suspicious of business's reluctance to make new investments, urged a massive antitrust campaign against monopolies. Others urged a return to the strategy of massive federal spending. Emergency spending bills in the spring of 1938 pumped new life into the WPA and the PWA. But Republican gains in the 1938 congressional elections made it harder than ever to get new reform measures through Congress.

There were a couple of important exceptions. The 1938 Fair Labor Standards Act established the first federal minimum wage (that paid employees twenty-five cents an hour) and set a maximum work week of forty-four hours for all employees engaged in interstate commerce. The National Housing Act of 1937, also known as the Wagner–Steagall Act, funded public housing construction and slum clearance and provided rent subsidies for low-income families. But by and large, by 1938 the reform whirlwind of the New Deal was over.

CONCLUSION

Far from being the radical program its conservative critics charged, the New Deal did little to alter fundamental property relations or the distribution of wealth. But the New Deal profoundly changed many areas of American life. Overall, it radically increased the role of the federal government in American lives and communities. Western and southern communities in particular were transformed. Relief programs and the Social Security system established at least the framework for a welfare state. The federal government guaranteed the rights of workers to join trade unions, and it set standards for minimum wages and maximum hours. In politics, the New Deal established the Democrats as the majority party. Some version of the Roosevelt New Deal coalition would dominate the nation's political life for another three decades.

The New Deal's efforts to end racial and gender discrimination were modest at best. Some of the more ambitious programs, such as subsidizing the arts or building model communities, enjoyed only brief moments of success. Other reform proposals, such as national health insurance, never got off the ground. Conservative counterpressures, especially after 1937, limited what could be changed.

Still, the New Deal made Washington a much greater center of economic regulation and political power, and the federal bureaucracy grew in size and influence. With the coming of World War II, the direct role of national government in shaping American communities would expand beyond the dreams of even the most ardent New Dealer.

CHRONOLOGY

1929	Stock market crash	**1935**	Second New Deal: Works Progress Administration, Resettlement Administration, National Labor Relations (Wagner) Act, Social Security Act
1930	Democrats regain control of the House of Representatives		Committee for Industrial Organization (CIO) established
1932	Reconstruction Finance Corporation established to make government credit available		Dust storms turn the southern Great Plains into the Dust Bowl
	Bonus Army marches on Washington		Boulder Dam completed
	Franklin D. Roosevelt elected president	**1936**	Roosevelt defeats Alfred M. Landon in reelection landslide
1933	Roughly 13 million workers unemployed		Sit-down strike begins at General Motors plants in Flint, Michigan
	First New Deal: Civilian Conservation Corps, Federal Emergency Relief Administration, Agricultural Adjustment Administration, Tennessee Valley Authority, National Recovery Administration, Public Works Administration	**1937**	General Motors recognizes United Automobile Workers
			Roosevelt's "court-packing" plan causes controversy
			Memorial Day Massacre in Chicago demonstrates the perils of union organizing
	Twenty-first Amendment repeals Prohibition (Eighteenth Amendment)		"Roosevelt recession" begins
1934	Indian Reorganization Act repeals Dawes Severalty Act and reasserts the status of Indian tribes as semisovereign nations	**1938**	CIO unions withdraw from the American Federation of Labor to form the Congress of Industrial Organizations
	Growing popularity of Father Charles E. Coughlin and Huey Long, critics of Roosevelt		Fair Labor Standards Act establishes the first federal minimum wage

REVIEW QUESTIONS

1. What were the underlying causes of the Great Depression? What consequences did it have for ordinary Americans, and how did the Hoover administration attempt to deal with the crisis?

2. Analyze the key elements of Franklin D. Roosevelt's first New Deal program. To what degree did they succeed in getting the economy back on track and offering relief to suffering Americans?

3. How did the second New Deal differ from the first? What political pressures did Roosevelt face that contributed to the new policies?

4. How did the New Deal reshape western communities and politics? What specific programs had the greatest impact in the region? How are these changes still visible today?

5. Evaluate the impact of the labor movement and radicalism on the 1930s. How did they influence American political and cultural life?

6. To what extent were the grim realities of the Depression reflected in popular culture? To what degree were they absent?

7. Discuss the long- and short-range effects of the New Deal on American political and economic life. What were its key successes and failures? What legacies of New Deal–era policies and political struggles can you find in contemporary America?

RECOMMENDED READING

Anthony J. Badger, *The New Deal: The Depression Years, 1933–1940* (1989). Recent and very useful overview that emphasizes the limited nature of New Deal reforms.

John Braeman et al., eds, *The New Deal: The State and Local Levels* (1975). Good collection of essays analyzing the workings of the New Deal in local communities throughout the nation.

Alan Brinkley, *The End of Reform: New Deal Liberalism in Recession and War* (1995). A sophisticated analysis of the political and economic limits faced by New Deal reformers from 1937 through World War II.

Lizabeth Cohen, *Making a New Deal: Industrial Workers in Chicago, 1919–1939* (1990). A brilliant study that demonstrates the transformation of immigrant and African American workers into key actors in the creation of the CIO and in New Deal politics and illuminates the complex relationship between ethnic cultures and mass culture.

Michael Denning, *The Cultural Front: The Laboring of American Culture in the Twentieth Century* (1997). A provocative reinterpretation of 1930s culture, emphasizing the impact of the Popular Front and its lasting influence on American modernism and mass culture.

Richard Lowitt, *The New Deal and the West* (1984). A comprehensive study of the New Deal's impact in the West, with special attention to water policy and agriculture.

Robert S. McElvaine, *The Great Depression: America, 1929–1941* (1984). The best one-volume overview of the Great Depression. It is especially strong on the origins and early years of the worst economic calamity in American history.

Lois Scharf, *To Work and to Wed* (1980). Examines female employment and feminism during the Great Depression.

Harvard Sitkoff, *A New Deal for Blacks* (1978). Focuses on the narrow gains made by African Americans from New Deal measures, as well as the racism that pervaded most government programs.

William Stott, *Documentary Expression and Thirties America* (1973). A very thoughtful account of the documentary impulse and its relationship to the political and social upheavals of the era.

Studs Terkel, *Hard Times* (1970). The best oral history of the Great Depression. It includes a very wide range of voices recalling life in the Depression era.

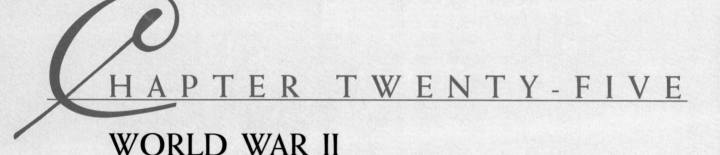

CHAPTER TWENTY-FIVE

WORLD WAR II

1941–1945

AMERICAN COMMUNITIES
Los Alamos, New Mexico

On Monday, July 16, 1945, at 5:29:45 A.M., Mountain War Time, the first atomic bomb exploded in a brilliant flash visible in three states. Within just seven minutes, a huge, multicolored, bell-shaped cloud soared 38,000 feet into the atmosphere and threw back a blanket of smoke and soot to the earth below. The heat generated by the blast was four times the temperature at the center of the sun, and the light produced rivaled that of nearly twenty suns. Within a second, the giant fireball hit the ground, ripping out a crater a half-mile wide and fusing the surrounding sand into glass. The shock wave blew out windows in houses more than 200 miles away. Within a mile of the blast, every living creature was killed—squirrels, rabbits, snakes, plants, and insects—and the smells of death persisted for nearly a month.

Very early that morning, Ruby Wilkening had driven to a nearby mountain ridge, where she joined several other women waiting for the blast. Wilkening worried about her husband, a physicist, who was already at the test site. No one knew exactly what to expect, not even the scientists who developed the bomb.

The Wilkenings were part of a unique community of scientists who had been marshaled for war. President Franklin D. Roosevelt, convinced by Albert Einstein and other physicists that the Nazis might successfully develop an atomic bomb, had inaugurated a small nuclear research program. Shortly after the United States entered World War II the scientists reported that, with sufficient support, they could produce an atomic weapon in time to affect the course of the conflict. The program, known as the Manhattan Project, was directed by the Army Corps of Engineers. By December 1942 a team headed by Italian-born Nobel Prize–winner Enrico Fermi had produced the first chain reaction in uranium under the University of Chicago's football stadium. Now the mission was to build a new, formidable weapon of war, the atomic bomb.

The government moved the key researchers and their families to Los Alamos in the remote and sparsely populated Sangre de Cristo Mountains of New Mexico, a region of soaring peaks, ancient Indian ruins, modern Pueblos, and villages occupied by the descendants of the earliest Spanish settlers. The scientists and their families arrived in March 1943. They occupied a former boys' preparatory school until new houses could be built. Some families doubled up in rugged log cabins or nearby ranches. Telephone service to the outside world was poor, and the mountain roads were so rough that changing flat tires became a tiresome but familiar routine. Construction of new quarters proceeded slowly, causing nasty disputes between the "long-hairs" (scientists) and the "plumbers" (army engineers) in charge of the grounds. Despite the chaos, outstanding American and European scientists eagerly signed up. Most were young, with an average age of twenty-seven, and quite a few were recently married. Many couples began their families at Los Alamos, producing a total of nearly a thousand babies between 1943 and 1949.

The scientists and their families formed an exceptionally close-knit community united by secrecy as well as antagonism toward the army. Most annoying was the military atmosphere. Homes and laboratories were cordoned off by barbed wire and guarded by military police. Everything, from linens to food packaging, was stamped with the words *Government Issue*. Security personnel followed the scientists whenever they left Los Alamos. The scientists' homes were wired for sound, and several scientists were reprimanded for discussing their work with their wives. All outgoing mail was censored. Well-known scientists commonly worked under aliases—Fermi became "Eugene Farmer"—and code names were used for such terms as atom, bomb, and uranium fission. Children registered without surnames at nearby public schools. Only a group thoroughly committed to the war effort could accept such restrictions on their personal liberty.

A profound feeling of urgency motivated the research team, which included refugees from Nazi Ger-

many and Fascist Italy and a large proportion of Jews. The leadership of California physicist J. Robert Oppenheimer created a scientific élan that offset the military style of commanding general Leslie Groves. Just thirty-eight, slightly built, and deeply emotional, "Oppie" personified the idealism that helped the community of scientists overcome whatever moral reservations they held about placing such an ominous weapon in the hands of the government.

Once a week Oppenheimer called together the heads of the various technical divisions to discuss their work in round-table conferences. From May to November 1944 the key issue was testing the bomb. Many scientists feared that the test might fail, and, with the precious plutonium scattered and lost, the entire project might be discredited. But as plutonium production increased, the Los Alamos team agreed to test "the gadget" on a site 160 miles away.

The unprecedented scientific mobilization at Los Alamos mirrored changes occurring throughout American society as the nation rallied behind the war effort. In addition to the 16 million men and women who left home for military service, nearly as many moved to take advantage of wartime jobs. Several states in the South and Southwest experienced huge surges in population. California alone grew by 2 million people, a large proportion from Mexico. Many broad social changes—such as the massive economic expansion in the West, the erosion of farm tenancy among black people in the South and white people in Appalachia, and the increased employment of married women—accelerated during the war. Although reluctant to enter the war, the United States emerged from under the weight of the Great Depression and became the leading superpower. The events of World War II, eroding old communities and creating new ones such as Los Alamos, transformed nearly all aspects of American society.

Los Alamos

KEY TOPICS

- The events leading to Pearl Harbor and declaration of war

- The marshaling of national resources for war

- American society during wartime

- The mobilization of Americans into the armed forces

- The war in Europe and Asia

- Diplomacy and the atomic bomb

THE COMING OF WORLD WAR II

The worldwide Great Depression accelerated a breakdown in the political order, which had been shaky since World War I. Production declined by nearly 40 percent, international trade dropped by as much as two-thirds, unemployment rose, and political unrest spread across Europe and Asia. Demagogues played on nationalist hatreds, fueled by old resentments and current despair, and offered solutions in the form of territorial expansion by military conquest.

Preoccupied with restoring the domestic economy, President Franklin D. Roosevelt had no specific plan to deal with the upsurge of conflict elsewhere in the world. Moreover, the majority of Americans strongly opposed entanglement in another world war. But as debate over diplomatic policy heated up, terrifying events overseas pulled the nation steadily toward military intervention.

The Shadows of War

War spread first across Asia. Militarist–imperialist leaders in Japan, which suffered economically from the loss of trade during the 1930s, were determined to make their nation the richest in the world. The Japanese Army seized control of Manchuria in 1931 and in 1932 installed a puppet government there. When reprimanded by the League of Nations, Japan simply withdrew from the organization. In 1937 Japan provoked a full-scale war with an invasion of northern China. When it seized control of the capital city of Nanking, Japan's army murdered as many as 300,000 Chinese men, women, and children and destroyed much of the city. Within the year Japan controlled all but China's western interior and threatened all of Asia and the Pacific.

Meanwhile, the rise of authoritarian nationalism in Italy and Germany cast a dark shadow over Europe. The economic hardships brought on by the Great Depression—and in Germany resentment over the harsh terms of Versailles Treaty that ended World War I—fueled the rise of demagogic mass movements. Glorifying war as a test of national virility, the Italian

Fascist dictator Benito Mussolini, who had seized power in 1922, declared, "We have buried the putrid corpse of liberty." In Germany, the National Socialists (Nazis), led by Adolf Hitler, combined militaristic rhetoric with a racialist doctrine of Aryan (Nordic) supremacy that claimed biological superiority for the blond-haired and blue-eyed peoples of northern Europe and classified nonwhites, including Jews, as "degenerate races."

Hitler, who had the backing of major industrialists such as the weapons manufacturer Krupp and the support of about a third of the German electorate, was appointed chancellor of Germany in 1933. With his brown-shirted storm troopers ruling the streets, Hitler quickly seized absolute authority, destroying opposition parties and effectively making himself dictator of the strongest nation in central Europe. Renouncing the disarmament provisions of the Versailles Treaty, he began to rebuild Germany's armed forces. In 1936 Italy allied with Germany to form the Rome-Berlin Axis. In November 1937 Hitler announced plans to obtain *Lebensraum*—living space and farmland for Germany's growing population—through territorial expansion. Already in 1935 Italy had sent troops the Ethiopia and formally claimed the impoverished African kingdom as a colony. The following year Hitler had sent troops to occupy the Rhineland, a region demilitarized by the Versailles Treaty, and prepared to advance on central Europe. In 1938 he annexed his native Austria to Germany.

Hitler next turned his attention to Czechoslovakia, a country that both Britain and France were pledged by treaty to assist. War seemed imminent. But Britain and France surprised Hitler by agreeing, at a conference in Munich the last week of September 1938, to allow Germany to annex the Sudetenland, a part of Czechoslovakia bordering Germany. In return, Hitler pledged to stop his territorial advance. In March 1939, however, Hitler seized the rest of Czechoslovakia.

By the fall of 1938, shocking details of Hitler's regime became known. After 1935, when Hitler published the notorious Nuremberg Laws denying Jews their civil rights, the campaign against the Jews became steadily more vicious. On the night of November 9, 1938, Nazi storm troopers rounded up Jews, beating them mercilessly and murdering an untold number. They smashed windows in Jewish shops, hospitals, and orphanages and burned synagogues to the ground. This attack became known as *Kristallnacht*, "the Night of Broken Glass." The Nazi government soon expropriated Jewish property and excluded Jews from all but the most menial forms of employment. Pressured by Hitler, Hungary and Italy also enacted laws against Jews.

Roosevelt Readies for War

While Americans looked on anxiously, the twists and turns of world events prompted President Franklin D. Roosevelt to ready the nation for war. In October 1937, he had called for international cooperation to "quarantine the aggressors." But a poll of Congress revealed that a two-thirds majority opposed economic sanctions, calling any such plan a "back door to war." Forced to draw back, Roosevelt nevertheless won from Congress $1 billion in appropriations to enlarge the navy.

Everything changed on September 1, 1939, when Hitler invaded Poland. Committed by treaty to defend Poland against unprovoked attack, Great Britain and France issued a joint declaration of war against Germany two days later. After the fall of Warsaw at the end of the month, the fighting slowed to a near halt. Even along their border, French and German troops did not exchange fire. From the east, however, the invasion continued. Just two weeks before Hitler overran Poland, the Soviet Union had stunned the world by signing a nonaggression pact with its former enemy. The Red Army now entered Poland, and the two great powers proceeded to split the hapless nation between them. Soviet forces then headed north, invading Finland on November 30. The European war had begun.

Calculating that the United States would stay out of the war, Hitler waged his brutal spring offensive, the *Blitzkrieg* (lightning war), against western Europe. Nazi troops first struck Germany's northern neighbors in April 1940. After taking Denmark and Norway, the Nazi armored divisions swept over Holland, Belgium, and Luxembourg and sent more than 338,000 British troops into retreat across the English Channel from Dunkirk. Hitler's army, joined by the Italians, easily conquered France in June 1940. Hitler now turned toward England. In the battle of Britain, Nazi bombers pounded population and industrial centers while U-boats cut off incoming supplies.

Even with Great Britain under attack, opinion polls indicated Americans' determination to stay out of the war. But most Americans, like Roosevelt himself, believed that the security of the United States depended on both a strong defense and the defeat of Germany. Invoking the Neutrality Act of 1939, which permitted the sale of arms to Britain, France, and China, the president clarified his position: "all aid to the Allies short of war." In May 1940 he began to transfer surplus U.S. planes and equipment to the Allies. In September the president secured the first peacetime military draft in American history, the Selective Service Act of 1940, which sent 1.4 million men to army training camps by July 1941.

President Roosevelt could not yet admit the inevitability of U.S. involvement, especially during an election year. His popularity had dropped with the "Roosevelt recession" that began in 1937, raising doubts about the possibility of an unprecedented third term. In his campaign he promised voters not to "send your boys to any foreign wars." Roosevelt and his vice-presidential candidate, Henry Wallace, won by a margin of 5 million popular votes over the Republican dark-horse candidate, Wendell L. Willkie of Indiana.

Roosevelt now moved more aggressively to aid the Allies in their struggle with the Axis powers. He proposed a bill that would allow the president to sell, exchange, or lease arms to any country whose defense appeared vital to U.S. security. Passed by Congress in March, 1941, the Lend-Lease Act made Great Britain the first beneficiary of massive aid. After Congress authorized the merchant marine to sail fully armed while conveying lend-lease supplies directly to Britain, a formal declaration of war was only a matter of time.

In August 1941 Roosevelt met secretly at sea off Newfoundland with British prime minister Winston Churchill to map military strategy and declare "common principles." Known as the Atlantic Charter, their proclamation specified the right of all peoples to live in freedom from fear, want, and tyranny.

Pearl Harbor

Throughout 1940 and much of 1941 the United States focused on events in Europe, but the war in Asia went on. Roosevelt, anticipating danger to American interests in the Pacific, had directed the transfer of the Pacific Fleet from bases in California to Pearl Harbor, on the island of Oahu, Hawai'i, in May 1940. Over the summer the United States expanded its embargo on trade with Japan. Japan responded on September 27 by formally joining Germany and Italy as the Asian partner of the Axis alliance.

The United States and Japan played for time. Roosevelt wanted to save his resources to fight against Germany, and Japan's leaders gambled that America's preoccupation with Europe might allow them to conquer all of Southeast Asia, including the French colonies in Indochina (Vietnam, Cambodia, and Laos) and the British possessions of Burma and India. When Japan occupied Indochina in July, 1941, however,

Roosevelt responded by freezing Japanese assets in the United States and cutting off its oil supplies.

Confrontation with Japan now looked likely. U.S. intelligence had broken the Japanese diplomatic code, and the president knew that Japan was preparing for war against the western powers. Roosevelt's advisers expected an attack in the southern Pacific or British Malaya sometime after November.

Early Sunday morning, December 7, 1941, Japanese planes caught American forces off guard at Pearl Harbor. Within two hours, Japanese pilots had destroyed nearly 200 American planes and badly damaged the fleet; more than 2,400 Americans were killed and nearly 1,200 wounded. On the same day, Japan struck U.S. bases on the Philippines, Guam, and Wake Island.

The next day, Congress heard Roosevelt predict that this day "will live in infamy." The president asked for a declaration of war against Japan. With only one dissenting vote—by pacifist Jeannette Rankin of Montana, who had voted against U.S. entry into World War I in 1917—Congress acceded. But the United States had not yet declared war on Japan's allies. Hitler obliged Roosevelt, appealing to the Reichstag on December 11 to support war against the "half Judaized and the other half Negrified" American nation. Mussolini joined him in the declaration, and the United States on the same day recognized that a state of war existed with Germany and Italy. World War II now began for Americans.

ARSENAL OF DEMOCRACY

Late in 1940 President Roosevelt called upon all Americans to make the nation "an arsenal of democracy." During the next three years, the economic machinery that had failed during the 1930s was swiftly retooled for military purposes, with dramatic results. The Great Depression suddenly ended.

Mobilizing for War

A few days after the United States declared war on Germany, Congress passed the War Powers Act, which established a precedent in executive authority that would endure long after the war's end. The president gained the power to reorganize the federal government and create new agencies, to establish programs censoring all news and information and abridging civil liberties, to seize property owned by foreigners, and even to award government contracts without competitive bidding.

Roosevelt promptly created special wartime agencies. At the top of his agenda was a massive reorientation and management of the economy, and an alphabet soup of new agencies arose to fill gaps in production.

In June 1942 the president created the Office of War Information (OWI) to coordinate information from the multiplying federal agencies and to engage the press, radio, and film industry in an informational campaign—in short, to sell the war to the American people.

The Federal Bureau of Investigation (FBI) was kept busy, its appropriation rising from $6 million to $16 million in just two years. The attorney general authorized wiretapping specifically in cases of espionage or sabotage, but the FBI used it extensively—and illegally—in domestic surveillance. The Joint Chiefs of Staff created the Office of Strategic Services (OSS) to assess the enemy's military strength, gather intelligence information, and oversee espionage activities. Its head, Colonel William Donovan, envisioned the OSS as an "adjunct to military strategy" and engaged leading social scientists to plot psychological warfare against the enemy.

President Franklin D. Roosevelt signs the declaration of war against Japan, December 8, 1941, a day after the attack on Pearl Harbor. Congressional leaders, many of whom had earlier hoped to keep the United States out of war, here unite around the president and his policies.

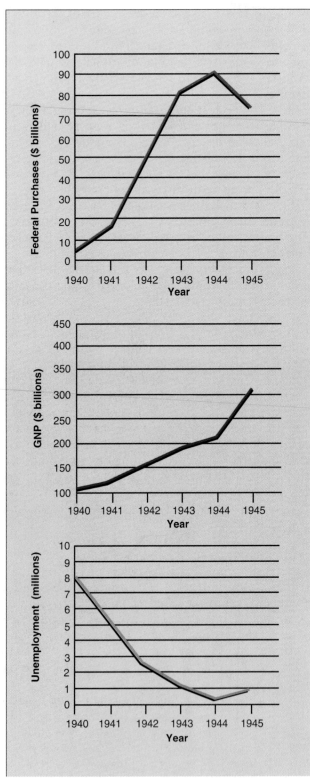

Effects of War Spending, 1940–1945 *Wartime spending had a multiplier effect on the U.S. economy. Government contracts with industry rapidly increased the gross national product, and the sharp upswing in production utilized all available workers and sharply reduced unemployment.*

Source: Figure adapted from *The Economic Transformation of America* by Robert L. Heilbroner and Aaron Singer, copyright © 1977 by Harcourt, Inc., reproduced by permission of the publisher.

It cost about $250 million a day to fight the war, and the federal government spent twice as much during the war as during its entire prior history. The federal budget grew to be ten times the size of the peacetime budget of the New Deal. The exception to this pattern of expansion was the New Deal itself. As President Roosevelt announced in 1942, "Dr. New Deal" had been replaced by "Dr. Win the War."

Economic Conversion

Neither military power nor strategy, many observers agreed, would prove to be the decisive factor: the United States would win the war by outproducing its enemies. Enjoying a sizable industrial base, abundant natural resources (largely free from interference by the war), and a civilian population large enough to increase its labor force without draining military energies, the nation could rise to the challenge. The war would inspire the most productive workforce in the world, lift the United States out of the Great Depression, and create the biggest economic boom in the history of any nation. But first the entire civilian economy had to be expanded and transformed for the production of arms and other military supplies.

By the summer of 1941 the federal government was pouring vast amounts into defense production, and six months after the attack on Pearl Harbor government allocations for equipment and supplies topped $100 billion, more than American firms had produced in any previous year. Facing war orders too large to fill, American industries were now primed for all-out production.

With better equipment and more motivation, American workers proved twice as productive as the Germans, five times as productive as the Japanese. No wonder the actual volume of industrial output expanded at the fastest rate in American history. Military production alone grew from 2 percent of the 1939 total gross national product to 40 percent of the 1943 total. "Something is happening," announced *Time* magazine, "that Adolf Hitler does not understand . . . it is the miracle of production."

Defense production transformed entire regions. This impact was strongest in the West, as the federal government poured in nearly $40 billion for military and industrial expansion in this major staging area for the Pacific war. California secured 10 percent of all federal funds, and by 1944 Los Angeles had become the nation's second largest manufacturing center, only slightly behind Detroit. The South also benefited from 60 of the army's 100 new camps. Its textile factories hummed: the army alone required nearly 520 million pairs of socks and 230 million pairs of pants. The economic boom lifted entire populations out of sharecropping and tenancy into well-paid industrial jobs in the cities and pumped unprecedented profits into southern business. Across the country the rural population decreased by almost 20 percent.

Despite a "Food for Freedom" program, American farmers could not keep up with the rising international demand or even the domestic market for milk, potatoes, fruits, and sugar. The Department of Agriculture reached its goals only in areas such as livestock production, where farmers were encouraged by skyrocketing wholesale prices for meat. The war also speeded the development of large-scale, mechanized production of crops, including the first widespread use of chemical fertilizers and pesticides. By 1945 farm income had doubled, but thousands of small farms had disappeared, never to return.

New Workers

The wartime economy brought an unprecedented number of new workers into the labor force. The *bracero* program, negotiated by United States and Mexico in 1942, opened to Mexicans short-term employment in trades previously closed to them, such as shipbuilding on the Pacific coast. Sioux and Navajos were hired in large numbers to help build military depots and training centers. African Americans found new opportunities in industry, and the number of black workers rose from 2,900,000 to 3,800,000.

The war most dramatically altered the wage-earning patterns of women. The female labor force grew by over 50 percent, reaching 19.5 million in 1945. The rate of growth proved especially high for white women over the age of thirty-five, and for the first time married women became the majority of female wage earners. The employment rate changed comparatively little for African American women; fully 90 percent had been in the labor force in 1940. However, large numbers of black women left domestic service for higher-paying jobs in manufacturing.

Neither government nor industry expected women to stay in their jobs when the war ended. Recruitment campaigns targeted "Mrs. Stay-at-Home" yet underscored the temporary aspect of her wartime service. "Rosie the Riveter" appeared in posters and advertisements as the model female citizen, but only "for the duration." In Washington, D.C., women bus drivers were given badges to wear on their uniforms that read: "I am taking the place of a man who went to war."

Compared to the Great Depression, when married women were barred from many jobs, World War II opened up new fields. The number of women automobile workers, for example, jumped from 29,000 to 200,000, and that of women electrical workers from 100,000 to 374,000. Polled near the end of the war, the overwhelming majority—75 percent—of women workers expressed a desire to keep working, preferably at the same jobs.

The major advances proved short-lived. As early as 1943 some industries began to design plans for laying off women as war production wound down. With jobs reserved for returning veterans, women in industry saw their numbers diminish rapidly; as many as 4 million lost their jobs between 1944 and 1946.

Wartime Strikes

Although 17 million new jobs were created during the war, the economic gains were unevenly distributed. Wages increased by as much as 50 percent but never as fast as profits or prices. This widely reported disparity produced one of the most turbulent periods in American labor history.

Labor strife began even before U.S. involvement in World War II. Only two weeks after the 1940 election, workers struck at the Vultee aircraft plant in Los Angeles. After the attorney general denounced the strikers as unpatriotic and the FBI began to harass participants, workers throughout the city walked off their jobs in sympathy with the aircraft workers.

More workers went on strike in 1941, before the United States entered the war, than in any previous year except 1919. Rising production orders and tightening labor markets made strikes feasible: jobs were plentiful, and business leaders, anticipating hefty profits, had reason to settle quickly. This climate prompted a militant union drive at Ford Motor Company's enormous River Rouge plant, and the United Auto Workers (UAW) emerged as one of the most powerful labor organizations in the world.

Once the United States entered the war, the major unions agreed to no-strike pledges for its duration. The National War Labor Board, with representatives from business and labor, encouraged employers to allow unions in their plants, and unions secured contracts that included automatic dues checkoff, high wages, and new fringe benefits such as pension plans. Total union membership increased from 10.5 million to 14.7 million, with women's share alone rising from 11 to 23 percent.

Unions also enrolled 1,250,000 African Americans, twice the prewar number. But many white workers resisted this change. "Hate strikes" broke out in plants across the country when African Americans were hired or promoted to jobs customarily held by white workers. For example, at a U.S. Rubber Company factory in Detroit, more than half the workers walked out in 1943 when African American women began to operate the machinery. Such strikes usually ended quickly because black workers refused to back down.

Rank-and-file union members staged other illegal strikes. The most dramatic, a walkout of more than a half-million coal miners in 1943 led by the rambunctious John L. Lewis, withstood the attacks of the government and the press. Roosevelt repeatedly ordered the mines seized, only to find, as Lewis retorted, that coal could not be mined with bayonets. The Democratic majority in Congress passed the first federal antistrike bill, giving the president power to penalize strikers, even to draft them. Yet the strikes grew in size and number, reaching a level greater than in any other four-year period in American history.

THE HOME FRONT

Most Americans thoroughly appreciated the burst of prosperity brought on by wartime production, but they also experienced food rationing, long workdays, and separation from loved ones. Alongside national unity ran deep conflicts on the home front. Racial and ethnic hostilities repeatedly flared up and on several occasions erupted into violence.

Families in Wartime

Despite the uncertainties of wartime, or perhaps because of them, men and women rushed into marriage. The surge in personal income caused by the wartime economic boom meant that many young couples could afford to set up their own households—something their counterparts in the 1930s had not been able to do. As one social scientist remarked at the time, "Economic conditions were ripe for a rush to the altar." For other couples, the prospect of separation provided the incentive. The U.S. Census Bureau estimated that between 1940 and 1943 at least a million more people married than would have been expected had there been no war. The marriage rate skyrocketed, peaking in 1946, but by 1946 the number of divorces also set records.

Housing shortages were acute, and rents were high. So scarce were apartments that taxi drivers, for an extra fee, became up-to-the-minute guides to vacancies. Able to set their own terms, landlords often discriminated against families with children and even more so against racial minorities.

Supplying a household was scarcely less difficult. Although retailers extended their store hours into the evenings and weekends, shopping had to be squeezed in between long hours on the job. Extra planning was necessary for purchasing government-rationed staples such as meat, cheese, sugar, milk, coffee, gasoline, and even shoes. Many women found it nearly impossible to manage both a demanding job and a household; this dual responsibility contributed to high turnover and absentee rates in factories.

The care of small children became a major problem. Wartime employment or military service often separated husbands and wives, leaving children in the hands of only one parent. But even when families stayed together, both adults often worked long hours, sometimes on different shifts. Although the War Manpower Commission estimated that as many as 2 million children needed some form of child care, federally funded day-care centers served less than 10 percent of defense workers' children.

Juvenile delinquency rose during the war. With employers often relaxing minimum age requirements for employment, many teenagers quit school for the high wages of factory jobs. In 1944 the U.S. Office of Education and the Children's Bureau inaugurated a back-to-school campaign. Local school boards appealed to employers to hire only older workers, and toward the end of the war the student dropout rate began to decline.

Public health improved greatly during the war. Forced to cut back on expenditures for medical care during the Great Depression, many Americans spent large portions of their wartime paychecks on doctors, dentists, and prescription drugs. But even more important were the benefits provided to the more than 16 million men inducted into the armed forces and their dependents. Nationally, incidences of such communicable diseases as typhoid fever, tuberculosis, and diphtheria dropped considerably, the infant death rate fell by more than a third, and life expectancy increased by three years. The death rate in 1942, excluding battle deaths, was the lowest in the nation's history.

The Internment of Japanese Americans

After the attack on Pearl Harbor, many Americans feared an invasion of the mainland and suspected Japanese Americans of secret loyalty to an enemy government. On December 8, 1941, the federal government froze the financial assets of those born in Japan, known as *Issei*, who had been barred from U.S. citizenship. Although a State Department intelligence report certified their loyalty, Japanese Americans, two-thirds of whom were American-born citizens, became the only ethnic group singled out for legal sanctions.

Charges of sedition masked long-standing racial prejudices. The press began to use the word "Jap" in headlines, and political cartoonists employed blatant racial stereotypes. Popular songs appeared with titles such as "You're a Sap, Mister Jap, to Make a Yankee Cranky." "The very fact that no sabotage has taken place to date," an army report suggested, with twisted logic, "is a disturbing and confirming indication that action will be taken."

On February 19, 1942, President Roosevelt signed Executive Order 9066, suspending the civil rights of Japanese Americans and authorizing the exclusion of approximately 110,000 men, women, and chil-

Byron Takashi Tsuzuki, Forced Removal, Act II, 1944. *This Japanese American artist illustrates the forced relocation of Japanese Americans from their homes to one of ten inland camps in 1942. About 110,000 Japanese Americans were interned during World War II, some for up to four years. Beginning in January 1945, they were allowed to return to the Pacific coast.*   Byron Takashi Tsuzuki. Forced Removal, Act II, 1944. Japanese American National Museum. Collection of August and Kitty Nakagawa.

The Japanese American Citizens League charged that racial animosity rather than military necessity had dictated the internment policy. Despite the protest of the American Civil Liberties Union and several church groups against the abridgment of the civil rights of Japanese Americans, the Supreme Court in *Korematsu v. U.S.* (1944) upheld the constitutionality of relocation on grounds of national security. By this time a program of gradual release was in place, although the last center, at Tule Lake, California, did not close until March 1946. In protest, nearly 6,000 Japanese Americans renounced their U.S. citizenship. Japanese Americans had lost homes and businesses valued at $500 million in what many historians judge the worst violation of American civil liberties during the war. Not until 1988 did the U.S. Congress vote reparations of $20,000 and public apology to each of the 60,000 surviving victims.

dren from mainly California, Oregon, Washington, and southern Arizona.

During the spring of 1942, Japanese American families received one week's notice to close up their businesses and homes before being transported to one of the ten internment camps managed by the War Relocation Authority. The guarded camps were located as far away as Arkansas, although the majority had been set up in isolated districts of Utah, Colorado, Idaho, Arizona, Wyoming, and California. Karl G. Yoneda described his quarters at Manzanar:

> There were no lights, stoves, or window panes. My two cousins and I, together with seven others, were crowded into a 25 × 30 foot room. We slept on army cots with our clothes on. The next morning we discovered that there were no toilets or washrooms. . . . We saw GIs manning machine guns in the watchtowers. The barbed wire fence which surrounded the camp was visible against the background of the snow-covered Sierra mountain range. "So this is the American-style concentration camp," someone remarked.

By August, virtually every West Coast resident who had at least one Japanese grandparent had been interned.

Civil Rights and Race Riots

Throughout the war, African American activists conducted a "Double V" campaign, mobilizing not only for Allied victory but for their own rights as citizens. "The army is about to take me to fight for democracy," one Detroit resident said, "but I would as leave fight for democracy right here." Black militants demanded, at a minimum, fair housing and equal employment opportunities. President Roosevelt responded in a lukewarm fashion, supporting advances in civil rights that would not, in his opinion, disrupt the war effort.

Before the United States entered the war, A. Philip Randolph, president of both the Brotherhood of Sleeping Car Porters and the National Negro Congress, had organized the March on Washington Movement. Eager to stop the movement, President Roosevelt met with Randolph, who proposed an executive order "making it mandatory that Negroes be permitted to work." Randolph reviewed several drafts before approving the text that became, on June 25, 1941, Executive Order 8802 banning discrimination in defense industries and government. Randolph called off the march but did not disband his all-black March on Washington organization. He remained determined to "shake up white America."

Other civil rights organizations formed during wartime to fight both discrimination and Jim Crow practices, including segregation in the U.S. armed forces. The interracial Congress of Racial Equality (CORE), formed by pacifists in 1942, staged sit-ins at Chicago, Detroit, and Denver restaurants that refused to serve African Americans. Meanwhile, membership in the National Association for the Advancement of Colored People (NAACP), which took a strong stand against discrimination in the military, grew from 50,000 in 1940 to 450,000 in 1946.

The struggle for equality took shape within local communities. In February 1942, when twenty black families attempted to move into new federally funded apartments adjacent to a Polish American community in Detroit, a mob of 700 white protesters halted the moving vans and burned a cross on the project's grounds. The police overlooked the white rioters but arrested black youths. Finally, two months later, 1,000 state troopers supervised the move of these families into the Sojourner Truth Homes, named after the famous abolitionist and former slave.

Racial violence reached its wartime peak during the summer of 1943, when 274 conflicts broke out in nearly fifty cities. In Detroit, twenty-five blacks and nine whites were killed and more than 700 were injured. Poet Langston Hughes, who supported U.S. involvement in the war, wrote:

> *Looky here, America*
> *What you done done—*
> *Let things drift*
> *Until the riots come*
>
> *. . . . .*
>
> *Yet you say we're fighting*
> *For democracy.*
> *Then why don't democracy*
> *Include me?*
>
> *I ask you this question*
> *Cause I want to know*
> *How long I got to fight*
> *BOTH HITLER—AND JIM CROW.**

Zoot-Suit Riots

On the night of June 4, 1943, sailors poured into nearly 200 cars and taxis to drive through the streets of East Los Angeles in search of Mexican Americans dressed in zoot suits. The sailors assaulted their victims at random,

*From Collected Poems *by Langston Hughes, copyright © 1994 by the Estate of Langston Hughes. Reprinted by permission of Alfred A. Knopf and Harold Ober Associates Incorporated.*

even chasing one youth into a movie theater and stripping him of his clothes while the audience cheered. Riots broke out and continued for five days.

Two communities had collided, with tragic results. The sailors had only recently been uprooted from their hometowns and regrouped under the strict discipline of boot camp. Now stationed in southern California while awaiting departure overseas, they came face to face with Mexican American teenagers wearing long-draped coats, pegged pants, pocket watches with oversized chains, and big, floppy hats. To the sailors, the zoot suit was not just a flamboyant fashion. Unlike the uniform the young sailors wore, the zoot suit signaled a lack of patriotism.

However, the zoot-suiters represented less than 10 percent of their community's youth. More than 300,000 Mexican Americans were serving in the armed forces, in numbers greater than their proportion of the draft-age population and in the most hazardous branches, the paratrooper and marine corps. Many others were employed in war industries in Los Angeles, which had become home to the largest community of Mexican Americans in the nation. For the first time Mexican Americans were finding well-paying jobs, and, like African Americans, they expected their government to protect them from discrimination.

In Los Angeles, military and civilian authorities eventually contained the zoot-suit riots by ruling several sections of the city off limits to military personnel. The Los Angeles City Council passed legislation making the wearing of a zoot suit in public a criminal offense. Many Mexican Americans feared that, after the government rounded up the Japanese, they would be the next group sent to internment camps.

Popular Culture and "The Good War"

Global events shaped the lives of American civilians but appeared to touch them only indirectly in their everyday activities. Food shortages, long hours in the factories, and even fears for loved ones abroad did not take away all the pleasures of full employment and prosperity. With money in their pockets, Americans spent freely at vacation resorts, country clubs, racetracks, nightclubs, dance halls, and movie theaters. Sales of books skyrocketed, and spectator sports attracted huge audiences.

Hollywood artists meanwhile threw themselves into a perpetual round of fundraising and morale-boosting public events. Movie stars called on fans to buy war bonds and to support the troops. Combat films such as *Action in the North Atlantic* made heroes of ordinary Americans under fire, depicting GIs of different races and ethnicities discovering their common humanity. Movies with antifascist themes, such as *Tender Comrade*, promoted friendship among Russians and

Americans, while films such as *Since You Went Away* portrayed the loyalty and resilience of families with servicemen stationed overseas.

Never to see a single battle, safeguarded by two oceans, many Americans nevertheless experienced the war years as the most intense of their entire lives. Popular music, Hollywood movies, radio programs, and advertisements—all screened by the Office of War Information—encouraged a sense of personal involvement in a collective effort to preserve democracy at home and to save the world from fascism. No one was excluded, no action considered insignificant. Even casual conversation came under the purview of the government, which warned that "Loose Lips Sink Ships."

MEN AND WOMEN IN UNIFORM

During World War I, American soldiers served for a brief period and in small numbers. A quarter-century later, World War II mobilized 16.4 million Americans into the armed forces. Although only 34 percent of men who served in the army saw combat—the majority during the final year of the war—the experience had a powerful impact on nearly everyone.

Creating the Armed Forces

Before the European war broke out in 1939, the majority of the 200,000 men in the U.S. armed forces were employed as military police, engaging in such tasks as patrolling the Mexican border or occupying colonial possessions, such as the Philippines. Neither the army nor the navy was prepared for the scale of combat necessitated by World War II. Only the Marine Corps, which had been planning since the 1920s to wrest control of the western Pacific from Japan, was poised to fight.

On October 16, 1940, National Registration Day, all men between the ages of twenty-one and thirty-six were legally obligated to register for military service. After the United States entered the war, the draft age was lowered to eighteen, and local boards were instructed to choose first from the youngest.

One-third of the men examined by the Selective Service were rejected. Surprising numbers were refused induction because they were physically unfit for military service, and nearly 1 million were rejected because of "neuropsychiatric disorders or emotional problems." At a time when only one American in four graduated from high school, induction centers turned away many conscripts because they were functionally illiterate.

But those who passed the screening tests joined the best-educated army in history: nearly half of white draftees had graduated from high school and 10 percent had attended college.

The officer corps, whose top-ranking members were from the Command and General Staff School at Fort Leavenworth, tended to be highly professional, politically conservative, and personally autocratic. General Douglas MacArthur, supreme commander in the Pacific theater, was said to admire the discipline of the German army and to disparage political democracy. On the other hand, General Dwight D. Eisenhower, supreme commander of the Allied forces in Europe, introduced a new spirit. Distrusted by MacArthur and many of the older brass, Eisenhower appeared to his troops a model of fair play, encouraging young men to follow him into the officer corps for idealistic rather than career reasons.

The democratic rhetoric of the war encouraged this transformation. A shortage of officers during World War I had prompted a huge expansion of the Reserve Officer Training Corps, but drilling and discipline alone did not create good officers. Racing to make up for the deficiency, Army Chief of Staff George Marshall opened schools for officer candidates. In 1942, in seventeen-week training periods, these schools produced more than 54,000 platoon leaders. Closer in sensibility to the civilian population, these new officers were the kind of leaders Eisenhower sought.

Most GIs (short for "government issue"), the vast majority of draftees, had limited contact with the officers at the higher levels and instead forged bonds with their company commanders and men within their own combat units.

Although Americans at home heard little about the human devastation during the first years of the war, the GIs at the front experienced firsthand the unprecedented brutality, fear, and agony produced by World War II. The prolonged stress of combat caused a sizable number of GIs to succumb to "battle fatigue." More than 1 million soldiers, more than three times the number who died in battle, suffered at one time or another from debilitating psychiatric symptoms. In France, where soldiers spent up to 200 days in the field without a break from fighting, thousands cracked, occasionally inflicting wounds upon themselves in order to be sent home.

Women Enter the Military

Before World War II women served in the armed forces mainly as nurses and clerical workers. With the approach of World War II, Massachusetts Republican congresswoman Edith Nourse Rogers proposed legislation for the formation of a women's corps. Although barred from combat, women were not necessarily protected from danger. Nurses accompanied the troops into combat in Africa, Italy, and France, treated men under fire, and dug and lived in their own foxholes.

More than 1,000 women flew planes, although not in combat missions.

The government feared the spread of "immorality" among women in the armed forces and closely monitored their conduct. They advised women to avoid drinking alcoholic beverages in public and to abstain from any kind of sexually promiscuous behavior. The Marine Corps even used intelligence officers to ferret out suspected lesbians or women who showed "homosexual tendencies" (as opposed to homosexual acts), both causes for dishonorable discharge.

Old Practices and New Horizons

The draft brought hundreds of thousands of young African American men into the army, where they would join all-black regiments commanded by white officers. Secretary of War Henry Stimson refused to challenge this policy, saying that the army could not operate effectively as "a sociological laboratory." African Americans nevertheless enlisted at a rate 60 percent above their proportion of the general population.

By 1944 black soldiers represented 10 percent of the army's troops, and overall approximately 1 million African Americans served in the armed forces during World War II. The majority served in the Signal, Engineer, and Quartermaster Corps, mainly in construction or stevedore work. Only a small minority were permitted to rise to fighting status and lower officer ranks, and only toward the end of the war when the shortage of infantry neared a crisis. An all-black tank squadron earned distinction in Germany. And despite the very small number of African Americans admitted to the Air Force, the 99th Pursuit Squadron gained high marks in action against the feared German air force, the *Luftwaffe*.

Throughout 1941 race riots broke out at training bases, especially in the South. Serving in segregated, low-prestige units, African Americans encountered discrimination at every point, from the army canteen to the religious chapels. Even the blood banks kept blood segregated by race (although a black physician, Dr. Charles Drew, had invented the process for storing plasma).

The army also grouped Japanese Americans into segregated units, sending most to fight far from the Pacific theater. Better educated than the average soldier, many Nisei soldiers served as interpreters and translators. When the army decided to create a Nisei regiment, more than 10,000 volunteers stepped forward. With an acceptance rate of one in five, the Nisei 442nd fought heroically in Italy and France and became the most decorated regiment in the war.

Despite segregation, the armed forces ultimately pulled Americans of all varieties out of their communities. Many Jews and other second-generation European immigrants, for example, described their stint in the military as an "Americanizing" experience. Large numbers of Indian peoples left reservations for the first time, approximately 25,000 serving in the armed forces. For many African Americans, military service provided a bridge to postwar civil rights agitation.

Many homosexuals also discovered a wider world. Despite the implementation of a policy disqualifying them from military service, most slipped through mass screening at induction centers. Moreover, the emotional pressures of wartime, especially the fear of death, encouraged close friendships, and homosexuals in the military often found more room than in civilian life to express their sexual orientation openly. In army canteens, for example, men often danced with one another, whereas in civilian settings they would have been subject to ridicule or even arrest for such activity.

Most soldiers looked back at the war, with all its dangers and discomforts, as the greatest experience they would ever know. As the *New Republic* predicted in 1943, they met fellow Americans from every part of the country and recognized for the first time in their lives "the bigness and wholeness of the United States."

Overseas Occupation

As a liberating or occupying force, Americans stationed overseas had a mixed record. Children especially welcomed the GIs, who brought candy and chewing gum. But civilians in areas not controlled by Axis powers often resented the presence of American troops, whose demands for entertainment could turn their communities into red-light zones for drinking and prostitution.

Few Britishers welcomed the nearly 3 million GIs who were stationed in their country between 1942 and 1945. "It is difficult to go anywhere in London without having the feeling that Britain is now Occupied Territory," complained novelist George Orwell in 1943.

The relationship between GIs and civilians was worse on the Continent. At first, the French welcomed the American troops as soldiers of liberation. But the Americans arrived in 1944, when several million Europeans were without homes and nearly everyone was living on the brink of starvation. The GIs themselves were war-weary or war-crazed, and not a few committed robberies or rapes in towns and villages en route to Paris.

In Belgium and southern Holland, however, where Nazi rule had been harsh, American soldiers were greeted as heroes. City restaurants were renamed "Cafe Texas" or "Cafe Alaska." Civilians cheered the Americans and eagerly shared—or traded sexual favors for—their supply of chewing gum, small cash, and cigarettes. Despite government-sponsored precautions, the rate of sexually transmitted disease ran at 42 per 1,000 soldiers.

THE WORLD AT WAR

During the first year of declared war, the United States remained on the defensive. Hitler's forces held the European Continent and pounded England with aerial bombardments while driving deep into Russia and across northern Africa to take the Suez Canal. The situation in the Pacific was scarcely better. Just two hours after the attack on Pearl Harbor, Japanese planes struck the main U.S. base in the Philippines and demolished half of the air force commanded by General Douglas MacArthur. Within a short time, MacArthur was forced to withdraw his troops to the Bataan Peninsula, admitting that Japan had practically seized the Pacific.

But the Allies enjoyed several important advantages: vast natural resources and a skilled workforce with sufficient reserves to accelerate the production of weapons and ammunitions, the determination of millions of antifascists throughout Europe and Asia, and the capacity of the Soviet Union to endure immense losses. Slowly at first, but then with quickening speed, these advantages made themselves felt.

Soviets Halt Nazi Drive

Within a generation, a revolution in weapons and tactics had changed the nature of military conflict. Unlike World War I, which was fought by immobile armies behind trenches and between bursts of machine gun fire, World War II took the form of offensive maneuvers punctuated by surprise attacks. Its chief weapons were tanks and airplanes, combining mobility and concentrated firepower, artillery, and explosives, which according to some estimates accounted for over 30 percent of the casualties. Major improvements in communication systems, mainly two-way radio transmission and radiotelephony enabling commanders to be in contact with division leaders, also played a decisive role from the beginning of the war.

Early on, Hitler had used these methods to seize the advantage, purposefully creating terror among the stricken populations of western Europe. He now aimed to conquer the Soviet Union before the United States entered the war. By 1941, however, he had already overextended his resources. Britain's Royal Air Force fought the *Luftwaffe* to a standstill, and Mussolini's weak army was pushed out of Ethiopia and Greece. Compelled to aid their Italian ally, German strategists delayed invading the Soviet Union to secure the Balkans. Suspecting that time was running out, Hitler ordered his troops to attack his former ally on June 22—too late to avoid the brutal Russian winter.

The burden of the war quickly fell on the Soviet Union. From June to September, Hitler's forces overran the Red Army, killing or capturing nearly 3 million soldiers and leaving thousands to die from exposure or starvation. But Nazi commanders did not count on civilian resistance. The Soviets rallied, cutting German supply lines and sending every available resource to Soviet troops concentrated just outside Moscow. After furious fighting and the onset of severe winter weather, the Red Army launched a massive counterattack, catching the freezing German troops off guard. For the first time, the Nazi war machine suffered a major setback.

Turning strategically away from Moscow, during the summer of 1942 German troops headed toward Crimea and the rich oil fields of the Caucasus. Still set on conquering the Soviet Union and turning its vast resources to his own use, Hitler decided to attack Stalingrad, a major industrial city on the Volga River. The Soviets suffered more casualties during the following battles than Americans did during the entire war. But intense house-to-house and street fighting and a massive Soviet counteroffensive took an even greater toll on the Nazi fighting machine. By February 1943 the German Sixth Army had met defeat, overpowered by Soviet war equipment and by numbers. More than 100,000 German soldiers surrendered.

Already in retreat but plotting one last desperate attempt to halt the Red Army, the Germans threw most of their remaining armored vehicles into action at Kursk, in the Ukraine, in July 1943. It quickly became the greatest land battle in history. More than 2 million troops and 6,000 tanks went into action. After another stunning defeat, the Germans had decisively lost the initiative. Their only option was to delay the advance of the Red Army against their homeland.

Meanwhile, the Soviet Union had begun to recover from its early losses, even as tens of millions of its own people remained homeless and near starvation. Assisted by the U.S. Lend-Lease program, by 1942 the Soviets were outproducing Germany in many types of weapons and other supplies. Nazi officers and German civilians alike began to doubt that Hitler could win the war. The Soviet victories had turned the tide of the war.

The Allied Offensive

In the spring of 1942, Germany, Italy, and Japan had commanded a territory extending from France to the Pacific Ocean. They controlled central Europe and a large section of the Soviet Union as well as considerable parts of China and the southwestern Pacific. But their momentum was flagging. American shipbuilding kept up with all the punishment Nazi submarines could dish out, and sub-sinking destroyers greatly reduced the submarines' range. Moreover, the United States far outstripped Germany in the production of landing craft and amphibious vehicles, two of the most important innovations of the war. Outnumbered by the Allies, the German air force was now limited to defensive action. On land, the United States and Great Britain had the trucks and jeeps to mount fully mobile armies, whereas German troops marched in and out of Russia with pack-horses.

Still, German forces were a mighty opponent on the European Continent. Fighting the Nazis there almost by themselves, the Soviets repeatedly appealed for the creation of a Second Front. By 1942 Josef Stalin became yet more urgent in calling for an Allied offensive against Germany from the West. The Allies chose another military venue: northward from Africa, through Italy, and toward Central Europe.

On the night of October 23–24, 1942, near El Alamein in the deserts of western Egypt, the British Eighth Army halted a major offensive by the German Afrika Korps, headed by General Edwin Rommel, the famed "Desert Fox." Although suffering heavy losses—approximately 13,000 men and more than 500 tanks—their forces destroyed the Italian North African Army and much of Germany's Afrika Korps. The Allies now launched Operation Torch. After staging the largest amphibious military landing to that date, after six months of driving across the North African coastline, the Allied troops entered Tunis in triumph. With the surrender of a quarter-million Germans and Italians in Tunisia in May 1943, the Allies controlled Africa. More important, they had secured a solid position in the Mediterranean and closed the trap on the European Axis forces.

During the North African campaign, the Allies announced the terms of victory as unconditional surrender. In January 1943, Roosevelt and Churchill had met in Casablanca in Morocco and ruled out any possibility of negotiation with the Axis powers. Roosevelt's supporters hailed the policy as a clear statement of goals, a promise to the world that the scourge of fascism would be completely banished. Stalin, who did not attend the meeting, criticized the policy, fearing that it would only increase the enemy's determination to fight to the end. Other critics similarly charged that the demand for total capitulation would prolong the war and lengthen the casualty list.

Allied aerial bombing further increased pressure on Germany. Many U.S. leaders believed that the air force possessed the ultimate weapon, "the mightiest bomber ever built," the B-17 Flying Fortress. The U.S. Army Air Corps described this precision bomber as a "humane" weapon, capable of hitting specific military targets and sparing the lives of civilians. But when weather or darkness required pilots to depend on radar for sightings, the potential error range expanded to nearly two miles, and it was impossible to distinguish clearly between factories and schools, or between mili-

tary barracks and private homes. American pilots preferred to bomb during daylight hours, while the British bombed during the night. Bombing missions over the Rhineland and the Ruhr successfully took out many German factories. But the Germans responded by relocating their plants, often dispersing light industry to the countryside.

Determined to break German resistance, the Royal Air Force redirected its main attack away from military sites to cities, including fuel dumps and public transportation. Hamburg was practically leveled. Between 60,000 and 100,000 people were killed, and 300,000 buildings were destroyed. Sixty other cities were hit hard, leaving 20 percent of Germany's total residential area in ruins. The very worst raid of the war—650,000 incendiary bombs dropped on the city of Dresden, destroying 8 square miles and killing 135,000 civilians—had no particular military value.

The Allied Invasion of Europe

During the summer of 1943, the Allies began their advance on southern Italy. On July 10 British and American troops stormed Sicily from two directions; they conquered the island in mid-August. King Vittorio Emmanuel dismissed Mussolini, calling him "the most despised man in Italy," and Italians, by now disgusted with the Fascist government, celebrated in the streets. While Allied troops began to drive northward, Italy surrendered unconditionally on September 8.

Hitler sent new divisions into Italy, occupied the northern peninsula, and effectively stalled the Allied campaign. When the European war ended, the enemies were still battling on the rugged Italian terrain.

Elsewhere in occupied Europe, armed uprisings against the Nazis spread. The brutalized inhabitants of Warsaw's Jewish ghetto repeatedly rose up against their tormentors during the winter and spring of 1943. Realizing that they could not hope to defeat superior forces, they finally sealed off their quarter, executed collaborators, and fought invaders, street by street and house by house. Scattered revolts followed in the Nazi labor camps, where military prisoners of war and civilians were being worked to death on starvation rations.

Partisans were active in many sections of Europe, from Norway to Greece and from Poland to France. Untrained and unarmed by any military standard, organized groups of men, women, and children risked their lives to distribute antifascist propaganda, taking action against rich and powerful Nazi collaborators.

Meanwhile, Stalin continued to push for a second front. Stalled in Italy, the Allies prepared in early 1944 to retake the continent with a decisive counterattack through France. American and British forces began by filling the southern half of England with military camps. All leaves were canceled.

World War II: The Allied Offensive

The offensive phase of the Allied campaign against the Axis unfolded late in the war. Major defeats in the Soviet Union and Africa deprived Germany of the resources needed to expand the war. The British and Americans, with an almost endless supply of materials and personnel, proceeded to overpower Germany and its European allies. Germans had ruled the skies early in the war. By 1943, Allied planes destroyed the German and Italian systems of transportation and supply, making cities almost unlivable. As British and Americans troops continued to pour into Europe, victory became inevitable.

Reprinted by permission of Mountain High Maps, Digital Wisdom, Inc., Tappahannock, VA.

Allied invasion plans finally went into action on D-Day, June 6, 1944. Under steady German fire the Allied fleet brought to the shores of Normandy more than 175,000 troops and more than 20,000 vehicles, an accomplishment unimaginable in any previous war. Although the Germans had responded slowly, anticipating an Allied strike at Calais instead, at Omaha Beach they had prepared their defense almost perfectly. Wave after wave of Allied landings met machine gun and mortar fire, and the tides filled with corpses and those pretending to be dead. Some 2,500 troops died, many before they could fire a shot. In the next six weeks, nearly 1 million more Allied soldiers came ashore, broke out of Normandy, and prepared to march inland.

As the fighting continued, all eyes turned to Paris, the premier city of Europe. Allied bombers pounded factories producing German munitions on the outskirts of the French capital. As dispirited German soldiers retreated, many now hoping only to survive, the French Resistance unfurled the French flag at impromptu demonstrations on Bastille Day, July 14. General Charles de Gaulle, accompanied by Allied troops, arrived in Paris on August 25 to become president of the reestablished French Republic.

One occupied European nation after another swiftly fell. But the Allied troops had only reached a resting place between bloody battles.

The High Cost of European Victory

In September 1944 Allied commanders searched for a strategy to end the war quickly. Missing a spectacular chance to move through largely undefended territory and on to Berlin, they turned south instead, aiming to open the Netherlands for Allied armies en route to Germany's industrial heartland. Faulty intelligence reports overlooked a German division at Arnhem, Holland, waiting with firepower and ready to cut the Allied paratroopers to pieces. By the end of the battle, the Germans had captured 6,000 Americans.

In a final, desperate effort to reverse the Allied momentum, Hitler directed his last reserves, a quarter-million men, at Allied lines in the Belgian forest of the Ardennes. After weeks of fighting, the Battle of the Bulge—named for the temporary dent in Allied lines—exhausted the German capacity for counterattack. After Christmas day 1944, the Germans fell back, retreating toward their own territory.

The end was now in sight. In March 1945 the Allies rolled across the Rhine and took the Ruhr valley, with its precious industrial resources. The defense of Germany, now hopeless, had fallen into the hands of young teenagers and elderly men. By the time of the German surrender, May 8, Hitler had committed suicide in a Berlin bunker and high Nazi officials were

planning their escape routes. The casualties of the Allied European campaign had been enormous, if still small compared to those of the Eastern Front: more than 200,000 killed and almost 800,000 wounded, missing, or dead in nonbattle accidents and unrelated illness.

The War in Asia and the Pacific

The war that had begun with Pearl Harbor rapidly escalated into scattered fighting across a region of the world far larger than all of Europe, stretching from Southeast Asia to the Aleutian Islands. Japan followed up its early advantage by cutting Burma's supply routes to China, crushing the British navy, and seizing the Philippines, Hong Kong, Wake Island, British Malaya, and Thailand. Although China officially joined the Allies on December 9, 1941, and General Stillwell arrived in March as commander of the China–Burma–India theater, the military mission there remained on the defensive. Meanwhile, after tenacious fighting at the Bataan Peninsula and on the island of Corregidor, the U.S. troops not captured or killed retreated to Australia.

At first, nationalist or anticolonial sentiment played into Japanese hands. Japan succeeded with only 200,000 men because so few inhabitants would fight to defend the British or French empires. But the new Japanese empire proved terrifyingly cruel. Nationalists from Indochina to the Philippines turned against the Japanese, establishing guerrilla armies that cut supply lines and prepared the way for Allied victory.

Six months after the disaster at Pearl Harbor, the United States began to regain naval superiority in the central Pacific and to halt Japanese expansion. In a carrier duel with spectacular aerial battles at the Battle of the Coral Sea on May 7 and 8, 1942, the United States blocked a Japanese threat to Australia. A month later, the Japanese fleet converged on Midway Island. American strategists, however, thanks to specialists who had broken Japanese codes, knew when and where the Japanese planned to attack. The two carrier fleets, separated by hundreds of miles, clashed at the Battle of Midway on June 4. American planes sank four of Japan's vital aircraft carriers and destroyed hundreds of planes, ending Japan's offensive threat to Hawai'i and the west coast of the United States.

But the war for the Pacific was far from over. By pulling back their offensive perimeter, the Japanese concentrated their remaining forces. Their commanders calculated that bitter fighting, with high casualties on both sides, would wear down the American troops. The U.S. command, divided between General Douglas MacArthur in the southwest Pacific and Admiral Chester Nimitz in the central Pacific, needed to develop a counterstrategy to strangle the Japanese import-based economy and to retake strategic islands closer to the homeland.

The Allies launched their counteroffensive campaign on the Solomon Islands and Papua, near New Guinea. American and Australian ground forces fought together through the jungles of Papua, while the marines prepared to attack the Japanese stronghold of Guadalcanal.

For the next two years, the U.S. navy and marine corps pushed to capture the tiny atolls from the well-armed Japanese forces. More than 1,000 Marines died in the campaign for the island of Tarawa in November 1943. A shrewd alternative plan of "island hopping" reduced casualties by concentrating on selected land battles and gradually opening a path to Japan through air and sea power.

In October 1944 General MacArthur led a force of 250,000 to the Philippines for what was expected to be the largest naval battle in history. Practically all that remained of the Japanese navy threw itself at American transports in Leyte Gulf. After three days of battle, the United States controlled the Pacific. But the accompanying ground war cost 100,000 Filipino lives and left Manila devastated.

The struggle for the island of Okinawa, on a direct line to Tokyo 800 miles to the northeast, proved even more bloody. The invasion, which began on April 1, 1945, was the largest amphibious operation mounted by Americans in the Pacific war. Waves of Japanese airborne *kamikaze* (or "divine wind") suicide missions carried only enough fuel for a one-way flight—with a 500-pound bomb. On the ground, U.S. troops used

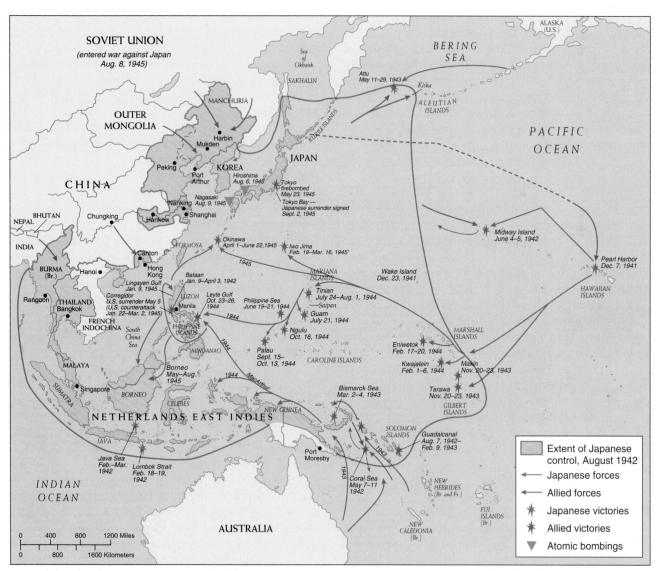

War in the Pacific   *Across an ocean battlefield utterly unlike the European theater, Allies battled Japanese troops near their homeland.*

flame-throwers, each mounted with three hundred gallons of napalm, against the dug-in Japanese. More Americans died or were wounded here than at Normandy. In all, the fighting killed more than 200,000 people.

Attacks on mainland Japan had begun to take their toll. U.S. submarines had drastically reduced the supply ships reaching Japan. After Guam had been taken, land-based American bombers could reach Tokyo and other Japanese cities with devastating results. Trapped in houses and apartments still built mostly of wood or bamboo, civilians faced massive fire-bombings that burned thousands alive and left hundreds of thousands more homeless.

Japan could not hold out forever. Without a navy or air force, the government could not even transport the oil, tin, rubber, or grain needed to maintain a military force. The Allies pressed for a quick unconditional surrender. Great Britain and particularly the United States had special reasons to hurry. Earlier seeking a commitment from the Soviet Union to invade Japan, they now looked beyond the war, determined to prevent the Red Army from taking any territories held by the Japanese. These calculations and the anticipation that an invasion would be extremely bloody set the stage for the use of a secret weapon that American scientists had been preparing: the atomic bomb.

THE LAST STAGES OF WAR

From the attack on Pearl Harbor until mid-1943, President Roosevelt and his advisers focused on military strategy rather than on plans for peace. But once the defeat of Nazi Germany appeared in sight, high government officials began to reconsider their diplomatic objectives. Roosevelt wanted both to crush the Axis powers and to establish a system of collective security to prevent another world war. He knew he could not succeed without the cooperation of the other key leaders, Stalin and Churchill.

During 1944 and 1945, the "Big Three" met to hammer out the shape of the postwar world. Although none of these nations expected to reach a final agreement, neither did they anticipate the speed and enormity of global events still to come. It soon became clear that only the mission of destroying the Axis held the Allies together.

The Holocaust

Not until the last stages of the war did Americans learn the extent of Hitler's atrocities. As part of his "final solution to the Jewish question," Hitler had ordered the systematic extermination of not only Jews but Gypsies, homosexuals, and others of "inferior races." Beginning in 1933 and accelerating after 1941, the Nazis murdered millions of people from Germany and the European nations they conquered.

During the war the U.S. government released little information on what came to be known as the Holocaust. Although liberal magazines such as the *Nation* and small committees of intellectuals pressed for attention to concentration camps, major news media such as the *New York Times* and *Time* magazine treated reports of camps and killings as minor news items. An earlier generation of journalists had helped to produce a climate of skepticism by reporting stories of German atrocity during World War I that proved in most cases to have been fabricated by the British. As late as 1943, only 43 percent of Americans polled believed that Hitler was systematically murdering European Jews.

Roosevelt and his advisers maintained that the liberation of European Jews depended primarily on a speedy and total Allied victory. When American Jews pleaded for a military strike against the rail lines leading to the notorious extermination camp in Auschwitz, Poland, the War Department replied that Allied armed forces would not be employed "for the purpose of rescuing victims of enemy oppression unless such rescues are the direct result of military operations conducted with the objective of defeating the armed forces of the enemy." In short, the government viewed civilian rescue as a diversion of precious resources.

Allied troops discovered the death camps when they invaded Germany and liberated Poland. When Eisenhower and General George S. Patton visited the Ohrdruf concentration camp in April 1945, they found barracks crowded with corpses and crematories still reeking of burned flesh. "I want every American unit not actually in the front lines to see this place," Eisenhower declared. "We are told that the American soldier does not know what he is fighting for. Now, at least, he will know what he is fighting *against*." At Buchenwald, in the first three months of 1944, over 14,000 prisoners were murdered. In all, 250,000 Gypsies, and 60,000 homosexuals, among others, had perished.

The Yalta Conference

In February 1945 Roosevelt held his last meeting with Churchill and Stalin at Yalta, a Crimean resort on the Black Sea. Seeking their cooperation, the president recognized that prospects for postwar peace also depended on compromise. Although diplomats avoided the touchy phrase "spheres of influence," it was clear that this principle guided all negotiations. Neither the United States nor Great Britain did more than object to the Soviet Union's plan to retain the Baltic states and part of Poland as a buffer zone to protect it against any future German aggression. In return, Britain planned to reclaim its empire in Asia, and the United States hoped to hold several Pacific islands in order to monitor any military resurgence in Japan. Stalin also affirmed his pledge to enter the war against Japan and approved plans for a future world organization, which Roosevelt championed.

The death of Franklin Roosevelt of a stroke on April 12, 1945 cast a dark shadow over all hopes for long-term, peaceful solutions to global problems. The president did not live to witness the surrender of Germany on May 8, 1945. And now, as new and still greater challenges were appearing, the nation's great pragmatic idealist was gone.

The Atomic Bomb

Roosevelt's death shook the fragile foundations of the Grand Alliance. His successor, Harry S. Truman, who had been a Kansas City machine politician, a Missouri judge, and a U.S. senator, lacked diplomatic experience as well as Roosevelt's personal finesse. Above all, the new president had no intention of making concessions to the war-devastated Soviets. Shortly after taking office, Truman announced to his secretary of state, "We must stand up to the Russians at this point and not be easy with them."

In this light, negotiations at the Potsdam Conference, held just outside Berlin from July 17 to August 2, 1945, lacked the spirited cooperation characteristic of Roosevelt's leadership. The American, British, and Soviet delegations had a huge agenda, including reparations, the future of Germany, and the status of other Axis powers such as Italy. They managed to agree to demand Japan's unconditional surrender and to try Nazi leaders as war criminals. But they were sharply divided over most other issues, exposing the breach in the Grand Alliance that foreshadowed the cold war.

It was during the Potsdam meetings that Truman first learned about the successful testing of an atomic bomb in New Mexico. Until this time, the United States had been pushing the Soviet Union to enter the Pacific war as a means to avoid a costly U.S. land invasion. But after Secretary of State Stimson received a cable reading "Babies satisfactorily born," U.S. diplomats concluded that they no longer needed assistance from the Soviet Union to bring the war to an end.

American diplomats knew that the emperor of Japan was prepared to end the fighting if the Allies would set aside the stipulation of unconditional surrender. At first, Truman considered accepting a slight modification, such as allowing the emperor to continue to head the Japanese nation. But the president also went forward with the plan to deploy the atomic bomb. As Truman later stated, he had no moral reservations about making this decision. He understood that the three bombs on hand had been developed specifically for this purpose. He therefore endorsed the principal outcome

of the Potsdam Conference, a warning to Japan to surrender immediately or face "complete and utter destruction."

On August 3, 1945, Japan wired its refusal to surrender. Three days later, the Army Air Force B-29 bomber *Enola Gay* dropped the bomb that destroyed the Japanese city of Hiroshima. Approximately 80,000 people died on August 6; in the following weeks thousands more died from radiation poisoning or burns; by 1950 the death toll reached 200,000. "I was greatly moved," Truman reported when he heard the news.

An editorialist wrote in the Japanese *Nippon Times*, "This is not war, this is not even murder; this is

On August 6, 1945, a U.S. B-29 *fighter plane dropped "Little Boy," an atomic bomb, on Hiroshima, killing nearly 80,000 Japanese civilians and injuring another 70,000. Three days later, "Fat Man" destroyed Nagasaki, killing 40,000 and injuring 60,000 more. On August 14, the government of Japan surrendered, bringing an end to the war.*

pure nihilism . . . a crime against God which strikes at the very basis of moral existence." In the United States, several leading religious publications echoed this view. The *Christian Century* interpreted the use of the bomb as a "moral earthquake" that made the long-denounced use of poison gas by Germany in World War I utterly insignificant by comparison.

Most Americans learned about the atomic bomb for the first time on August 7, when the news media reported the rampant destruction and death in Hiroshima. The surrender of the Japanese on August 14, after a second bomb destroyed Nagasaki, brought such relief that any implication other than military triumph dimmed. In Los Alamos, New Mexico, horns and sirens blared in exultation. Proud of his scientific accomplishment, Oppenheimer nevertheless reported that he was a "little scared of what I have made."

The decision to use the atomic bomb against Japan remains one of the most controversial aspects of the war. Although Truman stated in his memoirs, written much later, that he gave the order with the expectation of saving "a half a million American lives" in ground combat, no such official estimate exists. An intelligence document of April 30, 1946, states, "The dropping of the bomb was the pretext seized upon by all leaders as the reason for ending the war, but . . . [even if the bomb had not been used] the Japanese would have capitulated upon the entry of Russia into the war." There is no question, however, that the use of nuclear force did strengthen the U.S. diplomatic mission. It certainly intimidated the Soviet Union, which would soon regain its position as the major enemy of the United States. Truman and his advisers in the State Department knew that their atomic monopoly could not last, but they hoped that in the meantime the United States could play the leading role in erecting the structure of the new world order.

CONCLUSION

New weapons, such as massive air raids and the atomic bomb, had made warfare incomparably more deadly to both military and civilian populations. Between 40 and 50 million people died in World War II—four times the number in World War I—and half the casualties were women and children. American death tolls exceeded 405,000, the number of wounded 670,000. Slight compared to the death and injuries suffered by Allied troops and civilians from other Allied nations—more than 20 million Soviets died during the war—the human cost of World War II for Americans was second only to that of the Civil War.

Coming at the end of two decades of resolutions to avoid military entanglements, the war pushed the nation's leaders to the center of global politics and into risky military and political alliances that would not outlive the war. The United States emerged the strongest nation in the world, but in a world where the prospects for lasting peace appeared increasingly remote.

If World War II raised the nation's international commitments to a new height, its impact on ordinary Americans was not so easy to gauge. Many new communities formed as Americans migrated in mass numbers to new regions that were booming as a result of the wartime economy. Enjoying a rare moment of full employment, many workers new to well-paying industrial jobs anticipated further advances against discrimination. Exuberant at the Allies' victory over fascism and the return of the troops, the majority were optimistic as they looked ahead.

CHRONOLOGY

1931	September: Japan occupies Manchuria
1933	March: Adolf Hitler seizes power in Germany
	May: Japan quits League of Nations
1935	October: Italy invades Ethiopia
1935–37	Neutrality Acts authorize the president to deny American firms the right to sell or ship munitions to belligerent nations
1937	August: Japan invades China
	October: Franklin D. Roosevelt's quarantine speech calls for international cooperation against aggression
1938	March: Germany annexes Austria
	September: At Munich, France and Britain agree to German annexation of Sudeten Czechoslovakia
	November: *Kristallnacht,* Nazis attack Jews and destroy Jewish property
1939	March: Germany annexes remainder of Czechoslovakia
	August: Germany and the Soviet Union sign nonaggression pact
	September: Germany invades Poland; World War II begins
	November: Soviet Union invades Finland
1940	April–June: Germany's *Bliztkrieg* sweeps over Western Europe
	September: Germany, Italy, and Japan—the Axis powers— conclude a military alliance
	First peacetime military draft in American history
	November: Roosevelt is elected to an unprecedented third term
1941	March: Lend-Lease Act extends aid to Great Britain
	May: German troops secure the Balkans
	A. Philip Randolph plans March on Washington movement for July

	June: Germany invades Soviet Union
	Fair Employment Practices Committee formed
	August: Atlantic Charter announces "common principles" of the United States and Great Britain
	December: Japanese attack Pearl Harbor; United States enters the war
1942	February: Executive order mandates internment of Japanese Americans
	May–June: United States regains naval superiority in the battles of Coral Sea and Midway in the Pacific
	August: Manhattan Project begins
	November: United States stages amphibious landing in North Africa; Operation Torch begins
1943	January: Casablanca conference announces unconditional surrender policy
	February: Soviet victory over Germans at Stalingrad
	April–May: Coal miners strike
	May: German Afrika Korps troops surrender in Tunis
	July: Allied invasion of Italy
	Summer: Race riots break out in nearly fifty cities
1944	August: Liberation of Paris
	November: Roosevelt elected to fourth term
1945	February: Yalta Conference renews American–Soviet alliance
	February–June: United States captures Iwo Jima and Okinawa
	April: Roosevelt dies in office; Harry Truman becomes president
	May: Germany surrenders
	July–August: Potsdam Conference
	August: United States drops atomic bombs on Hiroshima and Nagasaki; Japan surrenders

REVIEW QUESTIONS

1. Describe the response of Americans to the rise of nationalism in Japan, Italy, and Germany during the 1930s. How did President Franklin D. Roosevelt ready the nation for war?

2. What role did the federal government play in gearing up the economy for wartime production?

3. How did the war affect the lives of American women?

4. Discuss the causes and consequences of the Japanese American internment program.

5. Describe the role of popular culture in promoting the war effort at home.

6. How did military service affect the lives of those who served in World War II?

7. What were the main points of Allied military strategy in Europe and Asia?

8. How successful were diplomatic efforts in ending the war and establishing the terms of peace?

RECOMMENDED READING

Stephen E. Ambrose, *D-Day, June 6, 1944: The Climactic Battle of World War II* (1994). A vivid and extremely readable, moment-by-moment reconstruction of the preparation and battle, relying heavily on the oral histories of American veterans.

Allan Berube, *Coming Out Under Fire: The History of Gay Men and Woman in World War Two* (1991). A study of government policy toward homosexuals during the war and the formation of a gay community. Berube offers many insights into the new opportunities offered homosexuals through travel and varied companionship and of the effects of sanctions against them.

John Morton Blum, *V Was for Victory: Politics and American Culture During World War II* (1976). A colorful narration of American society and culture during wartime. Blum seeks to recreate the patriotic spirit that quelled potential conflict among diverse groups during wartime.

Paul Boyer, *By the Bomb's Early Light: American Thought and Culture at the Dawn of the Atomic Age* (1985). An analysis of the intellectual and cultural assumptions in relation to atomic weaponry. Boyer examines the development of a political logic, on the part of President Harry Truman and others, that made use of atomic weapons against the Japanese inevitable.

Wayne S. Cole, *Roosevelt and the Isolationists, 1932–45* (1983). Shows the president and his critics sparring over foreign policy issues. Cole analyzes the complexities of liberal–conservative divisions over war and offers insights into the logic of conservatives who feared the growth of a permanent bureaucratic, militarized state.

Richard M. Dalfiume, *Desegregation of the U.S. Armed Forces: Fighting on Two Fronts, 1939–1953* (1969). Analyzes wartime race relations in the military. By examining the official mechanisms to end discrimination and the remaining patterns of racism in the armed forces, Dalfiume reveals how changing attitudes from the top ran up against old assumptions among enlisted men and women.

Roger Daniels, *Concentration Camps USA: Japanese Americans and World War II* (1981). Perhaps the best account of Japanese American internment. Daniels details the government programs, the experiences of detention and camp life, and the many long-term consequences of lost liberty.

Sherna Berger Gluck, *Rosie the Riveter Revisited: Women, the War, and Social Change* (1987). An oral history-based study of women workers during World War II. Gluck's interviewees reveal the diversity of experiences and attitudes of women workers as well as their common feelings of accomplishment.

Gerald F. Linderman, *The World Within War: America's Combat Experience in World War II* (1997). Emphasizes the less glamorous aspects of war, mainly the strains placed on the combat soldiers on the front lines. Linderman examines in especially close detail the grim experiences of army infantrymen and the marine riflemen who fought in the Pacific campaign.

Katrina R. Mason, *Children of Los Alamos: An Oral History of the Town Where the Atomic Age Began* (1995). Recollections of those who spent their childhood in Los Alamos. They describe their affection for the geographical setting as well as their sense of safety growing up in a community so well protected. They also comment on the diversity among the ethnic groups who populated the town and the pride they took in their parents' contribution to building the bomb and ending the war.

Neil R. McMillan, ed., *Remaking Dixie: The Impact of World War II on the American South* (1997). A collection of essays on the impact of World War II on the South with special attention to the experiences of African Americans and women. Several authors question the degree to which southern society was transformed by wartime mobilization.

Robert J. Moskin, *Mr. Truman's War: The Final Victories of World War II and the Birth of the Postwar World* (1996). A lively history of the final stages of World War II, including the surrender of Germany and the emergence of postwar foreign policy. Moskin provides an assessment of the impact of the war on social and economic conditions in the United States.

William M. Tuttle Jr., *"Daddy's Gone to War": The Second World War in the Lives of America's Children* (1993). Draws from 2,500 letters that the author solicited from men and women in their fifties and sixties about their wartime childhood memories.

David S. Wyman, *The Abandonment of the Jews: America and the Holocaust, 1941–1945* (1984). A detailed examination of U.S. immigration policy and response to Hitler's program of genocide. Wyman shows both the indifference of the Roosevelt administration to appeals for Allied protection of Jews and the inclinations of leading American Jewish organizations to stress the formation of a future Jewish state above the protection of European Jewry.

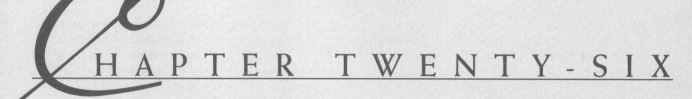

CHAPTER TWENTY-SIX

THE COLD WAR

1945–1952

AMERICAN COMMUNITIES
University of Washington, Seattle:
Students and Faculty Face the Cold War

I n May 1948, a philosophy professor at the University of Washington in Seattle answered a knock on his office door. Two state legislators, members of the state's Committee on Un-American Activities, entered. "Our information," they charged, "puts you in the center of a communist conspiracy."

The accused professor, Melvin Rader, had never been a communist. A self-described liberal, Rader drew fire because he had joined several organizations supported by communists.

Despite this disavowal, Rader was caught up in a Red Scare that curtailed free speech and political activity on campuses throughout the United States. At some universities, such as Yale, the Federal Bureau of Investigation (FBI) set up camp with the consent of the college administration, spying on students and faculty, screening credentials of job or scholarship applicants, and seeking to entice students to report on their friends or roommates. The University of Washington administration turned down the recommendation of the Physics Department to hire J. Robert Oppenheimer because the famed atomic scientist had become a vocal opponent of the arms race and the proliferation of nuclear weapons.

Although one state legislator claimed that "not less than 150 members" of the University of Washington faculty were subversives, the state's Committee on Un-American Activities turned up just six members of the Communist Party. These six were brought up before the university's Faculty Committee on Tenure and Academic Freedom, charged with violations ranging from neglect of duty to failing to inform the university administration of their party membership. Three were ultimately dismissed, while the other three were placed on probation.

What had provoked this paranoia? Instead of peace, a pattern of cold war—icy relations between the two superpowers—prevailed. Uneasy allies during World War II, the United States and the Soviet Union now viewed each other as archenemies.

If not for the outbreak of the cold war, this era would have marked one of the most fruitful in the history of higher education. The Servicemen's Readjustment Act, popularly known as the GI Bill of Rights, passed by Congress in 1944, offered stipends covering tuition and living expenses to veterans attending vocational schools or college. By the 1947–48 academic year, the federal government was subsidizing nearly half of all male college students. Between 1945 and 1950, 2.3 million students benefited from the GI Bill, at a cost of more than $10 billion.

At the University of Washington the student population in 1946 had grown by 50 percent over its prewar peak of 10,000, and veterans represented fully two-thirds of the student body. According to many observers, a feeling of community flourished among these war-weary undergraduates. Often the first in their families to attend college, they joined fellow students in campaigns to improve the campus. Married, often fathers of young children, they expected university administrators to treat them as adults. They wanted less supervision of undergraduate social life, more affordable housing, and better cultural opportunities. On some campuses, film societies and student-run cooperatives vied with fraternities and sororities as centers of undergraduate social activity.

The cold war put a damper on these community-building efforts. FBI director J. Edgar Hoover testified

Seattle

that the college campuses were centers of "red propaganda," full of teachers "tearing down respect for agencies of government, belittling tradition and moral custom and . . . creating doubts in the validity of the American way of life."

These extravagant charges were never substantiated, but several states, including Washington, enacted or revived "loyalty acts," obligating all state employees to swear in writing their loyalty to the United States and to disclaim membership in any subversive organization. Nationwide, approximately 200 faculty members were dismissed outright and many others were denied tenure. Thousands of students simply left school, dropped out of organizations, or changed friends after "visits" from FBI agents or interviews with administrators. The main effect on campus was the restraint of free speech generally and fear of criticizing U.S. racial, military, or diplomatic policies in particular.

This gloomy mood reversed the wave of optimism that swept Americans only a few years earlier. V-J Day, marking Victory over Japan, had erupted into a two-day national holiday of wild celebrations, complete with ticker-tape parades, spontaneous dancing, and kisses for returned GIs. Americans, living in the richest and most powerful nation in the world, finally seemed to have gained the peace they had fought and sacrificed to win. But peace proved fragile and elusive.

KEY TOPICS

- Prospects for world peace at end of World War II

- U.S. diplomatic policy during the cold war

- The Truman presidency

- Anticommunism and McCarthyism

- Cold war culture and society

- The Korean War

GLOBAL INSECURITIES AT WAR'S END

The war that had engulfed the world from 1939 to 1945 created an international interdependence that no country could ignore. The legendary African American folk singer Leadbelly (Huddie Ledbetter) added a fresh lyric to an old spiritual melody: "We're in the same boat, brother. . . . And if you shake one end you're going to rock the other." Never before, not even at the end of World War I, had hopes risen so strong for a genuine "community of nations."

"The American Century"

In 1941 Henry Luce, publisher of *Time, Life,* and *Fortune* magazines, had forecast the dawn of "the American Century." This bold pronouncement reflected the prevailing faith that, with the rest of the world in ruins, only the United States could establish the principles of world order.

Americans had good reason to be confident about their prospects for setting the terms of peace. Unlike Great Britain and France, the United States had not only escaped the ravages of military conflict but had actually prospered. By June 1945 the capital assets of manufacturing had increased 65 percent over prewar levels and were equal in value to approximately half the entire world's goods and services.

Yet the foundation of this vigorous economy appeared fragile. Above all, Americans feared the return of widespread unemployment. Economists understood that it was the massive government spending associated with wartime industry, rather than New Deal programs, that had ended the nightmare of the 1930s. A great question loomed: What would happen when wartime production slowed and millions of troops returned home?

Just to maintain the current level of growth, the United States needed an estimated $14 billion in exports—an unprecedented amount. Many business leaders even looked to the Soviet Union as a potential trading partner. With this prospect vanishing, Eastern European markets threatened, and large chunks of former colonial territories closed off, U.S. business and government leaders became determined to secure Western Europe for American trade and investment.

During the final stages of the war, Roosevelt's advisers laid plans to secure U.S. primacy in the postwar global economy. In July 1944 representatives from forty-four Allied nations met at Bretton Woods, New Hampshire, and established the International Bank for Reconstruction and Development (World Bank) and the International Monetary Fund (IMF) to facilitate the rebuilding of war-torn Europe and to assist the nations of Asia, Latin America, and Africa. By stabilizing exchange rates to facilitate expansion of international trade, the IMF would deter currency conflicts and trade wars, two maladies of the 1930s that were largely responsible for the political instability and national rivalries leading to World War II. As the principal supplier of funds for the IMF and the World Bank— over $7 billion to each—the United States could unilaterally shape the world economy by determining the allocation of loans.

The Soviet Union interpreted "the American Century," and especially its aggressive economic programs, as a return to the policy that had guided international affairs since the Russian Revolution: U.S. determination to destroy communism. For this reason, the USSR simply refused to join either the World Bank or the IMF. By spurning these financial institutions, the Soviet Union cut off the possibility of aid to its own people as well as to its Eastern European client states. Equally important, the USSR isolated itself economically.

The United Nations and Hopes for Collective Security

The dream of postwar international cooperation had been seeded by President Roosevelt. In late summer and fall 1944 at the Dumbarton Oaks Estate near Washington, D.C., and again in April 1945 in San Francisco, the Allies worked to shape the United Nations as an international agency that would arbitrate disputes among members as well as impede aggressors, by military force if necessary.

The UN represented all member nations through its General Assembly. But the "primary responsibility for the maintenance of international peace and security" lay exclusively with the Security Council, which comprised five permanent members (the United States, Great Britain, the Soviet Union, France, and Nationalist China) and six temporary members elected for two-year terms.

The UN's agency provided the war-torn countries of Europe and Asia with billions of dollars for medical supplies, food, and clothing. The UN also dedicated itself to protecting human rights, and its high standards of human dignity owed much to the lobbying of Eleanor Roosevelt. The president's widow served as one of the first delegates from the United States.

The Division of Europe

The Atlantic Charter of 1941 had recognized the right of all nations to self-determination and renounced all claims to new territories as the spoils of war. The Allied leaders themselves, however, violated the charter's main points before the war had ended by dividing occupied Europe into spheres of influence (see Chapter 25).

As long as Franklin Roosevelt remained alive, this kind of realism in world politics had seemed reconcilable with world peace. The president had balanced his own international idealism with his belief that the United States was entitled to extraordinary influence in Latin America and the Philippines, and that other great powers might have similar privileges or responsibilities elsewhere. Roosevelt believed that by offering economic assistance he might ease Stalin's fears and loosen the Soviet grip on conquered nations. But by the time of the Potsdam Conference in July 1945, the USSR had already consolidated its influence over most of Eastern Europe and the little Baltic states.

Hopes for cooperation further unraveled in Central Europe. France, Great Britain, the USSR, and the United States had divided Germany temporarily into four occupation zones, each governed by one of the Allied nations. But the Allies could not agree on long-term plans. Having borne the brunt of German aggression, France and the USSR both opposed reunification. The latter, in addition, demanded heavy reparations along with a limit on postwar reindustrialization. Roosevelt appeared to agree with the Soviets. But American business leaders, envisioning a new center for U.S. commerce, shared Churchill's hope of rebuilding Germany into a powerful counterforce against the Soviet Union and a strong market for U.S. and British goods.

The division of Germany forecast the shape of the new world order. West Germany became more and more "American," as the United States directed the reconstruction of its capitalist economy. Meanwhile, the Soviets dragged industrial equipment out of impoverished East Germany for their own domestic needs and imposed a harsh discipline upon the inhabitants.

"The main prize of the victory" over the Axis powers was, a State Department document had noted in November 1945, a "limited and temporary power to establish the kind of world we want to live in." But this prediction failed to account for the dissolution of the Grand Alliance. Winston Churchill, swearing to preserve the British colonial empire in a speech delivered in Fulton, Missouri, in February 1946, declared that "an iron curtain has descended upon the [European] continent." The dream of a community of nations had dissolved with the expansion of Soviet control over unwilling Eastern European citizens, but perhaps it had never been more than a fantasy contrived to maintain a fragile alliance amid the urgency of World War II.

THE POLICY OF CONTAINMENT

Harry Truman sorely lacked FDR's talent for diplomacy. More comfortable with southern or conservative Democrats than with polished New Dealers, the new president liked to talk tough and act defiantly. Just ten days after he took office, Truman complained that U.S.–Soviet negotiations had been a "one-way street." He vowed to "baby" them no longer.

Truman replaced Roosevelt's diplomatic advisers with a hard-line team. Drawing on the advice of policy experts around him, he aimed to establish U.S. leadership in the world through a race for power that would exhaust communist resources. In the short run, Truman determined to maintain U.S. military superiority and prevent communism from spreading outside the USSR. Containment, a doctrine uniting military, economic, and diplomatic strategies, now became the linchpin of U.S. foreign policy.

The Truman Doctrine

Truman showed his cards early in 1947 when a crisis erupted in the Middle East, a region considered a British sphere. When civil war broke out in Greece and Great Britain announced its plan to withdraw all economic and military aid, U.S. diplomatic leaders began to fear a move into this territory by the Soviet Union. They knew Stalin was not involved in this crisis, but they recognized that the USSR would derive enormous benefits from a Communist victory. Truman insisted that without U.S. intervention Greece and perhaps the entire oil-rich Middle East would fall under Soviet control.

To drum up support from a fiscally conservative Republican Congress for his plan to step in for the British, Republican Senator Arthur H. Vandenburgh of Michigan, chair of the Foreign Relations Committee, told the president he would have to "scare the hell out of the country."

In early March 1947 Truman swung into action. On March 12, appearing before a joint session of Congress, the president appealed for all-out resistance to a "certain ideology," wherever it appeared in the world. World peace and the welfare of all Americans depended, Truman insisted, on containing communism.

Congress approved his request to appropriate $400 million in economic and military aid for Greece and Turkey. The aid to Greece helped the monarchy and right-wing military crush the rebel movement. Truman's victory buoyed his popularity for the 1948 election. It also helped to generate support for a campaign against communism, both at home and abroad.

The significance of what became known as the Truman Doctrine far outlasted the events in the Mediterranean. Although critics such as Walter Lippmann described it as a "strategic monstrosity," requiring an endless diffusion of resources for military operations around the world, containment served as the cornerstone of U.S. foreign policy for the next several decades.

The Marshall Plan

The Truman Doctrine directly inspired the European Recovery Program, commonly known as the Marshall Plan. Introduced on June 5, 1947, by Secretary of State and former army chief of staff George C. Marshall, the plan aimed to reduce "hunger, poverty, desperation, and chaos" and to restore "the confidence of the European people in the economic future of their own countries and of Europe as a whole." Indirectly, the Marshall Plan aimed to turn back socialist and communist bids for power in northern and western Europe.

The Marshall Plan in effect brought the seventeen recipients of aid into a bilateral agreement with the United States. These Western European nations ratified the General Agreement on Tariffs and Trades (GATT), which reduced commercial barriers among member nations and opened all to U.S. trade.

Considered by many historians to be the most successful postwar U.S. diplomatic venture, the Marshall Plan created the climate for a viable capitalist economy in western Europe. Industrial production in that region rose by 200 percent between 1947 and 1952. Deflationary programs cut wages and increased unemployment, but profits soared and the standard of living improved.

The Marshall Plan drove a further wedge between the United States and the Soviet Union. Stalin denounced it as an American scheme to rebuild Germany and incorporate it into an anti-Soviet bloc. The President readily acknowledged that the Truman Doctrine and the Marshall Plan were "two halves of the same walnut."

The Berlin Crisis and the Formation of NATO

Once the Marshall Plan was in place, the strategy of containment began to take clear shape in Germany. In June 1948 the Western allies decided to incorporate the American, French, and British occupation zones into a single nation, the Federal Republic of West Germany. Stalin perceived this as yet another threat to Soviet security. On June 24, 1948, he responded by stopping all traffic to West Berlin, formally controlled by the Western allies but situated deep within Soviet-occupied East Germany.

The Soviet retaliation created both a crisis and an opportunity for confrontation. With help from the Royal Air Force, the United States began an airlift of historic proportions that delivered nearly 2 million tons of supplies to West Berliners. Finally, in May 1949, the Soviet Union conceded defeat and lifted the blockade. Within a few weeks, East Germany and West Germany were established as separate republics.

The Berlin crisis made a U.S.-led military alliance against the Soviets attractive to western European nations. In April 1949 ten European nations, Canada, and the United States formed the North Atlantic Treaty Organization (NATO), a mutual defense pact in which "an armed attack against one or more of them . . . shall be considered an attack against them all." NATO complemented the Marshall Plan, strengthening economic ties among the member nations by, according to one analyst, keeping "the Russians out, the Americans in, and the Germans down." It also deepened divisions between eastern and western Europe, making a permanent military mobilization on both sides almost inevitable.

Congress approved $1.3 billion in military aid, which involved the creation of U.S. Army bases and the deployment of American troops abroad. Critics warned that the United States could not afford to police all of Europe without sidetracking domestic policies and undercutting the UN. But opinion polls revealed strong support for Truman's tough line against the Soviets.

Between 1947 and 1949, the Truman administration had defined the policies that would shape the cold war for decades to come. The Truman Doctrine explained the ideological basis of containment, the Marshall Plan put into place its economic underpinnings in Western Europe, and NATO created the mechanisms for military enforcement. When NATO extended membership to re-armed West Germany, the Soviet Union responded by creating a counterpart to NATO, the Warsaw Pact, including East Germany.

The Cold War in Asia

Triumphant in Western Europe, Truman managed only a mixed record in Asia. The United States achieved its greatest success in occupied Japan. General Douglas MacArthur directed an interim government in a modest reconstruction program that included land reform, the creation of independent trade unions, abolition of contract marriages and granting of woman suffrage, sweeping demilitarization, and, eventually, a constitutional democracy that barred communists from all posts. In return for its sovereignty, granted in 1952, Japan agreed to house huge U.S. military bases, thus placing U.S. troops and weapons strategically close to the Soviet Union's Asian rim.

The situation in China could not be handled so easily. After years of civil war, the pro-Western Nationalist government of Jiang Jeishi (Chiang Kaishek)

collapsed. Jiang's troops were forced to surrender in mid-1949 to the Communists, led by Mao Zedong, who enjoyed the support of the Chinese countryside, where 85 percent of the population lived. By the end of the year the Nationalist government had withdrawn to the island of Formosa (Taiwan), leaving Mao the entire China mainland.

Since World War II, the United States had sent military and economic aid to Jiang despite his unpopularity in China. American officials warned him that without major reforms, the Nationalists were destined to lose the war. Moreover, they tried to convince Jiang to turn over the reins of government to a less corrupt group of moderates or to accept a coalition with Mao.

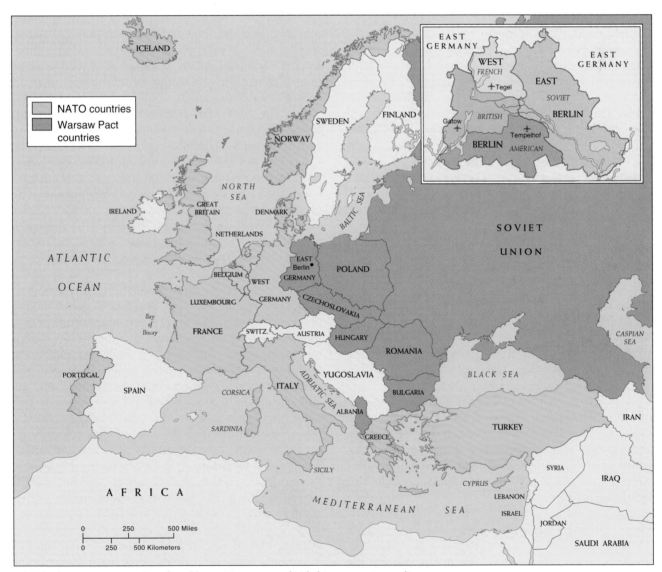

Divided Europe *During the cold war, Europe was divided into opposing military alliances, the North American Treaty Organization (NATO) and the Warsaw Pact (communist bloc).*

But when Jiang insisted on fighting, the United States broke off relations.

The news of China's "fall" to communism created an uproar in the United States. The Asia First wing of the Republican party, which envisioned Asia rather than Europe as the site of economic expansion, blamed the Truman administration for "losing" China and began to refer to the Democrats as the "party of treason."

After Stalin signed a formal alliance with Mao in February 1950, the rhetoric of the cold war became yet more pronounced. The perceived threat of "international communism" came to dominate American foreign policy for the next twenty years.

Atomic Diplomacy

The policy of containment depended on the ability of the United States to back up its commitments through military means, and Truman invested his faith in the U.S. monopoly of atomic weapons to pressure the Soviets to cooperate. The United States began to build atomic stockpiles and to conduct tests on the Bikini Islands in the Pacific. By 1950, as a scientific adviser subsequently observed, the United States "had a stockpile capable of somewhat more than reproducing World War II in a single day."

Despite warnings to the contrary by leading scientists, U.S. military analysts estimated it would take the Soviet Union three to ten years to produce an atomic bomb. In August 1949 the Soviet Union proved the U.S. military wrong by testing its own atomic bomb. "There is only one thing worse than one nation having the atomic bomb," prize-winning scientist Harold C. Urey said, "that's two nations having it."

Within a few years, both the United States and the Soviet Union had tested hydrogen bombs a thousand times more powerful than the weapons dropped on Hiroshima and Nagasaki in 1945. Both proceeded to stockpile bombs attached to missiles, inaugurating the fateful nuclear arms race that scientists had feared since 1945.

The United States and the Soviet Union were now firmly locked into the cold war. The nuclear arms race imperiled their futures, diverted their economies, and fostered fears of impending doom. Prospects for global peace had dissipated, and despite the Allied victory in World War II, the world had again divided into hostile camps.

THE TRUMAN PRESIDENCY

Truman's aggressive, gutsy personality suited the confrontational mood of the cold war. He linked the Soviet threat in Europe to the need for a strong presidency. Pressed to establish his own political identity,

"Give 'em Hell" Harry Truman successfully portrayed himself as a fierce fighter against all challengers, yet loyal to Roosevelt's legacy.

"To Err Is Truman"

Within a year of assuming office, Harry Truman rated lower in public approval than any twentieth-century president except Roosevelt's own predecessor, Herbert Hoover, who had been blamed for the Great Depression. The responsibilities of reestablishing peacetime conditions seemed to overwhelm the new president's administration.

In handling the enormous task of reconverting the economy to peacetime production, Truman appeared both inept and mean-spirited. The president faced millions of restless would-be consumers tired of rationing and eager to indulge themselves in shiny cars, new furniture, choice cuts of meat, and colorful clothing. The demand for consumer items rapidly outran supply, fueling inflation and creating a huge black market. When Congress proposed to extend wartime controls, Truman vetoed the bill and prices immediately began to skyrocket.

In 1945 and 1946, while homemakers protested rising prices, industrial workers struck in unprecedented numbers. Employers, fearing a rapid decline to Depression-level profits, determined to slash wages or at least hold them steady; workers wanted a bigger cut of the huge war profits they had heard about. The spectacle of nearly 4.6 million workers on picket lines alarmed the new president. In May 1946 Truman proposed to draft striking railroad workers and miners into the army. The usually conservative Senate killed this plan.

Congress defeated most of Truman's proposals for reconversion. One week after Japan's surrender, the president introduced a twenty-one–point program that included greater unemployment compensation, higher minimum wages, and housing assistance. Later he added proposals for national health insurance and atomic energy legislation. Congress turned back the bulk of these bills, passing the Employment Act of 1946 only after substantial modification. The act created a new executive body, the Council of Economic Advisors, which would confer with the president and formulate policies for maintaining employment, production, and purchasing power. But the measure did not guarantee full employment, thus undermining Truman's chief effort to advance beyond the New Deal.

Republicans, sensing victory in the upcoming off-year elections, asked the voters, "Had enough?" Apparently the voters had. They gave Republicans majorities in both houses of Congress and in the state capitols. In office, the Republicans set out to turn back the New Deal. And in a symbolic repudiation of

Roosevelt they passed an amendment establishing a two-term limit for the presidency.

The Republicans, dominant in Congress for the first time since 1931, prepared a full counteroffensive against organized labor. Unions had by this time reached their peak in size and prestige, with membership topping 15 million and encompassing nearly 40 percent of all wage earners. Concluding that labor had gone too far, the Republican Eightieth Congress passed the Taft–Hartley bill in 1947.

The Labor–Management Relations Act, as the measure was officially known, outlawed many practices approved by the Wagner Act of 1935 (see Chapter 24), such as the closed shop, the secondary boycott, and the use of union dues for political activities. It also mandated an eighty-day cooling-off period in the case of strikes affecting national safety or health. Taft–Hartley furthermore required all union officials to swear under oath that they were not communists—a cold war mandate that abridged freedoms ordinarily guaranteed by the First Amendment. Unions that refused to cooperate were denied access to the National Labor Relations Board, which arbitrated strikes and issued credentials to unions.

Truman regained some support from organized labor when he vetoed the Taft–Hartley Act, saying it would "conflict with important principles of our democratic society." However, Congress overrode his veto, and Truman himself went on to invoke the act against strikers.

The 1948 Election

Harry Truman had considered some of Roosevelt's advisers to be "crackpots and the lunatic fringe." By 1946 Truman had forced out the remaining social planners who had staffed the Washington bureaus for over a decade, including one of the best-loved New Dealers, Secretary of Interior Harold Ickes. Truman also fired the secretary of commerce, Henry Wallace, for advocating a more conciliatory policy toward the Soviet Union.

However, Wallace would not retreat and made plans to run against Truman for president. He pledged to expand New Deal programs by moving boldly to establish full employment, racial equality, and stronger labor unions. He also promised peace with the Soviet Union. As the 1948 election neared, Wallace appeared a viable candidate on the new Progressive party ticket until Truman accused him of being a tool of communists.

Meanwhile, Truman deftly repositioned himself to discredit congressional Republicans. He called for federal funds for education and new housing and a national program of medical insurance. Knowing the Republican Congress would kill all such proposals, the president called legislators into a fruitless special session

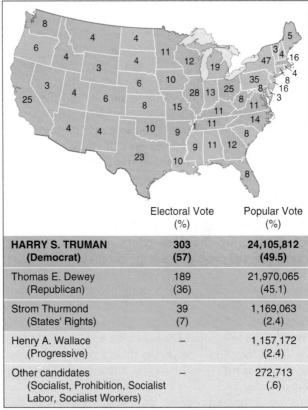

	Electoral Vote (%)	Popular Vote (%)
HARRY S. TRUMAN (Democrat)	**303** **(57)**	**24,105,812** **(49.5)**
Thomas E. Dewey (Republican)	189 (36)	21,970,065 (45.1)
Strom Thurmond (States' Rights)	39 (7)	1,169,063 (2.4)
Henry A. Wallace (Progressive)	–	1,157,172 (2.4)
Other candidates (Socialist, Prohibition, Socialist Labor, Socialist Workers)	–	272,713 (.6)

The Election of 1948   *Harry Truman holds up a copy of the* Chicago Tribune *with headlines confidently and mistakenly predicting the victory of his opponent, Thomas E. Dewey. An initially unpopular candidate, Truman made a whistle-stop tour of the country by train to win 49.5 percent of the popular vote to Dewey's 45.1 percent.*

in 1948 so that he could denounce the "do-nothing Congress."

To cut into Wallace's lead on civil rights, Truman issued executive orders in July 1948 desegregating the armed forces and banning discrimination in civil service jobs. When he endorsed a Democratic plank on racial equality, some 300 southern delegates bolted from the Democratic convention and formed a States' Rights ("Dixiecrat") ticket headed by Governor Strom Thurmond of South Carolina, known for his segregationist views. With the South as good as lost and popular New York governor Thomas E. Dewey heading the Republican ticket, Truman appeared hopelessly far from victory.

As the election neared, Truman managed to restore essential components of the New Deal coalition. He recognized the new state of Israel in May 1948, which helped prevent the defection of many liberal Jewish voters. The success of the Berlin airlift also buoyed Truman's popularity. After making a whistle-stop tour of the country by train, Truman won back Democrats outside the South and carried most states. Moreover, congressional Democrats returned to majorities in both houses.

The Fair Deal

Truman hoped that his election victory and the return of Democratic majorities in the House and Senate would allow him to translate campaign promises into concrete legislative achievements. But most of the president's plans were defeated in the new Congress by a powerful bloc of conservative southern Democrats and midwestern Republicans.

Congress passed a National Housing Act in 1949, promoting federally funded construction of low-income housing. It also raised the minimum wage and expanded the Social Security program. Otherwise, Truman made little headway. He and congressional liberals introduced a variety of bills to weaken segregationism: making lynching a federal crime, outlawing the poll tax, and prohibiting discrimination in interstate transportation. These measures were all defeated by southern-led filibusters. Proposals to create a national health insurance plan, provide federal aid for education, and repeal or modify Taft–Hartley remained bottled up in committees. Truman himself appeared to lose interest in the liberal agenda as the cold war took priority over domestic issues.

The Truman administration effectively used the threat of military confrontation between the United States and the Soviet Union to cut across conservative and liberal political lines. By the end of Truman's second term, defense allocations accounted for 10 percent of the gross national product, directly or indirectly employed hundreds of thousands of well-paid workers, and subsidized some of the nation's most profitable corporations. This vast financial outlay, guided through Congress by legislators seeking economic benefits for their constituents, created the rationale for permanent, large-scale military spending as a basic stimulus to economic growth.

THE COLD WAR AT HOME

The specter of a prolonged cold war with the USSR had encouraged many Americans, including the nation's leaders, to become obsessed with problems of national security, real or imagined, and to resort to extreme measures to solve them. Within a decade after World War II ended, a huge federal bureaucracy, dependent on government spending and surveillance at home and abroad, had greatly changed the relationship of the federal government to everyday affairs.

The National Security State

Shortly before World War II, the federal workforce totaled about 900,000 civilians, with about 10 percent engaged in security work. By war's end, the government employed nearly 4 million people, of whom 75 percent worked in national security agencies. The Pentagon, which had opened in 1943 as the largest office building in the world, housed the Joint Chiefs of Staff and 35,000 military personnel. The ties between the armed forces and the State Department grew closer as former military officers routinely began to fill positions in the State Department and diplomatic corps.

The National Security Act of 1947 laid the foundation for this expansion. The act established the Department of Defense and the National Security Council (NSC) to coordinate and administer defense policies and to advise the President. The Central Intelligence Agency (CIA), with roots in the wartime Office of Strategic Services, was established to obtain political, military, and economic information from around the world. Although information about the CIA was classified—that is, secret from Congress and the public—historians have estimated that the agency soon dwarfed the State Department in number of employees and size of budget.

On March 21, 1947, Truman signed Executive Order 9835, establishing the Federal Employee Loyalty Program. The program barred members of the Communist Party—as well as Fascists and anyone guilty of "sympathetic association" with either—from federal employment. Later amendments added homosexuals as potential security risks on the grounds that they might succumb to blackmail by enemy agents.

Many state and municipal governments enacted loyalty programs and required public employees, including teachers at all levels, to sign loyalty oaths. In all, some 6.6 million people underwent loyalty and security checks. Although no spies or saboteurs turned up, nearly 500 government workers were fired and nearly 6,000 more chose to resign.

OVERVIEW

MAJOR COLD WAR POLICIES

Policy	Date	Provisions
Truman Doctrine	1947	Pledged the United States to the containment of communism in Europe and elsewhere. The doctrine was the foundation of Truman's foreign policy. It impelled the United States to support any nation whose stability was threatened by communism or the Soviet Union.
Federal Employees Loyalty and Security Program	1947	Established by Executive Order 9835, this program barred communists and fascists from federal employment and outlined procedures for investigating current and prospective federal employees.
Marshall Plan	1947	U.S. program of aid to war-torn Europe, also known as the European Recovery Program. The Marshall Plan was a cornerstone in the U.S. use of economic policy to contain communism.
National Security Act	1947	Established Department of Defense (to coordinate the three armed services), the National Security Council (to advise the president on security issues), and the Central Intelligence Agency (to gather and evaluate intelligence data).
North Atlantic Treaty Organization (NATO)	1948	A military alliance of twelve nations formed to deter possible aggression of the Soviet Union against Western Europe.
NSC-68	1950	National Security Council Paper calling for an expanded and aggressive U.S. defense policy, including greater military spending and higher taxes.
Internal Security Act (also known as the McCarran Act and the Subversive Activities Control Act)	1950	Legislation providing for the registration of all communist and totalitarian groups and authorizing the arrest of suspect persons during a national emergency.
Immigration and Nationality Act (also known as McCarran-Walter Immigration Act)	1952	Reaffirmed the national origins quota system but tightened immigration controls, barring homosexuals and people considered subversive from entering the United States.

Attorney General Tom C. Clark aided this effort by publishing a list of hundreds of potentially subversive organizations selected by criteria so vague that any views "hostile or inimical to the American form of government" could make an organization liable for investigation and prosecution. Moreover, there was no right of appeal. The attorney general's list effectively outlawed many political and social organizations. Fraternal and cultural institutions, especially popular among aging European immigrants, were among the largest groups destroyed. The state of New York, for example, legally dismantled the International Workers' Order, which had provided insurance to nearly 200,000 immigrants. Only a handful of organizations had the funds to challenge the listing legally; most simply closed their doors.

In 1950 Congress overrode the president's veto to pass a bill that Truman called "the greatest danger to freedom of press, speech, and assembly since the Sedition Act of 1798." The Internal Security (McCarran) Act required communist organizations to register with the Subversive Activities Control Board and authorized the arrest of suspect persons during a national emergency. The Immigration and Nationality Act, sponsored by Republican senator Pat McCarran of Nevada and adopted in 1952, again over Truman's veto, barred people deemed "subversive" or "homosexual" from becoming citizens or even from visiting the United States. It also empowered the attorney general to deport immigrants who were members of communist organizations, even if they had become citizens. Challenged repeatedly on constitutional grounds, the Subversive Activities Control Board remained in place until 1973, when it was terminated.

The Red Scare in Hollywood

Anti-Communist Democratic representative Martin Dies of Texas, who had chaired a congressional committee on "un-American activities" since 1938, told reporters at a press conference in Hollywood in 1944:

> Hollywood is the greatest source of revenue in this nation for the Communists and other subversive groups. . . . Two elements stand out in . . . the making of pictures which extoll foreign ideology—propaganda for a cause which seeks to spread its ideas to our people[,] and the "leftist" or radical screenwriters.

A few years later, Dies's successor, J. Parnell Thomas, directed the committee to investigate supposed Communist infiltration of the movie industry.

Renamed and made a permanent standing committee in 1945, the House Un-American Activities Committee (HUAC) had the power to subpoena witnesses to testify anywhere in the United States and to compel answers on threat of contempt of Congress charges. In well-publicized hearings held in Washington in August 1947, HUAC found ample evidence of leftist sympathies but none of the subversive activity it alleged.

In 1947 the studios announced that no writer, technician, or actor who refused to denounce communism would be employed again, and HUAC encouraged testimony by "friendly witnesses" such as Ronald Reagan and Gary Cooper. The committee intimidated many who feared the loss of their careers into naming suspect former friends and co-workers in order to be cleared for future work in Hollywood.

A small but prominent minority refused to cooperate with the investigators. By claiming the freedoms of speech and association guaranteed by the First and Sixth Amendments to the Constitution, they became known as "unfriendly witnesses." A handful served prison sentences for contempt of Congress. Meanwhile, a blacklist persuaded advertisers to cancel their accounts with many radio and television programs considered friendly to the Soviet Union, the United Nations, and liberal causes. The Hollywood blacklist remained in effect until the 1960s, effectively limiting the production of films dealing with social or political issues.

Spy Cases

In August 1948 HUAC opened public hearings with a star witness: Whittaker Chambers, *Time* magazine editor and former communist, who confessed to spying for the Soviet Union during the 1930s. Chambers named as a fellow communist Alger Hiss, a veteran of Roosevelt's State Department, Roosevelt's adviser at Yalta, and at the time of the hearings president of the prestigious Carnegie Endowment for International Peace. A federal grand jury in January 1950 convicted Hiss of perjury only (for denying he knew Chambers), and he received a five-year prison term.

Many Democrats, including Truman himself, at first dismissed the allegations against Hiss—conveniently publicized at the start of the 1948 election campaign—as a red herring, a Republican maneuver to convince the public that Democrats had allowed communists to infiltrate the federal government. In 1954 Hiss was released from prison, still claiming his innocence.

The most dramatic spy case of the era involved Julius Rosenberg, former government engineer, and his wife, Ethel, who were accused of stealing and plotting to convey atomic secrets to Soviet agents. The government's case against the Rosenbergs rested on the testimony of their supposed accomplices, some of them secretly coached by the FBI. Nevertheless, in March 1951 a jury found them guilty of conspiring to commit espionage. Around the world the Rosenbergs were defended by citizens' committees and their convictions protested in large-scale demonstrations. Scientist Albert Einstein, the pope, and the president of France, among many prominent figures, all pleaded for clemency. The Rosenbergs maintained their innocence to the end, insisting they were being persecuted as Jews and for holding leftist political beliefs. They died in the electric chair on June 19, 1953.

McCarthyism

In a sensational Lincoln Day speech to the Republican Women's Club of Wheeling, West Virginia, on February 9, 1950, Republican senator Joseph R. McCarthy of Wisconsin announced that the United States had been sold out by the "traitorous actions of those who have been treated so well by the nation." These "bright young men who have been born with silver spoons in their mouths"—such as Secretary of State Dean Acheson, whom McCarthy called a "pompous diplomat in striped pants, with a phony English accent"—were part of a conspiracy, he charged, of more than 200 communists working in the State Department.

McCarthy refused to reveal names, however, and a few days later, after a drinking bout, he told persistent reporters: "I'm not going to tell you anything. I just want you to know I've got a pailful [of dirt] . . . and

I'm going to use it where it does me the most good." Although investigations uncovered not a single communist in the State Department, McCarthy led a flamboyant offensive against not only New Deal Democrats but the entire Truman administration with failing to defend the nation's security. His name provided the label for the entire campaign to silence critics of the cold war: McCarthyism.

Behind the blitz of publicity, the previously obscure junior senator from Wisconsin had struck a chord. Communism seemed to many Americans to be much more than a military threat—indeed, nothing less than a demonic force capable of undermining basic values. It compelled vigorous patriots to proclaim themselves ready for atomic warfare: "Better Dead Than Red." McCarthy also had help from organizations such as the American Legion and the Chamber of Commerce, prominent religious leaders, and union leaders.

Civil rights organizations faced the severest persecution since the 1920s. The Civil Rights Congress and the Negro Youth Council, for instance, were destroyed after frequent charges of communist influence. W. E. B. Du Bois, the renowned African American historian, and famed concert singer (and former All-American football hero) Paul Robeson had public appearances canceled and their right to travel abroad abridged.

In attacks on women's organizations and homosexual groups, meanwhile, anti-communist rhetoric cloaked deep fears about changing sexual mores. Aided by FBI reports, the federal government fired up to sixty homosexuals per month in the early 1950s. Undesirable discharges from the U.S. armed forces for homosexuality, an administrative procedure without appeal, also increased dramatically. Even noted liberal historian Arthur Schlesinger, Jr., suggested that critics of the cold war were not "real" men, or, perhaps, "real" women either.

Joseph McCarthy and his fellow red-hunters eventually burned themselves out. During televised congressional hearings in 1954, not only did McCarthy fail to prove wild charges of communist infiltration of the army, but in the glare of the television cameras he appeared deranged. Cowed for years, the Senate finally censured him for "conduct unbecoming a member."

AGE OF ANXIETY

"We have about 50 percent of the world's wealth," George Kennan noted in 1948, "but only 3.6 percent of its population." Very large pockets of poverty remained, and not all Americans benefited from the postwar abundance. Nonetheless, millions of Americans achieved middle-class status, often through programs subsidized by the federal government.

Prosperity did not dispel an anxious mood, fueled in part by the reality and the rhetoric of cold war and nuclear proliferation. To ease their apprehensions, many Americans turned their attention inward, focusing on a personal life they could understand and influence instead of the uncertainties of foreign affairs.

Even the ultimate symbol of postwar prosperity, the new home in the suburbs, did not simply reflect self-confidence. In 1950 the *New York Times* ran advertisements that captured a chilling quality of the boom in real estate: country properties for the Atomic Age located at least fifty miles outside major cities—the most likely targets, it was believed, of a Soviet nuclear attack. To protect their families in light of this possibility, many suburbanites built bomb shelters adjoining their homes. These underground structures reinforced with concrete and steel and outfitted with sufficient provisions to maintain a family for several weeks after an atomic explosion signaled a wide-spread anxiety about life in postwar American communities.

The tables turned on Senator Joseph McCarthy after he instigated an investigation of the U.S. Army for harboring communists. A congressional committee then investigated McCarthy for attempting to make the army grant special privileges to his staff aide, Private David Schine. During the televised hearings, Senator McCarthy discredited himself. In December 1954 the Senate voted to censure him.

The Two-Income Family

The postwar prosperity propelling the suburban boom helped to strengthen the domestic ideal of the nuclear family. Couples were marrying younger and producing more children than at any time in the past century. The U.S. Census Bureau predicted that this spurt would be temporary. To everyone's surprise, the birth rate continued to grow at a record pace, peaking at over 118 per 1,000 women in 1957. The "baby boom" lasted well into the 1960s.

Postwar prosperity also sparked a spending spree of trailblazing proportions. "The year 1946," *Life* magazine proclaimed, "finds the U.S. on the threshold of marvels, ranging from runless stockings and shineless serge suits to jet-propelled airplanes that will flash across the country in just a little less than the speed of sound." By the time Harry Truman left office two-thirds of all American households claimed at least one television set.

These two trends—the baby boom and high rates of consumer spending—encouraged a major change in the middle-class family. Having worked during World War II, often in occupations traditionally closed to them, many women wished to continue in full-time employment. Reconversion to peacetime production forced the majority from their factory positions, but most women quickly returned, taking jobs at a faster rate than men and providing half the total growth of the labor force. By 1952, 2 million more wives worked than during the war. However, the high-paying unionized jobs in manufacturing were gone. Instead, most women found minimum-wage jobs in the expanding service sector: clerical work, health care and education, and

restaurant, hotel, and retail services. Mothers of young children were the most likely to be employed. Older women whose children were grown might work because they had come to value a job for its own sake. Younger women often worked for reasons of "economic necessity"—that is, to maintain a middle-class standard of living that now required more than one income.

Even though most women sought employment primarily to support their families, they ran up against popular opinion and expert advice urging them to return to their homes. Public opinion registered resounding disapproval—by 86 percent of those surveyed—of a married woman's working if jobs were scarce and her husband could support her. Commentators even appealed for a return to an imaginary "traditional" family, where men alone were breadwinners and women stayed happily at home, as a bulwark against communism because most Soviet women worked in industry.

Popular magazines, television shows, and high-profile experts chimed in with similar messages. Talcott Parsons, the distinguished Harvard sociologist, delineated the parameters of the "democratic" family: husbands served as breadwinners while wives, "the emotional hub of the family," stayed home to care for their families. In the first edition of *Baby and Child Care* (1946), the child-rearing advice manual that soon outsold the Bible, Benjamin Spock similarly advised women to devote themselves full time, if financially possible, to their maternal responsibilities. "Women have many careers," another expert explained, "but only one vocation —motherhood."

Patterns of women's higher education reflected this conservative trend. Having made slight gains during World War II when college-age men were serving in the armed forces or working in war industries, women lost ground after the GI Bill created a huge upsurge in male enrollment. Women represented 40 percent of all college graduates in 1940 but only 25 percent a decade later.

With a growing number of middle-class women working to help support their families, these policies and prescriptions worked at cross-purposes. As early as 1947 *Life* magazine registered this concern in a thirteen-page feature, "American Woman's Dilemma." How could women comfortably take part in a world beyond the home and at the same time heed the advice of FBI director J. Edgar Hoover, who exhorted the nation's women to fight "the twin enemies of freedom—crime and communism" by fulfilling their singular role as "homemakers and mothers"?

Religion and Education

Cold war fears helped to make Baptist Billy Graham one of the most popular evangelical ministers of the era and star of the first major televised "crusades" for reli-

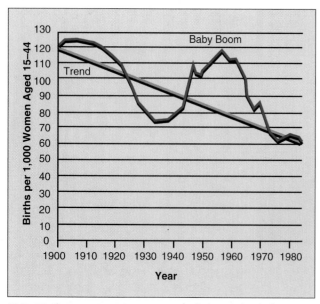

U.S. Birth Rate, 1930–1980 *The bulge of the "baby boom," a leading demographic factor in the postwar economy, stands out for this fifty-year period.*

gious revival. Born in Charlotte, North Carolina, in 1918, Graham had grown up believing that all doubts about the literal truth of the Bible were traps set by Satan. He gave a spiritual twist to cold war anxieties, warning against the decline of "God-centered homes" and the increased number of wives who tried to "wear the trousers" of the family. Politically, Graham aligned himself with the Republican Party and supported a large military budget to protect the United States, which he saw as the last hope of Christianity.

The message of anticommunism also permeated public education. In an era of higher education reshaped by the GI Bill, and of primary education expanding to meet the postwar baby boom, the nation invested more than funds in its school system. According to guidelines set down by the Truman administration, teachers were to "strengthen national security through education," specifically redesigning their lesson plans to illustrate the superiority of the American democratic system over Soviet communism.

Leading historians, such as Samuel Eliot Morison, insisted that fellow scholars shape their interpretations of the nation's past to highlight traditional values, especially the sanctity of private property. Some historians portrayed earlier critics of capitalism, such as the populists, as mentally unbalanced and dangerous to American democracy.

A fearless minority of scholars protested infringements on their academic freedom by refusing to sign loyalty oaths and by writing books pointing out the potential dangers of U.S. foreign and domestic policies of the cold war. But the chilling atmosphere, such as the political climate pervading on the campus of the University of Washington, made a far larger number reluctant to express opinions contrary to these ideas.

The Cultural Noir

The cold war years seemed to many observers a time of great psychic stress. Popular culture soon registered these anxieties. The genre of film *noir* (French for "black") deepened this mood into an aesthetic. These movies feature protagonists who are strangers or loners falsely accused of crimes. Feelings of frustration and loss of control seemed to come alive in tough, cynical characters played by actors such as Robert Mitchum and Barbara Stanwyck.

Drama and novels also described anxiety and alienation. Arthur Miller's drama *Death of a Salesman* (1949) vividly portrays American individualism as fatally self-destructive. J. D. Salinger's novel *Catcher in the Rye* (1951) described the mental anguish of a boy estranged from his materialistic parents.

Cold war anxiety manifested itself in a flurry of unidentified flying object (UFO or flying saucer) sightings. Dozens of private researchers claimed to have been contacted by aliens demanding that the earthlings cease atomic testing. The popular film *The Day the Earth Stood Still* (1951) carried the same message, in the form of a godlike being who warns earthlings to abandon their weaponry.

END OF THE DEMOCRATIC ERA

The cold war tensions that fostered the cultural *noir* continued to fester in Europe and pushed the United States and the Soviet Union to the brink of armed conflict during the Berlin Crisis. Yet it was a conflict in Asia that finally transformed their political and ideological competition into a war threatening to destroy the world. For Truman, the Korean War proved political suicide.

The Korean War

At the end of World War II, the Allies had divided the small peninsula of Korea, ceded by Japan, at the thirty-eighth parallel. Although all parties hoped to reunite the nation under its own government, the line between North and South hardened instead. The United States backed the unpopular government of Syngman Rhee (the Republic of Korea) and the Soviet Union sponsored a rival government in North Korea under Kim Il Sung.

On June 25, 1950, the U.S. State Department received a cablegram reporting a military attack on South Korea by the communist-controlled North. "If we are tough enough now," President Truman pledged, "if we stand up to them like we did in Greece three years ago, they won't take any next steps." The Soviet Union, on the other hand, regarded the invasion as Kim Il Sung's affair. Despite Soviet disclaimers, Truman sought approval from the UN Security Council to send in troops. Because of the absence of the Soviet delegate, who could have vetoed the decision, the Security Council agreed. Two-thirds of Americans polled approved the president's decision to send troops under the command of General Douglas MacArthur to South Korea.

Military events seemed at first to justify the president's decision. Seoul, the capital of South Korea, had fallen to North Korean troops within weeks of the invasion, and communist forces continued to push south until they had taken most of the peninsula. The situation appeared grim until Truman authorized MacArthur to carry out an amphibious landing at Inchon, which he did on September 15, 1950. With tactical brilliance and good fortune, the general orchestrated a military campaign that halted the communist drive. By October, UN troops had retaken South Korea.

Basking in victory, the Truman administration could not resist the temptation to expand the war aims. Hoping to prove the Democrats were not "soft" on

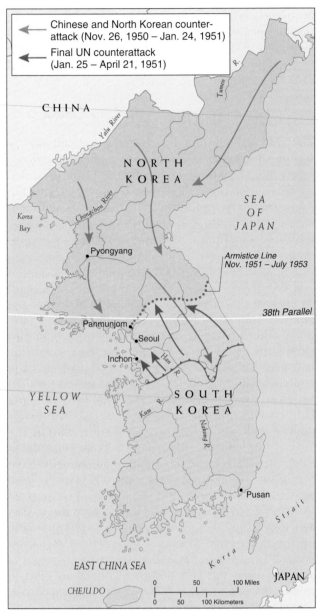

The Korean War   *The intensity of battles underscored the strategic importance of Korea in the cold war.*

Chinese attacked in human waves. MacArthur's force was all but crushed. The Chinese drove the UN troops back to South Korea, where they regrouped along the thirty-eighth parallel. By summer 1951 a stalemate had been reached very near the old border. Negotiations for a settlement went on over the next eighteen months amid heavy fighting.

MacArthur tried without success to convince Truman to prepare for a new invasion of communist territory. Encouraged by strong support at home, he continued to provoke the president by speaking out against official policy, calling for bombing of supply lines in China and a naval blockade of the Chinese coast—actions certain to lead to a Chinese–American war. Finally, on April 10, 1951, Truman dismissed MacArthur for insubordination and other unauthorized activities.

The Legacy of "The Sour Little War"

By instituting a peacetime draft in 1948 and then ordering American troops into Korea, Truman had bypassed congressional authority. Truman carefully referred to the military deployment not as a U.S. war but as a UN-sanctioned "police action."

The president derived his authority from NSC-68, a paper adopted by the National Security Council in April 1950. NSC-68 pledged the United States not only to drive back communist influence throughout the world but also to "foster the seeds of destruction within the Soviet Union." Its use demonstrated, as one historian observed, a "centralization of power" in which the entire government "had literally been compressed or consolidated into the president and his like-minded appointees."

The Korean War, which permitted Truman to activate NSC-68, also provided the president with the public rationale for a rapid and permanent military buildup, including the allocation of at least 20 percent of GNP to national defense. By 1952 the U.S. Army had grown to 3.6 million, or six times its size at the beginning of the conflict. At the same time, the federal government accelerated the development of nuclear bombs and weapons, including the first hydrogen bomb, tested in November 1952.

The outcome of the Korean War did nothing to improve Truman's case for rolling back communism. Negotiations and fighting proceeded in tandem until the summer of 1953, when a settlement was reached in which both North Korea and South Korea occupied almost the same territory as when the war began. Approximately 54,000 Americans died in Korea; the North Koreans and Chinese lost well over 2 million people. The UN troops had employed both "carpet bombing" (intense, destructive attack on a given area)

communism, the president and his advisors decided to roll back the communists beyond the thirty-eighth parallel. Until this point, China had not been actively involved in the war. But it now warned that any attempt to cross the dividing line would be interpreted as a threat to its own national security. Truman flew to Wake Island in the Pacific on October 15 for a conference with MacArthur, who assured the president of a speedy victory.

MacArthur had sorely miscalculated. Chinese troops massed just above the UN offensive line, at the Yalu River. Suddenly, and without any air support, the and napalm (jellied gasoline bombs), destroying most of the housing and food supplies in both Koreas. True to the pattern of modern warfare, which emerged during World War II, the majority of civilians killed were women and children. Nearly 1 million Koreans were left homeless.

For the United States, the Korean War extended the principle of containment far beyond Europe and enlarged the geographical range of the cold war to include the Far East. The war also lined up the People's Republic of China and the United States as unwavering enemies for the next twenty years and heightened U.S. commitment to Southeast Asia. Moreover, the Korean War did much to establish an ominous tradition of "unwinnable" conflicts that left many American soldiers and civilians skeptical of official policy.

In retrospect, many Americans recognized that Truman, in fighting communism in Korea, had pledged the United States to defend a corrupt government and a brutal dictator. Decades later the Korean War inspired the dark comedy *M*A*S*H*, adapted for television from the film written by Hollywood screenwriter Ring Lardner, Jr., who was sent to jail by HUAC during the Korean War for contempt of Congress. As late as 1990, members of Congress were still debating the terms of a Korean War memorial. "It ended on a sad note for Americans," one historian has concluded, "and the war and its memories drifted off into a void."

Truman's Downfall

There was only one burning issue during the election campaign of 1952: the Korean War. Opinion polls indicated widespread frustration with Truman's conduct of the war. His popularity had wavered continually since he took office in 1945, but it sank to an all-time low shortly after he dismissed MacArthur as commander of the UN troops in Korea. Congress received thousands of letters and telegrams calling for Truman's impeachment. "Oust President Truman" bumper stickers could be seen. MacArthur, meanwhile, returned home a hero, welcomed by over 7 million fans in New York City alone.

Popular dissatisfaction with Truman increased. Newspapers reported that officials in his administration had been dealing in 5 percent kickbacks for government contracts. Business and organized labor complained about the price and wage freezes imposed during the Korean War. A late-1951 Gallup poll showed the president's approval rating at 23 percent. In early 1952 Truman announced he would not run for reelection, a decision rare for a president eligible for another term.

In accepting political defeat and disgrace, Truman left the Democratic Party in disarray. The Democrats' best hope for victory now lay in convincing Dwight Eisenhower to run on their ticket, although his reputation as a moderate conservative suggested no continuity with party traditions. When Eisenhower politely refused their offers, Democratic leaders turned to the popular but uncharismatic governor of Illinois, Adlai E. Stevenson, Jr.

Admired for his honesty and intelligence, Stevenson offered no solutions to the conflict in Korea, the accelerating arms race, or the Cold War generally. Accepting the Democratic nomination, Stevenson candidly admitted that "the ordeal of the twentieth century is far from over," a prospect displeasing to voters aching for peace.

The Republicans made the most of the Democrats' dilemma. Without proposing any sweeping answers of their own, they pointed to all the obvious shortcomings of their opponents. When opinion polls showed that Dwight Eisenhower possessed an "unprecedented" 64 percent approval rating, and when "Ike" allowed himself to be "drafted" for the Republican nomination, his triumph within the party was certain. Republicans had waited too long for a White House victory.

Eisenhower styled himself the moderate. He wisely avoided the negative impressions made by the unsuccessful 1948 Republican candidate, Thomas Dewey, who had seemed as aggressive as Truman on foreign policy and simultaneously eager to overturn the New Deal domestic legislation. Eisenhower knew better: voters wanted peace and government-assisted prosperity. He neither threatened to widen the war nor supported the stalemate created by Truman. He appeared firm but not confrontational. He promised to end the Korean War with "an early and honorable" peace, although he did not go into specifics. Whenever he was tempted to address questions of finance or the economy, his advisers warned him: "The chief reason that people want to vote for you is because they think you have more ability to keep us out of another war."

Meanwhile, Eisenhower's vice-presidential candidate, Richard Nixon, waged a relentless and defamatory attack on Stevenson, calling him "Adlai the Appeaser" and the "Ph.D. graduate of Dean Acheson's cowardly College of Communist Containment." Senator Joseph McCarthy chimed in, proclaiming that with club in hand he might be able to make "a good American" of Stevenson. A month before the election, McCarthy went on network television with his requisite "exhibits" and "documents," this time purportedly showing that the Democratic presidential candidate had promoted communism at home and abroad. These outrageous charges kept the Stevenson campaign off balance.

The Republican campaign was itself not entirely free of scandal: Nixon had been caught accepting personal gifts from wealthy benefactors. Nixon chose to plead his case on national television. Describing his wife Pat's "good Republican cloth coat" and their modest style of living, he contritely admitted that he had indeed accepted one gift, a puppy named Checkers that his daughters loved and that he refused to give back. "The Poor Richard Show," as critics called the event, defused the scandal without answering the most important charges.

Eisenhower, meanwhile, continued to enchant the voters as a peace candidate. Ten days before the election he dramatically announced, "I shall go to Korea" to settle the war. Eisenhower received 55 percent of the vote and carried thirty-nine states, in part because he brought out an unusually large number of voters in normally Democratic areas. He won the popular vote in much of the South and in the northern cities of New York, Chicago, Boston, and Cleveland. Riding his coattails, the Republicans regained control of Congress. The New Deal coalition of ethnic and black voters, labor, northern liberals, and southern conservatives no longer commanded a majority.

CONCLUSION

Dwight Eisenhower's election diminished the intensity of the cold war mood without actually halting the conflict. "The Eisenhower Movement," wrote Walter Lippmann, was a "mission in American politics" to restore a sense of community among the American people. In a larger sense, many of the issues of the immediate post–World War II years seemed to have been settled, or put off for a distant future. The international boundaries of communism were frozen with the Chinese Revolution, the Berlin Blockade, and now the Korean War. Meanwhile, at home cold war defense spending had become a permanent part of the national budget, an undeniable drain on tax revenues but an important element in the government contribution to economic prosperity. If the nuclear arms race remained a cause for anxiety, joined by more personal worries about the changing patterns of family life, a sense of security nevertheless spread. Prospects for world peace had dimmed, but the worst nightmares of the 1940s had eased as well.

CHRONOLOGY

1941	Henry Luce forecasts the dawn of "The American Century"
1944	International Monetary Fund and World Bank founded at Bretton Woods
1945	Franklin D. Roosevelt dies; Harry Truman becomes president
	United Nations charter signed
	World War II ends
	Strike wave begins
	Truman proposes program of economic reforms
1946	Winston Churchill's Iron Curtain speech
	Republicans win control of Congress
	Benjamin Spock publishes *Baby and Child Care*
1947	Truman Doctrine announced
	Federal Employees Loyalty and Security Program established and attorney general's list of subversive organizations authorized
	Marshall Plan for European recovery announced
	Taft–Hartley Act restricts union activities
	National Security Act
	House Un-American Activities Committee hearings in Hollywood
1948	State of Israel founded
	Berlin blockade begins
	Henry Wallace runs for president on Progressive Party ticket
	Truman announces peacetime draft and desegregates U.S. army
	Truman wins election; Democrats sweep both houses of Congress
1949	Truman announces Fair Deal
	NATO created
	Communists led by Mao Zedong take power in China
	Berlin blockade ends
	Soviet Union explodes atomic bomb
1950	Alger Hiss convicted of perjury
	Senator Joseph McCarthy begins anticommunist crusade
	Adoption of NSC-68 consolidates presidential war powers
	Korean War begins
	Internal Security (McCarran) Act
1951	Truman dismisses General Douglas MacArthur
	Armistice talks begin in Korea
1952	Immigration and Nationality Act
	United States explodes first hydrogen bomb
	Dwight D. Eisenhower wins presidency; Richard Nixon becomes vice president
1953	Julius and Ethel Rosenberg executed for atomic espionage
	Armistice ends fighting in Korea
1954	Army–McCarthy hearings end
1955	Warsaw Pact created

REVIEW QUESTIONS

1. Discuss the origins of the cold war and the sources of growing tensions between the United States and the Soviet Union at the close of World War II.

2. Describe the basic elements of President Harry Truman's policy of containment. How did the threat of atomic warfare affect this policy?

3. Compare the presidencies of Franklin D. Roosevelt and Harry S. Truman, both Democrats.

4. Describe the impact of McCarthyism on American political life. How did the anticommunist campaigns affect the media? What were the sources of Senator Joseph McCarthy's popularity? What brought about his downfall?

5. How did the cold war affect American culture?

6. Discuss the role of the United States in Korea in the decade after World War II. How did the Korean War affect the 1952 presidential election?

7. Why did Dwight Eisenhower win the 1952 presidential election?

RECOMMENDED READING

Warren I. Cohen, *America in the Age of Soviet Power, 1945–1991* (1993). A volume in the "Cambridge History of American Foreign Relations" series, this study examines the origins of the cold war in policies ending World War II, including the breakup of the colonial empires, and concludes with the collapse of communism in the Soviet Union.

Martin Bauml Duberman, *Paul Robeson* (1988). A biography of the renowned African American singer and actor who was driven from the stage for political reasons. Duberman shows Robeson as a great artist but also a self-conscious representative of black rights who felt compelled to oppose U.S. foreign policy and suddenly lost his public career.

Townsend Hoopes and Douglas Brinkley, *FDR and the Creation of the U.N.* (1997). A concise account of the founding of the United Nations, from Franklin D. Roosevelt—whose "initiative and determination" laid the groundwork for world organization—to Harry S. Truman.

Joyce Kolko and Gabriel Kolko, *The Limits of Power: The World and United States Foreign Policy, 1945–1954* (1972). A detailed commentary on U.S. efforts to dictate world conditions that argues that the complexities of world politics, especially the rise of colonized nations toward independence, placed control outside American hands.

George Lipsitz, *A Rainbow at Midnight: Labor and Culture in the 1940s* (1994). A vivid account of economic and cultural hopes, uneasiness, and disappointments after World War II. Lipsitz shows how struggles for economic democracy were defeated and how popular culture—for example, country-and-western music and rock-n-roll, as well as stock car racing and roller derby—arose in blue-collar communities.

Elaine Tyler May, *Homeward Bound: American Families in the Cold War Era* (1988). A lively account of the effects on family life and women's roles of the national mood of "containment." May argues that government policy became part of a popular culture that solidified the cold war era's "feminine mystique."

David G. McCullough, *Truman* (1992). An uncritical rendition of Truman's personal life and political career. Through personal correspondence and other documents, McCullough details Truman's view of himself and the generally favorable view of him held by supporters of cold war liberalism.

Patrick McGilligan and Paul Buhle, *Tender Comrades: A Backstory of the Hollywood Blacklist* (1997). A collection of interviews with thirty-five victims of the Hollywood Blacklist, including some of the most important writers, directors, and film stars. The collection is especially valuable for its detailing of film production during the years of World War II and afterward, including the creation of *film noir.*

Joanne Meyerowitz, ed., *Not June Cleaver: Women and Gender in Postwar America, 1945–1960* (1994). A collection of essays that refute the common stereotype of women as homebound during the postwar era.

Victor S. Navasky, *Naming Names* (1980). A fascinating account of government informants, McCarthyism, and the blacklist. Navasky presents especially interesting treatments of academic life, where blacklisting made only a slight impact, and Hollywood, where McCarthyism changed American popular culture.

David M. Oshinsky, *A Conspiracy So Immense: The World of Joe McCarthy* (1983). A study of McCarthyism and the driving personality within it that presents a keen view of McCarthy as a product of his background and the political conditions of the time as well as a clever politician who found widespread support in the Republican Party.

Daniel Yergin, *Shattered Peace: The Origins of the Cold War and the National Security State* (1977). A lucid analysis of the motives of the Americans and the Soviets that led to a full-scale arms race, arguing that each side misinterpreted the motives of the other and thereby lost the opportunity to attain world peace.

CHAPTER TWENTY-SEVEN

AMERICA AT MIDCENTURY
1952–1963

AMERICAN COMMUNITIES
Popular Music in Memphis

The nineteen-year-old singer was peering nervously out over the large crowd. He knew that people had come to Overton Park's outdoor amphitheater that hot, sticky July day in 1954 to hear the headliner, country music star Slim Whitman. Sun Records, a local Memphis label, had just released the teenager's first record, and it had begun to receive some airplay on local radio. But the singer and his two bandmates had never played in a setting even remotely as large as this one. And their music defied categories: it wasn't black and it wasn't white; it wasn't pop and it wasn't country. But when he launched into his version of a black blues song called "That's All Right," the crowd went wild. "I came offstage," the singer later recalled, "and my manager told me that they was hollering because I was wiggling my legs. I went back out for an encore, and I did a little more, and the more I did, the wilder they went." Elvis Presley had arrived.

Elvis combined a hard-driving, rhythmic approach to blues and country music with a riveting performance style, inventing the new music known as rock 'n' roll. An unprecedented cultural phenomenon, rock 'n' roll was a music made largely for and by teenagers. In communities all over America, rock 'n' roll brought teens together around jukeboxes, at sock hops, in cars, and at private parties. It also demonstrated the enormous consumer power of American teens. Rock 'n' roll also embodied a postwar trend accelerating the integration of white and black music. This cultural integration prefigured the social and political integration won by the civil rights movement.

Like most American cities, the Memphis economy enjoyed a healthy growth during World War II, with lumber mills, furniture factories, and chemical manufacturing supplementing the cotton market as sources of jobs and prosperity. And like the rest of the South, Memphis was a legally segregated city; whites and blacks lived, went to school, and worked apart. Class differences among whites were important as well. Like thousands of other poor rural whites in these years, Elvis Presley had moved from Mississippi to Memphis in 1949, where his father found work in a munitions plant.

The Presleys were poor enough to qualify for an apartment in Lauderdale Courts, a Memphis public housing project. To James Conaway, who grew up in an all-white, middle-class East Memphis neighborhood, people like the Presleys were "white trash." Negroes, he recalled, were "not necessarily below the rank of a country boy like Elvis, but of another universe, and yet there was more affection for them than for some whites."

Yet in the cultural realm, class and racial barriers could be challenged. Elvis Presley grew up a dreamy, shy boy, who turned to music for emotional release and spiritual expression. He soaked up the wide range of music styles available in Memphis. The Assembly of God Church his family attended featured a renowned hundred-voice choir. Elvis and his friends went to marathon all-night "gospel singings" at Ellis Auditorium, where they enjoyed the tight harmonies and emotional style of white gospel quartets.

Elvis also drew from the sounds he heard on Beale Street, the main black thoroughfare of Memphis and one of the nation's most influential centers of African American music. In the postwar years, local black rhythm and blues artists like B. B. King, Junior Parker, and Muddy Waters attracted legions of black and white fans with their emotional power and exciting showmanship. At the Handy Theater on Beale Street, the teenaged Elvis Presley, like thousands of other white young people, heard black performers at the "Midnight Rambles"—late shows for white people only. Elvis himself performed along with black contestants in amateur shows at Beale Street's Palace Theater. Nat D. Williams, a prominent black Memphis disc jockey and music promoter, recalled how black audiences responded to Elvis's unique style. "He had a way of singing the blues that was distinctive. He could sing 'em not necessarily like a Negro, but he didn't sing 'em altogether like a typical white musician. . . . Always he had that certain humanness about him that Negroes like to put in their songs."

The expansion of the broadcasting and recording in-

dustries in the postwar years also contributed to the weakening of racial barriers in the musical realm. Two Memphis radio stations featured the hard-driving rhythm and blues music that was beginning to attract a strong following among young white listeners. These Memphis stations also featured spirituals by African American artists such as Mahalia Jackson and Clara Ward.

Elvis himself understood his debt to black music and black performers. "The colored folks," he told an interviewer in 1956, "been singing and playing it just like I'm doing now, man, for more years than I know. They played it like that in the shanties and in their juke joints and nobody paid it no mind until I goosed it up. I got it from them."

Dissatisfied with the cloying pop music of the day, white teenagers across the nation were increasingly turning to the rhythmic drive and emotional intensity of black rhythm and blues. They quickly adopted rock 'n' roll (the term had long been an African American slang expression for dancing and sexual intercourse) as their music. But it was more than just music: it was also an attitude, a celebration of being young, and a sense of having something that adult authority could not understand or control.

When Sun Records sold Presley's contract to RCA Records in 1956, Elvis became an international star. Records like "Heartbreak Hotel," "Don't Be Cruel," and "Jailhouse Rock" shot to the top of the charts and blurred the old boundaries between pop, country, and rhythm and blues. By helping to accustom white teenagers to the style and sound of black artists, Elvis helped establish rock 'n' roll as an interracial phenomenon. Institutional racism would continue to plague the music business—many black artists were routinely cheated out of royalties and severely underpaid—but the music of postwar Memphis at least pointed the way toward the exciting cultural possibilities that could emerge from breaking down the barriers of race. It also gave postwar American teenagers a newfound sense of community.

Memphis

KEY TOPICS

- Post–World War II prosperity

- Suburban life: ideal and reality

- The emergence of youth culture

- Television, mass culture, and their critics

- Foreign policy in the Eisenhower years

- John F. Kennedy and the promise of a New Frontier

AMERICAN SOCIETY AT MIDCENTURY

The Eisenhower Presidency

Dwight D. Eisenhower's landslide election victory in 1952 set the stage for the first full two-term Republican presidency since that of Ulysses S. Grant. During his eight-year administration, intellectuals and liberals found it easy to satirize and attack Eisenhower for his blandness, his frequent verbal gaffes, his vagueness, and his often contradictory pronouncements. But for Eisenhower, politics demanded conciliation and compromise more than devotion to principle and truth. "The public loves Ike," observed one journalist in 1959. "The less he does the more they love him. That, probably, is the secret. Here is a man who doesn't rock the boat."

In practice, this meant that Eisenhower wanted to run government in a businesslike manner while letting the states and corporate interests guide domestic policy and the economy. Eisenhower appointed nine businessmen to his first Cabinet. Former GM chief Charles Wilson served as secretary of defense and epitomized the administration's economic views with his famous aphorism "What's good for General Motors' business is good for America." In his appointments to the Federal Trade Commission, the Federal Communications Commission, and the Federal Power Commission, Eisenhower favored men congenial to the corporate interests they were charged with regulating. Eisenhower also secured passage in 1953 of the Submerged Lands Act, which transferred $40 billion worth of disputed offshore oil lands from the federal government to the Gulf states. This ensured a greater role for the states and private companies in the oil business and accelerated a trend toward the destruction of the natural environment.

At the same time, Eisenhower accepted the New Deal legacy of greater federal responsibility for social welfare. He rejected calls from conservative Republicans to dismantle the Social Security system. His administration agreed to a modest expansion of Social Security and unemployment insurance and small increases in the minimum wage. Ike also created the Department of Health, Education, and Welfare, appointing Oveta Culp Hobby as the second woman to hold a cabinet post. In agriculture Eisenhower continued the policy of parity payments designed to sustain farm prices. Between 1952 and 1960 Federal spending on agriculture jumped from about $1 billion to $7 billion.

After the Korean War ended in 1953, and again in 1958, when the unemployment rate reached 7.5 percent, the economy went into a recession. The administration refused to cut taxes or increase spending to stimulate growth. Eisenhower feared starting an inflationary spiral more than he worried about unemployment or poverty. By the time he left office, Eisenhower could proudly point out that real wages for an average family had risen 20 percent during his term. Combined with low inflation and steady, if modest, growth, the Eisenhower years meant greater prosperity for most Americans.

Subsidizing Prosperity

During the Eisenhower years the federal government played a crucial role in subsidizing programs that helped millions of Americans achieve middle-class status. The Federal Housing Administration (FHA), established in 1934, put the full faith and credit of the federal government behind residential mortgages and attracted new private capital into home building. A typical FHA mortgage required less than 10 percent for a down payment and spread low-interest monthly payments over thirty years.

Yet FHA policies also had longer-range drawbacks. FHA insurance went overwhelmingly to new residential developments. This hastened the decline of older inner-city neighborhoods. It was FHA policy to favor the construction of single-family projects while discouraging multiunit housing, to refuse loans for the repair of older structures and rental units, and to require for any loan guarantee an "unbiased professional estimate" rating the property, the prospective borrower, and the neighborhood. In practice, these estimates resulted in blatant discrimination against racially mixed communities.

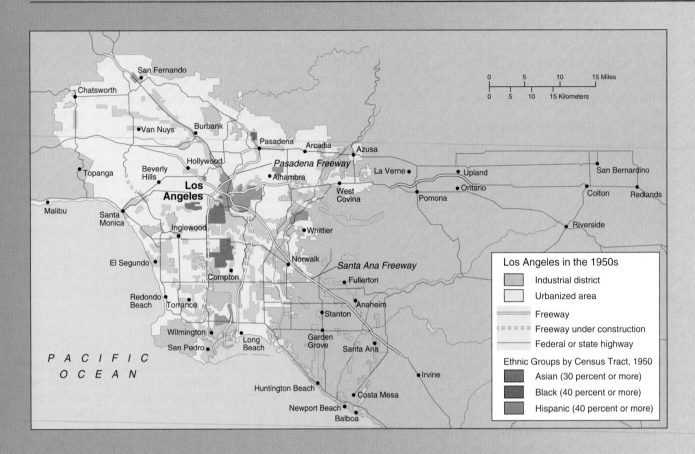

Los Angeles in the 1950s

- Industrial district
- Urbanized area
- Freeway
- Freeway under construction
- Federal or state highway

Ethnic Groups by Census Tract, 1950

- Asian (30 percent or more)
- Black (40 percent or more)
- Hispanic (40 percent or more)

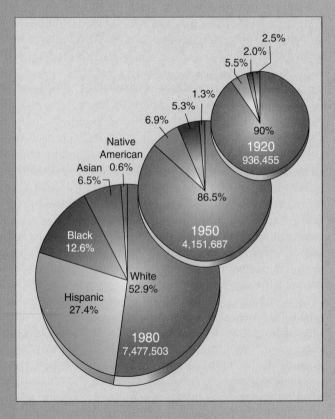

1920 936,455 — 90%, 5.5%, 2.0%, 2.5%

1950 4,151,687 — 86.5%, 6.9%, 5.3%, 1.3%

1980 7,477,503 — White 52.9%, Hispanic 27.4%, Black 12.6%, Asian 6.5%, Native American 0.6%

The Changing Face of Postwar Los Angeles

Los Angeles epitomized two postwar American trends: the rapid growth of western cities and the rapid expansion of the suburbs. Spurred by government funding, it boasted the highest per capita ownership of both private homes and automobiles for any American city. Federal tax policies subsidized home ownership, and loan guarantees through the Federal Housing Administration and the Veterans Administration made home mortgages available to millions. The state's Collier–Burns Act of 1947 committed gasoline taxes and auto registration fees to building a high-speed freeway system in metropolitan Los Angeles. The Federal Highway Act of 1956 supplemented these funds by incorporating some of the freeways into the national highway system. By 1960 Los Angeles had 250 miles of freeways. By the 1970s, about two-thirds of downtown Los Angeles was devoted to the automobile.

Postwar Los Angeles also evolved into one of the most ethnically diverse cities in the nation. What had been an overwhelmingly white Protestant population began to change during World War II with the influx of African American, Mexican, and Indian factory workers. By the 1970s Korean, Filipino, Vietnamese, and other Asian immigrants, along with newcomers from Mexico and Central America, had radically altered the city's ethnic character. But Los Angeles neighborhoods and suburbs remained largely segregated by race and ethnicity.

The revolution in American life wrought by the 1944 Servicemen's Readjustment Act, known as the GI Bill of Rights, extended beyond its impact on higher education (see Chapter 26). In addition to educational grants, the act provided returning veterans with low-interest mortgages and business loans, thus subsidizing the growth of suburbs as well as the postwar expansion of higher education. Through 1956, nearly 10 million veterans received tuition and training benefits under the act. Loans insured by the VA totaled more than $50 billion by 1962, providing assistance to millions of former GIs who started businesses.

The Federal Highway Act of 1956 gave another key boost to postwar growth, especially in the suburbs. By 1972 the program had become the single largest public works program in American history; 41,000 miles of highway were built at a cost of $76 billion. Federal subsidy of the interstate highway system stimulated both the automobile industry and suburb building. But it also accelerated the decline of American mass transit and older cities. By 1970 the nation possessed both the world's best roads and one of its worst public transportation systems.

The shadow of the cold war prompted the federal government to take new initiatives in aid for education. After the Soviet Union launched its first *Sputnik* satellite in the fall of 1957, American officials worried that the country might be lagging behind the Soviets in training scientists and engineers. The National Defense Education Act (NDEA) of 1958 allocated $280 million in grants for state universities to upgrade their science facilities. The NDEA also created $300 million in low-interest loans for college students, who had to repay only half the amount if they went on to teach in elementary or secondary school after graduation. The NDEA represented a new consensus on the importance of high-quality education to the national interest. It permanently shifted debate from whether there should be federal aid to education to what form that aid ought to take.

Suburban Life

The suburban boom strengthened the domestic ideal of the nuclear family as the model for American life. Suburban domesticity was usually presented as women's only path to happiness and fulfillment. This

Wife and children of the typical white, middle-class family greet the breadwinning father arriving home from work. Such images, which appeared frequently in popular magazines, idealized the home as the safe haven from the tensions of the office and enshrined the family as the source of happiness and security.

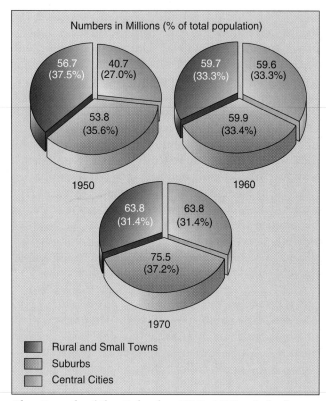

Numbers in Millions (% of total population)

1950

56.7 (37.5%) 40.7 (27.0%) 53.8 (35.6%)

1960

59.7 (33.3%) 59.6 (33.3%) 59.9 (33.4%)

1970

63.8 (31.4%) 63.8 (31.4%) 75.5 (37.2%)

■ Rural and Small Towns
■ Suburbs
■ Central Cities

The Growth of the Suburbs, 1950–1970 *Suburban growth, at the expense of older inner cities, was one of the key social trends in the twenty-five years following World War II. By 1970, more Americans lived in suburbs than in either inner cities or rural areas.*

Source: Adapted from U.S. Bureau of the Census, *Current Censuses,* 1930–1970 (Washington, D.C.: U.S. Government Printing Office, 1975).

cultural image often masked a stifling existence defined by housework, child care, and boredom. In the late 1950s Betty Friedan, a wife, mother, and journalist, began a systematic survey of her Smith College classmates. She found "a strange discrepancy between the reality of our lives as women and the image to which we were trying to conform." Friedan expanded her research and in 1963 published *The Feminine Mystique,* a landmark book that articulated the frustrations of suburban women and helped to launch the feminist movement.

Contemporary journalists, novelists, and social scientists contributed to the popular image of suburban life as essentially dull, conformist, and peopled exclusively by the educated middle class. Yet many new suburbs had a distinctively blue-collar cast, and self-segregation and zoning ordinances gave some others as distinctively an Italian, Jewish, or Irish ethnic identity as older urban neighborhoods. For millions of new suburbanites, architectural and psychological conformity was an acceptable price to pay for the comforts of home ownership, a small plot of land, and a sense of security and status.

The Expansion of Higher Education

American higher education experienced rapid growth after the war. The number of students enrolled in colleges and universities climbed from 2.6 million in 1950 to 3.2 million in 1960. It then more than doubled—to 7.5 million—by 1970, as the baby boom generation came of age.

Several factors contributed to this explosion. The GI Bill and the National Defense Education Act helped subsidize college education for millions of new students. Government spending on research and development in universities, especially for defense-related projects, promoted a postwar shift to graduate education and faculty research and away from traditional undergraduate teaching.

Colleges and universities by and large accepted the values of postwar corporate culture. By the mid-1950s, 20 percent of all college graduates had majored in business or other commercial fields. The college degree became a requirement for a whole range of expanding white-collar occupations in banking, insurance, real estate, advertising and marketing, and other corporate enterprises. Universities themselves were increasingly run like businesses, with administrators adopting the language of input–output, cost effectiveness, and quality control.

YOUTH CULTURE

The Youth Market

The term "teenager," describing someone between the ages of thirteen and nineteen, entered standard usage only at the end of World War II. Birth rates had accelerated gradually during the late 1930s and more rapidly during the war years. The children born in those years had by the late 1950s come of age in a society that, compared with that of their parents and the rest of the world, was uniquely affluent. Together, the demographic growth of teens and the postwar economic expansion created a burgeoning youth market.

The increasing uniformity of public school education also contributed to the public recognition of the special status of teenagers. In 1900 about one of every eight teenagers was in school; by the 1950s, the figure was six out of eight. Psychologists wrote guidebooks for parents, two prominent examples being Dorothy Baruch's *How to Live with Your Teenager* (1953) and Paul Landis's *Understanding Teenagers* (1955). Traditional sources of adult authority and socialization—the marketplace, schools, child-rearing manuals, the mass media—all reinforced the notion of teenagers as a special community, united by age, rank, and status.

"Hail! Hail! Rock 'n' Roll!"

In the recording industry, small, independent record labels led the way in aggressively recording local rhythm-and-blues artists. Atlantic, in New York, developed the most influential galaxy of artists, including Ray Charles, Ruth Brown, the Drifters, Joe Turner, LaVerne Baker, and the Clovers. Chess, in Chicago, had blues-based singer–songwriter–guitarists Chuck Berry and Bo Diddley. In New Orleans, Imperial had veteran pianist–singer Fats Domino and Specialty unleashed the outrageous Little Richard on the world. On radio, over jukeboxes, and in record stores, all of these African American artists "crossed over," adding millions of white teenagers to their solid base of black fans.

The older, more established record companies, such as RCA, Decca, MGM, and Capitol, had largely ignored black music, concentrating instead on popular music for the traditional adult market: pop ballads, novelty songs, and show tunes. Their response to the new trend was to offer slick, toned-down "cover" versions by white pop singers of rhythm-and-blues originals. Although African American artists enjoyed newfound mass acceptance, there were limits to how closely white kids could identify with black performers. Also, because of the superior promotional power of the major companies and the institutional racism in the music business, cover versions often outsold the originals.

The stage was thus set for the arrival of white rock-'n'-roll artists who could exploit the new sounds and styles. Elvis Presley burst upon the national scene and created as big a cultural convulsion as anyone in this century. With his carefully pomaded hair, flashy outfits, and sexy sneer, Elvis was a big hit with young female fans and a nightmare for their parents. Elvis reinvented American popular music. As a symbol of rebellious youth and the embodiment of youthful sexuality, Elvis revitalized American popular culture.

Almost Grown

Teenage consumers remade the landscape of popular music into their own turf. The dollar value of annual record sales nearly tripled between 1954 and 1959, from $213 million to $603 million. New teen magazines flourished, focused on the rituals, pleasures, and

This photo of Elvis Presley singing at a 1956 state fair in Memphis captured his dramatic stage presence. Performing with only a trio, his sound was spare but hard driving. Both the music and Presley's stage moves owed a great deal to African American rhythm-and-blues artists.

sorrows surrounding teenage courtship. Paradoxically, behavior patterns among white middle-class teenagers in the 1950s and early 1960s exhibited both a new kind of youth orientation and a more pronounced identification with adults.

Postwar affluence multiplied the number of two-car families, making it easier for sixteen-year-olds to win driving privileges formerly reserved for eighteen-year-olds. Among girls, the continuing decline in the age of menarche, combined with the sharp drop in the age of marriage after World War II, contributed to earlier dating, wearing of brassieres and nylon stockings, and use of cosmetics. These activities often began at twelve or thirteen rather than fifteen or sixteen. By the late 1950s eighteen had become the most common age at which American females married.

Many observers of the emerging youth culture were disturbed by an apparent decline of parental control. A psychiatrist writing in the *New York Times* described rock as "a cannibalistic and tribalistic kind of a music" and "a communicable disease." Many clergymen and church leaders declared it "the devil's music." Much of the opposition to rock 'n' roll, particularly in the South, played on long-standing racist fears that white females might be attracted to black music and black performers. The undercurrent beneath all this opposition was a deep anxiety over the more open expression of sexual feelings by both performers and audiences.

Paralleling the rise of rock 'n' roll was a growing concern with an alleged increase in juvenile delinquency. Gang fights, drug and alcohol abuse, car theft, and sexual offenses received the most attention. Highly publicized Senate hearings in 1955 and 1956 convinced much of the public that youthful criminals were terrorizing the country. Although crime statistics do suggest an increase in juvenile crime during the 1950s, particularly in the suburbs, the public perception of the severity of the problem was surely exaggerated.

MASS CULTURE AND ITS DISCONTENTS

Television: Tube of Plenty

No mass medium ever achieved such power and popularity as rapidly as television. The three main television networks—NBC, CBS, and ABC—grew directly from radio organizations. Nearly all TV stations were affiliated with one or more of the networks; only a handful of independent stations could be found around the country.

The television business, like radio, was based on the selling of time to advertisers who wanted to reach the mass audiences tuning into shows. Radio had offered entire shows produced by and for single sponsors, usually advertisers who wanted a close identification between their product and a star. Sponsors now bought scattered time slots for spot advertisements, rather than bankrolling an entire TV show.

Ad agencies switched their creative energy to producing slick thirty-second commercials rather than entertainment programs. A shift from broadcasting live shows to filming them opened up lucrative opportunities for reruns and foreign export. The total net revenue of the TV networks and their affiliated stations in 1947 was about $2 million; by 1957 it was nearly $1 billion.

Set largely among urban ethnic families, shows such as *I Remember Mama, The Goldbergs, The Life of Riley, Life with Luigi,* and *The Honeymooners* often featured working-class families struggling with the dilemmas posed by consumer society. By the late 1950s all of the urban ethnic comedy shows were off the air. A new breed of situation comedies presented affluent suburban WASP middle-class families who had very little contact with the outside world. Shows such as *Father Knows Best, Leave It to Beaver,* and *Ozzie and Harriet* epitomized the ideal suburban American family. Most plots focused on ethical crises, usually brought on by children's mischief and resolved by wise, kind, and bland fathers. Politics, social issues, cities, white ethnic groups, African Americans, and Latinos were virtually nonexistent.

Television and Politics

As in Hollywood, the cold war chill severely restricted the range of political discussion on television. An important exception was Edward R. Murrow's *See It Now* series on CBS, but that show was off the air by 1955. Television news did not come into its own until 1963, with the beginning of half-hour nightly network newscasts. Only then did television's extraordinary power to rivet the nation on a current crisis become clear.

Still, some of the ways that TV would alter the nation's political life emerged in the 1950s. Television made Democratic senator Estes Kefauver of Tennessee a national political figure through live coverage of his 1951 Senate investigation into organized crime. It also contributed to the political downfall of Senator Joseph McCarthy in 1954 by showing his cruel bullying tactics during Senate hearings into alleged subversive influence in the army. The 1952 election also brought the first use of TV political advertising for presidential candidates. Ever since then, television has come to dominate political polling, fundraising, and issues.

Culture Critics

The urge to denounce the mass media for degrading the quality of American life tended to unite liberal and conservative critics. Thus, Marxist writer Dwight MacDonald sounded an old conservative warning when he described "a tepid, flaccid Middlebrow Culture that threatens to engulf everything in its spreading ooze."

Critics of mass culture argued that the audiences for the mass media were atomized, anonymous, and detached. These critics undoubtedly overestimated the power of the media. They ignored the preponderance of research suggesting that most people watched and responded to mass media in family, peer group, and other social settings. The critics also missed the genuine vitality and creative brilliance to be found within mass culture: African American music; the films of Nicholas Ray, Elia Kazan, and Howard Hawks; the television of Ernie Kovacs; and the satire of *Mad* magazine.

One of the sharpest dissents from the cultural conformity of the day came from a group of writers known collectively as the Beats. Led by novelist Jack Kerouac and poet Allen Ginsberg, the Beats were a loose collection of writers who shared a distrust of the American virtues of progress, power, and material gain. Kerouac, born and raised in a working-class French Canadian family in Lowell, Massachusetts, coined the term "beat" in 1948. It meant for him a "weariness with all the forms of the modern industrial state." The Beat sensibility celebrated spontaneity, friendship, jazz, open sexuality, drug use, and the outcasts of American society.

Kerouac's novel *On the Road* became the Beat manifesto. Originally written in 1951, the novel was not published until 1957. Beat writers received a largely antagonistic, even virulent reception from the literary establishment. But millions of young Americans read

Jack Kerouac, founding voice of the Beat literacy movement in front of a neon lit bar, ca. 1950. Kerouac's public readings often to the accompaniment of live jazz music, created a performance atmosphere underlining the connections between his writing style and the rhythms and sensibility of contemporary jazz musicians.

their work and became intrigued by their alternative visions, which foreshadowed the mass youth rebellion and counterculture to come.

THE COLD WAR CONTINUED
The "New Look" in Foreign Affairs

Secretary of State John Foster Dulles gave shape to the "new look" in American foreign policy in the 1950s. Dulles had been involved in diplomatic affairs since World War I. He brought a strong sense of righteousness to his job, an almost missionary belief in America's responsibility to preserve the "free world" from "godless" communism. He was by far the most influential of Eisenhower's advisers, enjoying constant, direct access to the president.

Dulles articulated a more assertive policy toward the communist threat by calling not simply for containment but for a "rollback." The key would be greater reliance on America's nuclear superiority. The emphasis on massive retaliation, the administration claimed, would also facilitate cuts in the military budget. As Secretary of Defense Charles Wilson said, the goal was to "get more bang for the buck."

The limits of a policy based on nuclear strategy became painfully clear when American leaders faced tense situations with no clear alternative means of pressure. In the fall of 1956 Hungarians staged a general strike against their Soviet-dominated communist rulers, taking over the streets and factories in Budapest and other cities. Amid urgent appeals for American action, Eisenhower recognized that the Soviets would defend their own borders, and all of Eastern Europe as well, by all-out military force if necessary. The United States opened its gates to thousands of Hungarian refugees, but it refused to intervene when Soviet tanks and troops crushed the revolt.

The death of Joseph Stalin in 1953 and the worldwide condemnation of his crimes, revealed by his successor, Nikita Khrushchev, in 1956, gave Eisenhower fresh hope for a new spirit of détente between the two superpowers. Khrushchev made a twelve-day trip to America in 1959, a psychological thaw in the cold war.

In early 1960 Khrushchev called for another summit in Paris, to discuss German reunification and nuclear disarmament. Meanwhile, Eisenhower planned his own friendship tour of the Soviet Union. But in May 1960 the Soviets shot down an American U-2 spy plane gathering intelligence on Soviet military installations. The summit collapsed when Eisenhower refused Khrushchev's demands for an apology and an end to the spy flights.

The U-2 incident demonstrated the limits of personal diplomacy in resolving the deep structural rivalry between the superpowers. Although Eisenhower knew from earlier U-2 flights that the Soviet Union had undertaken no major military buildup, he had agreed with Congress to a hike of $2.5 billion in military spending in 1957. The launching of the first space-orbiting satellite by the Soviets in October 1957 provided a new incentive for expanded defense spending. *Sputnik* demonstrated Russian technological prowess and upset Americans' precarious sense of security. In Congress a bipartisan majority voted to increase the military budget by another $8 billion in 1958, thereby accelerating the arms race and helping to prop up the growing defense sector of the economy.

Covert Action

While the United States moderated its stance toward the Soviet Union and its eastern European satellites, it hardened its policies in the Third World. The need for anticommunist tactics short of all-out military conflict pushed the Eisenhower administration to develop new means of fighting the cold war. The premise rested on encouraging confusion or rivalry within the Communist sphere, and on destabilizing or destroying anticapitalist movements around the world.

The Central Intelligence Agency, created in 1947, was perfectly designed for this task. For CIA director Eisenhower named Allen Dulles, brother of the secretary of state and a former leader in the CIA's World War II precursor, the Office of Strategic Services (OSS). Mandated to collect and analyze information, the CIA did much more under Dulles's command. Thousands of covert agents stationed all over the world carried out a wide range of political activities. Some agents arranged large, secret financial payments to friendly political parties or to foreign trade unions opposed to socialist policies.

Intervening Around the World

The CIA produced a swift, major victory in Iran in 1953. The popular prime minister, Mohammed Mossadegh, had nationalized Britain's Anglo-Iranian Oil Company. The State Department worried that this precedent might encourage a trend toward nationalization throughout the oil-rich Middle East. Kermit Roosevelt, CIA chief in Iran, organized and financed an opposition to Mossadegh within the Iranian army and on the streets of Teheran. This CIA-led movement forced Mossadegh out of office and replaced him with Riza Shah Pahlavi. The Shah proved his loyalty to his American sponsors by renegotiating oil contracts so as to assure American companies of 40 percent of Iran's oil concessions.

The most publicized CIA intervention of the Eisenhower years took place in Guatemala, where a fragile democracy had taken root in 1944. President Jácobo Arbenz Guzmán, elected in 1950, aggressively pursued land reform and encouraged the formation of trade unions. Arbenz also challenged the long-standing dominance of the United Fruit Company by threatening to expropriate hundreds of thousands of acres that United Fruit was not cultivating. The company began intensive lobbying for U.S. intervention. United Fruit linked the land reform program to the evils of international communism, and the CIA spent $7 million training antigovernment dissidents based in Honduras.

On June 14, 1954, a U.S.-sponsored military invasion began. Guatemalans appealed in vain to the United Nations for help. Meanwhile, President Eisenhower publicly denied any knowledge of CIA activities. The appointed military leader, Carlos Castillo Armas, was assassinated in 1957, and a decades-long civil war ensued between military factions and peasant guerrillas.

In Indochina the United States provided France with massive military aid and CIA cooperation in its desperate struggle to maintain a colonial regime in Vietnam, fighting against the nationalist Vietminh movement led by communist Ho Chi Minh. When Vietminh forces surrounded 25,000 French troops at Dien Bien Phu in March 1954, France pleaded with the United States to intervene directly. But Eisenhower, recalling the difficulties of the Korean conflict, rejected this call.

At the same time, Eisenhower wanted to contain communism in Asia. The "loss" of Vietnam, he believed, would threaten other Southeast Asian nations, such as Laos, Thailand, the Philippines, and perhaps even India and Australia—the so-called domino theory. After the French surrender at Dien Bien Phu, a Geneva convention established a cease-fire and a temporary division of Vietnam along the seventeenth parallel into northern and southern sectors. The Geneva agreement called for reunification and national elections in 1956. The United States attended these sessions, along with the Soviet Union and China, but it refused to sign the accord.

South Vietnamese leader Ngo Dinh Diem, a former Japanese collaborator and a Catholic in a country that was 90 percent Buddhist, quickly alienated many peasants with his corruption and repressive policies. Both Diem and Eisenhower refused to permit the 1956 elections stipulated in Geneva because they knew popular hero Ho Chi Minh would easily win. By 1959 Diem's harsh and unpopular government in Saigon faced a civil war: thousands of peasants had joined guerrilla forces determined to drive him out. Eisenhower's commitment of advisers and economic aid to South Vietnam, based on firm belief in cold war assumptions, laid the foundation for the full-scale commitment of American ground troops in the early 1960s.

Ike's Warning: The Military–Industrial Complex

Throughout the 1950s small numbers of peace advocates in the United States had protested that the increasing reliance on nuclear weapons did not strengthen national security but rather threatened the entire planet with extinction. As he neared retirement, President Eisenhower came to share some of their anxiety and doubts about the arms race. He chose to devote his farewell address, delivered in January 1961, to warning the nation about the dangers of what he called the "military–industrial complex." The conjunction of a large military establishment and a large arms industry, Eisenhower noted, was new in American history. "The potential for the disastrous rise of misplaced power exists and will persist. We must never let the weight of this combination endanger our liberties or democratic processes."

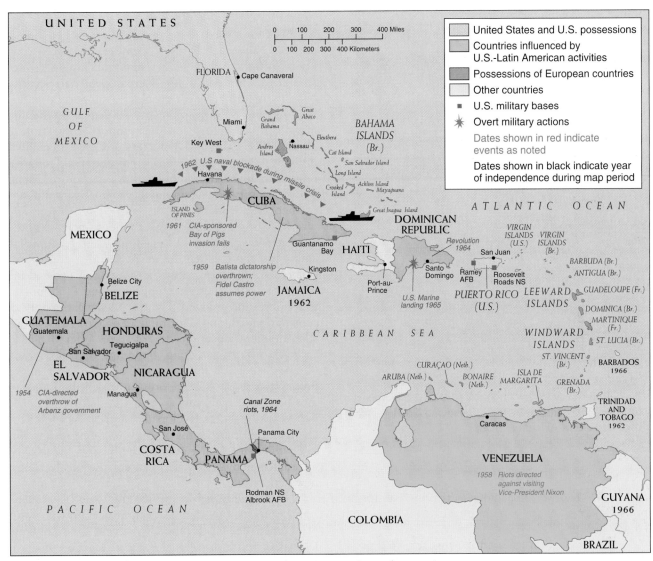

The U.S. in the Caribbean, 1948–1966   *U.S. military intervention and economic presence grew steadily in the Caribbean following World War II. After 1960, opposition to the Cuban Revolution dominated U.S. Caribbean policies.*

The old soldier understood perhaps better than most the dangers of raw military force. Eisenhower's public posture of restraint and caution in foreign affairs accompanied an enormous expansion of American economic, diplomatic, and military strength. Yet the Eisenhower years also demonstrated the limits of power and intervention in a world that did not always conform to the simple dualistic assumptions of cold war ideology.

JOHN F. KENNEDY AND THE NEW FRONTIER

The Election of 1960

No one could have resembled Dwight Eisenhower less in personality, temperament, and public image than John Fitzgerald Kennedy. The handsome son of a promi-

nent, wealthy Irish American diplomat, husband of a fashionable, trend-setting heiress, forty-two-year-old JFK embodied youth, excitement, and sophistication.

John F. Kennedy's political career had begun in Massachusetts, which elected him to the House in 1946 and then the Senate in 1952. Kennedy won the Democratic nomination after a bruising series of primaries in which he defeated party stalwarts Hubert Humphrey of Minnesota and Lyndon B. Johnson of Texas. Vice President Richard M. Nixon, the Republican nominee, was far better known than his younger opponent. The Kennedy campaign stressed its candidate's youth and his image as a war hero. During his World War II tour of duty in the Pacific, Kennedy had bravely rescued one of his crew after their PT boat had been sunk. Kennedy's supporters also pointed to his intellectual

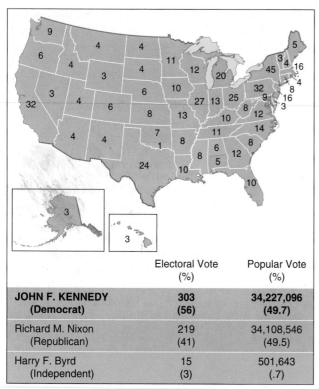

	Electoral Vote (%)	Popular Vote (%)
JOHN F. KENNEDY (Democrat)	**303 (56)**	**34,227,096 (49.7)**
Richard M. Nixon (Republican)	219 (41)	34,108,546 (49.5)
Harry F. Byrd (Independent)	15 (3)	501,643 (.7)

The Election of 1960 *Kennedy's popular vote margin over Nixon was only a little over 100,000, making this one of the closest elections in American history.*

ability. JFK had won the Pulitzer Prize in 1957 for his book *Profiles in Courage,* which in fact had been written largely by aides.

The election featured the first televised presidential debates. Nixon appeared unshaven and nervous through the camera, while Kennedy's confident manner and good looks added to his stature. Both candidates emphasized foreign policy. Nixon defended the Republican record and stressed his own maturity and experience. Kennedy hammered away at the "missile gap" with the Soviet Union and promised more vigorous executive leadership. The 1960 election moved television to the center of presidential politics, making image and appearance more critical than ever.

Kennedy squeaked to victory in the closest election since 1884. He won by a little over 100,000 votes out of nearly 69 million cast. Surrounded by prestigious Ivy League academics, Hollywood movie stars, and talented artists and writers, he imbued the presidency with an aura of celebrity. The new president's ringing inaugural address ("Ask not what your country can do for you—ask what you can do for your country") had special resonance for a whole generation of young Americans.

New Frontier Liberalism

Kennedy promised to revive the long-stalled liberal domestic agenda. His New Frontier advocated such liberal programs as a higher minimum wage, greater federal aid for education, increased Social Security benefits, medical care for the elderly, support for public housing, and various antipoverty measures. Yet the thin margin of his victory and the stubborn opposition of conservative southern Democrats in Congress made it difficult to achieve these goals. For example, Congress refused to enact the administration's attempt to extend Social Security and unemployment benefits to millions of uncovered workers.

Congress did approve a modest increase in the minimum wage (to $1.25 per hour), agreed to a less ambitious improvement in Social Security, and appropriated $5 billion for public housing. It also passed the Manpower Retraining Act, appropriating $435 million to train the unemployed. The Area Redevelopment Act provided federal funds for rural, depressed Appalachia. The Higher Education Act of 1963 offered aid to colleges for constructing buildings and upgrading libraries. One of the best-publicized New Frontier programs was the Peace Corps, in which thousands of mostly young men and women traveled overseas for two-year stints in undeveloped countries. As a force for change, the Peace Corps produced modest results. But as a vehicle for young people, the Peace Corps epitomized Kennedy's promise to direct the idealism of a new generation.

Kennedy helped revive the issue of women's rights with his Presidential Commission on the Status of Women, led by Eleanor Roosevelt. One concrete legislative result, the Equal Pay Act of 1963, made it illegal for employers to pay men and women different wages for the same job. The work of the commission contributed to a new generation of women's rights activism.

Kennedy took a more aggressive stance on stimulating economic growth and creating new jobs than had Eisenhower. His administration pushed lower business taxes through Congress, even at the cost of a higher federal deficit. The Revenue Act of 1962 encouraged new investment and plant renovation by easing tax depreciation schedules for business. Kennedy also gained approval for lower U.S. tariffs as a way to increase foreign trade. To help keep inflation down, Kennedy intervened in the steel industry in 1961 and 1962, pressuring labor to keep its wage demands low and management to curb price increases.

Kennedy also increased the federal commitment to a wholly new realm of government spending: the space program. The National Aeronautics and Space Administration (NASA) had been established under Eisenhower in response to the Soviet success with *Sputnik*. In 1961 Kennedy won approval for a greatly expanded space program with the goal of landing an American on the moon by the end of the decade. In space, if not on earth, the New Frontier might actually be reached.

Kennedy and the Cold War

During Kennedy's three years in office his approach to foreign policy shifted between aggressive containment and efforts to ease U.S.–Soviet tensions. Certainly when he first entered office, Kennedy and his chief aides considered it their main task to confront the communist threat. To head the State Department Kennedy chose Dean Rusk, a conservative former assistant to Truman's secretary of state, Dean Acheson. Secretary of Defense Robert McNamara, a Republican and Ford Motor Company executive, was determined to streamline military procedures and weapons buying. Allen Dulles, Eisenhower's CIA director, remained at his post. These and other officials believed with Kennedy that Eisenhower had timidly accepted stalemate when the cold war could have been won.

Between 1960 and 1962 defense appropriations increased by nearly a third, from $43 billion to $56 billion. Kennedy expanded Eisenhower's policy of covert operations, creating the elite Special Forces (Green Berets) as a supplement to CIA covert operations in counterinsurgency battles against Third-World guerrillas. The Special Forces reflected Kennedy's desire as president to acquire greater flexibility, secrecy, and independence in the conduct of foreign policy.

The limits of the Special Forces and covert action became apparent in Southeast Asia. In Laos, where the United States had ignored the 1954 Geneva agreement and installed a friendly military regime, the CIA-backed government could not defeat Soviet-backed Pathet Lao guerrillas. The president had to arrange with the Soviets to neutralize Laos. In neighboring Vietnam the situation proved more difficult. When Viet Cong guerrillas launched a civil war in South Vietnam against the U.S.-supported government in Saigon, Kennedy began sending hundreds of Green Berets and other military advisers to support the rule of Ngo Dinh Diem. In May 1961, in response to North Vietnamese aid to the Viet Cong, Kennedy ordered a covert action against Ho Chi Minh's government that included sabotage and intelligence gathering.

Kennedy accepted the analysis of two aides, General Maxwell Taylor and Walt Rostow, who saw the situation in Vietnam through purely cold war eyes, ignoring the inefficiency, corruption, and unpopularity of the Diem government. By 1963, with Diem's army unable to contain the Viet Cong rebellion, Kennedy had sent nearly 16,000 support and combat troops to South Vietnam. By then, a wide spectrum of South Vietnamese society had joined the revolt against the hated Diem, including highly respected Buddhist monks and their students. Americans watched in horror as television news reports showed footage of Buddhists burning themselves to death on the streets of Saigon—the ultimate protest against Diem's repressive rule. The South Vietnamese army, bloated by U.S. aid and weakened by corruption, continued to disintegrate. In the fall of 1963 American military officers and CIA operatives stood aside as a group of Vietnamese generals removed President Diem, killing him and his top advisers. It was the first of many coups that racked the South Vietnamese government over the next few years.

In Latin America Kennedy looked for ways to forestall various revolutionary movements that were gaining ground. The erosion of peasant land holdings had accelerated rapidly after 1950. Millions of impoverished peasants were forced to relocate to already overcrowded cities. In 1961 Kennedy unveiled the Alliance for Progress, a ten-year, $100 billion plan to spur economic development in Latin America. Kennedy intended the program as a kind of Marshall Plan that would benefit the poor and middle classes of the continent. But the expansion in export crops and in consumption by the tiny upper class did little to aid the poor or encourage democracy. The United States hesitated to challenge the power of dictators and extreme conservatives who were staunch anti-Communist allies. Thus, the alliance soon degenerated into just another foreign aid program, incapable of generating genuine social change.

The Cuban Revolution and the Bay of Pigs

The direct impetus for the Alliance for Progress was the Cuban Revolution of 1959, which loomed over Latin America. The U.S. economic domination of Cuba had continued through the 1950s. American-owned business controlled all of Cuba's oil production, 90 percent of its mines, and roughly half of its railroads and sugar and cattle industries. Havana, the island's capital, was an attractive tourist center for Americans, and U.S. crime syndicates shared control of the island's lucrative gambling, prostitution, and drug trade with dictator Fulgencio Batista. In the early 1950s a peasant-based revolutionary movement, led by Fidel Castro, began gaining strength in the rural districts and mountains outside Havana.

On New Year's Day 1959, after years of guerrilla warfare, the rebels entered Havana and seized power amid great public rejoicing. Castro's land reform program, involving the seizure of acreage from the tiny minority that controlled much of the fertile land, threatened to set an example for other Latin American

Vice President Lyndon B. Johnson took the oath of office as President aboard Air Force One after the assassination of John F. Kennedy, November 22, 1963. Onlookers included the grief-stricken Jacqueline Kennedy (right) and Lady Bird Johnson (left). This haunting photo captured both the shock of Kennedy's assassination and the orderly succession of power that followed.

countries. Although Castro had not joined the Cuban Communist Party, he turned to the Soviet Union after the United States withdrew economic aid. He began to sell sugar to the Soviets and soon nationalized American-owned oil companies and other enterprises. Eisenhower established an economic boycott of Cuba in 1960, then severed diplomatic relations.

Kennedy inherited from Eisenhower plans for a U.S. invasion of Cuba, including the secret arming and training of Cuban exiles. The CIA drafted the invasion plan, which was based on the assumption that a U.S.-led invasion would trigger a popular uprising of the Cuban people and bring down Castro. Kennedy went along with the plan, but at the last moment he decided not to supply an Air Force cover for the operation. On April 17, 1961, a ragtag army of 1,400 counterrevolutionaries led by CIA operatives landed at the Bay of Pigs, on Cuba's south coast. Castro's efficient and loyal army easily subdued them.

The debacle revealed that the CIA, blinded by cold war assumptions, had failed to understand the Cuban Revolution. There was no popular uprising against Castro. Instead, the invasion strengthened Castro's standing among the urban poor and peasants, already attracted by his programs of universal literacy and medical care. An embarrassed Kennedy reluctantly took the blame for the abortive invasion, and his administration was censured time and again by Third-World delegates to the United Nations. American

liberals criticized Kennedy for plotting Castro's overthrow, while conservatives blamed him for failing to carry out the plan. Despite the failure, Kennedy remained committed to getting rid of Castro and keeping up the economic boycott. The CIA continued to support anti-Castro operations and launched at least eight attempts to assassinate the Cuban leader.

The Missile Crisis

The aftermath of the Bay of Pigs led to the most serious confrontation of the cold war: the Cuban missile crisis of October 1962. Frightened by U.S. belligerency, Castro asked Soviet premier Khrushchev for military help. Khrushchev responded in the summer of 1962 by shipping Cuba a large amount of sophisticated weaponry, including intermediate-range nuclear missiles. In early October U.S. reconnaissance planes found camouflaged missile silos dotting the island. For the first time, American cities and military bases were potential targets for Soviet nuclear bombs, sited a mere ninety miles from Florida. Several Kennedy aides demanded an immediate bombing of Cuban bases, arguing that the missiles had decisively changed the strategic global advantage the United States had previously enjoyed.

Instead, Kennedy went on national television on October 22. He announced the discovery of the missile sites, demanded the removal of all missiles, and ordered a strict naval blockade of all offensive military equipment shipped to Cuba. He also requested an emergency meeting of the UN Security Council and promised that any missiles launched from Cuba would bring "a full retaliatory response upon the Soviet Union." For a tense week, the American public wondered whether nuclear Armageddon was imminent. Eyeball to eyeball, the two superpowers waited for each other to blink. On October 26–27 Khrushchev yielded, ordering twenty-five Soviet ships off their course to Cuba, thus avoiding a challenge to the American blockade. Khrushchev offered to remove all the missiles in return for a pledge from the United States not to invade Cuba. Khrushchev later added a demand for removal of American weapons from Turkey, equally close to the Soviet Union. On November 20, after weeks of delicate negotiations, Kennedy publicly announced the withdrawal of Soviet missiles and bombers from Cuba, pledged to respect Cuban sovereignty, and promised that U.S. forces would not invade the island.

The crisis had passed. The Soviets, determined not to be intimidated again, engaged in the largest weapons buildup in their history. For his part Kennedy, perhaps chastened by this flirtation with nuclear disaster, made important gestures toward détente with the Soviets. In a June 1963 address at American University, Kennedy called for a rethinking of cold war diplomacy. Shortly after, Washington and Moscow set up a hotline, or direct phone connection, to facilitate instant communication during times of crisis. More substantial was the Limited Nuclear Test Ban Treaty, signed in August by the United States, the USSR, and Great Britain. The treaty prohibited above-ground, outer space, and underwater nuclear weapons tests. Underground testing continued to accelerate for years. But the limited test ban represented an important landmark in arms control, as well as a psychological breakthrough in East–West relations.

The Assassination of President Kennedy

The assassination of John F. Kennedy on November 22, 1963, sent the entire nation into shock and mourning. Tens of millions watched his funeral on television, trying to make sense of the brutal murder. Although a special commission found the killing to be the work of a lone assassin, Lee Harvey Oswald, many Americans still doubt this conclusion. Kennedy's death gave rise to a host of conspiracy theories, none of which seems provable. We will never know what Kennedy might have achieved in a second term. But in his 1,000 days as president, he demonstrated a capacity to change and grow in office. Having gone to the brink at the missile crisis, he then managed to launch new initiatives toward détente. At the time of his death, relations between the United States and the Soviet Union were more amicable than at any time since the end of World War II. Much of the domestic liberal agenda of the New Frontier would be finally implemented by his successor, Lyndon B. Johnson, who dreamed of creating a Great Society.

CONCLUSION

America in 1963 still enjoyed the full flush of its postwar economic boom. To be sure, millions of Americans, particularly African Americans and Latinos, did not share in the good times. But millions of others had managed to achieve middle-class status since the early 1950s. An expanding economy, cheap energy, government subsidies, and a dominant position in the world marketplace had made the hallmarks of the "good life" available to more Americans than ever before. The postwar "American dream" promised home ownership, college education, secure employment at decent wages, affordable appliances, and the ability to travel—for one's children if not for one's self. The nation's public culture—its schools, mass media, politics, and advertising—presented a powerful consensus based on the idea that the American dream was available to all who would work for it.

The presidential transition from the grandfatherly Dwight Eisenhower to the charismatic John Kennedy symbolized for many a generational shift as well. By 1963 young people had more influence than ever before in shaping the nation's political life, its media images, and its burgeoning consumer culture. Kennedy himself inspired millions of young Americans to pursue public service and to express their political idealism. But even by the time of Kennedy's death, the postwar consensus and the conditions that nurtured it were beginning to unravel.

CHRONOLOGY

1952	Dwight D. Eisenhower is elected president
1953	CIA installs Riza Shah Pahlavi as leader of Iran
1954	Vietminh force French surrender at Dien Bien Phu
	CIA overthrows government of Jácobo Arbenz Guzmán in Guatemala
	United States explodes first deliverable hydrogen bomb
1955	Jonas Salk pioneers vaccine for polio
	James Dean stars in the movie *Rebel Without a Cause*
1956	Federal Highway Act authorizes national systems of highways
	Elvis Presley signs with RCA
	Eisenhower is reelected
	Allen Ginsberg publishes *Howl*
1957	Soviet Union launches *Sputnik*, first space-orbiting satellite
	Jack Kerouac publishes *On the Road*
1958	National Defense Education Act authorizes grants and loans to college students
1959	Nikita Khrushchev visits the United States
1960	Soviets shoot down U-2 spy plane
	John F. Kennedy is elected president
	Almost 90 percent of American homes have television
1961	President Kennedy creates Green Berets
	Bay of Pigs invasion of Cuba fails
1962	Cuban missile crisis brings the world to the brink of a superpower confrontation
1963	Report by the Presidential Commission on the Status of Women documents ongoing discrimination
	Limited Nuclear Test-Ban Treaty is signed
	President Kennedy is assassinated
	Betty Friedan publishes *The Feminine Mystique*

REVIEW QUESTIONS

1. How did postwar economic prosperity change the lives of ordinary Americans? Which groups benefited most, and which were largely excluded from this affluence?
2. What role did federal programs play in expanding economic opportunities?
3. Analyze the origins of postwar youth culture. How was teenage life different in these years from previous eras? How did popular culture both reflect and distort the lives of American youth?
4. How did mass culture become even more central to American everyday life in the two decades following World War II? What problems did various cultural critics identify with this trend?
5. How did cold war politics and assumptions shape American foreign policy in these years? What key interventions did the United States make in Europe and the third world?
6. Evaluate the domestic and international policies associated with John F. Kennedy and the New Frontier. What continuities with Eisenhower-era politics do you find in the Kennedy administration? How did JFK break with past practices?

RECOMMENDED READING

Erik Barnouw, *Tube of Plenty* (1982). The best one-volume history of television, with excellent material on the new medium's impact on cultural and political life.

James B. Gilbert, *A Cycle of Outrage* (1986). An insightful analysis of juvenile delinquency and its treatment by social scientists and the mass media during the 1950s.

Peter Guralnick, *Last Train to Memphis: The Rise of Elvis Presley* (1994). The best biography of Presley and a stunning portrait of the milieu that produced him.

Kenneth T. Jackson, *Crabgrass Frontier* (1985). The most comprehensive overview of the history of American suburbs. Jackson provides a broad historical context for understanding postwar suburbanization, and offers an excellent analysis of the impact of government agencies, such as the Federal Housing Administration.

George Lipsitz, *Time Passages* (1990). An illuminating set of essays charting developments in American popular culture, especially strong analysis of music and early television.

Elaine Tyler May, *Homeward Bound: American Families in the Cold War* (1988). A thoughtful social history linking family life of the 1950s with the political shadow of the cold war.

Gerald Nicosia, *Memory Babe: A Critical Biography of Jack Kerouac* (1983). Both the best biography of this key Beat writer and the best analysis of the Beat generation.

Chester Pach Jr. and Elmo Richardson, *The Presidency of Dwight D. Eisenhower*, rev. ed. (1991). A good recent overview of the Eisenhower administration.

Herbert Parmet, *JFK* (1983). A solid, balanced examination of the Kennedy presidency.

James T. Patterson, *Grand Expectations: Postwar America, 1945–1974* (1996). A comprehensive overview of postwar life that centers on the "grand expectations" evoked by unprecedented prosperity.

CHAPTER TWENTY-EIGHT

THE CIVIL RIGHTS MOVEMENT
1945–1966

AMERICAN COMMUNITIES
The Montgomery Bus Boycott:
An African American Community
Challenges Segregation

A steady stream of cars and pedestrians jammed the streets around the Holt Street Baptist Church in Montgomery, Alabama. By early evening a patient, orderly, and determined crowd of over 5,000 African Americans had packed the church and spilled over onto the sidewalks. Loudspeakers had to be set up for the thousands who could not squeeze inside. After a brief prayer and a reading from the Scripture, all attention focused on the twenty-six-year-old minister who was to address the gathering. "We are here this evening," he began slowly, "for serious business. We are here in a general sense because first and foremost we are American citizens, and we are determined to apply our citizenship to the fullness of its means."

Rosa Parks, a seamstress and well-known activist in Montgomery's African American community, had been arrested and put in jail for refusing to give up her seat to a white passenger. Montgomery's black community had long endured the humiliation of a strictly segregated bus system. Drivers could order a whole row of black passengers to vacate their seats for one white person. And black people had to pay their fares at the front of the bus and then step back outside and reenter through the rear door. The day of the mass meeting, over 30,000 African Americans had answered a hastily organized call to boycott the city's buses in protest of Parks's arrest.

Even before the minister concluded his speech, it was clear to all present that the bus boycott would continue for more than just a day. He laid out the key principles that would guide the boycott: nonviolence, Christian love, and unity. By the time he finished his brief but stirring address, the minister had created a powerful sense of communion. "If we are wrong, justice is a lie," he told the clapping and shouting throng. "And we are determined here in Montgomery to work and fight until justice runs down like water and righteousness like a mighty stream." Historians would look back at Montgomery, he noted, and have to say, " 'There lived a race of people, black people, fleecy locks and black complexion, of people who had the moral courage to stand up for their rights.' And thereby they injected a new meaning into the veins of history and of civilization."

The Reverend Dr. Martin Luther King, Jr., made his way out of the church amid waves of applause and rows of hands reaching out to touch him. His speech catapulted him into leadership of the Montgomery bus boycott, and it also proved him to be a prophet. But he had not started the movement. Parks herself had served for twelve years as secretary of the local NAACP chapter. She was a committed opponent of segregation and was thoroughly respected in the city's African American community. E. D. Nixon, president of the Alabama NAACP and head of the local Brotherhood of Sleeping Car Porters union, saw Mrs. Parks's arrest as the right case on which to make a stand. On December 5, Nixon brought together Montgomery's black ministers to coordinate a boycott of city buses. They formed the Montgomery Improvement Association (MIA) and chose King as their leader.

While Nixon organized black ministers, Jo Ann Robinson, an English teacher at Alabama State College, played a key role in spreading the word to the larger black community. Robinson led the Women's Political Council (WPC), an organization of black professional women founded in 1949. With her WPC allies, Robinson wrote, mimeographed, and distributed 50,000 copies of a leaflet telling the story of Parks's arrest and urging all African Americans to stay off city buses on December 5. Buoyed by the success of that protest, the MIA now faced the more difficult task of keeping the boycott going. Success depended on providing alternative transportation for the 30,000 to 40,000 maids, cooks, janitors, and other black people who needed to get to work.

The MIA coordinated an elaborate system of carpools, using hundreds of private autos and volunteer drivers to provide as many as 20,000 rides each day. Local authorities, shocked by the discipline and sense of purpose shown by Montgomery's African American community, refused to engage in serious negotia-

tions. With the aid of the NAACP, the MIA brought suit in federal court against bus segregation in Montgomery. Police harassed boycotters with traffic tickets and arrests. White racists exploded bombs in the homes of King and E. D. Nixon. The days turned into weeks, then months, but still the boycott continued.

The boycott reduced the bus company's revenues by two-thirds. In February 1956 city officials obtained indictments against King, Nixon, and 113 other boycotters under an old law forbidding hindrance to business without "just cause or legal excuse." A month later King went on trial as the first of the indicted defendants. A growing contingent of newspaper reporters and TV crews from around the country watched as the judge found King guilty, fined him $1,000, and released him on bond pending appeal. But on June 4, a panel of three federal judges struck down Montgomery's bus segregation ordinances as unconstitutional. Attorneys for Montgomery and the state of Alabama immediately appealed to the U.S. Supreme Court. On November 13 the Court affirmed the district court ruling. After eleven hard months and against all odds, the boycotters had won.

The struggle to end legal segregation took root in scores of southern cities and towns. African American communities led these fights, developing a variety of tactics, leaders, and ideologies. With white allies, they engaged in direct action protests such as boycotts, sit-ins, and mass civil disobedience, as well as strategic legal battles in state and federal courts. The movement was not without its inner conflicts. Tensions between local movements and national civil rights organizations flared up regularly. Within African American communities, long-simmering distrust between the working classes and rural folk on one hand and middle-class ministers, teachers, and business people on the other sometimes threatened to destroy political unity. There were generational conflicts between African American student activists and their elders. But overall, the civil rights movement created new social identities for African Americans and profoundly changed American society as a whole.

Montgomery

KEY TOPICS

- Legal and political origins of the African American civil rights struggle

- Martin Luther King's rise to leadership

- Student protesters and direct action in the South

- Civil rights and national politics

- Civil Rights Act of 1964 and Voting Rights Act of 1965

- America's other minorities

ORIGINS OF THE MOVEMENT

Civil Rights After World War II

The boom in wartime production spurred a mass migration of nearly a million black Southerners to northern cities. Although racial discrimination in housing and employment was by no means absent in northern cities, greater economic opportunities and political freedom continued to attract rural African Americans after the war. Black people gained significant influence in local political machines in such cities as New York, Chicago, and Detroit. In industrial unions such as the United Automobile Workers and the United Steel Workers, white and black workers learned the power of biracial unity in fighting for better wages and working conditions.

After the war, civil rights issues returned to the national political stage for the first time since Reconstruction. Black voters had already begun to switch their allegiance from the Republicans to the Democrats during the New Deal. A series of symbolic and substantial acts by the Truman administration solidified that shift. In 1946 Truman created a Presidential Committee on Civil Rights. Its report, *To Secure These Rights*, set out an ambitious program to end racial inequality. Recommendations included a permanent civil rights division in the Justice Department, voting rights protection, antilynching legislation, and a legal attack on segregated housing. Although he publicly endorsed nearly all the proposals of the new committee, Truman introduced no legislation to make them law.

Truman and his advisers walked a political tightrope on civil rights. They understood that black voters in several key northern states would be pivotal in the 1948 election. At the same time, they worried about the loyalty of white southern Democrats adamantly opposed to changing the racial status quo. In July 1948 the president made his boldest move on behalf of civil rights, issuing an executive order barring segregation in the armed forces. When liberals forced the Democratic National Convention to adopt a strong civil rights

plank that summer, a group of outraged Southerners walked out and nominated Governor Strom Thurmond of South Carolina for president on a States' Rights ticket. Thurmond carried four southern states in the election. But with the help of over 70 percent of the northern black vote, Truman managed—barely—to defeat Republican Thomas E. Dewey in November. The deep split over race issues would continue to rack the national Democratic Party for a generation.

During the war membership in the National Association for the Advancement of Colored People had mushroomed from 50,000 to 500,000. Working- and middle-class urban black people provided the backbone of this new membership. The NAACP conducted voter registration drives and lobbied against discrimination in housing and employment. Its Legal Defense and Education Fund, vigorously led by Thurgood Marshall, mounted several significant legal challenges to segregation laws. In *Morgan v. Virginia* (1946) the Supreme Court declared that segregation on interstate buses was an undue burden on interstate commerce. Other decisions struck down all-white election primaries, racially restrictive housing covenants, and the exclusion of blacks from law and graduate schools.

The NAACP's legal work demonstrated the potential for using federal courts in attacking segregation. But federal enforcement of court decisions was often lacking. In 1947 a group of black and white activists tested compliance with the *Morgan* decision by traveling on a bus through the Upper South. This Freedom Ride was cosponsored by the Christian pacifist Fellowship of Reconciliation (FOR) and its recent offshoot, the Congress of Racial Equality (CORE), which was devoted to interracial, nonviolent direct action. The riders met stiff resistance in North Carolina. A number were arrested and sentenced to thirty days on a chain gang for refusing to leave the bus.

Two symbolic firsts raised black expectations and inspired pride. In 1947 Jackie Robinson broke the color barrier in major league baseball, winning rookie-of-the-year honors with the Brooklyn Dodgers.

Robinson's courage in the face of fan and player hostility paved the way for the other black ballplayers, who soon followed him to the big leagues. In 1950 United Nations diplomat Ralph Bunche won the Nobel Peace Prize for arranging a Middle East armistice. However, Bunche later declined an appointment as undersecretary of state because he did not want to subject his family to the humiliating segregation laws of Washington, D.C.

Cultural change had political implications as well. Although black musicians had pioneered the development of swing, white bandleaders and musicians had reaped most of the recognition and money from the public. Artists such as Charlie Parker, Dizzy Gillespie, Thelonius Monk, Bud Powell, and Miles Davis revolted against the standard big band format of swing, preferring small groups and extended jam sessions. The new music, dubbed *bebop* by critics and fans, demanded a much more sophisticated knowledge of harmony and melody and featured more complex rhythms and extended improvisation. Serious about both their music and the way it was presented, these black artists refused to cater to white expectations of grinning, easygoing black performers.

The Segregated South

The 1896 Supreme Court ruling in *Plessy v. Ferguson* had sanctioned the principle of "separate but equal" facilities in southern life. In practice, segregation meant separate and unequal. A tight web of state and local ordinances enforced strict separation of the races in schools, restaurants, movie theaters, libraries, restrooms, even cemeteries. Fifty years of legal segregation meant inferior public schools, health care, and public lodging for the region's black people. There were no black policemen in the Deep South and only a handful of black lawyers. "A white man," one scholar observed, "can steal from or maltreat a Negro in almost any way without fear of reprisal, because the Negro cannot claim the protection of the police or courts."

In the late 1940s only about 10 percent of eligible southern black people voted, most of these in urban areas. A combination of legal and extralegal measures kept all but the most determined black people disenfranchised. Poll taxes, all-white primaries, and discriminatory registration procedures reinforced the belief that voting was "the white man's business." African Americans who insisted on exercising their right to vote, especially in remote rural areas, faced beatings, shootings, and lynchings.

Outsiders often noted the irony of Jim Crow laws (discussed in Chapter 20) coexisting with the most intimate contact between blacks and whites. The mass of black Southerners worked on white-owned plantations and in white households. The South's racial code forced African Americans to accept, at least outwardly, social conventions that reinforced their low standing with whites. A black person did not shake hands with a white person, enter a white home through the front door, or address a white person except formally.

Brown v. Board of Education

Since the late 1930s, the NAACP had chipped away at the legal foundations of segregation. Rather than making a frontal assault on the *Plessy* separate-but-equal rule, civil rights attorneys launched a series of suits seeking complete equality in segregated facilities. The aim of this strategy was to make segregation so prohibitively expensive that the South would be forced to dismantle it. In the 1939 case *Missouri v. exrel. Gaines*, the Supreme Court ruled that the University of Missouri law school must either admit African Americans or build another, fully equal law school for them. NAACP lawyers pushed their arguments further, asserting that equality could not be measured simply by money or physical plant. In *McLaurin v. Oklahoma State Regents* (1950), the Court agreed. Thurgood Marshall successfully argued that regulations forcing a black law student to sit, eat, and study in areas apart from white students inevitably created a "badge of inferiority."

By 1951, Marshall had begun coordinating the NAACP's legal resources for a direct attack on the sepa-

Signs designating "White" and "Colored" restrooms, waiting rooms, entrances, benches, and even water fountains were a common sight in the segregated South.

rate-but-equal doctrine. For a test case, he combined five lawsuits challenging segregation in public schools. The Supreme Court heard initial arguments on the cases, grouped together as *Brown v. Board of Education,* in December 1952.

In his argument before the Court, Thurgood Marshall tried to establish that separate facilities, by definition, denied black people their full rights as American citizens. He used evidence from psychologists and sociologists demonstrating that black children educated in segregated schools developed a negative self-image and low self-esteem. Chief Justice Earl Warren, eager for a unanimous decision, patiently worked at convincing two holdouts.

On May 17, 1954, Warren read the Court's unanimous decision aloud. "Does segregation of children in public schools solely on the basis of race . . . deprive the children of the minority group of equal educational opportunities?" The chief justice paused. "We believe that it does." He ended by directly addressing the constitutional issue. Segregation deprived the plaintiffs of the equal protection of the laws guaranteed by the Fourteenth Amendment. "We conclude that in the field of public education the doctrine of 'separate but equal' has no place. Separate educational facilities are inherently unequal. . . . Any language in *Plessy v. Ferguson* contrary to these findings is rejected."

African Americans and their liberal allies around the country hailed the decision and the legal genius of Thurgood Marshall. But the issue of enforcement soon dampened this enthusiasm. To gain a unanimous decision, Warren had to agree to let the Court delay for one year its ruling on how to implement desegregation. This second *Brown* ruling, handed down in May 1955, assigned responsibility for desegregation plans to local school boards. The Court left it to federal district judges to monitor compliance, requiring only that desegregation proceed "with all deliberate speed." Thus, although the Court had made a momentous and clear constitutional ruling, the need for compromise dictated gradual enforcement by unspecified means.

Crisis in Little Rock

Resistance to *Brown* took many forms. Most affected states passed laws transferring authority for pupil assignment to local school boards. This prevented the NAACP from bringing statewide suits against segregated school systems. Counties and towns created layers of administrative delays designed to stop implementation of *Brown.* Some school boards transferred public school property to new, all-white private "academies." State legislatures in Virginia, Alabama, Mississippi, and Georgia resurrected the nineteenth-century doctrines of "interposition" and "nullification," declaring their right to "interpose" themselves between the

people and the federal government. In 1956, 101 congressmen from the former Confederate states signed the Southern Manifesto, urging their states to refuse compliance with desegregation. President Eisenhower declined to publicly endorse *Brown,* contributing to the spirit of southern resistance. Privately, moreover, the president opposed the *Brown* decision.

In Little Rock, Arkansas, the tense controversy over school integration became a test case of state versus federal power. A federal court ordered public schools to begin desegregation in September 1957, and the local school board made plans to comply. But Governor Orval Faubus, facing a tough reelection fight, decided to make a campaign issue out of defying the court order. He dispatched Arkansas National Guard troops to Central High School to prevent nine black students from entering. For three weeks, armed troops stood guard at the school.

At first, President Eisenhower tried to intervene quietly, gaining Faubus's assurance that he would protect the nine black children. But when Faubus suddenly withdrew his troops, leaving the black students at the mercy of the white mob, Eisenhower had to move. On September 24 he placed the Arkansas National Guard under federal control and ordered a thousand paratroopers to Little Rock. The nine black students arrived in a U.S. Army car. With fixed bayonets, the soldiers protected the students as they finally integrated Little Rock High School. Eisenhower, the veteran military commander, justified his actions on the basis of upholding federal authority and enforcing the law. He made no endorsement of desegregation. Unfazed, Governor Faubus kept Little Rock high schools closed during the 1958–59 academic year to prevent what he called "violence and disorder."

NO EASY ROAD TO FREEDOM, 1957–1962

Martin Luther King and the SCLC

The 381-day Montgomery bus boycott made Martin Luther King a prominent national figure. King himself was an extraordinary and complex man. Born in 1929 in Atlanta, he enjoyed a middle-class upbringing as the son of a prominent Baptist minister. As a graduate student, he was drawn to the social Christianity of American theologian Walter Rauschenbusch, who insisted on connecting religious faith with struggles for social justice. Above all, King admired Mohandas Gandhi, a lawyer turned ascetic who had led a successful nonviolent resistance movement against British colonial rule in India.

A unique blend of traditional African American folk preacher and erudite intellectual, King used his passion and intelligence to help transform a community's pain into a powerful moral force for change. He recognized the need to exploit the momentum of the Montgomery movement. In early 1957, with the help of Bayard Rustin of the War Resister's League and other aides, he brought together nearly 100 black ministers to found the Southern Christian Leadership Conference (SCLC). The clergymen elected King president and his close friend, the Reverend Ralph Abernathy, treasurer. The SCLC called upon black people "to understand that nonviolence is not a symbol of weakness or cowardice, but as Jesus demonstrated, nonviolent resistance transforms weakness into strength and breeds courage in the face of danger."

Previously, the struggle for racial equality had been dominated by a northern elite focusing on legal action. The SCLC now envisioned the southern black church, preaching massive nonviolent protest, as leading the fight. But the organization failed to spark the kind of mass, direct-action movement that had made history in Montgomery. Instead, the next great spark to light the fire of protest came from what seemed at the time a most unlikely source: black college students.

Sit-Ins: Greensboro, Nashville, Atlanta

On Monday, February 1, 1960, four black freshmen from North Carolina Agricultural and Technical College in Greensboro sat down at the whites-only lunch counter in Woolworth's. They were refused service. Although they could buy goods there, black people were not allowed to eat in Woolworth's. The four students stayed at the counter until closing time. Word of their action spread quickly, and the next day they returned with over two dozen supporters. On the third day, students occupied sixty-three of the sixty-six lunch counter seats. By Thursday they had been joined by three white students from the Women's College of the University of North Carolina in Greensboro. Scores of sympathizers overflowed Woolworth's and started a sit-in down the street in S. H. Kress. On Friday hundreds of black students and a few whites jammed the lunch counters.

City officials, looking to end the protest, offered to negotiate in exchange for an end to demonstrations. But white business leaders and politicians proved unwilling to change the racial status quo, and the sit-ins resumed on April 1. In response to the April 21 arrest of forty-five students for trespassing, an outraged African American community organized an economic boycott of targeted stores. The boycott cut deeply into merchants' profits, and Greensboro's leaders reluctantly acceded. On July 25, 1960, the first African American ate a meal at Woolworth's.

During the next eighteen months 70,000 people—most of them black students, a few of them white allies—participated in sit-ins against segregation in dozens of communities. Over 3,000 were arrested. African Americans had discovered a new form of direct-action protest, dignified and powerful, that white people could not ignore. The sit-in movement also transformed participants' self-image, empowering them psychologically and emotionally.

In Nashville, Rev. James Lawson, a northern-born black minister, had led workshops in nonviolent resistance since 1958. Lawson gathered around him a group of deeply committed black students from Nashville colleges who wanted to end segregation through Christian idealism and Gandhian principles. In the spring of 1960 more than 150 Nashville students were arrested in disciplined sit-ins aimed at desegregating downtown lunch counters, and Lawson found himself expelled from the divinity school at Vanderbilt. The Nashville group developed rules of conduct that became a model for protesters elsewhere: "Don't strike back or curse if abused. . . . Show yourself courteous and friendly at all times. . . . Report all serious incidents to your leader in a polite manner. Remember love and nonviolence."

The most ambitious sit-in campaign developed in Atlanta, the South's largest and richest city, home to the region's most powerful and prestigious black community. Students from Morehouse, Spelman, and the other all-black schools that made up Atlanta University took the lead. Led by Julian Bond, the students formed the Committee on an Appeal for Human Rights. Over the summer they planned a fall campaign of large-scale sit-ins at major Atlanta department stores and a boycott of downtown merchants. Their slogan became "Close out your charge account with segregation, open up your account with freedom." In October 1960 Martin Luther King and thirty-six students were arrested when they sat down in the all-white Magnolia Room restaurant in Rich's Department Store. The campaign stretched on for months, and hundreds of protesters went to jail. The city's business leaders finally relented in September 1961, and desegregation came to Atlanta.

SNCC and the "Beloved Community"

The sit-in movement pumped new energy into the civil rights cause, creating a new generation of activists and leaders. Mass arrests, beatings, and vilification in the southern white press only strengthened the resolve of those in the movement. Students also had to deal with the fears of their families, many of whom had made great sacrifices to send them off to college.

The new student militancy also caused discord within black communities. The authority of local African American elites had traditionally depended on influence and cooperation with the white establishment. Student calls for freedom disturbed many

The second day of the sit-in at the Greensboro, North Carolina, Woolworth's lunch counter, February 2, 1960. From left: Joseph McNeil, Franklin McCain, Billy Smith, and Clarence Henderson. The Greensboro protest sparked a wave of sit-ins across the South, mostly by college students, demanding an end to segregation in restaurants and other public places.

community leaders worried about upsetting traditional patronage networks. The president of Southern University in Baton Rouge, the largest black college in the nation, suspended eighteen sit-in leaders in 1960 and forced the entire student body of 5,000 to reapply to the college so that agitators could be screened out.

An April 1960 conference of 120 black student activists in Raleigh, North Carolina, underlined the generational and radical aspects of the new movement. The meeting had been called by Ella Baker, executive director of the SCLC. For years Baker had played an important behind-the-scenes role in the civil rights cause, serving as a community organizer and field secretary for the NAACP before heading the staff of the SCLC. She understood the psychological importance of the students' remaining independent of adult control and encouraged the trend toward group-centered leadership among the students. With Baker's encouragement, the conference voted to establish a new group, the Student Nonviolent Coordinating Committee (SNCC).

SNCC's emphasis was on fighting segregation through direct confrontation, mass action, and civil disobedience. SNCC field workers initiated and supported local, community-based activity. Three-quarters of the first field workers were less than twenty-two years old. Leadership was vested in a nonhierarchical Coordinating Committee, but local groups were free to determine their own direction. SNCC people distrusted bureaucracy and structure; they stressed spontaneity and improvisation. Over the next few years SNCC was at the forefront of nearly every major civil rights battle.

The Election of 1960 and Civil Rights

The issue of race relations was kept from center stage during the very close presidential campaign of 1960. As vice president, Richard Nixon had been a leading Republican voice for stronger civil rights legislation. In contrast, Democratic nominee Senator John F. Kennedy had played virtually no role in the congressional battles over civil rights during the 1950s. But during the campaign, their roles reversed. Kennedy praised the sit-in movement as part of a revival of national reform spirit. He declared, "It is in the American tradition to stand up for one's rights—even if the new way is to sit down." Although the Republican platform contained a strong civil rights plank, Nixon minimized his own identification with the movement. In October, when Martin Luther King was jailed after leading a demonstration in Atlanta, Kennedy telephoned Coretta Scott King to reassure her and express his personal support. Kennedy's brother Robert telephoned the judge in the case and angrily warned him that he had violated King's civil rights and endangered the national Democratic ticket. The judge released King soon afterward.

News of this intervention did not gain wide attention in the white South, much to the relief of the Kennedys. The race was tight, and they knew they could not afford to alienate traditional white southern Democrats. But the campaign effectively played up the story among black voters all over the country. On election day, Kennedy won 70 percent of the black vote, which helped put him over the top in several critical states. Many civil rights activists optimistically looked forward to a new president who would have to acknowledge his political debt to the black vote.

But the very closeness of his victory constrained Kennedy on the race question. Democrats had lost ground in the House and Senate, and Kennedy had to worry about alienating conservative southern Democrats who chaired key congressional committees. Passage of major civil rights legislation would be virtually impossible. The new president told leaders such as Roy Wilkins of the NAACP that a strategy of "minimum legislation, maximum executive action" offered the best road to change. The president did appoint some forty African Americans to high federal positions, including Thurgood Marshall to the federal appellate court. He established a Committee on Equal Employment Opportunity, chaired by Vice President Lyndon B. Johnson, to fight discrimination in the federal civil service and in corporations that received government contracts.

Most significant, the Kennedy administration sought to invigorate the Civil Rights Division of the Justice Department. Robert Kennedy, the new attorney general, began assembling a staff of brilliant and committed attorneys, headed by Burke Marshall. He encouraged them to get out of Washington and get into the field wherever racial troubles arose. In early 1961, when Louisiana school officials balked at a school desegregation order, Robert Kennedy warned them that he would ask the federal court to hold them in contempt. When Burke Marshall started court proceedings, the state officials gave in. But the new, more aggressive mood at Justice could not solve the central political dilemma: how to move forward on civil rights without alienating white southern Democrats. Pressure from the newly energized southern civil rights movement soon revealed the true difficulty of that problem.

Freedom Rides

In the spring of 1961 James Farmer, national director of CORE, announced plans for an interracial Freedom Ride through the South. The goal was to test compliance with court orders banning segregation in interstate travel and terminal accommodations. CORE had just recently made Farmer its leader in an effort to revitalize the organization. He designed the Freedom Ride to induce a crisis, in the spirit of the sit-ins. CORE informed the Justice Department and the FBI of its plans, but received no reply.

On May 4 seven blacks and six whites split into two interracial groups and left Washington on buses bound for Alabama and Mississippi. As the two buses made their way south, incidents of harassment and violence were isolated. But when one bus entered Anniston, Alabama, on May 14 an angry mob surrounded it,

A Freedom Riders' bus burns after being firebombed in Anniston, Alabama, May 14, 1961. After setting the bus afire, whites attacked the passengers fleeing the smoke and flames. Violent scenes like this one received extensive publicity in the mass media and helped compel the Justice Department to enforce court rulings banning segregation on interstate bus lines.

smashing windows and slashing tires. Six miles out of town, the tires went flat. A firebomb tossed through a window forced the passengers outside. The mob then beat the Freedom Riders with blackjacks, iron bars, and clubs. A caravan of cars organized by the Birmingham office of the SCLC rescued the wounded. Another mob attacked the second bus in Anniston, leaving one Freedom Rider permanently brain-damaged.

In Birmingham a mob of forty whites attacked the bus that managed to get out of Anniston. Although police had been warned to expect trouble, they did nothing to stop the mob from beating the Freedom Riders with pipes and fists. Nor did they make any arrests. FBI agents observed and took notes but did nothing. The remaining Freedom Riders decided to travel as a single group on the next lap, from Birmingham to Montgomery, but no bus would take them. Stranded and frightened, they reluctantly boarded a special flight to New Orleans arranged by the Justice Department. On May 17 the CORE-sponsored Freedom Ride disbanded.

But that was not the end of the Freedom Rides. SNCC leaders in Atlanta and Nashville assembled a fresh group of volunteers to continue the trip. On May 20 twenty-one Freedom Riders left Birmingham for Montgomery. The bus station in the Alabama capital was eerily quiet and deserted as they pulled in. But when the passengers left the bus a mob of several hundred whites rushed them, yelling "Get those niggers!" and clubbing people to the ground. James Zwerg, a white Freedom Rider from the University of Wisconsin, had his spinal cord severed. As John Lewis, veteran of the Nashville sit-in movement, lay in a pool of blood, a policeman handed him a state court injunction forbidding interracial travel in Alabama. The mob indiscriminately beat journalists and clubbed John Siegenthaler, a Justice Department attorney sent to observe the scene.

The mob violence and the indifference of Alabama officials made the Freedom Ride page-one news around the country and throughout the world. The Kennedy administration, preparing for the president's first summit meeting with Soviet premier Nikita Khrushchev, saw the situation as a threat to its international prestige. The attorney general called for a cooling-off period, but Martin Luther King, James Farmer, and the SNCC leaders announced that the Freedom Ride would continue. When Robert Kennedy warned that the racial turmoil would embarrass the president in his meeting with Khrushchev, Ralph Abernathy of the SCLC replied, "Doesn't the Attorney General know that we've been embarrassed all our lives?"

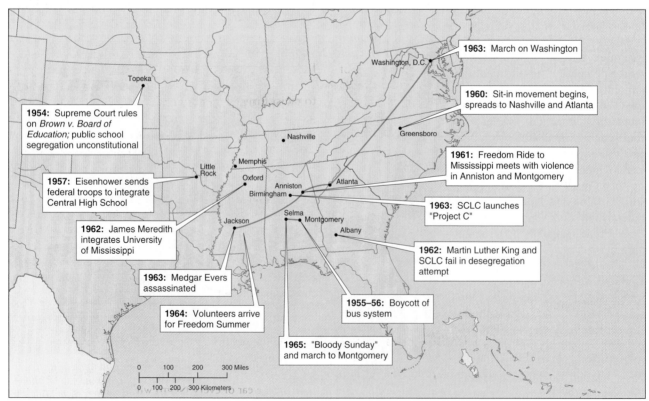

Map of the Civil Rights Movement   *Key battlegrounds in the struggle for racial justice in communities across the South.*

A bandaged but spirited group of twenty-seven Freedom Riders prepared to leave Montgomery for Jackson, Mississippi, on May 24. To avoid further violence Robert Kennedy arranged a compromise through Mississippi senator James Eastland. In exchange for a guarantee of safe passage through Mississippi, the federal government promised not to interfere with the arrest of the Freedom Riders in Jackson. This Freedom Ride and several that followed thus escaped violence. But more than 300 people were arrested that summer. Sticking to a policy of "jail, no bail," Freedom Riders clogged the prisons and faced harsh treatment that went largely unreported in the press. Their jail experiences turned most of them into committed leaders who formed the core of the student movement.

The Justice Department eventually petitioned the Interstate Commerce Commission to issue clear rules prohibiting segregation on interstate carriers. By creating a crisis, the Freedom Rides had forced the Kennedy administration to act. The Freedom Rides exposed the ugly face of southern racism to the world. At the same time, they reinforced white resistance to desegregation.

The Albany Movement: The Limits of Protest

Where the federal government chose not to enforce the constitutional rights of black people, segregationist forces tenaciously held their ground. In Albany, a small city in southwest Georgia, activists from SNCC, the NAACP, and other local groups formed a coalition known as the Albany Movement. Starting in October 1961 and continuing for over a year, thousands of Albany's black citizens marched, sat in, and boycotted as part of a citywide campaign to integrate public facilities and win voting rights. Over a thousand people spent time in jail. In December the arrival of Martin Luther King and the SCLC transformed Albany into a national symbol of the struggle.

But the gains at Albany proved minimal. Albany police chief Laurie Pritchett shrewdly deprived the movement of the kind of national sympathy won by the Freedom Riders. Pritchett filled the jails with black demonstrators, kept their mistreatment to a minimum, and prevented white mobs from running wild. "We met 'nonviolence' with 'nonviolence,'" he boasted.

By late 1962 the Albany Movement had collapsed, and Pritchett proudly declared the city "as segregated as ever." One activist summed up the losing campaign: "We ran out of people before he ran out of jails." Albany showed that mass protest without violent white counterprotest and direct federal intervention could not end Jim Crow.

In the fall of 1962 James Meredith, an Air Force veteran, tried to register as the first black student at the University of Mississippi. Governor Ross Barnett defied a federal court order and personally blocked Meredith's path at the admissions office. When Barnett refused to assure Robert Kennedy that Meredith would be protected, the attorney general dispatched 500 federal marshals to the campus. Over the radio, Barnett encouraged resistance to the "oppressive power of the United States," and several thousand whites, many of them armed, laid siege to the campus on September 30. A night of violence left 2 people dead and 160 marshals wounded, 28 from gunfire. President Kennedy ordered 5,000 army troops onto the campus to stop the riot. A federal guard remained to protect Meredith, who graduated the following summer.

THE MOVEMENT AT HIGH TIDE, 1963–1965

Birmingham

At the end of 1962 Martin Luther King and his SCLC allies decided to launch a new campaign against segregation in Birmingham, Alabama, the most segregated big city in America. After the failure in Albany, King and his aides were looking for a way to shore up his leadership and inject new momentum into the freedom struggle.

Working closely with local civil rights groups led by longtime Birmingham activist Rev. Fred Shuttlesworth, the SCLC carefully planned its campaign. The strategy was to fill the city jails with protesters, boycott downtown department stores, and enrage Public Safety Commissioner Eugene "Bull" Connor. In April King arrived with a manifesto demanding an end to racist hiring practices and segregated public accommodations and the creation of a biracial committee to oversee desegregation. Connor's police began jailing hundreds of demonstrators, including King himself, who defied a state court injunction against further protests.

Held in solitary confinement for several days, King managed to write a response to a group of Birmingham clergy who had deplored the protests. King's *Letter from Birmingham Jail* was soon widely reprinted and circulated as a pamphlet. It set out the key moral issues at stake, and scoffed at those who claimed the campaign was illegal and ill timed.

> We know through painful experience that freedom is never voluntarily given by the oppressor; it must be demanded by the oppressed. . . . For years now I have heard the word "Wait!" It rings in the ear of every Negro with a piercing familiarity. This "wait" has almost always meant "never."

After King's release on bail, the campaign intensified. In early May Bull Connor's forces began using high-powered water cannons, billy clubs, and snarling police dogs to break up demonstrations. Millions of Americans reacted with horror to the violent scenes from Birmingham shown on national television. Many younger black people, especially from the city's poor and working-class districts, began to fight back, hurling bottles and bricks at police. On May 10 mediators from the Justice Department negotiated an uneasy truce. The SCLC agreed to an immediate end to the protests. In exchange, businesses would desegregate and begin hiring African Americans over the next three months, and a biracial city committee would oversee desegregation of public facilities.

King claimed "the most magnificent victory for justice we've ever seen in the Deep South." But whites such as Bull Connor and Governor George Wallace denounced the agreement. When bombs rocked SCLC headquarters and the home of King's brother, a Birmingham minister, enraged blacks took to the streets and pelted police and firefighters with stones and bottles. President Kennedy ordered 3,000 army troops into the city and prepared to nationalize the Alabama Guard. The violence receded, and white businesspeople and politicians began to carry out the agreed-upon pact. But in September a bomb killed four black girls in a Birmingham Baptist church, reminding the city and the world that racial harmony was still a long way off.

The civil rights community now drew support from millions of Americans, black and white, who were inspired by the protesters and repelled by the face of southern bigotry. At the same time, Birmingham changed the nature of black protest. The black unemployed and working poor who joined in the struggle brought a different perspective from that of the students, professionals, and members of the religious middle class who had dominated the movement before Birmingham. They cared less about the philosophy of nonviolence and more about immediate gains in employment and housing and an end to police brutality. "Freedom now!" they cried.

JFK and the March on Washington

The growth of black activism and white support convinced President Kennedy that the moment had come to press for sweeping civil rights legislation. In June 1963 Alabama governor George Wallace threatened to personally block the admission of two black students to the state university. National Guard troops, placed under federal control by the president, ensured the students' safety and their peaceful admission into the University of Alabama.

It was a defining moment for Kennedy. On June 11 the president went on national television and

Reverend Dr. Martin Luther King, Jr., acknowledging the huge throng at the historic March on Washington for "jobs and freedom," August 28, 1963. The size of the crowd, the stirring oratory and song, and the live network television coverage produced one of the most memorable political events in the nation's history.

offered his personal endorsement of the civil rights activism. The next week Kennedy asked Congress for a broad law that would ensure voting rights, outlaw segregation in public facilities, and bolster federal authority to deny funds for programs that discriminated. After three years of fence sitting, Kennedy had finally committed his office and his political future to the civil rights cause.

Movement leaders lauded the president's initiative. Yet they understood that racial hatred still haunted the nation. Only a few hours after Kennedy's television speech, a gunman murdered Medgar Evers, leader of the Mississippi NAACP, outside his home in Jackson. To pressure Congress and demonstrate the urgency of their cause, a broad coalition of civil rights groups planned a massive nonviolent March on Washington.

The Kennedy administration originally opposed the march, fearing that it would jeopardize support for the president's civil rights bill in Congress.

LANDMARK CIVIL RIGHTS LEGISLATION, SUPREME COURT DECISIONS, AND EXECUTIVE ORDERS

Year	Decision, law or executive order	Significance
1939	*Missouri v. ex.rel. Gaines*	Required University of Missouri Law School either to admit African Americans or build another, fully equal law school
1941	Executive Order 8802 (by President Roosevelt)	Banned racial discrimination in defense industry and government offices; established Fair Employment Practices Committee to investigate violations
1946	*Morgan v. Virginia*	Ruled that segregation on interstate buses violated federal law and created an "undue burden" on interstate commerce
1948	Executive Order 9981 (by President Truman)	Desegregated the U.S. armed forces
1950	*McLaurin v. Oklahoma State Regents*	Ruled that forcing an African American student to sit, eat, and study in segregated facilities was unconstitutional because it inevitably created a "badge of inferiority"
1950	*Sweatt v. Painter*	Ruled that an inferior law school created by the University of Texas to serve African-Americans violated their right to equal protection and ordered Herman Sweatt to be admitted to University of Texas Law School
1954	*Brown v. Board of Education of Topeka I*	Declared "separate educational facilities are inherently unequal," thus overturning *Plessy v. Ferguson* (1896) and the "separate but equal" doctrine as it applied to public schools
1955	*Brown v. Board of Education of Topeka II*	Ordered school desegregation to begin with "all deliberate speed," but offered no timetable
1957	Civil Rights Act	Created Civil Rights Division within the Justice Department
1964	Civil Rights Act	Prohibited discrimination in employment and most places of public accommodation on basis of race, color, religion, sex, or national origin; outlawed bias in federally assisted programs; created Equal Employment Opportunity Commission
1965	Voting Rights Act	Authorized federal supervision of voter registration in states and counties where fewer than half of voting age residents were registered; outlawed literacy and other discriminatory tests in voter registration

But as plans for the rally solidified, Kennedy reluctantly gave his approval. Leaders from the SCLC, the NAACP, SNCC, the Urban League, and CORE—the leading organizations in the civil rights community—put aside their tactical differences to forge a broad consensus for the event. John Lewis, the young head of SNCC who had endured numerous brutal assaults, planned a speech that denounced the Kennedys as hypocrites. A. Philip Randolph, the acknowledged elder statesman of the movement, convinced Lewis at the last moment to tone down his remarks. "We've come this far," he implored. "For the sake of unity, change it."

On August 28, 1963, over a quarter of a million people, including 50,000 whites, gathered at the Lincoln Memorial to rally for "jobs and freedom." Americans from all walks of life joined the largest political assembly in the nation's history to that date. At the end of a long, exhilarating day of speeches and freedom songs, Martin Luther King stirred the crowd with his dream for America:

> I have a dream today that one day this nation will rise up and live out the true meaning of its creed: "We hold these truths to be self-evident— that all men are created equal." . . . When we let freedom ring, when we let it ring from every village and every hamlet, from every state and every city, we will be able to speed up that day when all of God's children, black men and white men, Jews and Gentiles, Protestants and Catholics, will be able to join hands and sing in the words of the old Negro spiritual, "Free at last! Free at last! Thank God almighty, we are free at last!"

LBJ and the Civil Rights Act of 1964

An extraordinary demonstration of interracial unity, the March on Washington stood as the high-water mark in the struggle for civil rights. But the assassination of John F. Kennedy on November 22, 1963, in Dallas threw an ominous cloud over the whole nation and the civil rights movement in particular. In the Deep South, many ardent segregationists welcomed the president's death because of his support for civil rights.

Lyndon Baines Johnson, Kennedy's successor, had never been much of a friend to civil rights. Johnson had built a career as one of the shrewdest and most powerful Democrats in Congress. Throughout the 1950s he had obstructed civil rights legislation and helped water down enforcement provisions, but as vice president he had ably chaired Kennedy's working group on equal employment. Civil rights activists looked upon Johnson warily as he took over the Oval Office.

As president, Johnson realized that he faced a new political reality, one created by the civil rights movement. Eager to unite the Democratic party and prove himself a national leader, he seized upon civil rights as a golden political opportunity. Throughout the early months of 1964, the new president let it be known publicly and privately that he would brook no compromise on civil rights.

Johnson exploited all his skills as a political insider. He cajoled, flattered, and threatened key members of the House and Senate. Working with the president, the fifteen-year-old Leadership Conference on Civil Rights coordinated a sophisticated lobbying effort in Congress. The House passed a strong civil rights bill in February by a 290–130 vote. The more difficult fight would be in the Senate, where a southern filibuster promised to block the bill or weaken it. But by June Johnson's persistence had paid off and the southern filibuster had collapsed.

On July 2, 1964, Johnson signed the Civil Rights Act of 1964. Every major provision had survived intact. This landmark law represented the most significant civil rights legislation since Reconstruction. It prohibited discrimination in most places of public accommodation; outlawed discrimination in employment on the basis of race, color, religion, sex, or national origin; outlawed bias in federally assisted programs; authorized the Justice Department to institute suits to desegregate public schools and other facilities; created the Equal Employment Opportunity Commission; and provided technical and financial aid to communities desegregating their schools.

Mississippi Freedom Summer

While President Johnson and his liberal allies won the congressional battle for the new civil rights bill, activists in Mississippi mounted a far more radical and dangerous campaign. In the spring of 1964 a coalition of workers led by SNCC launched the Freedom Summer project, an ambitious effort to register black voters and directly challenge the iron rule of segregation. Mississippi stood as the toughest test for the civil rights movement, racially and economically. It was the poorest, most backward state in the nation, and had remained largely untouched by the freedom struggle. African Americans constituted 42 percent of the state's population, but fewer than 5 percent could register to vote. Median black family income was under $1,500 a year, roughly one-third that of white families. A small white planter elite controlled most of the state's wealth, and a long tradition of terror against black people had maintained the racial caste system.

Bob Moses of SNCC and Dave Dennis of CORE planned Freedom Summer as a way of opening up this closed society to the glare of national publicity.

The project recruited over 900 volunteers, mostly white college students, to aid in voter registration, teach in "freedom schools," and help build a "freedom party" as an alternative to the all-white party of Mississippi Democrats. Organizers expected violence, which was precisely why they wanted white volunteers. Dave Dennis later explained their reasoning: "The death of a white college student would bring on more attention to what was going on than for a black college student getting it."

The predictions of violence proved accurate. On June 21, while most project volunteers were still undergoing training in Ohio, word arrived that three activists had disappeared in Neshoba County, Mississippi. Two white activists, Michael Schwerner and Andrew Goodman, and a local black activist, James Chaney, had gone to investigate the burning of a black church that was supposed to serve as a freedom school. Six weeks later, after a massive search belatedly ordered by President Johnson, FBI agents discovered the bodies of the three, buried in an earthen dam. Goodman and Schwerner had been shot once; Chaney had been severely beaten before being shot three times. Over the summer, at least three other civil rights workers died violently. Project workers suffered 1,000 arrests, 80 beatings, 35 shooting incidents, and 30 bombings in homes, churches, and schools.

Within the project there were simmering problems. Many black veterans of SNCC resented the affluent white volunteers, many of whom had not come to terms with their own racial prejudices. Sexual tensions between black male and white female volunteers also strained relations. A number of black and white women began to raise the issue of women's equality as a companion goal to racial equality. The day-to-day reality of violent reprisals, police harassment, and constant fear took a hard toll on everyone.

The project did manage to rivet national attention on Mississippi racism, and it got 60,000 black voters signed up to join the Mississippi Freedom Democratic party (MFDP). In August 1964 the MFDP sent a slate of delegates to the Democratic Convention looking to challenge the credentials of the all-white regular state delegation. Lyndon Johnson opposed the seating of the MFDP because he wanted to avoid a divisive floor fight. He was already concerned that Republicans might carry a number of southern states in November. But MFDP leaders and sympathizers gave dramatic testimony before the convention, detailing the racism and brutality in Mississippi politics. Led by vice presidential nominee Senator Hubert Humphrey, Johnson's forces offered a compromise that would have given the MFDP a token two seats on the floor. Bitter over what they saw as a betrayal, the MFDP delegates turned the offer down. Within SNCC, the defeat of the MFDP intensified disillusion with the Democrats and the liberal establishment.

Malcolm X and Black Consciousness

Growing frustration with the limits of nonviolent protest and electoral politics contributed to a more radical mood within SNCC. Younger civil rights activists found themselves more sympathetic to the militant rhetoric and vision articulated by Malcolm X. Since the late 1950s Malcolm had been the preeminent spokesman for the black nationalist religious sect, the Nation of Islam (NOI). The NOI had been founded in depression-era Detroit by Wallace D. Fard, and his disciple, Elijah Muhammad, had built it into an influential presence in northern urban black communities. Like the followers of Marcus Garvey in the 1920s (see Chapter 23), the NOI aspired to create a self-reliant, disciplined, and proud community—a separate "nation" for black people. During the 1950s the NOI (also called Black Muslims) successfully organized in northern black communities. It operated restaurants, retail stores, and schools as models for black economic self-sufficiency.

Malcolm Little had been born in 1925 and raised in Lansing, Michigan. His father, a preacher and a follower of black nationalist leader Marcus Garvey, was killed in a racist attack by local whites. Malcolm led a youthful life of petty crime, eventually serving a seven-year prison term for burglary. While in jail he educated himself and converted to the Nation of Islam. He took the surname "X" to mark his original African family name, lost through slavery. Emerging from jail in 1952, he became a dynamic organizer, editor, and speaker for the Nation of Islam. He encouraged his audiences to take pride in their African heritage and to consider armed self-defense rather than relying solely on nonviolence.

Malcolm ridiculed the integrationist goals of the civil rights movement. Black Muslims, he told audiences, do not want "to integrate into this corrupt society, but to separate from it, to a land of our own, where we can reform ourselves, lift up our moral standards, and try to be godly." In his best-selling *Autobiography of Malcolm X* (1965), he admitted that his position was extremist. "The black race here in North America is in extremely bad condition. You show me a black man who isn't an extremist," he argued, "and I'll show you one who needs psychiatric attention."

In 1964, troubled by personal scandals surrounding Elijah Muhammad (he faced paternity suits brought by two young female employees) and eager for a more political approach to improving conditions for blacks, Malcolm X broke with the Nation of Islam. He made a pilgrimage to Mecca, the holy city of Islamic religion, where he met Islamic peoples of all colors and underwent a "radical alteration in my whole outlook about 'white' men." He returned to the United States as El-Hajj Malik El-Shabazz, abandoned his black separatist views, and founded the Organization of Afro-American Unity.

On February 21, 1965, Malcolm X was assassinated during a speech at Harlem's Audubon Ballroom. His assailants were members of a New Jersey branch of the NOI, possibly infiltrated by the FBI. "More than any other person," remarked black author Julius Lester, "Malcolm X was responsible for the new militancy that entered The Movement in 1965." SNCC leader John Lewis thought Malcolm had been the most effective voice "to articulate the aspirations, bitterness, and frustrations of the Negro people," forming "a living link between Africa and the civil rights movement in this country." As much as anyone, Malcolm X pointed the way to a new black consciousness that celebrated black history, black culture, the African heritage, and black self-sufficiency.

Selma and the Voting Rights Act of 1965

Lyndon Johnson won reelection in 1964 by a landslide, capturing 61 percent of the popular vote. Of the 6 million black people who voted in the election, 2 million more than in 1960, an overwhelming 94 percent cast their ballots for Johnson. With Democrats in firm control of both the Senate and the House, Johnson and his staff began drafting a tough voting rights bill in late 1964, partly with an eye toward countering Republican gains in the Deep South by registering more black Democratic voters. Martin Luther King and the SCLC shared this goal of passing a strong voting rights law that would provide southern black people with direct federal protection of their right to vote.

Once again, movement leaders plotted to create a crisis that would arouse national indignation, pressure Congress, and force federal action. Selma, Alabama, because of its notorious record of preventing black voting, was selected as the target. Sensing that county sheriff Jim Clark might be another Bull Connor, King arrived in Selma in January 1965, just after accepting the Nobel Peace Prize in Oslo. King, the SCLC staff, and SNCC workers led daily marches on the Dallas County Courthouse, where hundreds of black citizens tried to get their names added to voter lists. By early February, Clark had imprisoned more than 3,000 protesters.

Despite the brutal beating of Rev. James Bevel, a key SCLC strategist, and the killing of Jimmie Lee Jackson, a young black demonstrator in nearby Marion, the SCLC failed to arouse the national indignation it sought. Consequently, in early March SCLC staffers called on black activists to march from Selma to Montgomery to deliver a list of grievances to Governor Wallace. On Sunday, March 7, while King preached to

his church in Atlanta, a group of 600 marchers crossed the Pettus Bridge on the Alabama River, on their way to Montgomery. A group of mounted, heavily armed county and state lawmen blocked their path and ordered them to turn back. When the marchers did not move, the lawmen attacked with billy clubs and tear gas, driving the protesters back over the bridge in a bloody rout. More than fifty marchers had to be treated in local hospitals.

The dramatic "Bloody Sunday" attack received extensive coverage on network television, prompting a national uproar. Demands for federal intervention poured into the White House from all over the country. King issued a public call for civil rights supporters to come to Selma for a second march on Montgomery. But a federal court temporarily enjoined the SCLC from proceeding with the march. King found himself trapped. He reluctantly accepted a face-saving

Voting rights demonstrators rallied in front of the state capitol in Montgomery, Alabama, March 35, 1965, after a four day, fifty-four mile trek from Selma. The original 3,000 marchers were joined by over 30,000 supporters by the end of their journey.

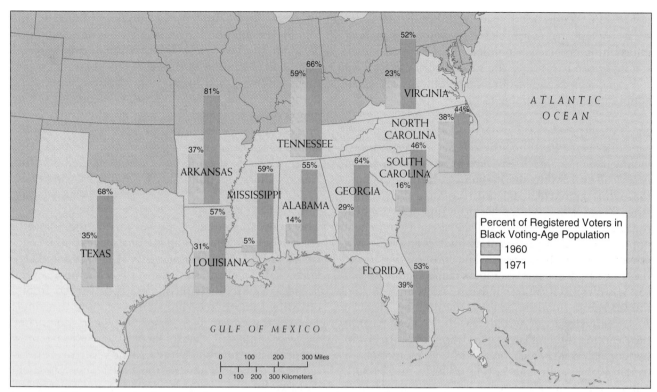

Impact of the Voting Rights Act of 1965   *Voter registration among African Americans in the South increased significantly between 1960 and 1971.*

compromise: in return for a promise from Alabama authorities not to harm marchers, King would lead his followers across the Pettus Bridge, stop, pray briefly, and then turn back. This plan outraged the more militant SNCC activists and sharpened their distrust of King and the SCLC.

But just when it seemed the Selma movement might die, white racist violence revived it. A gang of white toughs attacked four white Unitarian ministers who had come to Selma to participate in the march. One of them, Rev. James J. Reeb of Boston, died of multiple skull fractures. His death brought new calls for federal action. On March 15 President Johnson delivered a televised address to a joint session of Congress to request passage of a voting rights bill. In a stirring speech, the president fused the political power of his office with the moral power of the movement. "Their cause must be our cause, too. Because it is not just Negroes, but really all of us who must overcome the crippling legacy of bigotry and injustice. And," he concluded firmly, "we *shall* overcome." Johnson also prevailed upon federal judge Frank Johnson to issue a ruling allowing the march to proceed, and he warned Governor Wallace not to interfere.

On March 21 Martin Luther King led a group of more than 3,000 black and white marchers out of Selma on the road to Montgomery. Four days later they arrived at the Alabama statehouse. Their ranks had been swelled by more than 30,000 supporters, including hundreds of prominent politicians, entertainers, and black leaders.

In August 1965 President Johnson signed the Voting Rights Act into law. It authorized federal supervision of registration in states and counties where fewer than half of voting-age residents were registered. It also outlawed literacy and other discriminatory tests that had kept blacks disenfranchised. Between 1964 and 1968, black registrants in Mississippi leaped from 7 percent to 59 percent of the statewide black population; in Alabama, from 24 percent to 57 percent. In those years the number of southern black voters grew from 1 million to 3.1 million. For the first time in their lives, black Southerners in hundreds of small towns and rural communities could enjoy full participation in American politics. Ten years after the Montgomery bus boycott, the civil rights movement had reached a peak of national influence and interracial unity.

FORGOTTEN MINORITIES, 1945–1965

The historic injustices of slavery, racism, and segregation gave a moral and political urgency to the African American struggle for full citizenship rights. Yet other minorities as well had long been denied their civil rights. After World War II, Latinos, Indian peoples, and Asian Americans began making their own halting efforts to improve their political, legal, and economic status. By the late 1960s, the success of the black civil rights movement had inspired these minority groups to adopt more militant strategies of their own.

Mexican Americans

Mexican Americans in the West and Southwest included immigrants from Mexico who did not seek American citizenship and longtime citizens who found that white authorities did not recognize their rights. After World War II, several Mexican American political organizations sought to secure equal rights and equal opportunity for their community by stressing their own sense of American identity. The most important of these groups were the League of United Latin American Citizens (LULAC), founded in Texas in 1928, and the GI Forum, founded in Texas in 1948 by Mexican American veterans of World War II. Both emphasized the learning of English, assimilation into American society, improved education, and the promotion of political power through voting. LULAC successfully pursued two important legal cases that anticipated *Brown v. Board of Education*. In *Mendez v. Westminster*, a 1947 California case, and in the 1948 *Delgado* case in Texas, the Supreme Court upheld lower-court rulings that declared segregation of Mexican Americans unconstitutional. LULAC won another significant legal battle in the 1954 *Hernandez* decision, in which the Supreme Court ended the exclusion of Mexican Americans from Texas jury lists.

Mexican migration to the United States increased dramatically during and after World War II. During the war, the U.S. and Mexican governments created the *bracero* program, through which some 300,000 Mexicans entered the United States as temporary agricultural and railroad laborers. The program continued after the war as American agribusiness came to depend on hundreds of thousands of Mexicans as a key source of cheap farm labor. Most *braceros* endured harsh work, poor food, and substandard housing in the camps in which they lived. Some migrated into the newly emerging *barrio* neighborhoods in cities such as San Antonio, Los Angeles, El Paso, and Denver. Many *braceros* and their children became American citizens, but most returned to Mexico. Another stream of postwar Mexican immigrants were the *mojados*, or "wetbacks," so called because many swam across the Rio Grande River to enter the United States illegally.

In 1954 the Eisenhower administration launched the massive "Operation Wetback," in which Immigration Service agents tried to curb the flow of undocumented immigrants from Mexico. Over the next three years some 3.7 million allegedly illegal migrants were rounded up and sent back over the border. Immigration agents made little distinction between so-called illegals and *braceros* and Mexican American citizens. Many families were broken up, and thousands who had lived in the United States for a decade or more found themselves deported. Many deportees were denied basic civil liberties, such as due process, and suffered physical abuse and intimidation. Among Mexican Americans, Operation Wetback left a bitter legacy of deep mistrust and estrangement from Anglo culture and politics.

Puerto Ricans

The United States took possession of the island of Puerto Rico in 1898, during the final stages of the Spanish–American War. The Jones Act of 1917 granted U.S. citizenship to all Puerto Ricans. Over the next several decades, Puerto Rico's economic base shifted from a diversified, subsistence-oriented agriculture to a single export crop: sugar. U.S. absentee owners dominated the sugar industry. Puerto Rico's sugar industry grew enormously profitable, but few island residents benefitted from this expansion. By the 1930s, unemployment and poverty were widespread, and the island was forced to import its foodstuffs.

Small communities of Puerto Rican migrants had begun to form in New York City during the 1920s. The largest was on the Upper East Side of Manhattan: *el barrio* in East Harlem. During World War II, labor shortages led the federal government to sponsor the recruitment of Puerto Rican workers for industrial jobs in New Jersey, Philadelphia, and Chicago. But the "great migration" took place from 1945 to 1964.

The advent of direct air service between Puerto Rico and New York in 1945 made the city easily accessible. By 1970 there were about 800,000 Puerto Ricans in New York—more than 10 percent of the city's population. New Puerto Rican communities also took root in Connecticut, Massachusetts, New Jersey, and the Midwest.

The experience of Puerto Rican migrants both resembled and differed from that of other immigrant groups in significant ways. Like Mexican immigrants, Puerto Ricans were foreign in language, culture, and experience, yet unlike them they entered the United States as citizens. In New York, Puerto Ricans found themselves barred from most craft unions, excluded from certain neighborhoods, and forced to take jobs largely in the low-paying garment industry and service trades. Puerto Rican children were not well served by a public school system insensitive to language differences and too willing to track Spanish-speaking students into obsolete vocational programs.

By the early 1970s, Puerto Rican families were substantially poorer on average than the total population of the country, and they had the lowest median income of any Latino groups. The steep decline in manufacturing jobs and the garment industry in New York during the 1960s and 1970s hit the Puerto Rican community especially hard. So did the city's fiscal crisis, which brought sharp cuts in funding for schools, health care, libraries, government jobs, and other public services traditionally available to immigrant groups. The structural shift in the U.S. economy away from manufacturing and toward service and high-technology jobs reinforced the Puerto Rican community's goal of improving educational opportunities for its members. The struggle to establish and improve bilingual education in schools became an important part of this effort.

Indian Peoples

The postwar years also brought significant changes in the status and lives of Indian peoples. Congress reversed the policies pursued under the New Deal, which had stressed Indian sovereignty and cultural independence. Responding to a variety of pressure groups, including mining and other economic interests wishing to exploit the resources on Indian reservations, Congress adopted a policy known as "termination," designed to cancel Indian treaties and terminate sovereignty rights. In 1953 it passed House Concurrent Resolution 108, which allowed Congress to terminate a tribe as a political entity by passing legislation specific to that tribe. Supporters of termination had varied motives, but the policy added up to the return of enforced assimilation for solving the "Indian problem."

Between 1954 and 1962, Congress passed twelve termination bills covering more than sixty tribes, nearly all in the West. Even when tribes consented to their own termination, they discovered that dissolution brought unforeseen problems. For example, members of the Klamaths of Oregon and the Paiutes of Utah received large cash payments from the division of tribal assets. But after these one-time payments were spent, members had to take poorly paid, unskilled jobs to survive. Many Indian peoples became dependent on state social services and slipped into poverty and alcoholism.

Along with termination, the federal government gave greater emphasis to a relocation program aimed at speeding up assimilation. The Bureau of Indian Affairs encouraged reservation Indians to relocate to cities, where they were provided housing and jobs. For some, relocation meant assimilation, intermarriage with whites, and the loss of tribal identity. Others, homesick and unable to adjust to an alien culture and place, either returned to reservations or wound up on the margins of city life.

By the early 1960s Indians came to see the policy as geared mainly to exploiting resources on Indian lands. The National Congress of American Indians (NCAI), the leading national organization, condemned it, calling for a review of federal policies and a return to self-determination. The NCAI led a political and educational campaign that challenged the goal of assimilation and created a new awareness among white people that Indians had the right to remain Indians. When the termination policy ended in the early 1960s, it had affected only about 3 percent of federally recognized Indian peoples.

Taking their cue from the civil rights movement, Indian activists used the court system to reassert sovereign rights. Indian and white liberal lawyers, many with experience in civil rights cases, worked through the Native American Rights Fund, which became a powerful force in western politics. A series of Supreme Court decisions, culminating in *U.S. v. Wheeler* (1978), reasserted the principle of "unique and limited" sovereignty. The Court recognized tribal independence except where limited by treaty or Congress.

The Indian population had been growing since the early years of the century, but most reservations had trouble making room for a new generation. Indians suffered increased rates of poverty, chronic unemployment, alcoholism, and poor health. The average Indian family in the early 1960s earned only one-third of the average family income in the United States. Those who remained in the cities usually became "ethnic Indians," identifying themselves more as Indians than as members of specific tribes. By the late 1960s ethnic

George Gillette (left foreground), chairman of the Fort Berthold Indian Council, wept as Secretary of Interior J. A. Krug signed a contract buying 155,000 acres of the tribe's best land in North Dakota for a reservoir project, May 20, 1948. "The members of the tribal council sign this contract with heavy hearts," Gillette said.

Indians had begun emphasizing civil rights over tribal rights, making common cause with black people and other minorities. The National Indian Youth Council (NIYC), founded in 1960, tried to unite the two causes of equality for individual Indians and special status for tribes. But the organization faced difficult contradictions between a common Indian identity, emphasizing Indians as a single ethnic group, and tribal identity, stressing the citizenship of Indians in separate nations.

Asian Americans

The harsh relocation program of World War II devastated the Japanese American community on the West Coast (see Chapter 25). But the war against Nazism also helped weaken older notions of white superiority and racism. During the war the state of California had aggressively enforced an alien land law by confiscating property declared illegally held by Japanese. In November 1946 a proposition supporting the law appeared on the state ballot. But, thanks in part to a campaign by the Japanese American Citizens League (JACL) reminding voters of the wartime contributions of Nisei (second-generation) soldiers, voters overwhelmingly rejected the referendum. Two years later the Supreme Court declared the law unconstitutional, calling it "nothing more than outright racial discrimination."

The 1952 Immigration and Nationality Act (see Chapter 26) removed the old ban against Japanese immigration, and also made Issei (first-generation Japanese Americans) eligible for naturalized citizenship. Japanese Americans, who lobbied hard for the new law, greeted it with elation. By 1965 some 46,000 immigrant Japanese, most of them elderly Issei, had taken their citizenship oaths.

The Immigration and Nationality Act allowed immigration from the Asian-Pacific Triangle. It was nonetheless racially discriminatory, in that each country in Asia was permitted only 100 immigrants a year. In addition, the act continued the national origin quotas of 1924 for European countries. The civil rights struggle helped spur a movement to reform immigration policies.

In 1965 Congress passed a new Immigration and Nationality Act, abolishing the national origin quotas and providing for the admission each year of 170,000 immigrants from the Eastern Hemisphere and 120,000 from the Western Hemisphere. The new law set a limit of 20,000 per country from the Eastern Hemisphere—these immigrants to be admitted on a first-come, first-served basis—and established preference categories for professional and highly skilled immigrants.

The 1965 act would have a profound effect on Asian American communities, opening the way for a new wave of immigration. In the twenty years following the act the number of Asian Americans soared from 1 million to 5 million. Four times as many Asians settled in the United States in this period as in the entire previous history of the nation. This new wave also brought a strikingly different group of Asian immigrants. In 1960 the Asian American population was 52 percent Japanese, 27 percent Chinese, and 20 percent Filipino. In 1985, the composition was 21 percent Chinese, 21 percent Filipino, 15 percent Japanese, 12 percent Vietnamese, 11 percent Korean, 10 percent Asian Indian, 4 percent Laotian, and 3 percent Cambodian. These newcomers included significant numbers of highly educated professionals and city dwellers, a sharp contrast with the farmers and rural peoples of the past.

CONCLUSION

The mass movement for civil rights was arguably the most important domestic event of the twentieth century. The struggle that began in Montgomery in December 1955 ultimately transformed race relations in thousands of American communities. By the early 1960s this community-based movement had placed civil rights at the very center of national political life. It achieved its greatest successes by invoking the law of the land to destroy legal segregation and win individual freedom for African Americans. The Civil Rights Act of 1964 and the Voting Rights Act of 1965 testified to the power of an African American and white liberal coalition. Yet the persistence of racism, poverty, and ghetto slums challenged a central assumption of liberalism: that equal protection of constitutional rights would give all Americans equal opportunities in life. By the mid-1960s, many black people had begun to question the core values of liberalism, the benefits of alliance with whites, and the philosophy of nonviolence. At the same time, a conservative white backlash against the gains made by African Americans further weakened the liberal political consensus.

In challenging the persistence of widespread poverty and institutional racism, the civil rights movement called for deep structural changes in American life. By 1967, Martin Luther King was articulating a broad and radical vision linking the struggle against racial injustice to other defects in American society. "The black revolution," he argued, "is much more than a struggle for the rights of Negroes. It is forcing America to face all its interrelated flaws—racism, poverty, militarism, and materialism. It is exposing evils that are deeply rooted in the whole structure of our society." Curing these ills would prove far more difficult than ending legal segregation.

CHRONOLOGY

1941   Executive Order 8802 forbids racial discrimination in defense industries and government

1946   In *Morgan v. Virginia*, U.S. Supreme Court rules that segregation on interstate buses is unconstitutional

President Harry Truman creates the Committee on Civil Rights

1947   Jackie Robinson becomes the first African American on a major league baseball team

1948   President Truman issues executive order desegregating the armed forces

1954   In *Brown v. Board of Education*, Supreme Court rules segregated schools inherently unequal

1955   Supreme Court rules that school desegregation must proceed "with all deliberate speed"

Montgomery bus boycott begins

1956   Montgomery bus boycott ends in victory as the Supreme Court affirms a district court ruling that segregation on buses is unconstitutional

1957   Southern Christian Leadership Conference (SCLC) is founded

President Dwight Eisenhower sends in federal troops to protect African American students integrating Little Rock, Arkansas, high school

1960   Sit-in movement begins as four college students sit at a lunch counter in Greensboro, North Carolina, and ask to be served

Student Nonviolent Coordinating Committee (SNCC) founded

1961   Freedom Rides begin

1962   James Meredith integrates the University of Mississippi

The Albany movement fails to end segregation in Albany, Georgia

1963   SCLC initiates campaign to desegregate Birmingham, Alabama

Medgar Evers, leader of the Mississippi NAACP, is assassinated

March on Washington; Martin Luther King Jr. delivers his historic "I Have a Dream" speech

1964   Mississippi Freedom Summer project brings students to Mississippi to teach and register voters

President Johnson signs the Civil Rights Act of 1964

Civil rights workers Michael Schwerner, James Chaney, and Andrew Goodman are found buried in Philadelphia, Mississippi

Mississippi Freedom Democratic Party (MFDP) denied seats at the 1964 Democratic Presidential Convention

1965   SCLC and SNCC begin voter registration campaign in Selma, Alabama

Malcolm X is assassinated

Civil rights marchers walk from Selma to Montgomery

Voting Rights Act of 1965 is signed into law

REVIEW QUESTIONS

1. What were the key legal and political antecedents to the civil rights struggle in the 1940s and early 1950s? What organizations played the most central role? Which tactics continued to be used, and which were abandoned?

2. How did African American communities challenge legal segregation in the South? Compare the strategies of key organizations, such as NAACP, SNCC, SCLC, and CORE.

3. Discuss the varieties of white resistance to the civil rights movement. Which were most effective in slowing the drive for equality?

4. Analyze the civil rights movement's complex relationship with the national Democratic Party between 1948 and 1964. How was the party transformed by its association with the movement? What political gains and losses did that association entail?

5. What legal and institutional impact did the movement have on American life? How did it change American culture and politics? Where did it fail?

6. What relationship did the African American struggle for civil rights have with other American minorities? How—if at all—did these minorities benefit? Did they build their own versions of the movement?

RECOMMENDED READING

Taylor Branch, *Parting the Waters: America in the King Years, 1954–1963* (1988); *Pillar of Fire: America in the King Years, 1963–1965* (1998). A deeply researched and monumental narrative history of the southern civil rights movement organized around the life and influence of Rev. Martin Luther King, Jr.

Clayborne Carson, *In Struggle: SNCC and the Black Awakening of the 1960s* (1981). The most comprehensive history of the SNCC, arguably the most important civil rights organization. Carson stresses the evolution of SNCC's radicalism during the decade.

William Chafe, *Civilities and Civil Rights: Greensboro, North Carolina and the Black Struggle for Equality* (1980). Examines the community of Greensboro from 1945 to 1975. Chafe focuses on the "etiquette of civility" and its complex relationship with the promise of racial justice, along with black protest movements and relations between the city's blacks and whites.

David Chappell, *Inside Agitators: White Southerners in the Civil Rights Movement* (1994). The best recent analysis of white involvement in the movement.

Sara Evans, *Personal Politics: The Roots of Women's Liberation in the Civil Rights Movement and the New Left* (1979). A pathbreaking study showing the important connections between the struggle for black rights and the rebirth of feminism.

Aldon D. Morris, *The Origins of the Civil Rights Movement: Black Communities Organizing for Change* (1984). An important study combining history and social theory. Morris emphasizes the key role of ordinary black people, acting through their churches and other community organizations before 1960.

Howell Raines, *My Soul Is Rested: Movement Days in the Deep South Remembered* (1977). The best oral history of the civil rights movement, drawing from a wide range of participants and points of view. It is brilliantly edited by Raines, who covered the events as a journalist.

Jo Ann Gibson Robinson, *The Montgomery Bus Boycott and the Women Who Started It*, ed. David J. Garrow (1987). An important memoir by one of the key behind-the-scenes players in the Montgomery bus boycott. Robinson stresses the role of middle- and working-class black women in the struggle.

Mark Tushnet, *Making Civil Rights Law: Thurgood Marshall and the Supreme Court, 1936–1961* (1994). An in-depth examination of Marshall's critical role in leading the legal fight against segregation.

Robert Weisbrot, *Freedom Bound: A History of America's Civil Rights Movement* (1990). One of the best single-volume syntheses of the movement. Weisbrot is especially strong on the often turbulent relations between black activists and white liberals and the relationship between civil rights and broader currents of American reform.

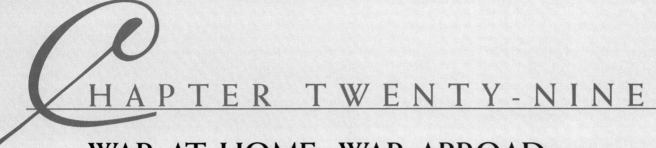

CHAPTER TWENTY-NINE

WAR AT HOME, WAR ABROAD

1965–1974

AMERICAN COMMUNITIES
Uptown, Chicago, Illinois

During Freedom Summer of 1964, while teams of northern college students traveled south to join voter registration campaigns among African Americans, a small group moved to Chicago to help the city's poor people to take control of their communities and demand better city services. They targeted a neighborhood known as Uptown, a one-mile-square section five miles north of the Loop, the city center. Four thousand people lived on just one street running four blocks, 20 percent of them on welfare. Chicago civic authorities had also selected this neighborhood for improvement. Designating it a Conservation Area, they hoped to upgrade the housing for middle-income families and, in effect, to clear out the current residents.

With the assistance of the Packinghouse Workers union, the students formed Jobs or Income Now (JOIN), opened a storefront office, and invited local residents to work with them to halt the city's plans. They spent hours and hours listening to people, drawing out their ideas, and helping them develop scores of programs. Confronting the bureaucracy of the welfare and unemployment compensation offices stood high on their list. They also campaigned against Mayor Richard Daley's policy of "police omnipresence," the fleet of squad cars and paddy wagons that continually patrolled the neighborhood. To curb police harassment, they demanded the creation of civilian review boards. They also helped community members to establish new social clubs, a food-buying cooperative, a community theater, and a health clinic.

Chicago JOIN was one of ten similar projects sponsored by Students for a Democratic Society (SDS). Impatient with the political drift of the nation, especially the cold war and chronic poverty, twenty-nine students from nine universities had met in June 1960 to form a new kind of campus-based political organization. In June 1962 in Port Huron, Michigan, its founding members had issued a declaration of principles, drafted mainly by graduate student Tom Hayden. "We are people . . . bred in at least modest comfort, housed now in universities," they opened, "looking uncomfortably to the world we inherit." The dire effects of poverty and social injustice were not the only things that dismayed them. As one organizer explained, programs such as JOIN were attempts to create a poor people's movement as well as a means for students themselves to live an authentic life outside the constraints of middle-class society.

SDS began with a campaign to reform the university, especially to disentangle the financial ties between campus-based research programs and the military-industrial complex. Later it expanded to the nation's cities, sending small groups of students to live and organize in the poor communities of Boston, Louisville, Cleveland, and Newark as well as Chicago.

Ultimately, few of these projects succeeded in mobilizing the poor into political action. Organizers learned quickly that they could not combat unemployment by protesting against local government. Nor did their campaigns for better city services, such as garbage collection or recreational facilities, necessarily build movements that lasted beyond the initial protest. Nevertheless, organizers did succeed in bringing many neighborhood residents "out of isolation and into community." By late 1967 SDS prepared to leave JOIN in the hands of the people it had organized, which was its goal from the beginning.

Initially, even Lyndon Baines Johnson promoted the ideal of civic participation. The Great Society, as the president called his domestic program, promised more than the abolition of poverty and racial inequality. In May 1964 at the University of Michigan, the president described his goal as a society "where every child can find knowledge to enrich his mind and to enlarge his talents."

By 1967 the Vietnam War had upset the domestic agendas of both SDS and the Johnson administration. If SDSers had once believed they could work with liberal Democrats to reduce poverty in the United States, now they threw their energies into the movement against the war in Vietnam. President Johnson, meanwhile, pursued a foreign policy that would swallow up the funding for his own plans for a war on poverty and precipitate a very different war at home, Americans against Americans. The dream of community did not vanish, but consensus appeared increasingly remote as the United States fought—and eventually lost—the longest war in its history.

Chicago

KEY TOPICS

- Widening U.S. involvement in the war in Vietnam

- The sixties generation and the antiwar movement

- Poverty and urban crisis

- The election of 1968

- The rise of liberation movements

- The Nixon presidency and the Watergate conspiracy

VIETNAM: AMERICA'S LONGEST WAR

The origins of the Vietnam War lead back to the Truman Doctrine and its chief goal of containing communism (see Chapter 26). After the defeat of the French by the communist forces of Ho Chi Minh in 1954, Vietnam had emerged as a major zone of cold war contention. President John Kennedy called it "the cornerstone of the Free World in Southeast Asia, the keystone in the arch, the finger in the dike," a barrier to the spread of communism throughout the region and perhaps the world. President Lyndon Johnson began his presidency on the same note. With American security at stake, he concluded, Americans had little choice but to fight.

Vietnam was not Valley Forge, however, and the United States ended up paying a huge price for its determination to turn back communism in Indochina. More than 50,000 Americans died in an unwinnable overseas war that only deepened divisions at home.

Johnson's War

Although President Kennedy had prepared the way by greatly increasing the number of military advisers in South Vietnam (see Chapter 27), it was his successor, Lyndon B. Johnson, who made the decision to engage the United States in a major war. At first, however, Johnson did not want to widen the war. Facing a presidential election in November 1964, he planned to focus on his domestic agenda, on building the Great Society.

Yet Johnson was determined to avoid the fate of President Harry Truman, who had bogged down politically by "losing" China to communism and producing a stalemate in Korea.

While the president continued to assure Americans that he would never "send American boys nine or ten thousand miles away from home to do what Asian boys ought to be doing for themselves," he and his advisers responded to the worsening situation in Vietnam by continuing covert military operations and secretly developing plans to deepen U.S. involvement.

They found their pretext on August 1, 1964, when North Vietnamese patrol boats attacked an American destroyer in the Gulf of Tonkin, off the coast of North Vietnam. Johnson warned North Vietnam of "grave consequences" of any further aggression. Three days later, amid a thunderstorm, the USS *Maddox* alleged that a second attack had occurred. Without waiting for confirmation, Johnson said in private, "We are not going to take it lying down."

On August 4, in a special televised address, President Johnson announced that he had ordered retaliatory measures. He next appealed to Congress for the authority to take whatever steps were necessary, including military force, to repel attacks on U.S. forces and to protect Southeast Asia. Secretly drafted six weeks before the incident, the Tonkin Gulf resolution passed the Senate with only two dissenting votes and moved unanimously through the House. It served as a declaration of war.

Ironically, Johnson campaigned for the presidency with a call for restraint in Vietnam. This strategy helped him win a landslide victory over conservative Republican Barry Goldwater. With the election behind him, Johnson faced a hard decision. The limited bombing raids had failed to slow the movement of the communist Vietcong forces across the border into the South. Meanwhile, the South Vietnamese government appeared near collapse. Faced with the prospect of a communist victory, the president chose to escalate U.S. involvement in Vietnam massively.

Deeper into the Quagmire

In early February 1965, Johnson found a rationale to justify massive bombing of the North. The Vietcong stormed the U.S. air base at Pleiku, killing 8 and wounding more than 100 Americans. Waving the list of casualties, Johnson rushed into an emergency meeting of the National Security Council to announce that the time had passed for keeping "our guns over the mantle and our shells in the cupboard." He ordered immediate reprisal bombing of North Vietnam and shortly after

Refugees, Binh Dinh Province, 1967. The massive bombing and ground combat broke apart the farming communities of South Vietnam, creating huge numbers of civilian casualties and driving millions into refugee camps or already overcrowded cities. Approximately 25 percent of the South Vietnamese population fled their native villages, many never to return.

authorized Operation Rolling Thunder, a campaign of gradually intensifying air attacks.

Once Rolling Thunder had begun, President Johnson found it increasingly difficult to hold the line against further escalations and to speak frankly with the American public about his policies. Initially, he announced that only two battalions of marines were being assigned to Danang to defend the airfields where the bombing runs began. But six weeks later 50,000 U.S. troops were in Vietnam. By November 1965 the total topped 165,000, and more troops were on the way. Even after Johnson authorized a troop buildup to 431,000 in mid-1966, victory was still nowhere in sight.

The strategy pursued by the Johnson administration and implemented by General William Westmoreland—a war of attrition—was based on the premise that continued bombing would eventually exhaust North Vietnam's resources. Meanwhile, in the South, U.S. forces would inflict both moral and military defeat on the Vietcong, forcing its soldiers to defect and supporters to scatter and thereby restoring political stability to the pro-Western government of South Vietnam. As Johnson once boasted, the strongest military power in the world surely could crush a communist rebellion in a country of peasants.

In practice, the United States wreaked havoc in South Vietnam, tearing apart its society and bringing ecological devastation to its land. Intending to locate and eradicate the support network of the Vietcong, U.S. ground troops conducted search-and-destroy missions throughout the countryside. They attacked villagers and burned their straw huts. In ferreting out Vietcong sympathizers, U.S. troops turned as many as 4 million people into refugees in their own land. By late 1968, the United States had dropped more than 3 million tons of bombs on Vietnam, more than the Allies had delivered during all World War II. The millions of gallons of herbicides used to defoliate suspected Vietcong camps and supply routes constituted the most destructive chemical warfare in history.

Several advisers had urged the president to take these decisions to the American people, even to declare a state of national emergency. But Johnson feared he would lose momentum on domestic reform, including his antipoverty programs, if he drew attention to his military policies. Seeking to avoid "undue excitement in the Congress and in domestic public opinion," he embarked on a course of intentional deceit.

The Credibility Gap

Johnson's popularity had surged at the time of the Tonkin Gulf resolution, skyrocketing in one day from 42 to 72 percent, according to a Louis Harris poll. But afterward it waned rapidly. The war dragged on. Every night network television news publicized the latest American body count. No president had worked so hard to control the news media, but by 1967 Johnson found himself badgered at press conferences by reporters who accused the president of creating a credibility gap.

Scenes of human suffering and devastation recorded by television cameras increasingly undermined the administration's moral justification of the war with claims that it was a necessary defense of freedom and democracy in South Vietnam. During the early 1960s network news had either ignored Vietnam or had been patriotically supportive of U.S. policy. Beginning with a report on a ground operation against the South Vietnamese village of Cam Ne by Morley Safer for CBS News in August 1965, however, the tenor of news reporting changed. Although government officials described the operation as a strategic destruction of "fortified Vietcong bunkers," the CBS *Evening News* showed pictures of Marines setting fire to thatched homes of civilians. After CBS aired Safer's report President Johnson complained bitterly to the news director. But more critical commentary soon followed. By 1967, according to a noted media observer, "every subject tended to become Vietnam." Televised news reports told of new varieties of American cluster bombs, which released up to 180,000 fiberglass shards, and showed the nightmarish effects of the defoliants used on forests in South Vietnam to uncover enemy strongholds.

Press coverage also became more skeptical of Johnson's policies. By 1967 independent news teams were putting aside the government's official releases. Harrison Salisbury, Pulitzer Prize–winning *New York Times* reporter, questioned the administration's claims of precision bombing, charging that U.S. planes had bombed the population center of Hanoi, capital of North Vietnam, and intentionally ravaged villages in the South. As American military deaths climbed more than 800 per month during the first half of 1967, newspaper coverage of the war focused yet more intently on such disturbing events.

The most vocal congressional critic of Johnson's war policy was Democratic senator J. William Fulbright of Arkansas, who chaired the Senate Foreign Relations Committee and had personally speeded the passage of the Tonkin Gulf resolution. A strong supporter of the cold war, Fulbright had decided that the war in Vietnam was unwinnable and destructive to domestic reform. At first he stood alone: in October 1966 only 15 percent of Congress favored a negotiated settlement. But Fulbright's *Arrogance of Power* (1966), which proposed a negotiated withdrawal from a neutralized Southeast Asia, became a best seller. Fulbright encouraged prominent Democrats in Congress, such as Frank Church, Mike Mansfield, and George McGovern, to put aside their personal loyalty to Johnson and oppose his conduct of the war. In 1967 Congress passed a nonbinding resolution appealing to the United Nations to help negotiate an end to hostilities. Meanwhile, some of the nation's most trusted European allies called for restraint.

The impact of the war, which cost Americans $21 billion per year, was also felt at home. Johnson encouraged Congress to levy a 10 percent surcharge on individual and corporate taxes. Later adjustments in the national budget tapped the Social Security fund, heretofore safe from interference. Inflation raced upward, fed by spending on the war. While Johnson replaced the advisers who questioned his policy, and as the number of casualties multiplied, a sizable number of Americans began to question his handling of the war.

A GENERATION IN CONFLICT

As the war in Vietnam escalated, Americans from all walks of life demanded an end to U.S. involvement. But between 1965 and 1971, its years of peak activity, antiwar activity had a distinctly generational character. At the forefront were the baby boomers who were just coming of age.

This so-called sixties generation, the largest generation in American history, was also the best educated so far. By the late 1960s, nearly half of all young adults between the ages of 18 and 21 were enrolled in college. In 1965 there were 5 million college students; in 1973 the number had doubled to 10 million. Public universities made the largest gains; by 1970 eight had more than 30,000 students apiece. These young people combined a massive protest against the war in Vietnam with a broader, penetrating critique of American society. Through music, dress, and even hairstyle, a large number expressed a deep estrangement from the values and aspirations of their parents' generation. As early as 1967, when opposition to the war had begun to swell, "flower children" were putting daisies in the rifle barrels of troops stationed to quash campus protests, providing an innocent counterpoint to the grim news of mass slaughter abroad.

These young adults believed they heralded a "culture of life" against the "culture of death" symbolized by the war. Campus organizations such as SDS, which had begun in the early 1960s as an attempt to build community, now turned against the government.

"The Times They Are A-Changin'"

The first sign of a new kind of protest was the free speech movement at the University of California at Berkeley in 1964. That fall, civil rights activists returned to the campus from Freedom Summer in Mississippi. They soon began to picket Bay Area stores that practiced discrimination in hiring and to recruit other students to join them. When the university administration moved to prevent them from setting up information booths on campus, eighteen groups protested, including the archconservative Students for Goldwater, claiming that their right to free speech had been abridged. The administration responded by sending police to break up the protest rally and arrest participants. University president Clark Kerr met with students, agreed not to press charges, and seemed to grant them a small space on campus for political activity. Then, under pressure from conservative regents, Kerr backed down and in November announced that the university planned to press new charges against the free speech movement's leaders. On December 2 a crowd of 7,000 gathered to protest this decision. Joining folk singer Joan Baez in singing "We Shall Overcome," a group of students marched toward the university's administration building, where they planned to stage a sit-in until Kerr rescinded his order. The police arrested nearly 800 students in the largest mass arrest in California history.

Mario Savio, a Freedom Summer volunteer and philosophy student, explained that the free speech movement wanted more than just the right to conduct political activity on campus. He spoke for many students when he complained that the university had become a faceless bureaucratic machine rather than a community of learning.

Across the country college students began to demand the right to participate more fully in structuring their own education. Brown University students, for example, demanded a revamp of the curriculum that would eliminate all required courses and make grades optional. Students also protested campus rules that treated students as children instead of as adults. After a string of campus protests, most large universities, including the University of California, relinquished *in loco parentis* (in the place of parents) policies and allowed students to live off-campus and to set their own hours.

Across the bay in San Francisco, other young adults staked out a new form of community—a counterculture. In 1967, "the Summer of Love," the population of the Haight–Ashbury district swelled by 75,000, as youthful adventurers gathered for the most celebrated "be-in" of the era. They congregated in the Haight for no other purpose but to listen to music, take drugs, and be with each other. In the fall, the majority returned to their own communities, often bringing with them a new lifestyle.

This generational rebellion took many forms, including a revolution in sexual behavior that triggered countless quarrels between parents and their maturing sons and daughters. During the 1960s more teenagers experienced premarital sex—by the decade's end three-quarters of all college seniors had engaged in sexual intercourse—and far more talked about it openly than in previous eras. "We've discarded the idea that the loss of virginity is related to degeneracy," one college student explained. Many heterosexual couples chose to live together outside marriage, a practice few parents condoned. A much smaller but significant number formed communes—approximately 4,000 by 1970—where members could share housekeeping and child care as well as sexual partners.

Psychedelic and other hallucinogenic drugs played a large part in this counterculture. Harvard professor Timothy Leary urged young people to "turn on, tune in, drop out" and also advocated the mass production and distribution of LSD (lysergic acid diethylamide), which was not criminalized until 1968. Marijuana, illegal yet readily available, often paired with rock music in a collective ritual of love and laughter. Singer Bob Dylan taunted adults with the lyrics of his hit single, "Everybody Must Get Stoned."

Music played a large part in defining the counterculture. Beginning in 1964, with the arrival of the British rock group the Beatles, popular music began to express a deliberate generational identity. Folk music, which had gained popularity on campuses in the early 1960s with the successful recordings of Peter, Paul, and

Mary, Phil Ochs, Judy Collins, and Joan Baez, continued to serve the voice of protest. Folk singer Bob Dylan issued a warning to parents:

> *Your sons and your daughters*
> *Are beyond your command*
> *Your old road is rapidly agin'.*
> *Please get out of the new one*
> *If you can't lend a hand*
> *For the times they are a-changin'.**

At a farm near Woodstock, New York, more than 400,000 people gathered in August 1969 for a three-day rock concert and to give witness to the ideals of the counterculture. Thousands took drugs while security officials and local police stood by.

The Woodstock Nation, as the counterculture was renamed by the media, did not actually represent the sentiments of most young Americans. But its attitudes and styles, especially its efforts to create a new community, did speak for the large minority seeking a peaceful alternative to the intensifying climate of war. "We used to think of ourselves as little clumps of weirdos," rock star Janis Joplin explained. "But now we're a whole new minority group." The slogan "Make Love, Not War" linked generational rebellion and opposition to the U.S. invasion of Vietnam.

From Campus Protest to Mass Mobilization

Three weeks after the announcement of Operation Rolling Thunder, peace activists called for a day-long boycott of classes so that students and faculty might meet to discuss the war. At the University of Michigan in Ann Arbor, more than 3,000 students turned out for sessions held through the night because administrators bowed to pressure of state legislators and refused to cancel classes. During the following weeks, "teach-ins" spread across the United States and as far away as Europe and Japan.

Students also began to protest against war-related research on their campuses. The expansion of higher education in the 1960s had depended largely on federally funded programs, including military research on counterinsurgency tactics and new chemical weapons. Student protesters demanded an end to these programs and, receiving no response from university administrators, turned to civil disobedience. In October 1967, the Dow Chemical Company, manufacturers of napalm, a form of jellied gasoline often used against civilians, sent job recruiters to the University of

*The Times They Are A-Changin'. Copyright © 1963, 1964 by Warner Bros. Music. Copyright renewed 1991 by Special Rider Music. All rights reserved. International copyright secured. Reprinted by permission.

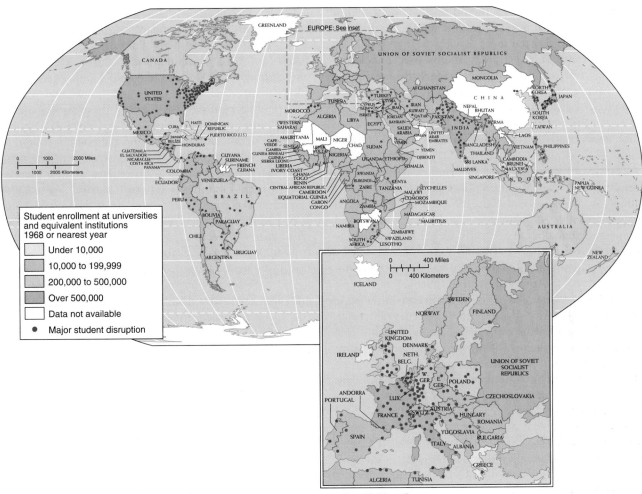

Antiwar Protests on College and University Campuses, 1967–1969 *Campus-based protests against the war in Vietnam, at first centered on the east coast and in California, spread to nearly every region of the country and around the world by the decade's end.*

Wisconsin at Madison despite warnings that a group of students would try to prevent them from conducting interviews. A few hundred students staged a sit-in at the building where the recruitment interviews were scheduled, and 2,000 onlookers gathered outside. Ordered by university administrators to disperse the crowd, the city's police broke glass doors, dragged students through the debris, and clubbed those who refused to move. Suddenly the campus erupted. Students chanted "Sieg Heil" at the police, who attempted to disperse them with tear gas and Mace. Undergraduate students and their teaching assistants boycotted classes for a week. During the next three years, hundreds of similar strikes took place on campuses in every region of the country.

Many student strikes merged opposition to the war with other campus and community issues. At Columbia University, students struck in 1968 against the administration's plans to build a new gymnasium in a city park used by residents of neighboring Harlem. In

the Southwest, Mexican American students demonstrated against the use of funds for military projects that might otherwise be allocated to antipoverty and educational programs.

In April 1967 the largest demonstration in American history to this time, at Sheep's Meadow in Manhattan's Central Park, drew more than 300,000 people to a day-long rally. Meanwhile, 60,000 protesters turned out in San Francisco. By summer, Vietnam Veterans Against the War began to organize returning soldiers and sailors, encouraging them to cast off the medals and ribbons they had won in battle.

The steadily increasing size of antiwar demonstrations provoked conservatives and prowar Democrats to take a stronger stand in support of the war. Several newspaper and magazine editorialists called for the arrest of antiwar leaders on charges of treason. Secretary of State Dean Rusk, appearing on NBC's *Meet the Press*, expressed his concern that "authorities in Hanoi" might conclude, incorrectly, that the majority of Americans did not back their president and that "the net effect of these demonstrations will be to prolong the war, not to shorten it."

Many demonstrators themselves concluded that mass mobilizations alone made little impact on U.S. policy. Some sought to serve as moral witness. Despite a congressional act of 1965 providing for a five-year jail term and a $10,000 fine for destroying a draft card, nearly 200 young men destroyed their draft cards at the April Sheep's Meadow demonstration and encouraged approximately a half-million more to resist the draft or refuse induction. Two Jesuit priests, Daniel and Philip Berrigan, raided the offices of the draft board in Catonsville, Maryland, in May 1968 and poured homemade napalm over records. Other activists determined to "bring the war home." An estimated 40,000 bombing incidents or bomb threats took place from January 1969 to April 1970; more than $21 million of property was damaged, and forty-three people were killed. The majority of the perpetrators never became known. Parallel wars were now being fought, one between two systems of government in Vietnam, another between the American government and masses of its citizens. The Americans sent to Vietnam were caught in between.

Teenage Soldiers

Whereas the average age of the World War II soldier was twenty-six, the age of those who fought in Vietnam hovered around nineteen. Until late 1969 the Selective Service Act—the draft—allowed male students to request educational deferments, and, overall, college graduates constituted only 12 percent of all soldiers and 9 percent of those in combat. Meanwhile, the army recruited hard in poor communities, advertising the armed forces as means of vocational training and social mobility. Working-class young men, disproportionately African American and Latino, were registered in large numbers under this program. High school dropouts were the most likely to be sent to Vietnam, and by far the most likely to die there. This disparity forced a rupture that would last well past the actual war.

Yet the soldiers were not entirely apart from the changes affecting their generation. GIs in significant numbers smoked marijuana, listened to rock music, and considered themselves part of the sexual revolution. But most resented the protests at home as the voice of privileged peers who did not have to fight. As the war dragged on, however, soldiers began to show their frustration and their desperation to escape psychologically. Flagrantly using heroin as well as the more "counter-cultural" marijuana and LSD both off and on duty, they often entered decades of personal addiction. Meanwhile, thousands of soldiers simply refused to enter battle, and hundreds took their revenge

with murderous results, "fragging" their commanding officers with grenades meant for the enemy. Some African American soldiers complained about being asked to fight "a white man's war" and sported helmets emblazoned with slogans like "No Gook Ever Called Me Nigger."

The nature of the war fed these feelings. U.S. troops entering South Vietnam expected a welcome from the people whose homeland they had been sent to defend. Instead, Americans encountered anti-American demonstrations and placards with messages such as "End Foreign Dominance of Our Country." Vietnamese civilians risked their lives to help drive the invaders out. Worse, armed guerillas refused to face American forces with vastly superior arms and air support. Instead, American soldiers had to chase their elusive enemies through deep swamps, crawled through dense jungles, found themselves covered with leeches and fire ants, and stumbled into deadly booby-traps. Through all this, they remained uncertain about who they should consider friend or foe. Patently false U.S. government press releases heralding glorious victories and grateful civilians not only fooled no one but deepened bitterness on the front lines.

Vietnam veterans returned to civilian life quietly and without fanfare, denied the glory earned by the soldiers of previous wars. They reentered a society badly divided over the cause for which they had risked their lives. Tens of thousands suffered debilitating physical injuries. Many more came home with drug dependencies or posttraumatic stress disorder, haunted and depressed by troubling visions and memories of atrocities. Many had trouble getting and keeping jobs; they lacked skills to cope with a shrinking industrial economy.

WARS ON POVERTY

During the early 1960s, the civil rights movement spurred a new awareness of and concern with poverty. What good was winning the right to sit at a lunch counter if one could not afford to buy a hamburger?

One of the most influential books of the times, Michael Harrington's *The Other America* (1962), added fuel to this fire. Harrington argued that one-fifth of the nation—as many as 40 to 50 million people—suffered from bad housing, malnutrition, poor medical care, and the other deprivations of poverty. He documented the miseries of what he called the "invisible land of the other Americans," the rejects of society who simply did not exist for affluent suburbanites or the mass media.

These arguments motivated President Johnson to expand the antipoverty program that he had inherited from the Kennedy administration. "That's my kind of program," he told his advisers. "It will help people. I want you to move full speed ahead on it." Ironically, it was another kind of war that ultimately undercut his aspiration to wage "an unconditional war on poverty."

The Great Society

In his State of the Union message in 1964, Johnson announced his plans to build a Great Society. Over the next two years, he used the political momentum of the civil rights movement and the overwhelming Democratic majorities in the House and Senate to push through the most ambitious reform program since the New Deal. In August 1964 the Economic Opportunity Act launched the War on Poverty. It established an Office of Economic Opportunity (OEO), which coordinated a network of federal programs designed to increase opportunities in employment and education.

The programs had mixed results. The Job Corps provided vocational training mostly for urban black youth considered unemployable. Housed in dreary barracklike camps far from home, trainees often found themselves learning factory skills that were already obsolete. The Neighborhood Youth Corps managed to provide work to about 2 million young people aged sixteen to twenty-one. But nearly all of these were low-paying, make-work jobs. Educational programs proved more successful. VISTA (Volunteers in Service to America) was a kind of domestic Peace Corps that brought several thousand idealistic teachers into poor school districts.

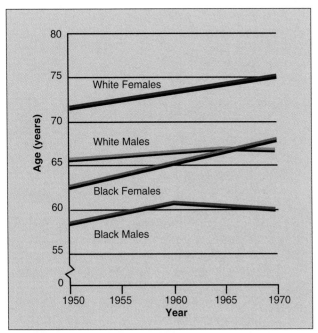

Comparative Figures on Life Expectancy at Birth by Race and Sex, 1950–1970 *Shifting mortality statistics suggested that the increased longevity of females increasingly cut across race lines, but did not diminish the difference between white people and black people as a whole.*

The most innovative and controversial element of the OEO was the Community Action Program (CAP). The program invited local communities to establish community action agencies (CAAs), to be funded through the OEO. The Economic Opportunity Act included language requiring these agencies to be "developed, conducted, and administered with the maximum feasible participation of residents of the areas and members of the groups served." In theory, as the SDS organizers had also believed, community action would empower the poor by giving them a direct say in mobilizing resources to attack poverty.

By 1966 the OEO was funding more than 1,000 CAAs, mostly in black neighborhoods of big cities. The traditional powers in cities—mayors, business elites, and political machines—generally resisted the CAP's promotion of institutional change. They looked at CAAs as merely another way to dispense services and patronage, with the federal government picking up the tab. A continual tug-of-war over who should control funding and decision making plagued the CAP in most cities, sparking intense power struggles that helped to cripple the antipoverty effort. Such was the case in Chicago, where Mayor Richard Daley demanded absolute control over the allocation of federal funds.

The most successful and popular offshoots of the CAP were the so-called national-emphasis programs, designed in Washington and administered according to federal guidelines. The Legal Services Program, staffed by attorneys, helped millions of poor people in legal battles with housing authorities, welfare departments, police, and slumlords. Head Start and Follow Through reached more than 2 million poor children and significantly improved the long-range educational achievement of participants. Comprehensive Community Health Centers—one-stop clinics—provided basic medical services to poor patients who could not afford to see doctors. Upward Bound helped low-income teenagers develop the skills and confidence needed for college. Birth control programs dispensed contraceptive supplies and information to hundreds of thousands of poor women.

But the root cause of poverty lay in unequal income distribution. The Johnson administration never committed itself to the redistribution of income or wealth. Spending on social welfare jumped from 7.7 percent of the gross national product in 1960 to 16 percent in 1974. But roughly three-quarters of social welfare payments went to the nonpoor. The largest sums went to Medicare, established by Congress in 1965 to provide basic health care for the aged, and to expanded Social Security payments and unemployment compensation.

The War on Poverty, like the Great Society itself, became a forgotten dream. "More than five years after the passage of the Economic Opportunity Act," a 1970 study concluded, "the war on poverty has barely scratched the surface. Most poor people have had no contact with it, except perhaps to hear the promises of a better life to come." Having made the largest commitment to federal spending on social welfare since the New Deal, Johnson could take pride in the gains scored in the War on Poverty. At the same time, he had raised expectations higher than could be reached without a more drastic redistribution of economic and political power. Even in the short run, the president could not sustain the welfare programs and simultaneously fight a lengthy and expensive war abroad.

Crisis in the Cities

With funds for new construction limited during the Great Depression and World War II, and the postwar boom taking place in the suburbs, the housing stock in the cities diminished and deteriorated. The Federal Housing Administration actually encouraged this trend by insuring loans to support the building of new homes in suburban areas. The federal government also encouraged "redlining," a common practice of lending agencies such as banks to draw a red line on a map around neighborhoods that would be blanketly denied building loans. In these mainly poor areas, the decline of adequate housing was sharp. Slumlords took advantage of this situation, collecting high rents while allowing their properties to deteriorate. City officials meanwhile appealed for federal funds under Title I of the 1949 Housing Act to upgrade housing. Designed as a program of civic revitalization, these urban renewal projects more often than not sliced apart poor neighborhoods with new highways, demolished them in favor of new office complexes, or, as in Chicago's Uptown, favored new developments for the middle class rather than the poor. In 1968 a federal survey showed that 80 percent of the residents who had been displaced under this program were nonwhite.

Along with housing, urban employment became increasingly inadequate to support the population. The industries and corporations that had lured working men and women to the cities a century earlier either automated their plants, thus scaling down the size of their workforces, or relocated to the suburbs or other regions, such as the South and Southwest, that promised lower corporate taxes and nonunion labor. Nationwide, military spending prompted by the escalation of the Vietnam War brought the unemployment rate down from 6 percent, where it was in 1960, to 4 percent in 1966, where it remained until the end of the decade. However, black unemployment was nearly

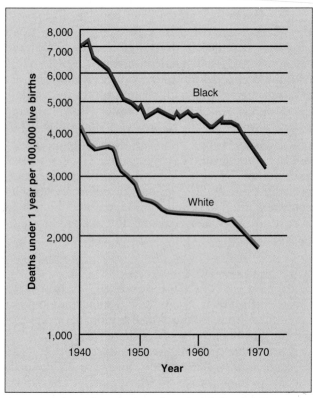

Comparative Figures on Infant Mortality by Race, 1940–1970 *The causes of infant mortality such as inadequate maternal diets, prenatal care, and medical services were rooted in poverty, both rural and urban. Despite generally falling rates of infant mortality, nonwhite people continued to suffer the effects more than white people.*

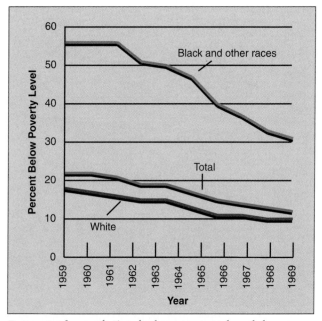

Percent of population below poverty level, by race, 1959–1969 Note: *The poverty threshold for a nonfarm family of four was $3,743 in 1969 and $2,973 in 1959.*

Source: *Congressional Quarterly, Civil Rights: A Progress Report*, 1971, p. 46.

twice that of whites. In northern cities, the proportion of the workforce employed in the higher-paying manufacturing jobs declined precipitously while the proportion working in minimum-wage service industries rose quickly. In short, African Americans were losing good jobs and steadily falling further behind whites.

Pollution, which had long plagued traffic-congested cities like Los Angeles and industrial cities like steel-producing Pittsburgh, became an increasingly pervasive urban problem. Cities like Phoenix that once had clean air began to issue smog alerts. Pointing to high levels of lead in the blood of urban children, scientists warned of the long-term threat of pollution to public health.

Despite deteriorating conditions, millions of Americans continued to move to the cities, mainly African Americans from the Deep South, white people from the Appalachian mountains, and Latinos from Puerto Rico. By the mid-1960s African Americans had become near majorities in the nation's decaying inner cities. The vast majority of these African Americans

fled rural poverty only to find themselves earning minimum wages at best and living in miserable, racially segregated neighborhoods.

Urban Uprisings

Urban pressures reached a boiling point, producing more than 100 uprisings during the "long, hot summers" between 1964 and 1968. The first major uprising erupted in August 1965 in the Watts section of Los Angeles. Here, the male unemployment rate hovered around 30 percent. Watts lacked health care facilities—the nearest hospital was twelve miles away—and although fewer than one-fifth of its residents owned cars, the city offered little public transportation. It took only a minor arrest to set off the uprising, which quickly spread fifty miles. Throwing rocks and bottles through store windows, participants reportedly shouted, "This is for Selma! This is for Birmingham!" and "Burn, baby, burn!" Nearly 50,000 people turned out, and 20,000 National Guard troops were sent in. After six days, 34 people lay dead, 900 were injured,

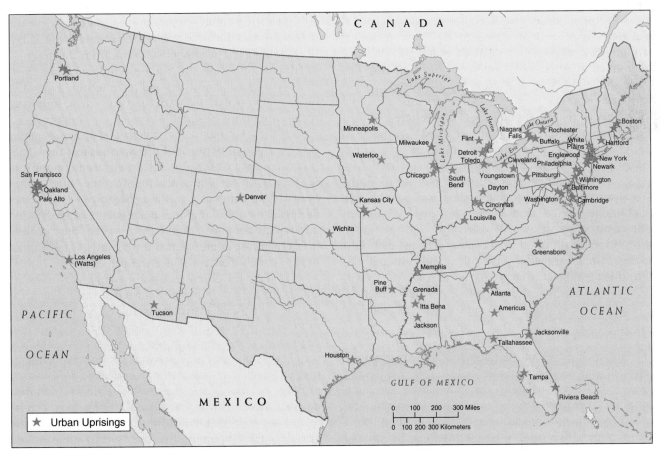

Urban Uprisings, 1965–1968 *After World War II urban uprisings precipitated by racial conflict increased in African American communities. In Watts in 1965 and in Detroit and Newark in 1967 rioters struck out at symbols of white control of their communities, such as white-owned businesses and residential properties.*

and 4,000 more had been arrested. Los Angeles chief of police William H. Parker blamed civil rights workers, the mayor accused communists, and both feigned ignorance when the media reported that white police assigned to "charcoal alley," their name for the Watts district, had for years called their nightsticks "nigger knockers."

The following summer, large-scale uprisings occurred in San Francisco, Milwaukee, Dayton, and Cleveland. On July 13, 1967, in Newark, New Jersey, a city with severe housing shortages and the nation's highest black unemployment rate, the beating and arrest of a black taxi driver by a white police officer provoked a widespread protest. Five days of looting and burning of white-owned buildings ended with twenty-five people killed by the bullets of police and the National Guard. One week later the Detroit "Great Rebellion" began. This time a vice squad of the Detroit police had raided a bar and arrested the after-hours patrons. Army tanks and paratroopers were brought in to quell the massive disturbance, which lasted a week and left 34 people dead and 7,000 under arrest.

The uprisings seemed at first to prompt badly needed reforms. After Watts, President Johnson set up a task force headed by Deputy Attorney General Ramsey Clark and allocated funds for a range of antipoverty programs. Several years later the Kerner Commission, headed by Governor Otto Kerner of Illinois, studied the riots and found that the participants in the uprisings were not the poorest or least-educated members of their communities. They suffered instead from heightened expectations sparked by the civil rights movement and Johnson's promise of a Great Society, expectations that were not to be realized.

But Congress ignored the commission's warning that "our nation is moving toward two societies, one black, one white—separate and unequal." Moreover, the costs of the Vietnam War left little federal money for antipoverty programs. Senator William Fulbright noted, "Each war feeds on the other, and, although the President assures us that we have the resources to win both wars, in fact we are not winning either of them."

1968

The urban uprisings of the summer of 1967 marked the apex of the most drawn-out violence in the United States since the Civil War. But rather than offering a respite, 1968 proved to be even more turbulent. The war in Vietnam, following one of the bloodiest, most destructive battles in its history, turned sour for most of Americans at home. By spring disillusionment deepened as two of the most revered political leaders were struck down by assassins' bullets. Once again protesters and police clashed on the nation's campuses and city streets, and millions of Americans asked what was wrong with their country. Why was it so violent? And the violence did not stop.

The Tet Offensive

On January 30, 1968, the North Vietnamese and their Vietcong allies launched the Tet Offensive (named for the Vietnamese lunar new year holiday), stunning the U.S. military command in South Vietnam. The Vietcong managed to push into the major cities and provincial capitals of the South, as far as the courtyard of the U.S. embassy in Saigon. The United States prevented the fall of Dien Bien Phu by staging massive air strikes, perhaps the most severe in military history. Despite this display of force, it took more than three weeks for U.S. troops to regain control. In the end, American casualties were comparatively modest—1,600 dead, 8,000 wounded—but the North Vietnamese and Vietcong suffered more than 40,000 deaths. Civilian casualties ran to the hundreds of thousands, and as many as 1 million South Vietnamese were reduced to refugees, their villages totally ruined.

The drama of the Tet Offensive had shattered the credibility of American officials, who had repeatedly predicted a quick victory over an unpopular enemy. Television and the press covered the events to the extent of showing U.S. personnel shooting from the embassy windows. Americans saw the beautiful, ancient city of Hue devastated almost beyond recognition. Television newscasters began to warn parents: "The following scenes might not be suitable viewing for children."

The United States had chalked up a major military victory during the Tet Offensive but lost the war at home. For the first time, polls showed strong opposition to the war, 49 percent concluding that the entire operation in Vietnam was a mistake. Meanwhile, in Rome, Berlin, Paris, and London, students and others turned out in huge demonstrations to protest U.S. involvement in Vietnam. At home, sectors of the antiwar movement began to shift from resistance to open rebellion.

The Tet Offensive also opened a year of political drama at home. Congress turned down a request for a general increase in troops issued by General Westmoreland. President Johnson, facing the 1968 election campaign, knew the odds were now against him. He watched as opinion polls showed his popularity plummet to an all-time low. After he squeaked to a narrow victory in the New Hampshire primary, Johnson decided to step down. On March 31 he announced he would not seek the Democratic Party's nomination. He also declared a bombing halt over North Vietnam and called Hanoi to peace talks, which began in Paris in May. Like Truman almost thirty years earlier, and despite his determination not to repeat that bit of history, Johnson had lost his presidency in Asia.

King, the War, and the Assassination

By 1968 the civil rights leadership stood firmly in opposition to the war, and Martin Luther King Jr. had reached a turning point in his life. Although pursued by the FBI through tapped telephones and malicious rumors—bureau chief J. Edgar Hoover swore to "destroy the burr-head"—King abandoned his customary caution in criticizing U.S. policy in Vietnam. In the fall of 1965 he began to connect domestic unrest with the war abroad, calling the U.S. government the "greatest purveyor of violence in the world today." As he became more militant in opposing the war, King lost the support of liberal Democrats who remained loyal to Johnson. King refused to compromise.

In the spring of 1968 King chose Memphis, Tennessee, home of striking sanitation workers, as the place to inaugurate a Poor People's Campaign for peace and justice. On April 4, 1968, as he stepped out on the balcony of his motel, King was shot in the head by a lone assassin, James Earl Ray.

Throughout the world crowds turned out to mourn King's death. Student Nonviolent Coordinating Committee leader Stokely Carmichael stormed, "When white America killed Dr. King, she declared war on us." Riots broke out in more than 100 cities. Chicago Mayor Richard Daley ordered his police to shoot to kill. In Washington, D.C., U.S. Army units set up machine guns outside the Capitol and the White House. By week's end, nearly 27,000 African Americans had been jailed.

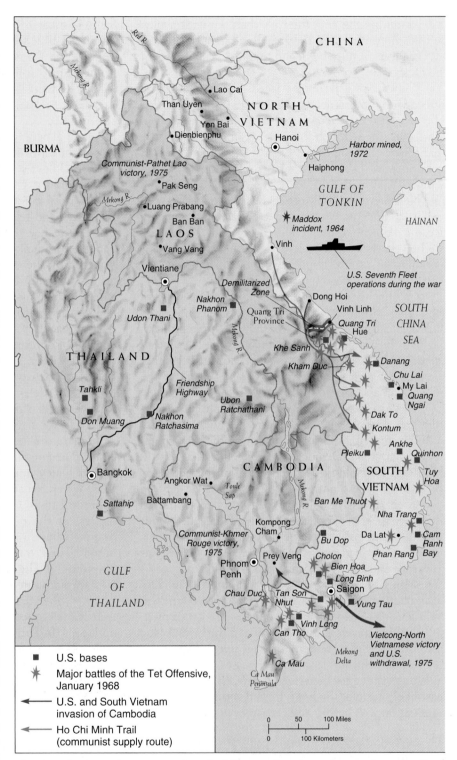

The Southeast Asian War *The Indo-Chinese subcontinent, home to long-standing regional conflict, became the center of a prolonged war with the United States.*

The Democratic Campaign

The dramatic events of the first part of the year had a direct impact on the presidential campaign. For liberals dissatisfied with Johnson's conduct of the war, and for African Americans suffering the loss of their greatest national leader, New York senator Robert F. Kennedy emerged as the candidate of choice. Kennedy had been moved by King's assassination to take up the cause of impoverished Americans more aggressively, and, like King, he had begun to interpret the war as a mirror of injustice at home. Kennedy insisted during the Tet Offensive that "our nation must be told the truth about this war, in all its terrible reality." On this premise he began to build a campaign for the Democratic nomination.

Ironically, Kennedy faced an opponent who agreed with him, Minnesota senator Eugene McCarthy. The race for the Democratic nomination positioned McCarthy, the witty philosopher, against Kennedy, the charismatic campaigner. McCarthy garnered support from liberal Democrats such as economist John Kenneth Galbraith and actors Joanne Woodward and Paul Newman. On college campuses his popularity with idealistic students was so great that his campaign became known as the "children's crusade." Kennedy reached out successfully to African Americans, Latinos, working-class whites, and liberal Democrats, and he won all but the Oregon primary.

Adroitly planning to unify the various wings of the Democratic Party behind him, Kennedy appeared unbeatable as June 4, the day of the California primary, dawned. But after the final tabulation of his victory came into his Los Angeles campaign headquarters that evening, Robert Kennedy was struck down by the bullet of an assassin, Jordanian Sirhan Sirhan.

Vice President Hubert H. Humphrey, a long-time presidential hopeful, was now the sole Democrat with the credentials to succeed Johnson. But his reputation as a cold war Democrat had become a liability. In the 1950s Humphrey had delivered stirring addresses for civil rights and antipoverty legislation, yet he also sponsored repressive cold war measures and supported huge defense appropriations that diverted needed funds from domestic programs. He fully supported the Vietnam War and had publicly scorned peace activists as cowardly and un-American. Incongruously calling his campaign "the Politics of Joy," Humphrey simultaneously courted Democrats who grimly supported the war and the King–Kennedy wing, which was sickened by it.

Humphrey skillfully cultivated the Democratic power brokers. Without entering a single state primary, he lined up delegates loyal to city bosses, labor leaders, and conservative southern Democrats. As the candidate least likely to rock the boat, he had secured his party's nomination well before delegates met in convention.

"The Whole World Is Watching!"

The events surrounding the Democratic convention in Chicago, August 21–26, demonstrated how deep the divisions within the United States had become. Antiwar activists had called for a massive demonstration at the delegates' hotel and at the convention center. The media focused, however, on the plans announced by the "Yippies," or Youth International Party, a largely imaginary organization of politicized hippies led by jokester and counterculture guru Abbie Hoffman. Yippies called for a Festival of Life, including a "nude-in" on Lake Michigan beaches and the release of a greased pig—Pigasus, the Yippie candidate for president. Still reeling from the riots following King's assassination, Chicago's Mayor Richard Daley refused to issue parade permits. According to later accounts, he sent hundreds of undercover police into the crowds to encourage rock throwing and generally incite violence so that retaliation would appear necessary and reasonable.

Daley's strategy boomeranged when his officers staged what a presidential commission later called a "police riot," randomly assaulting demonstrators, casual passersby, and television crews filming the events. For one of the few times in American history, the media appeared to join a protest against civil authorities. Angered by the embarrassing publicity, Daley sent his agents to raid McCarthy's campaign headquarters, where Democrats opposed to the war had gathered.

Inside the convention hall, a raging debate over a peace resolution underscored the depth of this division. Representative Wayne Hays of Ohio lashed out at those who substituted "beards for brains . . . [and] pot [for] patriotism." When the resolution failed, McCarthy delegates put on black armbands and followed folk singer Theodore Bikel in singing "We Shall Overcome." Later, as tear gas used against the demonstrators outside turned the amphitheater air acrid, delegates heard the beaming Humphrey praise Mayor Daley and Johnson's conduct of the Vietnam War. When Senator Abraham Ribicoff of Connecticut addressed the convention and protested the "Gestapo tactics" of the police, television cameras focused on Mayor Daley saying, "You Jew son of a bitch, . . . go home!" The crowd outside chanted, "The whole world is watching! The whole world is watching!" Indeed it was, through satellite transmission.

Protest and social strain spread worldwide. Across the United States the antiwar movement picked up steam. In Paris, students took over their campuses and workers occupied factories. Young people scrawled on the walls such humorous and half-serious slogans as "Be Realistic, Demand the Impossible!" Similar protests against authority occurred in eastern Europe. In Prague, Czechoslovakia, students wearing blue jeans and singing Beatles songs threw rocks at Soviet tanks. Meanwhile, demonstrations in Japan, Italy, Ireland, Germany, and England all brought young people into the streets to demand democratic reforms in their own countries and an end to the war in Vietnam.

THE POLITICS OF IDENTITY

The tragic events of 1968 brought whole sectors of the counterculture into political activism. With great media fanfare, gay liberation and women's liberation

OVERVIEW

PROTEST MOVEMENTS OF THE 1960S

Year	Organization/ Movement	Description
1962	Students for a Democratic Society SDS)	Organization of college students that became the largest national organization of left-wing white students. Calling for "participatory democracy," SDS involved students in community-based campaigns against poverty and for citizens' control of neighborhoods. SDS played a prominent role in the campaign to end the war in Vietnam.
1964	Free Speech Movement	Formed at the University of California at Berkeley to protest the banning of on-campus political fund-raising. Decried the bureaucratic character of the "multiuniversity" and advocated an expansion of student rights.
1965	Anti-Vietnam War Movement	Advocated grass-roots opposition to U.S. involvement in Southeast Asia. By 1970 a national mobilization committee organized a demonstration of a half-million protesters in Washington, D.C.
1965	*La raza*	A movement of Chicano youth to advance the cultural and political self-determination of Mexican Americans. *La raza* included the Brown Berets, which addressed community issues, and regional civil rights groups such as the Crusade for Social Justice, formed in 1965.
1966	Black Power	Militant movement that emerged from the civil rights campaigns to advocate independent institutions for African Americans and pride in black culture and African heritage. The idea of Black Power, a term coined by Stokely Carmichael, inspired the formation of the paramilitary Black Panthers.
1968	American Indian Movement (AIM)	Organization formed to advance the self-determination of Indian peoples and challenge the authority of the Bureau of Indian Affairs. Its most effective tactic was occupation. In February 1973 AIM insurgents protesting land and treaty violations occupied Wounded Knee, South Dakota, the location of an 1890 massacre, until the FBI and BIA agents drove them out.
1968	Women's Liberation	Movement of mainly young women that took shape following a protest at the Miss America Beauty Pageant. Impatient with the legislative reforms promoted by the National Organization for Women, founded in 1966, activists developed their own agenda shaped by the slogan "The Personal Is Political." Activities included the formation of "consciousness-raising" groups and the establishment of women's studies programs.
1968	Asian American Political Alliance (AAPA)	Formed at the University of California at Berkeley, the AAPA was one of the first pan-Asian political organizations to struggle against racial oppression. The AAPA encouraged Asian Americans to claim their own cultural identity and to protest the war against Asian peoples in Vietnam.
1969	Gay Liberation	Movement to protest discrimination against homosexuals and lesbians that emerged after the Stonewall Riots in New York City. Unlike earlier organizations such as the Mattachine Society, which focused on civil rights, Gay Liberationists sought to radically change American society and government, which they believed were corrupt.

movements emerged in the late 1960s. By the early 1970s young Latinos, Asian Americans, and Indian peoples had pressed their own claims. In different ways, these groups drew their own lessons from the nationalist movement that formed in the wake of Malcolm X's death: Black Power. Soon, "Brown Power," "Yellow Power," and "Red Power" became the slogans of movements constituted distinctly as new communities of protest.

Black Power

Derived from a century-long tradition of black nationalism, the key tenets of Black Power were self-determination and self-sufficiency. National conferences of activists, held annually beginning in 1966, adopted separatist resolutions, including a plan to partition the United States into black and white nations. Black Power also promoted self-esteem by affirming the unique history and heritage of African peoples.

The movement's boldest expression was the Black Panther Party for Self-Defense, founded in Oakland, California, in 1966 by Huey P. Newton and Bobby Seale. Armed self-defense was the Panthers' strategy, and they adopted a paramilitary style—black leather jackets, shoes, black berets, and firearms—that infuriated local authorities. Monitoring local police, a practice Panthers termed "patrolling the pigs," was their major activity. In several communities, Panthers also ran free breakfast programs for schoolchildren, established medical clinics, and conducted educational classes. For a time the Panthers became folk heroes in the black community. Persecuted by local police and the FBI—there were more than thirty raids on Panther offices in eleven states during 1968 and 1969—the Panthers were arrested, prosecuted, and sentenced to long terms in jail that effectively destroyed the organization.

Black Power nevertheless continued to grow during the late 1960s and became a multifaceted movement. The Reverend Jesse Jackson, for example, rallied African Americans in Chicago to boycott the A&P supermarket chain until the firm hired 700 black workers. A dynamic speaker and skillful organizer, Jackson encouraged African Americans to support their own businesses and services. His program, Operation Breadbasket, strengthened community control. By 1970 it had spread beyond Chicago to fifteen other cities.

Cultural nationalism became the most enduring component of Black Power. In their popular book *Black Power* (1967), Stokely Carmichael and Charles V. Hamilton urged African Americans "to assert their own definitions, to reclaim their history, their culture; to create their own sense of community and togetherness." Thousands of college students responded by calling for more scholarships and for more classes on African American history and culture.

The war in Vietnam contributed to the growing racial militancy in the United States. African Americans served on the front lines in Vietnam in disproportionate numbers, and many came to view the conflict as a "white man's war."

Meanwhile, trendsetters put aside Western dress for African-style dashikis and hairdos, and black parents gave their children African names. Many well-known African Americans such as Imamu Amiri Baraka (formerly LeRoi Jones), Muhammad Ali (formerly Cassius Clay), and Kwame Touré (formerly Stokely Carmichael) rejected their "slave names." The African holiday Kwanzaa began to replace Christmas as a seasonal family celebration. This deepening sense of racial pride and solidarity was summed up in the popular slogan "Black Is Beautiful."

Sisterhood Is Powerful

Like Black Power, the women's liberation movement attracted mainly young women, including many who had been active in civil rights, SDS, and campus antiwar movements. These women resented the sexist attitudes and behaviors of their fellow male activists. Impatient with the legislative reforms promoted by the National Organization for Women (NOW) and angered by the sexism of SNCC and SDS, these women proclaimed "Sisterhood Is Powerful." "Women are an oppressed class. Our oppression is total, affecting every facet of our lives," read the Redstocking Manifesto of 1969. "We are exploited as sex objects, breeders, domestic servants, and cheap labor."

The women's liberation movement developed a scathing critique of patriarchy, the power of men to dominate all institutions, from the family to business to the military to protest movements themselves. Patriarchy, they argued, was the prime cause of exploitation, racism, and war. Outraged and sometimes outrageous, radical feminists, as they called themselves, conducted "street theater" at the 1968 Miss America Beauty Pageant in Atlantic City, crowning a live sheep queen and "throwing implements of female torture" (bras, girdles, curlers, and copies of the *Ladies' Home Journal*) into a "freedom trash can."

The media focused on the audacious acts and brazen pronouncements of radical feminists, but the majority involved in the women's liberation movement were less flamboyant young women who were simply trying to rise above the limitations imposed on them because of their sex. Most of their activism took place outside the limelight in consciousness-raising (CR) groups. CR groups, which multiplied by the thousands in the late 1960s and early 1970s, brought women together to discuss the relationship between public events and private lives, particularly between politics and sexuality. Here women shared their most intimate feelings toward men or other women and established the constituency for the movement's most important belief, expressed in the aphorism "The personal is political." Believing that no aspect of life lacked a political dimension, women in these groups explored the power dynamics of the institutions of family and marriage as well as the workforce and government.

Participants in the women's liberation movement engaged in a wide range of activities. Some staged sit-ins at *Newsweek* to protest demeaning media depictions of women. Others established health clinics, day-care centers, rape crisis centers, and shelters for women fleeing abusive husbands or lovers. The women's liberation movement also had a significant educational impact. Feminist bookstores and publishing companies, such as the Feminist Press, reached out to eager readers. Scholarly books such as Kate Millett's *Sexual Politics* (1970) found a wide popular audience. By the early 1970s campus activists were demanding women's studies programs and women's centers. Like black studies, women's studies programs included traditional academic goals, such as the generation of new scholarship, but also encouraged personal change and self-esteem. Between 1970 and 1975, as many as 150 women's studies programs had been established. The movement continued to grow; by 1980 nearly 30,000 women's studies courses were offered at colleges and universities throughout the United States.

However, the women's liberation movement remained a bastion of white middle-class women. The appeal to sisterhood did not unite women across race or class or even sexual orientation. Lesbians, who charged the early leaders of NOW with homophobia, found large pockets of heterosexism in the women's liberation movement and broke off to form their own organizations. Although some African American women were outraged at the posturing of Black Power leaders such as Stokely Carmichael, who joked that "the only position for women in SNCC is prone," the majority remained wary of white women's appeals to sisterhood. African American women formed their own "womanist" movement to address their distinct cultural and political concerns. Similarly, by 1970 a Latina feminist movement had begun to address issues uniquely relevant to women of color in an Anglo-dominated society.

Gay Liberation

The gay community had been generations in the making but gained visibility during World War II (see Chapter 25). By the mid-1950s two pioneering homophile organizations, the Mattachine Society and the Daughters of Bilitis, were campaigning to reduce discrimination against homosexuals in employment, the armed forces, and all areas of social and cultural life. Other groups, such as the Society for Individual Rights, rooted themselves in New York's Greenwich Village, San Francisco's North Beach, and other centers of gay night life. But it was during the tumultuous 1960s that gay and lesbian movements encouraged many men and women to proclaim publicly their sexual identity: "Say It Loud, Gay Is Proud."

The major event prompting gays to organize grew out of repeated police raids of gay bars and harassment of their patrons. On Friday, June 27, 1969, New York police raided a well-known gay bar in Greenwich Village and provoked an uprising of angry homosexuals that lasted the entire night. The next day, Gay Power graffiti appeared on buildings and sidewalks throughout the neighborhood. The Stonewall Riot, as it was called, sparked a new sense of collective identity among many gays and lesbians and touched off a new movement for both civil rights and liberation. Gay men and women in New York City formed the Gay Liberation Front (GLF), announcing themselves as "a revolutionary homosexual group of men and women formed with the realization that complete sexual liberation for all people cannot come about unless existing social institutions are abolished. We reject society's attempt to impose sexual roles and definitions of our nature. We are stepping outside these roles and simplistic myths. We are going to be who we are." The GLF also took a stand against the war in Vietnam and supported the Black Panthers. It quickly adopted the forms of public protest, such as street demonstrations and sit-ins, developed by the civil rights movement and given new direction by antiwar protesters.

Changes in public opinion and policies followed. As early as 1967 a group of Episcopal priests had urged church leaders to avoid taking a moral position against same-sex relationships. The San Francisco–based Council on Religion and Homosexuality established a network for clergy sympathetic to gay and lesbian parishioners. In 1973 the American Psychiatric Association, which since World War II had viewed homosexuality as a treatable mental illness, reclassified it as a normal sexual orientation. Meanwhile, there began a slow process of decriminalization of homosexual acts between consenting adults. In 1975 the U.S. Civil Service Commission ended its ban on the employment of homosexuals.

The Chicano Rebellion

By the mid-1960s young Mexican Americans adopted the slang term *Chicano*, in preference to Mexican American, to express a militant ethnic nationalism. Chicano militants demanded not only equality with white people but cultural and political self-determination. Tracing their roots to the heroic Aztecs, they identified *la raza* (the race or people) as the source of a common language, religion, and heritage.

Between 1965 and 1969 the Chicano movement reached its peak. Students staged "blowouts" or strikes in East Los Angeles high schools to demand educational reform and a curricular emphasis on the history, literature, art, and language of Mexican Americans. Fifteen thousand students from five Los Angeles schools struck against poor educational facilities. The police conducted a mass arrest of protesters, and within a short time students in San Antonio and Denver were conducting their own blowouts, holding placards reading "Teachers, Sí, Bigots, No!" By 1969, on September 16, Mexican Independence Day, high school students throughout the Southwest skipped classes in the First National Chicano Boycott. Meanwhile, students organized to demand Mexican American studies on their campuses. In 1969, a group staged a sit-in at the administrative offices of the University of California–Berkeley, which one commentator called "the first important public appearance of something called Brown Power."

Chicano nationalism inspired a variety of regional political movements in the late 1960s. Several organizations, such as Corky Gonzales's Crusade for Justice, formed in 1965 to protest the failure of the Great Society's antipoverty programs. A former boxer and popular poet, Gonzales was especially well liked by barrio youth and college students. He led important campaigns for greater job opportunities and land reform throughout the Southwest well into the 1970s. In Colorado and New Mexico, the *Alianza Federal de Mercedes*, formed in 1963 by Reies López Tijerina, fought to reclaim land fraudulently appropriated by white settlers. The Texas-based *La Raza Unida* Party (LRUP), meanwhile, increased Mexican American representation in local government and established social and cultural programs.

Mexican American activists, even those who won local office, soon discovered that economic power remained out of community hands. Stifled by poverty, ordinary Mexican Americans had less confidence in the political process, and many fell back into apathy after early hopes of great, sudden change. Despite these setbacks, a sense of collective identity had been forged among many young people.

Red Power

Having battled government programs to terminate their tribal status (see Chapter 28), Indian peoples entered the 1960s determined to reassert themselves. The Civil Rights Act passed in 1968 restored the legitimacy of tribal laws on the reservations. Although economic and social reforms were limited by a shortage of antipoverty and educational funds, a movement to

Members of AIM *guard the door to the Bureau of Indian Affairs in Washington, D.C., during a week-long occupation in November 1972, meant to dramatize their grievances.*

build a sense of Indian identity spread widely among young people. In the 1970 census, many of the 800,000 respondents who identified themselves as Indians did so for the first time.

The American Indian Movement (AIM) was founded in 1968 by Chippewas George Mitchell and Dennis Banks. Like the Black Panthers, AIM was organized for self-defense, to protect Indians in Minneapolis from police harassment and brutality. The group's activities soon expanded to include a direct challenge of the Bureau of Indian Affairs's guidance over tribal life. Affirming Indian dignity while calling for greater economic opportunities and an end to police harassment, in 1969 the new militancy created national headlines when a group of young Indians occupied the deserted federal prison on Alcatraz Island in San Francisco Bay and demanded government funds for a cultural center and university.

The most dramatic series of events of the Red Power movement began in November 1972, when tribal members occupied the headquarters of the Bureau of Indian affairs for nearly a week. Soon AIM insurgents took over the site of the 1890 massacres at Wounded Knee, South Dakota, swearing to hold their position by force if necessary. Occupiers asked only that the federal government honor treaty rights. Instead, dozens of FBI agents invaded under shoot-to-kill orders, leaving two Indians dead and one federal marshal wounded.

Several tribes won in court, by legislation or by administrative fiat, small parts of what had been taken from them. Despite these victories, tribal lands continued to suffer from industrial and government dumping and other commercial uses. On reservations and in urban areas with heavy Indian concentrations, alcohol abuse and ill health remained serious problems.

The 1960s also marked the beginning of an "Indian Renaissance." New books such as Vine Deloria Jr.'s *Custer Died for Your Sins* (1969), Dee Brown's *Bury My Heart at Wounded Knee* (1971), and the classic *Black Elk Speaks* (1961), reprinted from the 1930s, reached millions of readers inside and outside Indian communities. A wide variety of Indian novelists, historians, and essayists, such as Pulitzer Prize–winning N. Scott Momaday and Leslie Silko, followed up these successes, and fiction and nonfiction works about Indian life and lore continued to attract a large audience.

The Asian American Movement

In 1968, students at the University of California at Berkeley founded the Asian American Political Alliance (AAPA), one of the first pan-Asian political organizations bringing together Chinese, Japanese, and Filipino American activists. Similar organizations soon appeared on campuses throughout California and spread quickly to the East Coast and Midwest.

These groups took a strong stand against the war in Vietnam, condemning it as a violation of the national sovereignty of the small Asian country. They also protested the racism directed against the peoples of Southeast Asia, particularly the practice common among American soldiers of referring to the enemy as "Gooks." This racist epithet, first used to denigrate Filipinos during the Spanish American War, implied that Asians were something less than human and therefore proper targets for slaughter. In response, Asian American activists rallied behind the people of Vietnam and proclaimed racial solidarity with their "Asian brothers and sisters."

Between 1968 and 1973, major universities across the country introduced courses on Asian American studies, and a few, such as the City College of New York, set up interdisciplinary departments. Meanwhile, artists, writers, documentary filmmakers, oral historians, and anthropologists worked to recover the Asian American past. Maxine Hong Kingston's *Woman Warrior: A Memoir of a Girlhood Among Ghosts* (1976) became the major best seller.

Looking to the example of the Black Panthers, young Asian Americans also took their struggle into the community. In 1968 activists presented the San Francisco municipal government with a list of grievances about conditions in Chinatown, particularly the poor housing and medical facilities, and organized a protest march down the neighborhood's main street. They led a community-wide struggle to save San Francisco's International Hotel, a low-income residential facility for mainly Filipino and Chinese men, which was ultimately leveled for a new parking lot.

Community activists ranging from college students to neighborhood artists worked in a variety of campaigns to heighten public awareness. The Redress and Reparations Movement, initiated by *Sansei* (third-generation Japanese Americans), for example, encouraged students to ask their parents about their wartime experiences and prompted older civil rights organizations, such as the Japanese American Citizens League, to bring forward the issue of internment. At the same time, trade union organizers renewed labor organizing among new Asian workers, mainly in service industries, such as hotel and restaurant work, and in clothing manufacturing. Other campaigns reflected the growing diversity of the Asian population. Filipinos, the fastest-growing group, organized to protest the destructive role of U.S.-backed Philippine dictator Ferdinand Marcos. Students from South Korea similarly denounced the repressive government in their homeland. Samoans sought to publicize the damage caused by nuclear testing in the Pacific Islands. Ultimately, however, in blurring intergroup differences, the Asian American movement failed to reach the growing populations of new immigrants, especially the numerous Southeast Asians fleeing their devastated homeland.

THE NIXON PRESIDENCY

The sharp divisions among Americans in 1968, caused to a large degree by President Johnson's policies in Vietnam, paved the way for the election of Richard Milhous Nixon. The new Republican president inherited not only an increasingly unpopular war but a nation riven by internal discord. Without specifying his plans, he promised a just and honorable peace in Southeast Asia and the restoration of law and order at home. Yet, once in office, Nixon puzzled both friends and foes. He ordered unprecedented illegal government action against private citizens while agreeing with Congress to enhance several welfare programs and improve environmental protection. He widened and intensified the war in Vietnam, yet made stunning moves toward détente with the People's Republic of China. An architect of the cold war in the 1950s, Nixon became the first president to foresee its end. Nixon worked hard in the White House, centralizing authority and reigning defiantly as an Imperial President—until he brought himself down.

The Southern Strategy

In 1968, Republican presidential contender Richard Nixon deftly built on voter hostility toward youthful protesters and the counterculture. He represented, he said, the "silent majority"—Americans who worked, paid taxes, and did not demonstrate, picket, or protest loudly, "people who are not haters, people who love their country." Recovering from defeats for the presidency in 1960 and the governorship of California in 1962, Nixon declared himself the one candidate who could restore law and order to the nation.

After signing the landmark Civil Rights Act of 1964, President Johnson said privately, "I think we just delivered the South to the Republicans for a long time to come." Republican strategists moved quickly to make this prediction come true. They also recognized the growing electoral importance of the Sunbelt, where populations grew with the rise of high-tech industries and retirement communities. A powerful conservatism dominated this region, home to a large number of military bases, defense plants, and an increasingly influential Protestant evangelism. Nixon appealed directly to these voters by promising to appoint to federal courts judges who would undercut liberal interpretations of civil rights and be tough on crime.

Nixon selected as his running mate Maryland governor Spiro T. Agnew, known for his vitriolic oratory. Agnew treated dissent as near treason. The 1968 campaign underscored the antiliberal sentiment

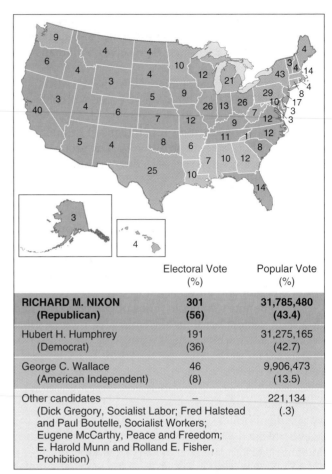

	Electoral Vote (%)	Popular Vote (%)
RICHARD M. NIXON (Republican)	**301 (56)**	**31,785,480 (43.4)**
Hubert H. Humphrey (Democrat)	191 (36)	31,275,165 (42.7)
George C. Wallace (American Independent)	46 (8)	9,906,473 (13.5)
Other candidates (Dick Gregory, Socialist Labor; Fred Halstead and Paul Boutelle, Socialist Workers; Eugene McCarthy, Peace and Freedom; E. Harold Munn and Rolland E. Fisher, Prohibition)	–	221,134 (.3)

The Election of 1968 *Although the Republican Nixon–Agnew team won the popular vote by only a small margin, the Democrats lost in most of the northern states that had voted Democratic since the days of FDR. Segregationist Governor George Wallace of Alabama polled more than 9 million votes.*

of the voting public. The most dramatic example was the relative success of Governor George Wallace's third-party bid for the presidency. Wallace took state office in 1963, promising white Alabamans "Segregation now! Segregation tomorrow! Segregation forever!" In 1968 he waged a national campaign around a conservative hate list that included school busing, antiwar demonstrations, and the urban uprisings. Winning only five southern states, Wallace nevertheless captured 13.5 percent of the popular vote.

The Nixon–Agnew team squeaked to victory, capturing the popular vote by the slim margin of 43.4 percent to Humphrey and Maine senator Edmund Muskie's 42.7 percent but taking nearly all the West's electoral votes. Bitterly divided by the campaign, the Democrats would remain out of presidential contention for decades, except when the Republicans suffered scandal and disgrace. The Republicans in 1968 had inaugurated a new political era.

Nixon's War

Nixon promised to bring "peace with honor." Despite this pledge, the Vietnam War raged for four more years before a peace settlement was reached.

Much of the responsibility for the prolonged conflict rested with Henry A. Kissinger. A dominating personality on the National Security Council, Kissinger insisted that the United States could not retain its global leadership by appearing weak to either allies or enemies. Brilliant and ruthless, Kissinger helped Nixon centralize foreign policy making in the White House. Together, they overpowered members of the State Department who had concluded that the majority of Americans no longer supported the war.

In public Nixon followed a policy of "Vietnamization." On May 14, 1969, he announced that time was approaching "when the South Vietnamese . . . will be able to take over some of the fighting." During the next several months, he ordered the withdrawal of 60,000 U.S. troops. Hoping to placate public opinion, Nixon also intended to "demonstrate to Hanoi that we were serious in seeking a diplomatic settlement." In private, with Kissinger's guidance, Nixon mulled over the option of a "knockout blow" to the North Vietnamese.

On April 30, 1970, Nixon made one of the most controversial decisions of his presidency; without seeking congressional approval, Nixon ordered U.S. troops to invade the tiny nation of Cambodia. Nixon had hoped in this way to end North Vietnamese infiltration into the South, but he had also decided to live up to what he privately called his "wild man" or "mad bomber" reputation. The enemy would be unable to anticipate the location or severity of the next U.S. strike, Nixon reasoned, and would thus feel compelled to negotiate.

Nixon could not have predicted the outpouring of protest that followed the invasion of Cambodia. The largest series of demonstrations and police–student confrontations in the nation's history took place on campuses and in city streets. At Kent State University in Ohio, twenty-eight National Guardsmen apparently panicked. Shooting into an unarmed crowd of about 200 students, they killed four and wounded nine. Ten days later, on May 14, at Jackson State University, a black school in Mississippi, state troopers entered a campus dormitory and began shooting wildly, killing two students and wounding twelve others. Demonstrations broke out on 50 campuses.

The nation was shocked. Thirty-seven college and university presidents signed a letter calling on the president to end the war. A few weeks later the Senate adopted a bipartisan resolution outlawing the use of funds for U.S. military operations in Cambodia, starting July 1, 1970. Although the House rejected the resolution, Nixon saw the writing on the wall. He had planned to negotiate a simultaneous withdrawal of North Vietnamese and U.S. troops, but he could no longer afford to hold out for this condition.

The president, still goaded by Kissinger, did not accept defeat easily. In February 1971 Nixon directed the South Vietnamese army to invade Laos and cut supply lines, but the demoralized invading force suffered a quick and humiliating defeat. Faced with enemy occupation of more and more territory during a major offensive in April 1972, Nixon ordered the mining of North Vietnamese harbors and directed B-52s on massively destructive bombing missions in Cambodia and North Vietnam.

Nixon also sent Kissinger to Paris for secret negotiations with delegates from North Vietnam. They agreed to a cease-fire specifying the withdrawal of all U.S. troops and the return of all U.S. prisoners of war. Knowing that these terms ensured defeat, South Vietnam's president refused to sign the agreement. On Christmas Day 1972, hoping for a better negotiating position, Nixon ordered one final wave of bomb attacks on North Vietnam's cities. To secure a halt to the bombing, the North Vietnamese offered to resume negotiations. But the terms of the Paris Peace Agreement, signed by North Vietnam and the United States in January 1973, differed little from the settlement Nixon could have procured in 1969, hundreds of thousands of deaths earlier. Commencing in March 1973, the withdrawal of U.S. troops left the outcome of the war a foregone conclusion. By December of that year the government of South Vietnam had no future.

In April 1975 North Vietnamese troops took over Saigon, and the communist-led Democratic Republic of Vietnam soon united the small nation. The war was finally over. It had cost the United States

---

In view of the developments since we entered the fighting in Vietnam, do you think the United States made a mistake sending troops to fight in Vietnam?

Yes	52%
No	39
No opinion	9

Interviewing Date 1/22–28/1969, Survey #774-K, Question #6/Index #45

Public Opinion on the War in Vietnam By 1969 *Americans were sharply divided in their assessments of the progress of the war and peace negotiations.*

Source: *The Gallup Poll: Public Opinion, 1935–1971* by George Gallup. Copyright © 1972 by American Institute of Public Opinion. Reprinted by permission of Random House, Inc.

58,000 lives and $150 billion. The country had not only failed to achieve its stated war goal but had lost an important post in Southeast Asia. Equally important, the policy of containment introduced by Truman had proved impossible to sustain.

While Nixon was maneuvering to bring about "peace with honor," the chilling crimes of war had already begun to haunt Americans. In 1971 the army court-martialed a young lieutenant, William L. Calley Jr., for the murder of at least twenty-two Vietnamese civilians during a 1968 search-and-destroy mission subsequently known as the My Lai Massacre. Calley's

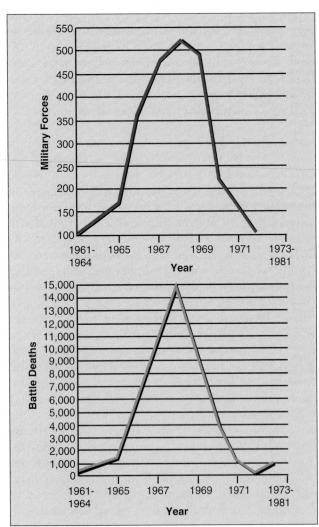

U.S. Military Forces in Vietnam and Casualties, 1961–1981 *The United States government estimated battle deaths between 1969 and 1973 for South Vietnamese troops at 107,504 and North Vietnamese and Vietcong at more than a half-million. Although the United States suffered fewer deaths, the cost was enormous.*

Source: U.S. Department of Defense, *Selected Manpower Statistics,* annual, and unpublished data; beginning 1981, National Archives and Records Service, "Combat Area Casualty File" (3-330-80-3).

platoon had destroyed a village and slaughtered more than 350 unarmed South Vietnamese, raping and beating many of the women before killing them. "My Lai was not an isolated incident," one veteran attested, but "only a minor step beyond the standard official United States policy in Indochina." Commander of the platoon at My Lai, Calley was first sentenced to life imprisonment before being given a reduced term of ten years. The secretary of the army paroled Calley after he served three years under house arrest in his apartment.

"The China Card"

Apart from Vietnam, Nixon's foreign policy defied the expectations of liberals and conservatives alike. Actually, he followed traditions of previous Republican moderates such as Herbert Hoover and Dwight Eisenhower, who had so effectively "proved" their anticommunism that they could conciliate international foes without undermining their popularity at home. Nixon added a new page, however, a policy of détente that replaced U.S.– Soviet bipolarity with multilateral relations. Nixon could cultivate relations with the People's Republic of China, a rising world power more rigidly communist than the Soviet Union, to form an alliance against the Soviet Union. And he could easily persuade the Soviet Union to cooperate on trade agreements, thus limiting the two nations' ruthless competition to control governments in Asia, the Middle East, and Africa. Opponents of the Vietnam War accused Nixon of double dealing, while conservatives howled at any compromise with communist governments. But Nixon persisted in his plans, anticipating an end to the cold war on American terms.

Playing "the China card" was the most dramatic of the president's moves. Early in his political career Nixon had avidly supported the archconservative China lobby. But as president he considered the People's Republic of China too important to be isolated by the West and too obviously hostile to the Soviet Union to be discounted as a potential ally.

"Ping-pong diplomacy" began in April 1971, when the Chinese hosted a table tennis team from the United States. Henry Kissinger embarked on a secret mission a few months later. Finally, in February 1972 Richard and Pat Nixon flew to Beijing, where they were greeted by foreign minister Zhou Enlai and a band playing "The Star-Spangled Banner."

It was a momentous and surprising event, one that marked a new era in East–West diplomacy. Nixon claimed that he had succeeded in bridging "16,000 miles and twenty-two years of hostility." The president's move successfully increased diplomatic pressure on the Soviet Union but simultaneously weakened the Nationalist Chinese government in Taiwan, which now slipped into virtual diplomatic obscurity.

Next the president arrived in Moscow to negotiate with Soviet leader Leonid Brezhnev, who was anxious about U.S. involvement with China and eager for economic assistance. Declaring, "There must be room in this world for two great nations with different systems to live together and work together," Nixon offered to sell $1 billion of grain to the Soviets. Winning the favor of American wheat farmers, this deal simultaneously relieved U.S. trade deficits and crop surpluses. Afterward, the Soviet leader became visibly more cautious about supporting revolutions in the third world. Nixon also completed negotiations of the Strategic Arms Limitation Treaty (SALT, known later as SALT I). A limited measure, SALT I represented the first success at strategic arms control since the opening of the cold war and a major public relations victory for the leaders of the two superpowers.

Nixon's last major diplomatic foray proved far less effective. The president sent Kissinger on a two-year mission of "shuttle diplomacy" to mediate Israeli–Arab disputes, ensure the continued flow of oil, and increase lucrative U.S. arms sales to Arab countries. The Egyptians and Israelis agreed to a cease-fire in their October 1973 Yom Kippur War, but little progress toward peace in the area was achieved.

Domestic Policy

Nixon deeply desired to restore order in American society. "We live in a deeply troubled and profoundly unsettled time," he noted. "Drugs, crime, campus revolts, racial discord, draft resistance—on every hand we find old standards violated, old values discarded." Despite his hostility to liberalism, however, Nixon had some surprises for conservatives. Determined to win reelection in 1972, he supported new Social Security benefits and subsidized housing for the poor and oversaw the creation of the Environmental Protection Agency and the Occupational Safety and Health Administration. Most notable was his support for the Family Assistance Plan, guided by Democratic adviser Daniel P. Moynihan, which proposed a minimal income for the poor in place of welfare benefits. Conservatives judged the plan too generous and liberals found it inadequate. Moreover, the plan was expensive. The bill died a bipartisan death.

Nixon also embraced a policy of fiscal liberalism. Early in 1971 he accepted the idea of deficit spending. Later that year he ordered a first: he took the nation off the gold standard. Subsequently, the dollar's value would float on the world market rather than being tied to the value of gold. His ninety-day freeze on wages, rents, and prices, designed to halt the inflation caused by massive spending on the Vietnam War, also closely resembled Democratic policies. Finally, Nixon's support of "black capitalism"—adjustments or quotas favoring minority contractors in construction projects—created an explosive precedent for set-aside programs later blamed on liberals.

However, Nixon lined up with conservatives on most civil rights issues and thus enlarged southern Republican constituencies. He accepted the principle of school integration but rejected the busing programs required to implement racial balance. His nominees to the Supreme Court were far more conservative than those appointed by Eisenhower. Warren E. Burger, who replaced Chief Justice Earl Warren, steered the Court away from the liberal direction it had taken since the 1950s.

One of the most newsworthy events of Nixon's administration was a distant result of President Kennedy's determination to outshine the Soviets in outer space (see Chapter 27). On July 21, 1969, the lunar module of *Apollo 11* descended to the moon's Sea of Tranquility. As millions watched on television, astronauts Neil Armstrong and Buzz Aldrin stepped out to plant an <u>American</u> flag and to bear the message, "We came in peace for all mankind."

WATERGATE

At times Richard Nixon expressed his yearning for approval in strange ways. A few days after the bombing of Cambodia in May 1970, he wandered out of the White House alone at 5:00 in the morning to talk to antiwar demonstrators. He tried to engage them in small talk about football and pleaded, "I know that probably most of you think I'm an SOB, but I want you to know I understand just how you feel." According to H. R. Haldeman, one of Nixon's closest advisers, the killings at Kent State deeply troubled the president.

Only a few months later Nixon ordered illegal wiretaps of news professionals. He also reaffirmed his support of Central Intelligence Agency (CIA) surveillance of U.S. citizens and organizations—a policy specifically forbidden by the CIA charter—and encouraged members of his administration to spy on Democrats planning for the 1972 election campaign. When news of these extralegal activities surfaced, one of the most canny politicians in American history found himself the first president since Andrew Johnson to face the likelihood of impeachment proceedings.

Foreign Policy as Conspiracy

Nixon's conduct of foreign policy offered early clues into his political character. Although he had welcomed the publicity surrounding his historic moves toward détente with the Soviet Union and normalized relations with China, Nixon generally handled the nation's foreign affairs in surreptitious fashion. But as opposition to the Vietnam War mounted in Congress, he began to face hard questions about this practice. As early as 1970 Republicans as well as Democrats had condemned covert operations in foreign countries. In response, the president, the Department of State, and the CIA developed plans to tighten security even further. Nixon issued a tough mandate against all leaks of information by government personnel, news specialists, or politicians.

At the time, apart from the highly publicized tour to China, Nixon revealed little about his policy for other parts of the globe. Unknown to most Americans, he accelerated arms supplies to foreign dictators, including the shah of Iran, Ferdinand Marcos of the Philippines, and the regime of Pieter William Botha in South Africa. His CIA assistants trained and aided SAVAK, the Iranian secret police force notorious for torturing political dissidents. They also stood behind the South African government in its effort to curtail the activities of the antiapartheid African National Congress. In Latin America, Nixon provided financial assistance and military aid to repressive regimes such as that of Anastasio Somoza of Nicaragua, notorious for its blatant corruption and repeated violations of human rights.

Still more controversial was Nixon's plan to overthrow the legally elected socialist government of Salvador Allende in Chile. With the assistance of nongovernment agencies, such as the AFL-CIO's American Institute for Free Labor Development, the CIA destabilized the regime by funding right-wing parties, launching demonstrations, and preparing the Chilean army for a coup. In September 1973, a military junta killed President Allende and captured, tortured, or murdered thousands of his supporters. Nixon and Kissinger warmly welcomed the new ruler, Augusto Pinochet, granting him financial assistance to restabilize the country.

Toward the end of Nixon's term, members of Congress who had been briefed on these policies began to break silence, and reports of clandestine operations flooded the media. Several former CIA agents issued anguished confessions of their activities in other countries. More troubling to Nixon, despite all his efforts the United States continued to lose ground as a superpower.

The Age of Dirty Tricks

As Nixon approached the 1972 reelection campaign, he tightened his inner circle of White House staff, who assisted him in withholding information from the public, discrediting critics, and engaging in assorted "dirty tricks." Circle members solicited illegal contributions for the campaign and laundered the money through Mexican bank accounts. They also formed a secret squad, "the plumbers," to halt the troublesome leaks of information. This team, headed by former CIA agent E. Howard Hunt and former FBI agent G.

Gordon Liddy, assisted in conspiracy at the highest levels of government.

The first person on the squad's "hit list" was Daniel Ellsberg, a former researcher with the Department of Defense, who in 1971 had turned over to the press secret documents outlining the military history of American involvement in Vietnam. The so-called Pentagon Papers exposed the role of presidents and military leaders in deceiving the public and Congress about the conduct of the United States in Southeast Asia. Nixon sought to bar publication by the *New York Times*, but the Supreme Court ruled in favor of the newspaper on the basis of the First Amendment. Within weeks, a complete version of the Pentagon Papers became a best-selling book, and in 1972 the *New York Times* won a Pulitzer Prize for the series of articles. Frustrated in his attempt to suppress the report, Nixon directed the Department of Justice to prosecute Ellsberg on charges of conspiracy, espionage, and theft. Meanwhile, Hunt and Liddy, seeking to discredit Ellsberg, broke into the office of his former psychiatrist. They found nothing that would make their target less heroic in the eyes of an increasingly skeptical public, and by 1973 the charges against Ellsberg were dropped after the Nixon administration itself stood guilty of misconduct.

Meanwhile, Nixon ran a skillful negative campaign charging George McGovern, the liberal Democrat who had won his party's nomination on the first ballot, with supporting "abortion, acid [LSD], and amnesty" for those who had resisted the draft or deserted the armed forces. The Republicans also informed the news media that McGovern's running mate, Senator Thomas Eagleton, had once undergone electric shock therapy for depression, thus forcing his resignation from the Democratic team. Voter turnout fell to an all-time low, and McGovern lost every state but Massachusetts. It was only later that bumper stickers read, "Don't Blame Me, I'm from Massachusetts."

The Committee to Re-Elect the President (CREEP) enjoyed a huge war chest and spent a good portion on dirty tricks designed to divide the Democrats and discredit them in the eyes of the voting public. The most ambitious plan—wiretapping the Democratic National Committee headquarters—backfired.

On June 17, 1972, a security team had tripped up a group of intruders hired by CREEP to install listening devices in the Washington, D.C., Watergate apartment and office complex where the Democrats were headquartered. The police arrested five men, who were later found guilty of conspiracy and burglary. Although Nixon disclaimed any knowledge of the plan, two *Washington Post* reporters, Bob Woodward and Carl Bernstein, followed a trail of evidence back to the nation's highest office.

Televised Senate hearings opened to public view more than a pattern of presidential wrongdoing: they showed an attempt to impede investigations of the Watergate case. Testifying before the committee, a former Nixon aide revealed the existence of secret tape recordings of conversations held in the Oval Office. After special prosecutor Archibald Cox refused to allow Nixon to claim executive privilege and withhold the tapes, the president ordered Cox's firing. This "Saturday Night Massacre," as it came to be called, further tarnished Nixon's reputation and swelled curiosity about the tapes. On June 24, 1974, the Supreme Court voted unanimously that Nixon had to release the tapes to a new special prosecutor, Leon Jaworski.

The Fall of the Executive

Although incomplete, the Watergate tapes proved sufficiently damning. The surviving portions documented Nixon's ravings against his enemies, including anti-Semitic slurs, and his conniving efforts to harass private citizens through federal agencies. The tapes also proved that Nixon had not only known about plans to cover up the Watergate break-in but had ordered it. In July 1974, the House Judiciary Committee adopted three articles of impeachment, charging Nixon with obstructing justice.

Charges of executive criminality had clouded the Nixon administration since his vice-president had resigned in disgrace. In 1972 Spiro Agnew had admitted accepting large kickbacks while governor of Maryland. Pleading no contest to this and to charges of federal income tax evasion, Agnew resigned from office in October 1973. Gerald Ford, a moderate Republican representative from Michigan, had replaced him and now stood in the wings while the president's drama unraveled.

Facing certain impeachment by the House of Representatives, Richard Nixon became, on August 9, 1974, the first U.S. president to resign from office.

CONCLUSION

The resignations of Richard Nixon and Spiro Agnew brought little relief to the feeling of national exhaustion that attended the Vietnam War. Although U.S. troops had pulled out in 1973 and the war officially ended in 1975, the accompanying mood did not dissipate but merely changed form. Bitterness lingered over the unprecedented—and, for many, humiliating—defeat. Moreover, confidence in the government's highest office was severely shaken. The passage of the War Powers Act in 1973, written to compel any future president to seek congressional approval for armed intervention abroad, dramatized both the widespread suspicion of presidential intentions and a yearning for peace. But the positive dream of community that had inspired Johnson, King, and a generation of student activists could not be revived. No other vision took its place.

In 1968 seven prominent antiwar protesters had been brought to trial for allegedly conspiring to disrupt the Democratic National Convention in Chicago. Just a few years later, the majority of Americans had concluded that presidents Johnson and Nixon had conspired to do far worse. They had intentionally deceived the public about the nature and fortunes of the war. This moral failure signaled a collapse at the center of the American political system. Since Dwight Eisenhower left office warning of the potential danger embedded in the military–industrial complex, no president had survived the presidency with his honor intact.

CHRONOLOGY

1964	President Lyndon Johnson calls for "an unconditional war on poverty"
	Tonkin Gulf resolution passes Congress
	The Economic Opportunity Act establishes the Office of Economic Opportunity
	Free speech movement gets under way at the University of California at Berkeley
	Johnson defeats conservative Barry Goldwater for president
1965	President Johnson authorizes Operation Rolling Thunder, the bombing of North Vietnam
	Teach-ins begin on college campuses
	First major march on Washington for peace is organized
	Watts uprising is the first of the major rebellions in black communities
1966	J. William Fulbright publishes *The Arrogance of Power*
	Uprisings break out in several cities
	Black Panther Party is formed
	National Organization for Women (NOW) is formed
1967	Antiwar rally in New York City draws 300,000
	U.S. supports Israel in Six-Day War
	Vietnam Veterans Against the War is formed
	Uprisings in Newark, Detroit, and other cities
	"Summer of Love"
1968	More than 500,000 U.S. ground troops are in Vietnam
	Tet Offensive in Vietnam, followed by international protests against U.S. policies
	Martin Luther King Jr. is assassinated; riots break out in more than 100 cities
	Vietnam peace talks begin in Paris
	Robert Kennedy is assassinated

	Democratic National Convention held in Chicago
	Richard Nixon elected president
	American Indian Movement (AIM) founded
1969	Woodstock music festival marks the high tide of the counterculture
	Stonewall Riot in Greenwich Village sparks the gay liberation movement
	Apollo 11 lands on the moon
1970	U.S. incursion into Cambodia sparks campus demonstrations; students killed at Kent State and Jackson State Universities
1971	Lieutenant William Calley Jr. is court-martialed for My Lai Massacre
	New York Times starts publishing the Pentagon Papers
1972	President Nixon visits China and Soviet Union
	Strategic Arms Limitation Treaty (SALT I) limits offensive intercontinental ballistic missiles
	Intruders attempting to "bug" Democratic headquarters in the Watergate complex are arrested
	Nixon is reelected in a landslide
	Christmas Day bombing of North Vietnam ordered by Nixon
1973	Paris Peace Agreement ends war in Vietnam
	FBI seizes Indian occupants of Wounded Knee, South Dakota
	Watergate burglars on trial; congressional hearings on Watergate
	CIA destabilizes elected Chilean government, which is overthrown
	Vice-President Spiro T. Agnew resigns
1974	House Judiciary Committee adopts articles of impeachment against Nixon
	Nixon resigns the presidency

REVIEW QUESTIONS

1. Discuss the events that led up to and contributed to U.S. involvement in Vietnam. How did U.S. involvement in the war affect domestic programs?

2. Discuss the reasons why the protest movement against the Vietnam War started on college campuses. Describe how these movements were organized and how the opponents of the war differed from the supporters.

3. Discuss the programs sponsored by Johnson's plan for a Great Society. What was their impact on urban poverty in the late 1960s?

4. What was the impact of the assassinations of Martin Luther King Jr. and Robert Kennedy on the election of 1968? How were various communities affected?

5. How were the "politics of identity" movements different from earlier civil rights organizations? In what ways did the various movements resemble one another?

6. Why did Richard Nixon enjoy such a huge electoral victory in 1972? Discuss his foreign and domestic policies. What led to his sudden downfall?

RECOMMENDED READING

Terry H. Anderson, *The Movement and the Sixties* (1995). A richly detailed and highly readable account of the political and cultural movements of the 1960s, beginning with an overview of the significance of the cold war and ending with an assessment of the impact of the various movements.

Loren Baritz, *Backfire: A History of How American Culture Led Us into Vietnam and Made Us Fight the Way We Did* (1985). A keen study of U.S. military policies and dissent within the military during the Vietnam War. Baritz shows how decisions for aggressive military policies in Vietnam divided poorer young men from middle- and upper-class men by sending to war those who did not or could not manage deferments.

Alexander Bloom and Wini Breines, eds., *Takin' It to the Streets: A Sixties Reader* (1996). A useful and popular anthology of documents from the time that emphasizes the connections of political and cultural developments.

Mary C. Brennan, *Turning Right in the Sixties: The Conservative Capture of the GOP* (1995). Challenges the conventional depiction of the 1960s as a time when liberal and radicals flourished. Brennan discusses the rise of conservatives within the Republican Party and their emergence as the dominant force in American politics by 1980. She focuses on grassroots organizations and their ability to appeal to discontented but generally apolitical Americans.

Susan J. Douglas, *Where the Girls Are: Growing Up Female with the Mass Media* (1994). A witty and perceptive interpretation of the images created for young women in the 1960s.

Neil Sheehan, *A Bright Shining Lie: John Paul Vann and America in Vietnam* (1988). A study of U.S. government deception of the public. Sheehan especially emphasizes the ways in which prowar messages played on false images of a noble and committed South Vietnamese government.

Athan Theoharis, *Spying on Americans* (1978). A sweeping view of the 1960s and early 1970s, including FBI and CIA investigations and "dirty tricks" against dissidents.

Fred Turner, *Echoes of Combat: The Vietnam War in American Memory* (1996). Examines the paradox of a war that many Americans hope to forget and the rise of a "memory industry" devoted to its preservation. Turner asks two main questions: What are Americans remembering? What are they trying to forget?

William L. Van Deburg, *New Day in Babylon: The Black Power Movement and American Culture, 1965–1975* (1992). A well-researched and lively study of the transformation of racial consciousness among African Americans.

Bob Woodward and Carl Bernstein, *The Final Days* (1976). Journalistic accounts of the Watergate cover-up by the news team that broke the first stories. The authors trace the series of events that led to the resignation of President Nixon.

Marilyn B. Young, *The Vietnam Wars, 1945–1990* (1991). An excellent overview of the involvement of the French and the American military and diplomatic forces in Vietnam from the 1910s to 1975, and of the various movements against them.

CHAPTER THIRTY

THE OVEREXTENDED SOCIETY

1974–1980

AMERICAN COMMUNITIES
Three Mile Island, Pennsylvania

On Wednesday, March 28, 1979, a series of mechanical problems and judgment errors at the nuclear generating facility at Three Mile Island (TMI), near Harrisburg, Pennsylvania, led to the loss of a reactor's protective blanket of water. As much as two-thirds of the nuclear core was uncovered, causing the formation of a dangerously explosive hydrogen bubble and a massive release of radioactive gas into the atmosphere and posing a danger of a catastrophic core meltdown. The plant director declared a site emergency and reported a "slight problem" to the governor at 7:40 A.M. By 9:00 A.M. President Jimmy Carter had been notified. The Associated Press issued a national news bulletin announcing a general emergency but stating (mistakenly) that no radiation had been released. Metropolitan Edison, which ran the TMI facility, denied the existence of any danger.

At 8:00 A.M. on Friday, when a higher-than-anticipated radiation level above a vent was recorded, staff at the Nuclear Regulatory Commission suggested an evacuation of people living near the plant. Fearing panic, the governor urged residents within ten miles of TMI to stay indoors with their windows shut. Only pregnant women and preschool children within five miles of the facility were advised to leave the area. Federal officials ordered the shipment to Pennsylvania of massive doses of potassium iodide, which, taken orally, saturates the thyroid gland and inhibits absorption of radiation. While nearly 150,000 residents fled their homes, President and Rosalynn Carter tried to reassure the striken community by visiting the site.

Ten days later, on Monday, April 9, Pennsylvania governor Richard Thornburgh announced that the danger of a meltdown had passed. The Nuclear Regulatory Commission, equally eager to end the crisis, reported that the size of the hydrogen bubble had decreased. The situation was now stable, the officials agreed. There was no longer any danger of explosion.

What had seemed an isolated event in one community grew quickly into a regional phenomenon with international repercussions. The world waited, as one newscaster put it, while "the danger faced by man for tampering with natural forces, a theme familiar from the myth of Prometheus to the story of Frankenstein, moved closer to fact from fantasy." During the crisis, millions of people living in eastern states downwind of TMI stayed glued to their televisions or radios. Ten days after the near-meltdown, elevated levels of radioactivity were found in milk supplies several hundred miles away. People throughout the mid-Atlantic area worried for months about consuming contaminated dairy products, meat, vegetables, and even jams or jellies coming from the agricultural region of central Pennsylvania. Massive demonstrations against nuclear power followed the accident, concluding in a rally of more than 200,000 people in New York City.

Closer to TMI, more than 1,000 people eventually became involved in legal claims of mental or physical harm. Protests and lawsuits against the plant's reopening continued for years, and its owner, General Public Utilities, teetered toward bankruptcy. Although steadfast proponents of nuclear energy argued that the events at TMI demonstrated that safety had prevailed even at the moment of the greatest potential danger, the scales had been tipped toward opponents of nuclear power plants.

The events at Three Mile Island capped a wave of community-based mobilizations against nuclear power. In 1975, a less serious accident at Brown's Ferry, Alabama, heightened public concern about safety. Broad coalitions, with members ranging from conservatives to liberals, from rural landowners to urban renters, formed to keep their communities safe from danger. Community groups defeated referendums to fund new nuclear facilities or rallied around candidates who promised to shut down existing ones. If few communities wanted nuclear power plants, fewer still were eager to accept the radioactive wastes they generated.

The economy itself helped slow the development of new plants. At the time of the TMI crisis, more than seventy generating plants had been built, producing altogether about 13 percent of the nation's electrical energy. Of the ninety-six still under construction and the thirty more planned, only a handful would ever be completed. The courts and regional authorities blocked the completed Shoreham plant on Long Island, New York, from going into operation. News of faulty construction and building-cost overruns sometimes topping 1,000 percent and amounting to hundreds of millions of dollars made local governments hesitant to back new projects.

The promoters of nuclear energy in the 1950s had billed it as a source of energy so cheap that utility companies would be able to "turn off the meter." Communities would bask in prosperity, enjoying the fruits of dramatic advances equal to those that followed the introduction of electricity itself seventy-five years earlier. As late as 1974 President Richard Nixon predicted that by 1980 nuclear power would free the United States of its dependence on foreign energy sources.

The end of the dream of unlimited, inexpensive, and safe nuclear energy was one of many disappointments in the 1970s that shattered the expectations of experts and ordinary citizens alike for a time of unsurpassed abundance. Faced with diminishing financial resources, environmental disasters, discredited political leaders, and international defeats, many Americans lowered their expectations. The cold war finally began to wind down, but international affairs remained turbulent. The Middle East, a major source of oil, was becoming the new battleground.

Three Mile Island

KEY TOPICS

- The economics and politics of "stagflation"
- The Carter presidency
- Crisis in the cities and in the environment

- Community politics and the rise of the New Right
- The Iran hostage crisis
- The Republican presidential victory in 1980

STAGFLATION

Americans in the 1970s faced skyrocketing prices, rising unemployment, and low economic growth. Economists called this novel condition "stagflation." By 1975 unemployment had reached nearly 9 percent, the highest since the Great Depression, and it remained close to 7 percent for most of the rest of the decade. Inflation, meanwhile, reached double-digit numbers.

The United States had reached a turning point in its economic history. The country suddenly found itself falling behind Western Europe and Japan. The standard of living in the United States dropped below that of Denmark, West Germany, Sweden, and Switzerland. Polls at the end of the 1970s revealed that a majority of Americans believed conditions would worsen.

The Oil Crisis

In October 1973 gasoline prices nearly doubled, jumping from forty to nearly seventy cents per gallon. Worse, many dealers ran out of supplies. Several states introduced emergency rationing programs.

Although the energy crisis began suddenly, it had been decades in the making. The United States, which used about 70 percent of all oil produced in the world, had found the domestic supply sufficient until the late 1950s. Rising demand from then on outstripped national reserves, and Americans found themselves dependent on foreign oil.

Although oil prices remained stable through most of the 1960s, rising political and military tensions in the Middle East threatened that stability. After Israel overwhelmed its Arab neighbors in the Six-Day War of 1967, Arab nations became increasingly bitter toward the United States and other Western supporters of Israel. Then came the Yom Kippur War of 1973, so named because it began with an Arab attack on Israel on that Jewish holy day. On October 17, 1973, the Organization of Petroleum Exporting Countries (OPEC), a cartel of mainly Arab oil producers, announced an embargo on oil shipments to Israel's allies, including the United States. A few weeks later

President Nixon announced, "We are heading toward the most acute shortage of energy since World War II." The embargo continued until March 18, 1974.

As oil prices continued to skyrocket through the 1970s, some angry motorists began to look suspiciously at U.S. oil companies. Skepticism grew as a congressional committee reported that American-owned Texaco Oil was withholding natural gas from the market and that Gulf Oil had overstated its crude oil costs and charged customers wildly inflated prices. Whatever the cause, whoever the scapegoat, the oil crisis played a major role in the economic downturn of 1974 and 1975, the worst since the Great Depression.

The Bill Comes Due

President Nixon appointed William Simon "energy czar," paving the way for the creation of the Department of Energy in 1977. Nixon also imposed emergency energy conservation measures. He ordered air travel cut by 10 percent and appealed to Congress to lower speed limits on state highways to fifty-five miles per hour and to extend daylight saving time into the winter months. State governments complied, turning down the thermostats in public buildings to sixty-eight degrees, reducing nonessential lighting, and restricting hours of service. Colleges and universities canceled midwinter sessions, and some factories voluntarily shortened the workday.

These conservation measures produced one unintended, positive result: a 23 percent reduction in highway deaths between 1973 and 1974 due to the lower speed limit. But children, meanwhile, returned home from school in the dark, workers shivered in their offices, and the poor and elderly succumbed to hypothermia in cold apartments.

With the cost of gasoline, oil, and electricity up, many other prices also rose, from apartment rents to telephone bills to restaurant checks. Inflation rose to 11 percent and assumed first place in a list of common worries, according to a 1974 poll; by 1980 it stood at 13.5 percent. The middle-class lifestyle that schoolteachers, secretaries, factory workers, and others had managed to create for themselves and their families on modest incomes became harder to maintain; for young families it was often impossible to achieve.

Falling Productivity

Many Americans had experienced the recessions of the 1950s, millions even remembered the Great Depression, but few were prepared to witness the death of entire sectors of basic industry. The problem, according to many experts, was not simply a result of dependence on foreign oil reserves. It had deeper roots—in the failure of American manufacturers to keep up with the rising industrial efficiency of Western Europe and Japan. As long as American manufacturers faced scant competition from abroad, they had little incentive to update their machinery or to establish management techniques that fully used the skills of younger, more educated managers and workers. American companies could meet large production quotas, but they could not fabricate high-quality goods at low cost.

Asian, Latin American, and European manufacturers offered consumers cheaper and better alternatives. Whereas the United States produced 60 percent of the world's steel in 1947, by 1975 American firms accounted for only 16 percent. Similar trends developed in related industries. Sales of American-made autos dropped by 11 million in 1973 and another 8 million in 1974. In high-tech electronics the United States scarcely competed against Japanese-produced televisions, radios, tape players, cameras, and computers.

To combat falling profits, some automakers turned to Mexico, Taiwan, South Korea, and the Philippines for cheaper labor. Many American automobiles were now "outsourced"—that is, made from parts produced abroad and imported into the United States as semifinished materials (which were subject to a lower tariff than finished goods).

A few American corporations tried to improve their production capacities by adopting the model of labor–management relations developed by their foremost competitors. "Quality work life" circles—American versions of Japanese factory teams—experienced far less success, however, than their Japanese counterparts. Older workers interpreted new management programs as an attempt to replace unions, and few new workers believed they would derive significant material benefits from the system. American industrial productivity continued to lag.

In agriculture the situation was equally grim. Ironically, a shortage of grain in the Soviet Union, Egypt, and the Third World during the 1970s hiked up agricultural prices and encouraged American farmers to produce a bounty of crops for export. But the huge increase in oil prices translated into higher gasoline and fertilizer costs, forcing farmers to borrow heavily from banks. Soon the high rates on borrowed money caught many farmers in a downward-spiraling debt cycle.

When overseas sales declined at the end of the 1970s, tens of thousands of farmers defaulted on loans and lost their farms to banks and credit companies. These failures often ended a way of life generations old. Many farmers survived only through part-time jobs in town. Many considered themselves fortunate if they could retire on the price offered by land developers, who turned their farms into suburban housing. Continuing soil erosion, high costs, and unstable prices offered a gloomy prospect for all but the leaders in corporate-style agribusiness, the 12 percent of farmers who made 90 percent of all farm income.

Blue-Collar Blues

In past decades labor unions had typically responded to inflation by negotiating new contracts or, if necessary, striking for higher pay. But by the 1970s the National Labor Relations Board was increasingly ruling in favor of management, making the formation of new union locals far more difficult. Between 1970 and 1982 the AFL-CIO lost nearly 30 percent of its membership, and its political influence dipped accordingly. Labor-backed measures now routinely failed in Congress, despite the Democratic majority.

The only real growth in organized labor took place among public employees, including teachers, civil service workers, and health professionals. However, their gains were often less than expected. During the 1970s local and state budgets sagged, due to inflation, lower revenues from business, and most of all a growing unwillingness of voters to shoulder a bigger tax burden.

By 1980 more than half of all married women and nearly 60 percent of mothers with children between the ages of six and seventeen were in the labor force. Yet despite these statistical changes, women had lost ground relative to men. In 1955 women earned 64 percent of the average wages paid to men; in 1980 they earned only 59 percent. The reason for this dip was that women were clustered in the clerical and service trades (among women professionals, teaching and nursing), where the lowest wages prevailed.

African American women made some gains. Through Title VII of the Civil Rights Act, outlawing discrimination by sex or race, and the establishment of the Equal Employment Opportunity Commission to enforce it, they managed to climb the lower levels of the job ladder. By 1980 northern black women's median earnings were about 95 percent of white women's earnings. Proportionately, slightly more black women than white were gainfully employed in technical, sales, and administrative jobs.

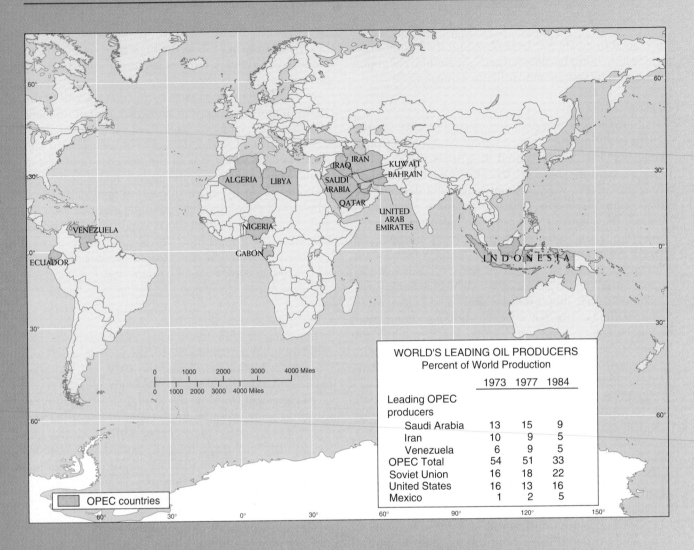

WORLD'S LEADING OIL PRODUCERS
Percent of World Production

	1973	1977	1984
Leading OPEC producers			
Saudi Arabia	13	15	9
Iran	10	9	5
Venezuela	6	9	5
OPEC Total	54	51	33
Soviet Union	16	18	22
United States	16	13	16
Mexico	1	2	5

OPEC countries

In contrast, Hispanic women, whose labor force participation leaped by 80 percent over the decade, were restricted to a very few, poorly paid occupations. Puerto Ricans found jobs in the garment industry of the Northeast; Mexican Americans more typically worked as domestics or agricultural laborers in the Southwest. Neither group earned much more than the minimum wage.

Sunbelt/Snowbelt

While the economic woes of the 1970s affected all sections of the country, regional differences became more pronounced. The Midwest and Northeast lost population and political influence as their economies slumped. The Sunbelt of the South, Southwest, and Far West, meanwhile, continued a trend begun during World War II (see Chapter 25). The economy of this region grew at a rate three times that of the rest of the nation.

By the 1970s the Sunbelt boasted a gross product greater than many nations and more cars, television sets, houses, and even miles of paved roads than the rest of the United States. Large influxes of immigrants from Latin America, the Caribbean, and Asia combined with the population shift of Americans from the depressed Northeast to boost the region's population.

The Sunbelt states had gained enormously from cold war defense spending as well as the allocation of Social Security funds. The number of residents over the age of sixty-five increased by 30 percent during the 1970s, reaching 26 million by 1980. Armed with retirement packages won decades earlier, huge "golden age" migrations created new communities in

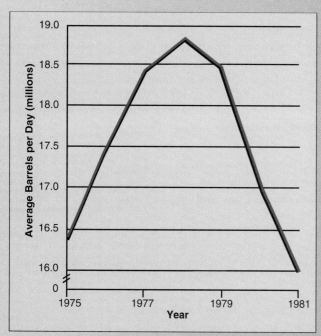

Decline of U.S. Oil Consumption, 1975–1981

Source: U.S. Department of Energy, *Monthly Energy Review*, June 1982.

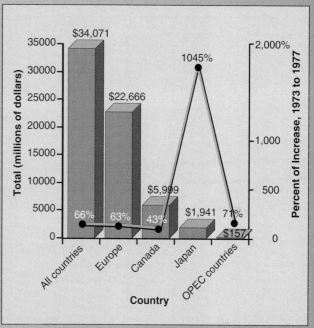

Foreign Direct Investment in the United States, 1977

Source: *Morgan Guaranty Survey*, September 1978.

1970s: Oil Consumption

OPEC successfully increased the world price of crude oil during the 1970s. Within a few years, all energy prices rose sharply in the United States. The resulting combination of inflation and recession prompted a new word for economic disorder: "stagflation."

These developments had two dramatic and unanticipated consequences. One was a sharp decline in U.S. oil consumption after 1978. High prices and shortages induced Americans to drive fewer miles and to switch off appliances when they weren't using them. In some cases the energy squeeze forced factories and businesses to close. A second consequence was increased foreign investment in the United States and with it, increased foreign ownership of U.S. businesses. Despite the role of the oil crisis in triggering this shift, only a small percentage of outside investment came from OPEC entrepreneurs. Most of it came from Europe, Canada, and Japan. Japanese investment in the United States increased more than tenfold between 1973 and 1977.

Florida, Arizona, and Southern California, pumping $8 billion per year into the Florida economy alone.

The South witnessed extraordinary changes in demographic and economic patterns. Southern cities reversed the century-long trend of out-migration among African Americans. In 1978 *Ebony* magazine listed the "ten best cities for Blacks"; five were the southern cities of Atlanta, Dallas, Houston, Baltimore, and Washington, all of them rigidly segregated only a few years earlier. For the first time, African Americans in large numbers returned south.

The Southwest and West changed yet more dramatically. Aided by air conditioning, water diversions, public improvements, and large-scale development, California became the nation's most populous state; Texas moved to third, behind New York. Former farms and deserts turned almost overnight into huge metropolitan areas dominated by automobile traffic and suburbs. Phoenix grew from 664,000 in 1960 to 1,509,000 in 1980, Las Vegas from 127,000 to 463,000.

The rapidly growing computer industry created California's Silicon Valley (named for the production of silicon chips), south of San Francisco, adding more than half a million jobs and billions of dollars of profit during the 1970s in Santa Clara County alone. Even when the number of lucrative defense contracts dropped off after the end of the Vietnam War, military outlays increased in high technology, with spin-offs in research and development centered in the Los Angeles area.

On the down side, much of the Sunbelt wealth tended to be temporary, producing a boom-and-bust economy. Corporate office buildings in cities such as Houston emptied almost as fast as they filled. Likewise,

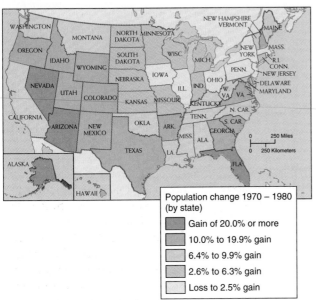

Population Shifts, 1970–1980   *Industrial decline in the Northeast coincided with an economic boom in the Sunbelt, encouraging millions of Americans to head for warmer climes and better jobs.*

textile and similarly labor-intensive industries that had earlier moved to the South for lower wages now relocated to Mexico, the Caribbean, or Asia. Even microchip processing, considered virtually a native Californian industry, gradually moved to Pacific islands and the Far East.

The Sunbelt's economic assets were also distributed very unevenly. Older Hispanic populations made only modest gains, and recent Mexican immigrants and Indian peoples survived on low incomes. Whereas eastern and midwestern states traditionally dependent on urban political machines and liberal voters spent significantly on public housing, education, and mass transit, the conservative Sunbelt states concentrated their tax and federal dollars on strengthening police forces, improving roads or sanitation systems for expanding suburbs, and creating budget surpluses.

The Snowbelt (or "Rustbelt"), as the Northeast and Upper Midwest came to be called, meanwhile suffered population losses following a sharp decline in industry. Of the nineteen metropolitan areas that lost population during the 1970s, all were old manufacturing centers, topped by New York, Cleveland, Pittsburgh, Boston, Philadelphia, and Buffalo. Reduced federal outlays compounded municipal budget crises, accentuating a feeling of defeat that prevailed in these areas.

New York City offered a spectacular example. A fiscal crisis in 1975 forced liberal mayor Abraham Beame to choose between wage freezes for public employees and devastating cuts and layoffs. Eventually,

with the municipal government teetering on the brink of bankruptcy, he chose both. In response to cutbacks in mass transit and the deterioration of municipal services, a large sector of the middle class left. At the same time, the number of poor in the city's population rose from 15 percent in 1969 to nearly 25 percent only fourteen years later.

"LEAN YEARS" PRESIDENTS

Gerald R. Ford and Jimmy Carter presided over a depressed economy and a nation of disillusioned citizens. Neither came up with a viable program to stimulate the economy. Carter admitted publicly that he doubted the government could solve this pressing problem, thus swelling the tide of voter apathy.

During the 1970s many Americans viewed electoral politics, especially at the federal level, as irrelevant to their lives. After the 1968 election, voter participation began a two-decade decline, with a little over half of eligible voters turning out for presidential elections.

"I'm a Ford, Not a Lincoln"

When Gerald Ford replaced Nixon as president in August 1974, an overwhelming majority of Americans reported that they supported the new president. But only a month after reassuring the public that "our long national nightmare is over," Ford turned around and pardoned Nixon for all the federal crimes he may have committed as president. Amid allegations that a deal had been struck, Ford irrevocably lost the nation's trust.

As president, Ford lacked a clear program and offered few initiatives to put the economy on the road to recovery. At best, he hoped to encourage slow but steady growth of the economy by keeping interest rates stable, raising taxes to reduce federal deficits, and above all restraining federal spending. His voluntary anti-inflation program, Whip Inflation Now, publicized by big red-and-white lapel buttons marked "WIN," failed to restore public confidence.

As rates of inflation and unemployment continued to soar, the midterm elections in 1974 added fifty-two Democrats to the House and four to the Senate, further eroding the Republican president's congressional support. Although Ford issued more vetoes of major bills than any other president in the twentieth century, Congress overrode most of them. Ford nevertheless swore to hold fast even against popular measures such as emergency job bills and education, health, and child nutrition programs. When New York City faced bankruptcy, Ford promised "to veto any bill that had as its purpose a federal bail-out." The New

York *Daily News* followed with the now famous headline "Ford to City: Drop Dead." When Congress united against him, the president relented.

The image that Ford conveyed was that of a pleasant person of modest ability. The press often caught him stumbling or mixing up his ideas.

First Lady Betty Ford, on the other hand, won the admiration of many Americans. She broke ranks with other Republicans to champion the Equal Rights Amendment. She once told a television reporter that she supported abortion rights, would not scold her adult daughter for having premarital sex, and probably would have tried marijuana herself if it had been in vogue when she was growing up. She also won praise for her courage in discussing her mastectomy for breast cancer and her voluntary entry into a substance abuse clinic for a drinking problem.

The 1976 Election

Despite his flagging popularity, Ford banked on his incumbency and put himself forward in 1976 as the Republican candidate for president. His chief Republican opponent was Ronald Reagan, a film and television actor and a former governor of California known widely for his conservative views. Most Republicans feared that a Reagan candidacy would push the party too far to the right and result in a landslide victory for the Democrats. Cautious in the aftermath of Watergate, the Republicans unenthusiastically nominated Ford and Senator Robert Dole of Kansas.

On the Democratic side, the public's mistrust of government was the most important factor in the selection of a presidential candidate. Jimmy Carter, a former one-term governor of Georgia, depicted himself as an antipolitician, an outsider, and someone who was independent of the Washington establishment. Carter's personal integrity was his chief qualification for the nation's highest office. Promising to apply the "Golden Rule . . . in all public matters," he further pledged, "I will never lie to you."

A moderate Democrat, Carter appealed to conservative and southern voters by playing up his credentials as a born-again Christian. At the same time he made fairly liberal statements on domestic policy, including civil rights, and favored a strong national defense. Carter also capitalized on the Nixon pardon with pointed references to the "Nixon–Ford Administration."

Carter and his running mate, Senator Walter Mondale of Minnesota, won the election with just over 50 percent of the popular vote and secured a 297-to-240 margin in the electoral college. Carter won more than 90 percent of the black vote, which provided his margin of victory in Pennsylvania, Ohio, and seven southern states. Apathy proved the most important factor. A record 46.7 percent of eligible voters, mainly the nation's poor, did not even bother to cast ballots.

The Carter Presidency

Jimmy Carter, the first president to come of age since World War II, remained an enigma to most political analysts. As a professed outsider, he never gained the confidence of congressional Democrats, let alone Republicans, and could never command their votes. To the contrary, he appeared uncertain and hesitant, a mirror image of the uneasiness that spread across the country in the late 1970s. Lacking an overarching political vision, Carter gradually shifted to the right.

The stalled economy resisted his best efforts, but Carter made his own mistakes. His tax reform measure of 1977 did little to help the middle classes; his energy bill, enacted in 1978, appeared to benefit the oil companies as much as consumers; and the health reform measures promised during his campaign failed altogether.

Carter's style reflected his managerial outlook as well as his lack of experience as a politician. He generally abstained from the customary bargaining with legislators. Lacking leadership ability, he tended to seek technical solutions to the country's enormous social problems. On occasion he got caught up in trivial detail, such as planning a players' schedule for the White House tennis courts. Overall, Carter relied on a

When Jimmy Carter took the oath of office in January 1977, he inherited an office dishonored by the Nixon–Ford administration. Hoping to dispel the political cynicism that had settled over the nation, he smiled broadly as he left the inaugural platform, bypassed his armored limousine, and walked hand-in-hand with Rosalynn Carter. Spectators cheered along the Pennsylvania Avenue parade route, greeting the new president's gesture as the symbolic end of an unhappy era.

small circle of advisers, mainly close friends from Georgia, and kept an unusually low profile for the nation's chief executive.

Although he appointed a higher percentage of women, African Americans, and Latinos to full-time federal appointments than any previous president and created a "superfund" to clean up abandoned toxic waste sites, Carter believed the nation faced problems that could not be solved by the redistribution of power and wealth that Democrats since FDR had advocated. He deregulated airlines, bringing fares down for millions of business and vacation travelers. He also removed the banks from congressional control, a policy change that inadvertently encouraged fraud, the granting of questionable loans, and eventually a round of disastrous bank failures.

Carter made no effort to renew the social welfare initiatives of his Democratic predecessor, Lyndon B. Johnson. Under Carter's administration, inner-city schools and health and social services declined. The federal funds that might have gone to poverty programs instead bolstered military spending. The press, aided by whistle-blowers working inside defense goods factories, found military spending loaded with fraud and abuse. Exposés of screwdrivers costing taxpayers fifty dollars each made Carter appear, despite his campaign promises, unable or unwilling to challenge corruption in government.

Inflation proved to be his worst enemy. As older Americans could recognize, half of all the inflation since 1940 had occurred in just ten years. Interest rates rose, driving mortgages out of reach for many would-be home buyers. Rents in many locations doubled, sales of automobiles and other consumer products slumped, and many small businesses went under. Tuition costs skyrocketed along with unemployment, and many young men and women who could neither afford to go to college nor find a job moved back home. Carter could not deliver on his promise to turn the economy around.

THE NEW POVERTY

Despite the diversion of federal funds to military spending during the Vietnam War, President Johnson's Great Society had brought a higher standard of living to many Americans. By the mid-1970s, however, it had become clear that many of these gains were short-lived. A contracting economy and persistent racism and sexism actually reversed these trends.

A Two-Tiered Society

During the 1970s Americans were healthier and living longer than at any time in history. Life expectancy rose from sixty years in 1930 to seventy-three years. The majority of Americans also enjoyed greater wealth. Real personal income had doubled since the late 1930s, and by 1977 median family income had reached $15,000.

The gap between rich and poor, however, was starting to grow wider. The wealthiest 20 percent of American families received about 40 percent of all income, while the poorest 20 percent received only about 5 percent. Nearly 26 million Americans—about 12 percent of the population—lived in poverty.

The widening gap between rich and poor was sharply defined by race. A disproportionate number of African Americans lived below the poverty line. Whereas 8.7 percent of whites lived in poverty in 1978, 30.6 of blacks and 21.6 percent of Hispanics did. The gains achieved by the civil rights movement and Great Society programs steadily eroded over the 1970s. In 1954, the year of the *Brown v. Board of Education* decision, black families earned about 53 percent of the income of white families. This figure rose to 60 percent in 1969 and peaked at 62 percent in 1975. By 1979 black family income had fallen back to about 57 percent of white family income. At the same time, residential segregation rose in most American cities.

The number of African Americans attending college peaked in 1976 at 9.3 percent of the black population, a 500 percent increase over the 1960 average. Implementing affirmative action mandates, major corporations began to recruit black college graduates, and a sizable number of African Americans found places in the professional, clerical, managerial, and technical realm. By the late 1970s one-third of all black workers had found white-collar employment.

But although 35 to 45 percent of African American families achieved middle-class status, the poor stayed behind in increasingly segregated urban neighborhoods and in jobs that did not pay a living wage. This trend dramatically affected the black community. Until the 1970s the majority of African Americans had held to common residential neighborhoods, institutions, and political outlooks. The growing income and residential disparity, which widened faster among blacks than among whites, eventually produced sharp differences among African Americans on social, economic, and political issues.

Toward the end of the decade, opportunities for advancement into the middle class dwindled. By 1980 fewer black students attended integrated schools than in 1954, except in the South, where about half the black students did. In 1975 a major clash between local white residents and black children occurred in Boston when a federally mandated busing plan was put into operation. By the end of the decade the busing controversy had nearly disappeared because federal judges hesitated to mandate such programs. But more important was the change in the racial composition of American cities. By 1980 big-city school systems served mainly African American and Latino children, making the issue of integration moot. By this time, the dropout rate of black teenagers had reached 50 percent in inner-city schools.

New legal rulings closed off important routes to employment in the professions. To ensure acceptance of a minimum number of minority students, the University of California–Davis Medical School had established a quota system. In 1973 and 1974 the school denied admission to Allan Bakke, a white student. Bakke sued the university for "reverse discrimination," claiming his academic record surpassed that of the sixteen minority students who were admitted. The U.S. Supreme Court handed down a five-to-four decision on June 18, 1978, stating that the use of an "explicit racial classification" in situations where no earlier discrimination had been demonstrated violated the equal protection clause of the Fourteenth Amendment. The Court ordered the University of California to admit Bakke to its medical school. Affirmative action programs could now operate only when "a legacy of unequal treatment" could be proved.

The Feminization of Poverty

Women as a group lost economic ground during the 1970s. Despite a growing rate of labor force participation, the majority of women gainfully employed did not earn a living wage. Even if employed, women usually lost ground following a divorce, especially as new no-fault divorce laws lowered or eradicated alimony. Moreover, the majority of men defaulted on child-support payments within one year of separation. Whereas divorced men enjoyed an average 42 percent increase in their standard of living, divorced women saw theirs drop by 73 percent. During the 1970s the number of poor families headed by women increased nearly 70 percent.

A sharp rise in teenage pregnancy reinforced this pattern. Many of these mothers were too young to have gained either the education or skills to secure jobs that would pay enough to support themselves and their children. Even with Aid to Families with Dependent Children (AFDC) payments and food stamps, it was impossible for these single mothers to keep their families above the poverty level. And with rising inflation, the real incomes of welfare recipients dropped in many states to a little over half their 1970 levels.

The National Advisory Council on Economic Opportunity issued a report in 1982 predicting that if these trends persisted, by the turn of the century female heads of households and their children would account for just about all the poor in the United States.

"A Permanent Underclass"

"Behind the [ghetto's] crumbling walls," *Time* magazine announced in 1977, "lives a large group of people who are more intractable, more socially alien and more hostile than almost anyone had imagined. They are the unreachables: the American underclass. . . ." Although the majority of poor Americans lived in rural areas and small towns, with Missouri, South Dakota, and Texas accounting for the nation's largest pockets of poverty, *Time* and other news media spotlighted the inner cities. "The underclass," in their discussions, became a metaphor for the deteriorating conditions of urban America.

The majority of African Americans, six out of ten, did live in central cities with high unemployment rates. With the drastic cutbacks of the 1970s, large numbers of municipal workers, which now included many African Americans and Puerto Ricans, were laid off. Jobs became as scarce as at any time since the 1930s.

The bleak prospects took a toll especially on young African Americans. A black child was twice as likely to die before reaching the first birthday than a white child and four times more likely to be killed between the ages of one and four. The high school dropout rate skyrocketed during the 1970s. Among dropouts, illiteracy, frequent arrests, alcohol and drug abuse, and long-term public welfare were endemic.

Sociologists also associated the growth of teenage poverty with a rise in crime. Rates of violent crimes, such as aggravated assault, robbery, rape, and murder, increased dramatically in all poor neighborhoods throughout the country. The number of serious crimes, such as burglary, car theft, and murder, perpetrated by children between the ages of ten and seventeen increased at an alarming rate.

Indian peoples remained the poorest and most disadvantaged of all racial or ethnic groups. They suffered from an excessive death rate: six times the national average from tuberculosis, and twenty-two times the national average from alcohol-related causes. Struggles to achieve tribal autonomy continued but were considerably slowed by neighboring whites who filed competing land and mineral claims. The Supreme Court, in *United States v. Wheeler,* ruled in 1978 that tribal sovereignty existed "only at the sufferance of Congress."

COMMUNITIES AND GRASS-ROOTS POLITICS

The mass demonstrations of the 1960s gave way to a different style of political mobilization centered squarely in communities. Unlike national elections, which registered increasing voter apathy, local campaigns brought people to the voting booth and into voluntary associations.

The New Urban Politics

In many cities, new groups came into political power. In several college towns, such as Berkeley, California, and Eugene, Oregon, both of which had been centers of student activism during the 1960s, student coalitions were formed to secure seats for their candidates on city councils. In 1973 labor unions, college students, and community groups in Madison, Wisconsin, elected a former student activist to the first of three terms as mayor.

African American candidates scored impressive victories during the 1970s. The newly elected African American mayor of Atlanta, Maynard Johnson, concluded that "politics is the civil rights movement of the 1970s." By 1978, 2,733 African Americans held elected offices in the South, ten times the number a decade earlier. Voters had elected African American mayors in New Orleans and Atlanta. In other parts of the country, black mayors, such as Coleman Young in Detroit and Richard Hatcher in Gary, held power along with many minor black officials.

Other racial or ethnic groups advanced more slowly, rarely in proportion to their actual numbers in the population. Mexican Americans had already won offices in little Crystal City, Texas, and in 1978 took control for the first time of a major city council, in San Antonio. They also scored electoral victories in other parts of Texas and in New Mexico and developed strong neighborhood or ward organizations in southern California. Puerto Ricans elected a handful of local officials in New York, mostly in the Bronx. Asian Americans advanced in similar fashion in parts of Hawai'i.

The fiscal crises of the 1970s nevertheless undercut these efforts to reform municipal government. Most of these new officials found themselves unable to make the sweeping changes they had promised during their campaigns. Temporary job programs could not counteract the effects of factory shutdowns and the disappearance of industrial jobs. Affirmative action programs aroused cries of "reverse discrimination" from angered whites who felt that minorities' progress had been registered at their expense. Although their support often dissipated when the cycle of poverty and violence could not be slowed, community-based mobilizations remained the political touchstone of the decade.

The City and the Neighborhood

The Community Development Act of 1974, signed by President Ford, combined federal grant programs for cities into a single program and put mayors and city managers directly in charge of spending. With grants totaling $8.4 billion over three years, city governments could allocate funds as they saw fit. These community development block grants encouraged citizens to take part in local planning efforts.

Groups of preservationists organized to save historical buildings and public spaces and formed land trusts to take over and refurbish old houses or turn vacant lots into neighborhood parks.

Local and national foundations joined federal agencies in funding Community Development Corporations (CDCs) through a series of antipoverty agencies. These community groups promoted "development banks" that would facilitate "sweat equity," that is, the granting of low-interest mortgage loans to buyers willing to rebuild or refurbish dilapidated housing themselves. They also acted to prevent local banks from closing when a neighborhood became mainly black.

In 1979 President Carter's National Commission on Neighborhoods compiled 200 specific recommendations to broaden and speed the development of local institutions. The long-range goal of such efforts, the Commission suggested, should be "to reorganize our society . . . to a new democratic system of grassroots involvement." But local advocacy groups were often caught up in creating the kinds of large-scale, well-funded projects that foundations and federal agencies desired rather than the projects they had originally intended to create. And even when local preservationists succeeded, "gentrification" often followed restoration, with poor residents displaced by "yuppies" (young upwardly mobile professionals) who craved the increasingly fashionable old homes.

The Endangered Environment

The discovery of high rates of cancer and birth defects in Love Canal, near Buffalo, New York, offered compelling evidence of a growing danger to many American communities. Here toxic wastes dumped by the Hooker Chemical Laboratory had oozed into basements and backyards, and homemaker Lois Gibbs organized a vigorous publicity campaign to draw attention to the grim situation. Meanwhile, outraged Florida residents realized that the damming of the Everglades for sugar production and housing developments, undertaken by the Army Corps of Engineers decades earlier, had degraded thousands of acres of land, eliminating natural filtration systems and killing millions of birds and other species.

Even before the energy crisis, many Americans had begun to make changes in their own ways of living. Many families began to save glass bottles and newspapers for reuse. Some began to reduce or eliminate the consumption of beef, which was far more costly to produce than the grains fed to cattle. Backyard vegetable gardens became popular, as did grocers who stocked organic foods, which were grown without pesticides or chemical fertilizers.

The environmentalist movement grew stronger on college campuses and in a handful of long-standing organizations, such as the Audubon Society and the Wilderness Society. The Sierra Club, formed in 1892 as a small society of Western mountain hikers, grew to 100,000 members in 1970 and a half million over the next decade. New groups sprang up in response to the energy crisis, often devoted to developing renewable energy sources such as solar power.

Cutting across nearly all population groups and regions, environmentalists reached such traditionally conservative areas as the Deep South with warnings of the dangers of toxic wastes, destruction of wetlands, and ruin of fishing industries. Sometimes campaigns succeeded in blocking massive construction projects such as nuclear energy plants; more often they halted small-scale destruction of a nature habitat or historic urban district. These campaigns made the public more aware of the consequences of private and government decisions about the environment. Responding to organized pressure groups, Congress passed scores of bills designed to protect endangered species, reduce pollution caused by automobile emissions, limit and ban the use of some pesticides, and control strip mining practices. The Environmental Protection Agency (EPA), established in 1970, grew to become the federal government's largest regulatory agency, the employer of over 10,000 people by the end of the decade.

Environmentalists enjoyed only limited success in bringing about large-scale changes in policy. Clean-air mandates passed by Congress for cities to deal with pollution problems were usually avoided. Despite the introduction of lead-free gasoline, the air in major metropolitan areas grew worse because automobile traffic increased at a very fast pace. Environmentalists lost an important campaign with the approval of the Alaska Pipeline, 800 miles of pipe connecting oil fields with refining facilities.

Small-Town America

A host of unresolved problems, ranging from air pollution to rising crime rates to higher taxes, encouraged a massive exodus from the nation's cities. Between 1970 and 1975, for every 100 people relocating to metropolitan areas, 138 moved out. Newer residential communities in small towns and in semirural or formerly rural areas grew at a fast pace, attracting retirees and others seeking solace or security.

Government programs such as mortgage guarantees and low-interest financing on individual homes promoted these large low-density developments of single-family houses. In many regions, the countryside gradually disappeared into "exurbia," a trend that population experts Peter A. Morison and Judith P. Wheeler attributed to the American "wish to love one's neighbor but keep him at arm's length." In opinion polls, large numbers of respondents reported that they wanted to live in a small town that was not a suburb but was still no more than thirty miles from a major city.

Soon even small towns developed their own suburbs, usually moderate-income tracts of ranch houses squeezed between older wood-frame colonial or Victorian farm houses. Federal subsidies for the construction of sewage and water lines, originally intended to aid rural communities, now became springboards for further development. Ironically, shopping malls on former farmland now drained commercial activity from the small-town centers, channeling the benefits of development to the chain stores rather than to local merchants.

Some communities organized to oppose these trends. Following the publication of E. F. Schumacher's *Small Is Beautiful* (1973), groups of people began to examine "bigness" and its toll on humanity. They principally sought to rebuild communities on a smaller scale and therefore campaigned to preserve the environment by opposing further development and the construction of new highways, nuclear energy generating plants, and toxic dumps. In Vermont, liberal "hippies" and "back-to-the-landers" joined traditionally conservative landowners to defeat a 1974 gubernatorial plan to attract developers. In other locales, such as the Berkshire Mountains, community land trusts were organized to encourage common ownership of the land. "From coast to coast," the *New York Times* reported, "environmental, economic and social pressures have impelled hundreds of cities and towns to adopt limitations on the size and character of their populations." To encourage public discussion of land-use issues, such as the use of open space or farms for commercial development, President Carter created the Small Community and Rural Development Policy group.

Some small towns, especially those without mild climates or nearby cities, did not prosper during the 1970s. In parts of Kansas, Iowa, and the Dakotas, where family farms failed at a high rate, other businesses also closed. A snowball effect resulted in rundown schools, inadequate medical care, and abandoned movie theaters and grocery stores. Only nursing homes and funeral parlors continued to thrive.

THE NEW CONSERVATISM

While many Americans concentrated their political energies in their communities, others organized to turn back the liberal Great Society programs. Sizable numbers of taxpayers resented the hikes required to fund government programs on behalf of minorities or to provide expanded social services for the poor. In 1978 California voters staged a "taxpayers' revolt," approving Proposition 13, which cut property taxes and government revenues for social programs and education. In other economically hard-pressed urban areas, white voters who resented the gains made by African Americans or Latinos formed a powerful backlash movement. Poles in Chicago, Irish in Boston, and Italians and Jews in Brooklyn, for example, organized to consolidate their political influence. By the end of the decade, the only substantial increase in voter participation was among conservatives.

The New Right

The political surge rightward in the 1970s united many traditional probusiness conservatives with a new constituency of alienated lower-class white voters. It gained intellectual respectability from neoconservatives, former liberals who blamed the social movements of the 1960s for the demoralization of the nation. The American Enterprise Institute and the Heritage Foundation, richly funded by major corporations, established major research centers for conservative scholars. These and other foundations also funded campus publications attacking welfare programs, affirmative action, and environmentalism.

The largest New Right constituency, however, united behind major conservative religious and political leaders to preserve and promote what they viewed as traditional values. Evangelical Christians became the backbone of key organizations such as the National Conservative Political Action Committee and, most especially, Moral Majority.

Conservatives were among the first political groups to employ direct mail. Greater success came from the work of televangelists. By the late 1960s televangelists such as Pat Robertson and Jim Bakker mixed conservative political messages with appeals to prayer. The *Old Time Gospel Hour,* featuring the Reverend Jerry Falwell, was broadcast by over 200 television stations and 300 radio stations each week. Christian broadcasters generally endorsed Falwell's faith that "the free-enterprise system is clearly outlined in the Book of Proverbs of the Bible." By the end of the decade more than 1,400 radio stations and 30 TV stations specialized in religious broadcasts and reached an audience of perhaps 20 million weekly.

Falwell formed the Moral Majority as a political lobbying group to advocate tough laws against homosexuality and pornography, a reduction of government services, especially welfare payments to poor families, and increased spending for a stronger national defense.

Archie Bunker (Carroll O'Connor) and Edith Bunker (Jean Stapleton) endowed television with a social and political complexity that previous situation comedies had scrupulously avoided. First broadcast in 1971, All in the Family featured a working-class family living in Queens, New York, trying to sort out their differences with Archie, the highly bigoted but lovable center of the household. Producer Norman Lear explained that the show "holds a mirror up to our prejudices. . . . We laugh now, swallowing just the littlest bit of truth about ourselves, and it sits there for the unconscious to toss about later."

Jesse Helms was the first major politician to appeal directly to the New Right and to build his own impressive fundraising empire with its help. A North Carolina journalist who had fought the integration of public schools and defended the Ku Klux Klan, he had often attacked Martin Luther King, Jr., as a Communist-influenced demagogue. Helms entered national politics as a Goldwater supporter in 1964 and ran for the Senate in 1972. Carried to victory with Nixon's success in North Carolina, Helms immediately promoted a host of conservative bills. He introduced legislation to allow automobile owners or dealers to disconnect mandatory antipollution devices. He also defended the Watergate break-ins as necessary to offset the "traitorous conduct" of antiwar activists. By 1978 he had raised $8.1 million, the largest amount ever, for his successful reelection campaign. Helms won few victories in the Senate but built a powerful, loyal, and wealthy following.

Anti-ERA, Antiabortion

The New Right rallied support for a balanced budget amendment to the Constitution, sought unsuccessfully to return prayers to public schools, and endorsed the Supreme Court's approval of the death penalty in 1977.

New Right's best-funded campaigns focused on restoring "traditional family values," destroyed, they said, by the women's liberation movement.

The defeat of the Equal Rights Amendment (ERA) stood at the top of the New Right agenda. Approved by Congress in March 1972, nearly fifty years after its introduction (see Chapter 22), the ERA stated "Equality of rights under the law shall not be denied or abridged by the United States or by any State on account of sex." Endorsed by the Democratic and Republican parties, the amendment appeared likely to be ratified by the individual states. Nearly all mainstream women's organizations, including the Girl Scouts of America, endorsed the ERA, as had first ladies Lady Bird Johnson, Betty Ford, and Rosalynn Carter. Even the AFL-CIO retracted its longstanding opposition and endorsed the amendment.

Cued by this groundswell in favor of the ERA, the New Right swung into action. Phyllis Schlafly, a self-described suburban housewife and popular conservative lecturer, headed the STOP ERA campaign, describing the amendment's supporters as "a bunch of bitter women seeking a constitutional cure for their personal problems." Conservatives mounted large, expensive campaigns in each swing state and overwhelmed pro-ERA resources. Although thirty-five states had ratified the ERA by 1979, the amendment remained three votes short of passage. Despite a three-year extension, the ERA died in 1982.

The New Right also waged a steady campaign against abortion, which the women's liberation movement had defined as a woman's right rather than a mere medical issue. In 1973 the Supreme Court had ruled in *Roe v. Wade* that state laws decreeing abortion a crime during the first two trimesters of pregnancy constituted a violation of a woman's right of privacy. Opponents of this decision rallied for a constitutional amendment defining conception as the beginning of life and argued that the "rights of the unborn" superseded a woman's right to control her own body. The Roman Catholic Church organized the first antiabortion demonstrations after the Supreme Court's decision and sponsored the formation of the National Right to Life Committee, which claimed 11 million members by 1980.

Antiabortion groups also picketed Planned Parenthood counseling centers, intimidating potential clients. They rallied against government-subsidized day-care centers and against sex education programs in public schools. A small minority turned to more extreme actions, bombing dozens of abortion clinics.

"The Me Decade"

The shift in the political winds of the 1970s registered not only the rise of the New Right but also the disengagement of a sizeable number of Americans from politics altogether. In 1976 novelist Tom Wolfe coined the phrase "the Me Decade" to describe an era obsessed with personal well-being, happiness, and emotional security. Health foods and diet crazes, a mania for physical fitness, and a quest for happiness through therapy involved millions of middle-class Americans. Historian Christopher Lasch provided his own label for this enterprise in the title of his best-selling book, *The Culture of Narcissism: American Life in an Age of Diminishing Expectations* (1978).

The rise of the "human potential movement" provided a vivid example of this trend. The most successful was Erhard Seminars Training (EST), a self-help program blending insights from psychology and mysticism. Founded by Werner Erhard (a former door-to-door encyclopedia salesperson), the institute taught individuals to form images of themselves as successful and satisfied. Through 60 hours of intensive training involving play acting and humiliation, participants learned one major lesson: "You are the one and only source of your experience. You created it." Priced at $400 for a series of two weekend sessions, EST peaked at 6,000 participants per month, grossing $25 million in revenue in 1980.

Transcendental meditation (TM) promised a shortcut to mental tranquility and found numerous advocates among Wall Street brokers, Pentagon officials, and star athletes. Techniques of TM were taught in more than 200 special teaching centers and practiced by a reputed 350,000 devotees.

Religious cults also formed in large numbers during the 1970s. The Unification Church, founded by the Korean Reverend Sun Myung Moon, extracted intense personal loyalty from its youthful disciples. Moon's financial empire, which included hundreds of retail businesses and the *Washington Times*, a conservative daily newspaper, proved very lucrative and kept his church solvent despite numerous lawsuits. By contrast, Jim Jones's People's Temple, an interracial movement organized in the California Bay Area, ended in a mass murder and suicide when Jones induced over 900 of his followers to take cyanide-laced Kool Aid in Guyana in 1978.

Popular music expressed and reinforced these trends. The songs of community and hope common in the late 1960s gave way to songs of despair or nihilism. Bruce Springsteen, whose lyrics lamented the disappearance of the white working class, became the decade's most popular new rock artist. At the same time, heavy metal bands such as Kiss as well as punk and new-wave artists underscored themes of decadence. Country and western music hit its peak with numerous new all-C&W radio stations. Willie Nelson sang melodic refrains reeking of loneliness or nostalgia and appealing to older, white, working-class Americans.

ADJUSTING TO A NEW WORLD

In April 1975 the North Vietnamese struck Saigon and easily captured the city as the South Vietnamese army fell apart without U.S. assistance. All fighting stopped within a few weeks, and Saigon was renamed Ho Chi Minh City. Vietnam was reunited under a government dominated by communists. For the Americans, this outcome underscored the futility of their involvement.

By the mid-1970s a new realism prevailed in U.S. diplomacy. Presidents Ford and Carter, as well as their chief advisers, acknowledged that the cost of fighting the Vietnam War had been high, speeding the decline of the United States as the reigning superpower. The realists shared with dissatisfied nationalists a single goal: no more Vietnams.

A Thaw in the Cold War

The military defeat in Vietnam forced the makers of U.S. foreign policy to reassess priorities. The United States must continue to defend its "vital interests," Ford's secretary of state Henry Kissinger declared, but must also understand that "Soviet–American relations are not designed for tests of manhood." Both nations had experienced a decline of power in world affairs. And both were suffering from the already enormous and relentlessly escalating costs of sustaining a prolonged cold war.

At the close of World War II, the United States could afford to allocate huge portions of its ample economic resources to maintaining and enlarging its global interests. Soon, however, military and defense expenses began to grow at a pace much faster than the economy itself. Whereas the Korean War cost around $69.5 billion, the Vietnam War cost $172.2 billion. Clandestine operations, alliance building, and weapons production accounted for trillions of dollars more.

Military spending at this level eventually took its toll on the American economy, especially as the federal government increasingly relied on deficit spending in an attempt to cover the bill. The federal debt, which stood at $257 billion in 1950, had jumped to $908 billion in 1980, and increasingly large parts of the federal budget went to paying just the interest on this debt. At the same time, military spending diverted funds away from programs that could have strengthened the economy. The results were disastrous. While the United States endured falling productivity levels and rates of personal savings, and a disappearing skilled workforce, other nations rushed ahead.

The Soviet Union, (whose economy suffered even greater setbacks from defense spending) joined the United States in moving toward détente. The signing of SALT I during Nixon's administration, followed by the U.S. withdrawal from Vietnam, encouraged new efforts to negotiate on strategic arms control. In November 1974 Ford and Brezhnev met in Vladivostok to set the terms of SALT II, and Carter secured the final agreement in 1979. However, the treaty failed to win confirmation from the Senate when the Soviet Union invaded Afghanistan in December 1979.

Although repeated conflicts in the Third World continued to slow the pace toward détente, leaders in both the United States and the Soviet Union recognized that their economic well-being depended on a reduction in defense spending.

Foreign Policy and "Moral Principles"

Historian Gaddis Smith has argued that "the four years of the Carter Administration were among the most significant in the history of American foreign policy in the twentieth century" because the whole legacy of a century of diplomatic relations came to bear on each major decision. For the first time since 1945 diplomacy tilted away from the cold war and toward global conflict over energy sources.

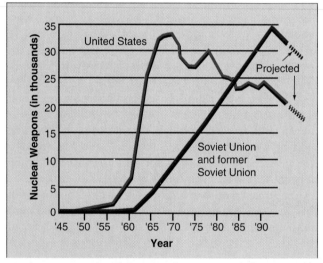

Nuclear Arsenals, the United States and the Soviet Union *During the cold war, both superpowers built up huge stockpiles of nuclear weapons, including sea and land missiles. President Lyndon Johnson began negotiations with the Soviet Union in an attempt to slow down the perilous nuclear arms race. In 1972, the Strategic Arms Limitation Treaty (SALT) set limits on offensive intercontinental ballistic missiles. SALT II, negotiated by President Carter in 1979, called for further reductions but failed to win approval in the U.S. Senate. Negotiations resumed under President Reagan and culminated in 1991 in the Strategic Arms Reduction Treaty (START), which included plans for the destruction of the stockpile of nuclear weapons.*

Source: James Sterngold, "Milestones of the Nuclear Era," New York Times, December 1, 1992, p. C10. Copyright © The New York Times Company; illustrations by Rebecca Perry and Martha hernandez; and the Bulletin of the Atomic Scientists.

Carter condemned policies that allowed the United States to support "right wing monarchs and military dictators" in the name of anticommunism. In 1976 a powerful human rights lobby pressured Congress to pass a bill that required the secretary of state to report annually on the status of human rights in all countries receiving aid from the United States and to cut off assistance to any country with a record of "gross violations." Carter's secretary of state, Cyrus R. Vance, and the assistant secretary for human rights and humanitarian affairs, Pat Derrian, worked effectively to punish or at least to censure repressive military regimes in Brazil, Argentina, and Chile. For the first time, leading U.S. diplomats spoke out against the South African apartheid regime.

But toward nations considered vital to U.S. interests, such as South Korea, the Philippines, and El Salvador, Carter put aside his principles to stabilize repressive regimes and dictatorship. In restoring formal diplomatic relations with the People's Republic of China in January 1979, Carter likewise overlooked the regular imprisonment of dissidents.

However, Carter did try to institute reforms at the CIA, particularly to halt the blatant intervention in the affairs of foreign governments. He appointed Admiral Stanfield Turner, a Rhodes scholar, as director and ordered a purge of the "rogue elephants" who had pursued covert operations in Southeast Asia during the Vietnam War. Under Turner, however, these reforms remained incomplete; they later proved temporary.

Carter scored his biggest moral victory in foreign affairs by paving the way for Panama to assume the ownership, operation, and defense of the Panama Canal Zone. Negotiations with Panama had begun during Johnson's administration, following riots by Panamanians against U.S. territorial rule in their country. Carter pressured the Senate to ratify new treaties in 1978 (by a vote of sixty-eight to thirty-two) that turned the Panama Canal over to Panama by the year 2000.

The Camp David Accords

Carter nearly triumphed in the Middle East. Early in his administration, Carter met privately with Israeli prime minister Menachem Begin to encourage conciliation

President Carter signs Mideast Peace treaty with Egyptian President Anwar Sadat and Israeli Prime Minister Menachem Begin in Washington, D.C., in March 1979. Considered Carter's greatest achievement in foreign policy, the negotiations resulted not only in the historic peace treaty but also in the Nobel Peace Prize for Begin and Sadat.

with Egypt. When negotiations between the two countries stalled in 1978, Carter brought Begin together with Egyptian president Anwar el-Sadat for a thirteen-day retreat at Camp David, Maryland.

The Camp David Accords, signed in September 1978, set the formal terms for peace in the region. Egypt became the first Arab country to recognize Israel's right to exist, as the two nations established mutual diplomatic relations for the first time since the founding of Israel in 1948. In return, Egypt regained control of the Sinai Penninsula, including important oil fields and airfields. Israel secured a virtually permanent guarantee of greatly enhanced U.S. military support. In 1979 Begin and Sadat shared the Nobel Prize for Peace.

But disappointment lay ahead. Carter staked his hopes for regional peace on the final achievement of statehood, or at least political autonomy, for Palestinians in a portion of their former lands now occupied by the Israelis. The accords specified that Israel would eventually return to its approximate borders of 1967. However, although Begin agreed to dismantle some Israeli settlements in the Sinai, the Israeli government continued to sponsor more and more Jewish settlements, expropriating Palestinian holdings. The final status of the Palestinians remained in limbo, as did that of Jerusalem, which many Christians and Muslims felt should be an autonomous holy city. Meanwhile Sadat grew increasingly isolated within the Arab world. In 1981 he was assassinated by Islamic fundamentalists.

CARTER'S "CRISIS OF CONFIDENCE"

Carter's modest victories in Middle East negotiations marked the final high point of his presidency. By 1979 it was clear that his domestic program for economic recovery had failed. To reassess his priorities, Carter withdrew with his staff to Camp David in July and emerged ten days later with a series of new energy proposals that Congress later rejected. But in his first public speech after the retreat, the president struck a nerve. The nation was experiencing a "crisis of confidence," he complained.

Carter's "malaise" speech backfired. His public approval rating hardly rose again from a trough of 26 percent. Many Americans resented the president for heaping blame on the public instead of taking responsibility for his own failures.

(Mis)Handling the Unexpected

As Carter's first term came to a close, multiple crises suddenly cut loose in foreign affairs. His secretary of state, Cyrus Vance, recommended well-planned negotiations to soothe Soviet–U.S. relations and resolve disagreements with Third World nations. National security adviser Zbigniew Brzezinski, a bitterly anti-

Communist Polish exile, adhered to cold war policies and interpreted events in even remote sections of Africa or South America as plays in a zero-sum game: wherever the United States lost influence, the Soviet Union gained, and vice versa. Mired in problems inherited from his predecessors, the president found himself disoriented by contradictory advice.

In 1979 the overthrow of the brutal Nicaraguan dictatorship of Anastasio Somoza, long-time ally of the United States, left Carter without a moderate successor to support. When the new Sandinista revolutionary government pleaded for help, Congress turned down Carter's request for $75 million in aid to Nicaragua. The Sandinistas aligned with Cuba and the Soviet Union and began to assist a revolutionary movement in El Salvador. The Carter administration continued to back the government in San Salvador even after the assassination of Oscar Romero, the Catholic archbishop who supported the revolutionaries. Following the rape and murder of four U.S. Catholic church women, apparently by the ultraright Salvadoran Armed Forces trained in the United States, peace activists and other Americans pleaded with Carter to withhold further military aid. Conservatives meanwhile demanded more funds to bolster the repressive anticommunist regime.

African nations vacillated between allying with the United States and courting the Soviet Union. In this tricky political territory, UN Ambassador (and former civil rights leader) Andrew Young, the first major African American diplomat assigned to Africa, scored an important victory in encouraging oil-rich Nigeria to resume economic relations with the United States. But Young could not persuade Carter to recognize the antiapartheid government of Angola, which had invited 20,000 Cuban troops to help in their fight against South Africa. Nor did Carter's and Young's criticisms of the South African regime, unaccompanied by any economic sanctions, satisfy black Africans. After Carter fired Young for having met secretly with the Palestine Liberation Organization (PLO), the president proved even less effective in negotiating with antiapartheid leaders.

The Soviet invasion of neighboring Afghanistan produced a major stalemate. Two Afghan military coups during the 1970s had troubled the Soviets, who feared that the United States might forge an alliance with a new right-wing government and create yet another border fortified with U.S. missiles. The war quickly bogged down, and Americans heard familiar stories, this time of Soviet soldiers using drugs and expressing disillusionment with their government.

President Carter responded to these events with his own corollary to the Monroe Doctrine. The so-called Carter Doctrine asserted the determination of the United States to protect its interests in yet another area of the world, the Persian Gulf. Carter acted on the advice of Brzezinski, who believed the Soviet Union would soon try to secure for itself a warm-water port on the Gulf, an area rich in oil and now vital to U.S. interests. The president backed up his policy by halting exports of grain and high technology to the Soviet Union, asking American athletes to boycott the 1980 Olympic Games in Moscow, and reinstituting registration for the military draft in the United States. The massive U.S. arms buildup of the 1980s was already under way.

By the end of Carter's first term, the cold war had once again heated up. With the economy still hurting, Carter called for yet another increase in the military budget. He also signed Presidential Directive 59, guaranteeing the arms alleged necessary to win a prolonged nuclear war. The prospect of peace and détente dried up.

The Iran Hostage Crisis

On November 4, 1979, Iranian fundamentalists seized the U.S. embassy in Tehran and held fifty-two employees hostage for 444 days. This event made President Carter's previous problems small by comparison.

For decades, U.S. foreign policy in the Middle East had depended on a friendly government in Iran.

After the CIA had helped to overthrow the reformist, constitutional government and installed the Pahlavi family in 1953, millions of U.S. dollars poured into the Iranian economy and the shah's armed forces. President Carter overlooked the rampant corruption in the shah's government and a well-organized opposition. By early 1979 a revolution led by Islamic fundamentalist Ayatollah Ruholla Khomeini had overthrown the shah.

When Carter allowed Mohammad Reza Pahlavi, the deposed shah, to enter the United States for treatment for cancer in November, a group of Khomeini's followers retaliated, storming the U.S. embassy and taking the staff as hostages.

Cyrus Vance assured Carter that only negotiations could free the Americans. Caught up in a reelection campaign and lobbied by Brzezinski for decisive action, Carter directed U.S. military forces to stage a nighttime helicopter rescue mission. But a sandstorm caused some of the aircraft to crash and burn, leaving eight Americans dead, their burned corpses displayed by the enraged Iranians. Short of all-out armed attack, which surely would have resulted in the hostages' death, the United States had used up its options.

The political and economic fallout was heavy. Cyrus Vance resigned, the first secretary of state in

Iranians demonstrate against the United States, burning an American flag and waving signs declaring "The U.S. is our enemy." The Iran hostage crisis, which began November 4, 1979, when a mob of Iranians seized the U.S. embassy in Tehran, contributed to Carter's defeat at the polls the following year. Despite a dramatic but failed helicopter rescue mission, fifty-two embassy employees were held hostage for 444 days.

sixty-five years to leave office over a political difference with a president. The price of oil rose by 60 percent. Carter had failed in the one area he had proclaimed central to the future of the United States: energy. He had also violated his own human rights policy, which was to be his distinctive mark on American foreign affairs.

The 1980 Election

Jimmy Carter began his campaign for renomination and reelection in what seemed the worst possible light. He had no significant accomplishments to stand on, not even a program for the future.

One more surprise dogged Carter. During May Fidel Castro invited thousands of Cubans, including political prisoners and petty criminals, to leave the island. Dubbed the "Marielitos," these Cuban refugees landed in Florida and demanded asylum. Unable to convince them to leave and unwilling to deport them, Carter established camps that were, inmates charged, inhumane.

Carter's bid for renomination depended more on his incumbency than his popularity. Delegates at the Democratic convention unenthusiastically endorsed Carter, along with running mate Walter Mondale. On the Republican side, former California governor Ronald Reagan had been building his campaign since his near-nomination in 1976. Former CIA director and Texas oil executive George Bush, more moderate than Reagan, became the Republican candidate for vice president. The Moral Majority, led by Reverend Jerry Falwell, placed itself squarely in Reagan's camp. Senator Jesse Helms's Congressional Club contributed $4.6 million to the Reagan campaign.

Reagan repeatedly asked voters, "Are you better off now than you were four years ago?" Although critics questioned Reagan's competence, the attractive, soft-spoken actor shrugged off criticisms while spotlighting the many problems besetting the country.

The Republican ticket cruised to victory. Carter won only 41.2 percent of the popular vote to Reagan's 50.9 percent. The Republicans won control of the Senate, for the first time since 1952 and with the largest majority since 1928. Still, barely half of the eligible voters had turned out in the 1980 election, bringing Ronald Reagan into office with a mandate of a thin 25 percent.

CONCLUSION

An era of quavering liberalism, but also of moderate conservatism, had come to an end. Gerald Ford's failure to set a new course either domestically or internationally had completed the Republican debacle of Richard Nixon's administration. Jimmy Carter, elected to office promising to restore public confidence in government, suffered repeated embarrassments and political defeats. Hopeful signs appeared mainly in local communities, in the form of campaigns for better schools, neighborhoods, and protection from toxic wastes. Grass-roots activism cut across political lines but stopped short of developing into a national movement.

As Carter's tenure in office came to a close, the economic problems that concerned most Americans continued to be exacerbated by military spending and dependence on foreign oil. The focus of U.S. foreign policy had begun to shift from the Soviet Union to the Middle East, where diplomatic conflict brought neither national security nor a fresh supply of low-cost crude oil. The erosion of America's industrial base meanwhile mirrored the nation's decline from unquestioned superpower status. Like the Soviet Union, the United States had paid too much for the cold war.

CHRONOLOGY

1973	*Roe* v. *Wade* legalizes abortion	**1978**	*Bakke v. University of California* decision places new limits on affirmative action programs
	Arab embargo sparks oil crisis in the United States		
	Construction of Alaska oil pipeline begins		Panama Canal Treaties arrange for turning the canal over to Panama by 2000
1974	Richard Nixon resigns presidency; Gerald Ford takes office		Camp David meeting sets terms for Middle East Peace
	President Ford pardons Nixon and introduces anti-inflation program		California passes Proposition 13, cutting taxes and government social programs
	Community Development Act funds programs for urban improvement	**1979**	Three Mile Island nuclear accident threatens a meltdown
1975	Unemployment rate reaches nearly 9 percent		Moral Majority is formed
	South Vietnamese government falls to communists		SALT II treaty is signed in Vienna but later stalls in the Senate
	Antibusing protests break out in Boston		Nicaraguan Revolution overthrows Anastasio Somoza
	New York City government declares itself bankrupt		Iranian fundamentalists seize the U.S. embassy in Tehran and hold hostages 444 days
1976	Percentage of African Americans attending college peaks at 9.3 percent and begins a decline		Soviets invade Afghanistan
	Tom Wolfe declares "the Me Decade"		Equal Rights Amendment, three states short of ratification, gets a three-year extension but eventually dies
	Jimmy Carter is elected president	**1980**	United States boycotts Olympic Games in Moscow
1977	President Carter announces human rights as major tenet in foreign policy		Ronald Reagan is elected president
	Department of Energy is established		

REVIEW QUESTIONS

1. Discuss the impact of the accident at the Three Mile Island nuclear plant on communities in the eastern states. How did fears generated by the near meltdown combine with anxieties provoked by the oil crisis?

2. Evaluate the significance of the major population shifts in the United States from the 1940s through the 1970s. How do these shifts relate to changes in the American economy? What was their impact on local and national politics?

3. Discuss the character of the "new poverty" of the 1970s. Why did the poor comprise mainly women and children?

4. Discuss the connections between the energy crisis and the rise of environmental movement during the 1970s.

5. Why was the 1970s dubbed "the Me Decade"? Interpret the decline of liberalism and the rise of conservative political groups. How did these changes affect Carter's role as president and his chances for reelection?

6. Was the Iran hostage crisis a turning point in American politics or only a thorn in Carter's reelection campaign?

RECOMMENDED READING

Peter N. Carroll, *It Seemed Like Nothing Happened* (1983). A broad overview of the 1970s, including its political and cultural aspects. Carroll captures the everyday lives of Americans, especially their frustrations over their failure to achieve according to their expectations, and finds a bitter comedy in the blunders of the era's mediocre political leaders.

Susan M. Hartmann, *From Margin to Mainstream: American Women and Politics Since 1960* (1989). An interpretation of women's growing role in American politics. Hartmann analyzes the important developments of the 1970s, most pointedly women's influence on the Democratic Party, and looks at the forces that pushed the Equal Rights Amendment through Congress but failed to see it ratified in the states.

Jerome L. Himmelstein, *To the Right: The Transformation of American Conservatism* (1990). The story of the decline of "Old Right" fiscal conservatives, isolationists, and Republican "centrists" during the 1970s and the rise of the "New Right" based in evangelical Protestantism. Himmelstein analyzes the New Right's ability to rally support for cold war foreign policy and the rollback of social welfare programs at both federal and state levels of government.

Michael B. Katz, *Improving Poor People: The Welfare State, the "Underclass," and Urban Schools as History* (1995). Provides a broad overview of the history of urban poverty, welfare policy, and public education. Katz examines the "underclass" debates of the 1970s as a function of the interaction between politics and economics within the postindustrial inner city.

William B. Quandt, *Camp David: Peacemaking and Politics* (1986). An insider's story of Jimmy Carter's greatest triumph. Quandt analyzes the Middle Eastern diplomacy as the centerpiece of Carter's otherwise unsuccessful program of world peace through negotiations and better understanding.

Edwin Schur, *The Awareness Trap: Self Absorption Instead of Social Change* (1977). A description of the various contemporary awareness movements. Schur includes detailed examples of how programs of self-improvement and religious mysticism appealed to people disoriented by social change and willing to pay money to find meaning in their lives.

James L. Sundquist, *The Decline and Resurgence of Congress* (1981). A close political study of changing relations between the two key branches of government. Sundquist underlines the revival of congressional strength after President Johnson's successful broadening of executive powers and the bipartisan tug of war that took place between Congress and its 1970s counterparts: the often haughty Nixon, the congressional-style "weak" president Gerald Ford, and the distant Jimmy Carter.

Andrew Szasz, *EcoPopulism: Toxic Waste and the Movement for Environmental Justice* (1994). A careful analysis of a turning point in federal regulation of toxic waste. Szasz shows how the prevention of pollution, previously considered a local issue, through strengthened state and federal regulations became a national issue and a springboard for the environmental movement.

Cyrus R. Vance, *Hard Choices: Critical Years of America's Foreign Policy* (1983). A former secretary of state's day-to-day recollections of his time in office during the Carter years. Vance, a career diplomat, reviews the crucial policy decisions concerning Afghanistan and the Middle East as well as the factors that caused him to resign from the Carter administration.

Winifred D. Wandersee, *On the Move: American Women in the 1970s* (1988). A highly readable overview of the changes that brought American women into political life but also kept them at the margins of power. This study includes a close description of the National Organization for Women as well as media personalities, such as Jane Fonda, who gave feminism a public face.

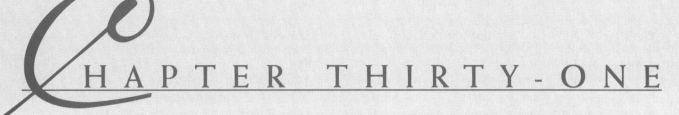

CHAPTER THIRTY-ONE

THE CONSERVATIVE ASCENDANCY
SINCE 1980

AMERICAN COMMUNITIES
Virtual Communities on the Electronic Frontier

When the moving van carrying lawyer Mike Godwin's possessions across the country from Cambridge, Massachusetts, to Washington caught fire, most of his belongings were destroyed. In a new city, with a new job, Godwin felt uprooted and alone. "I didn't know my new neighbors in Washington," he recalled, "but I knew who my cyberspace neighbors were." Godwin turned to his neighbors on the Whole Earth 'Lectronic Link (WELL), an electronic community of 8,000 based in Sausalito, California. Using his personal computer, Godwin posted news of his misfortune and expressed special concern over the loss of his books, which he had been collecting since his youth. He posted a list of the destroyed titles. "And for the next six months," he reported, "not a day went by that I didn't get a book, or a box of books, in the mail."

Cyberspace is the conceptual region occupied by people linked through computers and communications networks. It began with ARPANET, the first computer network, which was created by the Department of Defense in the early 1970s. Computer enthusiasts known as "hackers" created unexpected grass-roots spin-offs from ARPANET, including electronic mail, computer conferencing, and computer bulletin board systems.

In the mid-1980s the boom in cheap personal computers capable of linking to the worldwide telecommunications network began a population explosion in cyberspace. By then tens of thousands of researchers and scholars at universities and in private industry were linked to the Internet—the U.S. government-sponsored successor to ARPANET—through their institutions' computer centers. "Virtual communities" emerged from the Internet (or Net) whenever a group of users with a common interest reached a critical mass.

By 1998 there were more than 40 million cybercitizens in a variety of thriving virtual communities that suggested both the democratic and exploitative possibilities of cyberspace. WELL, for example, began in 1985 as a spin-off of the *Whole Earth Review*, a magazine with deep roots in the counterculture and ecology movements of the 1960s. Among its original goals were to make it easier for people in the San Francisco Bay area to communicate with one another, to provide sophisticated computer conferencing services, and to provide users who wanted it with electronic mail. Users were charged a small monthly fee plus an hourly rate for the time they spent "online." WELL initially attracted adventurous Bay area computer professionals and journalists, many of whom were given free accounts in exchange for "hosting" conversations. Passionate fans of the rock group the Grateful Dead—known as "Deadheads"—provided another early base of users.

WELL's subscriber use soon grew into the thousands. WELL was unusual among virtual communities in that it had a strong geographic locus, making it easier for members to meet "I.T.R.W."—in the real world—if they chose.

Although anger, feuds, and "flaming" with abusive interchanges were not unknown among WELL subscribers, the sense of community was strong. For many the virtual community replaced the more traditional centers of community like neighborhood, religious centers, and family. Those who faced illness or loss were consoled by "beams" from electronic well-wishers. WELL also posed a challenge to corporate-dominated communications media, and it offered a model for revitalizing citizen-based democracy.

In contrast, nationwide services such as Prodigy, Compuserve, and America Online evolved not from the grass roots but from corporate efforts to commercialize cyberspace. By the mid-1990s each counted between 500,000 and 2 million subscribers. Unlike WELL, they emphasized consumer serv-ices over interactive communication. For a flat monthly fee Prodigy users could play games, make airline reservations, sent electronic mail, and discuss issues in public forums. They also received a steady stream of advertising and had to agree to give Prodigy the right to edit public messages.

By blurring the lines between the public and private spheres, virtual communities created a whole new set of legal, political, and ethical issues that have yet to be fully resolved. Critics have pointed out that the same technology that permits citizens to communicate in new ways also opens them to government and corporate surveillance. As more and more intimate and private data about individuals move into cyberspace, the potential for abuse of that information increases.

Virtual communities are still in their infancy. They will continue to evolve as more Americans join them, although it is difficult to predict the forms they will take and the solutions to the problems they pose. Can the democratic promise of cyberspace be fulfilled, for example, if poverty or lack of education bar a substantial part of the American population from access to computer technology? The relentless commercialization of cyberspace accelerated in the late 1990s as millions of businesses explored the profit potential of selling goods and services over the Internet. (In 1994 the nonprofit organization that founded WELL sold it to California businessman Bruce Katz, who had made a fortune manufacturing Rockport shoes.) By 1998 there were some 320 million Web sites in the United States, representing everything from large corporations to fringe political groups to personal "home pages." At the close of the twentieth century, more and more Americans were finding—and inventing—versions of community on the electronic frontier of cyberspace.

KEY TOPICS

- Domestic policies under the Reagan administration

- Reagan era foreign policy: Soviet Union, Central America, Middle East

- Structural shifts in the economy and culture of the 1980s

- The growth of inequality

- The new immigration

- Contradictions and difficulties attending America's role in world affairs

- The Clinton presidency and the resurgent right

THE REAGAN REVOLUTION

The Great Communicator

Ronald Reagan was born in 1911 and raised in the small town of Dixon, Illinois. Reagan's father was a salesman and an alcoholic who had a tough time holding a job. His strong-willed mother was a fundamentalist Christian who kept the family together amid frequent moves. A WPA (Works Progress Administration) job for the father helped the Reagans survive the hard times of the Great Depression. Encouraged by his mother, Reagan began acting in church plays and in productions of Eureka College, from which he graduated in 1932.

In 1937 Reagan made a successful screen test with the Warner Brothers studio in Hollywood, and he began a movie acting career that lasted for a quarter century. He was never a big star, appearing in scores of mostly "B" movies. But Reagan became a skilled actor. On screen, he was tall, handsome, and affable, and his characters usually projected an optimistic and sunny personality.

While serving as president of the Screen Actors Guild from 1947 to 1952, Reagan became a leader of the anticommunist forces in Hollywood. He then began to distance himself from New Deal liberalism. In 1954 Reagan became host of a new national television program, *General Electric Theater*, and began a long stint as a national spokesman for GE. In this role he made numerous speeches celebrating the achievements of corporate America and emphasizing the dangers of big government, excessive liberalism, and radical trade unions.

Reagan switched his party affiliation to Republican and became a popular fundraiser and speaker for the California GOP. He took a leading role in conservative Republican Barry Goldwater's 1964 presidential campaign. A televised address on Goldwater's behalf thrust Reagan himself into national political prominence. The attack on big government was at the core of the Reagan message. He lashed out at growing bureaucracy and celebrated the achievements of entrepreneurs unfettered by government regulation or aid.

A group of wealthy, conservative southern Californians encouraged Reagan to run for office himself. These backers, most of whom had made fortunes in California real estate and the oil business, saw themselves as self-made men and shared a basic distrust of government intervention in the economy. With their financial and political support, Reagan defeated Democratic governor Edmund G. Brown in 1966 and won reelection in 1970. As governor, Reagan cut the state welfare rolls, placed limits on the increase of state employees, and funneled a large share of state tax revenues back to local governments. He vigorously attacked student protesters and black militants, thereby tapping into the conservative backlash against 1960s activism.

Reaganomics

During the Reagan presidency, supply-side economists dominated the administration's thinking and helped redirect American economic policy. Since the mid-1970s, supply-side theorists had urged a sharp break with the Keynesian policies that had been dominant since the New Deal era. Keynesians traditionally favored moderate tax cuts and increases in government spending to stimulate the economy and reduce unemployment during recessions. By putting more money in people's pockets, they argued, greater consumer demand would lead to economic expansion.

By contrast, supply-siders called for simultaneous tax cuts and reductions in public spending. This combination, they claimed, would give private entrepreneurs and investors greater incentives to start businesses, take risks, invest capital, and thereby create new wealth and jobs. Whatever revenues were lost in lower tax rates would be more than made up by the new growth. At the same time, spending cuts would keep the federal deficit under control and thereby keep

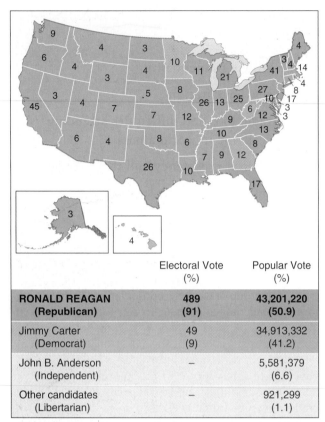

	Electoral Vote (%)	Popular Vote (%)
RONALD REAGAN (Republican)	**489 (91)**	**43,201,220 (50.9)**
Jimmy Carter (Democrat)	49 (9)	34,913,332 (41.2)
John B. Anderson (Independent)	–	5,581,379 (6.6)
Other candidates (Libertarian)	–	921,299 (1.1)

The Election of 1980   *Ronald Reagan won a landslide victory over incumbent Jimmy Carter, who managed to carry only six states and the District of Columbia. Reagan attracted millions of traditionally Democratic voters to the Republican camp.*

interest rates down. On the political level, supply-siders looked to reward the most loyal Republican constituencies: the affluent and the business community. At the same time, they hoped to reduce the flow of federal dollars received by two core Democratic constituencies: the recipients and professional providers of health and welfare programs.

Reagan quickly won approval for two key pieces of legislation based on these ideas. The Economic Recovery Tax Act of 1981, passed by a very willing Congress, cut income and corporate taxes by $747 billion over five years. It eliminated the distinction between earned and unearned income. This last measure proved a boon to the small and richest fraction of the population, which derives most of its income from rent, dividends, and interest.

With the help of conservative southern and western Democrats in the House, the administration also pushed through a comprehensive program of spending cuts known as the Omnibus Reconciliation Act of 1981. This bill mandated cuts of $136 billion for the period 1982–84, covering over 200 social and cultural programs. The hardest-hit areas included federal appropriations for education, the environment, synthetic fuels research, health, housing, urban aid, food stamps, and the arts. The conservative coalition in the House allowed only one vote on the entire package of spending cuts. This strategy allowed conservatives to slash appropriations for a wide variety of domestic programs in one fell swoop.

Reagan appointed conservatives to head the Environmental Protection Agency (EPA), the Occupational Safety and Health Administration (OSHA), and the Consumer Product Safety Commission (CPSC). These individuals abolished or weakened hundreds of rules governing business activity in the environment, workplace safety, and consumer protection, all in the name of efficiency and productivity.

Following the tenets of supply-side economics, Reagan weakened the Antitrust Division of the Justice Department, the Securities and Exchange Commission, and the Federal Home Loan Bank Board. Large corporations, Wall Street stock brokerages, investment banking houses, and the savings and loan banking industry were all allowed to operate with a much freer hand than ever before. By the late 1980s, the unfortunate consequences of this freedom would become apparent in a series of unprecedented scandals in the nation's financial markets and banking industry.

Military Buildup

During the 1980 election campaign, Reagan's calls to "restore America's defenses" helped reinforce the public perception that President Carter had dealt ineffectively with the Iranian hostage crisis. Reagan saw no contradiction between his campaign vows to cut the cost of government and the need to beef up defense spending. Along with reduced government spending and lowered tax rates, a stronger military posture was part of the ideological core of Reagan's worldview.

The Reagan administration greatly accelerated a trend already under way during the last two years of the Carter presidency: a sharp increase in defense spending. Secretary of Defense Caspar Weinberger and Secretary of State Alexander Haig persistently lobbied Congress, emphasizing the need for a stronger nuclear weapons capability. This included the MX, Cruise, and Pershing missiles. In 1983 President Reagan proclaimed his Strategic Defense Initiative (SDI), popularly called "Star Wars." He claimed, though few scientists agreed, that this enormously expensive project could use satellites and lasers to provide an impregnable shield against nuclear attack. Overall, the Reagan budgets for military spending totaled $1.6 trillion over five years.

Defense contracts meant the difference between prosperity and recession for blue- and white-collar workers, merchants, developers, and bankers in scores of communities. In 1983 California led all states with over $26 billion in military contracts, followed by New York ($9.6 billion), Texas ($8.2 billion), and Virginia ($7.1 billion). In 1980, 28 percent of federal spending went to housing, education, and urban and social services. By 1987, federal outlays for human resources totaled only 22 percent. In the same period, defense spending rose from 23 to 28 percent of the federal budget.

Recession, Recovery, Fiscal Crisis

The Reagan administration's economic policies had mixed results. A severe recession, the worst since the 1930s, gripped the nation in 1982. The official unemployment rate reached nearly 11 percent by the end of that year. Many communities, particularly in the industrial Midwest and Northeast, experienced depression-like conditions. In January 1983, 20,000 people lined up for hours in subfreezing weather to apply for 200 jobs at a Milwaukee auto-frame factory. American steelmakers operated at only about one-third of capacity.

By the middle of 1983 the economy had begun to recover. That year unemployment dropped to about 8 percent, and inflation was below 5 percent. The economy as a whole grew 3.6 percent, the biggest increase since the mid-1970s. Unemployment remained relatively low, and the stock market boomed, pushing the Dow Jones industrial average from 776 in August 1982 to an all-time high of 2,722 in August 1987. Inflation averaged just over 3 percent from 1982 to 1986. The administration took credit for the turnaround, hailing the supply-side fiscal policies that had drastically cut taxes and domestic spending. But critics pointed to other factors: the Federal Reserve Board's tight-money policies, the drastic drop in oil prices due to a worldwide energy glut, and the large military buildup that pumped hundreds of billions into the economy for defense spending.

The economic recovery produced more than 13 million new jobs between 1981 and 1986. But half of these paid less than $11,661, the federally defined poverty level for a family of four. Real family income rose nearly 11 percent from 1982 to 1986. But with average hourly earnings stagnant, most of this gain resulted from the addition of a second paycheck from a wife or child.

The supply-side formula also intensified an ominous fiscal crisis. Although President Reagan had promised to balance the budget, his policies brought on the exact opposite. The national debt grew from $907 billion in 1980 to over $2 trillion in 1986, more than the federal government had accumulated in its entire previous history. Expenditures for paying just the interest on the national debt reached 14 percent of the annual budget in 1988, double the percentage set aside in 1974.

In the Reagan years the fiscal crisis became a structural problem with newly disturbing and perhaps

Ronald and Nancy Reagan at the Inaugural Ball, January 20, 1981. The Reagans, supported by a circle of wealthy conservative friends from the business world and Hollywood, brought a lavish style to the White House that helped define the culture of the 1980s.

permanent implications for the American economy. Big deficits kept interest rates high, as the government drove up the cost of borrowing the money it needed to pay its own bills. Foreign investors, attracted by high interest rates on government securities, pushed up the value of the dollar in relation to foreign currencies. The overvalued dollar made it more difficult for foreigners to buy American products, while making overseas goods cheaper to American consumers. Basic American industries—steel, autos, textiles—thus found it more difficult to compete abroad and at home. In 1980 the United States still enjoyed a trade surplus of $166 billion. By 1987 the nation had an indebtedness to foreigners of $340 billion. Since World War I, America had been the world's leading creditor; in the mid-1980s it became its biggest debtor.

The Election of 1984

As the 1984 election approached, Democrats believed the president was politically vulnerable, especially on the economic issues of recession and the weakening of social programs. Many Americans also expressed fears over the nuclear weapons buildup of the early 1980s. Polls showed that over 70 percent of Americans favored a nuclear freeze with the Soviet Union.

By early 1984, Walter Mondale had emerged as the leading candidate for the Democratic nomination. As a senator from Minnesota and Jimmy Carter's vice president, Mondale had close ties with the party's liberal establishment. At the Democratic convention, Mondale named Representative Geraldine Ferraro of New York as his running mate, a first for women in American politics. Charismatic speakers such as the Reverend Jesse Jackson, a dynamic disciple of Martin Luther King, Jr., and Governor Mario Cuomo of New York stirred the convention, and many watching on television, with their appeals to compassion, fairness, and brotherhood. Opinion polls showed Mondale running even with Reagan. But the president's enormous personal popularity, along with the booming economy, overwhelmed the Democratic ticket. While Mondale emphasized the growing deficit and called attention to Americans left out of prosperity, Reagan cruised above it all. It was "morning again in America," his campaign ads claimed. Reagan won 59 percent of the popular vote and carried every state but Minnesota and the District of Columbia in one of the biggest landslides in American history.

REAGAN'S FOREIGN POLICY

The Evil Empire

Part of Reagan's success in the 1980 campaign lay in appeals to restoring America's will to assert itself in the post-Vietnam era. In a sharp turn from President Carter's focus on human rights and President Nixon's pursuit of détente, Reagan described the Soviet Union as "an evil empire . . . the focus of evil in the modern world." The president denounced the growing movement for a nuclear freeze, arguing that "we must find peace through strength."

Administration officials argued that the nation's military strength had fallen dangerously behind that of the Soviet Union during the 1970s. Critics disputed this, pointing out that the Soviet advantage in intercontinental ballistic missiles (ICBMs) was offset by American superiority in submarine-based forces and strategic aircraft. Nonetheless, the administration proceeded with plans designed to enlarge America's nuclear strike force.

The call for SDI introduced an unsettling new element into superpower relations. Reagan was SDI's most ardent proponent, and it eventually grew into a $17 billion research and development program. From the Soviet perspective, SDI looked like a potentially

offensive weapon that enhanced America's first-strike capability.

Central America

Declaring the "Vietnam syndrome" over, the president confidently reasserted America's right to intervene anywhere in the world to fight communist insurgency. The Reagan Doctrine, as this declaration was later called, assumed that social revolution anywhere must be directed and controlled by the Soviet Union and its allies. The Reagan Doctrine found its most important expression in Central America, where the United States hoped to reestablish its historical control over the Caribbean basin.

On the economic front, the Caribbean Basin Initiative (CBI) promised to stimulate the Caribbean economy by encouraging the growth of business corporations and a freer flow of capital through $350 million in U.S. aid. Yet the Congress refused to play by the rules of free trade, placing stiff tariffs and import quotas on shoes, leather goods, and sugar competing with U.S. products. Many Latin American businessmen opposed key parts of CBI, such as generous tax breaks for foreign investors. They feared that once large multinational corporations entered their markets, CBI would strengthen the kind of chronic economic dependency that had shaped so much of the region's past. In fact, indigenous history, internal political struggles, and the grinding poverty endured by the overwhelming majority of Central Americans counted for little in the administration's understanding of the region.

In El Salvador the Reagan administration encouraged a repressive regime dominated by the military and a handful of wealthy landowners to pursue a military victory over a coalition of rebel groups fighting for social revolution. Salvadoran soldiers received special training in North American camps and from U.S. advisers sent to El Salvador. Military aid jumped from $6 million in 1980 to $82 million in 1982, and El Salvador received more U.S. economic assistance than any other Latin American country. By 1983 right-wing death squads, encouraged by military elements within the regime, had tortured and assassinated thousands of opposition leaders, including Roman Catholic archbishop Oscar Romero. The election in 1984 of centrist president José Napoleon Duarte failed to end the bloody civil war. Some 53,000 Salvadorans, more than one out of every hundred, lost their lives in the conflict.

In Nicaragua the Reagan administration claimed that the revolutionary Sandinista government—which had come to power in 1979 after overthrowing the dictatorial regime of the Somoza family—posed "an unusual and extraordinary threat to the national security." U.S. officials accused the Sandinistas of shipping arms to antigovernment rebels in El Salvador. In December 1981

Reagan approved a $19 million CIA plan arming and organizing Nicaraguan exiles, known as Contras, to fight against the Sandinista government. As Reagan escalated this undeclared war, the aim became not merely the cutting of Nicaraguan aid to Salvadoran rebels but the overthrow of the Sandinista regime itself.

In 1984 the CIA secretly mined Nicaraguan harbors. When Nicaragua won a judgment against the United States in the World Court over this violation of its sovereignty, the Reagan administration refused to recognize the court's jurisdiction in the case and ignored the verdict. Predictably, the U.S. covert war pushed the Sandinistas closer to Cuba and the Soviet bloc. Meanwhile, U.S. grass-roots opposition to Contra aid grew more vocal and widespread. A number of U.S. communities set up sister city projects offering humanitarian and technical assistance to Nicaraguan communities. Scores of U.S. churches offered sanctuary to political refugees from Central America.

In 1984 Congress reined in the covert war by passing the Boland Amendment, forbidding government agencies from supporting "directly or indirectly military or paramilitary operations" in Nicaragua. Denied funding by Congress, President Reagan now turned to the National Security Council to find a way to keep the Contra war going. Between 1984 and 1986 the NSC staff secretly ran the Contra assistance effort, raising $37 million in aid from foreign countries and private contributors. In 1987 the revelation of this unconstitutional scheme exploded before the public as part of the Iran–Contra affair. This would become the most damaging political scandal of the Reagan years.

Glasnost and Arms Control

Meanwhile, momentous political changes within the Soviet Union set in motion a reduction in East–West tensions and ultimately the end of the cold war itself. Soviet premier Leonid Brezhnev, in power since 1964, died at the end of 1982. His successors, Yuri Andropov and Konstantin Chernenko, both died after brief terms in office. But in 1985 a new, reform-minded leader, Mikhail Gorbachev, won election as general secretary of the Soviet Communist Party. A lifelong Communist and a pure product of Soviet education and politics, Gorbachev represented a new generation of disenchanted party members. He initiated a radical new program of economic and political reform under the rubrics of *glasnost* (openness) and *perestroika* (restructuring).

Gorbachev and his advisers opened up political discussion and encouraged criticism of the Soviet economy and its political culture. The government released long-time dissidents such as Andrei Sakharov from prison and took the first halting steps toward profit-based, private initiatives in the economy. The "new

thinking" inspired an unprecedented wave of diverse, critical perspectives in Soviet art, literature, journalism, and scholarship. In Gorbachev's view, improving the economic performance of the Soviet system depended first on halting the arms race. Over 10 percent of the Soviet GNP went to defense spending, while the majority of its citizens still struggled to find even the most basic consumer items in shops. Gorbachev thus took the lead in negotiating a halt to the arms race with the United States.

The historical ironies were stunning. Reagan had made militant anticommunism the centerpiece of his political life, but between 1985 and 1988 Reagan had four separate summit meetings with the new Soviet leader. In October 1986 Reagan and Gorbachev met in Reykjavík, Iceland, but this summit bogged down over the issue of SDI. Reagan refused to abandon his plan for a space-based defensive umbrella. Gorbachev insisted that the plan violated the 1972 Strategic Arms Limitation Treaty (SALT I), and that SDI might eventually allow the United States to make an all-out attack on the Soviet Union.

After another year of tough negotiating, the two sides agreed to a modest treaty that called for comprehensive, mutual, on-site inspections. It provided an important psychological breakthrough. At one of the summits a Soviet leader humorously announced, "We are going to do something terrible to you Americans: we are going to deprive you of an enemy."

The Iran–Contra Scandal

In 1987 the revelations of the Iran–Contra affair laid bare the continuing contradictions and difficulties attending America's role in world affairs. The affair also demonstrated how overzealous and secretive government officials subverted the Constitution and compromised presidential authority under the guise of patriotism.

The Middle East presented the Reagan administration with its most frustrating foreign policy dilemmas. In October 1983 a terrorist bombing in marine barracks in Lebanon killed 241 American servicemen who were part of a U.S. force dispatched by Reagan to protect a weak government in the midst of a brutal civil war. After that the administration shied away from a long-term commitment of U.S. forces in the region.

Terrorist acts, including the seizing of Western hostages and the bombing of commercial airplanes and cruise ships, redefined the politics of the region. These were desperate attempts by small, essentially powerless sects, many of them splinter groups associated with the Palestinian cause or Islamic fundamentalism. In trying to force the Western world to pay attention to their grievances, they succeeded mostly in provoking outrage and anger. The Reagan administration insisted that behind international terrorism lay the sinister influence and money of the Soviet bloc, the Ayatollah Khomeini of Iran, and Libyan leader Muammar Qaddafi. In the spring of 1986 Reagan, eager to demonstrate his antiterrorist resolve, ordered the bombing of Tripoli in a failed effort to kill Qaddafi.

As a fierce war between Iran and Iraq escalated, the administration tilted publicly toward Iraq to please the Arab states around the Persian Gulf. But in 1986 the administration began secret negotiations with the revolutionary Iranian government. In exchange for help in securing the release of Americans held hostage by radical Islamic groups in Lebanon, the Reagan administration offered to supply Iran with sophisticated weapons for use against Iraq.

Subsequent disclosures elevated the arms-for-hostages deal into a major scandal. Some of the money from the deal had been secretly diverted into covert aid for the Nicaraguan Contras. The American public soon learned the sordid details from investigative journalists and through televised congressional hearings in the summer of 1987. In order to escape congressional oversight of the CIA, Reagan and CIA director William Casey essentially turned the National Security Council, previously a policy-coordinating body, into an operational agency. Under the direction of National Security Advisers Robert McFarlane and later Admiral John Poindexter, the NSC sold TOW and HAWK missiles to the Iranians, using Israel as a go-between. Millions of dollars from these sales were then given to the Contras in blatant and illegal disregard of the Boland Amendment.

In the televised congressional hearings, NSC staffer and marine lieutenant colonel Oliver North emerged as the figure running what he euphemistically called "the Enterprise." North defiantly defended his actions in the name of patriotism. Some Americans saw North as a hero. But most were appalled by his and Poindexter's blithe admissions that they had lied to Congress, shredded evidence, and refused to inform the president of details in order to guarantee his "plausible deniability." A blue-ribbon commission led by former senator John Tower concluded that Reagan himself "did not seem to be aware" of the policy or its consequences. But the Tower Report offered a stunning portrait of a president at best confused and far removed from critical policy-making responsibilities.

Ultimately, the Iran–Contra investigation raised more questions than it answered. The full role of CIA director Casey, who died in 1987, particularly his relationships with North and the president, remained murky. The role of Vice President George Bush remained mysterious as well, and it would return as an issue in the 1992 presidential election. Both North and Poindexter were convicted of felonies, but their convic-

Marine Lt. Col. Oliver North, *the key figure in the Iran–Contra affair, being sworn to testify before the special Senate committee investigating the scandal, July 7, 1987.*

tions were overturned by higher courts on technical grounds. Ronald Reagan pleaded ignorance. When pressed on what happened, he repeatedly claimed, "I'm still trying to find out."

In December 1992, following his own election defeat and six years after the scandal broke, President George Bush granted pardons to six key players in the Iran–Contra affair. The Bush pardons made it unlikely that the full truth about the arms-for-hostages affair would ever be known.

BEST OF TIMES, WORST OF TIMES

During the 1980s American communities experienced economic and social change in profoundly diverse ways. The decade witnessed the rapid expansion of new industries such as microelectronics, biotechnology, robotics, and computers. Simultaneously, old standbys such as steel and auto manufacturing declined more quickly than many could have imagined. Communities that had long depended on industry and manufacturing for their livelihood now struggled to create alternative job bases around newer service- and information-based enterprises.

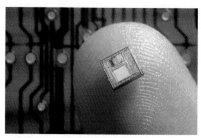

A silicon microchip, with imprinted circuit, on a finger. These tiny chips provided the basic building blocks for the rapid development of the computer industry.

Silicon Valley

Silicon Valley, a thirty- by ten-mile strip of Santa Clara County, achieved a special place in the American economy and imagination as the center of the microelectronics industry in the early 1980s. The name referred to the semiconductor chips, made of silicon, that provided the foundation for local high-technology firms. Semiconductors, containing complex integrated circuits, formed the brains of computers and the basic building blocks of modern electronics. Military contracts played a crucial role in the business during the 1950s and 1960s. In the 1970s a consumer electronics revolution fueled an explosive new wave of growth. Silicon Valley firms gave birth to pocket calculators, video games, home computers, cordless telephones, digital watches, and almost every other new development in electronics.

Silicon Valley became increasingly divided along geographic and class lines. The nearly all-white, all-male affluent managers and engineers tended to live in North County communities, such as Palo Alto, Mountain View, and Sunnyvale. Manual workers on assembly lines and in low-paying service jobs clustered in San Jose and Gilroy. Most of these were Latino, black, Vietnamese, Chinese, and Filipino men and women. The majority of Silicon Valley workers did not see or enjoy the affluent lifestyle publicized in the mass media; they constituted a cheap, nonunionized labor pool with an extremely high turnover rate. Public services in South County—schools, welfare, police and fire protection—were poor. Among Latino public school students in Santa Clara County, the dropout rate reached 50 percent in the mid-1980s.

By the early 1990s the Silicon Valley economy had matured. Stiff competition from computer companies in Japan, Korea, and Malaysia made it much more difficult for young entrepreneurs to start successful new companies. The leap from small, start-up company to large corporation was becoming more and more difficult.

Monongahela Valley

Across the continent, in western Pennsylvania, a different kind of economic transformation reshaped the industrial cities along the Monongahela River valley. In the 1980s the American steel industry suffered dramatic losses as the overvalued dollar hurt U.S. producers in two ways. They lost sales both directly, to cheaper imported steel, and indirectly as their domestic customers in steel-intensive industries (automobiles, machine tools) also lost sales to imports.

But much of the problem stemmed from the long-term failure of big steel companies to invest in modernizing their operations. Instead they redirected profits into buying chemical firms, shopping malls, and oil companies. In 1984 U.S. Steel's sales from steel accounted for just 34 percent of all revenues and only 9 percent of total operating income. This policy of disinvestment had a devastating impact on the people and communities who had helped build the nation's basic production industries.

On a hill about fifteen miles south of Pittsburgh sits Clairton, a small city of about 20,000. Clairton was once a bustling city of immigrants, with active Slavic, Italian, and Irish communities. At the end of World War II Clairton's coke works were the largest in the world, and its byproduct division made components for thousands of different products, including fertilizer, resin, and dyes. By the mid-1980s Clairton was suffering a permanent unemployment rate of about 35 percent, and it was bankrupt. The taxes once paid by U.S. Steel to the city dropped from $805,000 in 1980 to $331,000 in 1985. The entire thirteen-member police force had to be laid off. A state-appointed trustee handled Clairton's financial affairs. Several thousand people have moved out since 1980; others remain trapped and dependent on charity and food banks.

Some Mon Valley communities have made strides toward rebuilding around "postindustrial" enterprises. In Pittsburgh, on the former site of Jones & Laughlin Steel, state government, business, and local universities pooled resources to create a high-tech industrial park. Commercial tenants include ventures born of university research into biotechnology, robotics, and computer software. Pittsburgh's assets now include the world's largest robotics institute and the biggest research program on the industrial uses of artificial intelligence.

Indian Country

During the 1970s and 1980s Indians won a series of legal and political victories that cumulatively bolstered the principle of what the Supreme Court in *United States v. Wheeler* (1978) called "unique and limited" sovereignty. The federal government recognized tribal sovereignty except where limited by treaty or Congress. A series of court decisions defined precisely what those limits were. For example, tribes could tax corporations located on reservations, were exempted from paying state income taxes, and won greater powers for their own courts. In *United States v. John* (1978), the Court ruled that Indian tribes are essentially self-defined and can be dissolved only by their members, thus negating the policy of termination (see

Chapter 28). The 1983 Tribal Government Tax Status Act authorized tribes to be treated like states for certain purposes.

But this strengthening of the principle of self-determination had a limited impact on the lives of most Indians. The postwar trends toward urbanization and assimilation continued. By the 1980s more than half of the nation's Indian population lived in urban areas, with the largest communities in Los Angeles, Tulsa, Oklahoma City, and Phoenix. More than 50 percent of all Americans identifying themselves as Indians were married to non-Indians. On reservations, most tribes lacked the independence or authority of state governments because they continued to rely on federal funding.

This continued dependence on Washington was underscored in 1981 when the Reagan administration cut appropriations for Indians by a third. As Indians experienced the greatest per capita cut in federal programs of any American citizens, reservations saw a dramatic increase in unemployment and poverty. By the mid-1980s, for example, Navajo per capita income was $1,700, compared to $9,000 for the United States as a whole. In Arizona, a state with a large reservation population, more than a third of reservation Indians lived below the poverty line. On the Pine Ridge Reservation in South Dakota, some 18,000 Oglala Sioux lived amid corrosive poverty and an unemployment rate that averaged well above 50 percent. On Wyoming's Wind River Reservation about 8,000 Northern Arapaho and Eastern Shoshone Indians lived on land without any functioning economy except a few trading posts that brought in tourist dollars.

By the late 1980s a new source of income and economic power emerged for Indian tribes: gambling. An outgrowth of the drive for sovereignty rights, the Indian Gaming Regulatory Act of 1988 allowed tribes to operate any sort of gambling establishment that is legal in their state. Thus, if a church or social club can hold a "Las Vegas night," a tribe can run a casino. Within a few years at least seventy-five tribes in eighteen states had signed agreements with states to open reservation casinos.

For some tribes, the results proved spectacular. In Ledyard, Connecticut, the Mashantucket Pequots built Foxwoods, a full-scale gambling casino and hotel complex that not only brought riches to the tribe but also reshaped the economic landscape of surrounding communities. To build Foxwoods, the Mashantuckets borrowed $55 million from a Malaysian company that operated hotels and casinos in Asia. Under an agreement between Connecticut and the tribe, state agencies regulated the casino. All profits remained with the tribe after it reimbursed the state for money spent on regulation. The Mashantuckets paid no taxes to the state or federal governments.

Some people in the adjacent community of Ledyard, a traditional New England village of 15,000, worried about traffic congestion, pollution, and crime. Others expressed concern over the human tragedies caused by compulsive gambling. But the potential for Foxwoods to reverse southeastern Connecticut's disastrous economic decline dominated all discussion. No wonder, then, that more than 25,000 people applied for the 2,300 job openings at Foxwoods. At $3.75 an hour plus tips, dealers and cocktail waitresses would earn as much as $30,000 a year.

By 1998 Foxwoods was the single most profitable gambling casino in the United States, turning an estimated annual profit of more than $200 million on gross revenues of more than $400 million. The tribe could guarantee college tuition for all its children, world travel for its elders, and new homes for its 250 members. It hired its own archaeologist to help recover evidence of lost tribal history. Steady expansion resulted in 1200 hotel rooms, 300,000 square feet of casino space, and a new $135 million Mashantucket Pequot Museum and Research Center.

Foxwoods's success inspired other Indian peoples across the nation. In New Mexico the 600-year-old Sandia tribe renewed its culture with $16 million in annual gambling profits and helped revive the economy in Albuquerque.

Not all these ventures were bonanzas. The Wisconsin Winnebago tribe fell into near bankruptcy when its casinos were mismanaged by a corrupt businessman. But most shared the view of Reid A. Walker, an executive with the National Indian Gaming Association, who argued that reservation gambling had "brought us new hope. It's a renaissance for Indian country, giving us power to start our own programs in health care, infrastructure, education and more."

An Electronic Culture

In the 1980s, revolutions in computers and telecommunication changed the way people worked and played. They made the nation's cultural life more homogenous, and they played a greater role than ever in shaping politics. Many believed that the creation, processing, and sale of information and services had replaced the manufacturing and distribution of material goods as the most important and dynamic wealth-producing activities of the society.

The twin arrivals of cable TV and the videocassette recorder (VCR) expanded and redefined the power of television. By the end of the 1980s pay cable services and VCRs had penetrated roughly two-thirds of American homes. The VCR revolutionized the way people used their television sets, allowing them to organize program watching around their own schedules. People also used their television sets for playing video games and viewing Hollywood movies. Indeed, tape rental and sale for home viewing quickly replaced theater tickets as the main profit source for filmmakers.

A new cable channel called MTV (for Music Television) began in 1981 as a means of boosting record sales, but music videos, featuring popular music stars, soon became a new art form in themselves. Artists who best exploited music video, such as Madonna and Michael Jackson, achieved international superstar status. MTV also transformed smaller, cult musical forms such as rap and heavy metal into giant mass market phenomena. MTV pioneered an imaginative visual style, featuring rapid cutting, animation, and the sophisticated fusion of sound and image.

More than ever, television drove the key strategies and tactics defining American political life. Issues, positions, and debate all paled alongside the key question: how did it look on TV? Fewer citizens voted or took an active role in campaigns, and most relied on television coverage to make their choices. Televangelists such as Pat Robertson, Jimmy Swaggart, and Jim and Tammy Bakker attracted large audiences and built lucrative empires by preaching fundamentalist Protestantism over cable networks.

The dominant themes in popular culture were money, status, and power—the values embraced by the Reagan administration. The newly elected president himself set the tone when he responded to a reporter's question asking him what was best about America. "What I want to see above all," Reagan replied, "is that this remains a country where someone can always get rich." Many thousands of Americans made fortunes in the expansive and lucrative sectors of the economy: stock trading, real estate, business services, defense contracting, and high-tech industries. A step below the new rich were the "yuppies" (young upwardly mobile professionals), who were defined by their upscale consumer behavior. Yuppies ate gourmet foods, wore designer clothes, drove expensive automobiles, and lived in "gentrified" neighborhoods.

Hit TV series such as *Dallas* and *Dynasty* (and their imitators) focused on the family wars and business intrigues of oil tycoons and fashion queens. Shows such as *Lifestyles of the Rich and Famous* and *Entertainment Tonight* offered vicarious pleasures by taking viewers into the homes and on the shopping sprees of wealthy celebrities.

Tie-ins proliferated among films, television shows, advertising, newspapers and magazines, popular music, and politicians. A growing concentration of ownership among television networks, movie studios, publishers, and cable companies accelerated this trend. Demographic analysis created the most important "communities" in American life: communities of consumer choice, so that advertisers could define and target the right demographic community.

Epidemics: Drugs, AIDS, Homelessness

Drug addiction and drug trafficking took on frightening new dimensions in the early 1980s. The arrival of crack, a cheap, smokable, and highly addictive form of cocaine, made that drug affordable to the urban poor. As crack addiction spread, the drug trade assumed alarming new proportions both domestically and internationally. Crack ruined hundreds of thousands of lives and led to a dramatic increase in crime. The crack trade spawned a new generation of young drug dealers willing to risk jail and death for enormous profits. In city after city drug wars over turf took the lives of dealers and innocents, both caught in the escalating violence.

The Reagan administration declared a highly publicized "war on drugs" to bring the traffic under control. Critics charged that the war on drugs focused on supply from abroad when it needed to look at demand here at home. They urged more federal money for drug education, treatment, and rehabilitation. Drug addiction and drug use, they argued, were primarily health problems, not law enforcement issues.

In 1981 doctors in Los Angeles, San Francisco, and New York began encountering a puzzling new medical phenomenon. Young homosexual men were dying suddenly from rare types of pneumonia and cancer. The underlying cause was found to be a mysterious new viral disease that destroyed the body's natural defenses against illness, making its victims susceptible to a host of opportunistic infections. Researchers at the Centers for Disease Control (CDC) in Atlanta named the mysterious disease acquired immune deficiency syndrome (AIDS). The virus that causes AIDS is transmitted through semen or blood, but full-blown AIDS might not appear for years after initial exposure to the virus. Thus one could infect others without even knowing one had the disease. Although tests could determine whether one carried the AIDS virus, there was no cure. The preponderance of early AIDS victims were homosexual men infected through sexual contact. Many Americans thus perceived AIDS as a disease of homosexuals. But other victims became infected through intravenous drug use, blood transfusions, heterosexual transmission, or birth to AIDS-carrying mothers.

AIDS provoked fear, anguish, and anger. It also brought an upsurge of organization and political involvement. In city after city the gay community responded to the AIDS crisis with energy and determination. Most gay men changed their sexual habits, practicing "safe sex" to lessen the chances of infection. The Reagan administration largely ignored the epidemic. One important exception was Surgeon General C. Everett Koop, who urged a comprehensive sex education program in the nation's schools.

By the 1990s the fastest-growing group of AIDS victims were intravenous drug users, their sex

The AIDS Quilt in Washington, D.C., October 1992. The quilt project united thousands of individual memorials to AIDS victims into one power statement expressing the national sense of loss from the disease. Mourners were thus able to transcend their personal grief and connect with the larger movement to fight AIDS.

Who were the homeless? Analysts agreed that at least a third were patients who had been discharged from psychiatric hospitals amid the deinstitutionalization trend of the 1970s. Many more were alcoholics and drug addicts unable to hold jobs. But the ranks of the homeless also included female-headed families, battered women, Vietnam veterans, AIDS victims, and elderly people with no place to go. Some critics pointed to the decline in decent housing for poor people and the deterioration of the nation's health-care system as causes of homelessness.

Economic Woes

Congress sought to check burgeoning deficits, which had topped $200 billion in the annual budget for 1984. In late 1985, amid great fanfare, Congress enacted the Balanced Budget and Emergency Deficit Control Act, more popularly known by the names of its principal authors, Senators Phil Gramm and Warren Rudman. It mandated automatic spending cuts if the government failed to meet fixed deficit-reduction goals. Under the plan, congressional and presidential budget officials would forecast whether target reductions would be met. If not, the General Accounting Office would compile a list of across-the-board reductions, evenly divided between domestic and military programs. Gramm–Rudman targeted a deficit of $172 billion for 1986, with further reductions leading to a balanced budget by 1991.

But the deficit for 1986 reached $238 billion, some $66 billion over the target. In fact, the actual deficit was $283 billion, but Congress and the president took the $45 billion surplus from Social Security and other trust funds and spent it on government programs, thereby masking the true size of the deficit. This tactic of diverting trust funds to reduce the deficit became standard during the 1980s. Congress revised the Gramm– Rudman targets in 1987, but once again, the numbers did not add up. The 1991 deficit set a record at $269 billion; if the Social Security surplus was subtracted from government spending books, the real deficit totaled $321 billion.

On Wall Street, the bull market of the 1980s ended abruptly in the fall of 1987. The Dow Jones average of thirty leading industrial stocks had reached an

partners, and their babies. The AIDS epidemic spread rapidly among African Americans and Latinos as well. The revelations of AIDS infection in such well-known public figures as actor Rock Hudson and athletes Magic Johnson and Arthur Ashe helped remove some of the stigma and promoted AIDS awareness. More important were the continuing political and educational efforts mounted by groups such as the AIDS Coalition to Unleash Power (ACT-UP).

By 1997 some 612,000 Americans had contracted AIDS, of whom 379,000 had died. About 900,000 Americans were infected with the AIDS virus. But by 1995, although the infection rate remained steady, the death rate from AIDS began to drop. New drug treatments, such as AZT and protease inhibitors, slowed the disease's progress and relieved some symptoms. For those patients with access to these drugs, AIDS became a long-term chronic condition rather than an automatic death sentence. These treatments were enormously expensive, however, thus limiting their effectiveness against the epidemic.

Another chronic social problem plagued America during the 1980s. Often disoriented, shoeless, and forlorn, growing numbers of street people slept over heating grates, on subways, and in parks. Homeless people wandered city sidewalks panhandling and struggling to find scraps of food. Winters proved especially difficult.

all-time high of 2,722 at the end of August. There followed a gradual slide over the next few weeks and then a resounding crash. On October 19 the Dow lost an incredible 508 points in one day, almost 23 percent of its value. Analysts blamed the decline on computerized program trading, which automatically instructed money managers to sell stock-index futures when prices on the New York Stock Exchange fell below certain levels. Millions of Americans now feared that the 1987 crash would signal the onset of a great recession or even a depression.

Growing Inequality

The celebration of wealth, moneymaking, and entrepreneurship dominated much of 1980s popular culture, politics, and intellectual life. But grimmer realities lay under the surface. A variety of measures strongly suggested that the nation had moved toward greater inequality, that the middle class was shrinking, and that poverty was on the rise. Two of the most cherished basic assumptions about America—that life would improve for most people and their children and that a comfortable middle-class existence was available to all who worked for it—looked shaky by the early 1990s.

The very wealthy did extremely well during the 1980s. In 1989 the richest 1 percent of American households accounted for 37 percent of the nation's private wealth—up from 31 percent in 1983, a jump of almost 20 percent. This top 1 percent owned more than the bottom 90 percent of Americans.

The most affluent Americans made the biggest gains in family income as well. In 1980 the top 5 percent of families earned 15.3 percent of the nation's total income. By 1992 their share had grown to 17.6 percent, an increase of 15 percent; their average income was $156,000 a year. In 1980 the top 20 percent of families earned 41.6 percent of the nation's total. By 1992 their share had grown to 44.6 percent, an increase of about 7 percent, with an average income of $99,000 a year. In contrast, the bottom 40 percent of families had

16.7 percent of aggregate income in 1980. By 1992 their share had declined to 14.9 percent, a drop of nearly 11 percent, with an average income of about $16,500 a year.

The average weekly earnings of American workers declined from $373 in 1980 to $339 in 1992, and average hourly wages dropped from $10.59 to $9.87 (in 1990 dollars). Both these figures reflected the fact that most of the new jobs created during the 1980s were in low-paying service and manufacturing sectors. Millions of families now needed two wage earners to maintain middle-class status where formerly one would have sufficed.

The number and percentage of Americans living in poverty grew alarmingly during the decade. In 1979 the government classified about 26.1 million people as poor, 11.7 percent of the population. By 1992 the number of poor people had reached 36.9 million, or 14.5 percent of the population. That same year nearly 22 percent of all American children under eighteen lived in poverty, including 47 percent of all black children and 40 percent of all Hispanic children. Thirty-three percent of all African Americans lived in poverty, as did 29 percent of Hispanics. Female-headed households, comprising 13.7 million people, accounted for 37 percent of the poor.

END OF AN ERA?

The Election of 1988

For the 1988 campaign, Republicans nominated Vice-President George Bush. He embodied the eastern establishment, with a few twists. Son of an investment banker and senator from Connecticut, he moved to Texas after serving in World War II as a fighter pilot and finishing his education at Yale. Bush made money in the oil business and entered Texas Republican politics. He held a string of appointive offices under three presidents: head

SHARE OF TOTAL NET WORTH OF AMERICAN FAMILIES		
	1983	**1989**
Richest 1% of families	31%	37%
Next richest 9%	35	31
Remaining 90%	33	32

Source: The New York Times, April 21, 1992.

NUMBER OF POOR, RATE OF POVERTY, AND POVERTY LINE, 1979–1992		
	1979	**1992**
Millions of poor	26.1	36.9
Rate of poverty	11.7%	14.5%
Poverty line (family of four)	$7,412	$14,335

Source: U.S. Bureau of the Census, Current Population Reports: Consumer Income, Series P-60, Nos. 161 and 185, 1988, 1993. U.S. federal data compiled by Ed Royce, Rollins College.

of the National Republican Committee, UN ambassador, envoy to China, director of the CIA, and, finally, vice president. Bush promised to carry forward the policies of his patron, Ronald Reagan.

The Democratic nominee, Governor Michael Dukakis of Massachusetts, stressed competence over ideology and took credit for his state's economic boom. With Reagan retiring, Democrats believed they had a good chance to recapture the White House. At first, Dukakis led Bush in the polls. But Bush aggressively staked out his differences with Dukakis. Republican strategists created and ran a cynical and effective negative campaign that attacked Dukakis for vetoing a law requiring students to pledge allegiance to the flag, for opposing the death penalty and mandatory school prayer, and for being a "card-carrying member" of the American Civil Liberties Union. Most damaging was an ad campaign accusing Dukakis of being soft on crime by authorizing weekend furloughs for some Massachusetts prison inmates. One spot showed a black man named Willie Horton, serving time for rape and assault, who escaped during a furlough and committed another rape. The gut appeal to racist stereotypes was shocking and potent.

The 1988 election intensified the importance of image over substance in the nation's politics. The creation of daily sound bites and spin control by campaign aides seemed far more crucial than debate over issues. Bush and his running mate, Dan Quayle, won the popular vote by 54 to 46 percent and carried the electoral votes of forty out of fifty states. Above all, the election of 1988 signaled that more sophisticated levels of media manipulation and image making were the keys to success in presidential politics.

The New Immigration

Figures from the 1990 census confirmed what many Americans had observed over the previous decade in their communities and workplaces. The face of the nation was perceptibly changing. The Census Bureau estimated that 6 million legal and 2 million undocumented immigrants entered the country during the 1980s, second only to the 8.8 million immigrants who arrived between 1900 and 1910. More than a third of the nation's population growth over the decade—from 227 million to 248 million—came from immigration.

Hispanics and Asians led the accelerated trend toward cultural diversity. The Hispanic population increased by more than 50 percent. One out of every five immigrants living in the United States was Mexican-born, and Mexican Americans overall composed more than 60 percent of the Hispanic population identified in the 1990 census. Nearly a million Mexican Americans lived in Los Angeles alone. Large

Hispanic communities, including Cuban, Puerto Rican, Dominican, and Salvadoran Americans, also grew in New York City, Miami, and Chicago.

The decline of world oil prices had a devastating impact on the Mexican economy, worsening poverty and unemployment and spurring more people to seek a better life in the United States. Most Mexican Americans struggled in low-paying jobs and fought to hold onto their distinctive cultural heritage. Through education and business success, a significant number achieved middle-class status and wealth. But almost 20 percent of Mexican Americans lived below the poverty line.

The number of Asian Americans more than doubled, from 3.5 million to 7.3 million. Like earlier immigrant groups, new Americans from Korea, Vietnam, and the Philippines tended to cluster in their own communities and maintain a durable group identity. This social network explained the large numbers of Hmongs, a tribal group from Laos, drawn to Minneapolis and St. Paul by church-sponsored refugee programs. As a whole, Asian Americans made mobility through education a priority, along with pooling family capital and labor to support small businesses.

The Immigration and Nationality Act of 1965 gave preferential treatment to highly educated foreigners seeking professional opportunities in the United States. The 1965 act set limits of 120,000 immigrants per year from the Western Hemisphere and 170,000 from countries outside the Western Hemisphere. By the mid-1980s, growing concern over "illegal aliens" had become a hotly debated political issue, particularly in the Southwest. The Immigration Reform and Control Act of 1987 for the first time required employers to vouch for the legal status of their employees. At the same time, it offered an amnesty to all undocumented workers who had entered the country before 1982.

Anti-immigration sentiment re-emerged as a potent political force during the 1990s. Proposition 187, a referendum on California's ballot in 1994, called for making all undocumented aliens ineligible for any welfare services, schooling, and non-emergency medical care. It also required teachers and clinic doctors to report illegal aliens to the police. An economic recession during the early 1990s no doubt contributed to the state's increasingly anti-immigrant political mood. Proposition 187 passed by a 3–2 margin, but it was immediately challenged in the streets and in the courts. In 1998 a Los Angeles federal district court ruled that Proposition 187 unconstitutionally usurped federal authority over immigration policy. Despite this ruling, the national debate over immigration policy continued unabated.

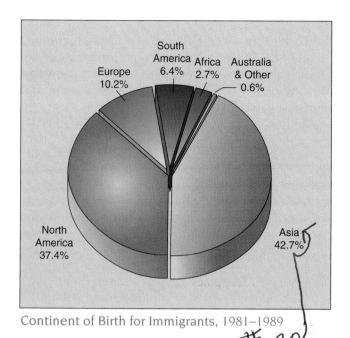

Continent of Birth for Immigrants, 1981–1989

 # 22

The Collapse of Communism

In the Soviet Union the political reforms initiated by Mikhail Gorbachev in the mid-1980s ultimately led to the dissolution of the Soviet state. By calling for a greater openness and a new spirit of democracy, Gorbachev boldly challenged the Communist Party establishment that had dominated Soviet life for three-quarters of a century. He also inspired open opposition to communist rule throughout Eastern Europe. The outright revolt against communist rule first gathered strength in Eastern European nations, then hit home in Moscow with stunning swiftness.

In June 1989 Poland held its first free elections since the communists took power following World War II, bringing an overwhelming victory for the Solidarity movement. In Hungary the Communist Party changed its name and called for a multiparty system, which in 1990 resulted in the election of a center–right government. In the fall of 1989 angry prodemocracy demonstrations forced out long-time Communist Party leaders in Czechoslovakia, Bulgaria, and Romania. Hungary opened its border with Austria, allowing the exit of East Germans gathered at the West German Embassy in Budapest. The Berlin Wall had suddenly been rendered irrelevant. East Germany was forced to open the Wall, which for thirty years had loomed as the ultimate symbol of cold war division. Popular protests and revelations of corruption forced East Germany's Communist Party leaders out of power and paved the way for German reunification the next year.

Political change in the Soviet Union had progressed more slowly. In 1987, on the seventieth

anniversary of the Russian Revolution, Gorbachev denounced Stalin, helping to legitimize growing criticism of censorship and organs of political repression such as the KGB. In March 1989 the Soviet Union held its first free elections since 1917, as a new Congress of People's Deputies replaced the old Communist Party–dominated Supreme Soviet.

In August 1991 the party's hardliners attempted a coup by placing Gorbachev under house arrest at his vacation home in the Crimea, reasserting control of the press, and banning street demonstrations. Boris Yeltsin, president of the Russian Republic, denounced Gorbachev's removal and urged thousands of Muscovites gathered outside the Parliament building to resist. The coup failed. Upon his return from the Crimea, Gorbachev resigned as head of the Communist Party and then banned it. As leader of Russia, the largest of the republics, Yeltsin now emerged as the most powerful political leader. On Christmas Day 1991 a weary and bitter Gorbachev resigned as president of the USSR and recognized the Commonwealth of Independent States. The Soviet Union had dissolved.

The Persian Gulf War

On August 2, 1990, 120,000 Iraqi troops backed by 850 tanks swept into neighboring Kuwait and quickly seized control of that tiny country. The motives of Saddam Hussein, Iraq's military dictator, were mixed. Like most Iraqis, Saddam believed that oil-rich Kuwait was actually an ancient province of Iraq, illegally carved away by British imperial agents in the 1920s as part of the dismemberment of the Ottoman Empire. Control of Kuwait would give Saddam control of its huge oil reserves, as well as Persian Gulf ports for his landlocked country. Oil rivalry within the Organization of Petroleum Exporting Countries (OPEC) was a factor as well. Iraq, which had just ended an exhausting and inconclusive eight-year war with Iran, bitterly resented Kuwait's production of oil beyond OPEC quotas, which had helped send the world price of oil plummeting.

The United States responded swiftly to news of the invasion. Its first concern was that Saddam might attack Saudi Arabia as well, which the United States had defined as vital to its interests as far back as 1943. On August 15 President Bush quickly ordered U.S. forces to Saudi Arabia and the Persian Gulf, calling it Operation Desert Shield. By the middle of October, some 230,000 American troops had been sent to the Persian Gulf.

In early November President Bush announced a change in policy to what he called "an offensive military option," and the U.S. troop deployment quickly doubled to over 400,000, reaching 580,000 by

U.S. Marines swept into Kuwait City, March 1991. After six weeks of intensive bombing and less than five days after the start of a massive ground offensive, U.S. and allied forces overwhelmed the Iraqi army and ended Saddam Hussein's occupation of Kuwait.

January 1991. Bush administration officials now demonized Saddam as another Hitler, and warned that he controlled a formidable fighting machine of over a million men. UN sanctions failed to budge Saddam from Kuwait, and the drift to war now looked inevitable. In January 1991 the Senate and the House vigorously debated a joint resolution authorizing the use of military force. Opponents urged the president to give the economic sanctions more time to force Iraq out, and they warned of the bloody cost of a drawn-out ground war against Saddam. They also pointed out that the United States had only recently supported Saddam (with economic aid, wheat exports, and arms sales) in his war with Iran. The resolution passed narrowly in the Senate (52 to 47), and more comfortably in the House (250 to 183).

A last-minute UN peace mission failed to break the deadlock. On January 16, 1991, President Bush announced the start of Operation Desert Storm. U.S. and Allied air forces began forty-two days of massive bombing of Iraqi positions in Kuwait, as well as Baghdad and other Iraqi cities. The ground war began on February 24, and it took only 100 hours to force Saddam out of Kuwait. Iraqi troops, most of whom were poor conscripts reluctant to fight, surrendered in droves. Saddam's military machine turned out to be far weaker than advertised. U.S. forces suffered only 184 casualties, compared with nearly 100,000 Iraqi deaths, mostly from bombing.

At home, the vast majority of Americans supported Operation Desert Storm; antiwar protests around the nation received scant media coverage. Unlike the coverage of Vietnam, Americans saw virtually no blood or death on their television screens. The Pentagon carefully controlled the release of silent film footage documenting precision bombing runs. On television these looked more like video games than bombing attacks. American military officials insisted that the bombing had been limited to Iraqi military targets. But subsequent investigations revealed the devastation of Iraq's electrical and communication systems, waterways, bridges, factories, and highways—in short, the nation's entire infrastructure.

To most Americans, the war seemed a welcome reassertion of the nation's military prowess and world leadership. Bush received a hero's welcome from a joint session of Congress in March. His approval rating with the public reached nearly 90 percent, higher than President Roosevelt's during World War II.

Yet nagging questions remained unanswered. Saddam himself survived, and the United States abandoned Iraqi opposition forces and Kurds after encouraging them to rebel. The United States had succeeded in restoring the government of Kuwait to power, but that government itself was an undemocratic feudal monarchy. The ecological damage in the Gulf region, mainly from Saddam's torching of Kuwaiti oil wells, was extensive. The massive bombing of Iraq led to a severe public health crisis and destroyed its economy. Human rights groups reported an appalling toll among civilians. The war brought an intense spirit of triumph to the people of the United States. But for the 18 million people of Iraq, heavily bombed and left with Saddam in power, it produced the worst possible outcome.

The Election of 1992

As President Bush's popularity soared following the Persian Gulf War, most political analysts believed he would win reelection easily. But as the glow of military victory faded, so did Bush's political fortunes. A harsh and lingering recession in 1991 and 1992 dominated the presidential election campaign. The recession was different from other post–World War II slumps in several ways. Although interest rates were low and theoretically should have encouraged investment, business continued to shrink rather than expand. The nation's manufacturers faced stiffer competition than ever, especially from Japan, Korea, and the industrialized nations of Europe. As unemployment climbed above 8 percent, consumer confidence and retail sales plummeted. The recession was unique in producing a large number of highly educated, white-collar unemployed, thrown out of work by declining real estate, financial, and computer industries.

The paradoxes of the Reagan–Bush years became apparent. Conservatives took credit for forcing the fall of communism and reviving America's military strength. Yet the fundamental international problem facing the country seemed to be the erosion of American economic competitiveness and the decline in real wages. In communities devastated by the loss of key industries, millions wondered whether the structural changes transforming the world economy meant an irreversible decline in the American standard of living. Conservatives had made cutting government spending a central premise of their appeal. But after twelve years of Republican rule the national debt stood at an astronomical $4 trillion and threatened to undermine the nation's economic future.

After a vigorous primary season the Democrats nominated Governor Bill Clinton of Arkansas. Clinton had begun his political life as a liberal, anti–Vietnam War Democrat. But after suffering defeat after his first term as Arkansas governor, he had remade himself politically as a centrist. Clinton's campaign for the nomination effectively adopted many of the conservative themes that had proved so popular for Republicans over the past twelve years. He called for "responsibility" from the recipients of social programs, spoke of the importance of stable families, promised to be tough on crime and bureaucracy, and stressed the need to encourage private investment to create new jobs.

A wild-card element in the 1992 election was the independent campaign of Texas billionaire H. Ross Perot. Perot had made a fortune with a data-processing company that had computerized Social Security and Medicare records in the 1960s and 1970s. He promoted his candidacy through appearances on television talk shows, hoping to bypass traditional media outlets and reach voters directly. With his folksy, East Texas twang, Perot appealed to the deep distrust and anger that millions felt toward the two major parties. He made the national debt his central issue, and he argued that a successful businessman like him was more qualified to solve the nation's economic woes than Washington insiders. Perot spent millions of dollars of his own money funding "volunteer" organizations in the fifty states. In July, with polls showing him running nearly even with Bush and Clinton, he abruptly announced that he was quitting the race. His reasoning was unclear. Two months later, in an effort to restore his damaged reputation, he was back in.

On election day Democrats recaptured the White House after twelve years of Republican control. Clinton won big, beating Bush 43 percent to 38 percent in the popular vote and 370 to 168 in the electoral vote. Although he carried no states, Perot garnered 19 percent of the popular vote, the strongest showing by a third-party candidate since Theodore Roosevelt in 1912.

Clinton won back many of the Reagan Democrats he had courted, and his campaign also broke the long Republican grip on the states of the trans-Mississippi West. With a solidly Democratic House and Senate, President Clinton called for an "American renewal" as he began his term.

"The Era of Big Government Is Over"

A self-styled new Democrat, President Clinton tempered his commitment to activist government with a strategy sensitive to widespread cynicism about Washington politics and big government in general. Although his party also controlled Congress, Clinton sought to distance himself from its liberal core. On several key domestic and foreign policy issues Clinton thus found himself fighting with Democrats nearly as much as with Republicans.

As part of a campaign strategy that promised a new government attentiveness to the "forgotten middle class," Clinton pledged a sweeping reform of the nation's health-care system. Nearly 40 million Americans had no health insurance at all. Many simply could not afford it, and others were denied coverage by private insurers because of preexisting conditions such as AIDS and heart disease. Sudden illness or long-term hospital care could wipe out the savings of the uninsured and underinsured. For millions of others, health insurance was tied to the workplace, and a loss or change of jobs threatened their coverage. National spending on health care had skyrocketed from roughly $200 billion in 1980 to more than $800 billion in 1992, constituting about one-seventh of the entire domestic economy.

Once in office Clinton appointed his wife, Hillary Rodham Clinton, to head a task force charged with preparing a sweeping legislative overhaul of health care. The complex plan that emerged from the task force in the fall of 1993 was difficult to understand and impossible to sell politically. Under this managed competition proposal, most Americans would obtain coverage through large purchasing groups called health-care alliances. Employers would be mandated to pay at least 80 percent of their employees' insurance premiums. Private insurance companies would remain at the center of the system.

Powerful forces attacked the Clinton administration's health-care plan immediately. The Chamber of Commerce and National Association of Manufacturers opposed the employer mandate provision. Republicans and conservative Democrats called for greater reliance on market forces and criticized the "big government" approach. Many of these members of Congress had received large campaign donations from political action committees associated with the pharmaceutical industry, insurance companies, and the American Medical Association. After a year of congressional wrangling, no plan was approved, and the president was forced to abandon his reform effort.

In foreign affairs Clinton focused on improving America's international trade position as the key to national economic growth. He pushed two important trade agreements through Congress, both of which built on efforts by the Reagan and Bush administrations to expand markets and encourage free trade. Approved in late 1993, the North American Free Trade Agreement (NAFTA) eased the international flow of goods, services, and investments among the United States, Mexico, and Canada by eliminating tariffs and other trade barriers. Supplemental agreements called for cooperation on environmental and labor concerns. The broad goal of NAFTA was to improve productivity and living standards through a freer flow of commerce in North America. It created the largest free trade zone in the world, comprising 360 million people and an annual gross national product of $6 trillion.

In 1994 Congress also approved the General Agreement on Tariffs and Trade (GATT), which slashed tariffs on thousands of goods throughout the world and phased out import quotas imposed by the United States and other industrialized nations. It also established the World Trade Organization to mediate commercial disputes among 117 nations. GATT supporters argued that the agreement would encourage global competition, thereby boosting American export industries and creating new high-wage jobs for American workers.

But NAFTA and GATT barely won approval after bruising congressional fights, and both found their strongest champions among Republicans. Many Democrats in Congress, especially those from traditionally liberal districts in the Northeast and Midwest, bitterly opposed the agreements, creating a strain within the party. Critics of GATT questioned the rosy predictions of a net gain in high-wage jobs. Increases in imports, they pointed out, would threaten hundreds of thousands of high-paying jobs in American industries such as automobiles and textiles. Opponents of NAFTA feared that the free trade agreements would mean an exodus of millions of jobs to Mexico because industries would be attracted there by its low wages and lax enforcement of workers' rights. They worried, too, that the environmental sections of the agreement were too weak to prevent Mexico from becoming a haven for corporate polluters.

In the first few years after the passage of NAFTA and GATT many of these fears seemed to be confirmed. Free trade with the United States was supposed to bring prosperity to Mexico. Instead, the peso collapsed, and the Mexican economy slipped into a serious depression. Meanwhile, a 1997 Department of Labor study concluded that some 142,000 U.S. and Canadian jobs had been lost as a direct result of NAFTA. Moreover, the report admitted, many American employers were using the threat of moving plants or facilities to Mexico as a weapon in wage negotiations with workers. There was also increasing evidence that environmental conditions along the U.S.–Mexican border were growing worse.

The failure of health-care reform and the debate over NAFTA revealed a Democratic Party deeply divided against itself. President Clinton's political position was also weakened by publicity attending his personal life. Paula Jones, a former Arkansas state employee, filed a sexual harassment suit against him. Nagging questions arose about real estate deals in which Clinton and his wife were involved while he was still governor of Arkansas—a scandal that became known as Whitewater. Responding to Republican charges that a former business partner of Clinton's had received favorable insider treatment in connection with a failed savings and loan company, the Attorney General eventually appointed an independent counsel, former judge Kenneth Starr.

Reacting to doubts about Clinton's character and leadership, voters in the 1994 congressional election rewarded Republicans with control of both the House and Senate for the first time in forty years—a disaster of historic proportions for Clinton and the Democratic Party. Congress was now dominated by a new breed of younger, ideologically more conservative Republicans. Their leader was the new House Speaker, Newt Gingrich of Georgia. First elected to Congress in 1978, Gingrich had quickly won a reputation as a formidable polemicist for the Republican Party's far right. A brilliant organizer and fund raiser, he had moved from the margins to the center of his party's power structure. With his scathing denunciations of big government, attacks on the counterculture of the 1960s, and celebration of entrepreneurship, Gingrich captured the heart of the Republican Party and emerged as potentially the most influential House Speaker in this century.

The Republicans exploited prevailing social conditions. As more and more working-class and middle-class voters expressed fear for their jobs and economic security in the new global economy, race and immigration loomed as effective "hot button" issues for political candidates. With attacks on welfare, affirmative action, and federal initiatives to aid education and the inner cities, conservatives exploited a continuing white backlash against the limited economic and political gains African Americans had achieved in the previous decades. No candidates addressed the deepening poverty and economic inequality that put one of every seven Americans, and one of every five children, below the poverty line.

The Republican victory at the polls allowed Gingrich to challenge Clinton as the key figure setting the nation's political agenda. His priorities were expressed in a set of proposals labeled the "Contract with America." Invoking the "hundred days" of Franklin D. Roosevelt's New Deal in 1933 (see Chapter 24), Gingrich promised to bring all these proposals to a vote in the House within 100 days. The House did indeed pass much of the Contract, including a large tax cut, an increase in military spending, cutbacks in federal regulatory power in the environment and at the workplace, a tough anticrime bill, and a sharp reduction in federal welfare programs. Differences with the Senate, however, and the threat of presidential veto thwarted Gingrich's plans and created conditions that allowed President Clinton to make a political comeback.

In December 1995 the Republican controlled Congress forced a shutdown of the federal government rather than accede to President Clinton's demand for changes in their proposed budget. The result was a public relations disaster for the Republicans. Gingrich's reputation plummeted, and after little more than a year as Speaker he had become one of the most unpopular figures in American politics.

of Kansas, Majority Leader of the Senate, was forced to move to his right to counter more conservative opponents such as commentator Patrick Buchanan and wealthy publisher Steve Forbes, who advocated replacing the income tax with a so-called "flat tax." Dole had the nomination locked up by June, but the bruising primary battles cost him the support of many voters who worried that Dole's positions were cut from the same cloth as Gingrich's "Contract with America."

Pursuing a strategy his advisers called "triangulation," the president successfully positioned himself above and between the interests of warring Democrats and Republicans. Welfare reform provided a prominent example of this strategy in action. Despite his attacks on the Republicans as radicals, Clinton opposed his own party's efforts to block a Republican plan to dismantle the federal welfare system in place since the New Deal. The new legislation—the Welfare Reform Act—abolished the sixty-year-old Aid to Families with Dependent Children program (AFDC). Poor mothers with dependent children would now have access to aid for only a limited period and only if they were preparing for or seeking work. When Congress passed the act in August of 1996, Clinton held a public signing ceremony and declared "an end to welfare as we know it."

The Election of 1996 and Clinton's Second Term

Meanwhile, Clinton undercut the Republicans by adapting many of their positions to his own. He endorsed the goal of a balanced federal budget and declared, in his January 1996 State of the Union message, that "the era of big government is over." With such deft maneuvers, the president set the theme for his 1996 reelection campaign, portraying himself as a reasonable conservative and the Republicans in Congress as conservative radicals. In a blitz of effective television ads, Democrats portrayed Republicans as reckless extremists bent on destroying the safety net of Social Security and Medicare and inattentive to the educational needs of children.

Leading Republicans, meanwhile, attacked each other as they fought to win their party's presidential nomination. In the state primaries leading up to the national convention, Robert Dole

The era of divided government at century's end meant that Democrats controlled the White House while Republicans dominated the Congress. Here President Bill Clinton talked to Senate Majority Leader Trent Lott (R-MS), as House Speaker Newt Gingrich (R-GA) looked on, during a White House meeting to discuss combating terrorism, July 29, 1996.

Clinton's greatest strength was a resurgent American economy. The recession that had plagued George Bush's presidency bottomed out in 1994, followed over the next two years by strong economic growth, a dramatic rise in the stock market, and a sharp decline in unemployment. Confounding the predictions of political pundits, who had pronounced his political death after the Republican congressional sweep of 1994, President Bill Clinton won a resounding reelection victory in November 1996. But it was a victory without coattails; the Republicans retained control of both houses of Congress. The era of big government may have ended, as Clinton had proclaimed, but the era of divided government would continue.

The conflict between the Democratic president and the Republican Congress reached historic proportions in 1998. Independent counsel Kenneth Starr delivered an explosive report of his investigation to the House Judiciary Committee. The Starr report focused entirely on an extramarital affair the president had conducted with a young White House intern, Monica Lewinsky. Starr claimed his office had discovered evidence of the affair while reviewing depositions from the Paula Jones lawsuit. The report outlined several potentially impeachable offenses, allegedly committed by the president in the course of trying to keep his affair with Lewinsky secret. These included lying under oath, witness tampering, and obstruction of justice. In October 1998, the House of Representatives voted along largely partisan lines to begin a full-scale, open-ended inquiry into possible ground for the impeachment of President Clinton. It was only the third time in American history that the House had taken such action.

Republicans expected the Lewinsky scandal and the impeachment inquiry to bolster their fortunes in the election of 1998, augmenting the gains the party out of power in the White House can traditionally expect in a midterm election. Indeed all summer and fall, virtually every professional pollster and media commentator predicted big Republican gains in the House and Senate. Instead, for the first time since 1934, the president's party added seats in a midterm election. The Democrats gained five seats in the House, cutting the Republican majority from 228–206 in the 105th Congress to 223–211 in the 106th. In the Senate, Republicans were unable to increase their 55–45 majority.

Voters no doubt had more on their minds than President Clinton's sex life. Democratic candidates benefited from continued strength in the economy, and they made effective appeals on a range of issues, from preserving Social Security and Medicare to protecting a woman's right to choose an abortion. Higher than expected turnout from such core constituencies as union members and African Americans (especially in the South) also contributed to the unexpectedly strong Democratic showing. The election also brought a shakeup in the Republican leadership. Newt Gingrich, under pressure from Republican colleagues angry about a campaign strategy that had narrowly focused on Clinton's impeachment problem, announced his resignation as Speaker of the House and from his seat in Congress. Ironically Gingrich, who had led the Republican resurgence in the 1990s, now appeared to be the first political victim of the Lewinsky scandal.

In the aftermath of the 1998 election, most politicians and analysts, and indeed most Americans, believed the impeachment inquiry to be at a dead end. But the House Judiciary Committee, after raucous televised debate, voted to bring four articles of impeachment—charging President Clinton with perjury, obstruction of justice, witness tampering, and abuse of power—to the full House. But unlike the bipartisan case the Judiciary Committee brought against Richard Nixon in 1974 (see Chapter 29), this time the votes were all along strictly party lines. Neither the 1998 election results, nor polls showing a large majority of Americans opposed to removing the president, curbed the Republican determination to push impeachment through the House. On December 19, 1998, for only the second time in American history, the full House voted to impeach a sitting president, passing articles along party lines charging Clinton with perjury and obstruction of justice and sending them to the Senate for trial. But none of the impeachment articles could muster even a simple majority in the Senate, much less the two-thirds required for conviction, thus leaving Clinton to finish out his second term. The impeachment drive could be understood as the culmination of divided government and the bitterly partisan turn American politics had taken since 1980.

Changing American Communities

The 1990 census showed that for the first time in U.S. history a majority of Americans lived within a large metropolitan area. The census defined a metropolitan area as "one or more counties including a large population nucleus and nearby communities that have a high degree of interaction." The census divided these areas into two groups: those with populations above 1 million and those with smaller populations. It revealed that nearly 125 million people out of a total population of 249 million lived within the thirty-nine large (over 1 million) metropolitan centers. Greater New York City, with more than 18 million people, was the largest of these areas, followed by Greater Los Angeles, with 14.5 million residents. The nation's fastest-growing large metropolitan areas were all in the West and South. These included Orlando, which grew by 53 percent in the 1980s, Phoenix (40 percent), Sacramento (34 percent),

San Diego (34 percent), Dallas–Fort Worth (32 percent), Atlanta (32 percent), and Los Angeles (26 percent).

This historic statistical shift stemmed directly from the expansion of the economy's service sector. The nation's postindustrial economy relied heavily on the growth of management, research and development, marketing, and distribution activities. These required the critical mass of educated people and services that could be found only in metropolitan areas. The proportion of the population with at least a college degree grew disproportionately in those areas, to 22.5 percent, compared with 13 percent in nonmetropolitan areas.

An enormous range of differences could be found both between and within metropolitan area communities. Recent immigrants brought a striking new multiculturalism to many coastal and Sunbelt "port of entry" communities, whereas smaller communities in the Midwest remained unchanged. In Greater Los Angeles, for example, half the population was Hispanic, black, or Asian, and 27 percent of the residents were foreign-born. But the community that many demographers called typical was Indianapolis, where less than 15 percent of the population was Hispanic, black, or Asian and less than 2 percent of the residents were foreign-born. A larger percentage of people lived in expanding metropolitan areas, but a larger proportion of metropolitan people lived in the suburbs. Metropolitan expansion created huge semiurban sprawls, which erased the boundaries between many towns. Population and job growth were concentrated at the geographic edges of metropolitan areas.

Whereas the traditional American city was built around a central business district, newer suburban cities grew up around a principal business or economic activity: a collection of computer companies, a large regional medical center, or a sports complex. Suburban cities have become even more economically specialized than the industrial centers of the nineteenth century. Yet their gains often meant losses for older cities. As core cities lost jobs and part of their tax base to suburban cities, it became more difficult for them to pay the costs of maintaining infrastructure and caring for the elderly, poor, and sick. While suburban cities often suffered from labor shortages, unemployment increased in the core cities, especially among African Americans and Latinos. Lack of adequate transportation and low-cost housing made it difficult for central-city residents to take advantage of new job opportunities in the suburban city.

CONCLUSION

In the late 1980s and early 1990s, as the nation faced competition from a tougher, more dynamic global economy, citizens, politicians, and business leaders had to rethink some of their most basic assumptions about the American way of life. American society became more stratified along lines of race and income. New immigrant groups, especially from Asia and Latin America, changed the face of the nation's neighborhoods, schools, and workplaces. New epidemics and spreading poverty threatened the public health of whole communities. New media technologies made cultural life more homogenized and made the manipulation of image more crucial than ever in both politics and entertainment.

During these decades the very notion of community itself, once defined entirely in terms of space, increasingly became a function of demographic categories. The proliferation of computer-based communication technologies made it easier to create communities centering in these categories, such as income, profession, education level, and consumption preferences. The mass media, advertisers, and political professionals all intensified their reliance on sophisticated marketing and polling techniques. Thus American culture defined and addressed its citizens less as whole human beings and more as the sums of statistical characteristics. At the same time, new technologies created "virtual communities" with the potential for new kinds of human relationships not defined by corporate values or even by physical familiarity. As American communities continue to evolve in response to a more global, service-oriented, and high-tech economy, they will no doubt be forced to seek both regional and international solutions to the problems posed by the twenty-first century.

CHRONOLOGY

1980	Ronald Reagan is elected president
1981	Reagan administration initiates major cuts in taxes and domestic spending
	Military buildup accelerates
	AIDS is recognized and named
	MTV and CNN start broadcasting as cable channels
1982	Economic recession grips the nation
	Nuclear freeze rally attracts 750,000 in New York City
1983	Reagan announces the Strategic Defense Initiative, labeled "Star Wars" by critics
	241 marines killed in Beirut terrorist bombing
	Marines land on Grenada and oust anti-American Marxist regime
1984	Reagan is reelected overwhelmingly
1985	Mikhail Gorbachev initiates reforms—*glasnost* and *perestroika*—in the Soviet Union
1986	Immigration Reform and Control Act addresses concerns about illegal aliens
	Democrats regain control of the Senate
1987	Iran–Contra hearings before Congress reveal arms-for-hostages deal and funds secretly and illegally diverted to Nicaraguan rebels
	Stock market crashes
	Reagan and Gorbachev sign INF Treaty
1988	George Bush is elected president
1989	Communist authority collapses in eastern Europe
1990	August: Iraqi invasion of Kuwait leads to massive U.S. military presence in the Persian Gulf
1991	January–February: Operation Desert Storm forces Iraq out of Kuwait
	Soviet Union dissolves into Commonwealth of Independent States
1992	Rodney King verdict sparks rioting in Los Angeles
	Bill Clinton is elected president
1993	Clinton administration introduces comprehensive health-care reform, but it fails to win passage in Congress
	Congress approves the North American Free Trade Agreement
1994	Republicans win control of Senate and House for first time in forty years
	Congress approves the General Agreement on Tariffs and Trade
1996	Congress passes Welfare Reform Act
	President Bill Clinton is reelected

REVIEW QUESTIONS

1. Describe the central philosophical assumptions behind Reaganomics. What were the key policies by which it was implemented? To what extent were these policies a break with previous economic approaches?

2. Evaluate Reagan–Bush-era foreign policy. What successes and failures stand out? Which problems from those years remain central or unsolved for today's policy makers?

3. Analyze the key structural factors underlying recent changes in American economic and cultural life. Do you see any political solutions for the growth of poverty and inequality?

4. Assess the growing political appeal of conservatism in American life. How would you explain its successes? What future do you see for the liberal tradition?

5. Is the United States entering a new era at the turn of the twenty-first century? What effects have the globalized economy and the fall of the Soviet Union had on American life?

RECOMMENDED READING

Donald Barlett and James B. Steele, *America: What Went Wrong* (1992). An expansion of the authors' series in the *Philadelphia Inquirer*. This book offers a mass of interesting data documenting the declining fortunes of the American middle class in the 1980s.

Sidney Blumenthal and Thomas B. Edsall, eds., *The Reagan Legacy* (1988). A collection of critical essays assessing the impact of Reagan's presidency on American society and culture.

Colin Campbell and Bert A. Rockman, eds., *The Clinton Presidency: First Appraisals* (1996). A wide-ranging collection of essays assessing the political historical significance of the Clinton administration.

Haynes Johnson, *Sleepwalking Through History* (1991). A readable, journalistic narrative of the Reagan presidency.

Michael T. Klare and Peter Kornbluh, eds., *Low Intensity Warfare* (1988). A valuable set of essays offering case studies of counterinsurgency and antiterrorist tactics during the 1980s.

Robert Lekachman, *Visions and Nightmares* (1987). An economist's view of Reagan's legacy, emphasizing the long-range impact of military spending, tax cuts, and the shrinking of social programs.

Nicolaus Mills, *Culture in an Age of Money* (1990). An acerbic account of the impact of corporate power and big money on the cultural life of the nation during the 1980s.

New York Times, The Downsizing of America (1996). A well-researched account detailing the devastating impact of corporate "downsizing" on American communities and families.

Kevin Phillips, *The Politics of Rich and Poor* (1990). A fascinating, superbly documented, and often brilliant analysis of the growth in economic inequality that characterized the 1980s. Phillips, a prominent Republican strategist, makes historical comparisons with the 1920s and the late nineteenth century to bolster his argument.

Howard Rheingold, *The Virtual Community* (1994). Very thoughtful examination of the promises and problems posed by the new computer-based technologies associated with "virtual communities."

Micah L. Sifry and Christopher Cerf, eds., *The Gulf War Reader* (1991). An excellent collection of historical essays, government documents, and political addresses that provides a comprehensive overview of the Persian Gulf War.

James B. Stewart, *Den of Thieves* (1991). A well-documented inside look at the people and events at the center of Wall Street's insider trader scandal. Stewart offers a detailed account of the shady financial practices of the 1980s.

During the last three quarters of the twentieth century, the character and sources of immigration to the United States changed radically. With America's growing power and prominence in the international arena, the laws governing immigration became increasingly tools of foreign policy. The social devastation of World War II and the ideological battles of the cold war created whole new categories of immigrant, such as that of political refugee. Recent immigration has also reflected the dynamic transformations in the economies of the United States and of the rest of the world. The national quotas established in the 1920s severely limited the flow of immigrants from Europe. But lawmakers, responding to the labor needs of industry and agriculture, had placed no barriers to newcomers from the Western Hemisphere. Thus, Canadians and Mexicans grew into the two largest national immigrant groups. Circular migration shaped the experience of these peoples; they were "transborder peoples," going frequently back and forth between their homelands and the United States. Dividing their political and cultural loyalties between the United States and their homelands, Mexicans and Canadians developed an ambiguous identity. As a result, they were slower to adopt U.S. citizenship than were other immigrants.

Some 1.4 million Canadians arrived in the United States between 1920 and 1960, with three quarters from British Canada (Ontario, Nova Scotia, New Brunswick) and one quarter from French Canada (Quebec). They settled close to the border, primarily in New England cities such as Boston, Lowell, Nashua, and Holyoke, as well as in the Great Lakes region. During the same period, more than 840,000 Mexicans arrived as permanent settlers and 4.7 million more as temporary guest workers. They headed mainly for the rich agricultural areas of southern California and the lower Rio Grande Valley of Texas. Many, however, looking for factory work, settled in big Midwestern industrial centers such as Chicago, Detroit, and Kansas City. In the Southwest, Mexicans tended to cluster in isolated *barrios*. In the midwest, in contrast, following the pattern of older European immigrant communities in big cities, they tended to assimilate more.

Perhaps more than any other group, Mexican immigrants were subject to the vagaries of the U.S. economy. The Great Depression drastically reduced the need for their labor and spurred a mass reverse migration. As many as half a million Mexicans were repatriated during the 1930s, often at the urging of local American officials who did not want Mexican aliens on public relief rolls. The onset of World War II brought a new demand for Mexican labor in agriculture and transportation. In 1942 the U.S. and Mexican governments revived the guest worker program of World War I. The *bracero* (farmhand) program admitted agricultural workers on short-term contracts; they were classified as foreign laborers, not immigrants. By 1947, some 200,000 *braceros* worked in twenty-one states, including 100,000 in California. Congress renewed the program after the war ended. By 1960 Mexicans made up more than one quarter of the nation's farm labor force.

Puerto Ricans, the third largest group of immigrants to the U.S. mainland from the Western Hemisphere, were a special case because, as U.S. citizens since 1917, they could come and go without restriction. Like Canadians and Mexicans, they helped fill the labor demand caused by the restriction of European immigration. Between 1945 and 1965 the Puerto Rican-born population jumped from 100,000 to roughly 1 million. The majority headed for New York City and surrounding communities.

Another growing class of immigrants consisted of refugees uprooted by World War II and the emergence of Communist regimes in Eastern Europe. A series of laws combined the historical notion of America as a haven for the world's oppressed with the new reality of cold war power politics. The Displaced Persons Act of 1948 was the first law in American history to set refugee policy as opposed to immigration policy. It provided 202,000 visas over a two-year period, allowing permanent settlement in the United States for refugees from fascist and Communist regimes. A 1950 amendment upped the number of visas to 341,000 annually. The Refugee Relief Act of 1953 authorized admission of 205,000 "nonquota" refugees, but limited these to people fleeing persecution from Communist regimes. In practice, this policy gave priority to refugees from the Baltic states and Eastern European Communist nations; only a minority admitted under the act were Jews or other victims of Hitler. Indeed, hundreds of former Nazis, including many scientists, were allowed in under the act in the interest of "national security."

In 1952, as a conservative counterpoint to the growth of refugee legislation, Congress passed the McCarran-Walter Act. Reaffirming the 1920s principle of discriminatory quotas based on national origin, the act specified that 85 percent of those admitted annually were to come from Northern and Western European countries. Yet McCarran-Walter also contained some important liberal innovations. It revoked the denial of admission based on race, and it allowed for small, token quotas for immigrants from China and Japan, ending the long-standing policy of Asian exclusion.

The Immigration Act of 1965, passed almost unnoticed in the context of the egalitarian political climate created by the Civil Rights movement, had revolutionary consequences, some of them unintended. The act abolished the discriminatory national origins quotas that had been in place since the 1920s. But it also limited immigration from the Western Hemisphere for the first time, allowing 120,000 annual visas from that region, compared to 170,000 from the Eastern Hemisphere. It continued the policy of selective admissions, but with important exceptions. Exempted from numerical quotas were immigrants seeking family reunification with American citizens or resident aliens. In addition, preferences to those with specialized job skills and training were extended to people from the nations of the Eastern Hemisphere.

The high priority given family reunification greatly increased the "chain migration" of people seeking to join relatives already in the United States. After 1965, Asian immigrants made up the fastest growing ethnic groups, with more than 1.5 million arriving during the 1970s, as opposed to roughly 800,000 from Europe. The new Asian migration included many professionals and well-educated technical workers. For example, immigrants from the Philippines and India included a high number of health care professionals, and many Chinese and Korean immigrants found work in professional and managerial occupations. At the same time, low-skilled and impoverished Asians poured into the "Chinatowns" and "Koreatowns" of cities like New York and Los Angeles, seeking work in restaurants, hotels, and garment manufacturing. The end of the Indochina War brought new refugees from Cambodia, Laos, and Vietnam. The 1965 act also created conditions that increased undocumented immigration from Latin America. The new limits on Western Hemisphere migration, along with simultaneous ending of the *bracero* program, tempted many thousands to enter the United States illegally. The Immigration and Naturalization Service arrested and deported 500,000 illegal aliens each year in the decade following the act, most of them from Mexico, Central America, and the Caribbean.

During the 1980s the rate of immigration accelerated. The estimated 6 million legal and 2 million undocumented immigrants who entered the United States during that decade was second only to the 8.8 million who had arrived between 1900 and 1910. By 1990, one out of every five immigrants living in the United States was Mexican-born, and Mexican Americans accounted for more than 60 percent of all Hispanics. Demographers predicted that by 2050 Hispanics would replace African Americans as the largest minority group in the nation. The number of Asian Americans more than doubled during the 1980s, from 3.5 million to 7.3 million. Nearly two out of every five Asian Americans lived in California, with 300,000 in Los Angeles' "Koreatown." Among recent immigrant groups, Asians—Vietnamese, Filipinos, Koreans, and Chinese—gained naturalization (citizenship) at the fastest rate. Asians totaled nearly 50 percent of all people naturalized in the 1980s. Unlike early-twentieth-century Asian migrants, the post-1965 newcomers were mostly intent on settling here permanently, and they migrated in family units. The new Asian immigrants also remade the small ethnic enclaves from earlier migrations, reinvigorating them with new energy, new capital, and a more explicit ethnic consciousness.

By the mid-1980s, growing concern over "illegal aliens" had become a hotly debated political issue, particularly in the Southwest. The Immigration Reform and Control Act of 1986 marked a break with past attempts to address this problem. Instead of mass deportation programs, the law offered an amnesty to all undocumented workers who had entered the country since 1982. Although opening the "front door" of admissions wider, the law also tried to shut the "back door" by imposing sanctions on employers who knowingly hired or recruited undocumented aliens. Yet no matter what Congress did, the desperate economic realities in Mexico and Central America continued to enlarge the flow of undocumented aliens. At the century's end, both American immigration policy and the immigrants now arriving look radically different than they did 75 years ago. Nativist sentiment and calls for greater immigration restriction are still powerful voices on the political scene, especially during economic downturns and within those states absorbing the bulk of new immigrants. Nativist appeals and campaigns will likely remain part of the American political landscape—but they have been defeated by the fundamental idea that immigration has ultimately strengthened America's economy, culture, and society. At the dawn of the new millennium, a glance at almost any American city, school, or workplace reinforces that point clearly.

West Indian-American Day Parade, Brooklyn New York, 1991

■ IN THEIR OWN WORDS

In 1984 Rosa Maria Urbina, a thirty-one-year-old widow from Juarez, Mexico, crossed the Rio Grande looking for work as a housecleaner in El Paso. She had hoped to earn enough money to take her three children out of an orphanage. José Luis, a Juarez farm worker, moved to El Paso permanently in 1981 at the age of twenty-two. The two married and made their life among El Paso's fifty thousand illegal immigrants, known in Mexican slang as *mojados*, or "wets," the river people.

José: The majority of the people in our apartment building have the same problem as my family. All of us are in El Paso without legal papers. I have been living here since 1981.

Rosa: I came in 1984, to find work. After José and I were married and we found a place to live, I brought my children from my previous marriage. We lived across the river in Juárez. But I was born further south, in Zacatecas.

José: My hometown is Juárez. Since I was nine years old, I've been coming to El Paso to work. At first I did gardening in people's yards, but I have stayed in El Paso constantly since 1981, going out to the fields to do farm work. I used to go to Juárez to visit my relatives at least one day each month. But in the last year, I haven't gone, because of the immigration law. To visit Juarez I have to swim across the river. I can't cross the bridge or the *migra* [Border Patrol officers] can catch me right there. . . .

Rosa: When I was a teenager, I worked as a hairdresser in a beauty salon, cutting hair. My first husband was a mechanic, fixing cars. We made a good living. But my husband spent the money he made drinking in the *cantinas.* And after a while, he wouldn't let me work, because I had young children to take care of. When he

died in 1984, he left me with nothing at all. . . . My children were nine, seven, and three years old. I had to find a way to pay rent and feed them.

At that time, the economy in Mexico had become horrible. Inflation was going crazy. The peso jumped to 500 per dollar. Today it is still climbing at 1,000 per dollar. I found a job working on an assembly line at a factory. We produced rubber gloves for hospitals and medical supplies like caps for syringes. I would go into work at 4:30 in the afternoon and stay until 2:00 A.M. I was paid only 7,000 pesos [$14] each week. That was not enough to feed my kids. And I didn't have any relatives or friends to watch the kids while I worked. So I had no other choice but to put them in a special institution, like an orphanage, for children without parents. This upset me very much. But with my husband dead, and no other form of support, there was nothing I could do.

My only hope was to cross the river to the United States. If I could find a job that paid enough money, my children could join me. I wanted them to have an education and a proper life . . . to be someone. . . .

Before I met José, I crossed back and forth across the river five days each week to my housekeeping jobs in El Paso. On weekends, I took my children out of the orphanage. Then I had to reluctantly return them to the orphanage on Sunday evenings and prepare to go back across the river.[1]

Wing Ng, a Cantonese woman born into a poor family, emigrated to California in 1975 at the age of twenty-three. She came alone, but had the sponsorship of her sister's friend in Los Angeles, as well as financial help from the YMCA for the airfare from Hong Kong. She soon relocated to New York's Chinatown.

The reason I wanted to come to the United States is that I heard it is really freedom. That's the first thing. And the second was the education. It's hard to get an education in China. Only the United States can support you to get a good education and a good life. My childhood was not happy. Too many children. Poor. I don't want that again. I graduated from high school but nothing can get you into college. Even though you have good grades and a good record you can never get into college in China. I don't know how it is now but in my experience, when I was young, during the Cultural Revolution, there were no colleges to get into. Every student who graduated from high school in 1968, 1970, around that time, was sent to work in the countryside, to become a farmer. . . .

I came first to California. Los Angeles. Then I came here to New York. I had some friends. They told me there were more opportunities to find a good job in

New York. To learn English. In Los Angeles everything is far away. You have to drive in a car for hours to get anywhere. There's not that much chance to get an education, to go to school, because of the distance between places. I stayed there just two weeks and then I came to New York.

When I got here I worked as a babysitter. I had a green card and I could have gotten another kind of job but I wanted to learn English. Even though you go to school, you are just listening a lot of the time, and I wanted a job where I could talk English. So I found a job with an American family. They talked to me and corrected me. Told me how to do things. I took care of their little boy. He was seven years old and very easy to take care of. I took him to the park on his bicycle or to the museum. For me it was very interesting. . . .

In February 1978, I started at City University, New York City Community College. There are many Chinese people there, many different races. Many, many. I have helped about twenty people go there myself. Told them it was a very good college, especially for data processing. I promised myself I will go on to a four-year college when I graduate but I do not know how long it will take. First I will get a job and then ask the boss to help me with my education. . . . That first year back in college was very difficult for me. I had to take any kind of job, just to get money. Type. Work in a restaurant. Whatever I could find.[2]

Questions

1. How do the immigrants' narratives reflect their encounters with new gender roles and possibilities in American life?
2. Discuss the importance of educational opportunities for immigrants. Why were these critical for some and not for others?
3. For many immigrants, the trip to the United States was only one of several migrations. What other kinds of migrations shaped their lives before they arrived here?
4. What do the immigrants' stories reveal about the role of economic instability in their decision to emigrate?

Sources

1. "Mojados (Wetbacks)", from *New Americans: An Oral History* by Al Santoli. Copyright © 1988 by Al Santoli. Used by permission of Viking Penguin, a division of Penguin Putnam, Inc.
2. From TODAY'S IMMIGRANTS, THEIR STORIES: A NEW LOOK AT THE NEWEST AMERICANS by Thomas Kessner and Betty Boyd Caroli, Copyright © 1982 by Thomas Kessner and Betty Boyd Caroli. Used with permission of Oxford University Press.

APPENDIX

THE DECLARATION OF INDEPENDENCE

When in the course of human events it becomes necessary for one people to dissolve the political bands which have connected them with another and to assume, among the powers of the earth, the separate and equal station to which the laws of nature and of nature's God entitle them, a decent respect to the opinions of mankind requires that they should declare the causes which impel them to the separation.

We hold these truths to be self-evident, that all men are created equal; that they are endowed by their Creator with certain unalienable rights; that among these are life, liberty, and the pursuit of happiness. That, to secure these rights, governments are instituted among men, deriving their just powers from the consent of the governed; that, whenever any form of government becomes destructive of these ends, it is the right of the people to alter or to abolish it, and to institute a new government, laying its foundation on such principles, and organizing its powers in such form, as to them shall seem most likely to effect their safety and happiness. Prudence, indeed, will dictate that governments long established should not be changed for light and transient causes; and, accordingly, all experience hath shown that mankind are more disposed to suffer, while evils are sufferable, than to right themselves by abolishing the forms to which they are accustomed. But when a long train of abuses and usurpations, pursuing invariably the same object, evinces a design to reduce them under absolute despotism, it is their right, it is their duty, to throw off such government and to provide new guards for their future security. Such has been the patient sufferance of these colonies, and such is now the necessity which constrains them to alter their former systems of government. The history of the present King of Great Britain is a history of repeated injuries and usurpations, all having, in direct object, the establishment of an absolute tyranny over these States. To prove this, let facts be submitted to a candid world:

He has refused his assent to laws the most wholesome and necessary for the public good.

He has forbidden his governors to pass laws of immediate and pressing importance, unless suspended in their operation till his assent should be obtained; and, when so suspended, he has utterly neglected to attend to them.

He has refused to pass other laws for the accommodation of large districts of people, unless those people would relinquish the right of representation in the legislature, a right inestimable to them and formidable to tyrants only.

He has called together legislative bodies at places unusual, uncomfortable, and distant from the depository of their public records, for the sole purpose of fatiguing them into compliance with his measures.

He has dissolved representative houses, repeatedly for opposing, with manly firmness, his invasions on the rights of the people.

He has refused, for a long time after such dissolutions, to cause others to be elected; whereby the legislative powers, incapable of annihilation, have returned to the people at large for their exercise; the state remaining, in the meantime, exposed to all the danger of invasion from without and convulsions within.

He has endeavored to prevent the population of these States; for that purpose, obstructing the laws for naturalization of foreigners, refusing to pass others to encourage their migration hither, and raising the conditions of new appropriations of lands.

He has obstructed the administration of justice by refusing his assent to laws for establishing judiciary powers.

He has made judges dependent on his will alone for the tenure of their offices and the amount and payment of their salaries.

He has erected a multitude of new offices and sent hither swarms of officers to harass our people and eat out their substance.

He has kept among us, in time of peace, standing armies, without the consent of our legislatures.

He has affected to render the military independent of, and superior to, the civil power.

He has combined with others to subject us to a jurisdiction foreign to our Constitution and unacknowledged by our laws, giving his assent to their acts of pretended legislation—

For quartering large bodies of armed troops among us;

For protecting them, by mock trial, from punishment for any murders which they should commit on the inhabitants of these States;

For cutting off our trade with all parts of the world;

For imposing taxes on us without our consent;

For depriving us, in many cases, of the benefit of trial by jury;

For transporting us beyond seas to be tried for pretended offences;

For abolishing the free system of English laws in a neighboring province, establishing therein an arbitrary government, and enlarging its boundaries, so as to render it at once an example and fit instrument for introducing the same absolute rule into these colonies;

For taking away our charters, abolishing our most valuable laws, and altering, fundamentally, the powers of our governments.

For suspending our own legislatures and declaring themselves invested with power to legislate for us in all cases whatsoever.

He has abdicated government here by declaring us out of his protection and waging war against us.

He has plundered our seas, ravaged our coasts, burnt our towns, and destroyed the lives of our people.

He is, at this time, transporting large armies of foreign mercenaries to complete the works of death, desolation, and tyranny already begun with circumstances of cruelty and perfidy scarcely paralleled in the most barbarous ages, and totally unworthy the head of a civilized nation.

He has constrained our fellow citizens, taken captive on the high seas, to bear arms against their country, to become the executioners of their friends and brethren, or to fall themselves by their hands.

He has excited domestic insurrections amongst us and has endeavored to bring on the inhabitants of our frontiers, the merciless Indian savages, whose known rule of warfare is an undistinguished destruction of all ages, sexes, and conditions.

In every stage of these oppressions, we have petitioned for redress in the most humble terms; our repeated petitions have been answered only by repeated injury. A prince whose character is thus marked by every act which may define a tyrant is unfit to be the ruler of a free people.

Nor have we been wanting in attention to our British brethren. We have warned them, from time to time, of attempts made by their legislature to extend an unwarrantable jurisdiction over us. We have reminded them of the circumstances of our emigration and settlement here. We have appealed to their native justice and magnanimity, and we have conjured them, by the ties of our common kindred, to disavow these usurpations, which would inevitably interrupt our connections and correspondence. They, too, have been deaf to the voice of justice and consanguinity. We must, therefore, acquiesce in the necessity which denounces our separation, and hold them, as we hold the rest of mankind, enemies in war, in peace, friends.

We, therefore, the representatives of the United States of America, in general Congress assembled, appealing to the Supreme Judge of the world for the rectitude of our intentions, do, in the name and by the authority of the good people of these colonies, solemnly publish and declare, that these united colonies are, and of right ought to be, free and independent states: that they are absolved from all allegiance to the British Crown, and that all political connection between them and the state of Great Britain is, and ought to be, totally dissolved; and that, as free and independent states, they have full power to levy war, conclude peace, contract alliances, establish commerce, and to do all other acts and things which independent states may of right do. And, for the support of this declaration, with a firm reliance on the protection of Divine Providence, we mutually pledge to each other our lives, our fortunes, and our sacred honor.

THE CONSTITUTION OF THE UNITED STATES OF AMERICA

We the people of the United States, in order to form a more perfect union, establish justice, insure domestic tranquillity, provide for the common defense, promote the general welfare, and secure the blessings of liberty to ourselves and our posterity, do ordain and establish this Constitution for the United States of America.

Article I

Section 1. All legislative powers herein granted shall be vested in a Congress of the United States, which shall consist of a Senate and House of Representatives.

Section 2. 1. The House of Representatives shall be composed of members chosen every second year by the people of the several States, and the electors in each State shall have the qualifications requisite for electors of the most numerous branch of the State legislature.

2. No person shall be a representative who shall not have attained to the age of twenty-five years, and been seven years a citizen of the United States, and who shall not, when elected, be an inhabitant of that State in which he shall be chosen.

3. Representatives and direct taxes[1] shall be apportioned among the several States which may be included within this Union, according to their respective numbers, which shall be determined by adding to the whole number of free persons, including those bound to service for a term of years, and excluding Indians not taxed, three fifths of all other persons.[2] The actual enumeration shall be made within three years after the first meeting of the Congress of the United States, and within every subsequent term of ten years, in such manner as they shall by law direct. The number of representatives shall not exceed one for every thirty thousand, but each State shall have at least one representative; and until such enumeration shall be made, the State of New Hampshire shall be entitled to choose three, Massachusetts eight, Rhode Island and Providence Plantations one, Connecticut five, New York six, New Jersey four, Pennsylvania eight, Delaware one, Maryland six, Virginia ten, North Carolina five, South Carolina five, and Georgia three.

4. When vacancies happen in the representation from any State, the executive authority thereof shall issue writs of election to fill such vacancies.

5. The House of Representatives shall choose their speaker and other officers; and shall have the sole power of impeachment.

Section 3. 1. The Senate of the United States shall be composed of two senators from each State, chosen by the legislature thereof,[3] for six years; and each senator shall have one vote.

2. Immediately after they shall be assembled in consequence of the first election, they shall be divided as equally as may be into three classes. The seats of the senators of the first class shall be vacated at the expiration of the second year, of the second class at the expiration of the fourth year, and of the third class at the expiration of the sixth year, so that one third may be chosen every second year; and if vacancies happen by resignation, or otherwise, during the recess of the legislature of any State, the executive thereof may make temporary appointments until the next meeting of the legislature, which shall then fill such vacancies.[4]

3. No person shall be a senator who shall not have attained to the age of thirty years, and been nine years a citizen of the United States, and who shall not, when elected, be an inhabitant of that State for which he shall be chosen.

4. The Vice President of the United States shall be President of the Senate, but shall have no vote, unless they be equally divided.

5. The Senate shall choose their other officers, and also a president pro tempore, in the absence of the Vice President, or when he shall exercise the office of the President of the United States.

6. The Senate shall have the sole power to try all impeachments. When sitting for that purpose, they shall be on oath or affirmation. When the President of the United States is tried, the chief justice shall preside: and no person shall be convicted without the concurrence of two thirds of the members present.

7. Judgment in cases of impeachment shall not extend further than to removal from office, and disqualification to hold and enjoy any office of honor, trust or profit under the United States: but the party convicted shall nevertheless be liable and subject to indictment, trial, judgment and punishment, according to law.

Section 4. 1. The times, places, and manner of holding elections for senators and representatives, shall be prescribed in each State by the legislature thereof; but the Congress may at any time by law make or alter such regulations, except as to the places of choosing senators.

2. The Congress shall assemble at least once in every year, and such meeting shall be on the first Monday in December, unless they shall by law appoint a different day.

Section 5. 1. Each House shall be the judge of the elections, returns and qualifications of its own members, and a majority of each shall constitute a quorum to do business; but a smaller number may adjourn from day to day, and may be authorized to compel the attendance of absent members, in such manner, and under such penalties as each House may provide.

2. Each House may determine the rules of its proceedings, punish its members for disorderly behavior, and, with the concurrence of two thirds, expel a member.

3. Each House shall keep a journal of its proceedings, and from time to time publish the same, excepting such parts as may in their judgment require secrecy; and the yeas and nays of the members of either House on any ques-

[1] See the Sixteenth Amendment.
[2] See the Fourteenth Amendment.
[3] See the Seventeenth Amendment.

[4] See the Seventeenth Amendment.

tion shall, at the desire of one fifth of those present, be entered on the journal.

4. Neither House, during the session of Congress, shall, without the consent of the other, adjourn for more than three days, nor to any other place than that in which the two Houses shall be sitting.

Section 6. 1. The senators and representatives shall receive a compensation for their services, to be ascertained by law, and paid out of the Treasury of the United States. They shall in all cases, except treason, felony, and breach of the peace, be privileged from arrest during their attendance at the session of their respective Houses, and in going to and returning from the same; and for any speech or debate in either House, they shall not be questioned in any other place.

2. No senator or representative shall, during the time for which he was elected, be appointed to any civil office under the authority of the United States, which shall have been created, or the emoluments whereof shall have been increased, during such time; and no person holding any office under the United States shall be a member of either House during his continuance in office.

Section 7. 1. All bills for raising revenue shall originate in the House of Representatives; but the Senate may propose or concur with amendments as on other bills.

2. Every bill which shall have passed the House of Representatives and the Senate, shall, before it become a law, be presented to the President of the United States; If he approves he shall sign it, but if not he shall return it, with his objections, to that House in which it shall have originated, who shall enter the objections at large on their journal, and proceed to reconsider it. If after such reconsideration two thirds of that House shall agree to pass the bill, it shall be sent, together with the objections, to the other House, by which it shall likewise be reconsidered, and if approved by two thirds of that House, it shall become a law. But in all such cases the votes of both Houses shall be determined by yeas and nays, and the names of the persons voting for and against the bill shall be entered on the journal of each House respectively. If any bill shall not be returned by the President within ten days (Sundays excepted) after it shall have been presented to him, the same shall be a law, in like manner as if he had signed it, unless the Congress by their adjournment prevent its return, in which case it shall not be a law.

3. Every order, resolution, or vote to which the concurrence of the Senate and the House of Representatives may be necessary (except on a question of adjournment) shall be presented to the President of the United States; and before the same shall take effect, shall be approved by him, or being disapproved by him, shall be repassed by two thirds of the Senate and House of Representatives, according to the rules and limitations prescribed in the case of a bill.

Section 8. The Congress shall have the power

1. To lay and collect taxes, duties, imposts, and excises, to pay the debts and provide for the common defense and general welfare of the United States; but all duties, imposts, and excises shall be uniform throughout the United States.

2. To borrow money on the credit of the United States;

3. To regulate commerce with foreign nations, and among the several States, and with the Indian tribes;

4. To establish a uniform rule of naturalization, and uniform laws on the subject of bankruptcies throughout the United States;

5. To coin money, regulate the value thereof, and of foreign coin, and fix the standard of weights and measures;

6. To provide for the punishment of counterfeiting the securities and current coin of the United States;

7. To establish post offices and post roads;

8. To promote the progress of science and useful arts, by securing for limited times to authors and inventors the exclusive right to their respective writings and discoveries;

9. To constitute tribunals inferior to the Supreme Court;

10. To define and punish piracies and felonies committed on the high seas, and offenses against the law of nations;

11. To declare war, grant letters of marque and reprisal, and make rules concerning captures on land and water;

12. To raise and support armies, but no appropriation of money to that use shall be for a longer term than two years;

13. To provide and maintain a navy;

14. To make rules for the government and regulation of the land and naval forces;

15. To provide for calling forth the militia to execute the laws of the Union, suppress insurrections and repel invasions;

16. To provide for organizing, arming, and disciplining the militia, and for governing such part of them as may be employed in the service of the United States, reserving to the States respectively, the appointment of the officers, and the authority of training the militia according to the discipline prescribed by Congress;

17. To exercise exclusive legislation in all cases whatsoever, over such district (not exceeding ten miles square) as may, by cession of particular States, and the acceptance of Congress, become the seat of the government of the United States, and to exercise like authority over all places purchased by the consent of the legislature of the State in which the same shall be, for the erection of forts, magazines, arsenals, dockyards, and other needful buildings; and

18. To make all laws which shall be necessary and proper for carrying into execution the foregoing powers, and all other powers vested by this Constitution in the government of the United States, or any department or officer thereof.

Section 9. 1. The migration or importation of such persons as any of the States now existing shall think proper to admit, shall not be prohibited by the Congress prior to the year one thousand eight hundred and eight, but a tax or duty may be imposed on such importation, not exceeding ten dollars for each person.

2. The privilege of the writ of habeas corpus shall not be suspended, unless when in cases of rebellion or invasion the public safety may require it.

3. No bill of attainder or ex post facto law shall be passed.

4. No capitation, or other direct, tax shall be laid, unless in proportion to the census or enumeration hereinbefore directed to be taken.[5]

5. No tax or duty shall be laid on articles exported from any State.

6. No preference shall be given by any regulation of commerce or revenue to the ports of one State over those of another: nor shall vessels bound to, or from, one State be obliged to enter, clear, or pay duties in another.

7. No money shall be drawn from the treasury, but in consequence of appropriations made by law; and a regular statement and account of the receipts and expenditures of all public money shall be published from time to time.

8. No title of nobility shall be granted by the United States: and no person holding any office of profit or trust under them, shall, without the consent of the Congress, accept of any present, emolument, office, or title, of any kind whatever, from any king, price, or foreign State.

Section 10. 1. No State shall enter into any treaty, alliance, or confederation; grant letters of marque and reprisal; coin money; emit bills of credit; make any thing but gold and silver coin a tender in payment of debts; pass any bill of attainder, ex post facto law, or law impairing the obligation of contracts, or grant, any title of nobility.

2. No State shall, without the consent of the Congress, lay any imposts or duties on imports or exports, except what may be absolutely necessary for executing its inspection laws: and the net produce of all duties and imposts laid by any State on imports or exports, shall be for the use of the treasury of the United States; and all such laws shall be subject to the revision and control of the Congress.

3. No State shall, without the consent of the Congress, lay any duty of tonnage, keep troops, or ships of war in time of peace, enter into any agreement or compact with another State, or with a foreign power, or engage in war, unless actually invaded, or in such imminent danger as will not admit of delay.

Article II

Section 1. 1. The executive power shall be vested in a President of the United States of America. He shall hold his office during the term of four years, and, together with the Vice President, chosen for the same term, be elected, as follows:

2. Each State shall appoint, in such manner as the legislature thereof may direct, a number of electors, equal to the whole number of senators and representatives to which the State may be entitled in the Congress: but no senator or representative, or person holding any office of trust or profit under the United States, shall be appointed an elector.

The electors shall meet in their respective States, and vote by ballot for two persons, of whom one at least shall not be an inhabitant of the same State with themselves. And they shall make a list of all the persons voted for, and of the number of votes for each; which list they shall sign and certify, and transmit sealed to the seat of the government of the United States, directed to the president of the Senate. The president of the Senate shall, in the presence of the Senate and House of Representatives, open all the certificates, and the votes shall then be counted. The person having the greatest number of votes shall be the President, if such number be a majority of the whole number of electors appointed; and if there be more than one who have such majority, and have an equal number of votes, then the House of Representatives shall immediately choose by ballot one of them for President; and if no person have a majority, then from the five highest on the list the said House shall in like manner choose the President. But in choosing the President, the votes shall be taken by States, the representation from each State having one vote; a quorum for this purpose shall consist of a member or members from two thirds of the States, and a majority of all the States shall be necessary to a choice. In every case after the choice of the President, the person having the greatest number of votes of the electors shall be the Vice President. But if there should remain two or more who have equal votes, the Senate shall choose from them by ballot the Vice President.[6]

3. The Congress may determine the time of choosing the electors, and the day on which they shall give their votes; which day shall be the same throughout the United States.

4. No person except a natural born citizen, or a citizen of the United States, at the time of the adoption of this Constitution, shall be eligible to the office of President; neither shall any person be eligible to the office who shall not have attained to the age of thirty-five years, and been fourteen years a resident within the United States.

5. In case of the removal of the President from office, or of his death, resignation, or inability to discharge the powers and duties of the said office, the same shall devolve on the Vice President, and the congress may by law provide for the case of removal, death, resignation or inability, both of the President and Vice President, declaring what officer shall then act as President, and such officer shall act accordingly until the disability be removed, or a President shall be elected.

6. The President shall, at stated times, receive for his services a compensation which shall neither be increased nor diminished during the period for which he shall have been elected, and he shall not receive within that period any other emolument from the United States, or any of them.

7. Before he enter on the execution of his office, he shall take the following oath or affirmation:—"I do

---

[5]See the Sixteenth Amendment.

[6]Superseded by the Twelfth Amendment.

solemnly swear (or affirm) that I will faithfully execute the office of President of the United States, and will to the best of my ability, preserve, protect and defend the Constitution of the United States."

Section 2. 1. The President shall be commander in chief of the army and navy of the United States, and of the militia of the several States, when called into the actual service of the United States; he may require the opinion in writing, of the principal officer in each of the executive departments, upon any subject relating to the duties of their respective offices, and he shall have power to grant reprieves and pardons for offenses against the United States, except in cases of impeachment.

2. He shall have power, by and with the advice and consent of the Senate, to make treaties, provided two thirds of the senators present concur; and he shall nominate, and by and with the advice and consent of the Senate, shall appoint ambassadors, other public ministers and consuls, judges of the Supreme Court, and all other officers of the United States, whose appointments are not herein otherwise provided for, and which shall be established by law; but the Congress may by law vest the appointment of such inferior officers, as they think proper, in the President alone, in the courts of laws, or in the heads of departments.

3. The President shall have power to fill up all vacancies that may happen during the recess of the Senate, by granting commissions which shall expire at the end of their next session.

Section 3. He shall from time to time give to the Congress information of the state of the Union, and recommend to their consideration such measures as he shall judge necessary and expedient; he may, on extraordinary occasions, convene both Houses, or either of them, and in case of disagreement between them with respect to the time of adjournment, he may adjourn them to such time as he shall think proper; he shall receive ambassadors and other public ministers; he shall take care that the laws be faithfully executed, and shall commission all the officers of the United States.

Section 4. The President, Vice President, and all civil officers of the United States, shall be removed from office on impeachment for, and conviction of, treason, bribery, or other high crimes and misdemeanors.

Article III

Section 1. The judicial power of the United States shall be vested in one Supreme Court, and in such inferior courts as the Congress may from time to time ordain and establish. The judges, both of the Supreme and inferior courts, shall hold their offices during good behavior, and shall, at stated times, receive for their services, a compensation, which shall not be diminished during their continuance in office.

Section 2. 1. The judicial power shall extend to all cases, in law and equity, arising under this Constitution, the laws of the United States, and treaties made, or which shall be made, under their authority;—to all cases of admiralty and maritime jurisdiction;—to controversies to which the United States shall be a party;[7]—to controversies between two or more States;—between a State and citizens of another State;—between citizens of different States;—between citizens of the same State claiming lands under grants of different States, and between a State, or the citizens thereof, and foreign States, citizens or subjects.

2. In all cases affecting ambassadors, other public ministers and consuls, and those in which a State shall be party, the Supreme Court shall have original jurisdiction. In all the other cases before mentioned, the Supreme Court shall have appellate jurisdiction, both as to law and fact, with such exceptions, and under such regulations as the Congress shall make.

3. The trial of all crimes, except in cases of impeachment, shall be by jury; and such trial shall be held in the State where the said crimes shall have been committed; but when not committed within any State, the trial shall be such place or places as the congress may by law have directed.

Section 3. 1. Treason against the United States shall consist only in levying war against them, or in adhering to their enemies, giving them aid and comfort. No person shall be convicted of treason unless on the testimony of two witnesses to the same overt act, or on confession in open court.

2. The Congress shall have power to declare the punishment of treason, but no attainder of treason shall work corruption of blood, or forfeiture except during the life of the person attained.

Article IV

Section 1. Full faith and credit shall be given in each State to the public acts, records, and judicial proceedings of every other State. And the Congress may by general laws prescribe the manner in which such acts, records and proceedings shall be proved, and the effect thereof.

Section 2. 1. The citizens of each State shall be entitled to all privileges and immunities of citizens in the several States.[8]

2. A person charged in any State with treason, felony, or other crime, who shall flee from justice, and be found in another State, shall on demand of the executive authority of the State from which he fled, be delivered up to be removed to the State having jurisdiction of the crime.

3. No person held to service or labor in one State under the laws thereof, escaping into another, shall, in consequence of any law or regulation therein, be discharged from such service or labor, but shall be delivered up on claim of the party to whom such service or labor may be due.[9]

Section 3. 1. New States may be admitted by the Congress into this Union; but no new State shall be formed or erected within the jurisdiction of any other State, nor any State be formed by the junction of two or more States, or parts of States, without the consent of the legislatures of the States concerned as well as of the Congress.

---

[7]See the Eleventh Amendment.
[8]See the Fourteenth Amendment, Sec. 1.
[9]See the Thirteenth Amendment.

2. The Congress shall have power to dispose of and make all needful rules and regulations respecting the territory or other property belonging to the United States; and nothing in this Constitution shall be so construed as to prejudice any claims of the United States, or of any particular State.

Section 4. The United States shall guarantee to every State in this Union a republican form of government, and shall protect each of them against invasion; and on application of the legislature, or of the executive (when the legislature cannot be convened) against domestic violence.

Article V

The Congress, whenever two thirds of both Houses shall deem it necessary, shall propose amendments to this Constitution, or, on the application of the legislatures of two thirds of the several States, shall call a convention for proposing amendments, which in either case shall be valid to all intents and purposes, as part of this Constitution, when ratified by the legislatures of three fourths of the several States, or by conventions in three fourths thereof, as the one or the other mode of ratification may be proposed by the Congress; Provided that no amendment which may be made prior to the year one thousand eight hundred and eight shall in any manner affect the first and fourth clauses in the ninth section of the first article; and that no State, without its consent, shall be deprived of its equal suffrage in the Senate.

Article VI

1. All debts contracted and engagements entered into, before the adoption of this Constitution, shall be as valid against the United States under this Constitution, as under the Confederation.[10]

2. This Constitution, and the laws of the United States which shall be made in pursuance thereof; and all treaties made, or which shall be made, under the authority of the United States, shall be the supreme law of the land; and the judges in every State shall be bound thereby, any thing in the Constitution or laws of any State to the contrary notwithstanding.

3. The senators and representatives before mentioned, and the members of the several State legislatures, and all executive and judicial officers, both of the United States and of the several States, shall be bound by oath or affirmation to support this Constitution; but no religious test shall ever be required as a qualification to any office or public trust under the United States.

Article VII

The ratification of the conventions of nine States shall be sufficient for the establishment of this Constitution between the States so ratifying the same.

Done in Convention by the unanimous consent of the States present the seventeenth day of September in the year of our Lord one thousand seven hundred and eighty-seven, and of the independence of the United States of America the twelfth. In witness whereof we have hereunto subscribed our names.

[Names omitted]

* * *

Articles in addition to, and amendment of, the Constitution of the United States of America, proposed by Congress, and ratified by the legislatures of the several States, pursuant to the fifth article of the original Constitution.

Amendment I [First ten amendments ratified December 15, 1791]

Congress shall make no law respecting an establishment of religion, or prohibiting the free exercise thereof; or abridging the freedom of speech, or of the press; or the right of the people peaceably to assemble, and to petition the government for a redress of grievances.

Amendment II

A well regulated militia, being necessary to the security of a free State, the right of the people to keep and bear arms, shall not be infringed.

Amendment III

No soldier shall, in time of peace be quartered in any house, without the consent of the owner, nor in time of war, but in a manner to be prescribed by law.

Amendment IV

The right of the people to be secure in their persons, houses, papers, and effects, against unreasonable searches and seizures, shall not be violated, and no warrants shall issue, but upon probable cause, supported by oath or affirmation, and particularly describing the place to be searched, and the persons or things to be seized.

Amendment V

No person shall be held to answer for a capital or otherwise infamous crime, unless on a presentment or indictment of a grand jury, except in cases arising in the land or naval forces, or in the militia, when in actual service in time of war or public danger; nor shall any person be subject for the same offense to be twice put in jeopardy of life or limb; nor shall be compelled in any criminal case to be a witness against himself, nor be deprived of life, liberty, or property, without due process of law; nor shall private property be taken for public use, without just compensation.

Amendment VI

In all criminal prosecutions, the accused shall enjoy the right to a speedy and public trial, by an impartial jury of the State and district wherein the crime shall have been committed, which district shall have been previously ascertained by law, and to be informed of the nature and cause of the accusation; to be confronted with the witnesses against him; to have compulsory process for obtaining witnesses in his favor, and to have the assistance of counsel for his defense.

---

[10]See the Fourteenth Amendment, Sec. 4.

Amendment VII

In suits at common law, where the value in controversy shall exceed twenty dollars, the right of trial by jury shall be preserved, and no fact tried by a jury shall be otherwise reexamined in any court of the United States, than according to the rules of the common law.

Amendment VIII

Excessive bail shall not be required, nor excessive fines imposed, nor cruel and unusual punishments inflicted.

Amendment IX

The enumeration in the Constitution of certain rights shall not be construed to deny or disparage others retained by the people.

Amendment X

The powers not delegated to the United States by the Constitution, nor prohibited by it to the States, are reserved to the States respectively, or to the people.

Amendment XI [January 8, 1798]

The judicial power of the United States shall not be construed to extend to any suit in law or equity, commended or prosecuted against one of the United States by citizens of another State, or by citizens or subjects of any foreign State.

Amendment XII [September 25, 1804]

The electors shall meet in their respective States, and vote by ballot for President and Vice President, one of whom, at least, shall not be an inhabitant of the same State with themselves; they shall name in their ballots the person voted for as President, and in distinct ballots, the person voted for as Vice President, and they shall make distinct lists of all persons voted for as President and of all persons voted for as Vice President, and of the number of votes for each, which lists they shall sign and certify, and transmit sealed to the seat of the government of the United States, directed to the President of the Senate;—The President of the Senate shall, in the presence of the Senate and House of Representatives, open all the certificates and the votes shall then be counted;—The person having the greatest number of votes for President, shall be the President, if such number be a majority of the whole number of electors appointed; and if no person have such majority, then from the persons having the highest numbers not exceeding three on the list of those voted for as President, the House of Representatives shall choose immediately, by ballot, the President. But in choosing the President, the votes shall be taken by States, the representation from each State having one vote; a quorum for this purpose shall consist of a member or members from two thirds of the States, and a majority of all the States shall be necessary to a choice. And if the House of Representatives shall not choose a President whenever the right of choice shall devolve upon them, before the fourth day of March next following, then the Vice President shall act as President, as in the case of the death or other constitutional disability of the President.

The person having the greatest number of votes as Vice President shall be the Vice President, if such number be a majority of the whole number of electors appointed, and if no person have a majority, then from the two highest numbers on the list, the Senate shall choose the Vice President; a quorum for the purpose shall consist of two thirds of the whole number of Senators, and a majority of the whole number shall be necessary to a choice. But no person constitutionally ineligible to the office of President shall be eligible to that of Vice President of the United States.

Amendment XIII [December 18, 1865]

Section 1. Neither slavery nor involuntary servitude, except as a punishment for crime whereof the party shall have been duly convicted, shall exist within the United States, or any place subject to their jurisdiction.

Section 2. Congress shall have power to enforce this article by appropriate legislation.

Amendment XIV [July 28, 1868]

Section 1. All persons born or naturalized in the United States, and subject to the jurisdiction thereof, are citizens of the United States and of the State wherein they reside. No State shall make or enforce any law which shall abridge the privileges or immunities of citizens of the United States; nor shall any State deprive any person of life, liberty, or property, without due process of law; nor deny to any person within its jurisdiction the equal protection of the laws.

Section 2. Representatives shall be apportioned among the several States according to their respective numbers, counting the whole number of persons in each State, excluding Indians not taxed. But when the right to vote at any election for the choice of electors for President and Vice President of the United States, representatives in Congress, the executive and judicial officers of a State, or the members of the legislature thereof, is denied to any of the male inhabitants of such State, being twenty-one years of age, and citizens of the United States, or in any way abridged, except for participating in rebellion, or other crime, the basis of representation there shall be reduced in the proportion which the number of such male citizens shall bear to the whole number of male citizens twenty-one years of age in such State.

Section 3. No person shall be a senator or representative in Congress, or elector of President and Vice President, or hold any office, civil or military, under the United States, or under any State, who having previously taken an oath, as a member of Congress, or as an officer of the United States, or as a member of any State legislature, or as an executive or judicial officer of any State, to support the Constitution of the United States, shall have engaged in insurrection or rebellion against the same, or given aid or comfort to the enemies thereof. But Congress may by a vote of two thirds of each House, remove such disability.

Section 4. The validity of the public debt of the United States, authorized by law, including debts incurred for payment of pensions and bounties for services in suppressing insurrection or rebellion; shall not be questioned.

But neither the United States nor any State shall assume or pay any debt or obligation incurred in aid of insurrection or rebellion against the United States, or any claim for the loss or emancipation of any slave; but all such debts, obligations, and claims shall be held illegal and void.

Section 5. The Congress shall have the power to enforce, by appropriate legislation, the provisions of this article.

Amendment XV [March 30, 1870]

Section 1. The right of citizens of the United States to vote shall not be denied or abridged by the United States or by any State on account of race, color, or previous condition of servitude.

Section 2. The Congress shall have power to enforce this article by appropriate legislation.

Amendment XVI [February 25, 1913]

The Congress shall have power to lay and collect taxes on incomes, from whatever source derived, without apportionment among the several States, and without regard to any census or enumeration.

Amendment XVII [May 31, 1913]

The Senate of the United States shall be composed of two senators from each State, elected by the people thereof, for six years; and each senator shall have one vote. The electors in each State shall have the qualifications requisite for electors of the most numerous branch of the State legislature.

When vacancies happen in the representation of any State in the Senate, the executive authority of such State shall issue writs of election to fill such vacancies: *Provided,* That the legislature of any State may empower the executive thereof to make temporary appointments until the people fill the vacancies by election as the legislature may direct.

This amendment shall not be so construed as to affect the election or term of any senator chosen before it becomes valid as part of the Constitution.

Amendment XVIII[1] [January 29, 1919]

After one year from the ratification of this article, the manufacture, sale, or transportation of intoxicating liquors within, the importation thereof into, or the exportation thereof from the United States and all territory subject to the jurisdiction thereof for beverage purposes is thereby prohibited.

The Congress and the several States shall have concurrent power to enforce this article by appropriate legislation.

This article shall be inoperative unless it shall have been ratified as an amendment to the Constitution by the legislatures of the several States, as provided in the constitution, within seven years from the date of the submission hereof to the States by Congress.

Amendment XIX [August 26, 1920]

The right of citizens of the United States to vote shall not be denied or abridged by the United States or by any State on account of sex.

Congress shall have the power to enforce this article by appropriate legislation.

Amendment XX [January 23, 1933]

Section 1. The terms of the President and Vice President shall end at noon on the 20th day of January and the terms of Senators and Representatives at noon on the 3d day of January, of the years in which such terms would have ended if this article had not been ratified; and the terms of their successors shall then begin.

Section 2. The Congress shall assemble at least once in every year, and such meeting shall begin at noon on the 3d day of January, unless they shall by law appoint a different day.

Section 3. If, at the time fixed for the beginning of the term of President, the President-elect shall have died, the Vice President-elect shall become President. If a President shall not have been chosen before the time fixed for the beginning of his term, or if the President-elect shall have failed to qualify, then the Vice President-elect shall act as President until a President shall have qualified; and the Congress may by law provide for the case wherein neither a President-elect nor a Vice President-elect shall have qualified, declaring who shall then act as President, or the manner in which one who is to act shall be selected, and such person shall act accordingly until a President or Vice President shall have qualified.

Section 4. The Congress may by law provide for the case of the death of any of the persons from whom, the House of Representatives may choose a President whenever the right of choice shall have devolved upon them, and for the case of the death of any of the persons from whom the Senate may choose a Vice President whenever the right of choice shall have devolved upon them.

Section 5. Sections 1 and 2 shall take effect on the 15th day of October following the ratification of this article.

Section 6. This article shall be inoperative unless it shall have been ratified as an amendment to the Constitution by the legislatures of three-fourths of the several States within seven years from the date of its submission.

Amendment XXI [December 5, 1933]

Section 1. The Eighteenth Article of amendment to the Constitution of the United States is hereby repealed.

Section 2. The transportation or importation into any State, Territory, or possession of the United States for delivery or use therein of intoxicating liquors in violation of the laws thereof, is hereby prohibited.

Section 3. This article shall be inoperative unless it shall have been ratified as an amendment to the Constitution by conventions in the several States, as provided in the Constitution, within seven years from the date of the submission thereof to the States by the Congress.

[1]Repealed by the Twenty-first Amendment.

Amendment XXII [March 1, 1951]

No person shall be elected to the office of the President more than twice, and no person who has held the office of President, or acted as President, for more than two years of a term to which some other person was elected President shall be elected to the office of the President more than once.

But this article shall not apply to any person holding the office of President when this article was proposed by the Congress, and shall not prevent any person who may be holding the office of President, or acting as President, during the term within which this article becomes operative from holding the office of President or acting as President during the remainder of such term.

This article shall be inoperative unless it shall have been ratified as an amendment to the Constitution by the legislatures of three-fourths of the several States within seven years from the date of its submission to the States by the Congress.

Amendment XXIII [March 29, 1961]

Section 1. The District constituting the seat of Government of the United States shall appoint in such manner as the Congress may direct.

A number of electors of President and Vice President equal to the whole number of Senators and Representatives in Congress to which the District would be entitled if it were a State, but in no event more than the least populous State; they shall be in addition to those appointed by the States, but they shall be considered, for the purposes of the election of President and Vice President, to be electors appointed by a State; and they shall meet in the District and perform such duties as provided by the twelfth article of amendment.

Section 2. The Congress shall have power to enforce this article by appropriate legislation.

Amendment XXIV [January 23, 1964]

Section 1. The right of citizens of the United States to vote in any primary or other election for President or Vice President, for electors for President or Vice President, or for Senator or Representative in Congress, shall not be denied or abridged by the United States or any State by reason of failure to pay any poll tax or other tax.

Section 2. The Congress shall have power to enforce this article by appropriate legislation.

Amendment XXV [February 10, 1967]

Section 1. In case of the removal of the President from office or of his death or resignation, the Vice President shall become President.

Section 2. Whenever there is a vacancy in the office of the Vice President, the President shall nominate a Vice President who shall take office upon confirmation by a majority of both Houses of Congress.

Section 3. Whenever the President transmits to the President pro tempore of the Senate and the Speaker of the House of Representatives his written declaration that he is unable to discharge the powers and duties of his office, and until he transmits to them a written declaration to the contrary, such powers and duties shall be discharged by the Vice President as Acting President.

Section 4. Whenever the Vice president and a majority of either the principal officers of the executive departments or of such other body as Congress may by law provide, transmit to the President pro tempore of the Senate and the Speaker of the House of Representatives their written declaration that the President is unable to discharge the powers and duties of his office, the Vice President shall immediately assume the powers and duties of the office as Acting President.

Thereafter, when the President transmits to the President pro tempore of the Senate and the Speaker of the House of Representatives his written declaration that no inability exists, he shall resume the powers and duties of his office unless the Vice President and a majority of either the principal officers of the executive departments or of such other body as Congress may by law provide, transmit within four days to the President pro tempore of the Senate and the Speaker of the House of Representatives their written declaration that the President is unable to discharge the powers and duties of his office. Thereupon Congress shall decide the issue, assembling within forty-eight hours for that purpose if not in session. If the Congress, within twenty-one days after receipt of the latter written declaration, or, if Congress is not in session, within twenty-one days after Congress is required to assemble, determines by two-thirds vote of both Houses that the President is unable to discharge the powers and duties of his office, the Vice President shall continue to discharge the same as Acting President; otherwise, the President shall resume the powers and duties of his office.

Amendment XXVI [June 30, 1971]

Section 1. The right of citizens of the United States who are eighteen years of age or older to vote shall not be denied or abridged by the United States or by any State on account of age.

Section 2. The Congress shall have power to enforce this article by appropriate legislation.

Amendment XXVII[12] [May 7, 1992]

No law, varying the compensation for services of the Senators and Representatives, shall take effect until an election of Representatives shall have intervened.

---

[12]James Madison proposed this amendment in 1789 together with the ten amendments that were adopted as the Bill of Rights, but it failed to win ratification at the time. Congress, however, had set no deadline for its ratification, and over the years—particularly in the 1980s and 1990s—many states voted to add it to the Constitution. With the ratification of Michigan in 1992 it passed the threshold of 3/4ths of the states required for adoption, but because the process took more than 200 years, its validity remains in doubt.

PRESIDENTS AND VICE PRESIDENTS

1. George Washington (1789)
   John Adams (1789)

2. John Adams (1797)
   Thomas Jefferson (1797)

3. Thomas Jefferson (1801)
   Aaron Burr (1801)
   George Clinton (1805)

4. James Madison (1809)
   George Clinton (1809)
   Elbridge Gerry (1813)

5. James Monroe (1817)
   Daniel D. Thompkins (1817)

6. John Quincy Adams (1825)
   John C. Calhoun (1825)

7. Andrew Jackson (1829)
   John C. Calhoun (1829)
   Martin Van Buren (1833)

8. Martin Van Buren (1837)
   Richard M. Johnson (1837)

9. William H. Harrison (1841)
   John Tyler (1841)

10. John Tyler (1841)

11. James K. Polk (1845)
    George M. Dallas (1845)

12. Zachary Taylor (1849)
    Millard Fillmore (1849)

13. Millard Fillmore (1850)

14. Franklin Pierce (1853)
    William R. King (1853)

15. James Buchanan (1857)
    John C. Breckinridge (1857)

16. Abraham Lincoln (1861)
    Hannibal Hamlin (1861)
    Andrew Johnson (1865)

17. Andrew Johnson (1865)

18. Ulysses S. Grant (1869)
    Schuyler Colfax (1869)
    Henry Wilson (1873)

19. Rutherford B. Hayes (1877)
    William A. Wheeler (1877)

20. James A. Garfield (1881)
    Chester A. Arthur (1881)

21. Chester A. Arthur (1881)

22. Grover Cleveland (1885)
    T. A. Hendricks (1885)

23. Benjamin Harrison (1889)
    Levi P. Morgan (1889)

24. Grover Cleveland (1893)
    Adlai E. Stevenson (1893)

25. William McKinley (1897)
    Garret A. Hobart (1897)
    Theodore Roosevelt (1901)

26. Theodore Roosevelt (1901)
    Charles Fairbanks (1905)

27. William H. Taft (1909)
    James S. Sherman (1909)

28. Woodrow Wilson (1913)
    Thomas R. Marshall (1913)

29. Warren G. Harding (1921)
    Calvin Coolidge (1921)

30. Calvin Coolidge (1923)
    Charles G. Dawes (1925)

31. Herbert C. Hoover (1929)
    Charles Curtis (1929)

32. Franklin D. Roosevelt (1933)
    John Nance Garner (1933)
    Henry A. Wallace (1941)
    Harry S. Truman (1945)

33. Harry S. Truman (1945)
    Alben W. Barkley (1949)

34. Dwight D. Eisenhower (1953)
    Richard M. Nixon (1953)

35. John F. Kennedy (1961)
    Lyndon B. Johnson (1961)

36. Lyndon B. Johnson (1963)
    Hubert H. Humphrey (1965)

37. Richard M. Nixon (1969)
    Spiro T. Agnew (1969)
    Gerald R. Ford (1973)

38. Gerald R. Ford (1974)
    Nelson A. Rockefeller (1974)

39. James E. Carter Jr. (1977)
    Walter F. Mondale (1977)

40. Ronald W. Reagan (1981)
    George H. Bush (1981)

41. George H. Bush (1989)
    James D. Quayle III (1989)

42. William J. Clinton (1993)
    Albert Gore (1993)

PRESIDENTIAL ELECTIONS

Year	Number of States	Candidates	Party	Popular Vote*	Electoral Vote[†]	Percentage of Popular Vote
1789	11	GEORGE WASHINGTON	No party designations		69	
		John Adams			34	
		Other Candidates			35	
1792	15	GEORGE WASHINGTON	No party designations		132	
		John Adams			77	
		George Clinton			50	
		Other Candidates			5	
1796	16	JOHN ADAMS	Federalist		71	
		Thomas Jefferson	Democratic-Republican		68	
		Thomas Pinckney	Federalist		59	
		Aaron Burr	Democratic-Republican		30	
		Other Candidates			48	
1800	16	THOMAS JEFFERSON	Democratic-Republican		73	
		Aaron Burr	Democratic-Republican		73	
		John Adams	Federalist		65	
		Charles C. Pinckney	Federalist		64	
		John Jay	Federalist		1	
1804	17	THOMAS JEFFERSON	Democratic-Republican		162	
		Charles C. Pinckney	Federalist		14	
1808	17	JAMES MADISON	Democratic-Republican		122	
		Charles C. Pinckney	Federalist		47	
		George Clinton	Democratic-Republican		6	
1812	18	JAMES MADISON	Democratic-Republican		128	
		DeWitt Clinton	Federalist		89	
1816	19	JAMES MONROE	Democratic-Republican		183	
		Rufus King	Federalist		34	
1820	24	JAMES MONROE	Democratic-Republican		231	
		John Quincy Adams	Democratic-Republican		1	
1824	24	JOHN QUINCY ADAMS	Democratic-Republican	108,740	84	30.5
		Andrew Jackson	Democratic-Republican	153,544	99	43.1
		William H. Crawford	Democratic-Republican	46,618	41	13.1
		Henry Clay	Democratic-Republican	47,136	37	13.2
1828	24	ANDREW JACKSON	Democrat	647,286	178	56.0
		John Quincy Adams	National-Republican	508,064	83	44.0
1832	24	ANDREW JACKSON	Democrat	687,502	219	55.0
		Henry Clay	National-Republican	530,189	49	42.4
		William Wirt	Anti-Masonic	} 33,108	7	} 2.6
		John Floyd	National-Republican		11	

*Percentage of popular vote given for any election year may not total 100 percent because candidates receiving less than 1 percent of the popular vote have been omitted.

[†]Prior to the passage of the Twelfth Amendment in 1904, the electoral college voted for two presidential candidates; the runner-up became Vice-President. Data from *Historical Statistics of the United States, Colonial Times to 1957* (1961), pp. 682–683, and *The World Almanac.*

PRESIDENTIAL ELECTIONS
(continued)

Year	Number of States	Candidates	Party	Popular Vote	Electoral Vote	Percentage of Popular Vote
1836	26	MARTIN VAN BUREN	Democrat	765,483	170	50.9
		William H. Harrison	Whig		73	
		Hugh L. White	Whig		26	
		Daniel Webster	Whig	739,795	14	49.1
		W. P. Mangum	Whig		11	
1840	26	WILLIAM H. HARRISON	Whig	1,274,624	234	53.1
		Martin Van Buren	Democrat	1,127,781	60	46.9
1844	26	JAMES K. POLK	Democrat	1,338,464	170	49.6
		Henry Clay	Whig	1,300,097	105	48.1
		James G. Birney	Liberty	62,300		2.3
1848	30	ZACHARY TAYLOR	Whig	1,360,967	163	47.4
		Lewis Cass	Democrat	1,222,342	127	42.5
		Martin Van Buren	Free-Soil	291,263		10.1
1852	31	FRANKLIN PIERCE	Democrat	1,601,117	254	50.9
		Winfield Scott	Whig	1,385,453	42	44.1
		John P. Hale	Free-Soil	155,825		5.0
1856	31	JAMES BUCHANAN	Democrat	1,832,955	174	45.3
		John C. Frémont	Republican	1,339,932	114	33.1
		Millard Fillmore	American ("Know Nothing")	871,731	8	21.6
1860	33	ABRAHAM LINCOLN	Republican	1,865,593	180	39.8
		Stephen A. Douglas	Democrat	1,382,713	12	29.5
		John C. Breckinridge	Democrat	848,356	72	18.1
		John Bell	Constitutional Union	592,906	39	12.6
1864	36	ABRAHAM LINCOLN	Republican	2,206,938	212	55.0
		George B. McClellan	Democrat	1,803,787	21	45.0
1868	37	ULYSSES S. GRANT	Republican	3,013,421	214	52.7
		Horatio Seymour	Democrat	2,706,829	80	47.3
1872	37	ULYSSES S. GRANT	Republican	3,596,745	286	55.6
		Horace Greeley	Democrat	2,843,446	*	43.9
1876	38	RUTHERFORD B. HAYES	Republican	4,036,572	185	48.0
		Samuel J. Tilden	Democrat	4,284,020	184	51.0
1880	38	JAMES A. GARFIELD	Republican	4,453,295	214	48.5
		Winfield S. Hancock	Democrat	4,414,082	155	48.1
		James B. Weaver	Greenback-Labor	308,578		3.4
1884	38	GROVER CLEVELAND	Democrat	4,879,507	219	48.5
		James G. Blaine	Republican	4,850,293	182	48.2
		Benjamin F. Butler	Greenback-Labor	175,370		1.8
		John P. St. John	Prohibition	150,369		1.5
1888	38	BENJAMIN HARRISON	Republican	5,447,129	233	47.9
		Grover Cleveland	Democrat	5,537,857	168	48.6
		Clinton B. Fisk	Prohibition	249,506		2.2
		Anson J. Streeter	Union Labor	146,935		1.3

*Because of the death of Greeley, Democratic electors scattered their votes.

PRESIDENTIAL ELECTIONS
(continued)

Year	Number of States	Candidates	Party	Popular Vote	Electoral Vote	Percentage of Popular Vote
1892	44	GROVER CLEVELAND	Democrat	5,555,426	277	46.1
		Benjamin Harrison	Republican	5,182,690	145	43.0
		James B. Weaver	People's	1,029,846	22	8.5
		John Bidwell	Prohibition	264,133		2.2
1896	45	WILLIAM MCKINLEY	Republican	7,102,246	271	51.1
		William J. Bryan	Democrat	6,492,559	176	47.7
1900	45	WILLIAM MCKINLEY	Republican	7,218,491	292	51.7
		William J. Bryan	Democrat; Populist	6,356,734	155	45.5
		John C. Woolley	Prohibition	208,914		1.5
1904	45	THEODORE ROOSEVELT	Republican	7,628,461	336	57.4
		Alton B. Parker	Democrat	5,084,223	140	37.6
		Eugene V. Debs	Socialist	402,283		3.0
		Silas C. Swallow	Prohibition	258,536		1.9
1908	46	WILLIAM H. TAFT	Republican	7,675,320	321	51.6
		William J. Bryan	Democrat	6,412,294	162	43.1
		Eugene V. Debs	Socialist	420,793		2.8
		Eugene W. Chafin	Prohibition	253,840		1.7
1912	48	WOODROW WILSON	Democrat	6,296,547	435	41.9
		Theodore Roosevelt	Progressive	4,118,571	88	27.4
		William H. Taft	Republican	3,486,720	8	23.2
		Eugene V. Debs	Socialist	900,672		6.0
		Eugene W. Chafin	Prohibition	206,275		1.4
1916	48	WOODROW WILSON	Democrat	9,127,695	277	49.4
		Charles E. Hughes	Republican	8,533,507	254	46.2
		A. L. Benson	Socialist	585,113		3.2
		J. Frank Hanly	Prohibition	220,506		1.2
1920	48	WARREN G. HARDING	Republican	16,143,407	404	60.4
		James M. Cox	Democrat	9,130,328	127	34.2
		Eugene V. Debs	Socialist	919,799		3.4
		P. P. Christensen	Farmer-Labor	265,411		1.0
1924	48	CALVIN COOLIDGE	Republican	15,718,211	382	54.0
		John W. Davis	Democrat	8,385,283	136	28.8
		Robert M. La Follette	Progressive	4,831,289	13	16.6
1928	48	HERBERT C. HOOVER	Republican	21,391,993	444	58.2
		Alfred E. Smith	Democrat	15,016,169	87	40.9
1932	48	FRANKLIN D. ROOSEVELT	Democrat	22,809,638	472	57.4
		Herbert C. Hoover	Republican	15,758,901	59	39.7
		Norman Thomas	Socialist	881,951		2.2
1936	48	FRANKLIN D. ROOSEVELT	Democrat	27,752,869	523	60.8
		Alfred M. Landon	Republican	16,674,665	8	36.5
		William Lemke	Union	882,479		1.9
1940	48	FRANKLIN D. ROOSEVELT	Democrat	27,307,819	449	54.8
		Wendell L. Willkie	Republican	22,321,018	82	44.8
1944	48	FRANKLIN D. ROOSEVELT	Democrat	25,606,585	432	53.5
		Thomas E. Dewey	Republican	22,014,745	99	46.0

PRESIDENTIAL ELECTIONS
(continued)

Year	Number of States	Candidates	Party	Popular Vote	Electoral Vote	Percentage of Popular Vote
1948	48	HARRY S. TRUMAN	Democrat	24,105,812	303	49.5
		Thomas E. Dewey	Republican	21,970,065	189	45.1
		J. Strom Thurmond	States' Rights	1,169,063	39	2.4
		Henry A. Wallace	Progressive	1,157,172		2.4
1952	48	DWIGHT D. EISENHOWER	Republican	33,936,234	442	55.1
		Adlai E. Stevenson	Democrat	27,314,992	89	44.4
1956	48	DWIGHT D. EISENHOWER	Republican	35,590,472	457*	57.6
		Adlai E. Stevenson	Democrat	26,022,752	73	42.1
1960	50	JOHN F. KENNEDY	Democrat	34,227,096	303[†]	49.9
		Richard M. Nixon	Republican	34,108,546	219	49.6
1964	50	LYNDON B. JOHNSON	Democrat	42,676,220	486	61.3
		Barry M. Goldwater	Republican	26,860,314	52	38.5
1968	50	RICHARD M. NIXON	Republican	31,785,480	301	43.4
		Hubert H. Humphrey	Democrat	31,275,165	191	42.7
		George C. Wallace	American Independent	9,906,473	46	13.5
1972	50	RICHARD M. NIXON[‡]	Republican	47,165,234	520	60.6
		George S. McGovern	Democrat	29,168,110	17	37.5
1976	50	JIMMY CARTER	Democrat	40,828,929	297	50.1
		Gerald R. Ford	Republican	39,148,940	240	47.9
		Eugene McCarthy	Independent	739,256		
1980	50	RONALD REAGAN	Republican	43,201,220	489	50.9
		Jimmy Carter	Democrat	34,913,332	49	41.2
		John B. Anderson	Independent	5,581,379		
1984	50	RONALD REAGAN	Republican	53,428,357	525	59.0
		Walter F. Mondale	Democrat	36,930,923	13	41.0
1988	50	GEORGE BUSH	Republican	48,901,046	426	53.4
		Michael Dukakis	Democrat	41,809,030	111	45.6
1992	50	BILL CLINTON	Democrat	43,728,275	370	43.2
		George Bush	Republican	38,167,416	168	37.7
		H. Ross Perot	United We Stand, America	19,237,247		19.0
1996	50	BILL CLINTON	Democrat	45,590,703	379	49.0
		Robert Dole	Republican	37,816,307	159	41.0
		H. Ross Perot	Reform	7,874,283		8.0

*Walter B. Jones received 1 electoral vote.

[†]Harry F. Byrd received 15 electoral votes.

[‡]Resigned August 9, 1974: Vice President Gerald R. Ford became President.

ADMISSION OF STATES INTO THE UNION

State	Date of Admission	State	Date of Admission
1. Delaware	December 7, 1787	26. Michigan	January 26, 1837
2. Pennsylvania	December 12, 1787	27. Florida	March 3, 1845
3. New Jersey	December 18, 1787	28. Texas	December 29, 1845
4. Georgia	January 2, 1788	29. Iowa	December 28, 1846
5. Connecticut	January 9, 1788	30. Wisconsin	May 29, 1848
6. Massachusetts	February 6, 1788	31. California	September 9, 1850
7. Maryland	April 28, 1788	32. Minnesota	May 11, 1858
8. South Carolina	May 23, 1788	33. Oregon	February 14, 1859
9. New Hampshire	June 21, 1788	34. Kansas	January 29, 1861
10. Virginia	June 25, 1788	35. West Virginia	June 20, 1863
11. New York	July 26, 1788	36. Nevada	October 31, 1864
12. North Carolina	November 21, 1789	37. Nebraska	March 1, 1867
13. Rhode Island	May 29, 1790	38. Colorado	August 1, 1876
14. Vermont	March 4, 1791	39. North Dakota	November 2, 1889
15. Kentucky	June 1, 1792	40. South Dakota	November 2, 1889
16. Tennessee	June 1, 1796	41. Montana	November 8, 1889
17. Ohio	March 1, 1803	42. Washington	November 11, 1889
18. Louisiana	April 30, 1812	43. Idaho	July 3, 1890
19. Indiana	December 11, 1816	44. Wyoming	July 10, 1890
20. Mississippi	December 10, 1817	45. Utah	January 4, 1896
21. Illinois	December 3, 1818	46. Oklahoma	November 16, 1907
22. Alabama	December 14, 1819	47. New Mexico	January 6, 1912
23. Maine	March 15, 1820	48. Arizona	February 14, 1912
24. Missouri	August 10, 1821	49. Alaska	January 3, 1959
25. Arkansas	June 15, 1836	50. Hawaii	August 21, 1959

DEMOGRAPHICS OF THE UNITED STATES

POPULATION GROWTH

Year	Population	Percent Increase
1630	4,600	
1640	26,600	478.3
1650	50,400	90.8
1660	75,100	49.0
1670	111,900	49.0
1680	151,500	35.4
1690	210,400	38.9
1700	250,900	19.2
1710	331,700	32.2
1720	466,200	40.5
1730	629,400	35.0
1740	905,600	43.9
1750	1,170,800	29.3
1760	1,593,600	36.1
1770	2,148,100	34.8
1780	2,780,400	29.4
1790	3,929,214	41.3
1800	5,308,483	35.1
1810	7,239,881	36.4
1820	9,638,453	33.1
1830	12,866,020	33.5
1840	17,069,453	32.7
1850	23,191,876	35.9
1860	31,443,321	35.6
1870	39,818,449	26.6
1880	50,155,783	26.0
1890	62,947,714	25.5
1900	75,994,575	20.7
1910	91,972,266	21.0
1920	105,710,620	14.9
1930	122,775,046	16.1
1940	131,669,275	7.2
1950	150,697,361	14.5
1960	179,323,175	19.0
1970	203,235,298	13.3
1980	226,545,805	11.5
1990	248,709,873	9.8
1996	265,557,000	6.8

Source: *Historical Statistics of the United States* (1975); *Statistical Abstract by the United States* (1991, 1997).
Note: Figures for 1630–1780 include British colonies within limits of present United States only; Native American population included only in 1930 and thereafter.

WORKFORCE

Year	Total Number Workers (1000s)	Farmers as % of Total	Women as % of Total	% Workers in Unions
1810	2,330	84	(NA)	(NA)
1840	5,660	75	(NA)	(NA)
1860	11,110	53	(NA)	(NA)
1870	12,506	53	15	(NA)
1880	17,392	52	15	(NA)
1890	23,318	43	17	(NA)
1900	29,073	40	18	3
1910	38,167	31	21	6
1920	41,614	26	21	12
1930	48,830	22	22	7
1940	53,011	17	24	27
1950	59,643	12	28	25
1960	69,877	8	32	26
1970	82,049	4	37	25
1980	108,544	3	42	23
1990	117,914	3	45	16
1995	124,900	3	46	15

Source: *Historical Statistics of the United States* (1975); *Statistical Abstract of the United States* (1991, 1996).

VITAL STATISTICS
(per thousands)

Year	Births	Deaths	Marriages	Divorces
1800	55	(NA)	(NA)	(NA)
1810	54.3	(NA)	(NA)	(NA)
1820	55.2	(NA)	(NA)	(NA)
1830	51.4	(NA)	(NA)	(NA)
1840	51.8	(NA)	(NA)	(NA)
1850	43.3	(NA)	(NA)	(NA)
1860	44.3	(NA)	(NA)	(NA)
1870	38.3	(NA)	9.6 (1867)	0.3 (1867)
1880	39.8	(NA)	9.1 (1875)	0.3 (1875)
1890	31.5	(NA)	9.0	0.5
1900	32.3	17.2	9.3	0.7
1910	30.1	14.7	10.3	0.9
1920	27.7	13.0	12.0	1.6
1930	21.3	11.3	9.2	1.6
1940	19.4	10.8	12.1	2.0
1950	24.1	9.6	11.1	2.6
1960	23.7	9.5	8.5	2.2
1970	18.4	9.5	10.6	3.5
1980	15.9	8.8	10.6	5.2
1990	16.7	8.6	9.8	4.7
1994	15.0	8.8	9.1	4.6

Source: *Historical Statistics of the United States* (1975); *Statistical Abstract of the United States* (1991, 1997).

RACIAL COMPOSITION OF THE POPULATION
(in thousands)

Year	White	Black	Indian	Hispanic	Asian
1790	3,172	757	(NA)	(NA)	(NA)
1800	4,306	1,002	(NA)	(NA)	(NA)
1820	7,867	1,772	(NA)	(NA)	(NA)
1840	14,196	2,874	(NA)	(NA)	(NA)
1860	26,923	4,442	(NA)	(NA)	(NA)
1880	43,403	6,581	(NA)	(NA)	(NA)
1900	66,809	8,834	(NA)	(NA)	(NA)
1910	81,732	9,828	(NA)	(NA)	(NA)
1920	94,821	10,463	(NA)	(NA)	(NA)
1930	110,287	11,891	(NA)	(NA)	(NA)
1940	118,215	12,866	(NA)	(NA)	(NA)
1950	134,942	15,042	(NA)	(NA)	(NA)
1960	158,832	18,872	(NA)	(NA)	(NA)
1970	178,098	22,581	(NA)	(NA)	(NA)
1980	194,713	26,683	1,420	14,609	3,729
1990	205,710	30,486	2,065	22,354	7,458
1996	219,749	30,503	2,288	28,269	9,743

Source: U.S. Bureau of the Census, *U.S. Census of Population: 1940*, vol. II, part 1, and vol. IV, part 1; *1950*, vol. II, part 1; *1960*, vol. I, part 1; *1970*, vol. I, part B; and *Current Population Reports*, P25-1095 and P25-1104; *Statistical Abstract of the United States* (1997), and unpublished data.

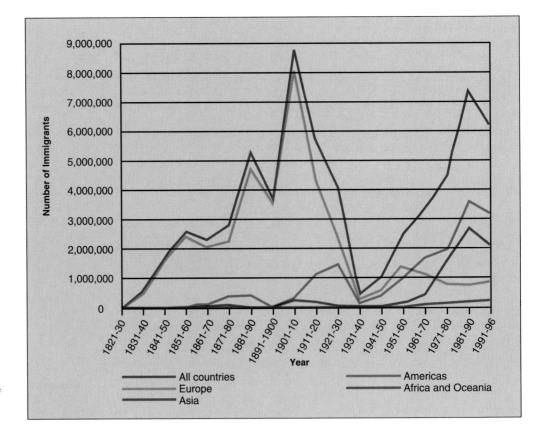

Immigration to the United States since 1820

Source: *Statistical Yearbook of the Immigration and Naturalization Service*, 1996.

THE ARTICLES OF CONFEDERATION AND PERPETUAL UNION*

Between the states of New Hampshire, Massachusetts-bay Rhode Island and Providence Plantations, Connecticut, New York, New Jersey, Pennsylvania, Delaware, Maryland, Virginia, North Carolina, South Carolina, and Georgia.

Article 1

The Stile of this Confederacy shall be "The United States of America".

Article 2

Each state retains its sovereignty, freedom, and independence, and every power, jurisdiction, and right, which is not by this Confederation expressly delegated to the United States, in Congress assembled.

Article 3

The said States hereby severally enter into a firm league of friendship with each other, for their common defense, the security of their liberties, and their mutual and general welfare, binding themselves to assist each other, against all force offered to, or attacks made upon them, or any of them, on account of religion, sovereignty, trade, or any other pretense whatever.

Article 4

The better to secure and perpetuate mutual friendship and intercourse among the people of the different States in this Union, the free inhabitants of each of these States, paupers, vagabonds, and fugitives from justice excepted, shall be entitled to all privileges and immunities of free citizens in the several States; and the people of each State shall have free ingress and regress to and from any other State, and shall enjoy therein all the privileges of trade and commerce, subject to the same duties, impositions, and restrictions as the inhabitants thereof respectively, provided that such restrictions shall not extend so far as to prevent the removal of property imported into any State, to any other State of which the owner is an inhabitant; provided also that no imposition, duties or restriction shall be laid by any State, on the property of the United States, or either of them.

If any person guilty of, or charged with, treason, felony, or other high misdemeanor in any State, shall flee from justice, and be found in any of the United States, he shall, upon demand of the Governor or executive power of the State from which he fled, be delivered up and removed to the State having jurisdiction of his offense.

Full faith and credit shall be given in each of these States to the records, acts, and judicial proceedings of the courts and magistrates of every other State.

Article 5

For the more convenient management of the general interests of the United States, delegates shall be annually appointed in such manner as the legislatures of each State shall direct, to meet in Congress on the first Monday in November, in every year, with a power reserved to each State to recall its delegates, or any of them, at any time within the year, and to send others in their stead for the remainder of the year.

No State shall be represented in Congress by less than two, nor by more than seven members; and no person shall be capable of being a delegate for more than three years in any term of six years; nor shall any person, being a delegate, be capable of holding any office under the United States, for which he, or another for his benefit, receives any salary, fees or emolument of any kind.

Each State shall maintain its own delegates in a meeting of the States, and while they act as members of the committee of the States.

In determining questions in the United States in Congress assembled, each State shall have one vote.

Freedom of speech and debate in Congress shall not be impeached or questioned in any court or place out of Congress, and the members of Congress shall be protected in their persons from arrests or imprisonments, during the time of their going to and from, and attendence on Congress, except for treason, felony, or breach of the peace.

Article 6

No State, without the consent of the United States in Congress assembled, shall send any embassy to, or receive any embassy from, or enter into any conference, agreement, alliance or treaty with any King, Prince or State; nor shall any person holding any office of profit or trust under the United States, or any of them, accept any present, emolument, office or title of any kind whatever from any King, Prince or foreign State; nor shall the United States in Congress assembled, or any of them, grant any title of nobility.

No two or more States shall enter into any treaty, confederation or alliance whatever between them, without the consent of the United States in Congress assembled, specifying accurately the purposes for which the same is to be entered into, and how long it shall continue.

No State shall lay any imposts or duties, which may interfere with any stipulations in treaties, entered into by the United States in Congress assembled, with any King, Prince or State, in pursuance of any treaties already proposed by Congress, to the courts of France and Spain.

No vessel of war shall be kept up in time of peace by any State, except such number only, as shall be deemed necessary by the United States in Congress assembled, for the defense of such State, or its trade; nor shall any body of forces be kept up by any State in time of peace, except such number only, as in the judgement of the United States in Congress assembled, shall be deemed requisite to garrison the forts necessary for the defense of such State; but every State shall always keep up a well-regulated and disciplined militia, sufficiently armed and accoutered, and shall provide and constantly have ready for use, in public stores, a due number of filed pieces and tents, and a proper quantity of arms, ammunition and camp equipage.

No State shall engage in any war without the consent of the United States in Congress assembled, unless such State be actually invaded by enemies, or shall have received certain advice of a resolution being formed by some nation of Indians to invade such State, and the danger is so imminent as not to admit of a delay, till the United States in Congress assembled can be consulted; nor shall any State grant commissions to any ships or vessels of war, nor letters of marque or reprisal, except it be after a declaration of war by the United States in Congress assembled, and then only against the Kingdom or State and the subjects thereof, against which war has been so declared, and under such regulations as shall be established by the United States in Congress assembled, unless such State be infested by pirates, in which case vessels of war may be fitted out for that occasion, and kept so long as the danger shall continue, or until the United States in Congress assembled shall determine otherwise.

Article 7

When land forces are raised by any State for the common defense, all officers of or under the rank of colonel, shall be appointed by the legislature of each State respectively, by whom such forces shall be raised, or in such manner as such State shall direct, and all vacancies shall be filled up by the State which first made the appointment.

Article 8

All charges of war, and all other expenses that shall be incurred for the common defense or general welfare, and allowed by the United States in Congress assembled, shall be defrayed out of a common treasury, which shall be supplied by the several States in proportion to the value of all land within each State, granted to or surveyed for any person, as such land and the buildings and improvements thereon shall be estimated according to such mode as the United States in Congress assembled, shall from time to time direct and appoint.

The taxes for paying that proportion shall be laid and levied by the authority and direction of the legislatures of the several States within the time agreed upon by the United States in Congress assembled.

Article 9

The United States in Congress assembled, shall have the sole and exclusive right and power of determining on peace and war, except in the cases mentioned in the sixth article; of sending and receiving ambassadors; entering into treaties and alliances, provided that no treaty of commerce shall be made whereby the legislative power of the respective States shall be restrained from imposing such imposts and duties on foreigners, as their own people are subjected to, or from prohibiting the exportation or importation of any species of goods or commodities whatsoever; of establishing rules for deciding in all cases, what captures on land or water shall be legal, and in what manner prizes taken by land or naval forces in the service of the United States shall be divided or appropriated; of granting letters of marque and reprisal in times of peace; appointing courts for the trial of piracies and felonies committed on the high seas and establishing courts for receiving and determining finally appeals in all cases of captures, provided that no member of Congress shall be appointed a judge of any of the said courts.

The United States in Congress assembled shall also be the last resort on appeal in all disputes and differences now subsisting or that hereafter may arise between two or more States concerning boundary, jurisdiction or any other causes whatever; which authority shall always be exercised in the manner following. Whenever the legislative or executive authority or lawful agent of any State in controversy with another shall present a petition to Congress stating the matter in question and praying for a hearing, notice thereof shall be given by order of Congress to the legislative or executive authority of the other State in controversy, and a day assigned for the appearance of the parties by their lawful agents, who shall then be directed to appoint by joint consent, commissioners or judges to constitute a court for hearing and determining the matter in question: but if they cannot agree, Congress shall name three persons out of each of the United States, and from the list of such persons each party shall alternately strike out one, the petitioners beginning, until the number shall be reduced to thirteen; and from that number not less than seven, nor more than nine names as Congress shall direct, shall in the presence of Congress be drawn out by lot, and the persons whose names shall be so drawn or any five of them, shall be commissioners or judges, to hear and finally determine the controversy, so always as a major part of the judges who shall hear the cause shall agree in the determination: and if either party shall neglect to attend at the day appointed, without showing reasons, which Congress shall judge sufficient, or being present shall refuse to strike, the Congress shall proceed to nominate three persons out of each State, and the secretary of Congress shall strike in behalf of such party absent or refusing; and the judgement and sentence of the court to be appointed, in the manner before prescribed, shall be final and conclusive; and if any of the parties shall refuse to submit to the authority of such court, or to appear or defend their claim or cause, the court shall nevertheless proceed to pronounce sentence, or judgement, which shall in like manner be final and decisive, the judgement or sentence and other proceedings being in either case transmitted to Congress, and lodged among the acts of Congress for the security of the parties concerned: provided that every commissioner, before he sits in judgment, shall take an oath to be administered by one of the judges of the supreme or superior court of the State, where the cause shall be tried, "well and truly to hear and determine the matter in question, according to the best of his judgement, without favor, affection or hope of reward:" provided also, that no State shall be deprived of territory for the benefit of the United States.

All controversies concerning the private right of soil claimed under different grants of two or more States, whose jurisdictions as they may respect such lands, and the States which passed such grants are adjusted, the said grants or either of them being at the same time claimed to have originated antecedent to such settlement of jurisdiction, shall on the petition of either party to the Congress of the United States, be finally determined as near as may be in the same manner as is before prescribed for deciding disputes respecting territorial jurisdiction between different States.

The United States in Congress assembled shall also have the sole and exclusive right and power of regulating the alloy and value of coin struck by their own authority, or by that of the respective States; fixing the standards of weights and measures throughout the United States; regulating the trade and managing all affairs with the Indians not members of any of the States; provided that the legislative right of any State within its own limits be not infringed or violated; establishing or regulating post offices from one State to another, throughout all the United States, and exacting such postage on the papers passing through the same as may be requisite to defray the expenses of the said office; appointing all officers of the land forces in the service of the United States, excepting regimental officers; appointing all the officers of the naval forces, and commissioning all officers whatever in the service of the United States; making rules for the government and regulation of the said land and naval forces, and directing their operations.

The United States in Congress assembled shall have authority to appoint a committee, to sit in the recess of Congress, to be denominated "A Committee of the States," and to consist of one delegate from each State; and to appoint such other committees and civil officers as may be necessary for managing the general affairs of the United States under their direction; to appoint one of their members to preside, provided that no person be allowed to serve in the office of president more than one year in any term of three years; to ascertain the necessary sums of money to be raised for the service of the United States, and to appropriate and apply the same for defraying the public expenses; to borrow money, or emit bills on the credit of the United States, transmitting every half year to the respective States an account of the sums of money so borrowed or emitted; to build and equip a navy; to agree upon the number of land forces, and to make requisitions from each State for its quota, in proportion to the number of white inhabitants in such State; which requisition shall be binding, and thereupon the legislature of each State shall appoint the regimental officers, raise the men and cloath, arm and equip them in a soldier-like manner, at the expense of the United States; and the officers and men so cloathed, armed and equipped shall march to the place appointed, and within the time agreed on by the United States in Congress assembled; but if the United States in Congress assembled shall, on consideration of circumstances judge proper that any State should not raise men, or should raise a smaller number of men than the quota thereof, such extra number shall be raised, officered, cloathed, armed and equipped in the same manner as the quota of such State, unless the legislature of such State shall judge that such extra number cannot be safely spared out in the same, in which case they shall raise, officer, cloath, arm and equip as many of such extra number as they judge can be safely spared. And the officers and men so cloathed, armed, and equipped, shall march to the place appointed, and within the time agreed on by the United States in Congress assembled.

The United States in Congress assembled shall never engage in a war, nor grant letters of marque or reprisal in time of peace, nor enter into any treaties or alliances, nor coin money, nor regulate the value thereof, nor ascertain the sums and expenses necessary for the defense and welfare of the United States, or any of them, nor emit bills, nor borrow money on the credit of the United States, nor appropriate money, nor agree upon the number of vessels of war, to be built or purchased, or the number of land or sea forces to be raised, nor appoint a commander in chief of the army or navy, unless nine States assent to the same: nor shall a question on any other point, except for adjourning from day to day be determined, unless by the votes of the majority of the United States in Congress assembled.

The Congress of the United States shall have power to adjourn to any time within the year, and to any place within the United States, so that no period of adjournment be for a longer duration than the space of six months, and shall publish the journal of their proceedings monthly, except such parts thereof relating to treaties, alliances or military operations, as in their judgment require secrecy; and the yeas and nays of the delegates of each State on any question shall be entered on the journal, when it is desired by any delegates of a State, or any of them, at his or their request shall be furnished with a transcript of the said journal, except such parts as are above excepted, to lay before the legislatures of the several States.

Article 10

The Committee of the States, or any nine of them, shall be authorized to execute, in the recess of Congress, such of the powers of Congress as the United States in Congress assembled, by the consent of the nine States, shall from time to time think expedient to vest them with; provided that no power be delegated to the said Committee, for the exercise of which, by the Articles of Confederation, the voice of nine States in the Congress of the United States assembled is requisite.

Article 11

Canada acceding to this confederation, and adjoining in the measures of the United States, shall be admitted into, and entitled to all the advantages of this Union; but no other colony shall be admitted into the same, unless such admission be agreed to by nine States.

Article 12

All bills of credit emitted, monies borrowed, and debts contracted by, or under the authority of Congress, before the assembling of the United States, in pursuance of the present confederation, shall be deemed and considered as a charge against the United States, for payment and satisfaction whereof the said United States, and the public faith are hereby solemnly pledged.

Article 13

Every State shall abide by the determination of the United States in Congress assembled, on all questions which by this confederation are submitted to them. And the Articles of this Confederation shall be inviolably observed by every State, and the Union shall be perpetual; nor shall any alteration at any time hereafter be made in any of them; unless such alteration be agreed to in a Congress of the United States, and be afterwards confirmed by the legislatures of every State.

These articles shall be proposed to the legislatures of all the United States, to be considered, and if approved of by them, they are advised to authorize their delegates to ratify the same in the Congress of the United States; which being done, the same shall become conclusive

---

*Agreed to in Congress November 15, 1777; ratified March 1781

PRESIDENTIAL ADMINSTRATIONS

The Washington Administration
(1789–1797)

Vice President	John Adams	1789–1797
Secretary of State	Thomas Jefferson	1789–1793
	Edmund Randolph	1794–1795
	Timothy Pickering	1795–1797
Secretary of Treasury	Alexander Hamilton	1789–1795
	Oliver Wolcott	1795–1797
Secretary of War	Henry Knox	1789–1794
	Timothy Pickering	1795–1796
	James McHenry	1796–1797
Attorney General	Edmund Randolph	1789–1793
	William Bradford	1794–1795
	Charles Lee	1795–1797
Postmaster General	Samuel Osgood	1789–1791
	Timothy Pickering	1791–1794
	Joseph Habersham	1795–1797

The John Adams Administration
(1797–1801)

Vice President	Thomas Jefferson	1797–1801
Secretary of State	Timothy Pickering	1797–1800
	John Marshall	1800–1801
Secretary of Treasury	Oliver Wolcott	1797–1800
	Samuel Dexter	1800–1801
Secretary of War	James McHenry	1797–1800
	Samuel Dexter	1800–1801
Attorney General	Charles Lee	1797–1801
Postmaster General	Joseph Habersham	1797–1801
Secretary of Navy	Benjamin Stoddert	1798–1801

The Jefferson Administration
(1801–1809)

Vice President	Aaron Burr	1801–1805
	George Clinton	1805–1809
Secretary of State	James Madison	1801–1809
Secretary of Treasury	Samuel Dexter	1801
	Albert Gallatin	1801–1809
Secretary of War	Henry Dearborn	1801–1809
Attorney General	Levi Lincoln	1801–1805
	Robert Smith	1805
	John Breckinridge	1805–1806
	Caesar Rodney	1807–1809
Postmaster General	Joseph Habersham	1801
	Gideon Granger	1801–1809
Secretary of Navy	Robert Smith	1801–1809

The Madison Administration
(1809–1817)

Vice President	George Clinton	1809–1813
	Elbridge Gerry	1813–1817
Secretary of State	Robert Smith	1809–1811
	James Monroe	1811–1817
Secretary of Treasury	Albert Gallatin	1809–1813
	George Campbell	1814
	Alexander Dallas	1814–1816
	William Crawford	1816–1817
Secretary of War	William Eustis	1809–1812
	John Armstrong	1813–1814
	James Monroe	1814–1815
	William Crawford	1815–1817
Attorney General	Caesar Rodney	1809–1811
	William Pinkney	1811–1814
	Richard Rush	1814–1817
Postmaster General	Gideon Granger	1809–1814
	Return Meigs	1814–1817
Secretary of Navy	Paul Hamilton	1809–1813
	William Jones	1813–1814
	Benjamin Crowninshield	1814–1817

The Monroe Administration
(1817–1825)

Vice President	Daniel Tompkins	1817–1825
Secretary of State	John Quincy Adams	1817–1825
Secretary of Treasury	William Crawford	1817–1825
Secretary of War	George Graham	1817
	John C. Calhoun	1817–1825
Attorney General	Richard Rush	1817
	William Wirt	1817–1825
Postmaster General	Return Meigs	1817–1823
	John McLean	1823–1825
Secretary of Navy	Benjamin Crowninshield	1817–1818
	Smith Thompson	1818–1823
	Samuel Southard	1823–1825

The John Quincy Adams Administration
(1825–1829)

Vice President	John C. Calhoun	1825–1829
Secretary of State	Henry Clay	1825–1829
Secretary of Treasury	Richard Rush	1825–1829
Secretary of War	James Barbour	1825–1828
	Peter Porter	1828–1829
Attorney General	William Wirt	1825–1829
Postmaster General	John McLean	1825–1829
Secretary of Navy	Samuel Southard	1825–1829

The Jackson Administration
(1829–1837)

Vice President	John C. Calhoun	1829–1833
	Martin Van Buren	1833–1837
Secretary of State	Martin Van Buren	1829–1831
	Edward Livingston	1831–1833
	Louis McLane	1833–1834
	John Forsyth	1834–1837
Secretary of Treasury	Samuel Ingham	1829–1831
	Louis McLane	1831–1833
	William Duane	1833
	Roger B. Taney	1833–1834
	Levi Woodbury	1834–1837
Secretary of War	John H. Eaton	1829–1831
	Lewis Cass	1831–1837
	Benjamin Butler	1837
Attorney General	John M. Berrien	1829–1831
	Roger B. Taney	1831–1833
	Benjamin Butler	1833–1837
Postmaster General	William Barry	1829–1835
	Amos Kendall	1835–1837
Secretary of Navy	John Branch	1829–1831
	Levi Woodbury	1831–1834
	Mahlon Dickerson	1834–1837

The Van Buren Administration
(1837–1841)

Vice President	Richard M. Johnson	1837–1841
Secretary of State	John Forsyth	1837–1841
Secretary of Treasury	Levi Woodbury	1837–1841
Secretary of War	Joel Poinsett	1837–1841
Attorney General	Benjamin Butler	1837–1838
	Felix Grundy	1838–1840
	Henry D. Gilpin	1840–1841
Postmaster General	Amos Kendall	1837–1840
	John M. Niles	1840–1841
Secretary of Navy	Mahlon Dickerson	1837–1838
	James Paulding	1838–1841

The William Harrison Administration
(1841)

Vice President	John Tyler	1841
Secretary of State	Daniel Webster	1841
Secretary of Treasury	Thomas Ewing	1841
Secretary of War	John Bell	1841
Attorney General	John J. Crittenden	1841
Postmaster General	Francis Granger	1841
Secretary of Navy	George Badger	1841

The Tyler Administration
(1841–1845)

Vice President	None	
Secretary of State	Daniel Webster	1841–1843
	Hugh S. Legaré	1843
	Abel P. Upshur	1843–1844
	John C. Calhoun	1844–1845
Secretary of Treasury	Thomas Ewing	1841
	Walter Forward	1841–1843
	John C. Spencer	1843–1844
	George Bibb	1844–1845
Secretary of War	John Bell	1841
	John C. Spencer	1841–1843
	James M. Porter	1843–1844
	William Wilkins	1844–1845
Attorney General	John J. Crittenden	1841
	Hugh S. Legaré	1841–1843
	John Nelson	1843–1845
Postmaster General	Francis Granger	1841
	Charles Wickliffe	1841
Secretary of Navy	George Badger	1841
	Abel P. Upshur	1841
	David Henshaw	1843–1844
	Thomas Gilmer	1844
	John Y. Mason	1844–1845

The Polk Administration
(1845–1849)

Vice President	George M. Dallas	1845–1849
Secretary of State	James Buchanan	1845–1849
Secretary of Treasury	Robert J. Walker	1845–1849
Secretary of War	William L. Marcy	1845–1849
Attorney General	John Y. Mason	1845–1846
	Nathan Clifford	1846–1848
	Isaac Toucey	1848–1849
Postmaster General	Cave Johnson	1845–1849
Secretary of Navy	George Bancrocft	1845–1846
	John Y. Mason	1846–1849

The Taylor Administration
(1849–1850)

Vice President	Millard Fillmore	1849–1850
Secretary of State	John M. Clayton	1849–1850
Secretary of Treasury	William Meredith	1849–1850
Secretary of War	George Crawford	1849–1850
Attorney General	Reverdy Johnson	1849–1850
Postmaster General	Jacob Collamer	1849–1850
Secretary of Navy	William Preston	1849–1850
Secretary of Interior	Thomas Ewing	1849–1850

The Fillmore Administration
(1850–1853)

Vice President	None	
Secretary of State	Daniel Webster	1850–1852
	Edward Everett	1852–1853
Secretary of Treasury	Thomas Corwin	1850–1853
Secretary of War	Charles Conrad	1850–1853
Attorney General	John J. Crittenden	1850–1853
Postmaster General	Nathan Hall	1850–1852
	Sam D. Hubbard	1852–1853
Secretary of Navy	William A. Graham	1850–1852
	John P. Kennedy	1852–1853
Secretary of Interior	Thomas McKennan	1850
	Alexander Stuart	1850–1853

The Pierce Administration
(1853–1857)

Vice President	William R. King	1853–1857
Secretary of State	William L. Marcy	1853–1857
Secretary of Treasury	James Guthrie	1853–1857
Secretary of War	Jefferson Davis	1853–1857
Attorney General	Caleb Cushing	1853–1857
Postmaster General	James Campbell	1853–1857
Secretary of Navy	James C. Dobbin	1853–1857
Secretary of Interior	Robert McClelland	1853–1857

The Buchanan Administration
(1857–1861)

Vice President	John C. Breckinridge	1857–1861
Secretary of State	Lewis Cass	1857–1860
	Jeremiah S. Black	1860–1861
Secretary of Treasury	Howell Cobb	1857–1860
	Philip Thomas	1860–1861
	John A. Dix	1861
Secretary of War	John B. Floyd	1857–1861
	Joseph Holt	1861
Attorney General	Jeremiah S. Black	1857–1860
	Edwin M. Stanton	1860–1861
Postmaster General	Aaron V. Brown	1857–1859
	Joseph Holt	1859–1861
	Horatio King	1861
Secretary of Navy	Isaac Toucey	1857–1861
Secretary of Interior	Jacob Thompson	1857–1861

16th

The Lincoln Administration
(1861–1865)

Vice President	Hannibal Hamlin	1861–1865
	Andrew Jackson	1865
Secretary of State	William H. Seward	1861–1865
Secretary of Treasury	Salmon P. Chase	1861–1864
	William P. Fessenden	1864–1865
	Hugh McCulloch	1865
Secretary of War	Simon Cameron	1861–1862
	Edwin M. Stanton	1862–1865
Attorney General	Edward Bates	1861–1864
	James Speed	1864–1865
Postmaster General	Horatio King	1861
	Montgomery Blair	1861–1864
	William Dennison	1864–1865
Secretary of Navy	Gideon Welles	1861–1865
Secretary of Interior	Caleb B. Smith	1861–1863
	John P. Usher	1863–1865

The Andrew Johnson Administration
(1865–1869)

Vice President	None	
Secretary of State	William H. Seward	1865–1869
Secretary of Treasury	Hugh McCulloch	1865–1869
Secretary of War	Edwin M. Stanton	1865–1867
	Ulysses S. Grant	1867–1868
	Lorenzo Thomas	1868
	John M. Schofield	1868–1869
Attorney General	James Speed	1865–1866
	Henry Stanbery	1866–1868
	William M. Evarts	1868–1869
Postmaster General	William Dennison	1865–1866
	Alexander Randall	1866–1869
Secretary of Navy	Gideon Welles	1865–1869
Secretary of Interior	John P. Usher	1865
	James Harlan	1865–1866
	Orville H. Browning	1866–1869

The Grant Administration
(1869–1877)

Vice President	Schuyler Colfax	1869–1873
	Henry Wilson	1873–1877
Secretary of State	Elihu B. Washburne	1869
	Hamilton Fish	1869–1877
Secretary of Treasury	George S. Boutwell	1869–1873
	William Richardson	1873–1874
	Benjamin Bristow	1874–1876
	Lot M. Morrill	1876–1877
Secretary of War	John A. Rawlins	1869
	William T. Sherman	1869
	William W. Belknap	1869–1876
	Alphonso Taft	1876
	James D. Cameron	1876–1877
Attorney General	Ebenezer Hoar	1869–1870
	Amos T. Ackerman	1870–1871
	G. H. Williams	1871–1875
	Edwards Pierrepont	1875–1876
	Alphonso Taft	1876–1877
Postmaster General	John A. J. Creswell	1869–1874
	James W. Marshall	1874
	Marshall Jewell	1874–1876
	James N. Tyner	1876–1877
Secretary of Navy	Adolph E. Borie	1869
	George M. Robeson	1869–1877
Secretary of Interior	Jacob D. Cox	1869–1870
	Columbus Delano	1870–1875
	Zachariah Candler	1875–1877

The Garfield Administration
(1881)

Vice President	Chester A. Arthur	1881
Secretary of State	James G. Blaine	1881
Secretary of Treasury	William Windom	1881
Secretary of War	Robert T. Lincoln	1881
Attorney General	Wayne MacVeagh	1881
Postmaster General	Thomas L. James	1881
Secretary of Navy	William H. Hunt	1881
Secretary of Interior	Samuel J. Kirkwood	1881

The Arthur Administration
(1881–1885)

Vice President	None	
Secretary of State	F. T. Frelinghuysen	1881–1885
Secretary of Treasury	Charles J. Folger	1881–1884
	Walter Q. Gresham	1884
	Hugh McCulloch	1884–1885
Secretary of War	Robert T. Lincoln	1881–1885
Attorney General	Benjamin H. Brewster	1881–1885
Postmaster General	Timothy O. Howe	1881–1883
	Walter Q. Gresham	1883–1884
	Frank Hatton	1884–1885
Secretary of Navy	William H. Hunt	1881–1882
	William E. Chandler	1882–1885
Secretary of Interior	Samuel J. Kirkwood	1881–1882
	Henry M. Teller	1882–1885

The Hayes Administration
(1877–1881)

Vice President	William A. Wheeler	1877–1881
Secretary of State	William M. Evarts	1877–1881
Secretary of Treasury	John Sherman	1877–1881
Secretary of War	George W. McCrary	1877–1879
	Alex Ramsey	1879–1881
Attorney General	Charles Devens	1877–1881
Postmaster General	David M. Key	1877–1880
	Horace Maynard	1880–1881
Secretary of Navy	Richard W. Thompson	1877–1880
	Nathan Goff, Jr.	1881
Secretary of Interior	Carl Schurz	1877–1881

The Cleveland Administration
(1885–1889)

Vice President	Thomas A. Hendricks	1885–1889
Secretary of State	Thomas F. Bayard	1885–1889
Secretary of Treasury	Daniel Manning	1885–1887
	Charles S. Fairchild	1887–1889
Secretary of War	William C. Endicott	1885–1889
Attorney General	Augustus H. Garland	1885–1889
Postmaster General	William F. Vilas	1885–1888
	Don M. Dickinson	1888–1889
Secretary of Navy	William C. Whitney	1885–1889
Secretary of Interior	Lucius Q. C. Lamar	1885–1888
	William F. Vilas	1888–1889
Secretary of Agriculture	Norman J. Colman	1889

The Benjamin Harrison Administration
(1889–1893)

Vice President	Levi P. Morton	1889–1893
Secretary of State	James G. Blaine	1889–1892
	John W. Foster	1892–1893
Secretary of Treasury	William Windom	1889–1891
	Charles Foster	1891–1893
Secretary of War	Redfield Proctor	1889–1891
	Stephen B. Elkins	1891–1893
Attorney General	William H. H. Miller	1889–1891
Postmaster General	John Wanamaker	1889–1893
Secretary of Navy	Benjamin F. Tracy	1889–1893
Secretary of Interior	John W. Noble	1889–1893
Secretary of Agriculture	Jeremiah M. Rusk	1889–1893

The Cleveland Administration
(1893–1897)

Vice President	Adlai E. Stevenson	1893–1897
Secretary of State	Walter Q. Gresham	1893–1895
	Richard Olney	1895–1897
Secretary of Treasury	John G. Carlisle	1893–1897
Secretary of War	Daniel S. Lamont	1893–1897
Attorney General	Richard Olney	1893–1895
	James Harmon	1895–1897
Postmaster General	Wilson S. Bissell	1893–1895
	William L. Wilson	1895–1897
Secretary of Navy	Hilary A. Herbert	1893–1897
Secretary of Interior	Hoke Smith	1893–1896
	David R. Francis	1896–1897
Secretary of Agriculture	Julius S. Morton	1893–1897

The McKinley Administration
(1897–1901)

Vice President	Garret A. Hobart	1897–1901
	Theodore Roosevelt	1901
Secretary of State	John Sherman	1897–1898
	William R. Day	1898
	John Hay	1898–1901
Secretary of Treasury	Lyman J. Gage	1897–1901
Secretary of War	Russell A. Alger	1897–1899
	Elihu Root	1899–1901
Attorney General	Joseph McKenna	1897–1898
	John W. Griggs	1898–1901
	Philander C. Knox	1901
Postmaster General	James A. Gary	1897–1898
	Charles E. Smith	1898–1901
Secretary of Navy	John D. Long	1897–1901
Secretary of Interior	Cornelius N. Bliss	1897–1899
	Ethan A. Hitchcock	1899–1901
Secretary of Agriculture	James Wilson	1897–1901

The Theodore Roosevelt Administration
(1901–1909)

Vice President	Charles Fairbanks	1905–1909
Secretary of State	John Hay	1901–1905
	Elihu Root	1905–1909
	Robert Bacon	1909
Secretary of Treasury	Lyman J. Gage	1901–1902
	Leslie M. Shaw	1902–1907
	George B. Cortelyou	1907–1909
Secretary of War	Elihu Root	1901–1904
	William H. Taft	1904–1908
	Luke E. Wright	1908–1909
Attorney General	Philander C. Knox	1901–1904
	William H. Moody	1904–1906
	Charles J. Bonaparte	1906–1909
Postmaster General	Charles E. Smith	1901–1902
	Henry C. Payne	1902–1904
	Robert J. Wynne	1904–1905
	George B. Cortelyou	1905–1907
	George von L. Meyer	1907–1909
Secretary of Navy	John D. Long	1901–1902
	William H. Moody	1902–1904
	Paul Morton	1904–1905
	Charles J. Bonaparte	1905–1906
	Victor H. Metcalf	1906–1908
	Truman H. Newberry	1908–1909
Secretary of Interior	Ethan A. Hitchcock	1901–1907
	James R. Garfield	1907–1909
Secretary of Agriculture	James Wilson	1901–1909
Secretary of Labor and Commerce	George B. Cortelyou	1903–1904
	Victor H. Metcalf	1904–1906
	Oscar S. Straus	1906–1909
	Charles Nagel	1909

The Taft Administration
(1909–1913)

Vice President	James S. Sherman	1909–1913
Secretary of State	Philander C. Knox	1909–1913
Secretary of Treasury	Franklin MacVeagh	1909–1913
Secretary of War	Jacob M. Dickinson	1909–1911
	Henry L. Stimson	1911–1913
Attorney General	George W. Wickersham	1909–1913
Postmaster General	Frank H. Hitchcock	1909–1913
Secretary of Navy	George von L. Meyer	1909–1913
Secretary of Interior	Richard A. Ballinger	1909–1911
	Walter L. Fisher	1911–1913
Secretary of Agriculture	James Wilson	1909–1913
Secretary of Labor and Commerce	Charles Nagel	1909–1913

The Wilson Administration
(1913–1921)

Vice President	Thomas R. Marshall	1913–1921
Secretary of State	William J. Bryan	1913–1915
	Robert Lansing	1915–1920
	Bainbridge Colby	1920–1921
Secretary of Treasury	William G. McAdoo	1913–1918
	Carter Glass	1918–1920
	David F. Houston	1920–1921
Secretary of War	Lindley M. Garrison	1913–1916
	Newton D. Baker	1916–1921
Attorney General	James C. McReyolds	1913–1914
	Thomas W. Gregory	1914–1919
	A. Mitchell Palmer	1919–1921
Postmaster General	Albert S. Burleson	1913–1921
Secretary of Navy	Josephus Daniels	1913–1921
Secretary of Interior	Franklin K. Lane	1913–1920
	John B. Payne	1920–1921
Secretary of Agriculture	David F. Houston	1913–1920
	Edwin T. Meredith	1920–1921
Secretary of Commerce	William C. Redfield	1913–1919
	Joshua W. Alexander	1919–1921
Secretary of Labor	William B. Wilson	1913–1921

The Harding Administration
(1921–1923)

Vice President	Calvin Coolidge	1921–1923
Secretary of State	Charles E. Hughes	1921–1923
Secretary of Treasury	Andrew Mellon	1921–1923
Secretary of War	John W. Weeks	1921–1923
Attorney General	Harry M. Daugherty	1921–1923
Postmaster General	Will H. Hays	1921–1922
	Hubert Work	1922–1923
	Harry S. New	1923
Secretary of Navy	Edwin Denby	1921–1923
Secretary of Interior	Albert B. Fall	1921–1923
	Hubert Work	1923
Secretary of Agriculture	Henry C. Wallace	1921–1923
Secretary of Commerce	Herbert C. Hoover	1921–1923
Secretary of Labor	James J. Davis	1921–1923

The Coolidge Administration
(1923–1929)

Vice President	Charles G. Dawes	1925–1929
Secretary of State	Charles E. Hughes	1923–1925
	Frank B. Kellogg	1925–1929
Secretary of Treasury	Andrew Mellon	1923–1929
Secretary of War	John W. Weeks	1923–1925
	Dwight F. Davis	1925–1929
Attorney General	Harry M. Daugherty	1923–1924
	Harlan F. Stone	1924–1925
	John G. Sargent	1925–1929
Postmaster General	Harry S. New	1923–1929
Secretary of Navy	Edwin Derby	1923–1924
	Curtis D. Wilbur	1924–1929
Secretary of Interior	Hubert Work	1923–1928
	Roy O. West	1928–1929
Secretary of Agriculture	Henry C. Wallace	1923–1924
	Howard M. Gore	1924–1925
	William M. Jardine	1925–1929
Secretary of Commerce	Herbert C. Hoover	1923–1928
	William F. Whiting	1928–1929
Secretary of Labor	James J. Davis	1923–1929

The Hoover Administration
(1929–1933)

Vice President	Charles Curtis	1929–1933
Secretary of State	Henry L. Stimson	1929–1933
Secretary of Treasury	Andrew Mellon	1929–1932
	Ogden L. Mills	1932–1933
Secretary of War	James W. Good	1929
	Patrick J. Hurley	1929–1933
Attorney General	William D. Mitchell	1929–1933
Postmaster General	Walter F. Brown	1929–1933
Secretary of Navy	Charles F. Adams	1929–1933
Secretary of Interior	Ray L. Wilbur	1929–1933
Secretary of Agriculture	Arthur M. Hyde	1929–1933
Secretary of Commerce	Robert P. Lamont	1929–1932
	Roy D. Chapin	1932–1933
Secretary of Labor	James J. Davis	1929–1930
	William N. Doak	1930–1933

The Franklin D. Roosevelt Administration
(1933–1945)

Vice President	John Nance Garner	1933–1941
	Henry A. Wallace	1941–1945
	Harry S. Truman	1945
Secretary of State	Cordell Hull	1933–1944
	Edward R. Stettinius, Jr.	1944–1945
Secretary of Treasury	William H. Woodin	1933–1934
	Henry Morgenthau, Jr.	1934–1945
Secretary of War	George H. Dern	1933–1936
	Henry A. Woodring	1936–1940
	Henry L. Stimson	1940–1945
Attorney General	Homer S. Cummings	1933–1939
	Frank Murphy	1939–1940
	Robert H. Jackson	1940–1941
	Francis Biddle	1941–1945
Postmaster General	James A. Farley	1933–1940
	Frank C. Walker	1940–1945
Secretary of Navy	Claude A. Swanson	1933–1940
	Charles Edison	1940
	Frank Knox	1940–1944
	James V. Forrestal	1944–1945
Secretary of Interior	Harold L. Ickes	1933–1945
Secretary of Agriculture	Henry A. Wallace	1933–1940
	Claude R. Wickard	1940–1945
Secretary of Commerce	Daniel C. Roper	1933–1939
	Harry L. Hopkins	1939–1940
	Jesse Jones	1940–1945
	Henry A. Wallace	1945
Secretary of Labor	Frances Perkins	1933–1945

The Truman Administration
(1945–1953)

Vice President	Alben W. Barkley	1949–1953
Secretary of State	Edward R. Stettinius, Jr.	1945
	James F. Byrnes	1945–1947
	George C. Marshall	1947–1949
	Dean G. Acheson	1949–1953
Secretary of Treasury	Fred M. Vinson	1945–1946
	John W. Snyder	1946–1953
Secretary of War	Robert P. Patterson	1945–1947
	Kenneth C. Royall	1947
Attorney General	Tom C. Clark	1945–1949
	J. Howard McGrath	1949–1952
	James P. McGranery	1952–1953
Postmaster General	Frank C. Walker	1945
	Robert E. Hannegan	1945–1947
	Jesse M. Donaldson	1947–1953
Secretary of Navy	James V. Forrestal	1945–1947

Secretary of Interior	Harold L. Ickes	1945–1946
	Julius A. Krug	1946–1949
	Oscar L. Chapman	1949–1953
Secretary of Agriculture	Clinton P. Anderson	1945–1948
	Charles F. Brannan	1948–1953
Secretary of Commerce	Henry A. Wallace	1945–1946
	W. Averell Harriman	1946–1948
	Charles W. Sawyer	1948–1953
Secretary of Labor	Lewis B. Schwellenbach	1945–1948
	Maurice J. Tobin	1948–1953
Secretary of Defense	James V. Forrestal	1947–1949
	Louis A. Johnson	1949–1950
	George C. Marshall	1950–1951
	Robert A. Lovett	1951–1953

The Eisenhower Administration
(1953–1961)

Vice President	Richard M. Nixon	1953–1961
Secretary of State	John Foster Dulles	1953–1959
	Christian A. Herter	1959–1961
Secretary of Treasury	George M. Humphrey	1953–1957
	Robert B. Anderson	1957–1961
Attorney General	Herbert Brownell, Jr.	1953–1958
	William P. Rogers	1958–1961
Postmaster General	Arthur E. Summerfield	1953–1961
Secretary of Interior	Douglas McKay	1953–1956
	Freed A. Seaton	1956–1961
Secretary of Agriculture	Ezra T. Benson	1953–1961
Secretary of Commerce	Sinclair Weeks	1953–1958
	Lewis L. Strauss	1958–1959
	Frederick H. Mueller	1959–1961
Secretary of Labor	Martin P. Durkin	1953
	James P. Mitchell	1953–1961
Secretary of Defense	Charles E. Wilson	1953–1957
	Neil H. McElroy	1957–1959
	Thomas S. Gates Jr.	1959–1961
Secretary of Health, Education, and Welfare	Oveta Culp Hobby	1953–1955
	Marion B. Folsom	1955–1958
	Arthur S. Flemming	1958–1961

The Kennedy Administration
(1961–1963)

Vice President	Lyndon B. Johnson	1961–1963
Secretary of State	Dean Rusk	1961–1963
Secretary of Treasury	C. Douglas Dillon	1961–1963
Attorney General	Robert F. Kennedy	1961–1963
Postmaster General	J. Edward Day	1961–1963
	John A. Gronouski	1963
Secretary of Interior	Stewart L. Udall	1961–1963
Secretary of Agriculture	Orville L. Freeman	1961–1963
Secretary of Commerce	Luther H. Hodges	1961–1963
Secretary of Labor	Arthur J. Goldberg	1961–1962
	W. Willard Wirtz	1962–1963
Secretary of Defense	Robert S. McNamara	1961–1963
Secretary of Health,	Abraham A. Ribicoff	1961–1962
Education, and Welfare	Anthony J. Celebrezze	1962–1963

The Lyndon Johnson Administration
(1963–1969)

Vice President	Hubert H. Humphrey	1965–1969
Secretary of State	Dean Rusk	1963–1969
Secretary of Treasury	C. Douglas Dillon	1963–1965
	Henry H. Fowler	1965–1969
Attorney General	Robert F. Kennedy	1963–1964
	Nicholas Katzenbach	1965–1966
	Ramsey Clark	1967–1969
Postmaster General	John A. Gronouski	1963–1965
	Lawrence F. O'Brien	1965–1968
	Marvin Watson	1968–1969
Secretary of Interior	Stewart L. Udall	1963–1969
Secretary of Agriculture	Orville L. Freeman	1963–1969
Secretary of Commerce	Luther H. Hodges	1963–1964
	John T. Connor	1964–1967
	Alexander B. Trowbridge	1967–1968
	Cyrus R. Smith	1968–1969
Secretary of Labor	W. Willard Wirtz	1963–1969
Secretary of Defense	Robert F. McNamara	1963–1968
	Clark Clifford	1968–1969
Secretary of Health,	Anthony J. Celebrezze	1963–1965
Education, and Welfare	John W. Gardner	1965–1968
	Wilbur J. Cohen	1968–1969
Secretary of Housing	Robert C. Weaver	1966–1969
and Urban Development	Robert C. Wood	1969
Secretary of Transportation	Alan S. Boyd	1967–1969

The Nixon Administration
(1969–1974)

Vice President	Spiro T. Agnew	1969–1973
	Gerald R. Ford	1973–1974
Secretary of State	William P. Rogers	1969–1973
	Henry S. Kissinger	1973–1974
Secretary of Treasury	David M. Kennedy	1969–1970
	John B. Connally	1971–1972
	George P. Shultz	1972–1974
	William E. Simon	1974
Attorney General	John N. Mitchell	1969–1972
	Richard G. Kleindienst	1972–1973
	Elliot L. Richardson	1973
	William B. Saxbe	1973–1974
Postmaster General	Winton M. Blount	1969–1971
Secretary of Interior	Walter J. Hickel	1969–1970
	Rogers Morton	1971–1974
Secretary of Agriculture	Clifford M. Hardin	1969–1971
	Earl L. Butz	1971–1974
Secretary of Commerce	Maurice H. Stans	1969–1972
	Peter G. Peterson	1972–1973
	Frederick B. Dent	1973–1974
Secretary of Labor	George P. Shultz	1969–1970
	James D. Hodgson	1970–1973
	Peter J. Brennan	1973–1974
Secretary of Defense	Melvin R. Laird	1969–1973
	Elliot L. Richardson	1973
	James R. Schlesinger	1973–1974
Secretary of Health,	Robert H. Finch	1969–1970
Education, and Welfare	Elliot L. Richardson	1970–1973
	Caspar W. Weinberger	1973–1974
Secretary of Housing	George Romney	1969–1973
and Urban Development	James T. Lynn	1973–1974
Secretary of Transportation	John A. Volpe	1969–1973
	Claude S. Banegar	1973–1974

The Ford Administration
(1974–1977)

Vice President	Nelson A. Rockefeller	1974–1977
Secretary of State	Henry A. Kissinger	1974–1977
Secretary of Treasury	William E. Simon	1974–1977
Attorney General	William Saxbe	1974–1975
	Edward Levi	1975–1977
Secretary of Interior	Rogers Morton	1974–1975
	Stanley K. Hathaway	1975
	Thomas Kleppe	1975–1977
Secretary of Agriculture	Earl L. Butz	1974–1976
	John A. Knebel	1976–1977
Secretary of Commerce	Frederick B. Dent	1974–1975
	Rogers Morton	1975–1976
	Elliot L. Richardson	1976–1977
Secretary of Labor	Peter J. Brennan	1974–1975
	John T. Dunlop	1975–1976
	W. J. Usery	1976–1977
Secretary of Defense	James R. Schlesinger	1974–1975
	Donald Rumsfeld	1975–1977
Secretary of Health,	Caspar Weinberger	1974–1975
Education, and Welfare	Forrest D. Mathews	1975–1977
Secretary of Housing	James T. Lynn	1974–1975
and Urban Development	Carla A. Hills	1975–1977
Secretary of Transportation	Claude Brinegar	1974–1975
	William T. Colemn	1975–1977

The Carter Administration
(1977–1981)

Vice President	Walter F. Mondale	1977–1981
Secretary of State	Cyrus R. Vance	1977–1980
	Edmund Muskie	1980–1981
Secretary of Treasury	W. Michael Blumenthal	1977–1979
	G. William Miller	1979–1981
Attorney General	Griffin Bell	1977–1979
	Benjamin R. Civiletti	1979–1981
Secretary of Interior	Cecil D. Andrus	1977–1981
Secretary of Agriculture	Robert Bergland	1977–1981
Secretary of Commerce	Juanita M. Kreps	1977–1979
	Philip M. Klutznick	1979–1981
Secretary of Labor	F. Ray Marshall	1977–1981
Secretary of Defense	Harold Brown	1977–1981
Secretary of Health,	Joseph A. Califano	1977–1979
Education and Welfare	Patricia R. Harris	1979
Secretary of Health	Patricia R. Harris	1979–1981
and Human Services		
Secretary of Education	Shirley M. Hufstedler	1979–1981

Secretary of Housing	Patricia R. Harris	1977–1979
and Urban Development	Moon Landrieu	1979–1981
Secretary of Transportation	Brock Adams	1977–1979
	Neil E. Goldschmidt	1979–1981
Secretary of Energy	James R. Schlesinger	1977–1979
	Charles W. Duncan	1979–1981

The Reagan Administration
(1981–1989)

Vice President	George Bush	1981–1989
Secretary of State	Alexander M. Haig	1981–1982
	George P. Shultz	1982–1989
Secretary of Treasury	Donald Regan	1981–1985
	James A. Baker III	1985–1988
	Nicholas F. Brady	1988–1989
Attorney General	William F. Smith	1981–1985
	Edwin A. Meese III	1985–1988
	Richard Thornburgh	1988–1989
Secretary of Interior	James Watt	1981–1983
	William P. Clark, Jr.	1983–1985
	Donald P. Hodel	1985–1989
Secretary of Agriculture	John Block	1981–1986
	Richard E. Lyng	1986–1989
Secretary of Commerce	Malcolm Baldridge	1981–1987
	C. William Verity, Jr.	1987–1989
Secretary of Labor	Raymond Donovan	1981–1985
	William Brock	1985–1987
	Ann D. McLaughlin	1987–1989
Secretary of Defense	Caspar Weinberger	1981–1987
	Frank C. Carlucci	1987–1989
Secretary of Health	Richard Schweiker	1981–1983
and Human Services	Margaret Heckler	1983–1985
	Otis R. Bowen	1985–1989
Secretary of Education	Terrel H. Bell	1981–1985
	William J. Bennett	1985–1988
	Laura F. Cavazos	1988–1989
Secretary of Housing	Samuel Pierce	1981–1989
and Urban Development		
Secretary of Transportation	Drew Lewis	1981–1983
	Elizabeth Dole	1983–1987
	James H. Burnley	1987–1989
Secretary of Energy	James Edwards	1981–1982
	Donald P. Hodel	1982–1985
	John S. Herrington	1984–1989

The Bush Administration
(1989–1993)

Vice President	J. Danforth Quayle	1989–1993
Secretary of State	James A. Baker III	1989–1992
	Lawrence S. Eagleburger	1992–1993
Secretary of Treasury	Nicholas F. Brady	1989–1993
Attorney General	Richard Thornburgh	1989–1991
	William P. Barr	1991–1993
Secretary of Interior	Manuel Lujan	1989–1993
Secretary of Agriculture	Clayton K. Yeutter	1989–1991
	Edward Madigan	1991–1993
Secretary of Commerce	Robert A. Mosbacher	1989–1992
	Barbara H. Franklin	1992–1993
Secretary of Labor	Elizabeth Dole	1989–1991
	Lynn M. Martin	1991–1993
Secretary of Defense	Richard B. Cheney	1989–1993
Secretary of Health and Human Services	Louis W. Sullivan	1989–1993
Secretary of Education	Laura F. Cavazos	1989–1991
	Lamar Alexander	1991–1993
Secretary of Housing and Urban Development	Jack F. Kemp	1989–1993
Secretary of Transportation	Samuel K. Skinner	1989–1992
	Andrew H. Card	1992–1993
Secretary of Energy	James D. Watkins	1989–1993
Secretary of Veterans Affairs	Edward J. Derwinski	1989–1993

The Clinton Administration
(1993–)

Vice President	Albert Gore, Jr.	1993–
Secretary of State	Warren M. Christopher	1993–1997
	Madeleine Albright	1997–
Secretary of Treasury	Lloyd M. Bentsen, Jr.	1993–1995
	Robert E. Rubin	1995–
Attorney General	Janet Reno	1993–
Secretary of Interior	Bruce Babbitt	1993–
Secretary of Agriculture	Mike Espy	1993–1995
	Daniel R. Glickman	1995–
Secretary of Commerce	Ronald H. Brown	1993–1996
	William M. Daley	1997–
Secretary of Labor	Robert B. Reich	1993–1997
	Alexis M. Hemman	1997–
Secretary of Defense	Les Aspin	1993–1994
	William Perry	1994–1996
	William S. Cohen	1996–
Secretary of Health and Human Services	Donna E. Shalala	1993–
Secretary of Education	Richard W. Riley	1993–
Secretary of Housing and Urban Development	Henry G. Cisneros	1993–1997
	Andrew Cuomo	1997–
Secretary of Energy	Hazel R. O'Leary	1993–1997
	Federico Peña	1997–
Secretary of Transportation	Federico Peña	1993–1997
	Rodney Slates	1997–
Secretary of Veterans Affairs	Jesse Brown	1993–

SUPREME COURT JUSTICES

Name*	Years on Court	Appointing President
JOHN JAY	1789-1795	Washington
James Wilson	1789-1798	Washington
John Rutledge	1790-1791	Washington
William Cushing	1790-1810	Washington
John Blair	1790-1796	Washington
James Iredell	1790-1799	Washington
Thomas Jefferson	1792-1793	Washington
William Paterson	1793-1806	Washington
JOHN RUTLEDGE†	1795	Washington
Samuel Chase	1796-1811	Washington
OLIVER ELLSWORTH	1796-1800	Washington
Bushrod Washington	1799-1829	J. Adams
Alfred Moore	1800-1804	J. Adams
JOHN MARSHALL	1801-1835	J.Adams
William Johnson	1804-1834	Jefferson
Brockholst Livingston	1807-1823	Jefferson
Thomas Todd	1807-1826	Jefferson
Gabriel Duvall	1811-1835	Madison
Joseph Story	1812-1845	Madison
Smith Thompson	1823-1843	Monroe
Robert Trimble	1826-1828	J. Q. Adams
John McLean	1830-1861	Jackson
Henry Baldwin	1830-1844	Jackson
James M. Wayne	1835-1867	Jackson
ROGER B. TANEY	1836-1864	Jackson
Philip P. Barbour	1836-1841	Jackson
John Cartron	1837-1865	Van Buren
John McKinley	1838-1852	Van Buren
Peter V. Daniel	1842-1860	Van Buren
Samuel Nelson	1845-1872	Tyler
Levi Woodbury	1845-1851	Polk
Robert C. Grier	1846-1870	Polk
Benjamin R. Curtis	1851-1857	Fillmore
John A. Campbell	1853-1861	Pierce
Nathan Clifford	1858-1881	Buchanan
Noah H. Swayne	1862-1881	Lincoln
Samuel F. Miller	1862-1890	Lincoln
David Davis	1862-1877	Lincoln
Stephen J. Field	1863-1897	Lincoln
SALMON P. CHASE	1864-1873	Lincoln
William Strong	1870-1880	Grant
Joseph P. Bradley	1870-1892	Grant

*Capital letters designate Chief Justices
†Never confirmed by the Senate as Chief Justice

SUPREME COURT JUSTICES
(continued)

Name*	Years on Court	Appointing President
Ward Hunt	1873-1882	Grant
MORRISON R. WAITE	1874-1888	Grant
John M. Harlan	1877-1911	Hayes
William B. Woods	1881-1887	Hayes
Stanley Matthews	1881-1889	Garfield
Horace Gray	1882-1902	Arthur
Samuel Blatchford	1882-1893	Arthur
Lucious Q. C. Lamar	1888-1893	Cleveland
MELVILLE W. FULLER	1888-1910	Cleveland
David J. Brewer	1890-1910	B. Harrison
Henry B. Brown	1891-1906	B. Harrison
George Shiras, Jr.	1892-1903	B. Harrison
Howel E. Jackson	1893-1895	B. Harrison
Edward D. White	1894-1910	Cleveland
Rufus W. Peckman	1896-1909	Cleveland
Joseph McKenna	1898-1925	McKinley
Oliver W. Holmes	1902-1932	T. Roosevelt
William R. Day	1903-1922	T. Roosevelt
William H. Moody	1906-1910	T. Roosevelt
Horace H. Lurton	1910-1914	Taft
Charles E. Hughes	1910-1916	Taft
EDWARD D. WHITE	1910-1921	Taft
Willis Van Devanter	1911-1937	Taft
Joseph R. Lamar	1911-1916	Taft
Mahlon Pitney	1912-1922	Taft
James C. McReynolds	1914-1941	Wilson
Louis D. Brandeis	1916-1939	Wilson
John H. Clarke	1916-1922	Wilson
WILLIAM H. TAFT	1921-1930	Harding
George Sutherland	1922-1938	Harding
Pierce Butler	1923-1939	Harding
Edward T. Sanford	1923-1930	Harding
Harlan F. Stone	1925-1941	Coolidge
CHARLES E. HUGHES	1930-1941	Hoover
Owen J. Roberts	1930-1945	Hoover
Benjamin N. Cardozo	1932-1938	Hoover
Hugo L. Black	1937-1971	F. Roosevelt
Stanley F. Reed	1938-1957	F. Roosevelt
Felix Frankfurter	1939-1962	F. Roosevelt
William O. Douglas	1939-1975	F. Roosevelt
Frank Murphy	1940-1949	F. Roosevelt
HARLAN F. STONE	1941-1946	F. Roosevelt
James F. Brynes	1941-1942	F. Roosevelt
Robert H. Jackson	1941-1954	F. Roosevelt
Wiley B. Rutledge	1943-1949	F. Roosevelt
Harold H. Burton	1945-1958	Truman
FREDERICK M. VINSON	1946-1953	Truman
Tom C. Clark	1949-1967	Truman

SUPREME COURT JUSTICES
(continued)

Name*	Years on Court	Appointing President
Sherman Minton	1949-1956	Truman
EARL WARREN	1953-1969	Eisenhower
John Marshall Harlan	1955-1971	Eisenhower
William J. Brennan, Jr.	1956-1990	Eisenhower
Charles E. Whittaker	1957-1962	Eisenhower
Potter Stewart	1958-1981	Eisenhower
Byron R. White	1962-1993	Kennedy
Arthur J. Goldberg	1962-1965	Kennedy
Abe Fortas	1965-1970	L. Johnson
Thurgood Marshall	1967-1991	L. Johnson
WARREN E. BURGER	1969-1986	Nixon
Harry A. Blackmun	1970-1994	Nixon
Lewis F. Powell, Jr.	1971-1987	Nixon
William H. Rehnquist	1971-1986	Nixon
John Paul Stevens	1975-	Ford
Sandra Day O'Connor	1981-	Reagan
WILLIAM H. REHNQIJIST	1986-	Reagan
Antonin Scalia	1986-	Reagan
Anthony Kennedy	1988-	Reagan
David Souter	1990-	Bush
Clarence Thomas	1991-	Bush
Ruth Bader Ginsburg	1993-	Clinton
Stephen Breyer	1994-	Clinton

PHOTO AND TEXT CREDITS

INDEX

Absolute Beginner's
ORIGAMI

Absolute Beginner's
ORIGAMI

The Simple Three-Stage Guide
to Creating Expert Origami

Nick Robinson

WATSON-GUPTILL PUBLICATIONS/NEW YORK

A QUARTO BOOK

Copyright © 1999, 2003 by Quarto Inc.

First published in 1999 in the United States
by Watson-Guptill Publications,
a division of VNU Business Media Inc.,
770 Broadway, New York, N.Y. 10003
www.wgpub.com

Library of Congress Control Number:
2005937861

ISBN 0-8230-0072-9

This book was designed and produced by
Quarto Publishing. plc
The Old Brewery
6 Blundell Street
London N7 9BH

Project editor Marnie Haslam
Editor Mike Stocks
Art editor Suzanne Metcalfe-Megginson
Designer Kevin Williams
Photography Martin Norris, Andrew Sydenham
Illustrator Terry Evans
Art director Moira Clinch
Assistant art director Penny Cobb
QUAR.AGO

Printed in China

First printing, 1999

1 2 3 4 5 6 / 11 10 09 08 07 06

CONTENTS

HOW TO USE THIS BOOK

ORIGAMI is the art of folding paper to produce lifelike, decorative, or even abstract designs. Most origami models start with a very simple folding sequence known as a base. The key to successful paperfolding is to understand the basic folding techniques, then to expand on your knowledge and expertise from there!

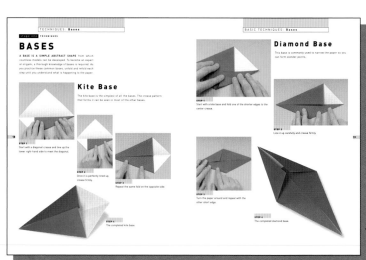

STAGE 1—BASIC TECHNIQUES

● Learn the basic folding techniques listed as "folds" and "bases."

● Follow the step-by-step instructions accompanied by color photographs.

● Practice each technique many times until you are confident.

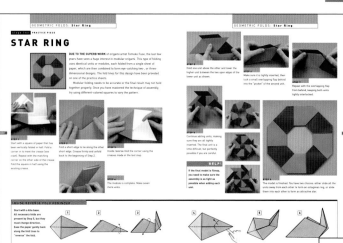

STAGE 2—PRACTICE PIECES

● Make simple origami models using the basic techniques learned in Stage 1.

● Follow the step-by-step instructions using a practice sheet of paper.

● The panel of illustrations at the bottom of the page will remind you how to make the base.

● See the Help! box for additional advice.

● Practice each design until you are confident.

● Ten sheets of practice paper with printed fold lines are provided for this stage.

STAGE 3—PROJECT

● Tackle the projects with confidence as you follow the step-by-step instructions.

● Don't forget to refer to the "reminder" panel at the bottom of the page and the Help! box, if you need assistance.

● A special sheet of colored origami paper is provided for each project.

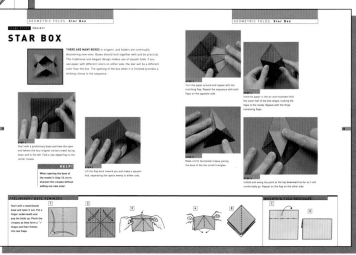

MATERIALS & EQUIPMENT

Of all the crafts or arts you might try, origami is, without doubt, the most economical—all you need is a piece of paper and your hands! In addition to a supply of paper, a well-lit desktop or table makes folding easier. As you build up a small collection of origami books, a bookshelf will become necessary. You can then display your best work on top of it.

Commercially available paper should be perfectly square, but if you buy larger sheets of paper, you will need to cut them down to size. There are two basic methods of doing this:

- Use a papercutter. This should be as big as possible for producing larger squares. Papercutters make life very easy, but they can be expensive.

- Use a craft knife on a cutting mat. The knife should have a retractable blade for safety reasons—some have "snap-off" blades, which are ideal. Cutting mats are inexpensive, and readily available at most craft shops.

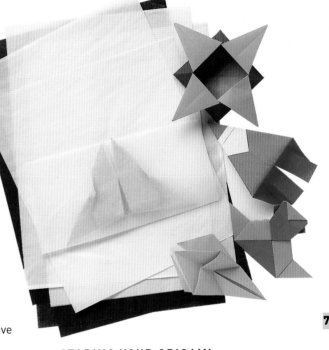

7

STORING YOUR ORIGAMI
Storing origami is a problem for experts and beginners alike. The most common solution is to wrap pieces carefully in tissue paper and keep them in a cardboard box.

CUTTING PAPER
Always be very careful when cutting paper, and if using a knife, safely store it away after use. To produce a square from a rectangle is not difficult—simply follow these three steps:

STEP 1
Start with a corner of the rectangle.

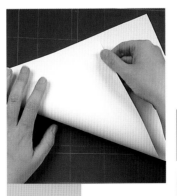

STEP 2
Fold the corner over to create a triangle. Line up the top edges evenly.

STEP 3
Trim off the remainder.

Selecting Paper

The type of paper you use to fold with will depend on what you want to do with the finished piece. If you are folding a model for the first time, plain paper will be fine. If you are going to exhibit your work in an art gallery or library, you will need to carefully consider the size, color, weight, and texture of the paper.

SIZE

The nature of paperfolding means that your end result will be many times smaller than the sheet of paper. If you want a finished model of a specific size, you will have to fold it first from a sample size of paper to see by how much it reduces. You can then work out how big your sheet of paper will need to be to produce the size of model you desire. Folding very large or very small models is very challenging, and an art in itself. However, with a little patience and practice, you will soon achieve the desired result.

COLOR AND PATTERN

Beginners will often fold from brightly colored paper regardless of the subject. Once you have mastered a particular design (which may mean folding it many, many times), you can then decide which color or pattern will suit it best. Remember, the choice is yours! Try not to use extremely bright colors that may distract from the model itself. A beautifully folded origami model should be impressive even when made from plain brown wrapping paper.

WEIGHT

The weight or thickness of the paper will determine which models you can fold from it. Complex folds are not suited to thick paper, since you won't be able to produce thin points or sometimes even fold the paper in half without tearing it! Thin paper may not be sturdy enough for models that rely on the strength of the paper to keep their shape. Standard photocopy paper is an ideal weight for folding, and you can buy it very cheaply.

TEXTURE

Thicker paper often has a distinct texture or feel to it. This can enhance the look of certain models and can add a pleasing tactile appeal to your finished design.

STANDARD ORIGAMI PAPER

On this page is a selection of sheets from a typical pack of origami paper. The sheets usually come in a wide assortment of colors, and measure 6 inches (15 cm) square, an ideal size for folding most designs.

FOIL PAPER (below)
Gold and silver are popular colors, but experience is required for the best results.

Paper Types

ORIGAMI PAPER
Most origami paper has a colored side and a plain white side, although you can find paper colored on both sides. A typical pack of paper contains sheets in several colors measuring 6 inches (15 cm) square, but other sizes are also sold. Over the past few years, an exciting range of patterns and finishes have been made available. Washi paper is handmade in Japan and uses a variety of traditional patterns and designs. The paper itself is quite soft in texture and is not suited to complex designs, but Washi paper will lend your work an authentic Oriental charm.

FOIL PAPER
You may have used this paper during arts and crafts at school—a sheet of white paper backed with a layer of shiny foil. You can find it in a variety of colors, although gold and silver are the most common. The larger rolls of foil paper are smooth, but you can buy many different embossed textures designed especially for origami. Kitchen foil is not suitable on its own, although some folders use spray-mount adhesive to glue a layer of tissue to either side of the aluminum foil. This laminate is known as "tissue-foil-tissue" and allows for very small, complex designs to be folded. All types of foil suffer from a serious drawback: It is almost impossible to change the direction of a crease once it is made.

WRAPPING PAPER
Most wrapping papers are excellent for folding, although you will usually need to cut them into smaller squares.

RECYCLED PAPER
The cheaper type of recycled paper is not suitable for folding, since it doesn't retain a sharp crease very well. In the best traditions of recycling, however, you will be able to find and reuse a huge range of papers such as handouts, computer paper, leaflets, posters, tickets, and many others. These are usually free and are ideal materials for practicing your designs.

PATTERNED AND WRAPPING PAPER
(below and right)
Achieve a unique or attractive look with patterned or wrapping paper. If it is only available in large sheets, simply cut it down to size.

START FOLDING

WHEN TO FOLD

The key to successful folding is taking your time. As with many activities, work that is done in a hurry is not usually very satisfying. Set aside sufficient time so that you don't feel rushed. Also, try to choose a time when you will have some peace and quiet; it's hard to work out difficult moves with lots of background noise. Some folders find that relaxing music helps them concentrate.

WHERE TO FOLD

Use a table with enough space for you to open the book and still have plenty of room for the paper and your elbows. Natural light is perhaps the best, but whatever lighting you use, make sure there is plenty of it. If you can arrange it so that the light is slightly to one side, the creases on the paper will show up more clearly.

HOW TO FOLD

Origami creases need to be made neatly and accurately; this is achieved by lining the paper up carefully and slowly before creasing. A few more seconds spent adjusting the paper will lead to a much more impressive result. When you progress to making complex designs, a small mistake on the first crease may mean that you can't finish the model!

Try to be aware of how the paper wants to behave; if you have to force it, you may be doing something wrong. If a crease begins to crumple, unfold that step immediately, flatten the paper, and try again, more gently.

USING THE SYMBOLS

One reason why origami has such an international appeal is because its folding instructions use a standard set of symbols. These symbols were created by the origami master Akira Yoshizawa and refined by an American, Samuel Randlett. The use of these symbols means that people all over the world can follow the instructions, regardless of the language they speak. The basic set of symbols is small, although many new symbols have been introduced over the years.

10

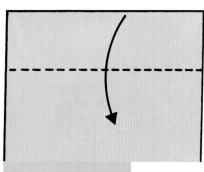

VALLEY FOLD

Shown above by a series of dashes— one side of the paper folds up and over.

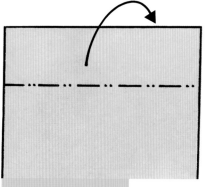

MOUNTAIN FOLD

Shown above by a dash and two dots— one side of the paper folds underneath the other.

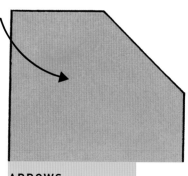

ARROWS

Shown above indicating the direction of the folding action.

BASIC FOLDS

FOLDING TECHNIQUES are the heart of origami. There is a logical progression to following the basic folds, and it is essential that you spend enough time practicing them until they come naturally to you. Once you have mastered these folds, you can begin to combine them into your own original creations!

Below and on pages 12-17 are the basic folding techniques you will need to complete the projects in this book. You should practice each fold using scrap paper until you thoroughly understand how it works. As you practice, alter distances and angles to see how they affect the end result.

Valley Fold

The valley fold is the fundamental starting point for all origami. Since it is a simple fold, try to make it perfect every time.

STEP 1
Lift one edge of the paper and fold it over to the opposite edge.

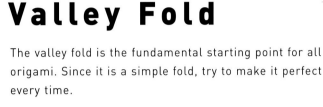

STEP 2
Line up the edges slowly and carefully—try to keep the lower half still and only move the top half.

STEP 3
Hold the layers in place with one hand and flatten the crease with the other, starting from the center and creasing outward (not shown). When you open up this fold, the raised sides of the paper will form a valley.

Mountain Fold

A mountain fold is the opposite of a valley fold. Since it is difficult to fold paper away from you and line it up neatly, you can turn the paper over and make a valley fold, then turn it over again to reverse the fold to make a mountain fold.

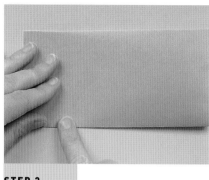

STEP 1

After making a valley fold, turn the paper over. Lift the bottom edge of the paper and fold it to meet the opposite edge using the same fold line, but changing the direction of the crease.

STEP 2

Make a firm crease along the fold line.

STEP 3

If you unfold the paper and set it on the table, the crease should form a distinct ridge that gives the fold a "mountain" appearance.

12

Location Crease

Sometimes you will need to make a fold that does not line up with an edge or corner. To do this we create a small crease known as a location crease. For example, you may need to fold to the center of a square but without making too many unnecessary creases.

STEP 1

Start with a sheet that has been vertically folded in half and unfolded again. Then fold the bottom of the sheet toward the top, but do not flatten the paper!

STEP 2

Line up the paper carefully, as if you were making a full crease, but instead, make a very small, gentle crease at the center.

STEP 3

Open out to reveal the location crease. The point where it meets the original crease is the center of the paper.

Squash Fold

This technique is very common in origami and its name is highly appropriate! If a squash fold starts to crumple, unfold it immediately, flatten the paper, and try again.

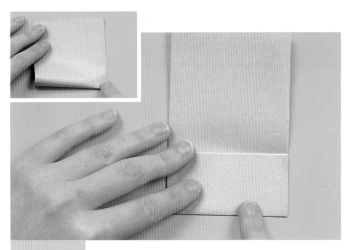

STEP 1

Start with a square that has been folded in half from left to right. Fold the bottom short edge to the opposite edge, but don't flatten the crease.

STEP 2

Make a small location crease at the halfway point (see inset), then unfold. Fold the same short edge to meet the location point and crease firmly.

STEP 3

Now lift the flap you have just made and start to open the two layers.

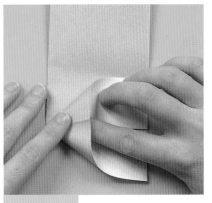

STEP 4

Slide your finger up between the layers until it meets the end. As your finger moves up, the top point of the flap will start to flatten outward. Put a finger on top of it and encourage it to flatten evenly. Use the center crease to make sure that it is lined up.

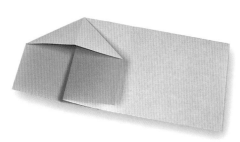

STEP 5

The completed squash fold.

Rabbit's Ear

This technique uses three separate creases to form a small triangular flap that can swing to both sides. It is often used to create ears, hence the name.

STEP 1

Fold one corner to the opposite corner, forming a triangle. Place a finger in the center of the folded edge and start to crease outward.

STEP 2

The completed diagonal crease.

STEP 3

Unfold the paper, then fold the lower left-hand edge to meet the diagonal crease along the center of the paper.

STEP 4

Crease it firmly and unfold.

STEP 5

Now repeat Steps 3 and 4 on the lower right-hand side and unfold.

14

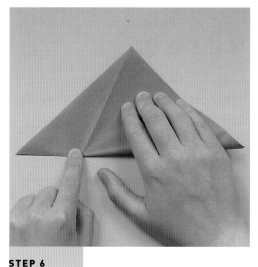

STEP 6

Rotate your paper 90-degrees clockwise and fold in half, but only crease outward from the left diagonal fold (as shown above).

STEP 7

Unfold and rotate your paper counter-clockwise back to the same position of Step 5. Lift the bottom left- and right-hand sides upward and fold inward.

STEP 8

This will cause the central flap to point upward.

15

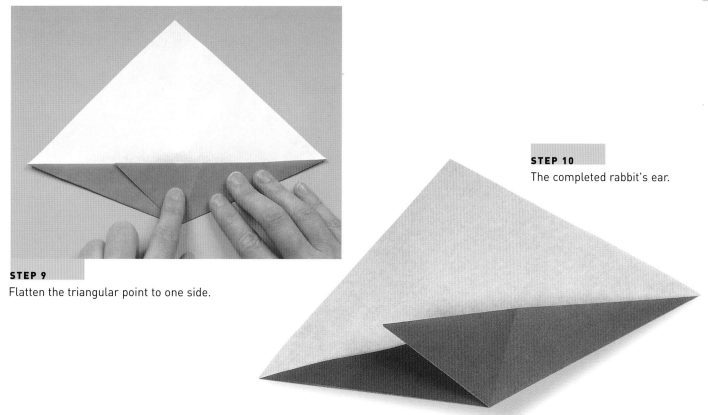

STEP 9

Flatten the triangular point to one side.

STEP 10

The completed rabbit's ear.

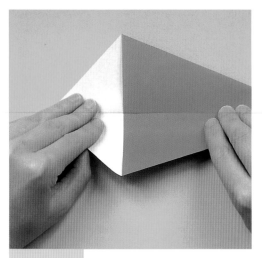

STEP 1
Start with a kite base (see page 18). Fold in half along the center crease...

Inside Reverse

This fold is called the inside reverse fold because you have to "reverse" two of its three creases. Since the paper moves inside, it becomes an inside reverse fold. The secret to a successful fold is to make the pre-crease in Step 3 firmly and neatly.

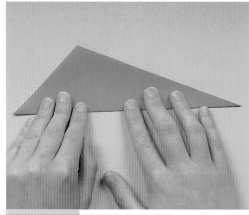

STEP 2
...like this.

STEP 3
Fold part of the sharp end at an angle, away from the long folded edge. The exact angle isn't important. Crease firmly.

16

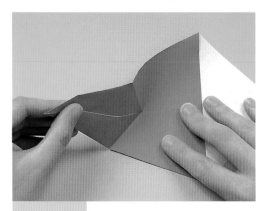

STEP 4
Unfold back to Step 1 and turn the paper around. All the creases for the reverse fold are present but some need to change direction. Fold the paper down using the lower of the two short creases. The paper won't lie flat at this stage.

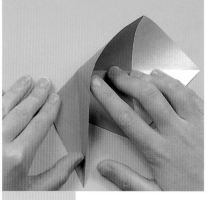

STEP 5
The original diagonal crease becomes a valley crease. The other short crease also has to change direction as the paper flattens down.

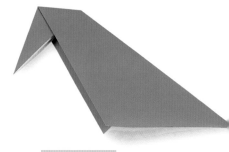

STEP 6
Reinforce the creases to complete the inside reverse fold.

Outside Reverse

This technique is similar to the inside reverse fold, but as you will see, once the fold is completed the "reversed" paper will lie on the outside.

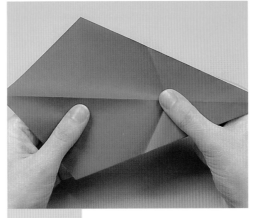

STEP 1

Start with a kite base (see page 18), folded in half as you did for the inside reverse fold. This time, swing the point at an angle away from the double-folded edge and flatten firmly. Note that this is the opposite direction to Step 3 of the inside reverse fold.

STEP 2

Open out to the underside of the kite base. One of the short creases is a valley (which we need); the other, a mountain crease, must be changed into a valley.

STEP 3

Start to fold the paper in half along the original diagonal, putting the short valley crease into place. The center crease of the reversed point also has to change direction.

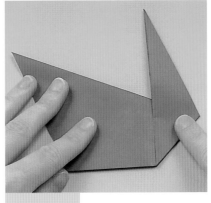

STEP 4

Here is the same fold shown from another angle. You can see how all three of the creases that make the reversed point become valley creases.

STEP 5

Flatten all the creases.

STEP 6

The completed outside reverse fold.

BASES

A BASE IS A SIMPLE ABSTRACT SHAPE from which countless models can be developed. To become an expert at origami, a thorough knowledge of bases is required. As you practice these common bases, unfold and refold each step until you understand what is happening to the paper.

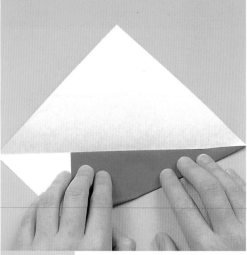

Kite Base

The kite base is the simplest of all the bases. The crease pattern that forms it can be seen in most of the other bases.

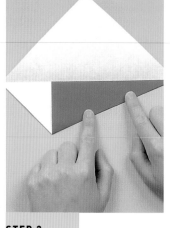

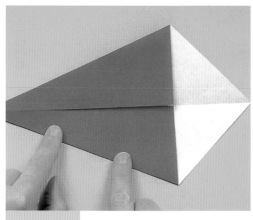

18

STEP 1
Start with a diagonal crease and line up the lower right-hand side to meet the diagonal.

STEP 2
Once it is perfectly lined up, crease firmly.

STEP 3
Repeat the same fold on the opposite side.

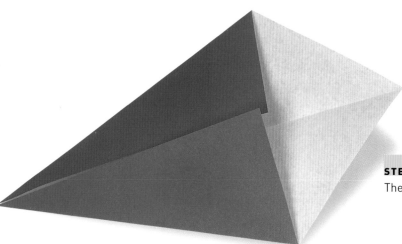

STEP 4
The completed kite base.

Diamond Base

This base is commonly used to narrow the paper so you can form slender points.

STEP 1
Start with a kite base and fold one of the shorter edges to the center crease.

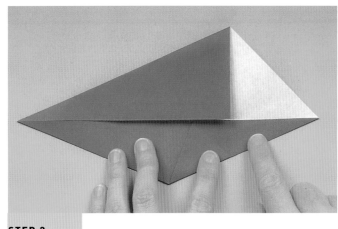

STEP 2
Line it up carefully and crease firmly.

STEP 3
Turn the paper around and repeat with the other short edge.

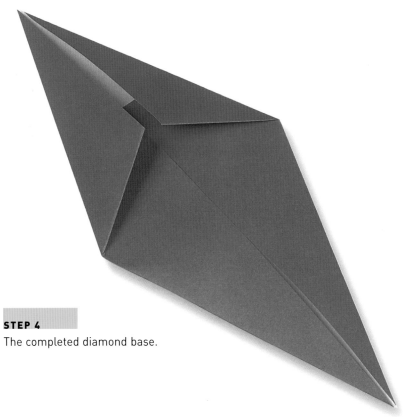

STEP 4
The completed diamond base.

Fish Base

The fish base is formed by creating two rabbit's ears on either side of a square. These flaps can then be squash- and petal-folded to form, for instance, legs.

STEP 1

Start with an upside-down kite base, sharp point toward you. Fold the sharp point to the opposite end...

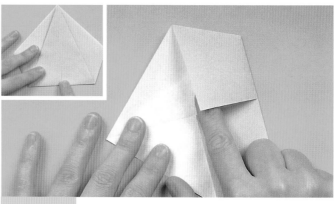

STEP 2

...and crease firmly (see inset). Turn the paper over and rotate it slightly. Put a finger inside one of the pockets and begin to open it up...

20

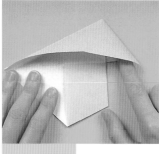

STEP 3

...so that the two raw edges line up along the center crease...

STEP 4

...like this. Flatten the paper neatly.

STEP 5

Repeat Steps 2-4 on the other side, making sure the raw edges line up neatly.

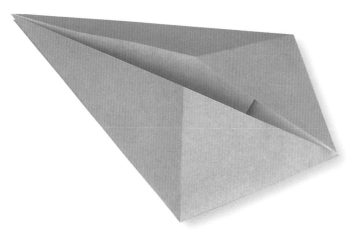

STEP 6

The completed fish base.

Waterbomb Base

This is the classic base for making the waterbomb that is familiar to many schoolchildren. If you turn it inside out, the same creases form a preliminary base.

STEP 1

Start with the intended base color facing upward. Fold the square in half and unfold.

STEP 2

Then fold the square in half from left to right and unfold.

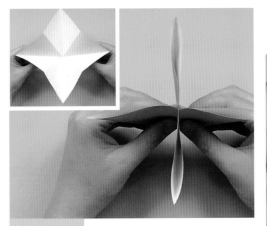

STEP 3

Turn the paper over to the other side and fold it from corner to corner to create a diagonal crease. Open and fold the opposite diagonal.

STEP 4

These are all the creases you need (see inset). Hold the paper underneath and gently press toward the center. The paper should easily fold into a star shape.

STEP 5

Flatten the paper so that there are two flaps on either side of the center fold. Reinforce the creases.

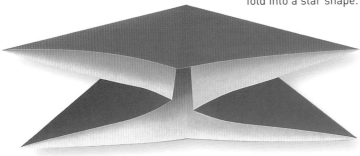

STEP 6

The completed waterbomb base.

Preliminary Base

The four corners of the square meet together in this base. It has proven to be an inspiring starting point for folders.

STEP 1

Start with a waterbomb base and begin to open it out.

STEP 2

When nearly open, put a finger underneath the center of the paper...

STEP 3

...and "pop" the creases inside out.

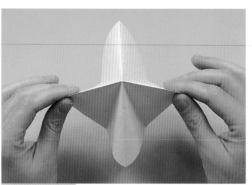

STEP 4

Finally, pinch the mountain creases on either side and begin to press these downward and together.

22

STEP 5

The paper will form into a shape like the flight of a dart. Flatten the paper so that there are two flaps on either side of the center fold.

STEP 6

The completed preliminary base.

Frog Base

This classic base provides an excellent opportunity to practice a number of folds.

STEP 1

Start with a waterbomb base (see page 21), with the open pocket toward you. Fold the bottom left-hand corner upward to meet the top corner.

STEP 2

Fold the top left edge in again to meet the center. Crease firmly and neatly!

STEP 3

Return the paper to its original position in Step 1. Slide your finger under the first layer and begin to lift and squash fold it evenly toward the center using the creases that are already present.

23

STEP 4

When the flap is squashed halfway, lift the tip of the bottom flap toward the top point, folding it at the horizontal crease. Allow the sides to fold inward...

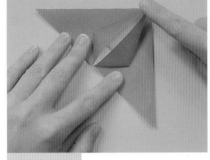

STEP 5

...making a petal fold (similar to that used in the bird base, see page 24).

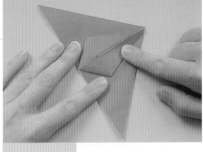

STEP 6

Flatten all the creases neatly. Repeat all steps on the other three corners.

STEP 7

The completed frog base.

Bird Base

This base has a delightful sequence of folds, creating four independent points that can be used to create a huge variety of subjects.

STEP 1

Start with a preliminary base, rotated so that the folded corner point is at the top. Fold the lower left-hand layer so that it lines up with the center crease.

STEP 2

Repeat on the right-hand side. Turn the paper over and repeat the same two folds.

STEP 3

Turn the paper around and fold the triangular flap upward...

24

STEP 4

...and crease firmly.

STEP 5

Turn the paper over from top to bottom and open the two top flaps (Steps 1 and 2) out again.

STEP 6

Then, lift the top layer up by the loose corner, holding the other flaps flat to the table...

STEP 7

...and swing it upward so that it starts to flatten on either side.

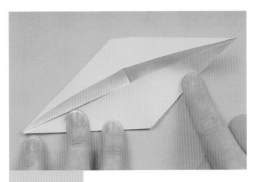

STEP 8

You will need to carefully change the direction of two creases as you flatten the sides.

STEP 9

Reinforce all the creases. You have just completed a "petal fold."

STEP 10

Turn the paper over and release the left and right flaps from underneath the triangular flap.

STEP 11

Lift the top flap upward and flatten as you did in Steps 6 to 9.

STEP 12

Both sides are now petal-folded. Then, fold both upper flaps down again.

STEP 13

The completed bird base.

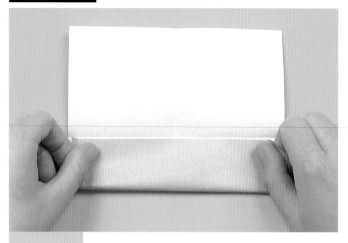

Windmill Base

This base differs from the others in that the corners form triangular flaps that can be swung to either side. This allows for a variety of shapes to be created with minimal effort.

STEP 1

Start with a square which has been folded in half both ways and unfolded. Fold the one edge to the center crease. Repeat this fold on the opposite edge so that both opposite edges now meet in the center of the paper.

STEP 2

Turn the paper sideways and fold the shorter edge to the center crease.

26

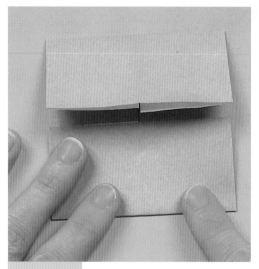

STEP 3

Turn the paper around and repeat with the opposite short edge, flattening carefully.

STEP 4

Rotate the paper 90-degrees and fold the bottom right-hand edge over to meet the vertical folded edge. Repeat on the three other edges.

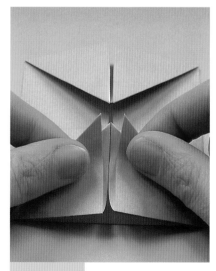

STEP 5

Hold the folded paper so that one set of triangles is facing you (as shown above), then lift a triangular flap upward, holding each side loosely between your finger and thumb.

STEP 6

Ease the outer layers away from each other, so that the inner triangle moves toward the center of the square.

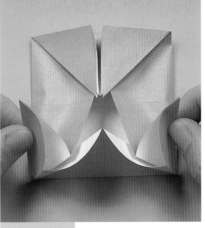

STEP 7

Continue pulling the two triangular flaps to the side until they come free.

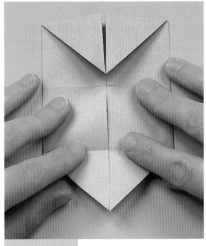

STEP 8

The paper flattens neatly and the two flaps fold downward to form a point. Repeat Steps 5 to 8 on the other end.

27

STEP 9

Crease firmly to reinforce the new folds.

STEP 10

The completed windmill base.

STAR

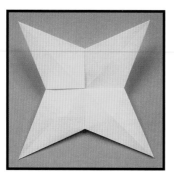

THE BIRD BASE is over one hundred years old and has proved to be very versatile, as it can be used to create a wide variety of subjects, including birds, snails, and people. This base is also suitable for creating several types of stars. The more advanced of these are three dimensional, but many, including the example here, are flat. This traditional design is ideal for practicing neat creasing and folding.

When making the squash fold, try to work with the paper rather than force it. If it starts to crumple, open the paper, flatten it, and try again. The fold lines for this design have been provided on one of the practice sheets.

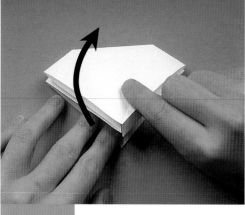

STEP 1
Make a bird base with the color inside as far as Step 5. Hold the lower layer flat to the table and lift the upper layer of paper, swinging it all the way over so it lies flat. This will cause the two inner flaps of the middle layer to point upward.

STEP 2
Put a finger inside one of the inner flaps and squash-fold it...

HELP!

Try to make the bird base as carefully as possible so that the edges of the star meet each other neatly.

STEP 3
...flattening carefully and evenly to either side. Repeat on the opposite side.

BIRD BASE REMINDER

Start with a preliminary base. After Step 2, turn over and repeat. Unfold the two flaps to complete Step 5.

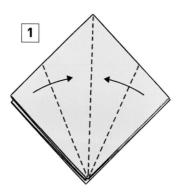

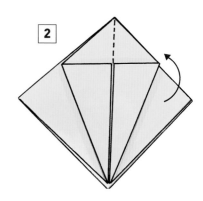

28

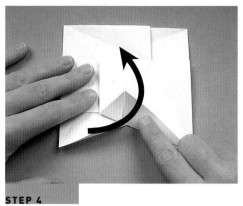

STEP 4

Turn the paper over and rotate it to the position shown. Fold one of the raw edges to the diagonal crease using an existing crease.

STEP 5

As it folds in, it will start to bring an adjoining edge with it. A new crease is formed pointing to the center as you carefully flatten the paper.

STEP 6

Make the same fold on the side to the right...

STEP 7

...and repeat on the remaining two raw edges. Flatten all the creases. Turn the paper over.

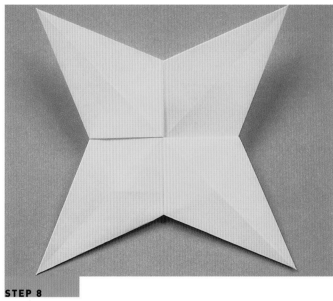

STEP 8

The completed star.

29

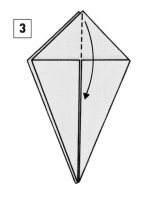

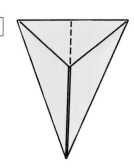

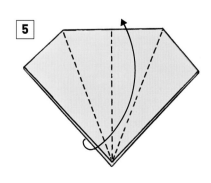

STAR RING

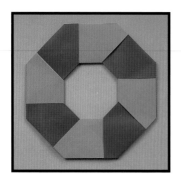

DUE TO THE SUPERB WORK of origami artist Tomoko Fuse, the last few years have seen a huge interest in modular origami. This type of folding uses identical units or modules, each folded from a single sheet of paper, which are then combined to form eye-catching two-, or three-dimensional designs. The fold lines for this design have been provided on one of the practice sheets.

Modular folding needs to be accurate or the final result may not hold together properly. Once you have mastered the technique of assembly, try using different-colored squares to vary the pattern.

30

STEP 1
Start with a square of paper that has been vertically folded in half. Fold a corner in to meet the crease (see inset). Repeat with the matching corner on the other side of the crease. Fold the square in half using the existing crease.

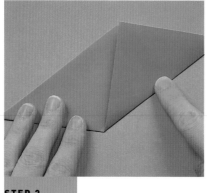

STEP 2
Fold a short edge to lie along the other short edge. Crease firmly and unfold back to the beginning of Step 2.

STEP 3
Inside reverse-fold the corner using the creases made in the last step.

STEP 4
The module is complete. Make seven more units.

INSIDE REVERSE FOLD REMINDER

Start with a kite base. All necessary folds are present by Step 5, but they must change direction. Ease the paper gently back along the fold lines to "reverse" the fold.

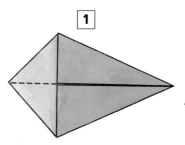

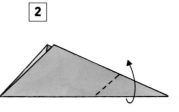

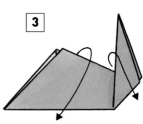

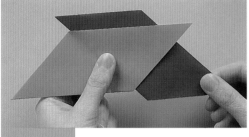

STEP 5

Hold one unit above the other and lower the higher unit between the two open edges of the lower unit as shown.

STEP 6

Make sure it is tightly inserted, then tuck a small overlapping flap behind into the "pocket" of the second unit.

STEP 7

Repeat with the overlapping flap from behind, keeping both units tightly interlocked.

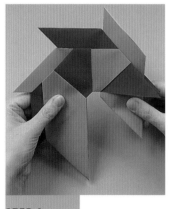

STEP 8

Continue adding units, making sure they are all tightly inserted. The final unit is a little difficult, but perfectly possible if you are careful.

HELP!

If the final model is flimsy, you need to make sure the assembly is as tight as possible when adding each unit.

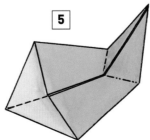

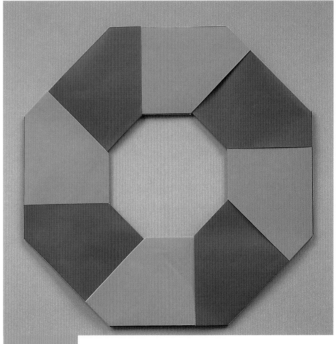

STEP 9

The model is finished. You have two choices: either slide all the units away from each other to form an octagonal ring, or slide them into each other to form an attractive star.

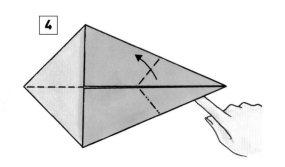

STAR BOX

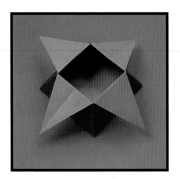

THERE ARE MANY BOXES in origami, and folders are continually discovering new ones. Boxes should lock together well and be practical. This traditional and elegant design makes use of squash folds. If you use paper with different colors on either side, the star will be a different color than the box. The opening of the box when it is finished provides a striking climax to the sequence.

STEP 1

Start with a preliminary base and have the open end (where the four original corners meet) facing down and to the left. Fold a raw-edged flap to the center crease.

HELP!

When opening the base of the model in Step 10, try to sharpen the creases without adding any new ones!

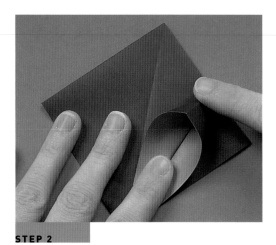

STEP 2

Lift the flap back toward you and make a squash-fold, separating the layers evenly to either side.

PRELIMINARY BASE REMINDER

Start with a waterbomb base and open it out. Put a finger underneath and pop the folds up. Pinch the creases as they form a "+" shape and then flatten into two flaps.

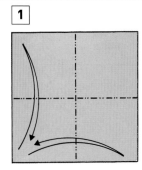

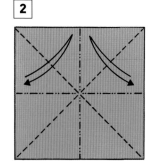

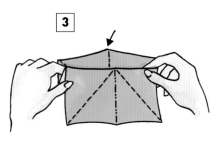

STEP 3

Turn the paper around and repeat with the matching flap. Repeat the sequence with both flaps on the opposite side.

STEP 4

Hold the paper in the air and mountain-fold the outer half of the kite shape, tucking the flaps to the inside. Repeat with the three remaining flaps.

STEP 5

Make a firm horizontal crease joining the base of the two small triangles.

STEP 6

Unfold and swing the point at the top downward as far as it will comfortably go. Repeat on the flap on the other side.

33

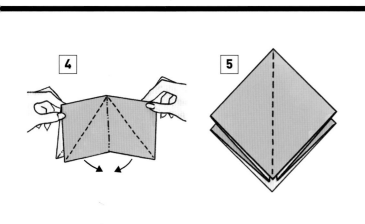

MOUNTAIN FOLD REMINDER

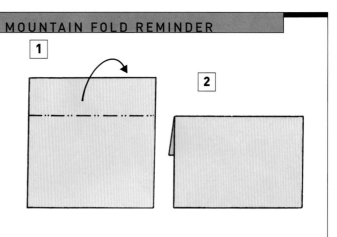

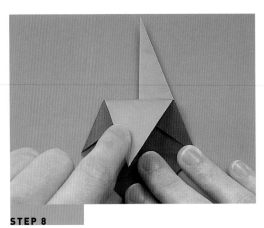

STEP 7

Fold the left-hand flap to the right...

STEP 8

...and swing the upper point downward as far as it will go.

34

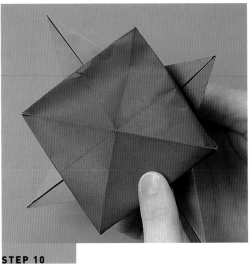

STEP 9

Fold the right flap to the left and repeat on the remaining point.

STEP 10

Nearly there now! Turn the paper upside down, place a finger inside the opening, then start to flatten the base into a neat square. Pinch the edges to help flatten the paper. Sharpen the creases around the base, turn the paper over, and you have a star box!

SQUASH FOLD REMINDER

Start with a square that has been folded in half. After folding to center, separate the two layers and "squash" the fold. Be sure to line up the squashed fold with the center crease.

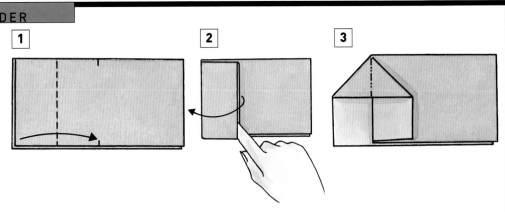

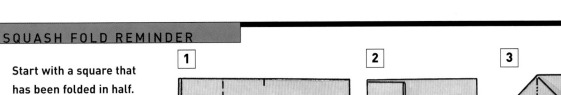

SWAN

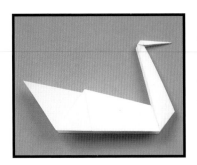

THE FLOWING LINES and pure white color of the swan has inspired folders for many years. This design is a simple, traditional model that uses two reverse folds to create the neck and head. The fold lines for this design have been provided on one of the practice sheets, but feel free to experiment with different proportions to create your own design.

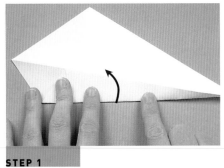

STEP 1

Start with an upside-down kite base. Fold a long edge to the center crease.

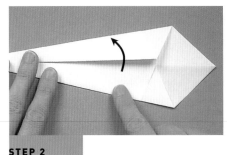

STEP 2

Turn the paper around and repeat with the other long edge.

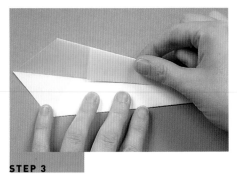

STEP 3

Mountain-fold the model in half along the center crease.

STEP 4

Starting at a point about halfway along the lower edge, swing the sharp point upward so that it angles back slightly.

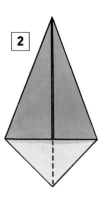

HELP!

When narrowing paper to a sharp point, you should take extra time to line the paper up carefully, or you may end up with a blunt beak.

KITE BASE REMINDER

Start with a diagonal crease and fold one side in to line up with the center crease. Repeat on the other side.

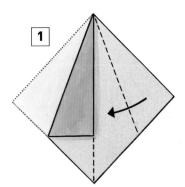

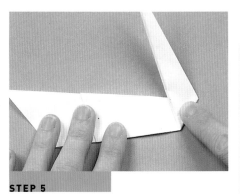

STEP 5

This will be the neck. Press the crease firmly and unfold.

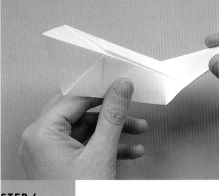

STEP 6

Open the two layers underneath the model and use the creases made in the last step to make an outside reverse fold.

STEP 7

Reinforce the reverse fold.

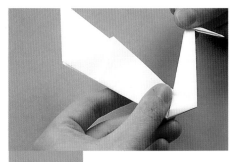

STEP 8

Fold the tip of the point forward to form a beak, crease firmly, and unfold.

STEP 9

Using the last crease, make another outside reverse-fold.

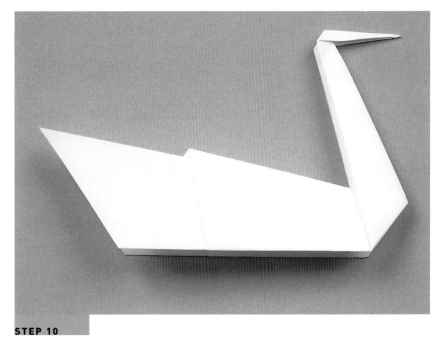

STEP 10

The completed swan.

37

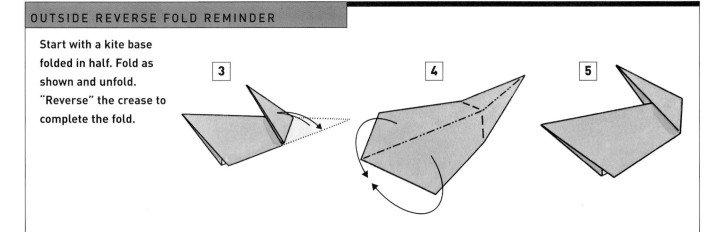

OUTSIDE REVERSE FOLD REMINDER

Start with a kite base folded in half. Fold as shown and unfold. "Reverse" the crease to complete the fold.

3

4

5

IRIS

THE FROG BASE can be used to make one or two classic designs—including the frog itself—but this iris is the most elegant and beautiful. The base is relatively complex because it is smaller than most other bases, so fold carefully! You can make use of a well-known paper-curling technique to encourage the petals to curve outward and downward.

Flower folds are an ideal opportunity to experiment with more exotic types of patterned paper.

HELP!

A neat result depends largely on accurate creasing, so take your time. Start with a larger square, then gradually reduce the size.

38

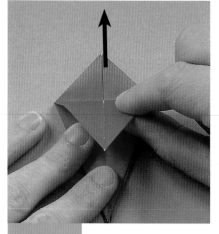

STEP 1
Start with a frog base, colored side outward. Lift all four loose flaps to point upward.

STEP 2
Narrow the lower side by folding the edge to the center.

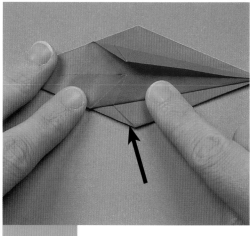

STEP 3
Turn the paper around and fold the matching edge in as well.

FROG BASE REMINDER

Start with a waterbomb base. Fold a bottom corner up, fold it in to the center again and unfold. Lift the flap, squash fold it halfway and make a petal fold. Repeat on all three corners.

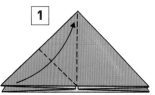

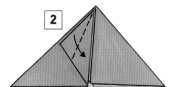

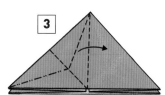

STEP 4

Repeat the last two steps on the three other flaps around the model.

STEP 5

Fold the top flap down as far as it will comfortably go. Repeat with the other three flaps.

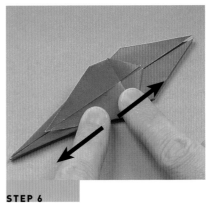

STEP 6

Gently pull these two flaps apart.

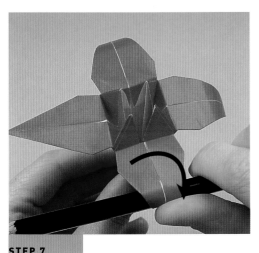

STEP 7

Wind each petal around a pencil so that they curl downward.

STEP 8

The completed iris.

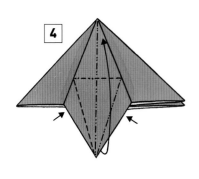

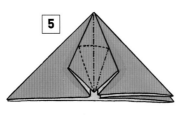

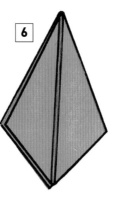

BUTTERFLY

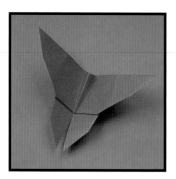

BUTTERFLIES are another popular subject for folders. Made from small squares of brightly colored paper, they can sometimes seem almost real. Try to fold with a light touch, or the model will look clumsy and heavy. The idea is to aim for a light, delicate appearance. The windmill base from which the butterfly is formed can be used for a large number of subjects.

Try swinging the windmill flaps in different directions to see if you can discover a new design "hidden" in the paper!

STEP 1

Start with a windmill base. Mountain-fold the top half of the paper behind.

HELP!

Keep the body of the butterfly firmly on the table when adding the body crease (Step 9).

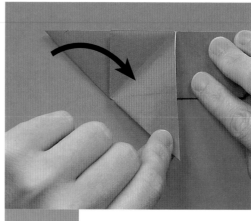

STEP 2

Swing a flap downward.

WINDMILL BASE REMINDER

Start with a preliminary base opened out. Follow the simple folding steps until Step 5. Pull the triangular flaps until the paper flattens and forms a point on each side.

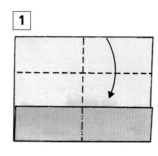

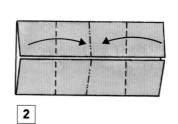

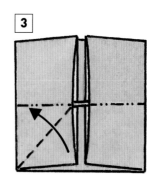

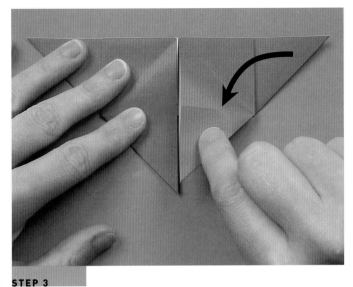

STEP 3

Repeat with the other flap.

STEP 4

To narrow the lower wing, fold in a corner.

STEP 5

Repeat on the other side.

STEP 6

Shape the upper wings in a similar fashion.

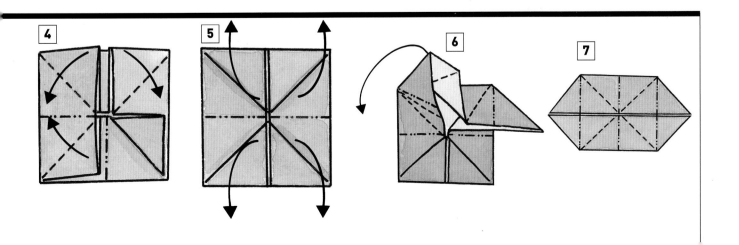

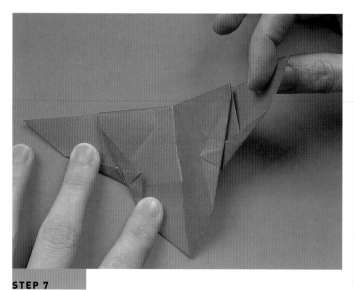

STEP 7

Valley-fold the model in half from right to left.

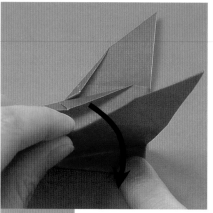

STEP 8

Then, valley-fold the top wing back at a slight angle.

42

STEP 9

Crease firmly and turn the paper over.

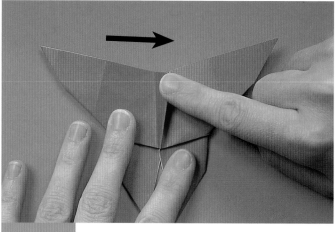

STEP 10

Swing the central flap to the right to reinforce it, then leave it pointing upward.

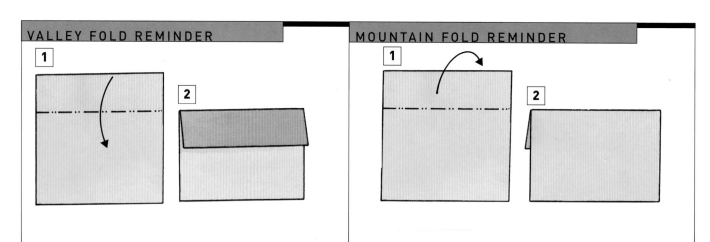

VALLEY FOLD REMINDER

MOUNTAIN FOLD REMINDER

stage two PRACTICE PIECE

WALLET

ORIGAMI is wonderful for making small, practical objects. Here is a small wallet in which you can keep money, photos, or even postage stamps, if you make it small enough! Try to choose a paper that is durable, so you can use it for many months. This design could make an ideal present for a friend. The fold lines for this design have been provided on one of the practice sheets.

44

STEP 1

Start with a windmill base, opened back out to the square. Valley-fold a corner to meet the intersection of three creases.

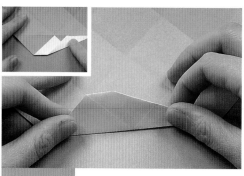

STEP 2

Fold half of the lower raw edge to meet the 45-degree crease (see inset)...then swing the whole corner in on that crease (main picture).

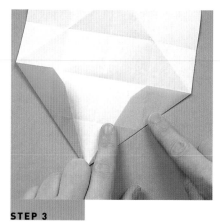

STEP 3

Rotate your paper to the left and repeat all the steps on the adjacent corner.

HELP!

When tucking the final flap inside, let the paper "curl" into the pocket rather than forcing it in (Step 8).

WINDMILL BASE REMINDER

Start with a preliminary base opened back to the square. Follow the simple folding steps until Step 5. Then pull the triangular flaps at one end until the paper flattens and forms a point. Repeat on other end.

1

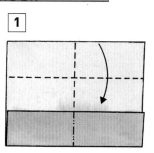

2

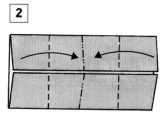

3

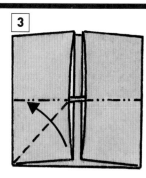

STEP 4

Turn the paper over. Fold the long raw edge down to the center crease.

STEP 5

Fold both of the short sides in to the center crease.

STEP 6

Turn the paper over, keeping the point at the top. Using an existing crease, valley-fold the bottom section away from you.

STEP 7

Turn the paper around again, then tuck the corner inside the pocket formed in Step 6. Make sure it folds in completely.

STEP 8

Mountain-fold the model in half down the center.

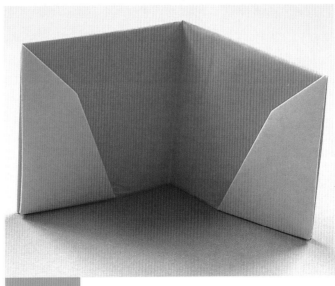

STEP 9

The completed wallet.

45

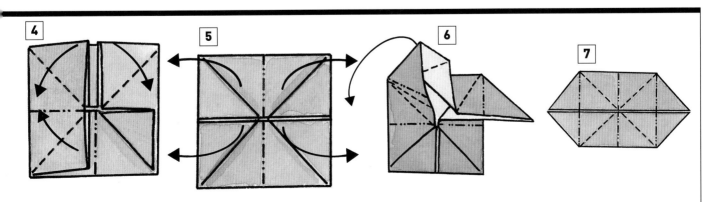

HEART

THE SINGAPORE FOLDER Francis Ow has written several books that deal solely with origami hearts. This design has a pleasing three-dimensional aspect and is also practical, since you can wear it by tucking it into a breast pocket.

The technique that allows us to create the shape of the heart is known as a "butterfly" lock, and it is an elegant method often used to make three-dimensional designs.

46

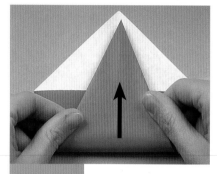

STEP 1
Start with a kite base folded with the colored side out. Fold the sharp corner to the opposite end.

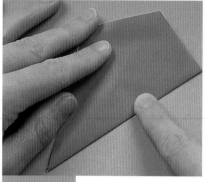

STEP 2
Rotate the paper 90-degrees to the left and valley-fold it in half away from you.

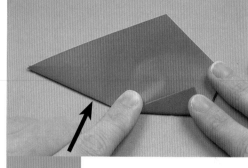

STEP 3
Fold a small flap over at the right-angled corner. Crease firmly and slowly, since the paper has several layers.

STEP 4
Unfold to the kite base and begin to form a rabbit's ear using the two halves of the central diamond creases that are nearest to you. The paper does not lie flat!

HELP!

Many of the steps are three-dimensional and must be folded off the table, so keep checking the next photo to see what you are aiming for.

RABBIT'S EAR FOLD REMINDER

Follow the simple folding instructions to Step 6, then rotate the point toward you and lift the paper, causing a verticle point to form. Flatten the point to one side.

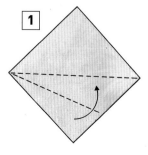

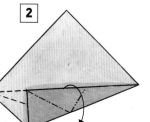

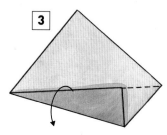

STEP 5

When the rabbit's ear is complete, start to bring its tip toward you.

STEP 6

Press in the center of the half diamond shape as you swing the sharp corner inward on the crease made in Step 1.

STEP 7

The paper will collapse naturally into this form. Blunt the tips of the outer corners by folding them in slightly...

STEP 8

...and the corners on the top.

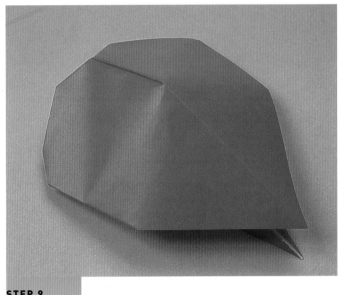

STEP 9

Turn the paper over to see the completed heart.

47

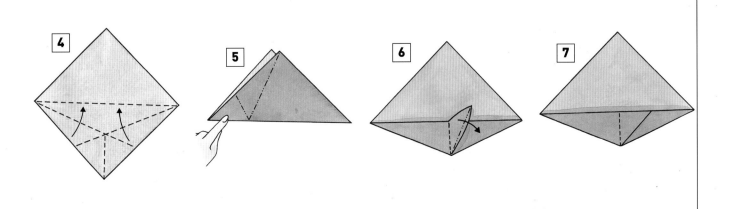

BOUTONNIERE

THIS TRADITIONAL DESIGN is a classic—simple, elegant, and beautiful. Many folders believe it is harder to capture a subject using simple lines than it is to create a more complex design with lots of detail. The boutonniere is an example of "climactic" folding, in which the final object is seen only at the last moment.

Try to find paper that is green on one side and a brighter color on the other. Spray adhesive is ideal for gluing two sheets together, but it must be used in a well-ventilated room.

STEP 1

Start with a preliminary base, with the color of the petals inside. Turn the base so that the open ends are facing away from you. Fold one of the sides with folded edges to lie along the vertical center crease.

STEP 2

Repeat on the adjacent flap.

PRELIMINARY BASE REMINDER

Start with a waterbomb base and open it out. Put a finger underneath the paper and pop the folds up. Pinch the creases as they form a "+" shape and then flatten into two flaps.

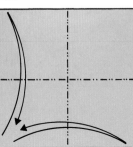

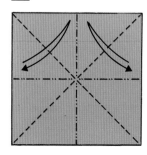

48

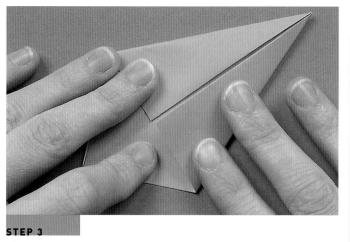

STEP 3

Then turn the paper over and fold both flaps to match.

STEP 4

Carefully fold the whole model in half along the center crease.

HELP!

When first making this design, you can add pre-creases for the reverse fold. Once you see what you are aiming for, try making it directly, as suggested (see Step 5).

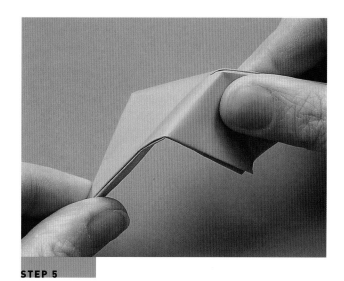

STEP 5

Turn the paper around so the longest edge is on top. Holding it in the air, pull the narrow point downward, adding an inside reverse fold directly into the paper. We don't pre-crease this fold because the paper is too thick. Use the next picture as a guide.

49

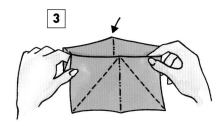

3

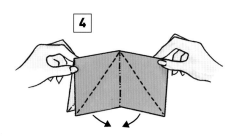

4

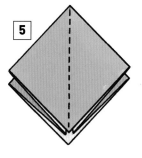

5

STEP 6

When the reverse fold is in place, crease it firmly.

STEP 7

Hold the paper loosely, then start to peel back the corner of the uppermost triangular flap.

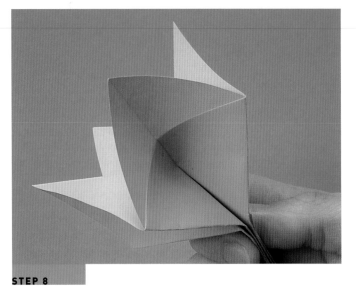

STEP 8

As you peel it back, the four petals suddenly spring out. Tighten the reverse fold again.

INSIDE REVERSE FOLD REMINDER

Just the last two steps shown here. Ease the paper gently back along the fold lines to "reverse" the fold.

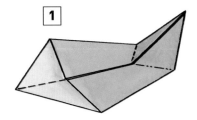

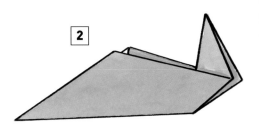

CARP

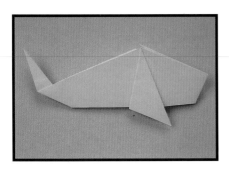

IN JAPAN, the carp symbolizes the will to succeed. On All Children's Day (May 5th), children make paper streamers from this basic design. This is one of the many simple models that can be made, not surprisingly, from a fish base! Some origami fish are highly detailed, but this one is a very basic but appealing design. The fold lines for this design have been provided on one of the practice sheets.

Using the carp as a starting point, can you create a fish of your own?

STEP 1

Start with a fish base. Lift the top flap and flatten the paper into a diamond.

STEP 2

Fold the diamond in half along the long center crease.

HELP!

If you make all pre-creases firmly, your reverse folds will be easier.

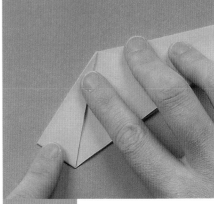

STEP 3

Take the right-hand point to the shallow point at the top. Crease firmly and unfold.

FISH BASE REMINDER

Start with an upside down kite base. Fold the sharp point to the opposite end, crease and turn over. Open the pockets and line up the center edges neatly.

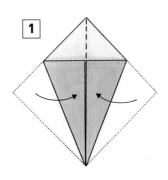

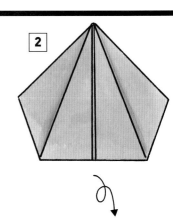

52

STEP 4

Then, make an inside reverse fold on that same crease.

STEP 5

There will now be two small triangular flaps. Fold each one to slightly past the verticle mark.

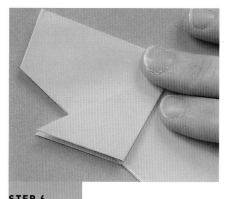

STEP 6

Fold the tip of the tail upward at a slight angle, crease and unfold.

STEP 7

Form the tail using an inside reverse fold.

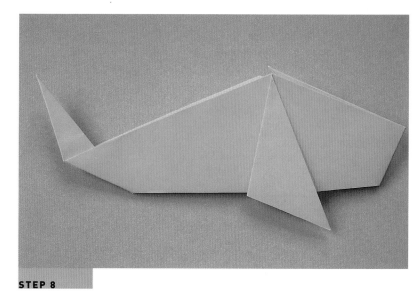

STEP 8

The completed carp.

53

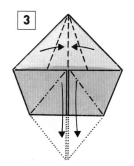

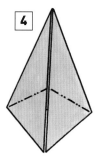

PAJARITA

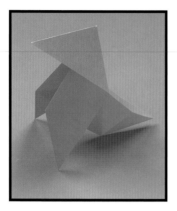

THE PAJARITA (Spanish for "little bird") has been an traditional symbol in Spain for many years. You can find it on airplanes, salt shakers, and even bars of chocolate! In origami, it is one of a long series of folds that uses the windmill base. The outside reverse fold that forms the head is also known as a "color-change," since it reveals the opposite side of the paper.

After you have completed the pajarita, unfold it and look carefully at the crease pattern. Try to work out how each crease is used in the final model. Analyzing crease patterns is a great help in creating new designs.

54

STEP 1

Start with a windmill base. Fold the top-left corner upward.

STEP 2

Mountain-fold the model in half, by folding the top-right corner behind to meet the bottom-left corner while pulling upward the top-left corner folded in Step 1.

STEP 3

This is the result.

WINDMILL BASE REMINDER

Start with a preliminary base opened out. Follow the simple folding steps until Step 5. Pull the triangular flaps until the paper flattens and forms a point on each side.

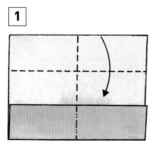

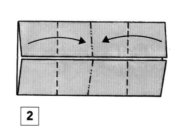

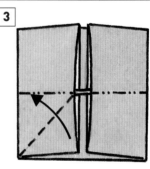

STEP 4

Begin to separate the layers at the top corner...

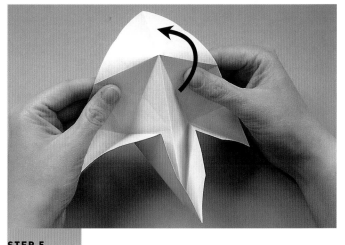

STEP 5

...then flip the corner inside out with an outside reverse fold.

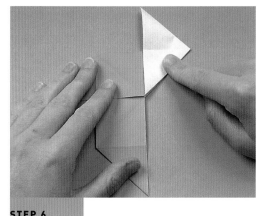

STEP 6

Flatten the head section, which will have a color change.

HELP!

Open the paper out as much as possible when forming the head—it will refold easily—if you have made the creases firmly (Step 5).

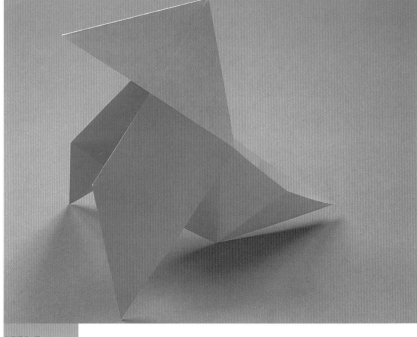

STEP 7

Separate the two front "wings" slightly to stand it up. The completed "pajarita."

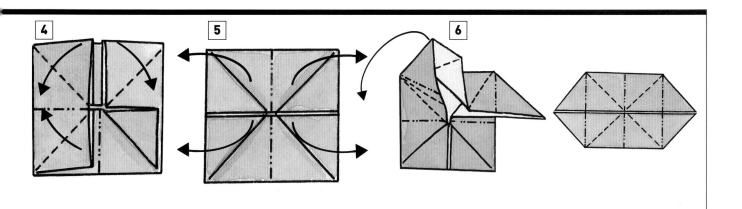

4 5 6

CUBE

THIS CLASSIC TOY has existed for many years and is well-known to schoolchildren as the "waterbomb" from which the base gets its name. However, it also forms an attractive fold for displaying on a mobile, particularly when it is folded from brightly colored paper.

STEP 1

Start with a waterbomb base with the raw edges toward you. Fold a bottom corner to the top of the triangle.

STEP 2

Fold the top of the triangle to the bottom, making a location crease at the halfway point. Unfold this flap.

STEP 3

Fold the outside corner of the triangle to meet the location crease at the center of the paper. Repeat with the other corner on this side and the two corners underneath.

WATERBOMB BASE REMINDER

Fold paper in half horizontally, vertically, and diagonally. Holding the paper underneath, gently press it into a star shape. Then flatten into a triangle with two flaps.

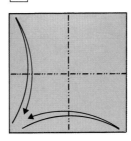
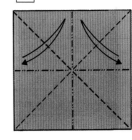

56

STEP 4

There are loose corners at the top of the model. Fold them down to the center to form a small triangle, twice on each side.

STEP 5

Fold the same triangle outward across the inside edge of the larger triangle, crease, and unfold.

STEP 6

Using the latest crease, begin to tuck the small triangle into the pocket of the larger triangle...

STEP 7

...like this. Repeat with the three other triangles.

57

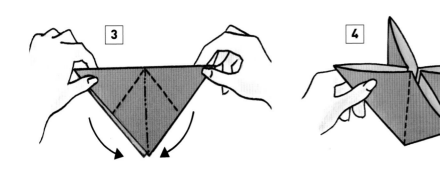

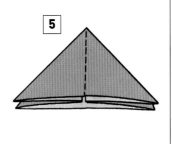

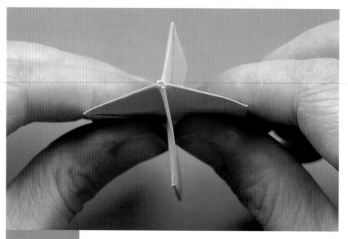

STEP 9

Spread the four flaps out to form a cross; then, holding two opposite flaps, blow into the small opening at the top of the model. As it inflates, use your fingers to help shape it into a rounded form.

STEP 8

Fold the nearest corner to the center, crease firmly and unfold. Repeat this action on the other corner.

58

STEP 10

Pinch the edges to make the form into a cube shape.

LOCATION CREASE REMINDER

Fold the paper in half vertically and unfold. Then fold the bottom to the top but only make a very small crease in the center.

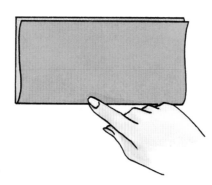

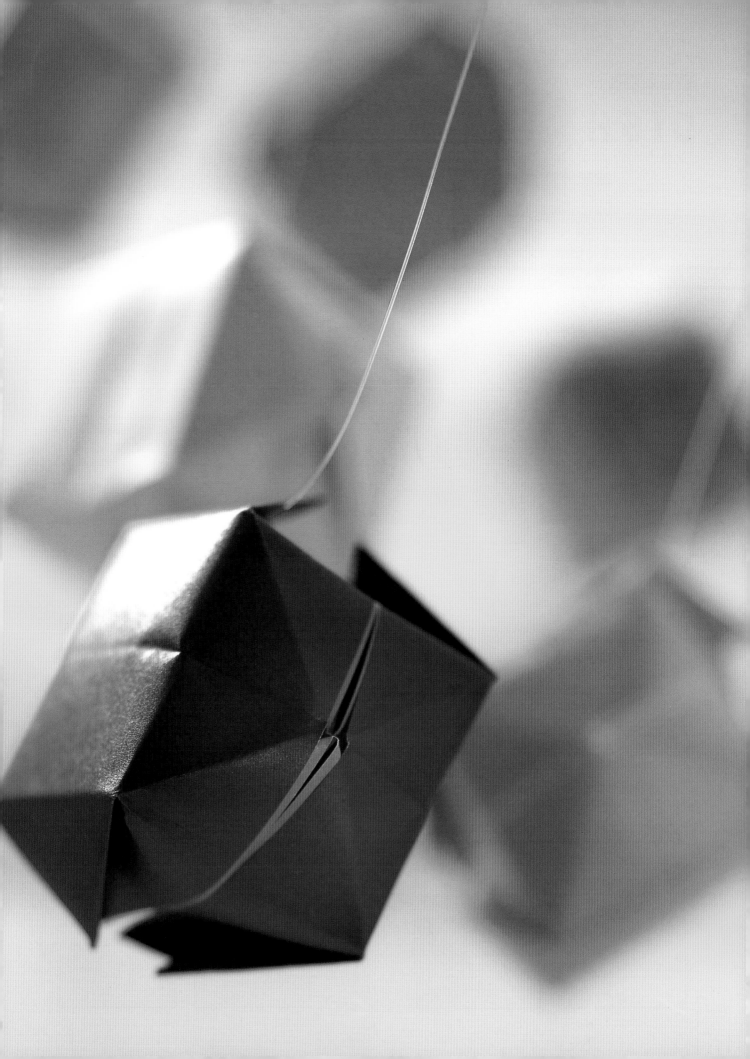

stage two **PRACTICE PIECE**

DISH

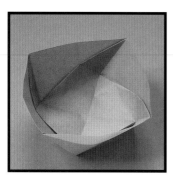

CREATED BY THE AUTHOR, this dish uses a simple locking technique to form the sides. The creases for this are done in advance, a technique known as "pre-creasing." You should make sure all pre-creasing is accurate. The fold lines for this design have been provided on one of the practice sheets.

Try to achieve smooth curves around the outside edges of the dish. By folding the mirror image of all the creases, you could create a dish that "twists" the other way.

STEP 1
Start with a square divided into sixteen smaller squares. Fold the nearest edge over to the center crease.

STEP 2
Fold the same edge over again, using the halfway crease. Then rotate the paper 180-degrees.

STEP 3
Make a crease that joins the top right outside corner with the center of your practice paper.

STEP 4
Unfold and fold the short raw edges on the right to meet the most recent crease made.

HELP!

If you struggle with the final lock, fold and unfold each corner in turn, so the paper knows where it is going.

VALLEY FOLD REMINDER

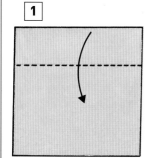

1

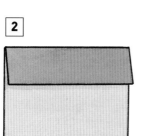

2

MOUNTAIN FOLD REMINDER

1

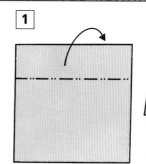

2

STEP 5

Open the paper out and repeat Steps 1 through 4 on the three other edges. Unfold once more, turn the paper over and fold in using the valley crease indicated below the right-hand thumb.

STEP 6

Lock it into place by folding the small triangle behind.

STEP 7

Repeat the previous two steps on the other three corners. Take care with the final corner.

STEP 8

Turn the dish over and smooth all its creases to give it a slightly circular feel.

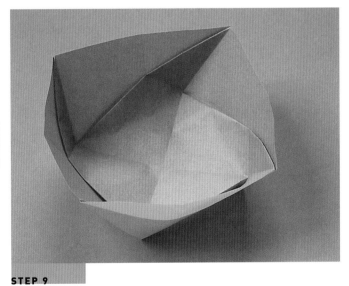

STEP 9

The completed dish.

61

LOCATION CREASE REMINDER

Fold the paper in half vertically and unfold. Then fold the bottom to the top but only make a very small crease at the fold mark at the center of the paper.

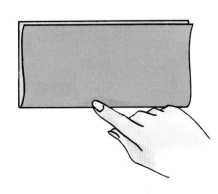

stage two **PRACTICE PIECE**

VALENTINE VASE

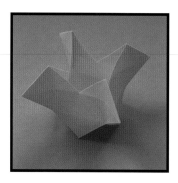

THIS DESIGN is by Pam Bisman from New Zealand. Note how the completed model holds itself together using the tension of the paper rather than complicated folding techniques. As with all origami, this design will look best if you fold neatly and accurately. It is interesting to see how the straight line creases can produce a model which appears to have curves.

Since the model incorporates a heart motif, you may want to use red or pink paper.

HELP!

Opening the layers is easiest if you do it in the air (Step 5).

STEP 1

Start with a windmill base, unfolded back to the original square. Alternatively, fold all quarter creases, then take each corner to the center and unfold. Fold a corner in to the first intersection of creases.

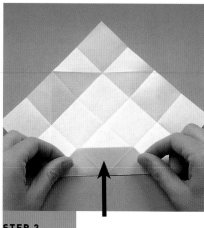

STEP 2

Fold over again on an existing crease. Repeat with the other three corners.

STEP 3

Take a corner to the opposite corner of the smaller internal square, but only crease the thinner central section.

WINDMILL BASE REMINDER

Start with a preliminary base opened back to the square. Follow the simple folding steps until Step 5. Then pull the triangular flaps at one end until the paper flattens and forms a point. Repeat steps on the other end.

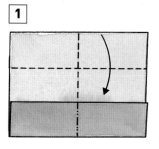

1

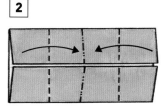

2

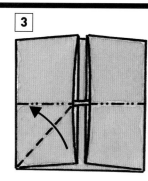

3

62

STEP 4

Repeat on the other three sides, then turn the paper over and fold all four corners to the center.

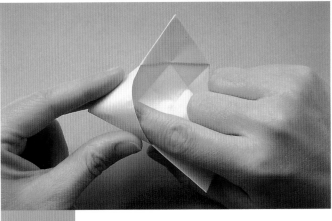

STEP 5

Turn over once more, then open out one of the pockets with your finger, gently pressing the sides together.

STEP 6

Repeat with the other three corners. The creases made in Steps 3 and 4 form the base of the vase.

STEP 7

The completed vase.

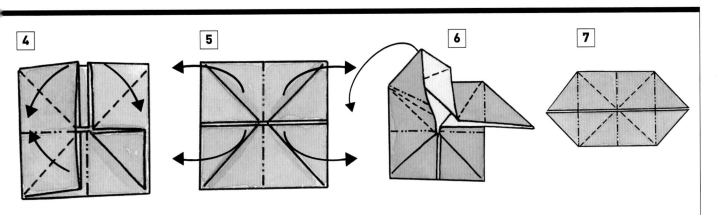

4   5   6   7

stage three PROJECT

BOOKMARK

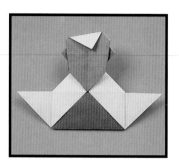

SINCE A BOOKMARK is such a simple concept (basically just a triangular pocket), it is a great subject to use when creating your first original models. Many will be purely functional, but this design adds a head and arms to make the bookmark more fun.

The folds that shape the hair and ears can be varied to suit your own taste.

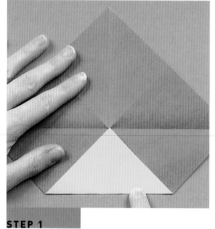

STEP 1

Start with a preliminary base, opened out to a square. The "head" color should be toward you. Fold each corner to the center, crease firmly, then unfold.

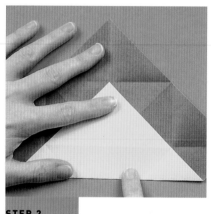

STEP 2

Fold each corner to the opposite quarter crease, crease firmly, then unfold. Leave the final crease in place.

HELP!

This design is quite challenging, so study the instructions and photographs carefully to fully understand each step. Be sure to tuck in the final flap carefully, or the paper may crumple (Step 15).

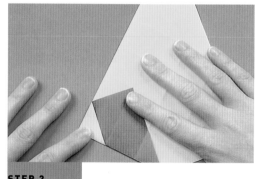

STEP 3

Turn the paper over and fold the left-hand corner to the center of the paper (where the creases meet).

64

PRELIMINARY BASE REMINDER

Start with a waterbomb base and open it out. Put a finger underneath and pop the folds up. Pinch the creases as they form a "+" shape and then flatten into two flaps.

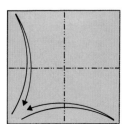

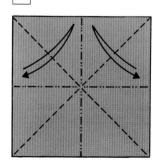

STEP 4

Fold the small triangle inward, crease firmly and unfold.

STEP 5

Make a valley fold using the crease at the center of the triangle, carefully squash-folding the corner. Repeat Steps 3 to 5 on the right-hand side.

STEP 6

Turn the paper over and inside reverse fold the right-hand outer section. The "arm" pops out during this step. Check the next photo as a guide. Repeat on the left-hand side.

STEP 7

Precrease and form a waterbomb base (see reminder below) in the top square section.

STEP 8

Turn the paper over and fold the two corners behind the head in toward the original center of the square.

STEP 9

Make two small pleats to form the ears—try to make them the same.

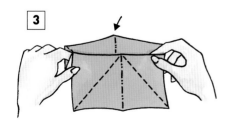

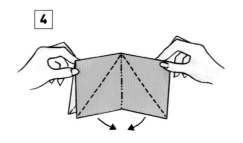

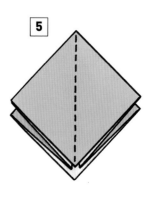

STEP 10

Turn the paper over and put your fingers inside the flaps of the body (as shown in inset), then open them fully out and squash-fold away from you. Fold the original corner to the first intersection of creases...

STEP 11

...then fold the flap over again on an existing crease (see inset). Pull down the top flap of the boat-shaped section, flattening the paper toward you. The result is shown in the main photo.

STEP 12

Fold a small corner down to form the hair and flatten all the creases. Your bookmark is complete!

SQUASH FOLD BASE REMINDER

Start with a square that has been folded in half. After folding to the center, separate the two layers and "squash" the fold. Be sure to line up the squashed fold with the center crease.

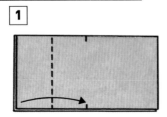

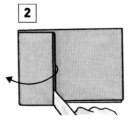

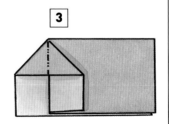

66

CHRISTMAS TREE

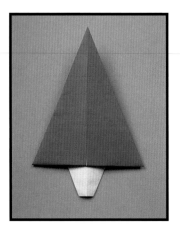

ONE OF THE SIMPLEST DESIGNS in this book, this charming tree is perfect for Christmas cards. If you make many trees, of varying sizes, they can be made into a realistic woodland montage. Altering the creases and rounding off the sharp points allows you to create several other types of tree. The fold lines for this design have been provided on one of the practice sheets.

HELP!

Because this design is so simple, you should concentrate on creating a perfect example every time!

STEP 1

Start with an upside-down kite base. Fold a small tip of the original corner inward.

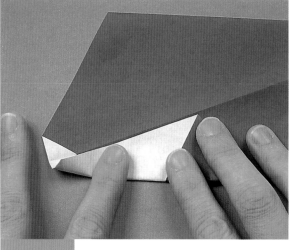

STEP 2

Fold a short raw edge to the center crease. Repeat on the other side.

KITE BASE REMINDER

Start with a diagonal crease and fold one side in to line up with the center crease. Repeat on the other side.

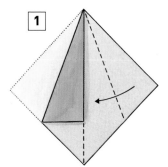

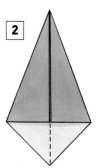

STEP 3

Fold in half between the widest corners, creasing firmly.

STEP 4

Valley-fold the blunt end back down so that half of it lies past the folded edge.

69

STEP 5

Turn the piece over to see the completed Christmas tree.

VALLEY FOLD REMINDER

To make a valley fold, simply fold the paper toward you and make a firm crease.

1

2

ENVELOPE

ENVELOPES HAVE BEEN USED for hundreds of years and much research has been carried out to study their history and use. There is even a group called ELFA (Envelope and Letter Folding Association) which publishes collections of envelope designs. The aim is always to create a practical design that keeps its contents secure. The fold lines for this design have been provided on one of the practice sheets.

Almost all the creases in this design can be altered to some extent. Try as many variations as you can think of.

STEP 1
Start with a square with both diagonals creased. Valley-fold a corner to the center, crease and unfold.

STEP 2
Make a similar fold placing the corner at the last crease made (as shown in inset). Fold this flap over on the existing crease.

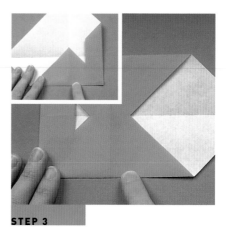

STEP 3
Rotate the paper to the position shown (see inset), then fold the corner inward to a point just past the center point. Turn the paper around and repeat on the opposite side. The two raw edges meet over the center crease.

HELP!

Start with a larger square if you plan to mail your envelope!

VALLEY FOLD REMINDER

To make a valley fold, simply fold the paper toward you and make a firm crease.

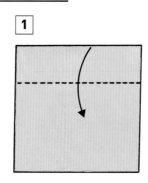

1

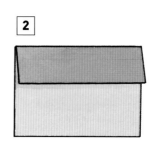

2

70

STEP 4

Fold the remaining corner to lie along the raw edges.

STEP 5

Rotate the paper 180-degrees and fold the same corner back out to the center of the top edge.

STEP 6

Then mountain-fold the whole of the loose flap behind on the crease made in Step 4.

STEP 7

Fold a corner of the same edge to where the raw edges meet. Repeat with the other corner.

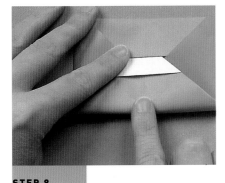

STEP 8

Carefully fold the pointed flap inside the small pocket.

STEP 9

Finally, press the fold flat and turn it around to see the completed envelope.

MOUNTAIN FOLD REMINDER

To make a mountain fold, simply fold the paper away from you and make a firm crease.

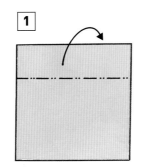

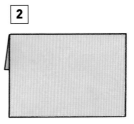

SANTA

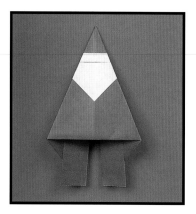

THIS DESIGN WAS CREATED by Minako Ishibashi from Japan. It is a fine example of how you can use origami to suggest a subject rather than to make a perfect copy of it; this Santa is clearly recognizable even with a minimum of features.

HELP!

Take care when narrowing the body at the final stages —the thicker layers of paper will crumple if you are not careful.

72

STEP 1

Start with a square that has a diagonal crease. Fold one end of the diagonal to the other and make a small location crease in the center and unfold (see inset). Then, fold a corner to the center (main picture).

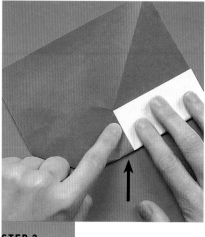

STEP 2

Turn the paper over and fold half of the short edge to the center crease.

STEP 3

Repeat the same fold on the other side of the short edge.

VALLEY FOLD REMINDER

To make a valley fold, simply fold the paper toward you and make a firm crease.

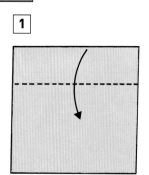

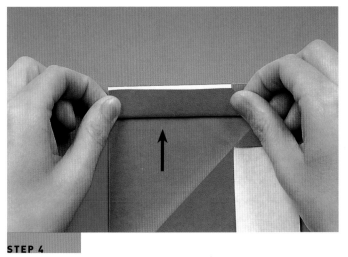

STEP 4

Fold the short edge in half back toward the outer edge so that only one color is visible.

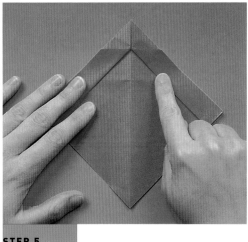

STEP 5

Repeat the previous step on the opposite side.

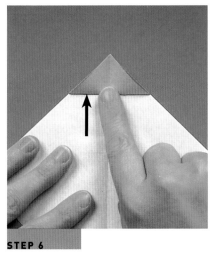

STEP 6

Turn the paper over and fold the inside corner of the small square to the outside corner. Crease firmly and unfold again.

STEP 7

Fold the same corner to the center of the square (see new foldmark).

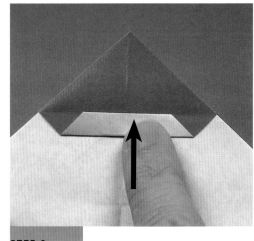

STEP 8

Fold the small triangle in half...

73

MOUNTAIN FOLD REMINDER

To make a mountain fold, simply fold the paper away from you and make a firm crease.

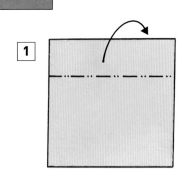

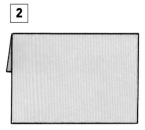

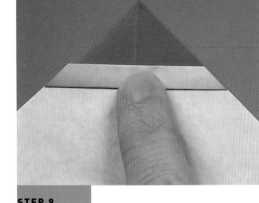

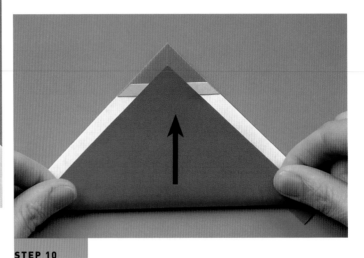

STEP 9

...then fold over again on the crease made in Step 5.

STEP 10

Fold the original corner to meet the opposite corner.

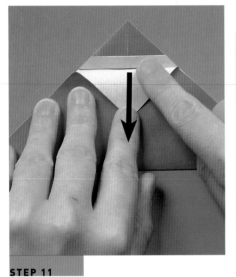

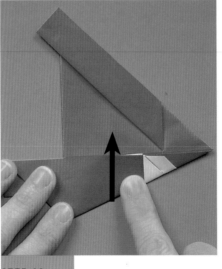

STEP 11

Fold the beard down just below the lining of the hat.

STEP 12

Turn over and fold a long edge to meet the center crease.

STEP 13

Repeat on the other side, pressing the model flat. The completed Santa!

LOCATION CREASE REMINDER

Fold the paper in half vertically and unfold. Then fold the bottom to the top but only make a very small crease in the center.

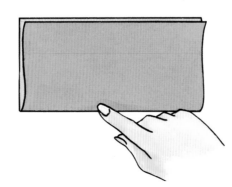

74

WOODPECKER

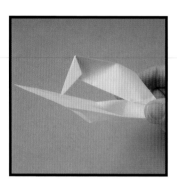

ORIGAMI MODELS that have some kind of movement or action have always been popular with both adults and children. This design uses a familiar technique for creating movement. The position and angle of the beak can be varied to taste. If you fold from crisp paper, quite a loud peck can be heard. The fold lines for this design have been provided on one of the practice sheets.

With just a few changes you can create a snapping beak instead. Try to come up with your own designs.

76

STEP 1

Start with an upside-down diamond base. Starting at the left-hand corner, fold the right-hand edge back along itself, but only crease as far as the center. Repeat on the left-hand side.

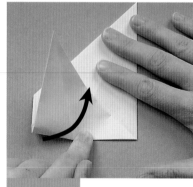

STEP 2

Turn the paper all the way around, then make the same folds at the other end. This will form a diamond-shaped crease pattern at the center.

HELP!

It is important to make all the creases sharp and neat for the best "pecking" action. Try to use crisp paper.

STEP 3

Turn the paper over and unfold two flaps at one end of the diamond base. Either end is fine. Fold both outside corners in to meet the two inner corners and crease firmly.

INSIDE REVERSE FOLD REMINDER

Start with a kite base. All the necessary folds are present by Step 5, but they must change direction. Ease the paper gently back along the fold lines to "reverse" the fold.

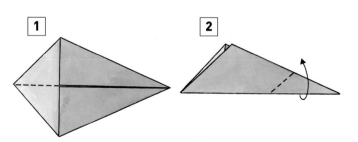

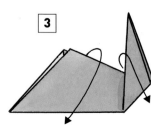

STEP 4

Pick the paper up and reinforce the diamond-shaped creases made in Steps 1 and 2 so that they pass through the extra layers.

STEP 5

Make an inside reverse fold to form a beak.

STEP 6

Fold either side of the beak downward, creasing firmly.

STEP 7

Hold the model by both sides (see inset) and gently press together to make the completed woodpecker peck!

77

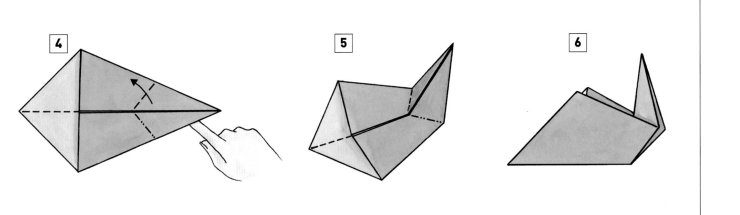

stage two PRACTICE PIECE

FLAPPING BIRD

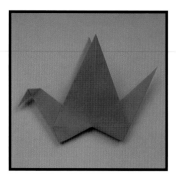

PERHAPS THE BEST known origami model after the paper airplane, this classic fold has been known for at least 150 years, possibly longer. The flapping action is guaranteed to enchant both children and adults whenever they see it. It can be folded quite rapidly with practice; the author made over 1,000 in a single day while raising money for charity! The fold lines for this design have been provided on one of the practice sheets.

HELP!

The tricky part is teaching the bird to flap. Try to curl the wings to encourage them to move and never pull too hard or too quickly.

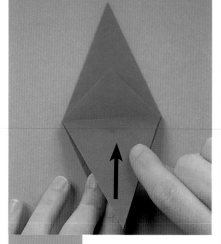

STEP 1
Start with a bird base. Fold the rear and front flaps upward.

STEP 2
There are two thin flaps; fold one upward at an angle, starting from the center of the paper. Use later pictures as guides. Crease firmly!

STEP 3
Make an inside reverse fold using the crease you have just made. Repeat with the other thin flap.

BIRD BASE REMINDER

Start with a preliminary base. After Step 2, turn over and repeat. Unfold two flaps and lift the top flap to complete Steps 5 and 6. Turn over and repeat last two steps.

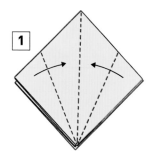

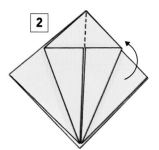

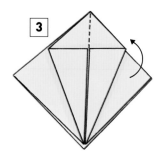

78

STEP 4

Fold a small section of one point over to form a beak. Crease firmly and unfold.

STEP 5

Make an inside reverse fold on that crease.

STEP 6

The completed flapping bird is ready for flight!

79

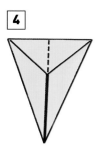

4

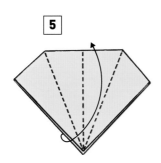

5

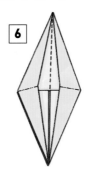

6

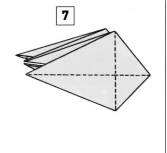

7

ACROBAT

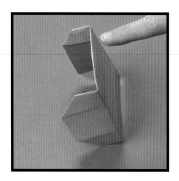

THIS DELIGHTFUL TOY was created by the late Seiro Takekawa, a Japanese folder who specialized in simple folds for children. The tumbling action seems simple also, but if you don't know the trick you won't be able to make it work every time!

The narrowing of the edges in Steps 4 and 5 needs to be quite precise for the fold to perform effectively.

STEP 1

Start with a square, colored side up. Fold the square in half, then open out.

HELP!

It doesn't matter if the edges overlap slightly in Step 7. The edges should be exactly at right angles for the fold to perform effectively (Step 8).

STEP 2

Fold both edges in to the center crease, opening one out again.

VALLEY FOLD REMINDER

To make a valley fold, simply fold the paper toward you and crease firmly.

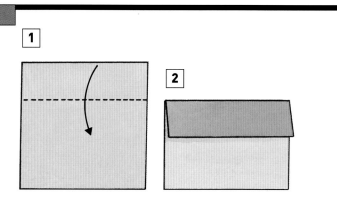

STEP 3
Fold both corners of the white section in to meet the inside edge. Repeat with the opposite side, folding the corners to meet the quarter crease.

STEP 4
Lift the outside folded edge in to meet the inside raw edge. Hold the corners in place as you flatten the crease.

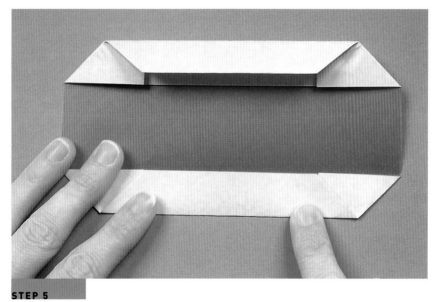

STEP 5
Turn the paper around and make a similar fold on the other edge.

81

MOUNTAIN FOLD REMINDER

To make a mountain fold, simply fold the paper away from you and crease firmly.

1

2

stage three PROJECT

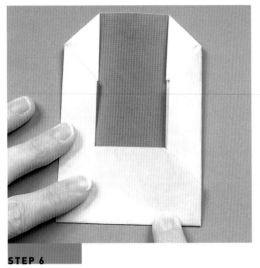

STEP 7

Rotate the paper again and repeat the fold with the other short edge.

STEP 6

Turn the paper sideways and fold the short edge in to the center. The crease lies along hidden edges of paper and so is easy to locate.

82

STEP 8

Open the short edges to halfway and stand the paper on its side, with the thicker side (it has double the layers) on top. Gently tip the paper over with your fingertip and it will perform a somersault. The trick is to then pick it up with the thinner side on top and invite your friend to try the same thing.

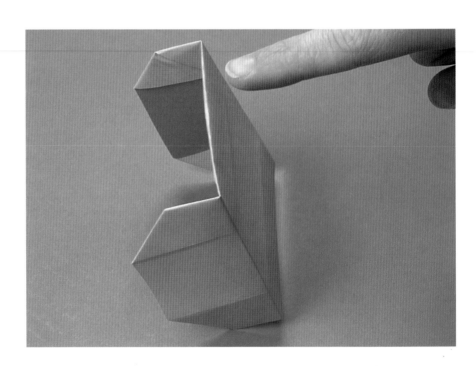

DIAMOND BASE REMINDER

Start with a kite base and fold both of the shorter edges to the center.

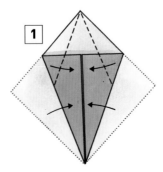

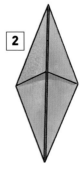

LIVELY CREATURES

THE WORLD OF NATURE has always been a rich source of inspiration for artists, and paper folders are no exception. Certain creatures, such as penguins, elephants, and dogs, are very popular, whereas others, such as slugs, hamsters, and cows, are very uncommon. Over the past few years there has been a growing interest in origami dinosaurs, including a number of skeletons! When creating your own designs, try to explore subjects that are not as common. That way, you are more likely to arrive at an original concept.

84

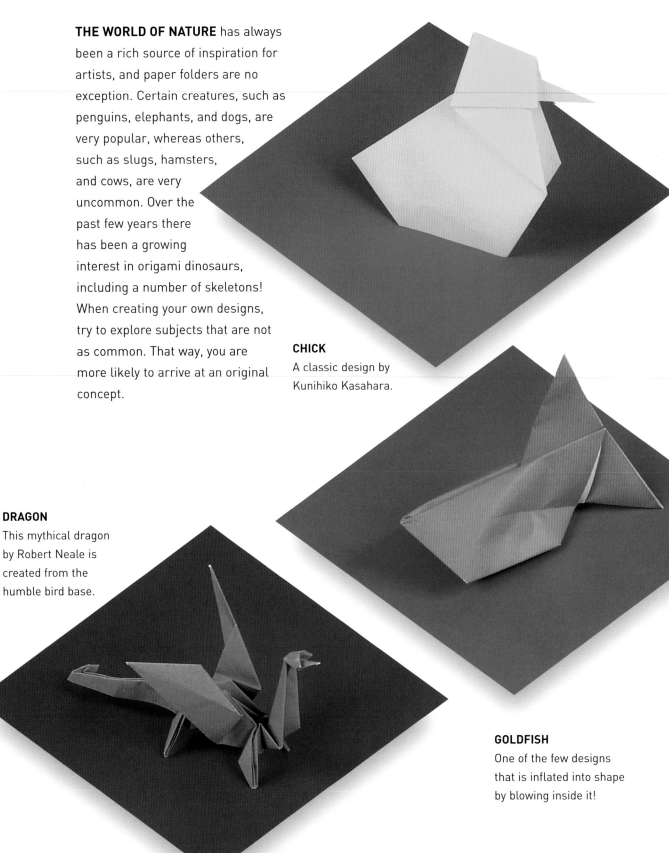

CHICK
A classic design by Kunihiko Kasahara.

DRAGON
This mythical dragon by Robert Neale is created from the humble bird base.

GOLDFISH
One of the few designs that is inflated into shape by blowing inside it!

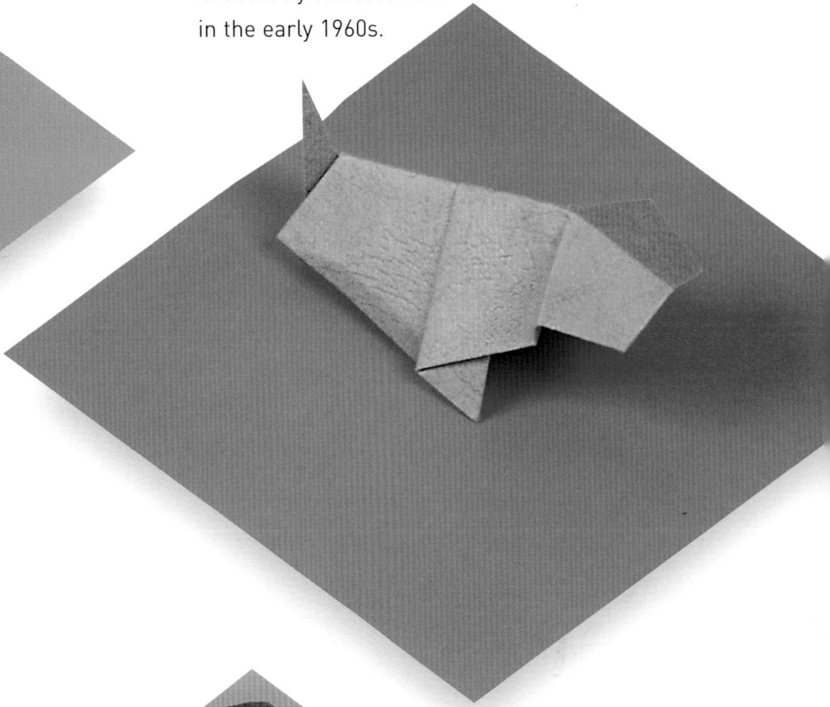

THURBER DOG
Created by Robert Neale
in the early 1960s.

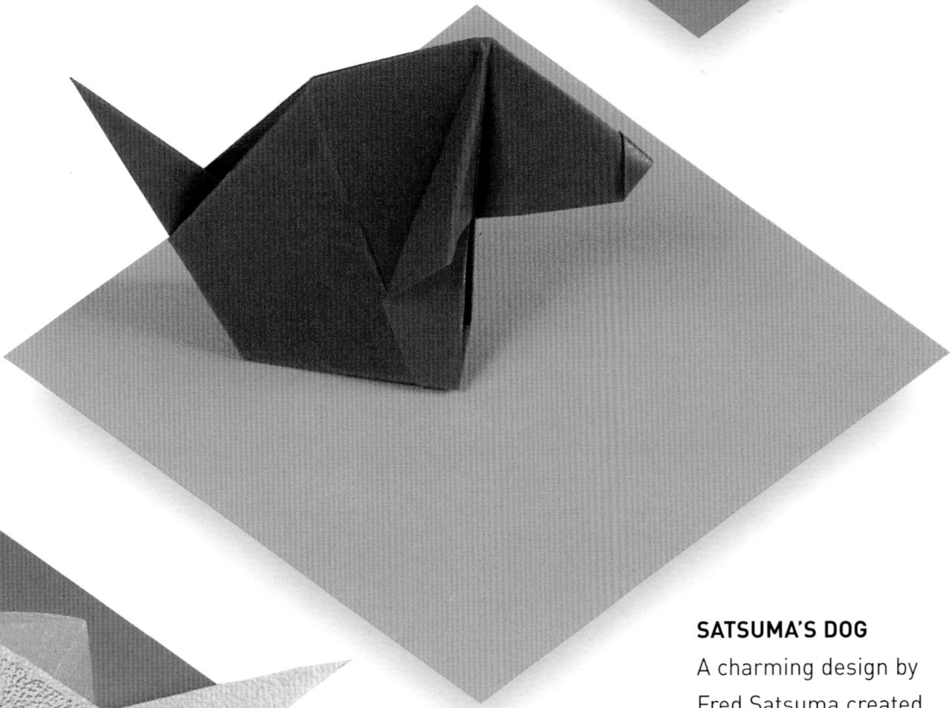

BABY BIRD
An original design by
the author showing
a baby bird in a nest.

SATSUMA'S DOG
A charming design by
Fred Satsuma created
in the 1990s.

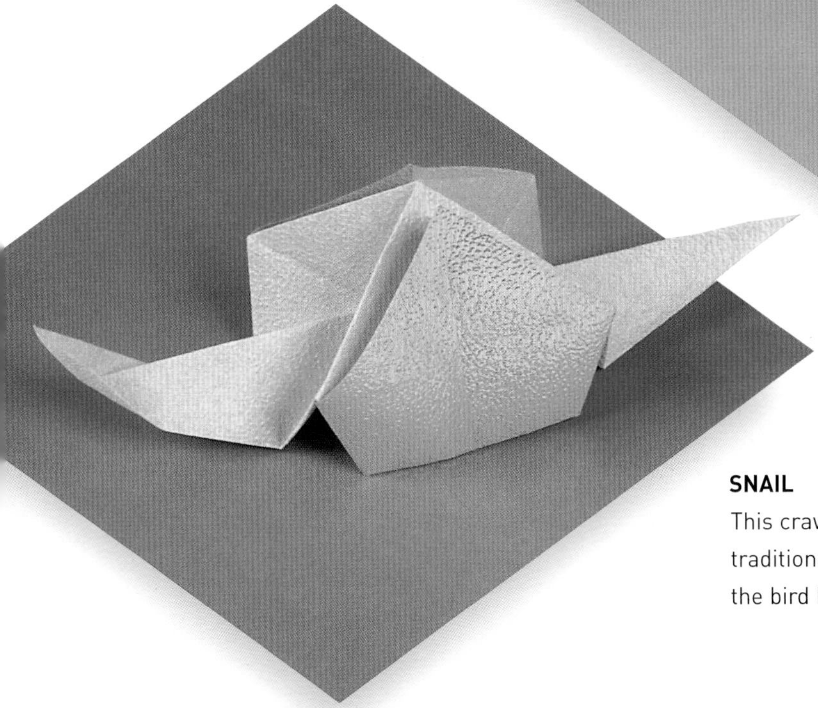

SNAIL
This crawling snail is a
traditional variation of
the bird base.

DISHES & BOXES

DISHES AND BOXES are the perfect challenge for origami folders—their methods are usually quite straightforward, and you can tell immediately whether you have been successful. Some containers are more decorative, with gentle curves and a pleasing elegance of shape, while others are purely practical. There are probably more origami designs in these subject areas than any others.

STUDIO 2
Inspired by the elegant lines of 1950s Hornsea Pottery.

LOUIS'S BOX
This box has a more complex design that "weaves" the sides together.

DECORATIVE DISH
A practical dish with decorative edges.

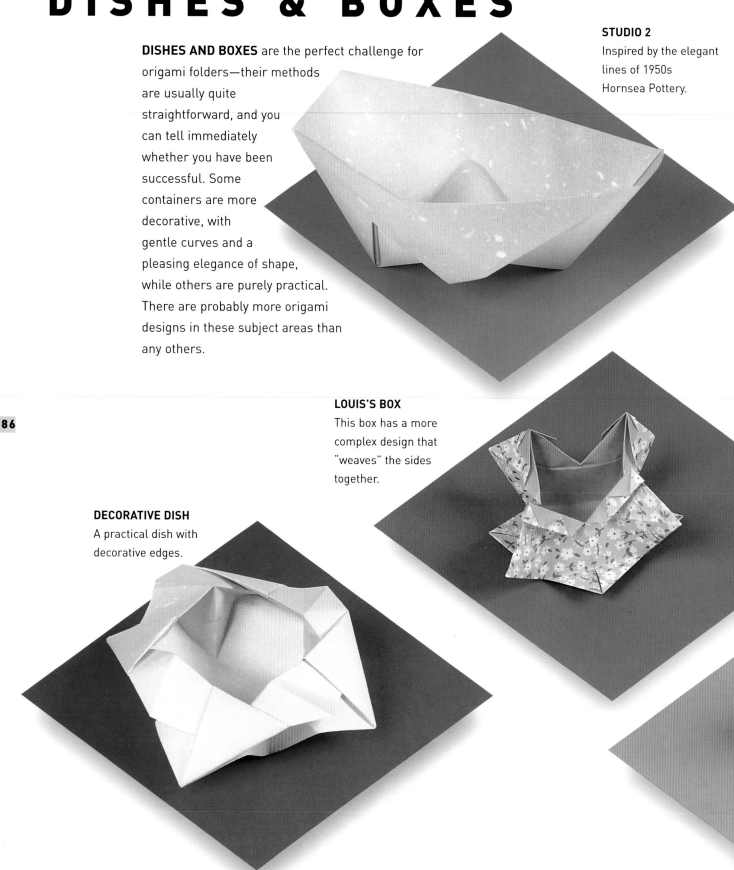

CLASSIC DISH
A classic design by
Philip Shen.

MINIMAL DISH
Here we see how minimal
folding can produce
beautiful lines.

DRINKING CUP
A sturdy and practical cup
by Paulo Mulatinho.

FACES & GEOMETRIC SHAPES

ORIGAMI FACES CAN BE simple or complex, but you should concentrate on the main features of the eyes, nose, and mouth for the best effects. Alongside the faces are some classic geometric shapes created by origami masters.

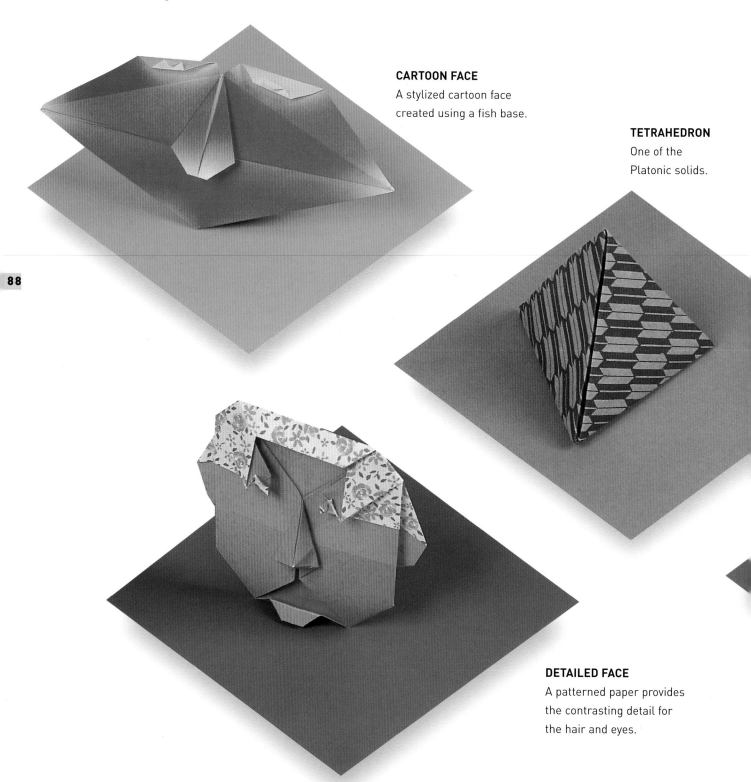

CARTOON FACE
A stylized cartoon face created using a fish base.

TETRAHEDRON
One of the Platonic solids.

DETAILED FACE
A patterned paper provides the contrasting detail for the hair and eyes.

BASIC FACE
A simple but easily
recognizable face design.

TRADITIONAL BOX
An early classic design
from Japan.

CUBE
A classic design by origami
master Shuzo Fujimoto.

UNIQUE & FUN SHAPES

THIS COLLECTION OF ORIGAMI designs reflects the varied nature of paperfolding. No subject is beyond the reach of a talented folder, and it is common for a shape to have some kind of personal connection to its designer. Think about your own personal interests and see if you are inspired to create a new design!

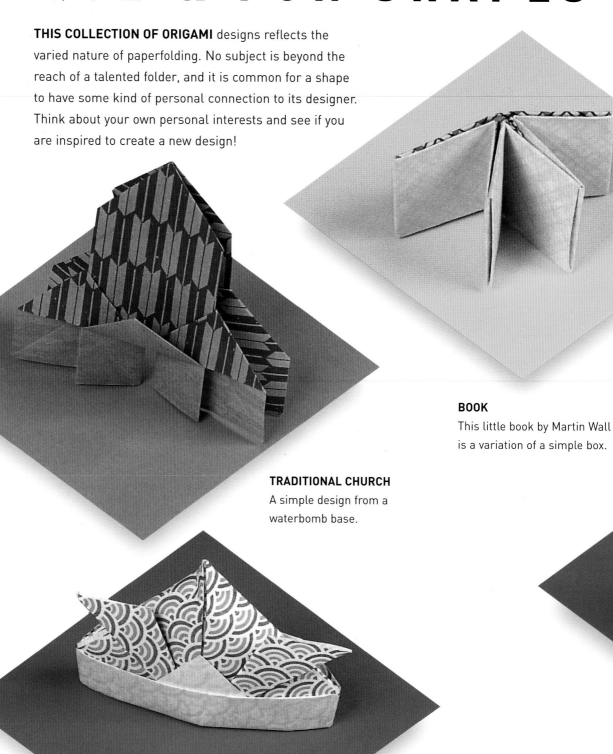

BOOK
This little book by Martin Wall is a variation of a simple box.

TRADITIONAL CHURCH
A simple design from a waterbomb base.

SAMURI HELMET
Another traditional design from Japan.

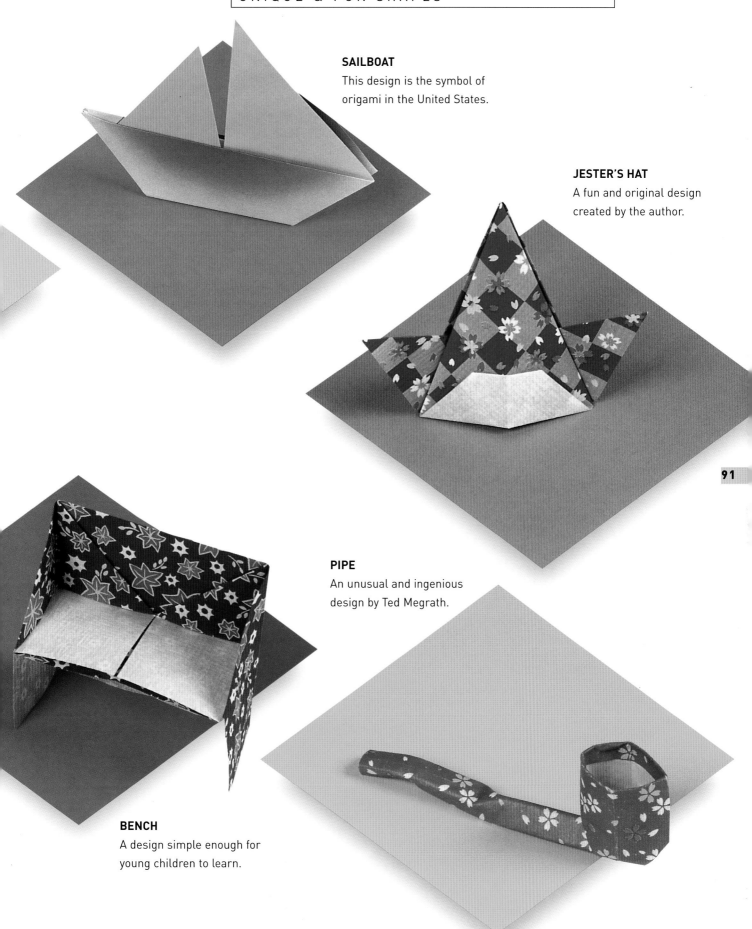

SAILBOAT
This design is the symbol of origami in the United States.

JESTER'S HAT
A fun and original design created by the author.

PIPE
An unusual and ingenious design by Ted Megrath.

BENCH
A design simple enough for young children to learn.

STARS & FLOWERS

IF YOU USE THE same technique on each corner of a
square, you are likely to arrive at a regular shape, such
as a star or flower. These designs lend themselves to
many variations in shape and color pattern, producing
designs that are usually very eye-catching.

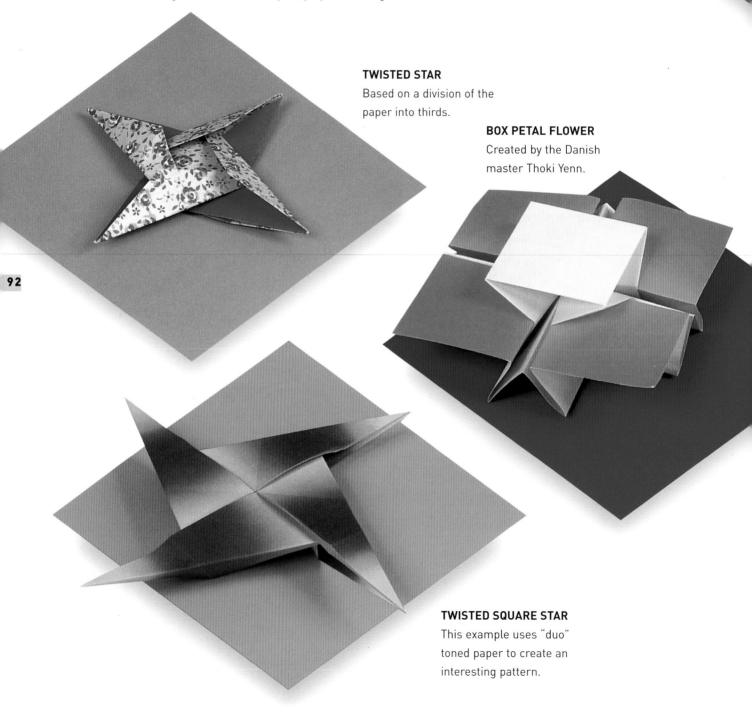

TWISTED STAR
Based on a division of the
paper into thirds.

BOX PETAL FLOWER
Created by the Danish
master Thoki Yenn.

TWISTED SQUARE STAR
This example uses "duo"
toned paper to create an
interesting pattern.

SIMPLE FLOWER
A flower design also known
as the Fortune Teller.

OPEN BLOSSOM FLOWER
One of Philip Shen's
masterpieces.

93

TWISTED STAR
This design utilizes both
sides of the paper to create
contrast.

INDEX

CREDITS

The following origami designs were created by these artists:

Star ring by Robert Neale, page 30; dish by Nick Robinson, page 60; Valentine vase by Pam Bisman, page 62; bookmark by Nick Robinson, page 64, Santa by Minako Ishibashi, page 72; acrobat by Seiro Takeawa, page 80; chick by Kunihiko Kasahara, page 84; dragon by Robert Neale, page 84; baby bird by Nick Robinson, page 85; Thurber Dog by Robert Neale, page 85; Satsuma's dog by Fred Satsuma, page 85; classic dish by Philip Shen, page 87; drinking cup by Paulo Mulatinho, page 87; cube by Shuzo Fujimoto, page 89; book by Martin Wall, page 90; jester's hat by Nick Robinson, page 91; pipe by Ted Megrath, page 90; box petal flower by Thoki Yenn, page 92; open blossom flower by Philip Shen, page 93.

INTERNATIONAL ORIGAMI ASSOCIATIONS

Origami is an art you can study on your own, but it's also a lot of fun to fold as part of a group! Here are two major origami organizations:

Origami USA (OUSA)
15 West 77th Street
New York, NY 10024-5192
USA
email: www.origami-usa.org

David Brill
British Origami Society
35 Corfe Crescent Hazel Grove
Stockport
Cheshire SK7 5PR
Tel: 0161 456 9975
email: www.rpmrecords.co.uk/bos